The European Union as an Area of Freedom, Security and Justice

This book presents a collection of essays on key topics and new perspectives on the EU's Area of Freedom, Security and Justice (AFSJ).

Europe's Area of Freedom, Security and Justice is of increasing importance in contemporary EU law and legislation. It is worthy of special research attention because of its high-stakes content (particularly from an individual and a state perspective) and because its development to date has tangentially thrown up some of the most important and contentious constitutional questions in EU law.

As the AFSJ becomes more and more intertwined with 'mainstream' EU law, this edited collection provides a timely analysis of the merger between the two. Showcasing a selection of work from key thinkers in this field, the book is organised around the major AFSJ themes of crime, security, border control, civil law cooperation and important 'meta' issues of governance and constitutional law. It also analyses the major constitutional and governance challenges such as variable geometry, institutional dynamics and interface with rights around data protection/secrecy/spying. In the concluding section of the book, the editors consider the extent to which the different facets of the AFSJ can be construed in a coherent and systematic manner within the EU legal system, as well as identifying potential future research agendas.

The European Union as an Area of Freedom, Security and Justice will be of great interest to students and scholars of European law and politics.

Maria Fletcher is Senior Lecturer in European Law at the University of Glasgow. Her research interests lie in the field of EU AFSJ law and EU constitutional law more generally. She is co-author of the first book published in English on *EU Criminal Law and Justice* (Edward Elgar, 2008, with Robin Lööf and William Gilmore) and has undertaken funded research and published widely on EU criminal, immigration and asylum and citizenship law.

Ester Herlin-Karnell is the Co-director of the VU Centre for European Legal Studies and Professor and Research Chair in EU Constitutional Law and Justice. She holds a DPhil from Oxford University. She has published widely on AFSJ law. Her recent publications include a monograph on the *Constitutional Dimension of European Criminal Law* (Hart Publishing, 2012).

Claudio Matera is Assistant Professor for the Chair of International and European Law and Government at the University of Twente (NL). His research and publications focus on the external dimension of the AFSJ.

Routledge Research in EU Law

Available titles in this series include:

The Habitats Directive in its EU Environmental Context
European Nature's Best Hope?
Charles-Hubert Born, An Cliquet, Hendrik Schoukens, Delphine Misonne, and Geert Van Hoorick

Global Data Protection in the Field of Law Enforcement
An EU Perspective
Cristina Blasi Casagran

Kadi on Trial
A Multifaceted Analysis of the Kadi Trial
Matej Avbelj, Filippo Fontanelli and Giuseppe Martinico

The Judge and the Proportionate Use of Discretion
A Comparative Administrative Law Study
Sofia Ranchordás & Boudewijn de Waard

European Agencies and Risk Governance in EU Financial Market Law
Paul Weismann

EU Health Systems and Distributive Justice
Towards New Paradigms for the Provision of Health Care Services?
Danielle Da Costa Leite Borges

EU Criminal Law and Policy
Values, Principles and Methods
Joanna Beata Banach-Gutierrez and Christopher Harding

The European Union as an Area of Freedom, Security and Justice
Maria Fletcher, Ester Herlin-Karnell and Claudio Matera

Forthcoming titles in this series include:

Retail Investor Protection under EU Law
Constantinos Tokatlides

The Right to Family Life in the European Union
Maribel González Pascual, Aida Torres Pérez

The European Union as an Area of Freedom, Security and Justice

Edited by
Maria Fletcher, Ester Herlin-Karnell
and Claudio Matera

Routledge
Taylor & Francis Group
LONDON AND NEW YORK

First published 2017
by Routledge

2 Park Square, Milton Park, Abingdon, Oxfordshire OX14 4RN
52 Vanderbilt Avenue, New York, NY 10017

Routledge is an imprint of the Taylor & Francis Group, an informa business

First issued in paperback 2018

British Library Cataloguing in Publication Data
A catalogue record for this book is available from the British Library

Library of Congress Cataloguing in Publication Data
Names: Fletcher, Maria (Law teacher), editor. | Herlin-Karnell, Ester, editor. | Matera, Claudio, editor.
Title: The European Union as an area of freedom, security and justice / edited by Maria Fletcher, Ester Herlin-Karnell and Claudio Matera.
Description: Abingdon, Oxon ; New York, NY : Routledge, 2017.
Identifiers: LCCN 2016027961| ISBN 9781138828575 (hardback) | ISBN 9781317573234 (adobe reader) | ISBN 9781317573227 (epub) | ISBN 9781317573210 (mobipocket)
Subjects: LCSH: Criminal justice, Administration of – European Union countries. | Justice, Administration of – European Union countries. | Freedom of movement – European Union countries.
Classification: LCC KJE9430 .E8954 2017 | DDC 345.24–dc23
LC record available at https://lccn.loc.gov/2016027961

ISBN: 978-1-138-82857-5 (hbk)
ISBN: 978-0-367-19345-4 (pbk)

Typeset in Galliard
by Out of House Publishing

Contents

Notes on contributors

Anneli Albi is Professor of European Law at the University of Kent (Canterbury, UK). She obtained her doctorate from the European University Institute in Florence (2003) and her law degree from the University of Tartu in Estonia. Professor Albi is the author of *EU Enlargement and the Constitutions of Central and Eastern Europe* (Cambridge University Press, 2005) and co-editor of *The European Constitution and National Constitutions: Ratification and Beyond* (Kluwer, 2006). She was recently awarded a five-year, €1.2 million European Research Council grant, in the framework of which a two-volume edited book, *The Role of National Constitutions in European and Global Governance*, will be published by TMC Asser Press in 2016. Among a variety of consultancy posts, Professor Albi has served for several years as an expert to the European Commission's Gender Equality Network.

Inés Armada graduated in law in 2009 and holds an LL.M from the College of Europe. After working as a criminal lawyer, she became a PhD researcher (FWO fellow, VUB-ULB) and did a research stay in Eurojust. She has written several articles on EU criminal law.

Helena Carrapiço is a lecturer in politics and international relations at Aston University. Her research focuses on European Union justice and home affairs, namely on organised crime policies, as well as on the external dimension of the Area of Freedom, Security and Justice. She holds a doctoral degree in social and political sciences from the European University Institute (Florence). She has a considerable number of publications in this area, the most recent ones being: *EU Borders and Shifting Internal Security: Technology, Externalization and Accountability* (edited with R. Bosson, Springer, 2015) and *The Governance of Online Expression in a Networked World: Free-Speech, Surveillance and Censorship* (edited with B. Farrand, Routledge, 2015).

Gerard Conway is a senior lecturer in law at Brunel University London, where he completed his PhD. He previously graduated from Uppsala University, Sweden; Kings Inns, Ireland; and the University of Limerick,

Ireland. Prior to commencing his PhD, he worked as a legal research officer in the Office of the Director of Public Prosecutions, Ireland (for almost three years); as a judicial researcher in the Four Courts, Dublin, Ireland (for nearly seven months); and as a legal trainee in the Department of Foreign Affairs, Ireland (for six months). He is the author of *The Limits of Legal Reasoning and the European Court of Justice* (Cambridge University Press, 2012) and *EU Law* (Routledge, 2015). His research interests are in the role and methodology of the European Court of Justice, EU constitutional law, EU and comparative criminal law, and legal theory.

Cathryn Costello is Andrew W. Mellon Associate Professor in International Human Rights and Refugee Law at the Refugee Studies Centre (RSC), Oxford, with a fellowship at St Antony's College. From 2003 to 2013, she was Francis Reynolds Fellow and Tutor in EU and Public Law at Worcester College, Oxford, during which time she also completed her DPhil studies on EU asylum and immigration law. She has taught a range of public, EU, labour and international courses on the Oxford undergraduate and postgraduate curriculum. She began her academic career in 1998 as Lecturer in European Law at the Law School, Trinity College Dublin, and from 2000 to 2003, she also held the position of Director of the Irish Centre for European Law. She has been a visiting professor at the University of San Francisco, a visiting research fellow at NYU School of Law, and at the Law School, University of Melbourne. Her research spans international and EU migration and refugee law. She has published on EU citizenship, mobility and human rights law, immigration detention, family migration and all aspects of the EU Common European Asylum System. Her publications include a monograph *The Human Rights of Migrants and Refugees in European Law* (Oxford University Press, 2016) and an edited collection (co-edited with Mark Freedland) on the intersection of labour and migration law, entitled *Migrants at Work: Migration and Vulnerability in Labour Law* (Oxford University Press, 2014). She is also the co-author of two recent studies for the European Parliament, *Study on Enhancing the Common European Asylum System and Alternatives to Dublin* (2015) and *Study on New Approaches, Alternative Avenues and Means of Access to Asylum Procedures for Persons Seeking International Protection* (2014).

Henri de Waele is Professor of International and European Law at Radboud University Nijmegen and currently also serves as Guest Professor of European Institutional Law at the University of Antwerp. He is affiliated as a senior fellow with the Center for European Integration Studies at the University of Bonn. He studied Dutch, international and European law in Nijmegen and Leuven, obtained his PhD from Radboud University, and was awarded the Diploma in European Union Law at the European University Institute (2009). He has published extensively on topics pertaining to the institutional law of the EU – covering, inter alia, issues of external relations, administration of justice, fundamental rights, judicial protection, Union citizenship – as well as on general principles of public international law.

Benjamin Farrand joined the University of Warwick School of Law in September 2015, having previously been Lecturer for Intellectual Property Law and Policy at the University of Strathclyde from April 2012. Farrand's research focuses predominantly on the interaction between law and politics, in particular in the development of copyright law and policy at the European level. Other research interests include contemporary issues in patent policy, internet law, regulatory theory and law and policy in human enhancement technologies. He published the book *Networks of Power in Digital Copyright Law and Policy: Political Salience, Expertise and the Legislative Process*. He holds a PhD in law from the European University Institute.

Massimo Fichera is Academy Research Fellow at the Network for European Studies, University of Helsinki. He was previously a postdoctoral fellow at the Faculty of Law, University of Helsinki. His interests lie in constitutional theory and the intersection between EU and international law. His most recent publication is *Polity and Crisis- Reflections on the European Odyssey* (Ashgate), co-edited with Kaarlo Tuori and Sakari Hänninen. He has been Visiting Fellow at the International Institute for the Sociology of Law, Oñati (Spain). Before joining the University of Helsinki, he completed his PhD at the University of Edinburgh and qualified as Avvocato in Italy.

Maria Fletcher is Senior Lecturer in European Law at the University of Glasgow. Her research interests lie in the field of EU AFSJ law and EU constitutional law more generally. She is co-author of the first book published in English on *EU Criminal Law and Justice* (Edward Elgar, 2008, with Robin Lööf and William Gilmore) and has published on EU criminal, immigration and asylum and citizenship law.

Ester Herlin-Karnell is the Co-director of the VU Centre for European Legal Studies and Professor and Research Chair in EU Constitutional Law and Justice. She holds a DPhil from Oxford University. She has published widely on AFSJ law. Her recent publications include a monograph on the *Constitutional Dimension of European Criminal Law* (Hart Publishing, 2012).

Dora Kostakopoulou is Professor of European Union Law, European Integration and Public Policy at the University of Warwick. Formerly, she was Jean Monnet Professor in European Law and European Integration and Co-director of the Institute of Law, Economy and Global Governance at the University of Manchester (2005–2011) and Professor of European Union Law and Director of the Centre for European Law at the University of Southampton (2011–2012). She has been British Academy, Thank

Offering to Britain Fellow (2003–2004) and recipient of an Innovation Award by the Arts and Humanities Research Council (2004–2005). She is the author of *Citizenship, Identity and Immigration in the European Union: Between Past and Future* (Manchester University Press, 2001) and *The Future Governance of Citizenship*, which was published by Cambridge University Press in 2008 (Law in Context Series). Her articles have appeared in the *Canadian Journal of Law and Jurisprudence*, *Columbia Journal of European Law*, *Oxford Journal of Legal Studies*, *Modern Law Review*, *European Law Journal*, *Journal of Common Market Studies*, *Political Studies*, *European Political Science*, *Journal of Ethnic and Migration Studies*, *Journal of European Public Policy*, *European Journal of Migration and Law*, *European Security*, *Perspectives on European Politics and Society*, *International Journal of Law in Context* and the *Journal of Political Philosophy*.

Vesna Lazic is Associate Professor on International Commercial Arbitration at the Utrecht University and a member of the staff at the T.M.C. Asser Institute in The Hague. In 2013, she was appointed Professor of the European Civil Procedure International at the University of Rijeka. Private international law, international dispute settlement, especially international commercial arbitration and international litigation, insolvency and commercial law are the fields of her particular interest and expertise. Her lectures and publications are particularly focused on the private international law instruments applicable within the EU Member States.

Dorota Leczykiewicz is Associate Professor of Law at the University of Oxford and an Official Fellow of St Peters College. She was previously a junior research fellow at Trinity College, Oxford, a Leverhulme Trust Early Career Fellow in the Oxford Law Faculty and a Marie Curie Fellow at the European University Institute in Florence. Her research focuses on constitutional and private law aspects of EU law, comparative law and theories of judicial reasoning. Together with Professor Stephen Weatherill she edited two collections of papers – *The Involvement of EU Law in Private Law Relationships* (Hart Publishing, 2013) and *The Images of the Consumer in EU Law: Legislation, Free Movement and Competition Law* (Hart Publishing, forthcoming). Her recent publications include 'Effectiveness of EU law before national courts' in A. Arnull and D. Chalmers (eds.), *Oxford Handbook of European Union Law* (Oxford University Press, 2015); 'Constitutional justice and judicial review of EU legislative acts', in G. de Búrca, D. Kochenov and A. Williams (eds.), *Europe's Justice Deficit? Beyond Good Governance* (Hart Publishing, 2014).

Claudio Matera is Assistant Professor for the Chair of International and European Law and Governance at the University of Twente, the Netherlands. His research and publications focus on the external dimension of the AFSJ.

Valsamis Mitsilegas is Professor of European Criminal Law, Director of the Criminal Justice Centre and, since 2012, Head of the Department of Law at Queen Mary University of London. From 2001 to 2005 he served as legal adviser to the House of Lords European Union Committee. His research interests and expertise lie in the fields of European criminal law; migration, asylum and borders; security and human rights, including the impact of mass surveillance on privacy; and legal responses to transnational crime, including organised crime and money laundering. He is the author of six monographs and over 100 articles and chapters in academic volumes. His latest books are *The Criminalisation of Migration in Europe* (Springer, 2015) and *EU Criminal Law After Lisbon* (Hart Publishing, 2016). He is a regular adviser to parliaments, governments and EU institutions including the European Commission, the European Parliament and the EU Fundamental Rights Agency. He has been appointed for a second term to the European Commission's Expert Group on Criminal Policy. He is co-coordinator of the European Criminal Law Academic Network and a member of the Management Board of the International Research Network on Migration and Crime.

Minos Mouzourakis is responsible for the coordination of the Asylum Information Database (AIDA) at the European Council on Refugees and Exiles (ECRE). Mouzourakis holds an MSc in refugee and forced migration studies from the University of Oxford and law degrees from University College London and Aix-Marseille Université. He has worked with NGOs in Greece and the UK and interned with the General Secretariat of the Council of the European Union and the Permanent Representation of Cyprus, where he participated in the legislative negotiations of the recast asylum package. He has also published widely on asylum-related issues such as the EU's Dublin System and conducted research for UNHCR, the European Parliament and the University of Oxford.

Steve Peers is Professor of Law at the University of Essex. Peers received a BA (Hons) in history from McMaster University (Canada) in 1988, an LLB from the University of Western Ontario (Canada) in 1991, an LLM in EU law from the London School of Economics in 1993, and a PhD from the University of Essex in 2001. His research interests include EU constitutional and administrative, justice and home affairs, external relations, human rights, internal market and social law. He has written more than 50 articles on many aspects of EU law in journals including the *Common Market Law Review*, *European Law Review*, *International and Comparative Law Quarterly*, *Yearbook of European Law* and the *Cambridge Yearbook of European Legal Studies*, as well as many chapters in books. He has worked as a consultant for the European Parliament, the European Commission, the Foreign and Commonwealth Office, the House of Lords Select Committee on the European Union and the Council of Europe, and contributed to the work of NGOs such as Amnesty International,

Justice, Statewatch, ILGA-Europe and the Immigration Law Practitioners' Association (ILPA).

Sara Poli is Associate Professor of European and International Law at the University of Pisa. She currently holds a Jean Monnet Chair in respect of a research project on 'Good governance principles within and outside the EU'. Her research interests include EU external relations, EU humanitarian aid policy, the EU's role in the management of emergencies, the external aspects of the Area of Freedom, Security and Justice and judicial remedies against counterterrorism measures.

Jorrit J. Rijpma is Associate Professor of European Law Leiden Law School in the Netherlands. His research focuses on the institutional dimension of justice and home affairs cooperation. He is a member of the standing committee of experts on international immigration, refugee and criminal law (Meijers Committee).

Ariadna Ripoll Servent is Junior Professor of Political Science and European Integration at the University of Bamberg. Her research interests include European institutions, decision-making, institutional and policy change as well as internal security policies. She has previously worked at the Institute for European Integration Research in Vienna, the University of Sussex and the College of Europe.

Eva Storskrubb is Marie Curie Research Fellow at the Faculty of Law, Uppsala University. She is also a practising lawyer with focus on cross-border commercial dispute resolution, currently on leave of absence from Roschier Attorneys, Stockholm. In addition to EU civil justice, her research interests include comparative procedural law, private international, EU free movement and arbitration.

Anne Weyembergh is a professor at the Université Libre de Bruxelles (ULB) and President of the Institute for European Studies (ULB). She teaches European criminal law, international criminal law, Belgian penal law (special part), methodology of research in criminal law and the Area of Freedom, Security and Justice. She founded and co-coordinates the European Criminal Law Academic Network (ECLAN). She has published numerous articles and co-edited several collective books in the field of EU criminal law

Irene Wieczorek is a PhD student at the Vrije Universiteit Brussels and at the Université Libre de Bruxelles (joint doctorate). She has been a visiting researcher at the European University Institute, at the University of Trento, where she was invited as a guest lecturer, and at the Max Planck Institute for Foreign and International Criminal Law. She was also an informal visiting student at the University of Cambridge. In July 2014, she was awarded the Diploma of the Academy of European Law (European University Institute) for an excellent examination paper. From

October 2011 to March 2012 she interned at the legal service and at the Italian desk at Eurojust, the Judicial Cooperation Unit of the European Union. She holds an MA in European Interdisciplinary Studies from the College of Europe (2011), an LLM, major European law, from Maastricht University (2010) and an LLM from Trento University (2010).

Foreword

The European integration project is no longer confined to economic and commercial matters relating to the establishment and functioning of the internal market. That project has evolved with the adoption of successive Treaty reforms so that it now aims to establish an Area of Freedom, Security and Justice (AFSJ), an objective that is expressly recognised in Article 3(2) of the Treaty on European Union.

By establishing an 'area of freedom', the authors of the Treaties sought to abolish border controls within the EU. Without prejudice to the police powers retained by the Member States, EU citizens should be able to move from one Member State to another in the same way as they move within a single Member State.

By creating an 'area of security', the authors of the Treaties sought to prevent criminals from relying on free movement as a means of pursuing their activities with impunity. Similarly, European businesses and consumers should be able to exercise cross-border activities with legal certainty as to the competent court for any dispute that may arise and as to the applicable law. The same should apply in the context of family law, where legal certainty is essential for couples and families who have exercised their right to free movement.

Accordingly, the authors of the Treaties decided that the exercise of free movement should not undermine the powers of the competent national court and the effectiveness of the applicable national laws. As internal borders disappear, the arm of the law should acquire a transnational reach.

Furthermore, the authors of the Treaties took the view that the abolition of internal borders should also bring about the 'Europeanisation' of external border controls, asylum and immigration policies. If free movement is to be facilitated by the elimination of internal borders, then it is imperative that the EU is entrusted with the necessary powers to adopt common standards that prevent third-country nationals who pose a threat to our security from entering the EU.

Last, but not least, in setting up an 'area of justice', the authors of the Treaties took the view that national courts were best placed to protect the fundamental rights of individuals. Indeed, it is a common feature of the constitutional traditions of the Member States that the judiciary – and not the political process – is entrusted with that task. Judicial dialogue and comity among national judiciaries were seen by the authors of the Treaties as the right avenue for the establishment and proper functioning of the AFSJ. That is why the establishment of such an area is, first and foremost, to be achieved through the mutual recognition of national judicial decisions.

Over the past two decades, the establishment and consolidation of the AFSJ have given rise to important questions that are not only specific to that area but have also served to define key features of the EU legal order as a whole. Notably, those questions relate to the vertical and horizontal allocation of powers between the EU and its Member States, to the balance between collective security and individual freedom, and to the degree of mutual trust between national judiciaries. Those questions show that the establishment and consolidation of the AFSJ have shifted the EU into a new constitutional paradigm that goes beyond market integration. Paraphrasing the title of this book, the EU must be seen as an AFSJ.

Edited by Dr Fletcher, Professor Herlin-Karnell and Dr Matera, this collection of essays makes a hugely valuable contribution to the existing literature on the AFSJ. By bringing together the expertise of its contributors, it does not come as a surprise that the book is an outstanding piece of scholarly work, providing very interesting insights to the way in which the EU has become an AFSJ.

Divided into six sections, this book provides a holistic study of the AFSJ. This is, first, because it puts forward a conceptual framework of the AFSJ that is based on a security discourse, while describing the main developments that have taken place in the AFSJ from prior to the Maastricht Treaty to the present day. Second, it examines at length the most salient aspects of judicial cooperation in civil and criminal matters, border control, asylum and immigration. Each of those areas is carefully studied from both a procedural and substantive perspective, paying special attention to the allocation of powers between the EU and its Member States, the principle of mutual recognition and the protection of fundamental rights. Third, the book is not limited to exploring the internal dimension of the AFSJ, but also examines the implications that flow from the fact that the EU may conclude international agreements with third countries in that area. The external dimension of the AFSJ raises important questions that relate to the principle of institutional balance, as well as to the dividing line between that dimension and the Common Foreign and Security Policy. Finally, the book looks at a new form of governance that has been developed in the AFSJ – i.e., the so-called 'network governance' that focuses on exploring the way in which national authorities are called upon to work together by trusting each other – and the challenges that such form of governance brings about. The book also devotes an entire chapter to examining how the Court of Justice has shaped the evolution of the AFSJ.

Throughout the book, the contributors do not limit themselves to describing the existing law and case law, but also provide thorough explanations as to the reasons why they believe that the EU legislator and the Court of Justice respectively reached a given outcome. Most importantly, in the light of the current refugee crisis, the ongoing terrorist threat and the rising importance of privacy in a digital world, they put forward innovative normative claims as to the way in which the AFSJ should evolve to overcome those challenges.

Written in a clear and entertaining style, this book succeeds in providing a solid analytical basis for future debates about the AFSJ. It is a thoughtful and rigorous study that addresses a challenging set of questions for scholars and students. Overall, it is an excellent contribution to the legal literature on European Union law and I warmly congratulate both the editors and contributors for it.

Professor Dr Koen Lenaerts
President of the Court of Justice of the European Union

1 Introduction

Maria Fletcher, Ester Herlin-Karnell and Claudio Matera

This edited collection explores Europe's Area of Freedom, Security and Justice (AFSJ) from a largely legal perspective. It attempts to do so holistically; in the sense that it offers both reflections on the range of policy fields that fall under the AFSJ umbrella and also analyses of the AFSJ as a phenomenon, from a variety of perspectives – including theoretical, institutional and constitutional. The AFSJ is worthy of special research attention because of its high-stakes content (particularly from an individual and a Member State perspective) and because its development to date has tangentially thrown up some of the most important and contentious constitutional questions in EU law – making it a focal point not only for AFSJ law academics and practitioners but also those with an interest in EU governance, human rights, EU citizenship and constitutionalism more generally. As the AFSJ becomes more and more intertwined with 'mainstream' EU law and given the various 'crises' currently facing the EU – from the migration crisis to the euro crisis to the increased terror threat – a critical assessment of responses and developments from the AFSJ perspective seems timely. Our aim for this edited collection is to offer a comprehensive look at AFSJ from this important vantage point and in so doing reflect on the past and future challenges of AFSJ law. In the following we set out to summarise the different parts of the book and explain how they are interlinked. The book consists of six parts all charting contemporary challenges in AFSJ law.

Part I introduces key concepts in the EU as an Area of Freedom, Security and Justice. This section sets the stage and identifies key issues in AFSJ law. In the first chapter, Steve Peers provides a helpful legal overview of the AFSJ domain. He traces institutional and policy evolution in key areas of justice and home affairs (JHA) law from prior to the Maastricht Treaty up to the present day. He suggests that today, particularly in light of recent terror attacks on EU territory and the recently escalated and ongoing EU 'migrant crisis', JHA law, and thus the AFSJ project, stands at a precipice in both institutional and substantive terms. While there is evidence that institutional changes heralded in by successive Treaty reforms have been accompanied by the development of a somewhat more liberal policy in some policy domains, EU responses in other areas of JHA law – particularly those developed more recently in response to the migration crisis – are rather less liberal. As for the future, he suggests, somewhat ominously, that the current crises create inherent tensions that will shape the EU's policy responses for years to come.

The next chapter, by Massimo Fichera, sketches out a theory for the Area of Freedom, Security and Justice. He explains how over the years a powerful and pervasive security discourse has unfolded, with an increasing focus on two functions, i.e., both *securing* the functioning or smooth operation of the internal market and ensuring a *secure* marketplace. Fichera discusses whether AFSJ as such can be constructed as having an autonomous meaning. Thereafter he defines the AFSJ as a space that claims to represent universal values and is characterised by a number of paradoxes, in particular a tension between its normative and its imperialistic facets. Finally, Fichera explores the notion of security as a technique of governance and compares it with the notions of freedom and justice, viewed as somewhat narrow and incomplete. In short, his chapter helps to set the scene for what we are actually debating in contemporary AFSJ law.

The connection between human rights and the AFSJ is explained and critiqued in the final chapter of Part I by Dorota Leczykiewicz. Human rights in the AFSJ sphere act not only, as in every area of EU law, as a standard against which Member State and EU action is assessed, but also as a prominent feature of the *acquis*, that is to say, many legislative acts have as their very purpose the enhancement of human rights protection. Even so, Leczykiewicz identifies how rights create tensions in the context of AFSJ and explains, with reference to individual policy spheres of activity, how the Court of Justice brings the protection received by human rights within EU law to bear on AFSJ law. The picture revealed is mixed but the trend is clear from these prominent findings; a resistance to intensive human rights review, the use of arguments of effectiveness of EU law to resist human rights arguments and only a limited use of the Charter of Fundamental Rights to infuse EU law in the AFSJ with human rights inspired content. Indeed the chapter argues that the Court's case law exhibits an extreme version of utilitarianism, which is incompatible with a corrective justice conception of human rights, underlying the ECHR and the Charter of Fundamental Rights.

Part II examines the sector specific area of criminal law, both procedural and substantive, within the AFSJ. It seeks to offer a constitutional and governance analysis of this field and focuses on two of the most auspicious and important criminal law initiatives, namely, the European Arrest Warrant and the proposal to develop judicial cooperation through the development of a European Public Prosecutor. Specifically, Anne Weyembergh and Inés Armada in their chapter chart the operation of mutual recognition by providing an impressive analysis of the law on the European Arrest Warrant and the European Investigation Order. They reflect on the most important features of the principle of mutual recognition order to identify if and how it contributes to the establishment of a true EU area of criminal justice. They conclude that the principle has undergone important changes, and that it faces numerous challenges in today's AFSJ. Anneli Albi then examines the constitutional questions facing the EU when enforcing supranational law in the national arena and what it means for the EU criminal law project. She queries the intentions of the EU and explains why a view from cooperative constitutionalism could offer a more fruitful pathway for EU integration in AFSJ matters. Specifically she discusses how the European Arrest Warrant system could be recalibrated towards a greater responsiveness to classic substantive constitutional values. Thereafter she explores two broader implications of the above argument for the future development of the EU's AFSJ. The first concerns the question whether in addition to changing legal thinking and the mindset in the field of constitutional law, autonomous EU law may have changed the legal thinking and vocabulary in the field of criminal law. The second is a broader discussion about harmonisation and the balance between uniformity and diversity in the field of criminal law in Europe.

In his chapter, Gerard Conway focuses on one of the most contentious and potentially transformative topics of EU criminal law; namely the European Public Prosecutor (EPP). He charts the history and current and ongoing developments related to the EPP, highlighting details of structure, competence, relationship with national authorities and the important question of accountability. In doing so Conway discusses the constitutional question of the adoption of an EPP and the question of accountability of the EPP.

EU developments in the realm of criminal procedure are investigated further in the final chapter of Part II by Valsamis Mitsilegas. He demonstrates convincingly that, notwithstanding the Treaty legal basis limitations and national concerns regarding an adverse impact of EU law on the diversity and integrity of national criminal justice systems, EU legislation on the rights of the individual in criminal procedure will have a transformative effect for the protection of human rights in Europe's area of criminal justice.

Next, Part III is focused on the topics of border controls, immigration, asylum and AFSJ paradigms. This part of the book addresses the challenges in EU security and border control and what it tells us about the AFSJ and in recent times, the EU as a 'crisis manager'. Jorrit Rijpma opens with a very topical chapter on Frontex, the European agency for the management of operational cooperation at the EU's external borders. Over the past decade, the agency has developed into an increasingly key actor in the management of the external borders of the Schengen area. Its tasks and resources have expanded in line with the consistent call for a reinforcement of the external borders of the EU at political level. Rijpma argues that the development of Frontex and a proposed future European System of Border Guards reveal a strong need to think more carefully about multilevel policing in the AFSJ and also the constitutional implications of further Europeanisation of executive powers in this field.

Dora Kostakopoulou and Ariadna Ripoll Servent continue with this constitutional theme in their chapter, which addresses the relationship between EU immigration law and the right to family life. They provide a critical assessment of the fundamental right to family reunification, and discuss how the Court of Justice of the European Union has limited the Member States' sovereign prerogatives in the field of migration law and tamed nationalist narratives. Their chapter examines and contrasts the regulation of family reunification in EU internal mobility law, on the one hand, and EU migration law, on the other. They reveal contrasting policy priorities and suggest that while 'communitarian egalitarianism' has characterised EU law and policy towards the family reunification of EU citizens, the family reunification of third-country nationals has been governed by a rival policy belief system; namely, by what may be termed 'restrictive collectivism'. Kostakopoulou and Ripoll Servent make a case for rethinking the restrictive family reunification rules applying to EU migration law and for the coherent application of the normative standards pertaining to the right to family reunion without differentiation on the basis of the sponsor's nationality.

Subsequently, Cathryn Costello and Minos Mouzourakis offer a pertinent legal analysis of the current and ongoing EU refugee 'crisis'. In doing so, they provide a chronological account of the development of asylum policies in EU law. Thereafter they identify the main structural shortcomings, namely (1) the lack of legal access routes to the EU to claim asylum, (2) tensions between legal duties at borders (such as *non-refoulement*, the prohibition on collective expulsion and other human rights obligations) and political discourse and framings of the nature of 'effective border controls' and (3) the pathologies of the asylum responsibility mechanism known as the Dublin System. Finally, they examine the legal responses adopted thus far to deal with the 'crisis' and ask and answer the question as to what went wrong with the Common European Asylum System. One might have hoped that the foundational flaws of the Common European Asylum System might be considered and addressed as part of the EU's response to the recent crisis, and yet, as they show, the recent proposals by the Commission seem all but designed to remedy those pitfalls.

Part IV focuses on civil justice as a particular policy area of the AFSJ. This area is often neglected in AFSJ literature, which as Eva Storskrubb points out in her chapter, is regrettable, since important parallels and fruitful comparisons can be made, especially between civil and criminal justice cooperation. Storskrubb's chapter provides a holistic 'health check' of civil justice cooperation today. She reminds us of the longstanding key constitutional and regulatory challenges identified in the field – most prominently competence and the cross-border 'struggle' and the absence of a coherent regulatory strategy – and questions whether they remain or have evolved. She identifies continued support for the cross-border limitation of scope in respect of *generic* EU civil justice measures but notes that this limitation has been breached in the context of several of the recently adopted *sector-specific* EU rules that regulate procedural issues, such that they also apply in purely domestic contexts. Such developments in the areas of consumer, intellectual property and competition law are examined in some detail. Storskrubb contends that this adoption of procedural rules within core substantive areas intended to support the internal market is remarkable; it raises queries related to national procedural autonomy and also to the relationship between market efficiency and (at least) AFSJ civil justice. Finally, reflections on mutual trust (as underpinning the mutual recognition basis for cooperation in this field) and the novel EU benchmarking of civil justice systems in the EU ultimately strengthen calls for increased regulatory awareness and debate from the justice community at large. Picking up from the mutual recognition regulatory framework, Vesna Lazic, in the second chapter in Part IV, offers a more in-depth analysis of one aspect of private international law cooperation in the EU context, namely the enforcement and recognition of judgments. She identifies different approaches to this topic across a range of relevant legislation – Regulation Brussels I and Brussels Ibis, Regulations European Enforcement Order, European Payment Order and Small Claims Procedure – and questions whether such diversity in legal regulation is desirable and can be justified. She furthermore reflects on how these differences impact on the legal protections of parties and offers some thoughts on how a greater degree of uniformity might be achieved in EU legal instruments.

The book then turns in Part V to the external dimension of the AFSJ and its impact. As the EU's AFSJ has developed, the externalisation of the different policies and disciplines that compose it has acquired a special place. Indeed, soon after the creation of the AFSJ itself, and in the aftermath of the 9/11 attacks, the European Council called upon the EU to integrate the AFSJ into the different instruments and policies of external action at the disposal of the Union. As a result of the growing number of security challenges that affect the Union on the one side and the emphasis on the externalisation of AFSJ objectives by the European Council on the other, the EU has become a proactive external actor in the different AFSJ fields

In this part of our volume, we asked the authors to take stock of some 16 years of EU external action in the AFSJ and look at how the externalisation of the AFSJ is related to the development of the AFSJ project at large and how this phenomenon affects or is affected by the EU integration process from a broader perspective. In his opening contribution, Claudio Matera looks at how the externalisation of the AFSJ has been developed and argues that, from the very beginning, the policy impetus has not paid attention to a number of constitutional principles and provisions, with the result that on more than one occasion the Court of Justice has intervened to solve disputes among institutional actors. At the same time, Matera shows that the externalisation of the AFSJ is also impacting the dynamics of EU external relations. Indeed, because of the special role that the EU plays in the AFSJ fields, external action in the AFSJ domains innovates the ways in which the EU enters agreements with third countries and international organisations, but also, in this case, often pushing the EU at the edges of its constitutional framework.

In the second contribution of this section, Sara Poli charts the EU antiterrorism policy and relations with the rest of the world. Her contribution offers a very updated and critical overview of the EU's anti-terrorism stance. Specifically, she examines the relationship between the Common Foreign and Security Policy and the AFSJ by focusing on the decision-making process and, in particular, on the strengthening of the democratic accountability in the negotiation and conclusion of international agreements designed to prevent and pursue terrorist activities and other forms of crime. She then considers whether the weakening of intergovernmentalism in the external dimension of the AFSJ has resulted in the fortification of the substantive human rights standards, in particular as far as data protection for European citizens is concerned.

Lastly in Part V, Maria Fletcher and Ester Herlin-Karnell examine the AFSJ through the lens of a particularly prominent and influential external relationship; that of the EU and the United States of America. It will reveal how the EU's security mission is shaping the internal face of the AFSJ while being largely influenced by transatlantic and indeed global dialogues. The chapter shows how the transatlantic relationship is deeply connected to both the *security* rationale and the *market* rationale and that this view provides the overall context in which to discuss AFSJ cooperation. These rationales and how they shape the regulatory environment are examined in relation to aspects of EU–US cooperation with regard to the fight against terrorism, namely terrorist financing, money-laundering and cybercrime regulation.[1] The chapter examines the current tricky question of data and rights protection in the context of data-sharing between the US and EU, particularly in light of mass-surveillance practices in the US. Security and market rationales and competences coexist messily here as the EU grapples with a global challenge that does not fit neatly into any particular policy 'box'. However, in light of recent CJEU cases of *Digital rights*[2] and the *Schrems*[3] the authors consider whether the EU might itself emerge as the norm-setter and global standard-bearer on data protection and privacy matters.

Finally, Part VI addresses legal challenges of network governance within the AFSJ. Because the EU cannot substitute its Member States to carry out the activities connected with the AFSJ project, the development of the EU *qua* AFSJ has been characterised by a new form of governance that can be conceptualised as network governance. Hence, the EU has been creating the AFSJ by networking not only the 28 Member States, but also their respective judicial and administrative authorities tasked with justice and home affairs matters. Therefore, the AFSJ project entails a peculiar method of governance and, as a result of this, further increments the legal challenges that the Union must address to deliver its citizens an Area of Freedom, Security and Justice. In the light of these observations, this part of the volume addresses

1 Note that this chapter does not address the transatlantic dimension of asylum and migration.
2 Case C-293/12, Opinion of Advocate General Cruz Villon delivered on 12 December 2013, judgment of 8 April 2014.
3 Case C-362/14, *Schrems*, judgment delivered on 6 October 2015, nyr.

the issue of network governance by looking at three distinct yet interconnected phenomena. The first issue addressed is the growing importance that AFSJ agencies have acquired in the AFSJ project. While the activities of the different agencies are analysed at various moments within the book,[4] the contribution by Irene Wieczorak takes its cue from the agencyfication of AFSJ activities to focus on the role that Eurojust has in the development of the AFSJ in the specific field of judicial cooperation in criminal matters. In her contribution, Wieczorak shows how the tensions between supranational and intergovernmental cooperation that have marked the AFSJ project since its beginning influence and condition the work of this agency. At the same time, Wieczorak suggests that, taking into account the ambitious project of the European Public Prosecutor's Office, the agency and its pull of expertise are an asset for the facilitation of cooperation among national authorities and more supranational integration.

The second chapter of this section looks at, possibly, the epitome of network governance challenges faced by the EU: cybersecurity. As Helena Carrapiço and Benjamin Farrand affirm in their introduction, 'given the world's degree of digital interdependence regarding communication commercial transactions and critical infrastructures, policymakers and citizens, in general, have come to perceive cyberspace as in need of protection'.[5]

At the same time, however, because of the 'lack of conceptual clarity, legal uncertainty and reliance on network governance with reluctant private stakeholder involvement … serves to create a significant gap between the expectations, competences and outcomes of the EU in this field of endeavour'.[6] In their chapter, the authors explore how the characteristics of cyberspace on the one side and the choice of relying upon coordinating agencies to fight cybercrime on the other have resulted in a fragmented regulatory picture in relation to which many unexplored facets remain to be analysed and addressed.

Finally, the last chapter of Section VI by Henri de Waele looks at the role that the Court of Justice has in this fragmented picture. In his contribution, de Waele first looks at the constitutional idiosyncrasies of the AFSJ in relation to decision-making, governance and enforcement before turning to the core of his chapter: the role of the Court of Justice on AFSJ matters. In his comprehensive overview, covering human rights protection and the division of competences, de Waele observes how the role of the Court has impacted the evolution of the AFSJ project itself. Yet, the contribution also suggests that the different regulatory gaps and ambiguities – especially in relation to the long-term direction of the AFSJ, on the one side, and the workload faced by the Court on the other one – may test the Court in an unprecedented manner.

4 See, for example, the contribution by Rijpma.
5 Helena Carrapiço and Benjamin Farrand, Part VI.
6 Ibid.

Conclusion

This edited collection seeks to introduce the reader to the perplexing and growing field of law in relation to the EU as an AFSJ. While the book focuses predominantly on legal perspectives, all contributions seek to embrace some interdisciplinarity; not as an end in itself but to encourage a more rounded and realistic reflection on the law. Despite the 'moving target' feature of contemporary AFSJ law, it is our hope that the contributions in the present volume will serve as an important reference source in the future for anyone trying to deepen her or his knowledge of AFSJ law (and its relationship to the rest of the EU project) with all its complexities.

Part I

The EU as an Area of Freedom, Security and Justice

2 The rise and fall of EU justice and home affairs law

Steve Peers

1 Introduction

More than other areas of EU law, EU justice and home affairs (JHA) law has had a complex history. The institutional rules have changed several times, apparently culminating, with the Treaty of Lisbon, in the application (with some exceptions) of the traditional 'Community method': a large role for the Commission, qualified majority voting in the Council, the joint decision-making power of the European Parliament, and full jurisdiction of the Court of Justice of the European Union (CJEU). Substantively, this change of institutional framework was, generally speaking, accompanied by the development of a somewhat more liberal policy.

However, in 2015–2016 this process was shaken by events: the huge increase in refugee and migrant flows and terrorist attacks in Paris and Brussels. In the spring of 2016, EU justice and home affairs law stands at a precipice in both institutional and substantive terms: is the solution to these crises more or less harmonisation at EU level? Do they call for a more liberal or more conservative policy?

This chapter traces the developments by looking first of all at the institutional evolution, then the policy evolution of the EU, in the main areas of JHA law (visas/borders, asylum, irregular migration, legal migration and criminal law).

2 Institutional evolution[1]

2.1 Prior to 1993

The EU's institutional framework for the adoption of JHA law has gone through several phases. First of all, there was a purely informal and intergovernmental phase, before the entry into force of the Maastricht

1 This chapter is partly adapted and updated from S. Peers, 'EU justice and home affairs law (non-civil)', in P. Craig and G. de Búrca (eds.), *The Evolution of EU Law* (2nd edn, Oxford University Press, 2011).

Treaty in November 1993. During this phase, some international treaties (Conventions) were concluded between Member States, largely within the framework of European Political Cooperation (EPC), mostly addressing criminal law issues. Generally speaking, this approach to cooperation proved ineffective, as the Conventions concerned were not ratified, except for the Dublin Convention on responsibility for asylum requests, which took seven years to enter into force, and earlier civil law Conventions, which were explicitly or implicitly linked to the EC legal order.[2] There was consistently no role given to the Community institutions as regards the negotiation of these Conventions, with the notable exception of jurisdiction for the Court of Justice to interpret the civil law Conventions – albeit subject to more restrictive jurisdictional rules than applied under the EEC Treaty.[3]

Outside the Community legal framework, but linked to the internal market project, the Schengen process began among a small number of Member States during this period.[4] In light of the opposition of some Member States to the substance of the Convention (the UK, Ireland and, at the time, Denmark), this approach proved more effective than intergovernmentalism among all Member States of the Community, as the Schengen system began between the States participating in it from 1995.

2.2 1993–1999

The next phase in this evolution could be described as formal intergovernmentalism, as applied during the Maastricht era (1993–1999). The original Treaty on European Union (TEU) provided for specific rules relating to JHA, but these rules established an essentially intergovernmental process, specifying that the Council could adopt by unanimity either Conventions or other acts, which were different from the ordinary Community law and not clearly defined.[5]

Unlike the pre-Maastricht period, there was an official role for the EC institutions other than the Council, but it was very limited. The Court of Justice was not awarded any mandatory jurisdiction, but rather there was the case-by-case possibility of giving it jurisdiction over dispute settlement or references from national courts as regards each third-pillar Convention.[6] In practice, the

2 [1997] OJ C 254 (Dublin Convention); [1998] OJ C 27/1 (Brussels Convention) and [1998] OJ C 27/34 (Rome Convention).

3 See the Protocols to these Conventions (ibid.).

4 1985 and 1990 Schengen Conventions ([2000] OJ L 239). See generally D. O'Keeffe, 'The Schengen Convention: a suitable model for European integration?' (1991) 11 *YEL* 185; J. Schutte, 'Schengen: its meaning for the free movement of persons in Europe' (1991) 28 *Common Market Law Review* 549.

5 See, inter alia, D. Curtin, 'The constitutional structure of the Union: a Europe of bits and pieces' (1993) 30 *Common Market Law Review* 17; P. Muller-Graff, 'The legal bases of the third pillar and its position in the framework of the Union Treaty' (1994) 29 *Common Market Law Review* 493.

6 Art K.3(2)(c), original TEU. No jurisdiction was possible as regards other third-pillar measures.

Court was given jurisdiction over two civil law Conventions concluded during this period, but Member States could not agree on a common approach as regards criminal law and policing Conventions. Instead, by way of compromise, they agreed on a multi-speed approach, by which Member States could opt to give the Court of Justice jurisdiction over references from all national courts, or from final courts only, or from no national courts at all.[7] As for the European Parliament (EP), it did not even have the right to be consulted on individual measures (even Conventions), but only the right to be 'regularly inform[ed]' of discussions and 'consult[ed]' by the Member State holding the rotating Council presidency on the 'principal aspects' of discussions.[8] The Commission had to share the right of initiative with individual Member States.

While the intergovernmental approach certainly preserved maximum control for Member States' governments, it arguably imposed significant limits on the effectiveness of EU action. Of the eight policing and criminal law conventions agreed during the Maastricht period, only six entered in force – and it took between four and 11 years to ratify these measures.[9] The legal effect of measures besides Conventions was unclear, and soft law was widely used instead, in particular as regards immigration and asylum law (except for the Dublin Convention on responsibility for asylum-seekers, which had been signed before the Maastricht Treaty anyway).

However, cooperation within the Schengen framework proved more effective during this period, despite sharing the intergovernmental approach, perhaps because it involved a more limited number of Member States that had agreed on the fundamental aspects of the cooperation concerned. The 1990 Schengen Convention was applied from March 1995, expanded to include more States, and implemented by means of a number of measures.

2.3 1999–2005

The next period, the initial 'Amsterdam era' (from the entry into force of the Treaty of Amsterdam to 2004–2005), could best be described as 'modified intergovernmentalism', as it retained the key features of the intergovernmental approach with some modest concessions to the Community method. First of all, the Treaty of Amsterdam transferred the issues of immigration and asylum law to the first pillar (Community law), in order to make use of the Community legal order, subject to special transitional rules.[10] But the rule of the Court of Justice was curtailed as regards references from national courts, with only final courts in each Member State able to send questions to the Court. In effect, these issues were still subject in the *political* sense to an intergovernmental regime.

7 See S. Peers, 'Who's judging the watchmen? The judicial system of the area of freedom, security and justice' (2000) 18 *YEL* 337.

8 Art K.6, original TEU.

9 For details see Peers, 'EU justice and home affairs law (non-civil)'.

10 Arts 67 and 68 EC.

The issues remaining in the third pillar (policing and criminal law) were subjected to even fewer elements of the Community legal order. The Commission gained a purely joint right of initiative with Member States, and the EP gained consultation power over nearly every measure,[11] but this was still a very limited role as compared to EC law. The jurisdiction of the Court of Justice was now subject to standard rules, which in effect entrenched the 'variable geometry' approach already agreed as regards the Court's jurisdiction before the Treaty of Amsterdam (as discussed above). There were new types of legal instruments in this area:[12] Framework Decisions, to be used to approximate national law, with exactly the same definition as a Directive, while ruling out direct effect; and Decisions, to be used for any other purpose other than approximation of national law, while again ruling out direct effect. In practice, these became the main form of EU criminal and policing law, with the use of Conventions and Protocols phased out.

Another key development was the integration of Schengen *acquis* (i.e., the Schengen Conventions and the measures implementing them) into the EU and EC legal order, while allowing the UK and Ireland to opt out of these rules in full or part.[13] Also, the UK, Ireland and Denmark were given a more general power to opt out of all EC immigration, asylum and civil law legislation. There was an underlying trade-off: the UK, Ireland and Denmark were willing to accept the expansion of the EC's role in this field if they could be exempted from the automatic application of it.

2.4 2005–2009

At the mid-point in the Amsterdam period (which lasted from 1999 to 2009), in approximately 2004–2005, a number of developments altered the institutional framework as regards EU JHA law, so that the remaining period might almost be considered a 'residual intergovernmental' period.

In the area of immigration and asylum law, the initial five-year transitional period came to an end on 1 May 2004, giving the Commission its full right of initiative, and extending the co-decision procedure (with qualified majority voting, QMV) to all visa legislation.[14] Soon afterward, co-decision (including QMV) was further extended to most other issues in this field, as from the start of 2005.[15] Also, in the meantime, the Treaty of Nice, which entered into force on 1 February 2003, had amended the decision-making rules so that the decision-making rules on most asylum matters would shift to QMV

11 Arts 34 and 37, previous TEU.

12 Art 34 TEU.

13 On the Schengen integration process, see generally D. Thym, 'Schengen law: a challenge for legal accountability in the European Union' (2002) 8 *ELJ* 218; S. Peers, '*Caveat emptor*? Integrating the Schengen *Acquis* into the European Union legal order' (2000) 2 *CYELS* 87.

14 Art 67(4) EC.

15 [2004] OJ L 396/45. See S. Peers, 'Transforming decision-making on EC immigration and asylum law' (2005) 30 *ELRev* 283.

and co-decision as soon as the Council adopted EC measures 'defining the common rules and basic principles' on asylum issues.[16] These changes meant that the EP was able to have a significant influence on the adoption of most legislation in this area after this point.[17]

On the other hand, no changes were made to the jurisdiction of the Court of Justice.[18] However, also beginning in 2005, the Court began to receive references from national courts as regards EC immigration and asylum law. Although it only received 11 such references from 2005 to 2009, the Court was nevertheless thereby able to begin to influence the interpretation of EC legislation in this area.[19]

The *quid pro quo* for these developments was the strengthening in practice of the British and Irish opt-outs from this field. In particular, those Member States now opted out of most irregular migration and asylum measures,[20] whereas they had generally opted into measures in these fields adopted up until 2004–2005. This process was exacerbated by rulings of the Court of Justice that required the Council lock the UK and Ireland out of new measures that related to provisions of the Schengen *acquis* (i.e., external border control), which the UK and Ireland had not opted in to, even if the new measures did not amend that original *acquis*.[21]

As for the third pillar, from 2005 to 2009, it still remained intergovernmental in principle, but this was changing in two ways. First of all, aspects of EU criminal law and policing policy were shifting to the first pillar, as regards in particular Community competence to adopt criminal sanctions

16 Art 67(5). On the interpretation of this clause, see the judgment in Case C-133/06 *EP v Council* [2008] ECR I-3189, which implies that the rules changed at the latest from 1 December 2005, when the last of the basic EC asylum laws was adopted.

17 The EP in particular played a notable role as regards negotiations on a Schengen Borders Code (Reg 562/2006, [2006] OJ L 105/1), the EU's visa code (Reg 810/2009, [2009] OJ L 243/1), the legislation establishing the second-generation Schengen Information System, or 'SIS II' (Reg 1987/2006, [2006] OJ L 381/4), and (more controversially), the so-called 'Returns Directive' on the rules governing expulsion of third-country nationals who have stayed irregularly (Dir 2008/115, [2008] OJ L 348/98).

18 The Commission's proposal to this end was not adopted: COM(2006) 346, 28 June 2006.

19 See, for instance, the judgments in Cases: C-465/07 *Elgafaji and Elgafaji* [2009] ECR I-921; C-578/08 *Chakroun* [2010] ECR I-1839; and C-357/09 PPU *Kadzoev* [2009] ECR I-11189.

20 As regards irregular migration, both member states opted out of the Returns Directive (n 17 above) and Dir 2009/52 on employment of irregular migrants ([2009] OJ L 168/24). As regards asylum, the UK and Ireland both opted out of the proposed new Directives on qualification for international protection and international protection procedures (COM(2009) 551 and 554, 21 Oct 2009), whereas both Member States had opted in to the prior measures (Dir 2004/83, [2004] OJ L 304/12 and Dir 2005/85, [2005] OJ L 326/13). As regards legal migration, the UK opted into a Regulation on third-country nationals' social security adopted in 2003 (Reg 859/2003, [2003] OJ L 124/1), but out of a proposal to replace that Regulation in 2007 (COM(2007) 439, 23 July 2007).

21 See Cases: C-77/05 *UK v Council* [2007] ECR I-11459; C-137/05 *UK v Council* [2007] ECR I-11459; and C-482/08 *UK v Council* [2010] ECR I-10413.

and rules on cooperation between law enforcement authorities and the private sector.[22] Second, first-pillar principles began to infiltrate the third pillar, particularly as regards indirect effect, the scope of the Court's jurisdiction[23] and the autonomous interpretation of third-pillar measures.[24] The Court also endorsed the replacement of Conventions by the forms of legislative acts introduced by the Treaty of Amsterdam.[25] There was also a fairly steady number of cases referred to the Court of Justice from national courts in this area.

2.5 *Treaty of Lisbon*

Finally, with the Treaty of Lisbon we see, at least at first sight, the triumph of the Community method in this area, with QMV and the ordinary legislative procedure (ex-co-decision) extended to legal migration[26] and most criminal law and policing issues;[27] the ordinary legislative procedure applied to the issues of visa lists and visa formats; full jurisdiction for the Court of Justice in all JHA areas;[28] the application of the usual legal

22 Cases C-170/03 *Commission v Council* [2005] ECR I-7879, C-440/05 *Commission v Council* [2007] ECR I-9097, and C-301/06 *Ireland v EP and Council* [2009] ECR I-593, although see Joined Cases C-317/04 and C-318/04 *EP v Council and Commission* [2006] ECR I-4721. In light of these rulings, the Council and EP adopted legislation exercising the EC's criminal law competence: Dirs 2008/99 on environmental crime ([2008] OJ L 328/28), 2009/123 on shipping pollution ([2009] OJ L 280/52), 2009/52 on employer sanctions for hiring irregular migrants (n 20 above). On these developments, see: E. Herlin-Karnell, 'Commission v council: some reflections on criminal law in the first pillar' (2007) 13 *EPL* 69; S. White, 'Harmonisation of criminal law under the first pillar' (2006) 31 *ELRev* 81; S. Peers, 'The community's criminal law competence: the plot thickens' (2008) 33 *ELRev* 399.

23 See respectively Cases **C-105/03 *Pupino* [2005] ECR I-5285 and** C-355/04 P *SEGI* [2007] ECR I-1657, and discussion in S. Peers, 'Salvation outside the church: judicial protection in the third pillar after the *Pupino* and *SEGI* judgments' (2007) 44 *Common Market Law Review* 883.

24 Case **C-66/08 *Koslowski* [2008] ECR I-6041; see earlier Joined Cases C-187/01 and C-345/01** *Gözütok and Brugge* [2003] ECR I-1345, on the interpretation of provisions of the Schengen *acquis* after their integration into the EU legal order.

25 Case C-303/05 *Advocaten voor de Wereld* [2007] ECR I-3633. Following this judgment, the Council replaced the Europol Convention and the Customs Information System Convention, and associated Protocols, with third-pillar Decisions ([2009] OJ L 121/37 and [2009] OJ L 323/20).

26 Arts 77–80 TFEU, in particular Art 79. Note, however, the requirement for unanimity and consultation of the EP as regards passports (Art 77(3) TFEU).

27 Arts 82–89 TFEU. The exceptions concern the European Public Prosecutor (Art 86) and police operations (Arts 87(3) and 89). Note also the 'emergency brake' procedure for some other aspects of criminal law (Arts 82(2) and 83).

28 Except for a limited restriction on jurisdiction as regards law enforcement issues: see Art 276 TFEU.

instruments (i.e., Regulations and Directives) to policing and criminal law matters; and the extensive revision of most competences in this area, particularly as regards immigration, asylum, and criminal law.[29] However, the application of the full Community method to policing and criminal law is limited by the continued possibility for a group of Member States to table initiatives to rival the Commission, although this possibility has rarely been invoked in practice.[30] There was also a five-year transitional period regarding the Court's jurisdiction over third-pillar measures adopted before the entry into force of the Treaty of Lisbon, although this expired in December 2014.[31]

In general, the initial impact of the amendments was a nearly complete application of the Community method in practice, unblocking discussions on measures where there had been a veto in Council, increasing the influence of the European Parliament over legislation, and enlarging the number of cases on immigration, asylum and civil law issues reaching the Court of Justice.[32]

Again, the Member States with misgivings about this change in the legal framework were bought off by opt-outs, this time extending to policing and criminal law matters.[33] In practice, the UK and Ireland have increasingly opted out of post-Lisbon JHA proposals.

3 Policy evolution

To what extent has EU JHA *policy* evolved over the years? This question will be assessed as regards five different policy areas in turn (visas/borders, asylum, irregular migration, legal migration and criminal law), by examining main trends in the development of those particular policy areas throughout the time periods (pre-Maastricht, Maastricht, early Amsterdam, late Amsterdam and post-Lisbon) discussed above.

29 Note in particular the limitation on the EU's immigration powers, as regards volumes of economic migrants coming from non-EU countries (Art 79(5) TFEU).

30 Art 76 TFEU. The provision was applied several times in the first six months after the Treaty of Lisbon entered into force: see the Member States' initiatives for Directives on the right to interpretation and translation in the framework of criminal proceedings ([2010] OJ C 69/1), on a European protection order ([2010] C 69/5), and for a European investigation order ([2010] OJ C 165/22). It has been invoked only once since, as regards the European Police College: [2014] OJ C 361/4.

31 Art 10 of the transitional protocol attached to the Treaty. For analysis, see S. Peers, 'Finally "fit for purpose?" The Treaty of Lisbon and the end of the third pillar legal order' (2008) 27 *Yearbook of European Law* 47.

32 For details, see S. Peers, 'Mission accomplished? EU justice and home affairs law after the Treaty of Lisbon' (2011) 48 *Common Market Law Review* 661.

33 For analysis, see S. Peers, 'In a world of their own? Justice and Home Affairs opt-outs and the Treaty of Lisbon' (2008–2009) 10 *CYELS* 383.

3.1 Visas and border controls

3.1.1 Prior to 1993

During the pre-Maastricht period, the focus was on the negotiation of the original 1985 Schengen Agreement and the 1990 Convention implementing that Agreement. The relevant provisions of the Schengen Convention clearly follow a customs union model, as applied to the free movement of goods by the EU (inter alia), consisting of a set of common controls at the external borders,[34] abolition of internal frontiers (a concept borrowed from the EU's internal market)[35] and freedom to travel for a three-month period between the participating States for those who are legally visiting or legally resident.[36] Notably, this model was endorsed by the Court of Justice, which took the view that the checks at internal borders could not be abolished until inter alia, common external border checks were established,[37] and that the simple rule of mutual recognition of other Member States' refusal decisions (established by the Schengen Information System, SIS) was acceptable, even (implicitly) without any harmonisation of the grounds for issuing SIS alerts for the refusal of entry.[38]

3.1.2 1993–1999

In the Maastricht period, the main focus in this area was applying and implementing the Schengen rules, after the application of the Convention as from March 1995. There was limited EU activity, due to the resistance of the UK to participate in this area. The EU's initial visa (black)list legislation was based on the Schengen list, with certain Commonwealth states removed due to UK opposition,[39] and attempts to agree an External Borders Convention with the UK's participation were unsuccessful.[40]

34 Arts 3–8 of the Schengen Convention (note 4 above), complemented by Arts 9–17 regarding visa policy.

35 Art 2 of the Convention (ibid.).

36 Arts 19–22 of the Convention (ibid.), known in practice as 'freedom to travel'. Compare to the internal free circulation of third-country goods in Art 29 TFEU (ex-Art 24 EC). See the comparison between the external and internal aspects of the various free movement regimes in S. Peers, 'EU Borders and Globalisation' in K. Groenendijk, E. Guild and P. Minderhoud (eds.), *In Search of Europe's Borders* (Kluwer, 2003), 45.

37 Case C-378/97 *Wijsenbeek* [1999] ECR I-6207.

38 Case C-503/03 *Commission v Spain* [2006] ECR I-1097. However, this judgment did establish limits as regards the application of the SIS where the free movement rights of EU citizens' third-country national family members were concerned.

39 Reg 2317/95, [1995] OJ L 234/1. See generally K. Hailbronner, 'Visa regulations and third-country nationals in EC law' (1994) 31 *Common Market Law Review* 969–995.

40 COM(93) 684, 10 Dec 1994 ([1994] OJ C 11/15).

3.1.3 1999–2009

Next, there was a modest uptake in activity during the early Amsterdam period, likely facilitated by the removal of Member States with objections to this policy from participation within it. The EU fully harmonised its visa lists as from 2001,[41] taking as a basis the high degree of Schengen harmonisation accomplished by 1998 and beginning to develop a distinctive EU policy in this area, putting one State on the EU blacklist due to concerns about security and irregular migration,[42] but putting other States on the EU whitelist due to enlargement policy, or in return for commitments relating to irregular migration.[43] At this point, the EU also began to develop a policy on visa reciprocity, i.e., expecting States on the whitelist to waive visa requirements for nationals of all Schengen States.[44]

There were more significant changes during the late Amsterdam period, after the application of QMV and co-decision to this entire policy area in 2004–2005. At this point, the Schengen rules concerning visas, border controls and the SIS were entirely replaced by EU legislation,[45] which established streamlined rules with a clearer legal status, also enhancing (as noted above) procedural rights and data protection rights.[46] An EC agency was created to assist Member States to manage the external borders (Frontex),[47] and a further agency was proposed to manage the EU's JHA databases, including SIS II.[48] The legislation to establish the Visa Information System (VIS), a database containing information on all visa applicants for use in particular by national consulates, was adopted in 2008,[49] and further uniformity of visa policy was established by means of a visa code.[50] Uniform EU rules on local border traffic treaties with neighbouring non-Member States were also drawn up.[51]

41 Reg 539/2001 ([2001] OJ L 81/1).

42 Colombia, which had previously been the one State on the 'greylist', i.e., about which Schengen States could not agree.

43 These States were Romania and Bulgaria, plus the entities of Hong Kong and Macao.

44 See the original Art 1(4), Reg 539/2001 (note 41 above).

45 See the legislation establishing the Schengen Borders Code, the visa code, and SIS II (note 17 above).

46 For example, individuals must be told about, and told the reason for, a refusal to issue a visa or a refusal to permit entry at the external border, and also have the right to information if they are listed in SIS II. They then have the right to appeal against such refusals or listings.

47 Reg 2007/2004 ([2004] OJ L 349/1), as amended by Reg 863/2007 ([2007] OJ L 199/30).

48 See the proposed Regulation establishing an agency to manage VIS, SIS II, and Eurodac, adopted after the entry into force of the Treaty of Lisbon: Reg 1077/2011 ([2011] OJ L 286/1).

49 Reg 767/2008 ([2008] OJ L 218/60).

50 Reg 810/2009 ([2009] OJ L 243/1).

51 Reg 1931/2006 ([2006] OJ L 405/1).

EU visa list legislation was also amended during this period to ensure greater uniformity as regards the exceptions from visa requirements and as regards quasi-British citizens.[52] The external aspect of the policy was developed by offering visa facilitation agreements (mostly) to neighbouring countries, in return for readmission agreements. These treaties reduced visa fees and simplified and sped up the issue of visas to the nationals of the countries concerned.[53] For Western Balkan States, and in future for Russia and other eastern neighbours, the EU went further and established visa liberalisation roadmaps that offered visa abolition in return for extensive policy commitments as regards managing migration and internal security.[54]

3.1.4 After 2009

Since the entry into force of the Treaty of Lisbon, EU visa and borders policy has been pulled in different directions. The full roll-out of the Visa Information System has been counterbalanced by more liberal visa policies, waiving visa requirements for a number of neighbouring and other middle-income countries in the interests of foreign policy, tourism or trade,[55] and proposing reforms of the EU visa code to the same effect.[56] Concerns about control of external borders have manifested in increased powers for Frontex,[57] and proposals for an entry–exit system.[58] The initial impact of the Arab Spring was an increase in the possibility for reimposing checks at the internal borders.[59]

The impact of increased levels of immigration in 2015 has shaken the Schengen system fundamentally, with many Member States reimposing checks at internal borders to stem the numbers of potential asylum-seekers reaching their territory. To address these concerns (and parallel fears about terrorism) the Commission has proposed additional checks at the external borders (including regular security checks on EU citizens) and the transformation of Frontex into an EU Border Guard,[60] and has raised the prospect

52 Reg 1932/2006 ([2006] OJ L 405/23).
53 See, for instance, the agreement with Ukraine: [2007] OJ L **332/66.**
54 See Reg 1244/2009 abolishing visa requirements as regards several Western Balkans States ([2009] OJ L 336/1).
55 See Regs 1091/2010 ([2010] OJ L 329/1), 1211/2010 ([2010] OJ L 339/6), 1289/2013 ([2013] OJ L 347/74), 259/2014 ([2014] OJ L 105/9) and 509/2014 ([2014] OJ L 149/67).
56 COM(2014) 164, 1 April 2014. See also the proposed touring visa Reg (COM(2014) 165, 1 April 2014).
57 Reg 1168/2011 amending Reg 2007/2004 establishing Frontex ([2011] OJ L 304/1).
58 COM(2013) 95, 27 February 2013; amended by COM(2016) 194, 6 April 2016.
59 Reg 1051/2013 amending borders code ([2013] OJ L 295/1); see also Reg 1052/2013 establishing Eurosur ([2013] OJ L 295/11).
60 COM(2015) 668 and 670, 15 December 2015.

of the reimposition of border checks for up to two years across many internal borders.[61]

Overall, before the migration crisis, which escalated in 2015 and is ongoing, the basic customs union model taken over from the Schengen framework was not fundamentally altered, but rather further refined, in order to establish greater uniformity as regards the outside world (the visa list policy, treaties on visa waivers, visa liberalisation and border traffic) and further free circulation within the EU (by means of enlarging the Schengen area as well as the categories of people who benefit from freedom to travel).[62] But the crisis has exposed the underlying differences between a customs union and an area of the free movement of persons, once the latter becomes subject to a perceived security and migration control deficit. It remains to be seen whether the attempts to address those concerns – which also relate to changes in asylum policy, discussed below – will be sufficient to save the central elements of the Schengen system.

3.2 *Asylum*

3.2.1 *Prior to 1999*

During the initial intergovernmental period, the Member States focused on the issue of asylum responsibility, adopting the Dublin Convention on this issue and adopting a small amount of soft law, starting out with Resolutions of Member States on perceived abuse of asylum procedures,[63] continuing (after the original TEU entered into force) with Council Resolutions or Joint Positions on aspects of asylum law.[64]

3.2.2 *1999–2009*

During the 'Amsterdam era', the orientation of EU asylum policy was changed significantly, first of all when the Tampere programme stipulated that the EU would establish a 'Common European Asylum System' (CEAS) in two phases.[65]

The first phase of legislation to establish the CEAS was proposed from 2000 to 2001 and adopted, after great political difficulty, between 2003 and

61 For details see COM(2016) 120, 4 March 2016.

62 Reg 265/2010 on long-stay visas ([2010] OJ L 85/1).

63 Unpublished in the OJ; see T. Bunyan, *Key Texts on Justice and Home Affairs in the European Union, Volume I* (Statewatch, 1997), 64 and 66; E. Guild and J. Niessen, *The Emerging Immigration and Asylum Law of the European Union: Adopted Conventions, Resolutions, Recommendations, Decisions and Conclusions* (Kluwer, 1996), 141, 161 and 177.

64 Resolution on asylum procedures ([1996] OJ C 274/13) and Joint Position on the definition of refugees ([1996] OJ L 63/2).

65 See generally H. Battjes, *European Asylum Law and International Law* (Martinus Nijhoff, 2006).

2005, at which point the decision-making rules shifted entirely to QMV and co-decision.[66] These measures – which especially comprised Directives on reception conditions for asylum-seekers, procedural rules in asylum cases and the definition and content of refugee and subsidiary protection status,[67] in parallel with further measures on asylum responsibility (which did not alter the fundamental precepts of the Dublin Convention)[68] – were widely criticised for setting low standards.[69] Nonetheless, in principle, the legislation concerned covered most of the subject-matter of asylum law.

3.2.3 After 2009

With the entry into force of the Treaty of Lisbon, there was a significant change in the EU's competence, providing now for the adopting of measures fully harmonising the law and enshrining the Tampere principles (i.e., creation of a Common European Asylum System and a uniform status valid throughout the Union) into the binding text of the Treaty. The second phase of the Common European Asylum System was ultimately established by legislation adopted between 2011 and 2013, which provides for a wider scope for EU asylum legislation, a greater degree of uniformity, significantly higher standards and the creation of an asylum support agency, the European Asylum Support Office.[70]

It is striking that although the initial model of an exclusive focus on asylum responsibility criteria was discarded in favour of a broader harmonisation agenda, nevertheless the rationale of 'preventing secondary movements' (i.e., the movement of asylum-seekers between Member States) remained at least one rationale for the adoption of the harmonisation measures, based on the assumption that one factor driving secondary movements was disparate treatment of asylum-seekers as regards substantive law, reception conditions and procedural rules. The underlying logic of the policy development was therefore still connected to *movement between Member States*, albeit the objective was to *deter or reduce* such movement, rather than *facilitate* it, as is the case with the visa and borders policies, and the EU internal market generally. Needless to say, the objective of reducing such movements at the same time

66 See Art 67(5) EC and Case C-133/06 (note 16 above).

67 Directives 2003/9 ([2003] OJ L 31/18), 2005/85 ([2005] OJ L 326/13), and 2004/83 ([2004] OJ L 304/12).

68 Regulation 343/2003, replacing the Dublin rules ([2003] OJ L 50/1; the 'Dublin II Regulation'), and Regulation 2725/2000 ([2000] OJ L 316/1), creating Eurodac, a system for the comparison of asylum-seekers' fingerprints, operational in 2003 ([2003] OJ C 5/2).

69 See, for instance, the ECRE position papers, online at: www.ecre.org/topics/ecre_agenda_for_europe (accessed 30 May 2016).

70 Dir 2011/95 ([2011] OJ L 343/11); Dirs 2013/32 and 33 ([2013] OJ L 180/60 and 96; Regs 603 and 604/ 2013 ([2013] OJ L 180/1 and 31); and Reg 439/2010 ([2010] OJ L 132/11. For a full account of recent EU developments in relation to asylum-seekers see Costello and Mouzourakis in this collection (Chapter 11).

as abolishing border controls between most Member States proved relatively futile, and the statistics showed only a modest increase in the low percentage of the asylum-seekers who were subject to the Dublin rules during the first phase of the CEAS.[71] The development of the Dublin rules was linked to the parallel strengthening of external border controls in that the Eurodac system requires Member States to take and transmit to the central database the fingerprints of all irregular migrants stopped at the external borders, because it is possible that such persons will subsequently apply for asylum in another Member State and the Dublin rules make the Member State that the person concerned entered irregularly responsible in most circumstances. But the number of persons fingerprinted due to irregular border crossing was at first very low, although it has gradually risen.[72]

The migration crisis of 2015–2016 led to an incoherent response from Member States, some aiming to prevent entry onto their territory while others welcomed it. The main response from the EU has been a commitment to relocate large numbers of people from the territory of Greece;[73] this has proved ineffective in practice. So the EU activated an alternative plan, aiming to return the vast majority of people to Turkey despite doubts about the effectiveness of this plan, or its compatibility with EU or human rights law.[74] The Commission has now promised (in effect) a third phase of the Common European Asylum System,[75] consisting of: reforms to the Dublin rules along the lines of the unsuccessful relocation regime; deterring secondary movement with harsh punishments; and lowering standards in the hope that fewer people will want to come to the EU at all. Time will tell whether the removals to Turkey and the latest plans (if implemented) will be effective or upheld by the courts.

3.3 *Irregular migration*

3.3.1 *Prior to 1999*

During the initial intergovernmental period, the EU's measures in this area consisted almost entirely of soft law,[76] except for a few provisions of the

71 COM(2007) 299 and SEC (2007) 742, 6 June 2007.

72 See the annual reports on Eurodac, starting with SEC (2004) 557, 5 May 2004 (for 2003).

73 Decisions 2015/1523 ([2015] OJ L 239/146) and 2015/1601 ([2015] OJ L 248/80).

74 EU–Turkey statement, 18 Mar 2016.

75 COM(2016) 197, 6 April 2016.

76 Recommendation of Immigration Ministers on 30 November/1 December 2002 on the main aspects of irregular migration policy (SN 4678/92, WGI 1266, 16 November 1992), published in Guild and Niessen, *The Emerging Immigration and Asylum Law of the European Union*, and in Bunyan, *Key Texts on Justice and Home Affairs*; Recommendation of Immigration Ministers on 1–2 June 2003 on in-country detection of irregular migration and irregular employment (SN 3017/93, WGI 1516, 25 May 1993, published in ibid.; see also [1996] OJ C 5/1 and [1996] OJ C 304/1); Recommendations on expulsion ([1996] OJ C 5/3, 5, and 7); Recommendations on a standard travel document (or laissez-passer) for use

Schengen Convention on carrier sanctions and facilitation of irregular entry and residence,[77] and a Decision on monitoring the implementation of some of the soft law.[78]

3.3.2 1999–2009

Originally, for the first few years following the entry into force of the Treaty of Amsterdam, the measures in this area were rather piecemeal. A first set of Directives building upon the Schengen *acquis* as regards carrier sanctions, facilitation of irregular entry and residence, and mutual recognition of expulsion decisions were all adopted by the Council by 2001–2002.[79] So was a Framework Decision on the criminal law aspects of trafficking in persons, replacing a pre-Amsterdam Joint Action on the same topic.[80] The Commission and Council then tried to elaborate a coherent policy in this field,[81] and subsequently adopted a number of specific measures: for instance, concerning pre-entry control (a Regulation on a network of immigration liaison officers and a Directive on the exchange of passenger data);[82] control on the territory (a Directive on the legal status of victims of trafficking in persons);[83] aspects of expulsion (a Directive on assistance for expulsions via air transit;[84] a Decision on financing expulsion measures;[85] and a Decision on joint expulsion flights);[86] along with measures on administrative cooperation measures (a Decision establishing an information and coordination network for Member States' migration management services).[87] The development of

in individual expulsions ([1996] OJ C 274/20), a standard bilateral readmission agreement ([1996] OJ C 274/21), and principles to be included in protocols to readmission agreements ([1996] OJ C 274/25); and Council Conclusions of 30 November 2004 on CIREFI ([1996] OJ C 274/50).

77 Arts 23, 24, 26 and 27 of the Convention (note 4 above). Of course the provisions of the Convention dealing with borders, visas and the SIS to some extent also aimed to prevent irregular migration.

78 [1996] OJ L 342/5.

79 Directives 2001/51 ([2001] OJ L 187/45), 2002/90 ([2002] OJ L 328/17, along with a Framework Decision on the criminal law aspects: [2002] OJ L 328/1), and 2001/40 ([2001] OJ L 149/34).

80 [2002] OJ L 203/1.

81 Commission Communication on irregular migration (**COM(2001) 672, 15 November 2001**), followed by a Council action plan ([2002] OJ C 142/23); Commission Green Paper on return policy (**COM(2002) 175, 10 April 2002, followed by Communication on the same topic: COM(2002) 564, 14 October 2002**), followed by a Council action plan (Council doc 14673/02, 25 November 2002). See also the subsequent reports on the development of the policy: **COM(2003) 323, 3 June 2003; SEC (2004) 1349, 25 October 2004; SEC (2006) 1010, 19 July 2006; and SEC (2009) 320, 9 March 2009.**

82 Reg 377/2004 ([2004] OJ L 64/1) and Dir 2004/82 ([2004] OJ L 261/24).

83 Dir 2004/81 ([2004] OJ L 261/19).

84 Dir 2003/110 ([2003] OJ L 321/26).

85 [2004] OJ L 60/55.

86 [2004] OJ L 261/28.

87 [2005] OJ L 83/48.

the SIS and other border control and visa measures were also intended to contribute to the control of irregular migration.

On the external front, the EU also developed a policy of agreeing bilateral readmission agreements, both to clarify aspects of the process of identifying returning nationals of the third States concerned, and in order to oblige each of those third States to take back persons who have merely transited through their territory. The EU ran into difficulty incentivising third States to sign agreements that were essentially solely in the EU's interest, but managed to overcome that difficulty in most cases by offering parallel visa facilitation agreements (with Balkan and ex-Soviet neighbours), visa waivers (for Hong Kong and Macao), anti-terrorist measures (for Sri Lanka) or money (for Pakistan). The EU also concluded Protocols to the UN Convention on organised crime, concerning smuggling and trafficking in persons.

After 2005, the EU adopted fewer but more wide-ranging measures in this area, notably the Returns Directive (which addresses the issues of detention of irregular migrants, expulsion procedures and treatment pending expulsion), and a Directive on employer sanctions for employment of irregular migrants, aiming to reduce the incentive (or 'pull') effect for irregular migrants to enter and stay in the EU.[88]

3.3.3 After 2009

There have been no significant legislative developments in this field since the Treaty of Lisbon. The biggest impact has been the case law of the CJEU on the EU's Returns Directive, which has focused on the underlying objective of removing irregular migrants from EU territory as effectively as possible. In some cases, this has meant more favourable treatment for the persons concerned, because the CJEU has ruled that detaining irregular migrants on the basis of criminal law delays their removal.[89] But in other cases, it has meant a ceiling being placed on more favourable treatment, because the Court found that failure to enforce removal was a breach of the Directive. In some cases, paradoxically, the Directive has been used to ground a right to stay for individuals. Therefore, despite the absence of any formal codification of the law, the CJEU's approach points toward a fuller harmonisation of standards.

3.4 Legal migration

3.4.1 Prior to 1999

During the initial intergovernmental period, only soft law was adopted on this topic, on the various categories of legal migrants (family reunion,

88 Dirs 2008/115 and 2009/52, notes 17 and 20 above.

89 On the Directive, see generally S. Peers, 'Irregular migrants: can humane treatment be balanced against efficient removal?' (2015) 16 *EJML* 289.

employment, self-employment, students) and on the status of long-term residents.[90] A Decision on follow-up was also adopted. However, a far-reaching proposal for a Convention on migration was not agreed by the Council.[91]

3.4.2 1999–2009

The Tampere programme set a broad agenda for harmonisation of legal migration policy, and established a principle of 'fair' treatment of legally resident third-country nationals, with equal treatment 'as far as possible'. However, it proved difficult to put these principles into practice during the initial period of EC competence (from 1999 to 2004), with key legislation proving difficult to negotiate and setting relatively low standards when agreed.[92] Moreover, it was entirely impossible to reach agreement on the issue of labour migration during this period.[93]

After 2005, even though there was no change to the decision-making rules applicable (i.e., unanimity still remained), it proved possible to relaunch attempts to adopt measures on labour migration,[94] with some degree of success as regards legislation on favoured categories of migrants (researchers and the highly skilled, the latter being the subject of the 'Blue Card'

90 For the Ministers' Resolution on family reunion, see SN 2828/1/93, not published in the Official Journal; see Guild and Niessen, *The Emerging Immigration and Asylum Law of the European Union*, 250–257. For the other Resolutions, see [1996] OJ C 274 and [1996] OJ C 80/2. See also the Resolutions on marriages of convenience ([1997] OJ C 382/1) and unaccompanied minors ([1997] OJ C 221/23) and the Decision on monitoring implementation ([1997] OJ C 11/1). For discussion, see M. Hedemann-Robinson, 'Third-country nationals, European Union citizenship and free movement of persons: a time for bridges rather than divisions?' (1996) 16 *YEL* 321; S. Peers, 'Building Fortress Europe: the development of EU migration law', (1998) 35 *Common Market Law Review* 1235.

91 COM(97) 387, 30 July 1997; [1997] OJ C 337/9. For more on the proposed Convention, see M. Hedemann-Robinson, 'From object to subject? Non-EC nationals and the draft proposal of the Commission for a Council Act establishing the rules for admission of third-country nationals to the Member States' (1998) 18 *YEL* 289.

92 In particular, see Directive 2003/86 on family reunion ([2003] OJ L 251/12), which was the subject of a challenge from the EP for setting standards that fell below minimum levels of human rights protection on several points (Case C-540/03 *EP v Council* [2006] ECR I-5769). See also Directive 2003/109 on long-term residents' rights ([2004] OJ L 16/44), which left Member States many options to restrict the equal treatment of long-term residents or to limit their movement between Member States, and Directive 2004/114 on admission of students and other non-economic migrants ([2004] OJ L 375/12), which is only optional for Member States as regards the three categories of persons other than students (school pupils, unpaid trainees and volunteers). See also Regulations 1030/2002 ([2002] OJ L 157/1) on residence permit formats and 859/2003 ([2003] OJ L 124/1) on social security equality for third-country nationals who move within the EU.

93 The wide-ranging Commission proposal on this issue (COM(2001) 386, 11 July 2001) was only discussed a few times in the Council's working parties.

94 See the Green Paper (COM(2004) 811, 11 January 2005) and policy plan (COM(2005) 669, 21 December 2005) on labour migration.

Directive).[95] But even here, the degree of harmonisation was limited, with Member States free to maintain or introduce parallel regimes as regards the admission of highly skilled workers.[96] Also, it became clear in the limited number of cases reaching the CJEU that the Court was inclined to raise the standards in this legislation by means of its interpretation.[97]

On the other hand, the unanimity requirement still limited attempts to further develop EU policy in this field. In particular, before the entry into force of the Treaty of Lisbon, it was impossible to agree legislation on a single permit and equal treatment for third-country national workers in general, or the extension of the long-term residents' legislation to include refugees and beneficiaries of subsidiary protection, or application of the new rules on social security to third-country national workers.[98]

3.4.3 After 2009

There has been a noticeable shift in EU policy since the entry into force of the Treaty of Lisbon, entailing the shift to QMV and the ordinary legislative procedure, as well as the redefinition of EU competence to include the development of a common migration policy. The exceptions to equal treatment in social security have been removed:[99] the long-term residents' Directive has been extended in scope;[100] Directives on a single permit and workers' equal treatment, seasonal workers and intra-corporate transferees have been adopted;[101] and a major reform of the Directives on students and researchers has been agreed.[102]

While EU immigration law originally followed a 'social policy' model of setting minimum standards, it has increasingly diverged from that model. First of all, the EU's immigration legislation increasingly has a free movement element, setting out specific rules governing the secondary movement of the relevant categories of third-country nationals between Member States.[103]

95 Dirs 2005/71 ([2005] OJ L 289/15) and 2009/50 ([2009] OJ L 155/17).
96 Art 3(4), Dir 2009/50 (ibid.).
97 In Case C-540/03 (note 92 above), the Court emphasised that Member States applying the impugned exceptions to the family reunion Directive could only apply those exceptions on a case-by-case basis, rather than rejecting all applications that fell within the scope of these exceptions automatically. In *Chakroun* (note 19 above), the Court interpreted the 'social assistance' condition for authorising family reunion narrowly.
98 See respectively: COM(2007) 638, 23 Oct 2007; COM(2007) 298, 6 June 2008; and COM(2007) 439, 23 July 2007.
99 Reg 1231/2010 ([2010] OJ L 344/1).
100 Directive 2011/51 applying the long-term residents' Directive to refugees and beneficiaries of subsidiary protection ([2011] OJ L 132/1).
101 Directives 2011/98 ([2011] OJ L 343/1), 2014/36 ([2014] OJ L 94/375) and 2014/66 ([2014] OJ L 157/1).
102 Directive 2016/801 ([2016] OJ L132/21).
103 See, for instance, Arts 14–23 of the long-term residents' Directive (note 92 above); Arts 18–19 of the Blue Card Directive (note 95 above); Art 8 of the students' Directive (note 92 above); and Art 13 of the researchers' Directive (note 95 above).

Second, the more recent EU legislation frequently confines Member States' power to set higher standards to only specific provisions of immigration Directives.[104] These two trends bring EU immigration policy more clearly in line with an internal market model, as EU internal market law often facilitates free movement between Member States on the basis of common standards of regulation.[105]

3.5 Criminal law

3.5.1 Prior to 1999

Prior to the Treaty of Amsterdam, the field of criminal law had already been subject to a number of Conventions, agreed not ratified, during the informal intergovernmental period of JHA integration prior to 1993. There had also been modest success agreeing measures on this subject within the Schengen framework as regards extradition, mutual assistance (concerning cooperation between criminal courts, in particular the movement of evidence), *ne bis in idem* (the cross-border 'double jeopardy' rule, preventing prosecution in a second Member State after a final judgment for the same acts in a first Member State) and the transfer of prisoners.[106]

During the formal intergovernmental period (1993–1999), the Member States reached agreement on a limited number of conventions (concerning extradition, corruption, fraud and driving disqualification), plus a few Joint Actions regarding substantive criminal law (as regards drug trafficking, racism, trafficking in persons and sexual exploitation, private corruption and organised crime).[107] Overall, the results of this process were still modest, taking into account the delays in ratification of Conventions and the unclear legal effect of Joint Actions.

3.5.2 1999–2009

During the 'Amsterdam era', after the early adoption of a Convention and Protocol on mutual assistance, Conventions were eschewed in favour of Framework Decisions on criminal law matters, the use of which was ultimately bolstered by the Court of Justice as regards both their legal effect and their

104 See, for instance, Art 4(2) of the Blue Card Directive (note 95 above).

105 However, see Kostakopoulou and Ripoll Servent in this collection (Chapter 10) on the contrasting policy priorities between EU internal mobility law and EU migration law on the matter of family reunification.

106 Arts 48–69 of the Convention (note 4 above).

107 See: [1996] OJ L 185/5 (racism); [1996] OJ L 342/6 (drug trafficking); [1997] OJ L 63/2 (trafficking in persons and sexual exploitation); [1997] OJ L 167/1 (synthetic drugs); [1998] OJ L 333/1 (money-laundering); [1998] OJ L 351/1 (organised crime); and [1998] OJ L 358/2 (private corruption).

capacity to replace prior Conventions.[108] A Decision was used to establish Eurojust, the EU prosecutors' agency.[109]

As for the substance of measures in this area, the foundations were laid in 1999–2001 for the establishment of the principle of mutual recognition in criminal matters, enshrined in the Tampere programme as the central principle at the heart of EU criminal law.[110] Following the impetus of the 11 September 2001 terrorist attacks, the development of EU criminal law hit its high point between 2001 and 2004, in particular as regards the agreement on Framework Decisions on the European Arrest Warrant (EAW) and terrorism within three months of the attacks.[111]

The EAW proved to be the template for the adoption of a number of other mutual recognition measures, each setting out the principle that Member States must recognise the decisions of another Member State's criminal authorities as regards a particular matter, subject to a limited number of grounds for refusal, detailed rules on procedures (such as time limits and standard forms) and vague provisions on human rights. Compared to the measures that they replaced (in most cases, existing Council of Europe Conventions), the EU measures contained fewer grounds for refusal, in particular obliging Member States to surrender their own nationals pursuant to an EAW (replacing the traditional possibility for Member States to refuse to extradite their own nationals, enshrined in many Member States' constitutions)[112] and abolishing, for a lengthy list of crimes, the principle of 'dual criminality', i.e., the principle that judicial cooperation could usually only take place where the act in question was criminal in both States concerned.

This was followed in short order by Framework Decisions on the freezing of assets and evidence in 2003 and on the recognition of non-custodial criminal judgments in 2005.[113] However, the traditional reserve of Member States concerning these matters, in part as a consequence of national constitutional challenges to the EAW, was already reasserting itself: the second of

108 See *Pupino* and *Advocaten voor de Wereld* (notes 23 and 25 above) and see Weyembergh and Armada in this collection (Chapter 5).

109 [2002] OJ L 63, as amended by [2003] OJ L 245/44 and by [2009] OJ L 138/14.

110 See the Council work programme on mutual recognition ([2001] OJ C 12/10), the earlier Commission communication on the issue (COM(2000) 495, 26 July 2000) and discussion of the development of the principle in S. Peers, 'Mutual recognition and criminal law in the European Union: has the Council got it wrong?', (2004) 41 *Common Market Law Review* 5 at 7–10.

111 The measures were formally adopted in 2002: [2002] OJ L 190/1 and [2002] OJ L 164/3. Contrary to a widespread 'Euromyth', neither measure was even under discussion before 11 September 2001; rather the Commission brought forward the release of its planned proposals on these matters to the end of September 2001. The agreement on these measures within ten weeks is therefore even more impressive.

112 See E. Guild and L. Marin, *Still Not Resolved? Constitutional Issues of the European Arrest Warrant* (Wolf, 2009).

113 [2003] OJ L 196/45 and [2005] OJ L 76/16.

these measures took longer to negotiate and then its adoption was subject to a lengthy delay due to national parliamentary scrutiny. And while the national implementation of the EAW in practice has been judged a success,[114] the implementation of these later two measures has been judged disappointing.[115]

This slowdown continued over the period from 2005 to 2009, resulting in further lengthy negotiations and delays due to parliamentary scrutiny (and in many cases, extended transposition periods) as regards a further batch of mutual recognition measures: Framework Decisions on the recognition of confiscation orders,[116] the transfer of custodial sentences,[117] probation and parole,[118] the European Evidence Warrant[119] and pre-trial supervision orders.[120] Member States also insisted on watering down the abolition of the dual criminality principle in many of these measures, and retaining a number of other grounds for refusal, resulting in a complex patchwork of legal requirements, although as regards one issue (the rules regarding *in absentia* trials) standard provisions were later agreed for all the relevant measures.[121] There were also closely connected measures on the recognition of other Member States' criminal convictions,[122] and the transfer of criminal records information between Member States.[123]

As regards the related issue of conflicts of jurisdiction, there was great difficulty agreeing on anything at all, with a failure to agree on proposed Framework Decisions updating the double jeopardy rules or regulating the transfer of criminal proceedings,[124] and adoption only of a very weak measure on information and consultation as regards possible conflicts of jurisdiction.[125] There was an even more profound failure to adopt any measures on the high-profile issue of suspects' rights, with a proposed Framework Decision failing to be adopted despite several years of effort.[126] However, as with the issue of labour migration, this topic was relaunched by means of an alternative strategy of tackling the issue piecemeal: a 'roadmap' for tackling procedural rights on a case-by-case basis was adopted by the Council,[127] and

114 See COM(2007) 407 and SEC (2007) 979, 11 July 2007.
115 See COM(2008) 885, 22 December 2008 and COM(2008) 888, 22 December 2008.
116 [2006] OJ L 328/59.
117 [2008] OJ L 327/27.
118 [2008] OJ L 337/102.
119 [2008] OJ L 350/72.
120 [2009] OJ L 294/20.
121 Framework Decision ([2009] OJ L 81/24).
122 [2008] OJ L 220/32.
123 See initially the Decision on this issue ([2005] OJ L 322/23), and subsequently the Framework Decision and Decision ([2009] OJ L 93/23 and 33).
124 [2003] OJ C 100/24 and [2009] OJ C 219/7.
125 Framework Decision ([2009] OJ L 328/42).
126 COM(2004) 328, 28 April 2004.
127 Resolution ([2009] OJ C 295/1).

agreement was soon reached on the first measure, concerning translation and interpretation rights for criminal suspects.[128]

On the other hand, it proved much easier to agree Framework Decisions on the more populist subject of crime victims' rights,[129] and on national confiscation proceedings (the latter linked to the mutual recognition measure on the same issue).[130] Moreover, despite the limits on the Court of Justice's jurisdiction in this area, the Court began to become engaged in the particular issues of double jeopardy, the EAW and crime victims' rights.

As regards substantive criminal law, the main focus of the EU's action was the review of pre-Amsterdam Joint Actions and their replacement by Framework Decisions.[131] A number of Framework Decisions were also adopted in new areas (besides terrorism): counterfeiting the euro,[132] payment card fraud and counterfeiting,[133] the facilitation of illegal entry and residence,[134] and attacks on information systems;[135] the two adopted measures relating to environmental crime and shipping pollution were both annulled by the Court of Justice.[136] It must be pointed out that the Treaty framework only permitted the EU to establish minimum standards as regards substantive criminal law. Nevertheless, the Framework Decisions were an advance on the prior Joint Actions in particular due to their enhanced legal effect, clearer drafting and the rules on minimum penalties that Member States should impose. Towards the end of the Amsterdam era, further steps were taken; the Framework Decision on terrorism was amended to add further crimes to reflect a Council of Europe Convention.[137]

3.5.3 After 2009

Following the entry into force of the Treaty of Lisbon, there have been few new mutual recognition measures: a European Protection Order (cross-border movement of victim protection orders) and a European Investigation Order

128 COM(2009) 338, 8 July 2009 (Commission proposal); Council doc 14792/09, 23 October 2009 (Council agreement). The measure was not adopted before the entry into force of the Treaty of Lisbon for procedural reasons.
129 [2001] OJ L 82/1.
130 [2005] OJ L 68/49.
131 See the Framework Decisions on money-laundering ([2001] OJ L 182/1), trafficking in humans ([2002] OJ L 203/1), corruption in the private sector ([2003] OJ L 192/54), the sexual exploitation of children and child pornography ([2004] OJ L 13/44), drug trafficking ([2004] OJ L 335/8), organised crime ([2008] OJ L 300/42), and racism and xenophobia ([2008] OJ L 328/55).
132 [2000] OJ L 140/1.
133 [2001] OJ L 149/1.
134 [2002] OJ L 328/1. As noted above, however, this measure replaced the prior Art 27 of the Schengen Convention.
135 [2005] OJ L 69/67.
136 See note 22 above.
137 [2008] OJ L 330/21.

(replacing existing measures concerning the cross-border movement of evidence).[138] As regards suspects' rights, the Council roadmap has been largely implemented in the form of six Directives: four adopted, another agreed and another under negotiation.[139] The victims' rights framework has been updated, in the form of a Directive on this issue.[140]

In the field of substantive criminal law, the EU has adopted Directives, replacing the prior Framework Decisions, on trafficking in persons, sexual offences against children, counterfeiting currency and attacks on information systems.[141] In light of the financial crisis, the EU also adopted criminal law legislation in a new field: market abuse by bankers.[142] Proposals for Directives to replace the prior measures on EU fraud and terrorism are under discussion.[143] Broadly speaking, these measures extend the scope of criminalisation, amend the rules on jurisdiction, and (in several cases) add rules on victim protection.

Overall, the mutual recognition model for the development of EU criminal law has shown in practice a profound tension between harmonisation of law (both procedural and substantive) and the mutual recognition principle, along with battles over human rights issues, the institutional framework and the constitutional protections of Member States.[144] After the Treaty of Lisbon, the EU focused far more on addressing criminal justice more broadly, intensifying its legislation addressing victims and for the first time addressing suspects' rights too. Time will tell whether this shift in focus will be effective in light of renewed concerns about terrorist threats.

4 Conclusions

As might be expected, the move toward the 'Community' model of supranational decision-making, legal instruments and jurisdiction of the Court of Justice has had some influence on the evolution of policy in this area. The second-generation legislation on visas and borders issues would have been much more difficult to adopt without applying QMV in this area from 2004/2005, and the development of EU immigration law and criminal law has already visibly been assisted by the removal of vetoes in these areas by the Treaty of Lisbon. The European Parliament has had a clear impact also on the areas of asylum, legal migration and criminal law since the Treaty of

138 Directives 2011/99 ([2011] OJ L 338/2) and 2014/41 ([2014] OJ L 130/1).

139 Directives: 2012/13 ([2012] OJ L 142/1); 2013/48 ([2013] OJ L 294/1); and 2016/343 ([2016] OJ L 65/1); and proposals in COM(2013) 822 and 824, 27 November 2013 and see also Mitsilegas (Chapter 8) in this collection.

140 Directive 2012/29, [2012] OJ L 315/57.

141 Directives: 2011/36 ([2011] OJ L 101/1); 2011/92 ([2011] OJ L 335/1); 2013/40 ([2013] OJ L 218/8); and 2014/62 ([2014] OJ L 151/1).

142 Directive 2014/57 ([2014] OJ L 173/179).

143 COM(2012) 363, 11 July 2012 and COM(2015) 625, 2 December 2015.

144 See, for instance, V. Mitsilegas, *EU Criminal Law* (Hart Publishing, 2009).

Lisbon, and the role of the Court of Justice has grown since its increase in jurisdiction.

Yet some of these areas of EU law are under obvious strain in light of the migration and refugee crisis. The tensions underlying the EU's Dublin System, which was intrinsically linked to the Schengen system, could not be maintained when far more people arrived. Both systems were effectively suspended, for now at least, with the search now focusing on a combination of more harmonisation, more EU-level control and lower standards as a means of deterring people from arriving and removing them if they do. As this strategy unfolds – that is, more EU and more restrictive – the role of the European Parliament and CJEU in accepting, amending or rejecting these developments will be crucial. While the initial post-Lisbon move toward further liberalisation was perfectly consistent with a bigger role for the EU institutions that broadly favoured that development, the crisis now creates an inherent tension that will likely categorise the EU's response to the crisis in the years to come.

3 Sketches of a theory of Europe as an Area of Freedom, Security and Justice

Massimo Fichera

Introduction

In the eyes of many detractors of the EU project, the creation and progress of Area of Freedom, Security and Justice (AFSJ) law may look like little more than window-dressing. They would perhaps insist that AFSJ plays at most a marginal role in the architecture of European integration, and their conviction that the economic dimension has always been prominent might seem strengthened by the fact that exceptional measures to handle the financial crisis of the Eurozone have been in the limelight recently. While sharing much of the criticism that is levelled at the AFSJ as such (for example, as regards the imbalance towards measures of proceduralisation[1]), I would like to argue that to belittle the significance of the AFSJ may be missing the point. In fact, the AFSJ represents the most important recent stage of development in European constitutionalism. Its relevance lies beyond its mere incorporation in the so-called Community pillars and goes to the heart of EU reflexivity, because it helps us to understand better the nature of the EU process of polity-building.[2] Over the years, a powerful and pervasive security discourse has been unfolded, with an increasing focus on two functions, i.e., both *securing* the functioning or smooth operation of the internal market[3]

1 By 'measures of proceduralisation' here I mean measures that emphasise effectiveness at the expense of fundamental rights. See, for example, S. Peers, 'Salvation outside the church: judicial protection in the third pillar after the *Pupino* and *Segi* judgments' (2007) 44 *Common Market Law Review* 883. On the compatibility between automaticity and fundamental rights, see V. Mitsilegas, 'The limits of mutual trust in Europe's Area of Freedom, Security and Justice: from automatic inter-state cooperation to the slow emergence of the individual' (2012) 31 *Yearbook of European Law* 319.

2 Reflexivity has been a constant feature of the EC/EU. As Preuβ observed, 'from its very beginning the Community possessed institutions which allowed it self-observation and self-evolution'. See U.K. Preuβ, 'Citizenship in the European Union: a paradigm for transnational democracy?' in D. Archibugi, D. Held and M. Köhler (eds.), *Re-imagining Political Community – Studies in Cosmopolitan Democracy* (Polity Press, 1998) 138.

3 On the use of Article 114 TFEU, 'regulatory powers' and financial crime, see E. Herlin-Karnell, 'Constructing Europe's Area of Freedom, Security and Justice through the framework of "regulation": a cascade of market-based challenges in the EU's fight against financial crime' (2015) 16 *German Law Journal* 49.

and ensuring a *secure* marketplace. On the one hand, the internal market needs to be socially embedded in order to acquire a properly European character. On the other hand, the EU project needs to be preserved at all costs in the face of new forms of crisis – and new forms of crisis emerge because of new forms of insecurity and threat, from ecological to financial to, ultimately, a crisis of intelligibility.[4] In the face of multiple crises, the AFSJ acquires a distinctive meaning, because security functions as the precondition for the existence of the internal market. The double supporting function of the AFSJ mentioned above is even more evident in the newly adopted EU Justice Agenda.[5] Moreover, the AFSJ can be identified as a space by means both of a territorial claim and a fabrication of symbols.[6]

The AFSJ as a space is in reality a claim to universality, beneath which lie remarkable contradictions that affect the heart of the European liberal project, i.e., a project based on the liberalisation of a peaceful market and the internal and external projection of its values as universal. In the radicalised version of this project, market values have almost absolute priority and may trump conflicting values.[7] The AFSJ consists, in other words, in a simultaneous reinterpretation of Europe not merely as a legal and political, but mainly as a *moral* space, which, through the security discourse, tends to expand both internally and externally. All keystones of EU integration, including citizenship, the four freedoms, the notion of uniform and effective implementation of EU law, and so on, are exposed to the expansion of the security discourse. Read through these lenses, the AFSJ thus acquires both an existential and an imperialistic dimension that have perhaps not yet been analysed sufficiently.

This chapter is structured as follows. The first section questions whether the AFSJ as such can be constructed as having an autonomous meaning. The second section defines the AFSJ as a space that claims to represent universal values and is characterised by a number of paradoxes, in particular a tension between its normative and its imperialistic facets. Finally, the third section explores the notion of security as a technique of governance and compares it with the notions of freedom and justice, which are viewed as somewhat narrow and incomplete.

1 The partially autonomous meaning of freedom, security and justice

The AFSJ holds high promises for its citizens. By promoting value-laden policies and legislation that are very close to the heart of a fully fledged

4 J. Clam, 'What is a crisis?' in P. Kjaer, G. Teubner and A. Febbrajo (eds.), *The Financial Crisis in Constitutional Perspective: The Dark Side of Functional Differentiation* (Hart Publishing, 2011) 189.

5 Communication from the Commission – *The EU Justice Agenda for 2020: Strengthening Trust, Mobility and Growth within the Union* 11 March 2014, COM(2014) 144 final.

6 See, for example, European Council Conclusions, Brussels, 27 June 2014 EUCO 79/14.

7 A. Somek, *Individualism* (Oxford University Press, 2008).

constitutional community, the AFSJ has progressively become one of the mainstays of European constitutionalism in the new millennium.[8] Yet its proclamations and seemingly triumphant pace of development have had to muddle through one of the most perilous stages of European integration, marked by financial turmoil, terrorist attacks, geopolitical tensions with Europe's neighbours and democratic conundrums. Never has the EU's very existence been under challenge as in recent years. Similarly, never has the EU's nature been questioned as much, from a variety of perspectives.[9]

Despite these hurdles, the AFSJ programme has steadily evolved into a complex set of institutions, agencies, legislative initiatives and principles, complete with a self-referential vocabulary of complacency and efficiency that is in sharp contrast with the deep loss of legitimacy and appeal that the EU is currently experiencing.[10] At this juncture, it seems thus natural to wonder whether freedom, security and justice have acquired an autonomous meaning and weight in the context of EU constitutionalism. The answer is that, in essence, they do not possess a full autonomy either as concepts or as values.

This statement does not suggest that the AFSJ is not a relevant area of EU law. On the contrary, as indicated above, the AFSJ represents the most important step in the process of constitutionalisation of the EU in recent years. Both national and EU identity-building have been affected considerably by the unrolling of the AFSJ agenda and many significant constitutional tensions in various spheres of State sovereignty have taken place as regards AFSJ-related issues.[11] The Treaty of Lisbon has codified the key changes in this area as a result of the decisive step from intergovernmental to Community decision-making and resolved some of these tensions; for example, as regards the legal basis of some EU instruments.[12] Yet there are many reasons that lead us to the conclusion that freedom, security and justice have only partial legal and political autonomy.[13]

Legally, the AFSJ performs a double supporting function. First of all, the AFSJ's wide-ranging scope encompassing delicate areas such as family matters, civil law, criminal law and immigration, ensures the *smooth* operation

8 S. Peers, *EU Justice and Home Affairs Law* (3rd edn, Oxford University Press, 2011).

9 Of course, the democratic deficit argument has been one of the most popular in academic circles. See, for example, R. Bellamy, 'Democracy without democracy? Can the EU's democratic "outputs" be separated from the democratic "inputs" provided by competitive parties and majority rule?' (2010) 17 *Journal of European Public Policy* 2.

10 See, for example, Communication from the Commission, *The EU Justice Agenda for 2020: Strengthening Trust, Mobility and Growth within the Union*, Strasbourg, 11 March 2014, COM(2014) 144 final, par. 2: 'Since the entry into force of the Lisbon Treaty [...] substantial progress has been made towards a better functioning common European area of justice' and par. 5: 'by 2020, justice and citizens' rights should know no borders in the EU'.

11 Case C–402/05 P and C–415/05 P *Kadi and Al Barakaat International Foundation v Council and Commission* [2008] ECR I–6351.

12 E. Herlin-Karnell, 'Light weapons and the dynamics of Article 47 EU: the EC's armoury of ever expanding competences' (2008) 71 *Modern Law Review* 998.

13 More optimism about the autonomy of AFSJ in A. Gibbs, *Constitutional Life and Europe's Area of Freedom, Security and Justice* (Ashgate, 2011).

of a common socially embedded marketplace. This objective is constantly promised yet remains undelivered.[14] As a matter of fact, for a market society to be sustainable, socioeconomic activities need to be embedded at least partially in non-market relations: yet this process of integration is never immune from struggles and ceaseless transformation; modern society's crisis has thus been linked to the 'dis-embeddedness' of real estate, labour, capital.[15] The Court of Justice of the European Union (CJEU) has emerged as a promoter of social embeddedness[16] and the AFSJ has an important role as a partially distinct regime in the process of EU polity-building.

Smooth operation of the common marketplace is achieved mostly through *proceduralisation*, both in civil and criminal matters.[17] For example, Article 81 TFEU has formally extended EU competence to include access to justice, the development of alternative methods of dispute settlement and judicial training. Moreover, the EU's power to legislate in judicial cooperation in civil matters (one of the areas falling within the AFSJ ambit) is a case in point. Here we may notice that a slight change has been brought about by the Treaty of Lisbon. The EU needs no longer show that a specific action is 'necessary for the proper functioning of the internal market'.[18] Judicial cooperation in civil matters having cross-border implications shall include harmonising legislation, '*particularly* when necessary for the proper functioning of the internal market'.[19] This indicates a broader scope for EU action in this field, although market principles still retain a considerable weight. In the context of mutual recognition in civil, commercial and criminal matters, for example, clearly the emergence of effectiveness as a master principle signals the strict subordination of inter-State cooperation to market paradigms, by abolishing the *exequatur* and other formalities impeding the free and speedy movement of judicial decisions.[20]

Additionally, precisely because social struggles always emerge, especially as regards the primary factors of production (land or real estate, labour,

14 This seems to be inherent to the process of EU integration. See, for example, P.F. Kjaer, *Constitutionalism in the Global Realm: A Sociological Approach* (Routledge, 2014) 124–125: 'the integration process proves that the liberalist quest for a free-flowing economic system capable of operating detached from the rest of society is a mirage. Nonetheless, there is a widespread perception [...] that European integration *does* lead to dis-embeddedness'.

15 K. Polanyi, *The Great Transformation: The Political and Economic Origins of Our Time* (Beacon Hill Press, 1944). He argued that re-embedding stages follow dis-embedding stages and are characterised by regulations focusing on non-economic values. Some provisions of the TEU, for example, Article 3 (3) on the social market economy, may be interpreted in this light.

16 J. Caporaso and S. Tarrow, 'Polanyi in Brussels: supranational institutions and the transnational embedding of markets' (2009) 63 *International Organization* 593.

17 See contributions by A. Albi and E. Storskrubb in this volume.

18 Article 65 TEC.

19 Article 81 TFEU, emphasis added.

20 On effectiveness, see, for example, E. Herlin-Karnell, *The Constitutional Dimension of European Criminal Law* (Hart Publishing, 2012).

capital), the AFSJ performs a second function: that of ensuring a *secure* marketplace. The European marketplace must be secure because it needs to operate smoothly, and for this to occur, it must be preserved at all costs.[21] As will be seen better in the next section, security has an existential facet that deeply affects the practices shaping the European public sphere.

To be sure, the AFSJ is permeated by a security discourse that is visible mostly in the case law of the CJEU and in policy documents.[22] However, security also has an expansive nature, as it tends to cover many areas of law and thus embraces both the internal market and the concepts of freedom and justice, which, as a result, are read through the lens of security.[23]

In other words, the dominance of the security dimension means that security turns into the precondition for the exercise of free movement. Free movement rights can only be exercised fully if they are not threatened or undermined by criminality. At the same time, free movement rights must be *secure*, i.e., free from measures that unreasonably constrain individual freedom. Yet, not only from a legal but also from a political perspective, the AFSJ is only partially autonomous from market paradigms and a number of political obligations, such as solidarity, social justice and protection, have not been fulfilled by the EU. In this respect, it has been noted that 'by stepping up identity checks in order to identify the undocumented migrants, using biometric technology, excluding them from social rights, discouraging their regularisation and imposing sanctions on those who hire them, states assign migrants to a subordinate status and undermine principled commitments'.[24]

In fact, freedom of movement is not a full form of political freedom, as it fails to include the participatory elements of political citizenship.[25] Benjamin Constant maintained that, while ancient freedoms were to be interpreted as the possibility to share collective power actively and continuously, modern

21 See, for example, as regards the Eurozone, Mario Draghi's speech at the Global Investment Conference, London, 26 July 2012 'the ECB is ready to do whatever it takes to preserve the euro', www.ecb.europa.eu/press/key/date/2012/html/sp120726.en.html.

22 See, for example, C-380/09 P *Melli Bank plc v Council of the European Union*, 13 March 2012, nyr; Case C-145/09 *Land Baden Württenberg v Panagiotis Tsakouridis* [2010] ECR I-11979; European Security Strategy, *A Secure Europe in a Better World*, Brussels, 12 December 2003; Communication from the Commission, *An Open and Secure Europe: Making it Happen*, Brussels, 11 March 2014, COM(2014) 154 final.

23 See, for example, the 1998 Vienna Action Plan, which notes that freedom includes the 'freedom to live in a law-abiding environment in the knowledge that public authorities are using everything in their individual and collective power […] to combat and contain those who seek to deny or abuse that freedom', Vienna Action Plan [1999] OJ C 19/1, 23 January 1999 par. 6. On the expansive nature of security, see M. Fichera, 'Security issues as an existential threat to the community', in M. Fichera and J. Kremer (eds.), *Law and Security in Europe: Reconsidering the Security Constitution* (Intersentia, 2013) 85.

24 D. Kostakopoulou, 'The Area of Freedom, Security and Justice and the political morality of migration and integration', in H. Lindahl, *A Right to Inclusion and Exclusion? Normative fault lines of the EU's Area of Freedom, Security and Justice* (Hart Publishing, 2009) 185.

25 M. Fichera, 'Criminal law beyond the state: the European model' (2013) 19 *European Law Journal* 174, 193.

freedoms should be interpreted instead as the possibility to enjoy security in the private sphere. In this sense, in his view, the expansion of the private sphere might undermine citizens' political rights.[26] From this perspective, it is no surprise that the EU model of internal market currently privileges individuals, such as the jobholder or the entrepreneur, who aim to conquer a private space where they can fulfil their life project in a secure and peaceful environment. There is little or no opportunity to foster political interaction with other individuals *as EU citizens* or with the public authorities.[27] What is missing is a public sphere that all citizens can access, so that public opinion is formed in an environment free from any sort of control.[28] Although cooperation in criminal matters and European criminal law are being developed at an increased speed, there is no public forum where a debate on right and wrong can take place. Instead, the prevailing paradigms seem to be that of the free market and individual self-fulfilment within that same marketplace. A full, more thorough notion of freedom and justice would entail the possibility to exercise direct participatory freedom, in the sense of constituent power.[29]

Despite the relevance conferred upon the AFSJ in the Treaty of Lisbon and in the Charter of Fundamental Rights (CFR), not only freedom but also justice has been conceived narrowly, mainly as access to justice and judicial cooperation across the EU territory.[30] After all, the substantive legitimacy of a political community is premised not only upon the establishment of the rule of law, but also upon subjecting the rule of law to popular self-determination, i.e., a people's freedom to determine one's own constitutional form.[31]

Despite its progress over the decades, a contradiction can thus be identified in the European liberal project. At the very moment in which it promises individual self-realisation by permitting the circulation of capital, people, labour and services (and encouraging a regime of the rational self, i.e., an autonomous and conscientious being, who pursues goals having an immediate effect on his private life), the European liberal project also fails to achieve its promises. It heralds an era of justice and freedom beyond the market, and yet leaves aside the consideration that 'the market depends upon and produces a mode of economic life grounded in a certain freedom – of production, of

26 B. Constant, *De la liberté des anciens compare à celle des modernes*, Discours prononcé à l'Athénée Royal de Paris (1819).

27 Fichera, 'Criminal law beyond the state' (2013) 19 *European Law Journal* 174, n25.

28 J. Habermas, *The Structural Transformation of the Public Sphere: An Inquiry into a Category of Bourgeois Society* (MIT Press, 1991). As a matter of fact, public debate on European issues has increased during the financial crisis.

29 'Constituent power' is a power that constitutes the State. It is traditionally meant that the people are the source of a constitution's authority. See, for example, T. Paine, 'The rights of man', in *The Great Works of Thomas Paine. Complete. Political and Theological* (D.M. Bennett, 1878). This idea, however, is strongly contested.

30 See Fichera, 'Criminal law beyond the state', n25, 177 and Article 67 TFEU.

31 See, for example, J. Tully, 'The unfreedom of the moderns in comparison to their ideals of constitutional democracy' (2002) 65 *Modern Law Review* 204.

consumption – but simultaneously relates persons only as isolated buyers and sellers of goods'.[32] The economic and financial crisis of the EU has just demonstrated how flimsy the triumphalist vocabulary of the AFSJ can be.

The new EU Justice Agenda adjusts its vocabulary to the post-crisis changed context, yet reasserting the AFSJ's dual market-supporting role. Thus 'EU Justice policy has become also a support for economic recovery, growth and structural reforms' and 'improving the independence, quality and efficiency of national justice systems is part of the economic adjustment programmes'.[33] At the same time, the EU Justice Agenda sets out the far-reaching goal of promoting trust, mobility and growth by 2020 and elevates trust to the highest rank, as 'the bedrock upon which EU justice policy should be built'.[34] This formulation designates a vindication of legitimation and autonomy, which, as will be seen in the next section, is incomplete.

2 The AFSJ as a space

The AFSJ is a space in which common values are promoted as mainstays of a transnational polity. At the heart of this rhetoric of space, there exists a territorial claim and a symbolic claim, i.e., a fabrication of symbols fostering legitimacy.[35] Beneath these claims, four paradoxes can be identified. As discussed below, these paradoxes are indicative of the true nature of the AFSJ, i.e., a space dominated by the security discourse. Hence, the typical image conveyed by the EU is that of a 'privileged' region of the world, in which universal liberal values are implemented. This has significant consequences for the configuration of EU law and governance.

The first paradox concerns the freedom to move in this space. Because they are qualified as 'EU citizens', 'residents' or 'third-country nationals', people as individuals are assigned a place by EU law, which they may change according to their needs and ambitions. Yet even the current formulation of freedom of movement is, in a sense, narrowly conceived. This is the sort of freedom that is heralded by rulings such as *Viking Line* and *Laval*,[36] in which considerations of proportionality and balance always open the way for ambiguous assessments of the extent to which the right to collective action and freedom of establishment should be weighed together – and indeed, raising the question whether they *should* be weighed together. It is the very application of a strict proportionality

32 N. Rose, *Powers of Freedom: Reframing Political Thought* (2nd edn, Cambridge University Press, 2004) 66.

33 Communication from the Commission, *The EU Justice Agenda for 2020: Strengthening Trust, Mobility and Growth within the Union*, Strasbourg, 11 March 2014, COM(2014) 144 final, para 2.

34 Ibid. See Joined Cases *N. S. and M. E. a.o.* C-411/10 and C-493/10 Judgment of 21 December 2011, nyr.

35 P. Twomey, 'Constructing a secure space: the Area of Freedom, Security and justice', in D. O'Keeffee and P. Twomey (eds.), *Legal Issues of the Amsterdam Treaty* (Hart Publishing, 1999) 359.

36 Cases C-438/05 *Viking Line* [2007] ECR I-10779; C-341/05 *Laval un Partneri* [2007] ECR I-11767.

test that is problematic here.[37] Subjecting socioeconomic rights to balance runs against the substance of those rights and thus conflicts with the claim to justice that is made within the European space. To be sure, no formulation of significant concepts such as freedom, security and justice can be neutral. At the very moment that a space is assumed to be a neutral, all-encompassing *locus* where liberal values are enhanced, there emerges the contradiction deriving from the impossibility of constructing such space without avoiding conflicts and, as a result, *having to decide* on those conflicts in one sense or another.

The second paradox emerges in the formulation of a secure space. The very act of founding the EU is essentially an act of space-fencing, which is simultaneously an opening to the world. This further paradox is articulated by the recent Communication of the European Commission's motto 'An open and secure Europe: making it happen'.[38] Europe as an AFSJ can only be fully secure if it exercises restraint over its openness, thus performing an act of exclusion – yet setting boundaries does not make the line between inclusion and exclusion any clearer. In fact, the distinction between what is included and what is excluded (which is a constitutional distinction) is never settled once and for all. As Lindahl observes, 'a legal space is never entirely a community's own place', simply because boundaries 'cannot exclude without including, nor include without excluding'.[39]

The third paradox resides in the construction of the AFSJ as a form of territorial *unity*. The AFSJ is grounded in a plethora of national (and subnational) cultural and socio-legal realities and each of these realities exercises identity claims.[40] Because the AFSJ is inevitably bound up with identity issues, there emerge between and underneath the domestic and the supranational level constant tensions (as will be seen later in this chapter), which the principle of subsidiarity and the division of competences may only partially assuage. It should be borne in mind that the EU is expanding towards the east and the south: the issue of EU enlargement also inevitably produces tensions and potential conflicts of values.

The fourth paradox can be found in the universalistic (and, in a sense, imperialistic) ambition of the EU as an AFSJ.[41] I argue that the AFSJ as a space embodies a claim to the universality of its values and that this very claim

37 C. Barnard, 'Social dumping or dumping socialism?' (2008) 67 *CLJ* 262.

38 Communication from the Commission, *An Open and Secure Europe: Making it Happen*, Brussels, 11 March 2014, COM(2014) 154 final.

39 H. Lindahl, 'Breaking promises to keep them: immigration and the boundaries of distributive justice', in H. Lindahl (ed.), *A Right to Inclusion and Exclusion? Normative Fault Lines of the EU's Area of Freedom, Security and Justice* (Hart Publishing, 2009) 137.

40 The opt-out regime is just the most evident example of this. See Protocol n. 21 on the position of the United Kingdom and Ireland in respect of the Area of Freedom, Security and Justice, Protocol n. 22 on the position of Denmark and Protocol n. 19, addressed to those countries which have incorporated the Schengen acquis into their legislation, but are not EU Member States (Iceland, Norway, Switzerland) OJ C 115 9 May 2008.

41 This is, at any rate, how I interpret EU official rhetoric. See, for example, Communication from the Commission, *The EU Justice Agenda for 2020 – Strengthening Trust, Mobility and Growth within the Union*, Strasbourg, 11 March 2014, COM(2014) 144 final, para 4: 'special attention

unveils some significant contradictions within the European liberal project. The AFSJ consists, in this sense, in a reinterpretation of Europe not merely as a legal and political, but mainly as a *moral* space. This reinterpretation is dominated by a powerful security discourse. In other words, the space in which freedom, security and justice are promoted is represented as a special, 'privileged' place, which is therefore, in a sense, *sacralised*. In the proclamation of the EU as an AFSJ, it is implicit that this 'privileged' space is legally, politically and morally distinct from other regions in the world where there might be *un*freedom, *in*security and *in*justice. The idea behind the EU as an AFSJ is that European values – such as democracy, freedom and the rule of law – are meant to be universal, because they are inherently superior to other values, and should therefore be exported and shared across the globe.[42]

In fact, the AFSJ (especially its external dimension) is inextricably linked with the Common Foreign and Security Policy (CFSP). Both the AFSJ and the CFSP are part of a security discourse that is centred on a few essential features: multilateralism; the connection between the internal and external dimension of security; the existence of defined and undefined threats that may emerge anywhere in the world.[43]

Reference to threats is common in the official documents. This is particularly evident in the European Security Strategy as well as in the Communication from the European Commission on a Strategy for the External Dimension of the Area of Freedom, Security and Justice.[44] Here the emphasis is on threats that can originate from outside Europe and on the need to promote the values of freedom, security and justice in third countries. Similarly, the Stockholm Programme refers to a 'Europe in a globalized world' and a 'reinforced external dimension', which involve cooperation with third countries across the globe and international organisations and the capacity to manage threats, including technological and natural catastrophes.[45] Recent documents confirm this trend, as will be pointed out further below.

In reality, this self-representation of the EU reflects a philosophy of history marked by a rational, universal idea of progress that looks quite unrealistic. It seeks to portray the image of man as capable of dominating nature. Danger is everywhere, but mankind can somehow control the events and calculate and eliminate any risk.[46] Risk assessment and the policy of prevention are the

will be devoted to the promotion of effective justice systems, in particular in enlargement and neighbouring countries'.

42 On new forms of imperialism, see J. Tully, *Public Philosophy in a New Key: Imperialism and Civic Freedom* (Cambridge University Press, 2009)

43 See Part V of this book.

44 European Security Strategy, *A Secure Europe in a Better World*, Brussels, 12 December 2003; Communication from the Commission, *A Strategy on the External Dimension of the Area of Freedom, Security and Justice*, Brussels, 12 October 2005, COM(2005) 491 final.

45 European Council, *The Stockholm Programme: An Open and Secure Europe Serving and Protecting Citizens*, 4 May 2010, OJ C 115.

46 See, for example, U. Beck, *Risk Society: Towards a New Modernity* (Sage, 1992); A. Giddens, 'Risk and responsibility' (1999) 62 *Modern Law Review* 1.

tools of a new, transnational bureaucracy that stands above State borders and promises the advent of a new world.

Security plays a key role in the imagery employed by the EU. Security as a discourse permeates the inner core of the AFSJ and, due to its expansive nature, it reaches out and embraces many important areas of EU law. As noted above, its existential connotation materialises itself in the language of external threats and cuts across environmental law, technology, national and European identity and, ultimately, the internal market and the *raison d'être* of the creation of the European liberal project as a project that ideally eliminates the possibility of war among European countries.

In other words, the expansion of the notion of security corresponds to a double expansion of the EU's reach, which is at the same time geographical (outward-looking) and substantive (inward-looking). The security discourse speaks to the innermost fears of the population at large. On the one hand, instability and disorder hover around Europe and must be harnessed. Thus 'widening gaps in prosperity and climate change are drivers for both voluntary mobility on a larger scale and forced displacement resulting in pressure on EU's external borders. The EU has to engage more effectively with neighbouring countries, both East and South, and those further afield to address the root causes of irregular and forced migration', as well as 'strengthen partnerships with third-countries in the field of migration and mobility'.[47] On the other hand, 'promoting an approach based on prevention and law enforcement [...] should also encourage greater synergies between Home Affairs and other policy areas related to internal security, such as transport, the internal market, the customs union, research and development, the digital market, civil protection and external relations'.[48] Through and as a consequence of the security discourse, the EU as a polity *in fieri* penetrates into all components of individual lives. Security turns, *à la* Foucault, into a technique of governance, an apparatus of control over the population, over its biological processes and private conduct.[49]

The self-representation of the EU through the external and internal dimensions of the AFSJ (in connection with the CFSP) is thus that of a promoter of the rule of law and human rights, offered as goods to be sold to neighbouring countries, which, in turn, enter the 'zone of influence' of the EU. Internal and external security are, as a result, tied up together indissolubly.[50] In fact,

47 Communication from the Commission, *An Open and Secure Europe: Making it Happen*, see note 22 above.

48 Ibid.

49 M. Foucault, *Security, Territory, Population: Lectures at the Collège de France 1977–1978* (trans. G Burchell, Palgrave Macmillan, 2009).

50 D. Bigo, 'The European internal security field stakes and rivalries in a newly developing area of police intervention', in M. Anderson and M. den Boer (eds.), *Policing Across National Boundaries* (Pinter, 1994) 164; D. Bigo, 'Internal and external security(ies), the Möbius ribbon', in M. Albert, D. Jacobson and Y. Lapid, (eds.), *Identities, Borders and Orders*

'the levels of instability in many third countries threaten democracy, the rule of law and human rights within the countries but could also have important impacts on the EU': this is why the EU provides assistance in law enforcement capacity-building, the promotion of the rule of law and good governance.[51]

There are echoes of Carl Schmitt's theory of *large space* in this portrayal,[52] although the Schmittian *large space* presupposes substantive homogeneity, which can be observed only to a limited extent in the European region. In Schmittian terms, pluralism is inconceivable within a political community, but only outside it. However, the AFSJ agenda, as noted above, does possess some imperialistic undertones, which enhance the contradictions of the European liberal project. For how can the EU normative project preserve its own original claims and *at the same time* promote enlargement? What (if any) are the borders of Europe's normativity? In other words, where does Europe end, not merely in a geographical sense? As the EU enlargement programme is scrupulously implemented, the territory of the EU includes an ever-greater variety of political and cultural communities. In addition, new agreements are struck and new interactions forged.[53] As the EU liberal agenda proclaims its value pluralism, it constantly risks turning into sheer, faceless functionality.

The existential dimension of the EU appears also internally, when not only threats such as terrorism, organised crime, but also ordinary crimes, are presented as a fact of life, addressed by strengthening and sharpening criminal law tools, which would ultimately serve the goal of effective implementation of EU law. Configuring the AFSJ as a space in which imperialistic and functional elements are disguised under a thin veil of normativity means that constructing freedom, security and justice as 'common constitutional commitments' made over time, as has instead been suggested, may be harder than expected.[54] This is especially true once we are prepared to admit that 'security has become the "super-good", the ultimate felt need which collective life must deliver and which forms the basis upon which our collective life is governed'.[55]

(University of Minnesota Press, 2001) 96; D. Bigo, 'When two become one: internal and external securitisations in Europe', in M. Kelstrup and M.C. Williams (eds.), *International Relations Theory and The Politics of European Integration. Power, Security and Community* (Routledge, 2000) 174; W. Rees, 'Inside out: the external face of EU internal security policy' (2008) 30 *Journal of European Integration* 97.

51 Communication from the Commission, *An Open and Secure Europe.*

52 See, for example, C. Schmitt, *The Nomos of the Earth in the Jus Publicum Europeaum* (first published 1950, trans. G.L. Ulmen, Telos Press Ltd., 2003); M. Fichera, 'Carl Schmitt and the new world order: a view from Europe', in M. Arvidsson, L. Brännström and P. Minkkinen (eds.), *The Contemporary Relevance of Carl Schmitt: Law, Politics, Theology* (Routledge, 2015) 165.

53 See, for example, Press Release, 'EU trade chief following EU-US trade deal stock taking: good progress, time to go the extra mile', at http://trade.ec.europa.eu/doclib/press/index.cfm?id=1028 (accessed 30 May 2016).

54 Gibbs, *Constitutional Life and Europe's Area of Freedom, Security and Justice.*

55 Ibid., 67.

The securitisation of citizenship is one of the most salient features of the process of EU polity-building and sacralisation of space depicted above. Member States may restrict the right of free movement and residence on grounds of, inter alia, public policy and public security, as long as measures taken in this field are proportionate and merely based on the personal conduct of the individual concerned – moreover, this conduct must constitute a genuine, present and sufficiently serious threat to a fundamental interest of society.[56] EU citizens and their family members can only be expelled on serious grounds of public policy and public security.

Yet the security discourse is always a double-edged weapon. Although the principle of proportionality plays an important role in the decision of concrete cases, imperative reasons of national security often count as a trump card. For example, in *Tsakouridis*, committing an offence was a sufficient ground for expelling a citizen, even if the Greek national, born in Germany, was deeply integrated into society (and, in the specific case, had resided on the territory of a Member State for the previous ten years) as long as the test of proportionality was met.[57] The CJEU had no qualms about finding that criminality 'could reach a level of intensity that might directly threaten the calm and physical security of the population as a whole or a large part of it'.[58] A crime can be sometimes so heinous as to justify expulsion, even when it is confined to a domestic act, as in *PI*, concerning an Italian national who had repeatedly committed sexual abuse of a minor who was a family member.[59] Here security as apparatus probes into individuals' private sphere, although the definition of the canons of criminality is ultimately left to the Member State's margin of appreciation.

However, the security discourse can be far more prominent. More in general, the securitisation of citizenship facilitates 'the discursive and sometimes literal mutation of the citizen into the foreigner'.[60] It produces 'the "alien within" in order to cast him or her out, figuratively and literally'.[61]

The AFSJ as a space (in Schmittian political theology terms) ultimately risks turning into an elitist space, where holding or acquiring EU citizenship is almost like winning a platinum club card. A club in which individual conduct is supposed to be in line with the standardised conduct of the constructed EU citizen, i.e., the perfectly rational individual, who maximises his or her behaviour and pursues the 'safe haven' – the place where the job

56 Article 27 Council Directive (EC) 2004/38 on the right of citizens of the Union and their family members to move and reside freely within the territory of the Member States [2004] OJ L 158/77.

57 Case C-145/09 *Land Baden Württenberg v Panagiotis Tsakouridis* [2010] ECR I-11979.

58 Ibid., paras 45–47.

59 Case C-348/09 *PI v Oberbürgermeisterin Der Stadt Remscheid*, Bailii [2012] EUECJ.

60 A. Macklin, 'The securitisation of dual citizenship', in T. Faist and P. Kivisto (eds.), *Dual Citizenship in Global Perspective- From Unitary to Multiple Citizenship* (Palgrave Macmillan, 2007) 42.

61 Ibid., 62.

market requires him or her to be. Indeed, every EU citizen may acquire a right of residence in another Member State, provided he or she is a worker (or has sufficient resources and a comprehensive health insurance).[62]

Products, capital and services must also move around in accordance with the criteria of effectiveness and rationality. Accordingly, for example, Article 86 of the TFEU provides for a European Public Prosecutor's Office, which has the power to investigate and prosecute EU-related fraud and other offences affecting the EU's financial interests. The EU's internal mechanism produces its own guarantees of maximisation.

Of course, a *sacred* space must be governed, and security is just one of the possible mechanisms of governance in the postmodern world. Every sacralisation begins with the act of sacralising, i.e., of singling out something as sacred and exercising power over and through it. Those who perform the act of sacralising are also those who possess the power of naming. In other words, every technique of governance begins as a linguistic exercise.

3 Security as a technique of governance

Security is a quintessential underpinning of a polity. It is present in various forms in key provisions of the US Constitution and several other modern constitutions across the world.[63] Yet, inevitably, the concept of security evokes something more than textual representations. As may have become apparent from the previous sections, the power and efficacy of the security discourse lie, beyond its pageantry, in its capacity to conjure up the most rudimentary, primeval and concrete needs of both collectives and individuals. There exists a psychology of power underneath the claim by a public authority that citizens can be protected not only here and now, but also in the long run, in such a way that citizens are free to pursue their life projects. It is through the security discourse that public authorities establish deep connections with the consciousness of the population and acquire an ability to manage social life. The same occurs also at the EU level. It has been observed that security accomplishes a variety of constitutional functions, sometimes in contradiction with each other: not only polity-building, but also restrictive; not only internal to a constitution, but also outside it.[64] Understood thus not merely as a bundle of provisions in the new Treaty of Lisbon, but in its substantive and meta-legal dimension, security entails a demand for coherence, unity and order.[65] Conceived not simply as an immediate, instrumental public

62 Council Directive 2004/38, note 56 above, Article 7. The right of residence for more than three months is accorded also for the purposes of following a course of study, including vocational training.

63 H.H. Koh, *The National Security Constitution: Sharing Power after the Iran-Contra Affair* (Yale University Press, 1990); J. Mazzone, 'The security constitution' (2005–2006) 53 *UCLA Law Review* 29.

64 K. Tuori, 'A European security constitution?' in M. Fichera and J. Kremer (eds.), *Law and Security in Europe* (Intersentia, 2013) 39.

65 Ibid.

good (where the good resides in the fact of sharing), but also in its social, constitutive and ultimately axiomatic dimension, security is increasingly being characterised as a global public good – although its 'institutional matrix' remains 'anchored in states as the primary motors of common action and sources of institutional initiative both within and beyond their boundaries'.[66]

However, nowadays we may observe that the Treaty of Lisbon has enabled the process of EU polity-building further by abolishing the distinction between pillars, and, at the same time, keeping a balance between the supranational interest and the safeguards of national competences. The transitional measures indicated in Article 10(1) of Protocol 36 of the Treaty of Lisbon ceased to produce effects on 1 December 2014 and the Lisbon AFSJ innovative provisions are now fully in place, although the legal effects of all former third-pillar instruments will continue until they are amended, repealed or annulled (Article 9 of Protocol 36 of the Treaty of Lisbon). On the one hand, the CJEU's jurisdiction covers almost all elements of the AFSJ; the European Commission is now able to launch Article 258 of the TFEU infringement proceedings against a Member State that breaches its obligation to implement EU law in this field; the CFR has been made legally binding; qualified majority voting has been extended to more policy areas; an 'ordinary legislative procedure' has been set up and the powers of the European Parliament have been strengthened. On the other hand, the CJEU cannot scrutinise the validity or proportionality of law enforcement operations or the exercise of municipal responsibilities concerning law and order and internal security; unanimity is still required for certain sensitive areas; Member States retain a right of legislative initiative together with the Commission in some situations. The AFSJ should therefore be seen also as a way of dealing with Europe's complexity and multilevel realities.

The question of the balance between the domestic and the supranational level is expressed in a significant way by the scope of application of the CFR. After Lisbon, the CJEU has felt the need to emphasise that the principle of primacy of secondary EU law over national law applies also to the AFSJ. This implies, as ruled in *Melloni*, that Article 53 CFR should *not* be interpreted as permitting a Member State to enforce its own standards of protection of human rights, when they are higher than those set in the CFR and, by virtue of that, disapply EU law, which is in line with the CFR but falls foul of domestic constitutional law.[67] The idea behind this ruling is that there should be no room for manoeuvre left to the domestic level when it comes to enforcing the uniform standards of protection of human rights as established by EU law – in this specific case, the Framework Decision on the European Arrest Warrant (EAW).[68] Yet there is no apparent reason why the guarantees

66 I. Loader and N. Walker, *Civilising Security* (Cambridge University Press, 2007) 264.

67 Case C-399/11 *Melloni* Judgment of 26 February 2013, nyr paras 56–58. See contributions by Albi (Chapter 6) and Mitsilegas (Chapter 8) in this volume.

68 Council Framework Decision (JHA) 2002/584 on the European Arrest Warrant and the surrender procedures between Member States [2002] OJ L 190/1.

incorporated in domestic constitutions should be dismissed so easily. The EAW as the showpiece of the mutual recognition agenda represents thus another noteworthy site of tension between spheres of competence. It is interesting to observe that *Melloni* was the first reference for preliminary ruling made by the Spanish Constitutional Court, just as *Jeremy F* was the first reference made by the French Conseil Constitutionnel.[69]

The AFSJ, in this sense, pursues an objective of coherence and uniformity of application, and thus a model that goes beyond mere inter-State cooperation. EU criminal law in particular has been showing some signs of a shift from a 'dialogic' (mainly based on inter-State cooperation) towards what has been termed a 'eunomic' model (which emphasises supranational integration).[70]

Indeed, in rationalistic types of analysis, it is often stressed that 'if the contribution to security reflects only what each state perceives to be in its own interest, the overall level of security is likely to be below what is needed to ensure ongoing stability in every state'.[71] Cooperation, common action and coherence are therefore often proclaimed and encouraged in EU policy documents.

However, it is a fact that many Member States have failed to implement EU Framework Decisions, or have implemented them in inhomogeneous ways.[72] In addition, what can be currently observed in the AFSJ landscape is a form of fragmented institutionalism. This is confirmed by the so-called 'enhanced cooperation' provisions and, even more clearly, by the opt-in/opt-out arrangements. In particular, under Protocols 21 and 22 the UK, Ireland and Denmark are free to decide whether they wish to participate in the adoption of a new measure or in the amendment of an existing one, or simply withdraw their participation at any stage of the legislative procedure. Moreover, Protocol 19 is addressed to those countries that have incorporated the Schengen *acquis* into their legislation, but are not EU Member States (Iceland, Norway and Switzerland).

In light of the considerations above, can we safely assume that the AFSJ has achieved coherence? Walker distinguishes between different types of

69 *Tribunal Constitucional*, Auto, Pleno, ATC 86/2011 9 de junio de 2011; Case C-168/13 PPU *Jeremy F v Premier Ministre*, Judgment of 30 May 2013, nyr; *Conseil Constitutionnel* Décision n. 2013–314 QPC du 14 juin 2013. In *Jeremy F* the substantive issue concerned the extent to which the right to an effective remedy is ensured by the EAW Framework Decision. The CJEU looked at Article 13 ECHR and Article 47 CFR and concluded that there is no obligation upon Member States to provide for a second level of jurisdiction to review the lawfulness of the detention.

70 M. Fichera, 'Criminal law beyond the state: the European model' (2013) 19 *European Law Journal* 174.

71 Mazzone, 'The security constitution' 39.

72 V. Mitsilegas, 'The Area of Freedom, Security and Justice from Amsterdam to Lisbon: challenges of implementation, constitutionality and fundamental rights', in J. Laffranque (ed.), *The Area of Freedom, Security and Justice, Including Information Society Issues: Reports of the XXV FIDE Congress, Tallinn 2012* (Tartu University Press, 2012) 21.

coherence, and argues that, although thematic, historical and institutional coherence are lacking, at least policy and constitutional coherence are being developed.[73] While this may be acknowledged, we should also be prepared to admit that this only occurs under the umbrella of an overwhelming security dimension. Similarly, although it is true that the AFSJ does not merely have a reactive, but also a proactive and polity-building function,[74] the deep rationale behind it is still that of building up and managing regimes of the self that are disconnected from considerations of due process and institutional constraints. The outrage caused by the recent surveillance cases[75] perhaps disregards the ostensible breach of basic constitutional principles that are nevertheless constantly asserted as foundational for the EU.

To be sure, security is not the only dimension that is fostered in AFSJ law. The CJEU has had a significant role in promoting the idea of a space where special conditions of freedom and justice are guaranteed as a beneficial effect of the *status* of EU citizen. Indeed, the claim to universality that is expressed by Europe as an AFSJ – and therefore as a space where rights and values ought to be distributed fairly – can only be fully effective if justice and freedom considerations are also factored in at least to some extent. This operation is performed mostly by the CJEU, which in its case law refers ever more explicitly to European Court of Human Rights (ECtHR) standards, CFR's scope of application and the constitutional traditions of the Member States or, simply, to Article 20 of the TFEU on citizenship. The idea is that the citizen should be put at the heart of the process of European integration, although Member States have perhaps not been given enough voice on the matter.[76]

For example, in *Ruiz Zambrano*[77] the Court clarified that EU law precludes a Member State from refusing third-country nationals a right of residence and a work permit, when their minor children are EU citizens, who are entitled to free movement rights *even if they have not yet exercised them in practice.*[78] Here again we may detect a sign of the sacralisation of the European space: whoever belongs to this space is entitled to special privileges, which are supposedly

73 N. Walker, 'In search of the Area of Freedom, Security and Justice: a constitutional odyssey', in N. Walker (ed.), *Europe's Area of Freedom, Security and Justice* (Oxford University Press, 2004) 3, 5–9; see also V. Mitsilegas, *European Criminal Law* (Hart Publishing, 2009).

74 Ibid., 13.

75 See, for example, Joined Cases C-293/12 and C-594/12 *Digital Rights Ireland and Seitlinger a.o.*, Judgment of 8 April 2014 nyr.

76 The European Commission has recently emphasised in its Communications the link between citizenship, fundamental rights and the AFSJ. See, for example, Communication from the Commission, *An Area of Freedom, Security and Justice Serving the Citizen*, 10 June 2009, COM(2009) 262 final. See also European Council, *The Stockholm Programme: An Open and Secure Europe Serving and Protecting Citizens*, 4 May 2010, OJ 2010 C 115/1.

77 Case C-34/09 *Gerardo Ruiz Zambrano v Office national de l'emploi* [2011] I-01177.

78 See instead Council Directive 2004/38 above note 56, Preamble, point 3: 'Union citizenship should be the fundamental status of nationals of the Member States when they exercise their right of free movement and residence', which codified previous case law, such

bestowed according to criteria of justice.[79] The status of EU citizenship needs to be protected as such. Simply being present in this space *qua* EU citizen, even when the individual is not moving from his or her country of origin, is sufficient to activate EU citizenship rights: the rights of residence of the children produce effects that are reflected on their non-EU citizen parents.[80]

Moreover, in the context of the circulation and residence of individuals on EU territory, the freedom and justice dimension rules out the possibility of national or regional legislation treating third-country nationals who are long-term residents differently from EU citizens when it comes to the allocation of funds for housing benefits.[81] Although Member States may limit the application of the principle of equal treatment established by Directive 2003/109/EC, long-term residents ought to enjoy the same level of core benefits as nationals.[82] In addition, the meaning and scope of core benefits ought to be established by looking at the objective of the Directive, which is the integration of third country nationals who have resided legally and continuously in the Member State.[83]

In other cases, considerations of freedom and justice have led the CJEU to conclude that, in order to assess exhaustively the compatibility of a national provision with the CFR, a national court ought to be able to disapply a provision contrary to a fundamental right guaranteed by the CFR in all cases, and not only when the infringement is manifest from the text of the Charter or the case law relating to it. The national court may, in its assessment task, look beyond the domestic statute that implements a particular piece of EU legislation.[84] In fact, as the CJEU specified further in *Siragusa*, 'the concept of "implementing Union law", as referred to in Article 51 of the Charter, requires a certain degree of connection above and beyond the matters

as Case **C-184/99,** *Rudy Grzelczyk v Centre public d'aide sociale d'Ottignies-Louvain-la-Neuve* **[2001] ECR** I-06193; C-413/99 *Baumbast and R v Secretary of State for the Home Department* [2002] I-07091; C-148/02 *Carlos Garcia Avello v Belgian State* [2003] I-11613; C-200/02 *Kunqian Catherine Zhu and Man Lavette Chen v Secretary of State for the Home Department* [2004] I-09925.

79 Some commentators argue that *Ruiz Zambrano* is an example of poor legal reasoning: see, for example, K. Hailbronner and D. Thym, 'Case C-34/09, Gerardo Ruiz Zambrano v. Office national de l'emploi (ONEm), Judgment of the Court of Justice (Grand Chamber) of 8 March 2011' (2011) 48 *Common Market Law Review* 1253.

80 See subsequent cases adjusting the Court's approach on this: Case C-434/09 *Shirley McCarthy v Secretary of State for the Home Department* [2011] ECR I-03375; C-256/11 *Dereci, Heiml, Kokollari, Maduike and Stevic v Bundesministerium fur Inneres*, Judgment of 15 November 2011; C-40/11 *Yoshikazu Iida v Stadt Ulm*, Judgment of 8 November 2012, nyr; Joined Cases C-356/11 and C-357/11 *O, S and L*, Judgment of 6 December 2012, nyr.

81 Case C-571/10 *Kamberaj v Istituto per l'Edilizia Sociale per la Provincia Autonoma di Bolzano a.o.* para 93; Council Directive (EC) 2003/109 concerning the status of third-country nationals who are long-term residents [2004] OJ L 16.

82 Case C-571/10 paras 83–84.

83 Case C-571/10 para 90. See also Council Directive (EC) 2003/86 on the right to family reunification, [2003] OJ L 251.

84 Case C-617/10 *Åklagaren v Hans Åkerberg Fransson*, Judgment of 26 February 2013, nyr.

covered being closely related or one of those matters having an indirect impact on the other'.[85] National courts, when assessing the level of respect of fundamental rights by a national legal system, are thus invited to consider the whole context in which a specific provision of EU law is located.

The concept of family has also been gradually revisited and extended in EU law according to the paradigms of justice and freedom, as confirmed by the Citizenship Directive.[86] Article 2 of the Directive defines 'family member' broadly, by including the registered partner if registered partnership is treated as equivalent to marriage by the legislation of the host Member State. Moreover, the situation of those who do not fall within the definition of 'family member' should still be taken into account as much as possible for the purposes of entry and residence (Preamble points 5 and 6).[87] Despite this, domestic and European courts in the field of same-sex marriage are examining situations of potential breach of equal treatment and/or free movement principles.[88]

The essence of justice and freedom should also transpire from the proclaimed principle of mutual recognition and the free circulation of judgments. Yet again, as mentioned earlier, it is the narrow conception of justice and freedom that prevails, mostly in a procedural sense; for example, in the provisions of the TFEU on judicial cooperation in civil and criminal matters and in the secondary legislation. Perhaps we should start recognising the perpetual gap that exists between announcing the AFSJ as a transnational polity and delivering it as an objective of government. It is now readily admitted that 'the EU presents extraordinary obstacles to the accomplishment of a transnational theory of justice'.[89] However, there is little point in supporting the virtues of the rule of law, its enabling and restraining functions,[90] if it is not maintained at the same time that what counts is on what foundations the rule of law stands. Once the veil of the security discourse is pierced, it should be evident that the process of polity-building at the EU level is marked by the inescapable tension between its imperialistic and its normative facets – and this aspect is perhaps overlooked too easily. The recent Aranyosi and Căldăraru[91] ruling on the European Arrest Warrant – in which the Court confirmed mutual trust as a rebuttable, rather than an absolute presumption – having previously done

85 Case C-206/13 *Siragusa*, Judgment of 6 March 2014, nyr, para 24.

86 Council Directive 2004/38, note 56 above; on the relationship between the AFSJ, citizenship of the EU and family law see the contributions by Kostakopoulou and Ripoll Servent (Chapter 10) and Peers (Chapter 2) in this book.

87 Council Directive (EC) 2004/38, note 56 above.

88 See, for example, Case C-267/12 *Frédéric Hay v Crédit agricole mutuel de Charente-Maritime et des Deux-Sèvres*, Judgment of 12 December 2013, nyr (equal treatment in the context of employment benefits).

89 S. Douglas-Scott, 'The problem of justice in the European Union: values, pluralism, and critical legal justice' in J. Dickson and P. Eleftheriadis (eds.), *Philosophical Foundations of European Union Law* (Oxford University Press, 2012) 412, 447.

90 Ibid., 446 (and the previous sections on the notion of 'critical legal justice').

91 Joined Cases C-404/15 and C-659/15 Aranyosi and Căldăraru nyr.

so in the asylum law domain[92] and in its Opinion on the accession to the ECHR[93] – might have an important impact on the configuration of the EU as an AFSJ. With the establishment of a clear duty upon Member States to build up barriers to mutual recognition where there is serious risk of violation of fundamental rights the Court encourages a coherent, deontological and rights-oriented approach to the AFSJ.

Conclusions

In the early 1990s, when the ASFJ was in its infancy, few would have imagined it would have gone so far in terms of both material scope and amount of legislation in such a short period of time.[94] While many aspects still need to be further developed, it is already possible to flesh out some crucial features that allow us to shed some light not only on AFSJ *per se*, but also, and more significantly, on the nature of the EU liberal project.

It would be naïve to assume that the proclamation of AFSJ as a secure space where free individuals, products, services, money, as well as judicial decisions, can circulate smoothly, is neutral. On the contrary, this proclamation is an expression of a security discourse that has a thick relevance as the projection of a universal claim made by the EU. In other words, the EU as a space of freedom, security and justice has both an internal and an external dimension. Externally, the EU offers to its new members, its candidates and neighbours an image of guardian of the rule of law, in exchange for increasing influence and reach. Internally, the security discourse stretches towards a wide range of branches of EU law, covering the internal market, transport, the environment, external relations, the economic and financial provisions, and so on. Security's expansive nature does not necessarily swallow freedom and justice, but, rather it reshapes them through its own language.

Freedom, security and justice are in fact not fully autonomous concepts, but must be read as a function of the internal market. While announcing the promotion and protection of the rule of law and human rights, the reality is that the AFSJ's existential and imperialistic dimensions risk turning it into a sacred space, where a secure inside is shielded from an insecure outside. One consequence of this is that both freedom and justice acquire a narrow meaning, devoid of their political potential. The AFSJ as a space and security as a technique of governance represent attempts to handle EU's social complexity at the expense of its coherence. Thus, ultimately, the EU faces this struggle between its normative and its imperialistic facets – and the economic and financial crisis, if anything, has merely made this all the more evident.

92 Joined Cases N. S. and M. E. a.o. C-411/10 and C-493/10, Judgement of 21 December 2011, nyr.

93 CJEU Opinion 2/13 EU:C:2014:2454 par. 191.

94 This area of EU law was initially called 'Justice and Home Affairs' in the Treaty of Maastricht, 29 July 1992, OJ C 191/1.

Bibliography

Archibugi, D., Held, D. and Köhler, M., *Re-imagining Political Community: Studies in Cosmopolitan Democracy* (Polity Press, 1998)

Barnard, C., 'Social dumping or dumping socialism?' (2008) 67 *CLJ* 262

Beck, U., *Risk Society: Towards a New Modernity* (Sage, 1992)

Bigo, D., 'The European internal security field stakes and rivalries in a newly developing area of police intervention', in M. Anderson and M. den Boer (eds.), *Policing Across National Boundaries* (Pinter, 1994) 164

Bigo, D., 'Internal and external security(ies), the Möbius ribbon', in M. Albert, D. Jacobson and Y. Lapid (eds.), *Identities, Borders and Orders* (University of Minnesota Press, 2001) 96

Bigo, D., 'When two become one: internal and external securitisations in Europe', in M. Kelstrup and M.C. Williams (eds.), *International Relations Theory and the Politics of European Integration: Power, Security and Community* (Routledge, 2000) 174

Brown, W., *Walled States, Waning Sovereignty* (MIT Press, 2010)

Caporaso, J. and Tarrow, S., 'Polanyi in Brussels: supranational institutions and the transnational embedding of markets' (2009) 63 *International Organization* 593

Clam, J., 'What is a crisis?' in P. Kjaer, G. Teubner and A. Febbrajo (eds.), *The Financial Crisis in Constitutional Perspective: The Dark Side of Functional Differentiation* (Hart Publishing, 2011)

Constant, B., *De la liberté des anciens compare à celle des modernes*, Discours prononcé à l'Athénée Royal de Paris (1819)

Dickson, J. and Eleftheriadis, P. (eds.), *Philosophical Foundations of European Union Law* (Oxford University Press, 2012)

Douglas-Scott, S., 'The problem of justice in the European Union: values, pluralism, and critical legal justice', in J. Dickson and P. Eleftheriadis (eds.), *Philosophical Foundations of European Union Law* (Oxford University Press, 2012) 412

Fichera, M., 'Criminal law beyond the state: the European model' (2013) 19 *European Law Journal* 174

Fichera, M., *The Implementation of the European Arrest Warrant in the European Union: Law, Policy and Practice* (Intersentia 2011)

Fichera, M., 'Schmitt and the new world order: a view from Europe', in M. Arvidsson, L. Brännström and P. Minkkinen (eds.), *The Contemporary Relevance of Carl Schmitt: Law, Politics, Theology* (Routledge, 2015) 165

Fichera, M., 'Security issues as an existential threat to the community', in M. Fichera and J. Kremer (eds.), *Law and Security in Europe: Reconsidering the Security Constitution* (Intersentia, 2013) 85

Fichera, M. and Kremer, J. (eds.), *Law and Security in Europe: Reconsidering the Security Constitution* (Intersentia, 2013)

Foucault, M., *Security, Territory, Population: Lectures at the Collège de France 1977–1978* (trans. G Burchell, Palgrave Macmillan, 2009)

Gibbs, A., *Constitutional Life and Europe's Area of Freedom, Security and Justice* (Ashgate, 2011)

Giddens, A., 'Risk and responsibility' (1999) 62 *Modern Law Review* 1

Habermas, J., *The Structural Transformation of the Public Sphere: An Inquiry into a Category of Bourgeois Society* (MIT Press, 1991)

Hailbronner, K. and Thym, D., 'Case C-34/09, Gerardo Ruiz Zambrano v. Office national de l'emploi (ONEm), Judgment of the Court of Justice (Grand Chamber) of 8 March 2011' (2011) 48 *Common Market Law Review* 1253

Herlin-Karnell, E., *The Constitutional Dimension of European Criminal Law* (Hart Publishing, 2012)

Herlin-Karnell, E., 'Constructing Europe's Area of Freedom, Security and Justice through the framework of "regulation": a cascade of market-based challenges in the EU's fight against financial crime' (2015) 16 *German Law Journal* 49

Herlin-Karnell, E., 'Light weapons and the dynamics of Article 47 EU: the EC's armoury of ever expanding competences' (2008) 71 *Modern Law Review* 998

Kjaer, P., Teubner, G. and Febbrajo, A. (eds.), *The Financial Crisis in Constitutional Perspective: The Dark Side of Functional Differentiation* (Hart Publishing, 2011)

Koh, H.H., *The National Security Constitution: Sharing Power after the Iran-Contra Affair* (Yale University Press, 1990)

Kostakopoulou, D., 'The Area of Freedom, Security and Justice and the political morality of migration and integration', in H. Lindahl (ed.), *A Right to Inclusion and Exclusion? Normative Fault Lines of the EU's Area of Freedom, Security and Justice* (Hart Publishing, 2009) 185

Laffranque, J. (ed.), *The Area of Freedom, Security and Justice, Including Information Society Issues: Reports of the XXV FIDE Congress, Tallinn 2012* (Tartu University Press, 2012)

Lindahl, H., 'Breaking promises to keep them: immigration and the boundaries of distributive justice', in H. Lindahl (ed.), *A Right to Inclusion and Exclusion? Normative Fault Lines of the EU's Area of Freedom, Security and Justice* (Hart Publishing, 2009) 137

Lindahl, H., *A Right to Inclusion and Exclusion? Normative Fault Lines of the EU's Area of Freedom, Security and Justice* (Hart Publishing, 2009)

Loader, I. and Walker, N., *Civilising Security* (Cambridge University Press, 2007)

Macklin, A., 'The securitisation of dual citizenship', in T. Faist and P. Kivisto (eds.), *Dual Citizenship in Global Perspective- From Unitary to Multiple Citizenship* (Palgrave Macmillan, 2007) 42

Mazzone, J., 'The security constitution' (2005–2006) 53 *UCLA Law Review* 29

Mitsilegas, V., 'The Area of Freedom, Security and Justice from Amsterdam to Lisbon: challenges of implementation, constitutionality and fundamental rights', in J. Laffranque (ed.), *The Area of Freedom, Security and Justice, Including Information Society Issues: Reports of the XXV FIDE Congress, Tallinn 2012* (Tartu University Press, 2012) 21

Mitsilegas, V., *European Criminal Law* (Hart Publishing, 2009)

Mitsilegas, V., 'The limits of mutual trust in Europe's Area of Freedom, Security and Justice: from automatic inter-state cooperation to the slow emergence of the individual' (2012) 31 *Yearbook of European Law* 319

O'Keeffee, D. and Twomey, P. (eds.), *Legal Issues of the Amsterdam Treaty* (Hart Publishing, 1999)

Paine, T., 'The rights of man', in *The Great Works of Thomas Paine. Complete. Political and Theological* (D.M. Bennett, 1878)

Peers, S., *EU Justice and Home Affairs Law* (3rd edn, Oxford University Press, 2011)

Peers, S., 'Salvation outside the church: judicial protection in the third pillar after the *Pupino* and *Segi* judgments' (2007) 44 *Common Market Law Review* 883

Polanyi, K., *The Great Transformation: The Political and Economic Origins of Our Time* (Beacon Hill Press, 1944)
Rees, W., 'Inside out: the external face of EU internal security policy' (2008) 30 *Journal of European Integration* 97
Rose, N., *Powers of Freedom: Reframing Political Thought* (2nd edn, Cambridge University Press, 2004)
Schmitt, C., *The Nomos of the Earth in the Jus Publicum Europeaum* (first published 1950, trans. G.L. Ulmen, Telos Press Ltd., 2003)
Somek, A., *Individualism* (Oxford University Press, 2008)
Tully, J., 'The unfreedom of the moderns in comparison to their ideals of constitutional democracy' (2002) 65 *Modern Law Review* 204
Tuori, K., 'A European security constitution?' in M. Fichera and J. Kremer (eds.), *Law and Security in Europe: Reconsidering the Security Constitution* (Intersentia, 2013) 39
Twomey, P., 'Constructing a secure space: the Area of Freedom, Security and Justice', in D. O'Keeffee and P. Twomey (eds.), *Legal Issues of the Amsterdam Treaty* (Hart Publishing, 1999) 359
Walker, N. (ed.), *Europe's Area of Freedom, Security and Justice* (Oxford University Press, 2004)
Walker, N., 'In search of the Area of Freedom, Security and Justice: a constitutional odyssey', in N. Walker (ed.), *Europe's Area of Freedom, Security and Justice* (Oxford University Press, 2004) 3

Case law

Joined Cases C-404/15 and C-659/15 *Aranyosi* and *Căldăraru*, nyr
Case C-206/13 *Siragusa*, Judgment of 6 March 2014, nyr
Case C-267/12 *Frédéric Hay v Crédit agricole mutuel de Charente-Maritime et des Deux-Sèvres*, Judgment of 12 December 2013, nyr
Case C-168/13 PPU *Jeremy F v Premier Ministre*, Judgment of 30 May 2013, nyr
Case C-399/11 *Melloni*, Judgment of 26 February 2013, nyr
Case C-617/10 *Åklagaren v Hans Åkerberg Fransson*, Judgment of 26 February 2013, nyr
Joined Cases C-356/11 and C-357/11 *O, S and L*, Judgment of 6 December 2012, nyr
Case C-40/11 *Yoshikazu Iida v Stadt Ulm*, Judgment of 8 November 2012, nyr
Joined Cases *N. S. and M. E. a.o.* C-411/10 and C-493/10, Judgment of 21 December 2011, nyr
Case C-256/11 *Dereci, Heiml, Kokollari, Maduike and Stevic v Bundesministerium fur Inneres*, Judgment of 15 November 2011, nyr
Case C-434/09 *Shirley McCarthy v Secretary of State for the Home Department* [2011] ECR I-03375
C-380/09 P *Melli Bank plc v Council of the European Union*, 13 March 2012, nyr
Case C-348/09 *PI v Oberbürgermeisterin Der Stadt Remscheid*, Bailii [2012] EUECJ
Case C-34/09 *Gerardo Ruiz Zambrano v Office national de l'emploi* [2011] I-01177
Case C-145/09 *Land Baden Württenberg v Panagiotis Tsakouridis* [2010] ECR I-11979
Case C–402/05 P and C–415/05 P *Kadi and Al Barakaat International Foundation v Council and Commission* [2008] ECR I–6351

Case C-438/05 *Viking Line* [2007] ECR I-10779
Case C-341/05 *Laval un Partneri* [2007] ECR I-11767
Case C-200/02 *Kunqian Catherine Zhu and Man Lavette Chen v Secretary of State for the Home Department* [2004] I-09925
Case C-148/02 *Carlos Garcia Avello v Belgian State* [2003] I-11613
Case C-413/99 *Baumbast and R v Secretary of State for the Home Department* [2002] I-07091
Case C-184/99 *Rudy Grzelczyk v Centre public d'aide sociale d'Ottignies-Louvain-la-Neuve* [2001] ECR I-06193
Tribunal Constitucional, Auto, Pleno, ATC 86/2011 9 de junio de 2011
Conseil Constitutionnel Décision n. 2013–314 QPC du 14 juin 2013
CJEU Opinion 2/13 EU:C:2014:2454

Official documents

Communication from the Commission, *An Area of Freedom, Security and Justice Serving the Citizen*, 10 June 2009, COM(2009) 262 final
Communication from the Commission, *The EU Justice Agenda for 2020 – Strengthening Trust, Mobility and Growth within the Union*, Strasbourg, 11 March 2014 COM(2014) 144 final
Communication from the Commission, *An Open and Secure Europe: Making it Happen*, Brussels, 11 March 2014, COM(2014) 154 final
Communication from the Commission, *A Strategy on the External Dimension of the Area of Freedom, Security and Justice*, Brussels, 12 October 2005, COM(2005) 491 final
Council Directive (EC) 2003/86 on the right to family reunification (2003) OJ L 251
Council Directive (EC) 2003/109 concerning the status of third country nationals who are long term residents (2004) OJ L 16
Council Directive (EC) 2004/38 on the right of citizens of the Union and their family members to move and reside freely within the territory of the Member States (2004) OJ L 158/77
Council Framework Decision (JHA) 2002/584 on the European Arrest Warrant and the surrender procedures between Member States (2002) OJ L 190/1
European Council, *The Stockholm Programme – An Open and Secure Europe Serving and Protecting Citizens*, 4 May 2010 OJ C 115
European Council Conclusions, Brussels, 27 June 2014 EUCO 79/14
European Security Strategy, *A Secure Europe in a Better World*, Brussels, 12 December 2003
Press Release, 'EU trade chief following EU-US trade deal stock taking: good progress, time to go the extra mile' at http://trade.ec.europa.eu/doclib/press/index.cfm?id=1028
Treaty of Maastricht, 29 June 1992 OJ C 191/1
UK Immigration Act 2014, c. 22
Vienna Action Plan (1999) OJ C 19/1, 23 January 1999

4 Human rights and the Area of Freedom, Security and Justice

Dorota Leczykiewicz

The sphere of EU activity described as the creation of the Area of Freedom, Security and Justice (AFSJ), first formalised by the Treaty of Amsterdam, is defined to encompass three policy areas: free movement of persons accompanied by appropriate external border controls and common rules on asylum and immigration; prevention of crime; and judicial cooperation in criminal and civil matters.[1] The Treaty on the Functioning of the EU in the first provision of the title dedicated to this field proclaims that the Union shall constitute an Area of Freedom, Security and Justice, but adds that this is to be accomplished 'with respect for fundamental rights and the different legal systems and traditions of the Member States'.[2] So it is the Treaty itself that imposes on EU measures in the AFSJ the requirement of complying with 'fundamental rights'. This entails that Member States' action in the AFSJ should observe national and international laws protecting human rights. Moreover, because such action of the Member States falls within 'the scope of Union law', they have to comply also, as an independent matter of EU law, with 'fundamental rights', guaranteed and protected by that law.[3]

1 Article 67(2)-(4) TFEU.

2 Article 67(1) TFEU. Note also the centrality of fundamental rights in the European Council's Stockholm Programme, 'An open and secure Europe serving and protecting citizens', OJ C 115, 4 May 2010, p. 1.

3 See below on the distinction between 'human rights' and 'fundamental rights' as understood in this chapter. The 'scope of Union law' in the AFSJ is not the same for all Member States. According to Protocol No. 21 to the Treaty of Lisbon, the UK and Ireland do not take part in the adoption of measures in the AFSJ and 'none of the provisions of Title V of Part Three of the Treaty on the Functioning of the European Union [the Title on the AFSJ], no measure adopted pursuant to that Title, no provision of any international agreement concluded by the Union pursuant to that Title, and no decision of the Court of Justice interpreting any such provision or measure shall be binding upon or applicable in the United Kingdom or Ireland' (Article 2). However, according to Article 3, the UK and Ireland may opt-in to individual measures, take part in their adoption and be bound by them. A similar, although not identical, arrangement applies in the case of Denmark on the basis of Protocol No. 22. See also Protocol No. 36 on transitional provisions; M. Fletcher, 'Schengen, the European Court of Justice and flexibility under the Lisbon Treaty: balancing the United Kingdom's "ins" and "outs"' (2009) 5 *European Constitutional Law Review* 74.

The purpose of this chapter is to discuss the connection between human rights and the AFSJ. Generally, we can identify two modes of interaction. First, the EU adopts acts whose overt purpose is to enhance human rights protection. So while human rights are not an independent EU policy, improving their protection often constitutes one of the main goals of measures enacted by the EU in the AFSJ. Second, given the place of human rights among Union values,[4] human rights constitute standards against which the EU's and the Member States' action falling in the AFSJ is assessed. This second mode of interaction between human rights and the AFSJ is characterised by challenges arising from the plurality of sources of human rights protection in the EU. Alongside the Charter of Fundamental Rights, which became officially binding with the Treaty of Lisbon,[5] EU law has protected human rights also by means of 'general principles' inspired by common constitutional traditions of the Member States and the European Convention on Human Rights (ECHR). It follows that already at the textual level, the EU system of human rights protection comprises an EU document – the Charter of Fundamental Rights, the national constitutions and the ECHR. Moreover, there are a number of international law documents that protect human rights to which EU law explicitly refers or that have a bearing on the issues regulated by the AFSJ Acts. Human rights that have been officially recognised as part of EU law are its 'fundamental rights'. This means that in order to investigate the protection of human rights in the AFSJ, one has to study the law relating to EU 'fundamental rights'.

This chapter will focus on the protection received by human rights within EU law in the context of the AFSJ. The importance of this question arises from the fact that national authorities and courts are bound by EU law, have to accord it primacy in the event of conflict with national rules, and have to ensure full effectiveness of EU measures. So it is a crucial question for anyone interested in human rights whether the EU has internally developed adequate standards of protection. The EU is not a party to the ECHR,[6] so violations of human rights in the AFSJ can be challenged before the Strasbourg court only as transgressions of the Member States. As I will explain, occasionally there may arise a conflict between human rights protection offered by EU law and that offered by national constitutions. In such cases, we speak of 'constitutional conflict' and its resolution in favour of the (lower) EU standard may

4 See Article 2 TEU.

5 According to Article 6(1) TEU: 'The Union recognises the rights, freedoms and principles set out in the Charter of Fundamental Rights of the European Union of 7 December 2000, as adapted at Strasbourg, on 12 December 2007, which shall have the same legal value as the Treaties.'

6 According to Article 6(2), the EU was meant to accede to the ECHR. However, the Court of Justice ruled in Opinion 2/13 of the Full Court of 18 December 2014 that the draft agreement on the accession of the EU to the ECHR was not compatible with Article 6(2) TEU and with Protocol No. 8 relating to Article 6(2) TEU.

leave us with the impression that the Court of Justice is not taking human rights seriously.[7] The Charter of Fundamental Rights, which has now become a focal point of the discussion about human rights standards in EU law, is more likely than 'general principles' to trigger conflicts between the national and the EU's level of protecting human rights. It is a centralised regime with a strong federalising effect. Moreover, the Charter, as a document using the notion of 'rights' and focusing on the individual, creates tensions with characteristically utilitarian programmes furthered by the EU. This is visible in particular within the AFSJ. Fundamental rights arguments present a different logic, largely incompatible with the objectively defined goals of the EU in this sphere, such as crime prevention, mutual recognition of judgments or the management of irregular migration. Tensions are also more frequent in the AFSJ than in other policy areas of the EU because this is where the positive law is a result of very difficult compromises among the Member States. The consequence of that is that acts adopted in the AFSJ leave Member States much discretion and, while they are bound to observe EU fundamental rights when they exercise this discretion, proportionality is often left to the assessment of national courts.

As it has been already made clear above, in the AFSJ both the EU and the Member States may potentially violate human rights. An effective and complete system of protection requires mechanisms ensuring compliance with human rights standards both from the EU's and the Member States' institutions. This system has to encompass a legality and a correctness review[8] and measures ensuring formal and practical access to a court, such as the right of standing, access to legal aid, legal representation, access to evidence and the respect of the right to the defence. One of the most important issues concerns the character of the review carried out by the competent court (due process versus substantive review) and the intensity of that review, in particular in the light of limitations to which EU fundamental rights may be subjected.[9]

7 J. Coppel and A. O'Neill, 'The European Court of Justice: taking rights seriously?' (1992) 12 *Legal Studies* 228; D. Leczykiewicz, 'Constitutional conflicts and the third pillar' (2008) 33 *European Law Review* 230. See also S. Douglas-Scott, 'The rule of law in the European Union – putting the security into the Area of Freedom, Security and Justice' (2004) 29 *European Law Review* 219.

8 The powers of the Court of Justice of the EU to review Member States' action are predominantly indirect and take the form of compatibility review whereby the Court of Justice by authoritative interpretation of EU law rules on whether a particular national rule, decision or practice is 'precluded' by that law (see Article 367 TFEU). According to Article 276 TFEU, in exercising its powers regarding judicial cooperation in criminal matters and police cooperation, the Court of Justice has no jurisdiction to review the validity or proportionality of operations carried out by the police or other law-enforcement services of a Member State or the exercise of the responsibilities incumbent upon Member States with regard to the maintenance of law and order and the safeguarding of internal security.

9 According to the Court's case law, 'fundamental rights' do not constitute 'unfettered prerogatives'. See for example, Case C-394/07 *Marco Gambazzi v Daimler Chrysler Canada Inc. and CIBC Mellon Trust Company* [2009] ECR I-2563, para 29. According to Article 52(1)

Moreover, there is a question of whether individuals should possess under EU law the right of appeal against a first-instance court judgment in cases falling within the AFSJ, or whether this matter should be more appropriately regulated by individual Member States according to their respective traditions of procedural and remedial law. Finally, there is a question of the role of human rights in creating exceptions to objective obligations imposed on Member States and their institutions, such as the duty to recognise a judgment of another Member State's court. In this chapter, I will discuss these issues by looking successively at individual spheres of EU activity in the AFSJ. I will start by looking at asylum and migration, then discuss prevention of crime with a particular focus on judicial cooperation in criminal matters, and finish by considering the human rights issues arising in the context of judicial cooperation in civil matters.

1 Asylum and immigration

EU asylum policy is characterised by a broad margin of discretion left to the Member States.[10] The first human rights issue at stake here is the protection of refugees and other migrants coming from outside of the EU. The large number of migrants from third countries attempting to enter the territory of the EU, both legally and illegally, creates a practical challenge for the Member States. This challenge is particularly acute in the case of illegal migrants fleeing turmoil in Africa and the Middle East, who tend to enter the EU through a small number of Mediterranean countries. The boats on which they come often need to be rescued and the migrants offered assistance or detained. This causes practical problems for states through which migrants enter the EU and raises also the question of the EU's *legal* responsibility. Failure to rescue a sinking vessel carrying irregular migrants can be regarded as a human rights violation. Equally, the EU could be seen as violating human rights through inaction if it fails to organise a system of rescue and support enabling individual Member States to cope with the obligation to save migrants endangered by the conditions in which smugglers bring them

of the Charter, '[a]ny limitation on the exercise of the rights and freedoms recognised by this Charter must be provided for by law and respect the essence of those rights and freedoms. Subject to the principle of proportionality, limitations may be made only if they are necessary and genuinely meet objectives of general interest recognised by the Union or the need to protect the rights and freedoms of others.' See D. Leczykiewicz, '"Constitutional justice" and judicial review of EU legislative acts', in G. de Búrca, D. Kochenov and A. Williams (eds.), *Europe's Justice Deficit? Beyond Good Governance* (Hart Publishing, 2015) 97; M. Fichera and E. Herlin-Karnell, 'The margin of appreciation test and balancing in the Area of Freedom Security and Justice: a proportionate answer for a Europe of rights?' (2013) 19 *European Public Law* 759.

10 On the EU asylum policy, see F. Cherubini, *Asylum Law in the European Union* (Routledge, 2014); S. Peers, E. Guild, M. Garlick and V. Moreno-Lax, *EU Immigration and Asylum Law* (Text and Commentary, Volumes 1–3; Brill Nijhoff, 2012 and 2015).

to Europe.[11] Moreover, the EU can be seen to be under a duty arising from its human rights commitments to take active steps to solve the political and military conflicts that create the floods of migration.

Two issues make the discussion of human rights in the context of the EU's migration and asylum policy difficult.[12] First of all, it is necessary to separate moral arguments from legal arguments. As a matter of law, there is no human right to live in Europe. If such a right was recognised in law, the Member States would have to admit every migrant regardless of his or her circumstances, in particular whether or not they properly qualify as refugees. The entitlement to residence in the EU has to be obtained either in reliance on EU legislative acts regulating migration and asylum of third-country nationals or on the basis of national laws.[13] The policy choice made by the EU vis-à-vis illegal immigrants (or those who have not obtained residence in the way described above) is that of their return to the home country.[14] The earliest point in time where the question of human rights protection arises as an issue of EU law is when the migrant first encounters an authority of an EU Member State. This is when human rights obligations of the Member States stemming from EU law become activated, in so far as those acts come within the scope of Union law.[15]

11 See the Statement of the Special Meeting of the European Council on 23 April 2015, which describes 'the situation in the Mediterranean' as 'a tragedy' and as a 'humanitarian emergency'. See also Commission's Recommendation of 8 June 2015 on a European resettlement scheme, C(2015) 3560 final.

12 For more on the challenges facing EU asylum and migration policy, see N. El-Enany, 'EU asylum and immigration law under the Area of Freedom, Security and Justice', in A. Arnull and D. Chalmers (eds.), *Oxford Handbook of European Union Law* (Oxford University Press, 2015) 867.

13 Some Member States have resettlement schemes, under which they admit migrants from outside of the EU. The Commission made a recommendation to the Member States for the EU-wide resettlement scheme: Commission Recommendation (EU) 2015/914 of 8 June 2015 on a European resettlement scheme, OJ L 148, 13 June 2015, p. 32. This is part of the Commission's European Agenda on Migration – Communication from the Commission to the European Parliament, the Council, the European Economic and Social Committee and the Committee of the Regions 'A European Agenda On Migration' COM(2015) 240 final, which aims to prevent further losses of migrants' lives at sea by providing additional funding to Frontex joint search and rescue operations. The Recommendation also claims that a resettlement scheme is a way of avoiding displaced persons in need of protection having to resort to the criminal networks of smugglers and traffickers. The proposed resettlement scheme would cover 20,000 migrants over the period of two years and apply only to those who qualify for 'international protection', i.e., refugees.

14 According to the Stockholm Programme, note 2 above, Point 6.1.6., 'an effective and sustainable return policy is an essential element of a well-managed migration system within the Union. The Union and the Member States should intensify the efforts to return illegally residing third-country nationals.'

15 This is true also with respect to Poland and the UK, which through Protocol (No. 30) on the application of the Charter to Poland and to the United Kingdom, OJ 2010 C 83, p. 313, decided to restrict some internal effects of the Charter of Fundamental Rights. The wording of the Protocol does not support a conclusion that its consequence is an opt-out from the Charter. That Poland and the UK were not exempted from the obligation to comply with the

The second issue that makes the discussion of human rights in the context of the migration and asylum policy difficult concerns the conflicting interests among the Member States. States through which irregular migrants enter the territory of the EU and the migrants themselves often have similar priorities. Irregular migrants in general want to apply for asylum. However, they rarely want to do that in a country through which they have entered the EU (for example, Italy or Greece). Member States through which they entered the EU do not want to become responsible for a large number of migrants. Therefore, they may be reluctant to take administrative or police action, and may in fact allow migrants to abscond, so that they can transfer to another Member State (the migrant's destination state). As negotiations on the European relocation scheme have shown, the Member States' attitude differ depending on whether they are a transfer state or a destination state, or a state that due to its sparing social assistance policy is not an attractive destination for migrants.

1.1 A human right to asylum

While international law instruments are not unequivocal, it is possible to claim that there is a human right to asylum.[16] It is granted to people fleeing persecution or serious harm in their own country and therefore in need of international protection (refugees).[17] Article 18 of the Charter of Fundamental Rights guarantees this right 'with due respect for the rules of the Geneva Convention of 28 July 1951 and the Protocol of 31 January 1967 relating to the status of refugees' and in accordance with the EU Treaties. Despite this statement, the person's individual fundamental right to asylum depends on the fulfilment of a number of requirements. The central one is

Charter was confirmed by the Court of Justice in Joined cases C-411/10 and C-493/10 *NS v Secretary of State for the Home Department and ME v Refugee Applications Commissioner and Minister for Justice, Equality and Law Reform* [2011] ECR I-13905, para 120. Poland and the UK remain also bound by the general principles of EU law protecting fundamental rights, insofar as their actions fall within the scope of Union law.

16 See Article 14 of the Universal Declaration of Human Rights. The right to asylum is mentioned in the Preamble to the 1951 UN Geneva Convention Relating to the Status of Refugees but not in its main text. It is a constitutional right in many Member States of the EU.

17 Granting asylum in specified situations is an international obligation of the Member States, first recognised in the 1951 UN Geneva Convention Relating to the Status of Refugees. Article 1.A.2 of the Convention defines as a refugee 'any person who: owing to a well-founded fear of being persecuted for reasons of race, religion, nationality, membership of a particular social group, or political opinion, is outside the country of his nationality, and is unable to or, owing to such fear, is unwilling to avail himself of the protection of that country'. An almost identical definition is included in Directive 2011/95/EU of the European Parliament and of the Council of 13 December 2011 on standards for the qualification of third-country nationals or stateless persons as beneficiaries of international protection, for a uniform status for refugees or for persons eligible for subsidiary protection, and for the content of the protection granted, OJ L 337, 20 December 2011, p. 9, Article 2(d).

being subjected to the risk of suffering 'serious harm'.[18] A threat to civilian life showing the risk of suffering 'serious harm' has to be individual, although the Court of Justice interpreted this condition expansively 'as covering harm to civilians irrespective of their identity, where the degree of indiscriminate violence characterising the armed conflict taking place … reaches such a high level that substantial grounds are shown for believing that a civilian, returned to the relevant country or, as the case may be, to the relevant region, would, solely on account of his presence on the territory of that country or region, face a real risk of being subject to the serious threat referred in … the Directive'.[19] The competent authorities' task is to determine whether a given migrant possesses the right, i.e., qualifies as a refugee (is entitled to international protection). This is why the procedural safeguards are so crucial in the context of asylum and the migrant's right to remain in the EU. All measures adopted by the EU in the field of asylum constitute jointly the 'Common European Asylum System'.[20]

Unsuccessful asylum-seekers are deported from the EU to their home country, unless it is not 'safe'. Otherwise, they are returned to the Member State that has become responsible for them.[21] The concept of a safe third country is regulated by Article 38 of Directive 2013/32/EU.[22] If a Member State is not satisfied that a person seeking protection will be treated according

18 According to Article 15 of Directive 2011/95/EU, serious harm consists of: '(a) the death penalty or execution; or (b) torture or inhuman or degrading treatment or punishment of an applicant in the country of origin; or (c) serious and individual threat to a civilian's life or person by reason of indiscriminate violence in situations of international or internal armed conflict.'

19 Case C-465/07 *Meki Elgafaji and Noor Elgafaji v Staatssecretaris van Justitie* [2009] ECR I-921, para 35.

20 The term is used in Article 78 TFEU. See also Communication from the Commission to the Council and the European Parliament establishing a framework programme on Solidarity and the Management of Migration Flows for the period 2007–2013, COM(2005)123 final.

21 Regulation (EU) No 604/2013 of the European Parliament and of the Council of 26 June 2013 establishing the criteria and mechanisms for determining the Member State responsible for examining an application for international protection lodged in one of the Member States by a third-country national or a stateless person, OJ L 180, 29 June 2013, p. 31 ('Dublin Regulation'). The regulation is based on the 'safe country' principle, which creates a presumption that all Member States are safe for the purpose of returning illegal migrants. According to Recital 3 of the Regulation: 'Member States, all respecting the principle of *non-refoulement*, are considered as safe countries for third-country nationals.'

22 Directive 2013/32/EU of the European Parliament and of the Council of 26 June 2013 on common procedures for granting and withdrawing international protection, OJ L 180, 29 June 2013, p. 60. Annex I to the Directive states: 'A country is considered as a safe country of origin where, on the basis of the legal situation, the application of the law within a democratic system and the general political circumstances, it can be shown that there is generally and consistently no persecution as defined in Article 9 of Directive 2011/95/EU, no torture or inhuman or degrading treatment or punishment and no threat by reason of indiscriminate violence in situations of international or internal armed conflict. In making this assessment, account shall be taken, inter alia, of the extent to which protection is provided against persecution or mistreatment by: (a) the relevant laws and regulations of the country

to principles listed in the Annex to the Directive, it cannot return them because the third country should not be considered 'safe'.[23] Returning a migrant to a country that was incorrectly considered 'safe' constitutes a violation of his or her human rights. It also constitutes a violation of the Charter of Fundamental Rights, which in Article 19(2) states that '[n]o one may be removed, expelled or extradited to a State where there is a serious risk that he or she would be subjected to the death penalty, torture or other inhuman or degrading treatment or punishment'.

1.2 Human rights issues arising in the asylum examination procedure

Article 51(1) of the Charter, which makes this document binding on the Member States when they are 'implementing Union law',[24] as well the case law of the Court of Justice, which makes EU law's general principles of fundamental rights applicable to Member States when they act within the scope of Union law,[25] means that on the Member State processing an asylum application and deciding on a removal rests a duty to deal with the application in such a way so as not to violate EU fundamental rights. The aforementioned Dublin Regulation provides rules for establishing the Member State formally responsible for examination of the asylum application. It should be stressed that, as will be explained below, also the state that is not formally responsible for examining the asylum application under the Dublin Regulation is under a duty to act in a way compatible with EU fundamental rights. According to Articles 7–17, the criteria that Member States need to use when they

and the manner in which they are applied; (b) observance of the rights and freedoms laid down in the European Convention for the Protection of Human Rights and Fundamental Freedoms and/or the International Covenant for Civil and Political Rights and/or the United Nations Convention against Torture, in particular the rights from which derogation cannot be made under Article 15(2) of the said European Convention; (c) respect for the *non-refoulement* principle in accordance with the Geneva Convention; (d) provision for a system of effective remedies against violations of those rights and freedoms.'

23 These principles are: '(a) life and liberty are not threatened on account of race, religion, nationality, membership of a particular social group or political opinion; (b) there is no risk of serious harm as defined in Directive 2011/95/EU; (c) the principle of *non-refoulement* in accordance with the Geneva Convention is respected; (d) the prohibition of removal, in violation of the right to freedom from torture and cruel, inhuman or degrading treatment as laid down in international law, is respected; and (e) the possibility exists to request refugee status and, if found to be a refugee, to receive protection in accordance with the Geneva Convention.'

24 See Case C-617/10 *Åklagaren v Hans Åkerberg Fransson*, Judgment of 26 February 2013, para 19, where the Court held that 'the fundamental rights guaranteed in the legal order of the European Union are applicable in all situations governed by European Union law … if [national] legislation falls within the scope of European Union law, the Court, when requested to give a preliminary ruling, must provide all the guidance as to interpretation needed in order for the national court to determine whether that legislation is compatible with the fundamental rights the observance of which the Court ensures'.

25 See above.

determine which of them is responsible for examining the application include considerations intended to ensure the protection of minors, joint examination of applications of members of the same family, and the processing of the application by the state with which the applicant already has a connection.

According to Article 18(1) of the Dublin Regulation, 'the Member State responsible' has a duty not only to examine the application and issue a decision but also to take charge of the applicant for whose application it is responsible and take back those applicants who have fled to another Member State. It follows that the criteria that determine which state is responsible for examining the application also determine in which state the applicant should remain. This provides additional justification for why the criteria need to take account of whether the applicant is a minor, where the family members of the applicant are located, and in which state the greatest number of his or her family members have filed an asylum application. We can see that these criteria are aimed at ensuring that the same Member State becomes responsible for processing applications of all migrating family members, and that their applications will be considered jointly. This means that migrating families can be kept together or be reunited within one Member State.[26] It is, however, unclear whether Articles 7–17 laying down the criteria of determining the state responsible create any individual rights. It could be argued that failure to take them into account leading to an incorrect designation of the responsible state constitutes not only a breach of the Regulation but also an infringement of the fundamental right to family life.

The Dublin Regulation sets out the procedure of determining the Member State responsible. It regulates also the taking charge and the taking back procedure. The person concerned has to be notified about the decision to transfer him to another Member State.[27] Articles 26 and 27 guarantee the right to an effective remedy in the form of an appeal or review, in fact and in law, before a court of a tribunal. These provisions codify the right included in Article 47 of the Charter of Fundamental Rights and previously protected by the general principle of effective judicial protection.[28] Given that the Regulation leaves Member States a lot of leeway and in no way prevents them

26 According to Article 12 of Directive 2013/33/EU, 'Member States shall take appropriate measures to maintain as far as possible family unity as present within their territory, if applicants are provided with housing by the Member State concerned. Such measures shall be implemented with the applicant's agreement.'

27 Article 26 of the Dublin Regulation.

28 Unlike many other EU measures, the Regulation includes a series of provisions on how the Member States are to realise that right, i.e., what they should provide in their national laws. They are obliged to provide for a 'reasonable' period of time within which the person concerned may bring an appeal or an application of a review, the appeal or review has to confer upon the person concerned the right to remain in the Member State pending the outcome of the appeal or review or at least the possibility of requesting the suspension of the implementation of the transfer decision. The Member States have to ensure access to free legal and linguistic assistance, when the applicant cannot afford the costs or at least on the same

from offering more generous rights enabling easier access to an effective remedy, it is unlikely that the Regulation could be challenged as incompatible with the fundamental rights of an effective remedy and of access to a court. It is however a persisting issue how Articles 26 and 27 should be interpreted, in particular in the light of the fact that they do not demand a suspensive effect, do not require free legal assistance in every case, do not create a right to appeal from the judicial decision in the first instance, and do not specify what time period at the minimum could be regarded as 'reasonable'.

Apart from remedial and procedural rights, another difficult issue concerns the applicant's freedom in the Member State considering his or her application. The Dublin Regulation allows Member States to hold asylum-seekers in detention, although applying for asylum cannot be the only reason for detaining the applicant.[29] Instead, detention should be a response to a significant risk of absconding, especially in the time before the person is transferred to another Member State. The right to challenge detention is guaranteed by Article 26 of Directive 2013/32/EU.[30]

More detailed issues of detention are regulated by Directive 2013/33/EU,[31] which lays down standards for the reception of applicants for international protection. Generally, applicants are guaranteed the freedom to move freely within the territory of the host Member State or within an area assigned to them by that Member State.[32] Under Article 17, Member States have to ensure that material reception conditions are available to applicants for international protection. The Member States should provide an adequate standard of living for applicants, guaranteeing their subsistence and protecting their physical and mental health. Applicants have to contribute to the costs of their subsistence and protection only if they have sufficient resources; for example, if they have been working for a reasonable period of time. If housing is provided, it has to offer an adequate standard of living, protection of the applicant's family life, the possibility of communicating with relatives, legal advisors and other representatives, including their physical access. Member States have also a duty to ensure physical safety of applicants, protection from harassment and access to at least emergency health care and essential treatment of illnesses and serious mental disorders.

Applying for asylum cannot be the only reason why the person is detained.[33] The Member State is entitled to detain the applicant only on the basis of an

conditions as those on the basis of which legal assistance is generally accorded. However, legal assistance may be offered only in cases with a tangible prospect of success. Moreover, the Regulation creates a duty to inform about the remedial rights under national law.

29 Article 28(1).

30 See note 22 above.

31 Directive 2013/33/EU of the European Parliament and of the Council of 26 June 2013 laying down standards for the reception of applicants for international protection, OJ L 180, 29 June 2013, p. 96, the so-called 'Reception Conditions Directive'.

32 Article 7(1).

33 Article 8(1).

individual assessment of each case, if other less coercive alternative measures cannot be applied effectively, and only in order to determine or verify his or her identity or nationality, to determine those elements on which the application for international protection is based that could not be obtained in the absence of detention, in particular when there is a risk of absconding. Detention can also be used if necessary for taking of the decision on the applicant's right to enter the territory and when required by national security or public order. The decision to detain the applicant can be taken by a judicial or an administrative authority, but when it is taken by an administrative authority, the Member State has to provide for a speedy judicial review of the lawfulness of detention. Detained applicants are to be kept in specialised facilities or, if in prison, separately from ordinary prisoners, and should have channels of communication with their family members, legal advisors and other representatives.[34] The Member States have to look after their health, including mental health.[35]

Directive 2013/32/EU[36] lays down the procedures applicable in asylum cases. The Directive ensures protection of fundamental rights of asylum-seekers by providing them with a set of concrete rights, particularly important in a system based on the idea of a single procedure (one responsible state). Of particular importance is the goal of ensuring objective and impartial examination of applications, without undue delay, access to legal assistance and special procedural guarantees in the case of some applicants. All applications must be examined on the substance. Decisions taken on an application for international protection, the decisions concerning a refusal to reopen the examination of an application after its discontinuation, and the decisions on the withdrawal of refugee or subsidiary protection status have to be reviewable. In this way, the Directive guarantees respect for the fundamental right to an effective remedy before a court or tribunal.

Of much practical significance for asylum-seekers is Article 9 of the Directive, which creates a right to remain in the Member State pending the examination of the application until the determining authority has made a decision in accordance with the relevant procedures.[37] Article 20 of the

34 Article 10.

35 Article 11(1).

36 For more on Directive 2013/32/EU, see C. Costello and E. Hancox, 'The Recast Asylum Procedures Directive 2013/32/EU: caught between the stereotypes of the abusive asylum seeker and the vulnerable refugee', in V. Chetail, P. De Bruycker and F. Maiani (eds.), *Reforming the Common European Asylum System: The New European Refugee Law* (Martinus Nijhoff, 2015).

37 There is an exception to this right under Article 41 of Directive 2013/32/EU in the case of subsequent applications lodged merely in order to delay or frustrate the enforcement of a decision that would result in the applicant's imminent removal from that Member State or another application following a final decision considering a first subsequent application inadmissible or after a final decision to reject that application as unfounded. Member States may rely on the exception only where the determining authority considers that a return

Directive grants asylum-seekers the right to free legal assistance and representation on request and defines its minimal scope,[38] but Member States are entitled to refuse it to those who have sufficient resources or where, in case of the applicant's appeal, it is considered by a court or tribunal or other competent authority that the appeal has no tangible prospect of success. However, the applicant has the right to challenge the refusal.[39] Article 25 guarantees protection of unaccompanied minors, including more restrictive conditions under which the Member State is entitled to deport a minor. Similar and additional rights of minors vis-à-vis detention are also guaranteed by Article 11 of Directive 2013/33/EU.

1.3 *Reception conditions, human rights and the responsibility of a Member State to examine an asylum application*

As explained above, the state that examines and takes decisions on an application for international protection made by an asylum-seeker is the 'responsible' state under the Dublin Regulation. The package of EU measures regulating asylum entrusts the 'responsible state' not only with the duty to examine the application according to prescribed rules, but also with a duty to take charge of the applicants themselves. As we have seen, the responsible state has to take back such an applicant when so requested by another Member State and provide adequate reception conditions. This creates a very heavy burden on these few EU states through which irregular migrants enter the EU, because according to Article 13(1) of the Dublin Regulation, in the case of irregular migrants, the Member States into which the migrant has crossed the border from a third country becomes the 'responsible' state. It follows that some Member States, due to a large number of irregular migrants, limited resources, absence of an adequate system for dealing with irregular migration, can find it difficult to cope with the requirements of EU law, including the duty to respect, in the case of asylum-seekers, their fundamental rights in the conditions of living offered to them. The Dublin Regulation, as well as its predecessor, Regulation 343/2003,[40] includes a 'discretionary clause' (Article 17), which entitles the Member States to

decision will not lead to direct or indirect *refoulement* in violation of that Member State's international and Union obligations.

38 The legal assistance has to include the preparation of the required procedural documents and participation in the hearing before a court or tribunal of first instance on behalf of the applicant (Article 20(1)).

39 Article 20(3) and Article 21(2).

40 Council Regulation (EC) No 343/2003 of 18 February 2003 establishing the criteria and mechanisms for determining the Member State responsible for examining an asylum application lodged in one of the Member States by a third-country national, OJ L 50, 25 February 2003, p. 1. The discretionary clause was included in Article 3(1), which, just like Article 17 of the Dublin Regulation, entitled the Member States to examine an application even if they were not the responsible state under the general rules of the Regulation.

examine an application even where they are not the 'responsible state' under general rules. The Member State that decides to examine an application for international protection pursuant to this paragraph becomes the Member State responsible and assumes aforementioned obligations associated with that responsibility.

An EU state that has been facing large numbers of asylum-seekers, exceeding the capacities of its asylum system, is Greece. In 2011 the European Court of Human Rights in case *MSS v Belgium and Greece*[41] held that the conditions of detention and the living conditions of asylum-seekers in Greece were to be regarded as a violation of Article 3 of the ECHR.[42] The Court concluded that there was a risk of direct or indirect *refoulement* to the home country of asylum applicants without any serious examination of their applications. This fact, in the absence of an effective judicial remedy, constituted violation of Article 13 in conjunction with Article 3.[43] The European Court of Human Rights also found that a state that returned the migrant to Greece, as the country that under the general rules was the 'responsible' state, also violated Article 3 of the ECHR because by doing so it had exposed him or her to the risks linked to the identified deficiencies in the Greek asylum system and to detention and living conditions that were in breach of Article 3 of the ECHR.

In the *NS*[44] case, the Court of Justice of the EU was asked about the consequences of the human rights violations in Greece for the operation of the European Common Asylum System. The Court had to determine whether any additional obligations stemmed, as a matter of EU law, from the Member States' duty to respect fundamental rights for a Member State in which an asylum application had been lodged and where the applicant was present but which was not under general rules the 'responsible' state, from the Member State's duty to respect the applicant's fundamental rights. On the facts, the Court had to decide whether the UK and Ireland were supposed to give effect to EU rules on the responsible state and transfer applicants back to Greece, even where it had been established that such a transfer would expose the asylum-seeker to having his or her fundamental rights violated. Under EU law, all Member States were presumed to be observing the standards laid down by that law, including fundamental rights. It followed that the Member States were bound by the principle of mutual trust and had to follow the formal rules of the Dublin Regulation. If, however, the principle no longer

41 Judgment of 21 January 2011, Application No 30696/09.

42 Article 3 ECHR: 'No one shall be subjected to torture or to inhuman or degrading treatment or punishment.'

43 Article 13 ECHR: 'Everyone whose rights and freedoms as set forth in this Convention are violated shall have an effective remedy before a national authority notwithstanding that the violation has been committed by persons acting in an official capacity.'

44 Joined cases C-411/10 and C-493/10 *NS v Secretary of State for the Home Department and ME v Refugee Applications Commissioner and Minister for Justice, Equality and Law Reform* [2011] ECR I-13905.

applied, the Member States would have to take account of the actual human rights situation in the responsible state and possibly use their discretionary powers exceptionally to identify themselves as the 'responsible' state.

The Court of Justice chose a solution that retained elements of the principle of mutual trust but at the same time avoided a situation where individuals were returned to a country where it was very likely that their human rights would be violated. Thus, the Court distinguished two situations affecting states infringing human rights. The first concerned a state in which a transferee may suffer some infringement of human rights but there are no systemic flaws in the asylum procedure and in reception conditions. The second situation concerned a state with respect to which there were substantial grounds for believing that it suffered from systemic flaws in its asylum procedure and in reception conditions, resulting in inhuman or degrading treatment. In the former case the transfer was permitted, in the latter it was prohibited by EU fundamental rights.[45] In paragraphs 88 and 89 of the judgment, the Court noted that a situation similar to those at issue in the cases before it had been the subject of a judgment of the European Court of Human Rights. The Court observed that 'the extent of the infringement of fundamental rights described in that judgment shows that there existed in Greece, at the time of the transfer of the applicant MSS, a systemic deficiency in the asylum procedure and in the reception conditions of asylum seekers'.[46] So it could be said that the UK and Ireland knew or should have known of the systemic deficiencies in Greece. The Court thereby created a duty for the Member State in which the application was lodged, which knew or had to have known of the systemic deficiencies in the 'responsible state', to use its discretionary powers to continue examining the criteria set out in the Regulation in order to establish whether another Member State could be identified as 'responsible', and accept responsibility for the asylum application if the responsible state could not be designated on the basis of these criteria.[47] The exception to the principle of mutual trust, based, as the Court claimed in paragraph 93, on the principle of solidarity, was nevertheless created only for 'exceptional situations' defined as 'a mass influx of displaced persons'.

Another issue is the scope of entitlements offered to illegally staying third-country nationals as far as their reception conditions are concerned. Also here, fundamental rights can be used to broaden that scope. In *Abdida*,[48]

45 Ibid., para 86.

46 The substantive evidence on which the Court of Justice relied included the regular and unanimous reports of international non-governmental organisations bearing witness to the practical difficulties in the implementation of the Common European Asylum System in Greece, the correspondence sent by the United Nations High Commissioner for Refugees (UNHCR) to the Belgian minister responsible, and also the Commission reports on the evaluation of the Dublin System and the proposals for recasting Regulation No. 343/2003 in order to improve the efficiency of the system and the effective protection of fundamental rights (*MSS v Belgium and Greece*, § 347–350).

47 *NS* (note 44 above), paras 96–97.

48 Case C-562/13 *Centre public d'action sociale d'Ottignies-Louvain-la-Neuve v Moussa Abdida*, Judgment of 18 December 2014.

the applicant argued that he had a right to emergency medical assistance and social assistance equal to that offered to nationals of the state where he was located. According to Article 14(1) of Directive 2008/115/EC on the return of the illegally staying third-country nationals, the Member States are not required to make provision for emergency health care and essential treatment of illness or for basic needs, but are only asked to ensure that the principle of access to emergency health care and essential treatment of illness is taken into account 'as far as possible'. Nevertheless, the Court interpreted this provision to mean that the Member States are required to provide emergency health care and essential treatment of illness, and that effectiveness of these rights required that the applicant was provided for his basic needs.[49] The Court held, however, that it was for the Member States to determine 'the form in which such provision for the basic needs of the third country national concerned [was] to be made', as long as it was sufficient for the person to be able to avail himself of emergency health care and essential treatment of illness during the period in which his removal from the Member States is postponed following their appeal from the return decision.[50]

1.4 The right to family life of regular migrants and refugees

A separate human rights issue, which concerns both regular migrants from third countries and recognised refugees, is the possibility of their unification with families still residing in third countries. This matter is regulated by the Family Reunification Directive.[51] Recital 4 presents family reunification as necessary in making family life possible, while Recital 5 asks the Member States to give effect to the provisions of the Directive without discrimination on the basis of sex, race, colour, ethnic or social origin, genetic characteristics, language, religion or beliefs, political or other opinions, membership of a national minority, fortune, birth, disabilities, age or sexual orientation. Under the Directive, the Member States are required to authorise family reunification of the spouse and children of 'the sponsor'. A third-country national can be a 'sponsor' if he or she holds a residence permit issued by a Member State for a period of validity of at least one year and has reasonable prospects of obtaining the right of permanent residence.[52]

According to Article 4(6), Member States may request that applications for family reunification of minor children are submitted before the age of

49 Ibid., para 60.
50 Ibid., para 61.
51 Council Directive 2003/86/EC of 22 September 2003 on the right to family reunification, OJ 2003 L 251, p. 12.
52 Article 3 of the Directive. The Member States are free to decide whether they wish to include among those entitled to reunification with a third-country national already present in their territory the relatives in the direct ascending line, adult unmarried children, unmarried or registered partners or, in the event of a polygamous marriage, minor children of a further spouse and the sponsor.

15, if so provided for by its existing legislation on the date of the implementation of the Directive. If the application is submitted after the age of 15, the Member States that have decided to apply this derogation may authorise the entry and residence of such children on grounds other than family reunification. The Member States may also limit the right to family reunification of children over the age of 12, whose primary residence is not with the sponsor. According to paragraph 3 of Article 4, the Member States may, before authorising entry and residence under the Directive, verify whether a minor above the age of 12 meets a condition for integration provided for by its legislation if the condition existed on the date of implementation of the Directive. The right to family reunification is, moreover, conditional on the sponsor showing that he or she has adequate accommodation, sickness insurance for himself or herself and the family members, and stable and regular resources sufficient to maintain the family without recourse to the social assistance systems of the Member State. These requirements do not apply to refugees, and neither do the restrictions concerning the refugee's children's age or the minimum period of residence in the Member State. The Member States have to ensure that the sponsor and/or the members of his/her family have the right to mount a legal challenge where an application for family reunification is rejected or a residence permit is either not renewed or is withdrawn or removal is ordered.[53] The UK, Ireland and Denmark are not bound by the Directive.

The Directive was subjected to a validity challenge on the ground of its incompatibility with the right to family life in an action brought before the Court of Justice by the European Parliament.[54] The challenge concerned restrictions imposed on the reunification of minor children above the age of 12 (where the integration requirement may apply) and above the age of 15 (with respect to which the Member States are entitled not to accept the applications at all). The Court held that Article 4(1) of the Directive could not be regarded as running counter to the right to family life because the margin of appreciation it left for the Member States corresponded to that accorded to states by the European Court of Human Rights, and because the Directive required the Member States to consider the issues with due regard to the best interests of minor children.[55] The requirement concerning the integration condition was presented by the Court to protect the applicant child and not the Member State's discretion in allowing reunification. This was a problematic interpretation of the function of the requirement, given that the concept of integration had not been defined in the Directive. In paragraph 70, the Court insisted, however, that '[t]he fact that the concept of integration [was] not defined [could not] be interpreted as authorising

53 Article 18.

54 Case C-540/03 *Parliament v Council* [2006] I-5769.

55 Ibid., paras 62–63.

the Member States to employ that concept in a manner contrary to general principles of Community law, in particular to fundamental rights'. The Court also rejected a challenge to the same provision of the Directive based on a breach of the duty to respect the best interests of a child and on the ground of age discrimination.[56] Twelve years was not considered to be an arbitrary limit because, in the Court's view, the criterion corresponded to 'a stage in the life of a minor child when the latter has already lived for a relatively long period in a third country without the members of his or her family, so that integration in another environment was liable to give rise to more difficulties'.[57] The limitation on the right of minor children above the age of 15 was also held legal because the Member States were merely free from a duty to consider applications brought by children above that age. The Court concluded that this derogation did not mean that the application could simply be rejected. The Member State continued to be 'obliged to examine the application in the interests of the child and with a view to promoting family life'.[58] In this way, the Court saved the validity of the relevant provisions of the Directive. The Member States' entitlement not to consider an application at all was converted into a duty to examine the application in the light of the general principles of fundamental rights. Only where these were not infringed would the Member State retain the power to reject an application brought by a minor child above the age of 15.

1.5 Removal of illegal migrants and penalties for illegal migration

It is not incompatible with EU fundamental rights for the Member States to remove illegally staying third-country nationals from their territory. In fact, apart from Denmark, Ireland and the UK, which do not participate in this regime, EU Member States are obliged to remove such migrants as a matter of EU law. The matter is regulated by Directive 2008/115/EC ('Return Directive').[59] Article 1 of the Directive lays down the common standards and procedures binding on the Member States 'in accordance with fundamental rights as general principles of Community law as well as international law, including refugee protection and human rights obligations'. The Directive requires the Member States to take decisions on a case-by-case basis and in reliance on objective criteria, the consideration going beyond the mere

56 Ibid., paras 73–74.
57 Ibid., para 74.
58 Ibid., para 88.
59 Directive 2008/115/EC of the European Parliament and of the Council of 16 December 2008 on common standards and procedures in Member States for returning illegally staying third-country nationals, OJ L 348, 24 December 2008, p. 98. The Directive replaced Article 23 of the CISA, i.e., the Convention implementing the Schengen Agreement of 14 June 1985 between the governments of the States of the Benelux Economic Union, the Federal Republic of Germany and the French Republic on the gradual abolition of checks at their common borders, OJ L 239, 22 September 2000, p. 19.

fact of illegal stay.[60] National legislation should define the basic conditions of subsistence of illegal migrants who cannot yet be removed, who also need to be provided with written confirmation of their situation so that they can explain their situation in case of checks. Article 7 of the Directive gives preference to a voluntary, rather than forced, departure of an illegally staying third-country national. A return decision should provide for a period between seven to 30 days for that possibility.[61] However, the Member States are entitled not to grant a period for voluntary departure or grant a shorter period if there is a risk of absconding, if an application for a legal stay has been dismissed as manifestly unfounded or fraudulent, or if the person concerned poses a risk to public policy, public security or national security.[62] According to the Court's case law, the voluntary departure protects fundamental rights of the illegally staying third-country national.[63] It follows that the risk to public policy has to be assessed on a case-by-case basis, in order to ascertain whether the personal conduct of the third-country national concerned poses a genuine and present risk to public policy and should not be assumed or stem from a general practice.[64]

The Return Directive also imposes on the Member States the obligation to comply with the principle of proportionality in the use of coercive measures and detention.[65] According to the Directive, detention is justified only to prepare the return or carry out the removal process and if the application of less coercive measures would not be sufficient. In detention, third-country nationals have the right to be treated in a humane and dignified manner with respect for their fundamental rights and in compliance with international and national law. They should be kept in specialised detention facilities, not prisons.[66] As for coercive measures, they need to be laid down in national legislation in accordance with fundamental rights. Member States are under a duty to respect the dignity and physical integrity of the third-country national. Minors and families are to be detained only as a measure of last resort and families should be provided with accommodation ensuring their privacy.[67] Article 5 requires Member States to take due account when deciding on the

60 Recital 6.

61 According to Article 7(1) of the Directive, 'Member States may provide in their national legislation that such a period shall be granted only following an application by the third-country national concerned'.

62 Article 7(4).

63 Case C-554/13 *Z. Zh. v Staatssecretaris voor Veiligheid en Justitie and Staatssecretaris voor Veiligheid en Justitie*, Judgment of 11 June 2015, para 48.

64 Ibid., para 50.

65 Articles 8(4) and 15 of the Directive. According to the case law of the European Court of Human Rights, the principle of proportionality requires that the detention of a person against whom a deportation or extradition procedure is underway should not continue for an unreasonable length of time; that is, its length should not exceed that required for the purpose pursued (*Saadi v United Kingdom*, 29 January 2008, § 72 and 74).

66 Article 16.

67 Article 17.

removal and in the process of removal, of the best interests of the child, the right to family life and the state of health of the third-country national. Article 14 more specifically asks the Member States to maintain family unity with family members present in their territory, provide emergency health care and essential treatment and take account of the special needs of vulnerable persons. According to the Return Directive, decisions on removal should state factual and legal reasons and inform about available legal remedies, which have to include an effective remedy to appeal or seek review before bodies with a power temporarily to suspend the enforcement of the decision on removal.[68]

A number of cases before the Court of Justice raised the question of implications of the fundamental rights obligations of the Member States in the context of the duty to remove illegal migrants. They concerned the power of the Member States to impose 'penalties', in particular a prison sentence for the fact of illegal stay. In *El Dridi* the Court ruled that the Member States could not provide for a custodial sentence on the sole ground that a third-country national continued to stay illegally on their territory after the period granted him to leave the state had expired.[69] A custodial sentence was held incompatible with the Directive's objective, which aims at the removal of illegally staying migrants and not their retention in prisons. This was confirmed in *Achughbabian*,[70] a case concerning an illegal migrant who was placed in police custody beyond 48 hours. The Court clarified that the Directive did not preclude the law of a Member State from classifying an illegal stay as an offence and laying down penal sanctions to deter and prevent such an infringement of the national rules on residence.[71] Third-country nationals could be placed in detention with a view to determining whether or not their stay was lawful, and could be placed in police custody to prevent them from fleeing before their situation was clarified. But a custodial sentence and the preceding criminal proceedings delayed the removal and thus went against the Directive's objective.

It follows from these judgments that the Court is opposed to the broadening of measures with which the Member States could fight illegal migration. The Return Directive opted for removal vis-à-vis the imposition of criminal penalties as the appropriate solution to the problem of illegal migration, and the Court strengthened that choice by precluding Member States'

68 Article 13.

69 Case C-61/11 PPU *Criminal proceedings against Hassen El Dridi, alias Karim Soufi* [2011] ECR I-3015, para 58.

70 Case C-329/11 *Alexandre Achughbabian v Préfet du Val-de-Marne* [2011] ECR I-12695, para 37: 'the imposition and enforcement of a sentence of imprisonment during the course of the return procedure provided for by Directive 2008/115 do not contribute to the carrying through of the removal which that procedure is intended to achieve, namely, the physical transportation of the person concerned out of the Member State concerned. Such a sentence does not therefore constitute a "measure" or a "coercive measure" within the meaning of Article 8 of Directive 2008/115.'

71 Ibid., para 28.

possibility to impose a custodial penalty. The rulings could thus be perceived as protecting illegally staying third-country nationals' liberty. However, in its reasoning, the Court elected to rely not on this argument but on the effectiveness of the removal procedure laid down by the Directive. This choice of grounds has implications for other cases. In *Zaizoune*,[72] the Court examined national legislation providing for the possibility of replacing a removal of an illegally staying third-country national with a financial penalty as a form of leniency shown by the Member State in the absence of aggravating factors justifying the removal. From a human rights perspective, this would be a more favourable solution because it enabled the individual to remain in the territory of an EU state. The Court held, however, that the state was not authorised to impose financial penalties in the place of a removal. The objective of Directive 2008/115/EC was to remove illegally staying third-country nationals from the territory of the Member States. More favourable national provisions had to be compatible with the Directive's objective, and a financial penalty as an alternative to removal was not because it delayed the return of the illegal migrant.[73]

1.6 *The right to be heard and the right to an effective remedy in asylum and return proceedings*

Article 47 of the Charter of Fundamental Rights guarantees everyone 'whose rights and freedoms guaranteed by the law of the Union are violated [...] the right to an effective remedy before a tribunal'. Article 41 of the Charter guarantees as part of the right to good administration the right to be heard, but that right, under a strict interpretation of that provision, is enforceable only against Union institutions, bodies and offices, and not against the Member States. However, the right to an effective remedy is strongly correlated with the right of defence, which the Court has interpreted to include the right to be heard.[74] These Charter rights are concretised in the context of the immigration and asylum policy in secondary law. Above, I have already described the legislative safeguards of the right to an effective

72 Case C-38/14 *Subdelegación del Gobierno en Gipuzkoa – Extranjería v Samir Zaizoune*, Judgment of 23 April 2015.

73 Ibid., paras 38 and 40. The prohibition on imposing on an illegally staying third-country national of a custodial sentence does not mean that the person cannot be detained, if further circumstances, beyond the illegal stay, exist. The Return Directive offers less strict conditions than those applying in the case of asylum-seekers. In Case C-534/11, *Mehmet Arslan v Policie ČR, Krajské ředitelství policie Ústeckého kraje, odbor cizinecké policie*, Judgment of 30 May 2013, the Court had to decide which conditions applied in the case of third-country nationals without a residence permit who applied for asylum. The Court held that a person who has applied for asylum could not be considered 'illegally staying' and the Return Directive did not apply until the outcome of the action brought by the applicant in relation to their request for international protection was known (para 48).

74 Case C-166/13 *Sophie Mukarubega v Préfet de police and Préfet de la Seine-Saint-Denis*, Judgment of 5 November 2014, para 45.

remedy and the right to be heard in the context of decisions concerning the responsible state and detention.[75] In this section, I will discuss the legislative safeguards offered to the right to an effective remedy in the context of the most important decisions taken by the Member States from the perspective of a third-country national wishing to stay in the EU – a decision to refuse asylum and a decision to remove the person from the EU.

Article 46 of Directive 2013/32/EU guarantees the right to an effective remedy before a court or tribunal against any decision taken on an asylum application, including a decision considering an application to be unfounded or inadmissible, a refusal to reopen the examination of an application, or a decision to withdraw international protection. 'An effective remedy', according to the same Article, has to provide for a full and *ex nunc* examination of both facts and points of law, in appeals procedures before a court or tribunal of at least first instance. The time limits imposed by the Member State cannot render the exercise of the right to an effective remedy impossible or excessively difficult. Member States are obliged to allow applicants to remain in the territory until the time limit within which they could exercise their right to an effective remedy has expired and, when such a right has been exercised within the time limit, pending the outcome of the remedy. Where the application was held by the challenged decision to be 'manifestly unfounded' or inadmissible, a court of the Member State has the power to rule whether or not the applicant may remain on the territory of that state.

Directive 2013/32/EU, as well as its predecessor, Directive 2005/85/EC,[76] did not guarantee the right to two instances of judicial proceedings (the right to appeal against a first-instance court judgment). Neither did it specify which of the decisions taken in the course of asylum proceedings should be regarded as 'decisions taken on an asylum application' and therefore covered by the right to an effective remedy guaranteed by the Directive. It follows that the Member States retain a broad margin of procedural autonomy.[77] Nevertheless, it could be argued that the legislative safeguards should be interpreted expansively, the rights expressly guaranteed should be assured 'full effect' and that the principle of effective judicial protection has to be observed also in cases not explicitly mentioned in the Directive.

The Court considered these issues in *Samba Diouf*.[78] The case concerned a challenge against an administrative decision to direct the applicant's case under national law to an accelerated procedure. Decisions taken

75 For more on this topic, see M. Reneman, *EU Asylum Procedures and the Right to an Effective Remedy* (Hart Publishing, 2014).

76 Council Directive 2005/85/EC of 1 December 2005 on minimum standards on procedures in Member States for granting and withdrawing refugee status. OJ 2005 L 326, p. 13.

77 On the procedural safeguards offered by the law of the UK, see S. Craig and M. Fletcher, 'The supervision of immigration and asylum appeals in the UK – taking stock' (2012) 24 *International Journal of Refugee Law* 60.

78 Case C-69/10 *Brahim Samba Diouf v Ministre du Travail, de l'Emploi et de l'Immigration* [2011] ECR I-7151.

in that procedure were reviewable but only by a court of first instance. No further appeal was envisaged under national law. The national court asked the Court of Justice whether Directive 2005/85/EC, interpreted in light of the right to an effective remedy, precluded a national law that allowed asylum cases to be dealt with through an accelerated procedure if there was no remedy against the decision to direct a case to such a procedure and if this decision deprived the applicant of the right to appeal from the judgment taken by a court reviewing the decision taken on the asylum application. The Court of Justice did not extend the right to an effective remedy onto the decision to direct the applicant's case to an accelerated procedure because it regarded that decision as merely preparatory.[79] The national court was nevertheless reminded of its duty to interpret national procedural law consistently with EU law to ensure that some review of the choice of the accelerated procedure was made possible, as demanded by the right to an effective remedy.[80] The Court was also not prepared to use the principle of effective judicial protection or Article 47 of the Charter to create a right to appeal, which was not explicitly guaranteed by the Directive.[81] The case clearly shows the limits of the arguments based on fundamental rights, in particular if reliance on them was to lead to the imposition of a duty on the Member States to create new remedies under national law.[82]

Observance of the right to be heard is an element of due process. It is a procedural right, which may affect the validity of a decision taken in its violation.[83] As explained above, the decision to return a third-country national to the third country is often preceded by a decision rejecting his or her asylum application. Alternatively, third-country nationals apply for a residence permits under national law and if they are refused, the state is in principle under a duty to remove them from the EU. The question that arose in *Mukarubega*[84] was whether the person concerned had to be heard twice, before the asylum decision and separately before the return decision, or it was sufficient to hear the person only once, before the asylum application was rejected. The Court held that it was sufficient if the applicant was heard only once, i.e., before the decision on the legality of stay was adopted.[85] The Court pointed out that:

79 Ibid., paras 43 and 55–58.

80 Ibid., paras 59–61.

81 Ibid., para 69.

82 Case 158/80 *Rewe-Handelsgesellschaft Nord mbH and Rewe-Markt Steffen v Hauptzollamt Kiel* [1981] ECR 1805; Case C-13/01 *Safalero Srl v Prefetto di Genova* [2003] ECR I-8679.

83 See for example, Joined cases C-402/05 P and C-415/05 P *Yassin Abdullah Kadi and Al Barakaat International Foundation v Council and Commission* [2008] ECR I-6351, where the Court invalidated an EU Regulation because the applicant's procedural rights have not been respected.

84 Case C-166/13 *Sophie Mukarubega v Préfet de police, Préfet de la Seine-Saint-Denis*, Judgment of 5 November 2014.

85 Ibid., para 60. It follows that under EU law, as interpreted by the Court of Justice, there is no duty to hear the applicant specifically on the subject of the return (ibid., para 82).

> the right to be heard before the adoption of a return decision cannot be used in order to re-open indefinitely the administrative procedure, for the reason that the balance between the fundamental right of the person concerned to be heard before the adoption of a decision adversely affecting that person and the obligation of the Member States to combat illegal immigration must be maintained.[86]

In *N and R*,[87] the Court explained the consequences of the breach of the right to be heard. It ruled that such an infringement results in annulment of the decision only if, had it not been for that irregularity, the outcome of the procedure 'might have been different'.[88] Any other interpretation would undermine the effectiveness of the return policy of the Directive.

A slightly different picture of the obligations of the Member States stemming from the right to be heard in the context of a return decision emerges from the Court's judgment in *Boudjlida*.[89] The case concerned the third-country national's right to be given a period of reflection before he submitted observations to the authority before being heard on his return to a third country, and the right to legal representation of his choice. The Court confirmed that the right to be heard in principle relates to the information about the legality of the stay and not the correctness of the return decision.[90] However, under Directive 2008/115/EC, the Member States have a duty to consider various other circumstances before they issue a return decision, such as the possible existence of a residence permit issued by another Member State or the best interest of the child.[91] They also need to respect the principle of *non-refoulement*. Furthermore, as the Court held in paragraph 51, 'the right to be heard before the adoption of a return decision implies that the competent national authorities are under an obligation to enable the person concerned to express his point of view on the detailed arrangements for his return, such as the period allowed for departure and whether return is to be voluntary or coerced'. However, the right to be heard did not entail that the person was given a period for reflection before the person submitted his or her observations, i.e., the illegally staying third-country nationals do not have to be warned prior to interview that the authority is contemplating adopting a return decision against them.[92] The Member States were also not required to provide free

86 Ibid., para 71.
87 Case C-383/13 PPU *MG, NR v Staatssecretaris van Veiligheid en Justitie*, Judgment of 10 September 2013.
88 Ibid., para 38.
89 Case C-249/13 *Khaled Boudjlida v Préfet des Pyrénées-Atlantiques*, Judgment of 11 December 2014.
90 Ibid., para 47.
91 Articles 5 and 6 of the Return Directive.
92 *Boudjlida*, note 89 above, para 55.

legal assistance to those who are 'being heard' but the applicant was entitled to legal representation at his or her own expense 'provided that the exercise of that right does not affect the due progress of the return procedure and does not undermine the effective implementation of Directive 2008/115'.[93]

Also, the principle of *non-refoulement* has important implications for the possibility to create a suspensive effect vis-à-vis decisions of national authorities that are not covered by EU secondary law. For example, in *Abdida*,[94] the applicant's request for a residence permit on medical grounds was rejected. He challenged the decision and argued that his return should be suspended until the outcome of the appeal is decided because his (immediate) return to the country of origin was incompatible with the principle of *non-refoulement* and Article 47 of the Charter. The applicant maintained that his country did not have adequate medical infrastructure for caring for persons suffering from his illness. As explained above, Article 19(2) of the Charter stated that no one should be removed to a state where there is a serious risk that he or she would be subjected to inhuman or degrading treatment.

The Court of Justice in its judgment first referred to the case law of the European Court of Human Rights, which has ruled that non-nationals subject to a decision authorising their removal could not claim any entitlement to remain in the territory of a state in order to continue to benefit from medical, social or other forms of assistance and services provided by that state.[95] In accordance with the case law of the European Court of Human Rights, the decision to remove a foreign national suffering from a serious illness to a country where the facilities for the treatment are inferior could be incompatible with Article 2 ECHR only in very exceptional cases 'where the humanitarian grounds against removal are compelling'.[96] It followed that also under Directive 2008/115/EC, interpreted in the light of the Charter and the jurisprudence of the European Court of Human Rights, a return of a third-country national suffering from a serious illness to a country in which appropriate treatment was not ensured was prohibited, albeit in very limited circumstances, and therefore the individual had to be granted a remedy with suspensive effect, so as to ensure that the return decision is not enforced before a competent authority had examined the alleged infringement of the Directive.[97]

93 Ibid., paras 64–65 and 70.

94 Case C-562/13 *Centre public d'action sociale d'Ottignies-Louvain-La-Neuve v Moussa Abdida*, Judgment of 18 December 2014.

95 Ibid., para 47.

96 *N v the UK*, no. 26565/05, § 42, ECHR 2008.

97 Ibid., paras 49–50.

2 Combating crime

The AFSJ policy focused on prevention of crime in practice involves coordination and cooperation between police and judicial authorities of the Member States.[98] According to Article 82(1) of the TFEU, the judicial cooperation is based on the principle of mutual recognition of judgments and judicial decisions. A number of principles protecting human rights, either directly or indirectly, are relevant in the crime prevention strand of the EU's AFSJ.[99] They include ***nullum crimen sine lege***, non-retroactivity of criminal provisions,[100] presumption of innocence,[101] proportionate penalties[102] and absence of penalties incompatible with the right to life and human dignity, as well as a number of procedural principles, such as that of a fair trial, the right of the defence and ***ne bis in idem***, discussed more fully below. The EU's objective of effective cooperation between criminal justice systems of the Member States, and especially the mutual recognition of judicial decisions – such as those requesting the cross-border surrender of an accused person or the giving effect to a penalty imposed by a court of another Member State – raise independent concerns in the light of human rights, in particular in the light of the principle of legality, equal treatment and access to a court. The collection of personal data in order to combat crime could in itself be seen as an infringement of the right to private life and privacy unless justified by a specific legitimate purpose.[103]

The Treaty of Lisbon addressed the most glaring deficiency of human rights protection in this field – absence of jurisdiction of the Court of Justice in issues concerning police and judicial cooperation in criminal matters

98 Articles 81–83 TFEU.

99 E. Herlin-Karnell, 'Constitutional principles in the Area of Freedom, Security and Justice', in D. Acosta Arcarazo and C. Murphy (eds.), *EU Security and Justice Law* (Hart Publishing, 2014) 38.

100 See Article 7 of the ECHR: 'No one shall be held guilty of any criminal offence on account of any act or omission which did not constitute a criminal offence under national or international law at the time when it was committed. Nor shall a heavier penalty be imposed than the one that was applicable at the time the criminal offence was committed.' Article 49(1) of the EU Charter also adds: 'If, subsequent to the commission of a criminal offence, the law provides for a lighter penalty, that penalty shall be applicable.'

101 Article 48(1) of the Charter: 'Everyone who has been charged shall be presumed innocent until proved guilty according to law.'

102 Article 49(3) of the Charter: 'The severity of penalties must not be disproportionate to the criminal offence.'

103 According to Article 8 of the Charter: '1. Everyone has the right to the protection of personal data concerning him or her. 2. Such data must be processed fairly for specified purposes and on the basis of the consent of the person concerned or some other legitimate basis laid down by law. Everyone has the right of access to data which has been collected concerning him or her, and the right to have it rectified. 3. Compliance with these rules shall be subject to control by an independent authority.'

(PJCCM), and in particular concerning the validity of EU acts adopted within that policy.[104] After the Treaty of Amsterdam, PJCCM constituted the entirety of the so-called 'third pillar' with its own typology of measures.[105] The main human rights deficiency in the third pillar concerned a very limited jurisdiction of the Court of Justice with respect to these measures. For example, Common Positions used by the EU to impose on the Member States the duty to freeze funds of individuals could not be challenged at all. The Court's solution to this problem was at best partial. In the *Segi* case,[106] concerning an organisation that claimed to have suffered damage as a result of being included in a list of individuals and entities whose funds were to be frozen,[107] the Court was asked to review the rejection of its claim for compensation by the then Court of First Instance against the principle of effective judicial protection. The Court used this opportunity to make Common Positions reviewable in a limited way. The Court insisted that national courts, when they can, should refer questions to it concerning Common Positions in order to verify whether, in the light of their content, they were correctly adopted as 'Common Positions', i.e., as measures not producing legal effects in relation to third parties.[108]

Now, after the Lisbon Treaty and a five-year transitional period that has passed since its entry into force, all acts concerning police and judicial cooperation in criminal matters are subjected to review by the Court of Justice.[109] This review is no longer conditional upon Member States' acceptance of the Court's jurisdiction.[110] Moreover, acts that before Lisbon fell within the scope of the third pillar have become reviewable on direct application by individuals, whose standing moreover is extended by a changed wording of Article 263 TFEU (ex-Article 230 EC).[111]

104 For more on the persisting gaps in the effective protection of human rights in EU law, see D. Leczykiewicz, '"Effective judicial protection" of human rights after Lisbon: should national courts be empowered to review EU secondary law?' (2010) 35 *European Law Review* 326.

105 In the third pillar, the EU could adopt: Common Positions, Framework Decisions and Decisions. Only the latter two could create legal effects for third parties. Under Article 35 EU, the Court of Justice could review only them and not Common Positions, used by the EU to impose on the Member States the duty to freeze the funds of listed individuals. Yet the EU Treaty did not envisage direct actions or an action for damages with respect to Common Positions, nor with respect to other third-pillar measures. Moreover, a request for a preliminary ruling with respect to Framework Decisions and Decisions was admissible only where the Member State of the court before which the case was pending had made a declaration accepting the Court's jurisdiction (Article 35 EU).

106 Case C-355/04 P *Segi, Araitz Zubimendi Izaga and Aritza Galarraga v Council* [2007] ECR I-1657.

107 Council Common Position 2001/931/CFSP of 27 December 2001 on the application of specific measures to combat terrorism, OJ L 344, 28 December 2001, p. 93.

108 *Segi*, note 106 above, para 54.

109 Articles 263 and 267 TFEU.

110 See Article 276 TFEU and Article 24 TEU.

111 Article 263(4) TFEU: 'Any natural or legal person may, under the conditions laid down in the first and second paragraphs, institute proceedings against an act addressed to that

2.1 The European Arrest Warrant

The European Arrest Warrant (EAW) Framework Decision[112] is probably the most controversial document of the pre-Lisbon 'third pillar'. The Framework Decision was adopted exclusively by the Council because under the pre-Lisbon provisions of the EU Treaty, the European Parliament was not involved. The EAW enables a speedy simplified extradition procedure between the Member States with respect to offences listed in Article 2(2) of the Framework Decision.[113] For this purpose, it relies on the mechanism of mutual recognition of arrest warrants issued by courts of the Member States. The executing state receives a warrant issued by another state's court and is obliged to arrest and surrender the person accused in the issuing Member State of committing one of the listed offences, regardless of their nationality. However, neither Article 2 nor other provisions of the Framework Decision define the listed offences. This means that the answer to the question of whether the EAW mechanism can be used in a given case depends on how the offences are defined in the criminal law of the issuing state. Furthermore, the executing state is not allowed to verify whether the act with respect to which the EAW has been issued in the other Member State constitutes a crime also in this state, the feature that is referred to as the abolition of the requirement of double criminality. This raises concerns relating to the principles of legality and equality before the law.

Another controversial issue of the EAW Framework Decision concerns the warrants issued for the execution of a custodial sentence. The measure requires the Member States to execute such warrants even where the judgment imposing the custodial sentence was delivered in proceedings in which the convicted person did not take part (proceedings *in absentia*). Such proceedings are in some states regarded as incompatible with the right to a fair trial. The 2009 amendment of the Framework Decision[114] improves the

person or which is of direct and individual concern to them, and against a regulatory act which is of direct concern to them and does not entail implementing measures.'

112 Council Framework Decision 2002/584/JHA of 13 June 2002 on the European Arrest Warrant and the surrender procedures between Member States – Statements made by certain Member States on the adoption of the Framework Decision, OJ L 190, 18 July 2002, p. 1.

113 The list includes participation in a criminal organisation, terrorism, trafficking in human beings, sexual exploitation of children and child pornography, illicit trafficking in narcotic drugs and psychotropic substances, illicit trafficking in weapons and explosives, corruption, laundering of the proceeds of crime, counterfeiting currency, murder, grievous bodily injury, illicit trade in human organs and tissue, kidnapping, illegal restraint and hostage-taking, but also fraud, computer-related crime, environmental crime, facilitation of unauthorised entry and residence, racism and xenophobia, counterfeiting and piracy of products, trafficking in stolen vehicles.

114 Council Framework Decision 2009/299/JHA of 26 February 2009 amending Framework Decisions 2002/584/JHA, 2005/214/JHA, 2006/783/JHA, 2008/909/JHA and 2008/947/JHA, thereby enhancing the procedural rights of persons and fostering the

measure's credentials against the right to a fair trial. After the amendment, the Framework Decision provides that the executing judicial authority may refuse to execute a EAW issued for the purpose of executing a custodial sentence if the convicted person did not appear in person at the trial. This discretion is, however, excluded in three sets of circumstances, including when the person was summoned in due time and informed that a decision might be handed down if he or she did not appear for the trial, or when he or she had given a mandate to a legal counsellor to defend him or her at the trial and was so defended. In these circumstances, the national court is under an obligation to execute the EAW and is not allowed to impose any additional conditions.

The EAW Framework Decision was the subject of high-profile litigation before both the Court of Justice of the EU and a number of national constitutional courts.[115] In 2005, the Belgian Cour d'Arbitrage referred a case to the Court of Justice, in which the applicant, Advocaten voor de Wereld, sought the annulment of a national measure implementing the Framework Decision.[116] The main challenge concerned the principle of legality and the right to equal treatment. According to the applicant, the measure enabled an unjustified difference in treatment as between individuals depending on whether they acted in the executing Member State or outside that state, which related to the absence of definitions of the offences covered by the Framework Decision. The Court's judgment has been generally received with disappointment due to its circular reasoning. The Court simply declares, without much justification, that neither the absence of definitions nor the abolition of the requirement of double criminality in the Framework Decision infringed the principles of non-discrimination and of legality in criminal matters. According to the Court, because the Framework Decision did not provide definitions of the listed offences and, in particular instances, it would be the law of the issuing Member State supplying the definitions whose content must respect the principle of legality, the Framework Decision itself did not infringe the principle of legality.[117] The Court's response to the challenge based on the principle of equal treatment was even more dismissive. In the Court's view, since the pre-Lisbon EU Treaty had not envisaged harmonisation of criminal law as a prerequisite of the EAW, the absence of definitions could not violate the principle of equal treatment. It was precisely the absence of definitions that prevented the Framework Decision from being challenged on the ground of lack of competence, and the problem of differential treatment did not arise given the level of trust between the Member States. To the extent

application of the principle of mutual recognition to decisions rendered in the absence of the person concerned at the trial, OJ L 81, 27 March 2009, p. 24.

115 Leczykiewicz, 'Constitutional conflicts and the third pillar', note 7 above.

116 Case C-303/05 *Advocaten voor de Wereld VZW v Leden van de Ministerraad* [2007] ECR I-3633.

117 Ibid., paras 52–53.

that some divergence in the treatment of individuals accused of crimes in different Member States did occur, it was objectively justified, and therefore did not lead to a violation of fundamental rights.[118] The *Advocaten* judgment shows that the Court is prepared to use superficial analysis, circular reasoning and irrelevant arguments (the need to respect the EU's limited competence 'proves' compatibility with fundamental rights) in order to preserve the validity of an EU measure.

The same approach is visible in a more recent challenge to the validity of the EAW Framework Decision in *Melloni*.[119] This time, the case concerned the duty to execute a warrant issued for the purpose of enforcing a custodial sentence issued in proceedings *in absentia*. Mr Melloni was convicted of fraud in a trial conducted in Italy in his absence. Some years later he was arrested by the Spanish police and a EAW was issued by the Italian court requesting Spanish authorities to surrender Mr Melloni. The Spanish court authorised the surrender, after which Mr Melloni lodged a petition for a constitutional protection before the Spanish Constitutional Court. He claimed that if he was surrendered to Italy, Article 24(2) of the Spanish Constitution guaranteeing the right to a fair trial would be violated. The right to a fair trial, as protected by the Spanish Constitution, entailed that he should not be surrendered without Spain imposing on Italy a condition that he would be able to challenge the result of his Italian trial, a possibility that did not exist under Italian law. The Spanish Constitutional Court interpreted Article 24(2) of the Spanish Constitution to mean that extradition to countries that allowed convictions *in absentia* without making surrender conditional upon the convicted party being able to challenge the conviction would be 'an "indirect" infringement of the requirements deriving from the right to a fair trial'. The protection offered by the Spanish Constitution was much broader than that offered by the EAW Framework Decision even after the 2009 amendment, which harmonises *exhaustively* the grounds on the basis of which recognition of decisions of courts of other Member States following a trial at which the person concerned did not appear in person may be refused.

The conflict between the Spanish Constitution and the EAW Framework Decision led the Spanish Constitutional Court to ask the Court of Justice of the EU for interpretation of the obligations of national courts under EU law. A further dimension of complexity in the case stemmed from Article 53 of the Charter, according to which '[n]othing in the Charter shall be interpreted as restricting or adversely affecting human rights and fundamental freedoms as recognised, in their respective fields of application, by Union law … and by the Member States' constitutions'. A federalist reading of this provision treats it as a simple confirmation of the status quo in the sense that national protection of human rights remains unchallenged only in the fields falling outside

118 Ibid., para 58.
119 Case C-399/11 *Stefano Melloni v Ministerio Fiscal*, Judgment of 26 February 2013.

the scope of EU law. Within that scope, the EU standard prevails because it benefits from the principle of primacy of Union law. However, the provision of Article 53 of the Charter could also be interpreted as guaranteeing the supremacy of national constitutional norms protecting human rights in situations where the level of protection offered by EU law is lower. On this latter reading, the Spanish court could refuse to surrender Mr Melloni because EU secondary law required Spain to restrict a human right recognised by its Constitution.

The Court of Justice in its judgment did not contemplate this latter possibility. Instead, it reformulated the question as concerning the validity of the relevant provision of the EAW Framework Decision (Article 4a). And here the Court found no deficiencies. The objective of the EAW Framework Decision, which was held to be the improvement of mutual recognition of judicial decisions,[120] justified the restrictions imposed on national courts' competence to refuse the execution of a EAW in a situation where the person being surrendered was unable to apply for a retrial.[121] The Court's view of the right to a fair trial is very limited.[122] The Court offered no discussion as to why the objective of the improvement of mutual recognition of judicial decisions was a legitimate reason (an aim of the public interest). The mere fact

120 Ibid., paras 62–63.

121 The Court's review of the measure is very light-touch. The Court's conclusion as to the measure's compatibility with the Charter is reached without any proportionality review, which could be seen in itself as a violation of Article 52(1) of the Charter. Second, the Court interprets the scope of a Charter right (Article 47 on the right to a fair trial) in the light of an act of secondary law and not vice versa. The right to a fair trial receives protection in EU law only within the limits delineated by Article 4a of the EAW Framework Decision. The fundamental right does not constitute an independent standard of review. Third, national constitutions are denied any role in the interpretation of the Charter right. According to the Court, national authorities and courts can apply national standards of protection of fundamental rights, a possibility envisaged by Article 53 of the Charter, only insofar as 'the level of protection provided for by the Charter, as interpreted by the Court, and the primacy, unity and effectiveness of EU law [were] not thereby compromised' (para 60). This means that EU secondary law prevails over state constitutions. Whenever application of national constitutional standards would affect effectiveness of an EU Act, national courts have to refrain from using them. Member States' courts are effectively prohibited from 'casting doubt on the uniformity of the standard of protection of fundamental rights as defined in that framework decision' (para 63).

122 This is visible in particular when one compares the Court's approach to the right to a fair trial with that of the European Court of Human Rights. In *Sejdovic v Italy*, Judgment of the Grand Chamber of 1 March 2006, application no 56581/00, the European Court of Human Rights held at § 81 that 'the object and purpose of the Article [Article 6(1) of the Convention] taken as a whole show[ed] that a person "charged with a criminal offence" [was] entitled to take part in the hearing'. At §§ 54–58 of *Stoichkov v Bulgaria*, Judgment of 24 March 2005, application no 9808/02, the European Court of Human Rights held that the duty to guarantee the right of a criminal defendant to be present in the courtroom – either during the original proceedings or in a retrial – '[ranked] as one of the essential requirements of Article 6' of the Convention and that the refusal to reopen proceedings conducted in the accused's absence, without any indication that the accused had waived his

that the Treaty provisions on the AFSJ envisage mutual recognition of judicial decisions does not mean that it is a legitimate aim. More properly, it is only a means to an end of well-functioning criminal justice system effectively apprehending, prosecuting and punishing those endangering the societal values and the safety of European citizens and thus safeguarding the public interest.

The importance of the judgment in *Melloni* goes beyond the particular facts of the case or the EU measure in question, especially where the same unwillingness to take account of fundamental rights had already been exhibited by the Court in an earlier case, *Radu*.[123] The reference from a national court tested the possibility of relying by the executing court on fundamental rights in order to refuse the execution of a EAW.[124] The Court rejected that possibility. The judgment should be contrasted with the opinion of AG Sharpston, who argued that fundamental rights could provide a basis for a decision not to execute a warrant.[125] Considering when the duty to refuse the execution of a EAW might arise, she referred to the Court's judgment in *NS* and proposed the following criterion: 'the deficiency or deficiencies in the trial process should be such as fundamentally to destroy its fairness', with the onus of proof on the requested person to show that the objections to the transfer 'are substantially well-founded', a circumstance to be assessed by the executing national court.[126] The Court of Justice disagreed with this interpretation of the EAW Framework Decision and with the role of EU fundamental rights assigned therein.[127] Unquestionably, the desire to ensure

or her right to be present during the trial, was a 'flagrant denial of justice' rendering the proceedings 'manifestly contrary to the provisions of Article 6 or the principles embodied therein'.

123 Case C-396/11, *Proceedings relating to the execution of European arrest warrants issued against Ciprian Vasile Radu*, Judgment of 29 January 2013.

124 The concrete problem related to the fact that the accused, Mr Radu, had not been notified about the charges against him, had not been subpoenaed in respect of them and was in fact unable to defend himself in proceedings, which led to a conviction. These considerations did not overtly fall within the range of circumstances in which the judicial authority of the executing Member State either must (Article 3) or may (Article 4) refuse to execute a European arrest warrant. According to Article 1(3) of the EAW Framework Decision, the measure 'shall not have the effect of modifying the obligation to respect fundamental rights and fundamental legal principles as enshrined in Article 6 of the Treaty on European Union'.

125 Opinion of AG Sharpston of 18 October 2012, para 70.

126 Ibid., paras 83 and 85.

127 The Court held that neither Article 47 nor Article 48 of the Charter of Fundamental Rights required that the requested person was heard by the issuing court before the warrant was issued if its purpose was the conducting of a criminal prosecution in the other Member State. The Court reasoned that 'an obligation for the issuing judicial authorities to hear the requested person before such a European arrest warrant [was] issued would inevitably lead to the failure of the very system of surrender provided for by Framework Decision 2002/584 and, consequently, prevent[ed] the achievement of the area of freedom, security and justice, insofar as such an arrest warrant must have a certain element of surprise, in

the effectiveness of the system of surrender had a huge gravitational pull for the Court.

Whether the matter concerns the validity of the EAW Framework Decision or the softening of its edges through interpretation, it is clear that the Court is not prepared to carry out an intensive review of measures falling within the AFSJ and their consequences. This is a cause for concern because the AFSJ is where we would expect judicial scrutiny to be the most thorough. What the judgments reveal is the Court's intention to harmonise human rights standards in all fields falling within the scope of Union law. For some states, this will mean the lowering of protection. This explains why the Court is hostile to national rules offering more generous protection. So for example in the *F* case,[128] concerning, inter alia, the right to appeal against a judicial decision executing a EAW, the Court held that EU fundamental rights did not compel Member States to set up a second level of jurisdiction.[129] But it did not follow that they were free to introduce the right to appeal under any conditions. The right could not lead to a violation of the strict time limits imposed by the Framework Decision for the execution of a warrant.[130]

2.2 *Access to a lawyer*

The directive on access to a lawyer in criminal proceedings,[131] adopted on the basis of Article 82(2) TFEU,[132] is one of the measures envisaged by the EU's Roadmap for strengthening of procedural standards,[133] whose function

particular in order to stop the person concerned from taking flight' (para 39). The Court held that it was for the court executing the EAW to ensure that the right to be heard was observed (paras 40–41).

128 Case C-168/13 PPU *Jeremy F v Premier Minister*, Judgment of 30 May 2013.

129 The Court of Justice referred to the case law of the European Court of Human Rights to point out that the ECHR does not compel the Contracting States to set up a second level of jurisdiction for the examination of the lawfulness of decisions related to the applicant's extradition (ibid., para 43), and observed that the same principle followed from its own case law concerning asylum applications. See *Samba Diouf*, note 78 above, para 69.

130 *Jeremy F*, note 128 above, para 65.

131 Directive 2013/48/EU of the European Parliament and of the Council of 22 October 2013 on the right of access to a lawyer in criminal proceedings and in European arrest warrant proceedings, and on the right to have a third party informed upon deprivation of liberty and to communicate with third persons and with consular authorities while deprived of liberty, OJ L 294, 6 November 2013, p. 1. The Directive is to be transposed by the Member States by 27 November 2016. Ireland, the UK and Denmark did not take part in the adoption of the Directive and are not bound by it.

132 Article 82(2) TFEU provides for the establishment of minimum rules applicable in the Member States so as to facilitate mutual recognition of judgments and judicial decisions and police and judicial cooperation in criminal matters having a cross-border dimension. That Article refers to 'the rights of individuals in criminal procedure' as one of the areas in which minimum rules may be established.

133 Resolution of the Council of 30 November 2009 on a Roadmap for strengthening procedural rights of suspected or accused persons in criminal proceedings, OJ C 295, 4 December 2009, p. 1. Two other measures that have been adopted pursuant to the Roadmap are

was to improve the level of confidence and trust among the Member States in each other's criminal justice systems. The purpose of the Directive is to lay down rules implementing the right to a fair trial. This Directive introduces the right of access to a lawyer in criminal proceedings and the right to have a third party informed upon deprivation of liberty and to communicate with third persons and with consular authorities while deprived of liberty. An important contribution of the Directive is the creation of the right of access to a lawyer in EAW proceedings.[134]

Controversial from a human rights perspective is the exclusion from the Directive's scope of minor offences, which are defined as offences for which sanctions are imposed by an authority other than a court having jurisdiction in criminal matters and with respect to which deprivation of liberty cannot be imposed as a sanction.[135] The Directive sets only minimum rules and the Member States may extend the rights set out in this Directive in order to provide a higher level of protection but only insofar as the higher level of protection does not constitute an obstacle to the mutual recognition of judicial decisions. The Directive lays down the time from which the right of access to a lawyer has to be ensured and guarantees confidentiality of communication between suspects or accused persons and their lawyers. In the EAW proceedings, under Article 10, the right of access to a lawyer concerns the executing state, which is also under a duty to take steps to facilitate the requested person's access to a lawyer in the issuing state.[136] The Directive does not regulate access to legal aid, which remains the competence of the Member States.

2.3 *Mutual recognition of judgments*

Mutual recognition of judgments delivered in the context of criminal proceedings is the cornerstone of the EU's policy of judicial cooperation in criminal matters. It is based on the assumption of equivalence and trust among the Member States. So while there is no harmonisation of criminal

Directive 2010/64/EU of the European Parliament and of the Council of 20 October 2010 on the right to interpretation and translation in criminal proceedings, OJ L 280, 26 October 2010, p. 1, and Directive 2012/13/EU of the European Parliament and of the Council of 22 May 2012 on the right to information in criminal proceedings, OJ L 142, 1 June 2012, p. 1. On the Roadmap, see C. Rijken, 'Re-balancing security and justice: protection of fundamental rights in police and judicial cooperation in criminal matters' (2010) 47 *Common Market Law Review* 1455.

134 Article 2(2).

135 Article 2(4).

136 Where the requested person wishes to exercise the right to appoint a lawyer in the issuing Member State and does not already have such a lawyer, the competent authority in the executing Member State shall promptly inform the competent authority in the issuing Member State. The competent authority of the issuing Member State shall, without undue delay, provide the requested person with information facilitating appointment of a lawyer in that state. Article 10(4)–(6).

procedure, national courts are expected to trust that in other Member States, fundamental values, such as human rights, are respected and that procedures are structured in a way ensuring the protection of essential interests, including the right to the defence, access to documents, the right to an effective remedy and the principle of proportionality. The objective of the system of mutual recognition of judgments is the improvement of their enforceability.

Financial penalties have their own Framework Decision 2005/214/JHA,[137] which extends the principle of mutual recognition to decisions taken by an authority of the issuing state other than a court in respect of acts that are punishable under the national law of the issuing state by a financial penalty. Recognition of such decisions is demanded if the person concerned has had an opportunity to have the case tried by a court having jurisdiction in particular *in criminal matters*.[138] This requirement ensures that the exception to the rule that only judicial decisions are to be automatically enforceable in another Member State does not affect the rights of the person on whom the penalty was imposed. AG Sharpston convincingly interpreted this additional safeguard to be understood substantively, as concerning the procedural rights and other guarantees that individuals traditionally obtain in the context of criminal proceedings.[139] So it is not the labelling of proceedings or the name of the court that are of significance but the rights of the accused in the procedure that it uses. If they correspond to what is required by human rights instruments in the case of proceedings leading to the imposition of a criminal penalty the decision may and has to be recognised in another Member State. The Court has agreed with this approach.[140] It held that the relevant issue was whether the court or tribunal had applied a procedure that satisfied 'the essential characteristics of criminal procedure'.[141] In assessing characteristics of the national court in question, the Court attached importance to the fact that the appeal before that court had a suspensory effect and that the court applied a criminal procedure requiring compliance with the procedural safeguards appropriate in criminal matters, among them being the principle *nulla poena sine lege*, the principle that culpability should arise only where there was capacity or criminal responsibility and the principle that the penalty must be in proportion to the degree of responsibility and to the facts.[142]

137 Council Framework Decision 2005/214/JHA of 24 February 2005 on the application of the principle of mutual recognition to financial penalties, OJ L 76, 22 March 2005, p. 16.
138 Article 1 (emphasis added).
139 Case C-60/12 *Proceedings concerning the enforcement of a financial penalty issued against Marián Baláž*, Opinion of AG Sharpston of 18 July 2013.
140 Ibid., Judgment of 14 November 2013.
141 Ibid., para 42.
142 Ibid., paras 39–41.

2.4 *Protection of victims of crimes*

Another Roadmap adopted in the AFSJ by the Council had as its objective the strengthening of rights and protection of victims in criminal proceedings.[143] A number of measures have been adopted within its framework, including the Victims' Rights Directive,[144] the Directive on the European Protection Order in criminal matters[145] and the Regulation on mutual recognition of protection orders in civil matters.[146] Among various entitlements in the Victims' Rights Directive, many of which depend on the Member States' legislative action, the most important are the participation rights in criminal proceedings.[147] Victims are also granted a right to ask for a review of a decision not to prosecute.[148] The Directive also protects their rights of privacy.[149]

The Directive is particularly engaged with vulnerable victims. It imposes on the Member States a duty to ascertain victims' vulnerabilities, identify their specific needs and decide on appropriate measures.[150] According to Article 22(4), children are presumed to be 'vulnerable victims' and are moreover offered special protection measures, in particular those relating to the taking of testimonies from them, confidentiality and the scope of questioning. The Directive's predecessor, Framework Decision 2001/220/JHA[151] – and in particular its Article 8(4), which laid down a duty to ensure that victims, particularly those most vulnerable, were protected 'from the effects of giving evidence in open court' – was instrumental in the broadening of obligations of national courts vis-à-vis child victims. In *Pupino*,[152] the Court held that

143 Resolution of the Council of 10 June 2011 on a Roadmap for strengthening the rights and protection of victims, in particular in criminal proceedings OJ C 187, 28 June 2011, p. 1.

144 Directive 2012/29/EU of the European Parliament and of the Council of 25 October 2012 establishing minimum standards on the rights, support and protection of victims of crime, OJ L 315, 14 November 2012, p. 57.

145 Directive 2011/99/EU of the European Parliament and of the Council of 13 December 2011 on the European protection order establishes a mechanism for the mutual recognition of protection measures in criminal matters between Member States, OJ L 338, 21 December 2011, p. 2.

146 Regulation (EU) No 606/2013 of the European Parliament and of the Council of 12 June 2013 on mutual recognition of protection measures in civil matters, OJ L 181 of 29 June 2013, p. 4.

147 They include the right to provide evidence, access to legal aid under conditions specified by national law, or the right to receive compensation preferably within criminal proceedings.

148 Article 11.

149 Article 21. The right to privacy covers the victim's personal characteristics and the images of them and their family members. Furthermore, Member States are required to ensure that competent authorities may take all lawful measures to prevent public dissemination of any information that could lead to the identification of a child victim. With respect to freedom of information, the Member States are asked to encourage the media to adopt self-regulatory measures.

150 Article 22.

151 Council Framework Decision 2001/220/JHA of 15 March 2001 on the standing of victims in criminal proceedings, OJ L 82, 22 March 2001, p. 1.

152 Case C-105/03 *Criminal proceedings against Maria Pupino* [2005] ECR I-5285.

even if under national law it would not be possible to take the testimony of children under special arrangements otherwise provided for proceedings concerning sexual offences, the use of that procedure should be enabled on the ground that national law was to be interpreted 'so far as possible in the light of the wording and purpose of the Framework Decision in order to attain the result which it pursues'.[153] It is possible that Articles 22 to 24 of the Victims' Rights Directive will have a similar effect.

2.5 *Protection of personal data*

Issues of the adequate protection of personal data in the AFSJ arise in two contexts regulated by EU law – the gathering of data for border controls and the gathering, processing and sharing of data for the purpose of crime prevention and prosecution. In 2008, the Council adopted a Framework Decision on the protection of personal data processed in the framework of police and judicial cooperation in criminal matters.[154] It has also adopted a Directive under the internal market competence, overtly intending to regulate the cross-border flow of data, but in reality imposing a duty on telecommunications companies to collect mobile phone data useful for crime prevention and as evidence in criminal proceedings.[155] This Directive was

153 Ibid., paras 43 and 56. The Court did not, however, create a right in victims to demand the special arrangements. Case C-507/10 *Criminal proceedings against X* [2011] ECR I-14241.

154 Council Framework Decision 2008/977/JHA of 27 November 2008 on the protection of personal data processed in the framework of police and judicial cooperation in criminal matters, OJ L 350, 30 December, 2008, p. 60.

155 Directive 2006/24/EC of the European Parliament and of the Council of 15 March 2006 on the retention of data generated or processed in connection with the provision of publicly available electronic communications services or of public communications networks and amending Directive 2002/58/EC, OJ L 105, 13 April 2006, p. 54. Directive 2002/58/EC of the European Parliament and of the Council of 12 July 2002 concerning the processing of personal data and the protection of privacy in the electronic communications sector, OJ L 201, 31 July 2002, p. 37, harmonises provisions of the Member States required to ensure an equivalent level of protection of fundamental rights and freedoms, and in particular the right to privacy and to confidentiality, with respect to the processing of personal data in the electronic communication sector and to ensure the free movement of such data and of electronic communication equipment and services in the European Union. Directive 2006/24/EC restricts those rights in a harmonised way by laying down the obligation on the providers of publicly available electronic communications services or of public communications networks to retain certain data that are generated or processed by them. In Case C-301/06 *Ireland v Parliament and Council* [2009] ECR I-593, the Court held that Directive 2006/24/EC was correctly adopted on the basis of Article 95 EC (now Article 114 TFEU) because its provisions were 'essentially limited to the activities of service providers and do not govern access to data or the use thereof by the police or judicial authorities of the Member States' (para 80). See E. Herlin-Karnell, 'Case C-301/06, Ireland v. Parliament and Council, Judgment of the Court (Grand Chamber) of 10 February 2009' (2009) 46 *Common Market Law Review* 1667. However, Article 1(1) of Directive 2006/24/EC states that its objective is to ensure that the data are available for the purpose of the investigation, detection and prosecution of serious crime, as defined by each Member State in its national law. In Joined cases C-293/12 and C-594/12 *Digital Rights Ireland Ltd v Minister for Communications,*

famously annulled by the Court of Justice in *Digital Rights Ireland*[156] on the ground that the interference with the right to privacy and the protection of personal data was 'particularly serious' and was not justified. While the Directive did not violate the essence of the rights, it interfered with fundamental rights in a disproportionate manner. According to the Court, 'the EU legislation in question must lay down clear and precise rules governing the scope and application of the measure in question and imposing minimum safeguards so that the persons whose data have been retained have sufficient guarantees to effectively protect their personal data against the risk of abuse and against any unlawful access and use of that data'.[157] The Directive was held invalid because, among other deficiencies, it failed to lay down objective criteria by which to determine the limits of the access of the competent national authorities to the data and their subsequent use for crime prevention and detention and in criminal proceedings, and to restrict it only to these purposes.[158] The Court ruled that in view of the extent and seriousness of the interference with the fundamental rights, only offences that could be considered sufficiently serious justified the interference. It also required that access to the data by the competent national authorities should be made dependent on prior review carried out by a court or an independent administrative body whose task would be to restrict accesses only to uses that were strictly necessary.[159] Furthermore, the Court had reservations concerning the length of time data were to be retained and the sufficiency of safeguards insuring their security and confidentiality.[160]

The gathering of data for the purpose of border controls, in particular the introduction of a biometric passport by the EU, on the whole proved less controversial.[161] In *Schwartz*,[162] the Court held that the processing of data

Marine and Natural Resources and Kärntner Landesregierung, Judgment of 8 April 2014, the Court held that '[t]he material objective of that directive was to contribute to the fight against serious crime and thus, ultimately, to public security' (para 41).

156 Note 155 above.

157 Ibid., para 57.

158 Ibid., paras 60–61.

159 Ibid., para 62.

160 The Directive did not demand from telecommunications services providers a high level of protection and security in terms of technical and organisational measures and allowed them to choose the level of security on the basis of economic considerations, did not demand from them the irreversible destruction of the data at the end of the period, that the data be retained with the EU where it could be subjected to the control of an independent authority on the basis of EU law (paras 67–68).

161 The security features including biometric identifiers for the passports and travel documents of the Member States are harmonised by the Council Regulation (EC) No 2252/2004 of 13 December 2004 on standards for security features and biometrics in passports and travel documents issued by Member States, OJ L 385, 29 December 2004, p. 1, amended by Regulation (EC) No 444/2009 of the European Parliament and of the Council of 6 May 2009, OJ 2009 L 142, p. 1; corrigendum: OJ 2009 L 188, p. 127. The designation of the authorities and bodies authorised to have access to the data contained in the storage medium of documents is generally a matter for national legislation.

162 Case C-291/12 *Michael Schwarz v Stadt Bochum*, Judgment of 17 October 2013.

in the form of fingerprints pursues an objective of general interest recognised by the Union, i.e., the prevention of the falsification of passports and their fraudulent use, and is therefore justified.[163] On the other hand, the Court refused to exercise a human rights competence in a case concerning the use of biometric data gathered on the occasion of passport applications for purposes other than border controls.[164] The Court held that because the Regulation did not require a Member State to guarantee that the data will be used only for the purpose of border controls, it was up to national law to determine whether the data could be used also for other purposes.[165] As a result, the matter was regarded not to fall within the scope of the Regulation and lay outside the scope of EU law. That meant that the Charter of Fundamental Rights did not apply and that the Court had no jurisdiction to assess Member States' actions' compatibility with fundamental rights.

2.6 Ne bis in idem

Article 50 of the Charter of Fundamental Rights states: 'No one shall be liable to be tried or punished again in criminal proceedings for an offence for which he or she has already been finally acquitted or convicted within the Union in accordance with the law.'[166] This right before the Charter functioned as a general principle of Union law of *ne bis in idem*, whose more formal source was Article 54 of the Convention implementing the Schengen Agreement (CISA).[167] Article 3 of the EAW Framework Decision obliges a judicial authority of the Member State of execution to refuse to execute a EAW if 'the executing judicial authority is informed that the requested person has been finally judged by a Member State in respect of the same acts provided that, where there has been sentence, the sentence has been served or is currently being served or may no longer be executed under the law of the sentencing Member State.' The Framework Decision

163 Ibid., paras 36–38.

164 Joined cases C-446/12 to C-449/12 *W. P. Willems v Burgemeester van Nuth, H. J. Kooistra v Burgemeester van Skarsterlân, M. Roest v Burgemeester van Amsterdam and L. J. A. van Luijk v Burgemeester van Den Haag*, Judgment of 16 April 2015.

165 Ibid., para 48.

166 For more on Article 50 of the Charter and the *ne bis in idem* principle more broadly, see J. Tomkin, 'Article 50 – right not to be tried or punished twice in criminal proceedings for the same criminal offence', in S. Peers, T. Harvey, J. Kenner and A. Ward (eds.), *The EU Charter of Fundamental Rights: A Commentary* (Hart Publishing, 2014) 1373.

167 The Convention implementing the Schengen Agreement of 14 June 1985 between the governments of the States of the Benelux Economic Union, the Federal Republic of Germany and the French Republic on the gradual abolition of checks at their common borders, OJ 2000 L 239, p. 19, signed on 19 June 1990 at Schengen. Protocol (No. 19) to the Lisbon Treaty on the Schengen *acquis* integrated the Convention into the framework of the European Union, OJ 2008 C 115, p. 290, now annexed to the TEU, by authorising 25 Member States to implement closer cooperation among themselves in areas covered by the Schengen *acquis*.

2009/948/JHA[168] introduces procedures aimed at preventing parallel criminal proceedings. Under Article 5(1), a competent authority of a Member State has reasonable grounds to believe that parallel proceedings are being conducted in another Member State, it is to contact the competent authority of that other Member State to confirm the existence of such parallel proceedings, with a view to initiating consultations aimed at avoiding the adverse consequences arising from such parallel proceedings, which may, where appropriate, lead to the concentration of the criminal proceedings in one Member State.

Article 54 of the CISA provides:

> A person whose trial has been finally disposed of in one Contracting Party may not be prosecuted in another Contracting Party for the same acts provided that, if a penalty has been imposed, it has been enforced, is actually in the process of being enforced or can no longer be enforced under the laws of the sentencing Contracting Party.

It is important to note the discrepancy between the wording of Article 50 of the Charter and that of Article 54 of the CISA.[169] While the Charter refers to 'an offence' for which an individual has already been finally acquitted or convicted, the CISA speaks of the same 'acts' in respect of which a finally disposed trial has taken place in another Member State. The wording of the Charter suggests that it is the legal classification of the act that matters for the applicability of the right not to be tried or punished twice, which is generally a less favourable approach for the accused. In *Van Esbroeck*,[170] the Court defined the concept of 'the same acts' within the meaning of Article 54 of the CISA as referring to the nature of the acts, and not their legal classification.[171] In paragraph 34, the Court linked the *ne bis in idem* principle to the right to freedom of movement, which is now also a right guaranteed by the Charter (Article 45). The Court held that the only relevant criterion for the application of Article 54 of the CISA was identity of the material acts, understood in the sense of the existence of a set of concrete circumstances

168 Council Framework Decision 2009/948/JHA of 30 November 2009 on prevention and settlement of conflicts of exercise of jurisdiction in criminal proceedings, OJ 2009 L 328, p. 42.

169 The Charter replicates Article 4(1) of Protocol No. 7 to the ECHR, which states that: 'No one shall be liable to be tried or punished again in criminal proceedings under the jurisdiction of the same State for an offence for which he has already been finally acquitted or convicted in accordance with the law and penal procedure of that State.' This provision has been interpreted by the European Court of Human Rights to bind states only internally and not internationally. The CISA and Article 50 of the Charter impose the principle of *ne bis in idem* also as *between* the Member States. It follows that territorially they offer more extensive protection. See Tomkin, 'Article 50 ', note 166 above.

170 Case C-436/04 *Criminal proceedings against Leopold Henri Van Esbroeck* [2006] ECR I-2333.

171 Ibid., para 27.

that were inextricably linked together in time, in space and by their subject-matter.[172] In *Kraaijenbrink*,[173] the Court restricted the scope of the right by excluding from the definition of 'the same acts' acts linked together solely by the same criminal intention.

In *Spasic*,[174] the Grand Chamber of the Court was asked to review in the light of Article 50 of the Charter the subjection in Article 54 CISA of the *ne bis in idem* principle to the condition that, upon conviction and sentencing, the penalty imposed 'has been enforced', is 'actually in the process of being enforced' or 'can no longer be enforced'. The Court considered the condition legitimate because its objective was to prevent a situation in which a person definitively convicted and sentenced in one state can no longer be prosecuted for the same acts in another state, and therefore ultimately remains unpunished, only because the first state conducted criminal proceedings and sentenced the person but has not enforced the sentence.[175] The Court did not, however, use the opportunity in *Spasic* to clarify the aforementioned terminological discrepancy between Article 54 of the CISA and Article 50 of the Charter.

In other judgments, the Court also defined the scope of the application of the *ne bis in idem* right. It could be relied on also where the enforcement of the penalty was time-barred,[176] where prosecution of the offence was time-barred,[177] where the judgment of acquittal resulted exclusively from the fact that there was insufficient evidence to prosecute,[178] or where further prosecution was barred due to a decision of the prosecuting authority to discontinue criminal proceedings against an accused person because he or she has fulfilled certain obligations such as the paying of a sum of money determined by the prosecuting authority.[179] The *ne bis in idem* principle applied also where the finding that there were no grounds to refer a case to a trial court precluded under national law the bringing of new criminal proceedings in respect of the same acts against the person to whom that finding applied, unless new facts and/or evidence against that person came to light.[180] However, a decision to suspend proceedings that under the national law did not definitely bar

172 Ibid., paras 36–38.

173 Case C-367/05 *Criminal proceedings against Norma Kraaijenbrink* [2007] ECR I-6619.

174 Case C-129/14 PPU *Criminal proceedings against Zoran Spasic*, Judgment of 27 May 2014.

175 Ibid., para 63.

176 Case C-297/07 *Klaus Bourquain* [2008] ECR I-9425.

177 Case C-467/04 *Criminal proceedings against Giuseppe Francesco Gasparini* [2006] ECR I-9199.

178 Case C-150/05 *Jean Leon Van Straaten v Staat der Nederlanden and Republiek Italië* [2006] ECR I-9327, para 61. Because Article 54 of the CISA makes no reference to the content of the judgment which 'finally disposes' the trial in another state, the acquitting judgment enabling reliance on the provision may result from mere lack of evidence.

179 Joined cases C-187/01 and C-385/01 *Criminal proceedings against Hüseyin Gözütok and Klaus Brügge* [2003] ECR I-1345.

180 Case C-398/12 *Criminal proceedings against M.*, Judgment of 5 June 2014.

prosecution was not held to generate the *ne bis in idem* effect.[181] Also in the context of the EAW, a decision not to prosecute or not to pass on information to the investigation judge, taken in the interest of the investigation – for example, in order to be able to break up a drug trafficking network and arrest the other persons involved – not precluding the criminal proceedings did not guarantee a mandatory refusal to execute the warrant.[182]

3 Judicial cooperation in civil matters

Recognition and enforcement of judgments in civil and commercial cases was originally based on a treaty signed by the then six members of the European Community, i.e., the 1968 Brussels Convention.[183] The Convention was replaced by an act of EU secondary law – the Brussels I Regulation.[184] Both acts have laid down rules governing the jurisdiction of courts and the recognition and enforcement of judgments in civil and commercial matters. Human rights issues arising in the context of the judicial cooperation in civil matters concern a broad range of topics and interests. On the one hand, we encounter applicants who have tried to use the right to an effective remedy to alter the rules on jurisdiction by encouraging the Court to reject the consequences of *lis pendens* in the case of proceedings pending before a court of the Member State which has been held to violate the right to a judicial decision within a reasonable time. On the other hand, we have parties who argue that fundamental rights may create a special exception to the duty to recognise a judgment of another Member State. Finally, we have the controversial cases concerning matters of marriage and parental responsibility, where mutual recognition of judicial decisions may require national courts to act against the best interest of the child.

3.1 Length of proceedings

According to the second paragraph of Article 47 of the Charter of Fundamental Rights, '[e]veryone is entitled to a fair and public hearing within a reasonable time by an independent and impartial tribunal previously established by law. Everyone shall have the possibility of being advised, defended and represented.' Article 6(1) ECHR also guarantees the right to a fair and public hearing by an independent and impartial tribunal established by law 'within a reasonable time'. Some of the Member States are notorious for the

181 Case C-491/07 *Criminal proceedings against Vladimir Turanský* [2008] ECR I-11039.

182 Case C-261/09 *Gaetano Mantello* [2010] ECR I-11477.

183 1968 Brussels Convention on jurisdiction and the enforcement of judgments in civil and commercial matters, consolidated version – OJ L 299, 31 December 1972, p. 32.

184 Council Regulation (EC) No 44/2001 of 22 December 2000 on jurisdiction and the recognition and enforcement of judgments in civil and commercial matters, OJ L 12, 16 January 2001, p. 1.

excessive length of proceedings before their courts. In the AFSJ, excessively long proceedings are not only in themselves a breach of a fundamental right but could also have implications for EU rules preventing parallel proceedings on the same subject-matter in two different Member States. According to Article 25 of the Brussels I Regulation, a court of a Member State seised with respect to a claim over which a court of another Member State has exclusive jurisdiction should declare of its own motion that it has no jurisdiction. According to Article 27(1), '[w]here proceedings involving the same cause of action and between the same parties are brought in the courts of different Member States, any court other than the court first seised shall of its own motion stay its proceedings until such time as the jurisdiction of the court first seised is established'. This provision is problematic from a human rights perspective, in particular where the court that has been seised is located in a state known to violate the reasonable time requirement of Article 6(1) ECHR. An argument can be made that human rights require a modification of obligations stemming from Article 27(1) of the other courts seised, in particular of the court that actually has a jurisdiction over the dispute. The duty to ensure that proceedings are concluded within a reasonable time could create an exception to the obligation to stay proceedings.

The Court of Justice had an opportunity to consider such a possibility in the *Gasser* case.[185] It concerned a contract law dispute with respect to which an Austrian court had jurisdiction. One of the contracting parties started proceedings before an Italian court, where the length of proceedings frequently violates the ECHR. The Court of Justice was asked to rule on whether the excessive and general slowness of legal proceedings in a contracting state where the court first seised was established was liable to affect, when interpreted in the light of fundamental rights, the duty to stay proceedings of a court of another Member State, also seised regarding the same dispute. The Court held that the duty to stay proceedings was not affected. It reasoned that an interpretation that would enable the setting aside of the duty to stay proceedings would be manifestly contrary both to the letter and spirit and to the aim of the Convention, which it defined as the prevention of a situation where a judgment of another Member State's court was not recognised on account of its irreconcilability with a judgment given in proceedings between the same parties in the state where recognition was sought.[186]

3.2 *Mutual recognition of judgments*

Just as in the context of criminal proceedings, also in civil matters there arises a question of the obligations of the Member States vis-à-vis a decision of a court of another Member State that was taken in breach of

185 Case C-116/02 *Erich Gasser GmbH v MISAT Srl* [2003] ECR I-14693.
186 Ibid., para 70.

fundamental rights or whose consequences, if the decision was recognised, would lead to a violation of those rights of an individual. EU law recognises the right to a fair legal process; a power of national courts to examine the quality of proceedings before they recognise a judgment delivered in these proceedings would enhance the protection of this right. The problem for the Court of Justice is that the existence of such a power goes against the principle of mutual trust and confidence among the civil justice systems of the EU.[187] As a result, the Court has decided to allow only a limited power of national courts to refuse recognition of a judgment of another Member State's court when the proceedings infringed the right to a fair trial.[188] In *Gambazzi*,[189] a case arising in relation to the enforcement in Italy of a judgment given in the UK, the Court of Justice held that the court of the state in which enforcement is sought could take into account the fact that the court of the state of the origin of a decision ruled on the applicant's claims without hearing the defendant, who was excluded from the proceedings on the grounds that he had not complied with the obligations imposed by an order made earlier in the same proceedings. The power could be exercised, however, only 'if, following a comprehensive assessment of the proceedings and in the light of all the circumstances, it appear[ed] to [the recognising court] that that exclusion measure constituted a manifest and disproportionate infringement of the defendant's right to be heard'.[190] While the exclusion order could in principle be justified by the public interest of ensuring the fair and efficient administration of justice, its capacity to justify the infringement of the right to a fair trial depended on whether the exclusion was a proportionate response. The Court pointed out that it was relevant whether the defendant had the opportunity to be heard before the order was made and had the right to challenge it and the right to appeal against the court's final decision.[191]

The national courts' power to review the quality of proceedings against the right to a fair trial covers also decisions affecting the *lis pendens* of a case. In *Eurofood*,[192] the Court of Justice accepted the discretion of a Member State not to recognise insolvency proceedings opened in another Member State where the decision to open the proceedings was taken in flagrant breach of the fundamental right to be heard, which a person concerned by such

187 A. Frąckowiak-Adamska, 'Time for a European "full faith and credit clause"' (2015) 52 *Common Market Law Review* 191.

188 In Case C-283/05 *ASML Netherlands BV v Semiconductor Industry Services GmbH (SEMIS)* [2006] ECR I-12041, the Court held the objective of ensuring the free movement of judgments in civil and commercial matters could not be attained by undermining in any way the right to a fair hearing (paras 23–24).

189 *Gambazzi*, note 9 above.

190 Ibid., para 48. The applicant was excluded from proceedings because he had failed to comply with numerous court orders (para 31).

191 Ibid., paras 42 and 44–45.

192 Case C-341/04 *Eurofood IFSC Ltd* [2006] ECR I-3813.

proceedings enjoys under EU fundamental rights law.[193] The ruling was facilitated by the content of Article 26 of the Insolvency Regulation,[194] according to which the Member State may refuse to recognise insolvency proceedings opened in another Member State or to enforce a judgment handed down in the context of such proceedings 'where the effects of such recognition or enforcement would be manifestly contrary to that State's public policy, in particular *its fundamental principles or the constitutional rights and liberties of the individual*'.[195] The Court considered whether recognising a decision issued in violation of the right to be heard could at all be regarded as going against public policy and held that it could, unless it was justified and protected by a right to an effective remedy.

Article 34 of the Brussels I Regulation now explicitly states that a national court should not recognise a judgment given 'in default of appearance, if the defendant was not served with the document which instituted the proceedings or with an equivalent document in sufficient time and in such a way as to enable him to arrange for his defence, unless the defendant failed to commence proceedings to challenge the judgment when it was possible for him to do so'.[196] In *Trade Agency*,[197] a case concerning the recognition and enforcement in Latvia of a judgment in default delivered for the claimant in the UK, the Latvian Supreme Court asked the Court of Justice to determine what requirements were imposed on national courts deciding on the recognition and enforcement of judgments delivered in proceedings in which the defendant did not participate and which had disposed of the substance of a dispute without examining the subject-matter of the claim solely because the defendant did not reply to the claim served to them. The Court held that the objective pursued by English rules was capable of justifying a restriction of the right to a fair trial on the condition that it was not manifestly disproportionate, which is to be assessed by the national court.[198] As a result, the national court was allowed to refuse to recognise and enforce the judgment only if it appeared 'after an overall assessment of the proceedings and in the light of all the relevant circumstances, that that judgment [was] a manifest and disproportionate breach of the defendant's right to a fair trial referred to in the second paragraph of Article 47 of the Charter, on account of the impossibility of bringing an appropriate and effective appeal against it'.[199]

193 Ibid., para 66.

194 Council Regulation (EC) No 1346/2000 of 29 May 2000 on insolvency proceedings, OJ L 160, 30 June 2000, p. 1.

195 Emphasis added.

196 Article 34(2) of the Regulation.

197 Case C-619/10 *Trade Agency Ltd v Seramico Investments Ltd*, Judgment of 6 September 2012.

198 Ibid., paras 58–59.

199 Ibid., para 62.

3.3 *Marriage and parental responsibility*

A group of judgments whose enforcement is also ensured by EU rules adopted as part of the AFSJ concerns parental rights.[200] Under the EU Regulation, national courts are under a duty to recognise judgments relating to parental responsibility without the need for a declaration of enforceability and without any possibility of opposing its recognition. Recital 21 of the Regulation states that 'the grounds for non-recognition should be kept to the minimum'. The Regulation applies in cases of child abduction, i.e., a 'wrongful removal' of a child defined as his or her removal in breach of custody rights acquired under the law of the Member State where the child was habitually resident immediately before the removal or retention. In those situations, the judgment on parental responsibility issued by one Member State's court, usually followed by a judgment ordering the child's return, is used by the parent with custody rights to start proceedings before the court of another Member State, the one where the child is currently located, with the aim to obtain the child's return to that parent. Under Article 10, in case of wrongful removal of the child, the courts of the Member State where the child was habitually resident immediately before the wrongful removal retain jurisdiction until the child has acquired a habitual residence in another Member State.

The matter of the child's return to another state is regulated by the Hague Convention of 25 October 1980 on the Civil Aspects of International Child Abduction. Under Article 12 of the 1980 Hague Convention:

> Where a child has been wrongfully removed or retained in terms of Article 3 and, at the date of the commencement of the proceedings before the judicial or administrative authority of the Contracting State where the child is, a period of less than one year has elapsed from the date of the wrongful removal or retention, the authority concerned shall order the return of the child forthwith. The judicial or administrative authority, even where the proceedings have been commenced after the expiration of the period of one year referred to in the preceding paragraph, shall also order the return of the child, unless it is demonstrated that the child is now settled in its new environment.

Under Article 13b of the 1980 Hague Convention, the requested state is not bound to order the return of the child if 'there is a grave risk that his or her return would expose the child to physical or psychological harm or

200 The matter is regulated by Council Regulation (EC) No 2201/2003 of 27 November 2003 concerning jurisdiction and the recognition and enforcement of judgments in matrimonial matters and the matters of parental responsibility, OJ L 338, 23 December 2003, p. 1. Its objective is to promote the recognition and enforcement of judgments given in another Member State on the basis of the principle of mutual trust.

otherwise place the child in an intolerable situation'. The requested state can also refuse to order the return of the child if it finds that the child objects to being returned and has attained an age and degree of maturity at which it is appropriate to take account of his or her views. These provisions aim at ensuring that decisions on the child's return take account of his or her best interest. The best interest of the child is a principle recognised by the Charter of Fundamental Rights.[201] Under the 1980 Hague Convention, the child's interest is understood as entailing that he or she is not returned to a parent with custody rights if the child could as a result suffer physical or psychological harm, the return is against the child's wishes or, on the expiry of a one-year period, if the child has settled into a new environment.

Under Article 60 of the EU Regulation, that Regulation takes precedence in relations between the Member States over the 1980 Hague Convention. The Regulation additionally requires that the courts issuing decisions relating to the child's return give the child the opportunity to be heard during the proceedings unless this appears inappropriate having regard to his or her age or degree of maturity.[202] However, a court cannot refuse to return a child on the basis of Article 13b of the 1980 Hague Convention if it is established that adequate arrangements have been made to secure the protection of the child after his or her return.[203] Thus, the Regulation effectively nullifies the protection offered to children by the 1980 Hague Convention,[204] which is difficult to understand in the light of the fact that the Regulation's recitals claim that the Regulation is based on the idea that the best interests of the child must prevail and that it seeks to ensure 'respect for the fundamental rights of the child, as set out in Article 24 of the Charter of Fundamental Rights'.[205] Unfortunately, the Court's view of the main objective of the Regulation is very different. In *Rinau*, the Court ruled that the particular objective of the Regulation was to deter from abducting children and to obtain the child's return without delay.[206] It follows that a refusal to recognise another Member State's court judgment of parental responsibility because it is in the best interest of the child to remain where she or he currently resides, is, in the Court's view, incompatible with the Regulation. The issue is further complicated by the fact that judgments on parental responsibility are not infrequently

201 Article 24(2) of the Charter states: 'In all actions relating to children, whether taken by public authorities or private institutions, the child's best interests must be a primary consideration.' Article 24(3) provides: 'Every child shall have the right to maintain on a regular basis a personal relationship and direct contact with both of his or her parents, unless that is contrary to his or her interests.'

202 Article 11(2) of the Regulation.

203 Article 11(4).

204 Article 23 allows the Member States to refuse recognition 'if it is manifestly contrary to the public policy of the Member State in which recognition is sought, taking into account the best interests of the child'.

205 Recitals 12–13 and 33.

206 In Case C-195/08 PPU *Inga Rinau* [2008] ECR I-5271, para 52.

delivered for the parent whose nationality is the same as that of the court taking the decision, and against the parent with a nationality of another Member State, and in possible disregard of the best interest of the child. The Court had an opportunity to respond to this challenge in *Detiček*,[207] but in a quite shocking judgment, it decided to put effectiveness of the Regulation above the best interest of the child in question.

Detiček concerned enforcement proceedings brought before a Slovenian court for return of Antonella, the daughter of Ms Detiček of Slovenian nationality, residing in Slovenia, and Mr Sgueglia of Italian nationality, residing in Italy. Under a provisional order of the Italian court Antonella on her return to Italy was to be placed in a children's home. Ms Detiček applied for provisional custody of Antonella before the Slovenian court. Mr Sgueglia challenged that order before the same court, which made a reference to the Court of Justice, asking whether the Slovenian court, by way of exception, had jurisdiction to take protective measures. Normally, only the court with jurisdiction as to the substance (here the Italian court) could take protective measures and if no additional powers were allowed to the Slovenian court, it would have to enforce these protective measures. The answer to the question depended on the application of the requirement of urgency in Article 20 of the Regulation,[208] and in particular on the finding of whether urgency could arise due to a change of circumstances since the first court had taken a provisional measure giving sole custody of the child to the father.[209]

The Court observed that the change in circumstances stemmed from the fact that Antonella had in the meantime settled into the new environment in Slovenia. However, the Court disagreed that such a change of circumstances was grounds for finding that the case is urgent within the meaning of Article 20 because it would run counter to the principle of mutual recognition of judgments and Article 31 of the Regulation, which prohibits any review as to the substance of a judgment whose enforcement is sought.[210] The Court held at paragraph 47:

> If a change of circumstances resulting from a gradual process such as the child's integration into a new environment were enough, under Article

207 Case C-403/09 PPU *Jasna Detiček v Maurizio Sgueglia* [2009] ECR I-12193.

208 Under Article 20(1) of Regulation 2201/2003, the courts of a Member State may take provisional measures 'in urgent cases' also where the court of another Member State has jurisdiction as to the substance of the matter. Under Article 20(2), '[the provisional] measures shall cease to apply when the court of the Member State having jurisdiction under this Regulation as to the substance of the matter has taken the measures it considers appropriate'.

209 The Slovenian court established that Antonella was settled in her social environment in Slovenia. The return to Italy with enforced placement in a children's home would be contrary to her welfare as that would cause irreversible physical and psychological trauma. In addition, during the judicial proceedings in Slovenia, Antonella had expressed the wish to remain with her mother. If the 1980 Hague Convention applied between the Member States, the Slovenian court could on these grounds refuse to issue an order of return.

210 Ibid., paras 44–46.

> 20(1) of Regulation No 2201/2003, to entitle a court not having jurisdiction as to the substance to adopt a provisional measure amending the measure in matters of parental responsibility taken by the court with jurisdiction as to the substance, any delay in the enforcement procedure in the requested Member State would contribute to creating the conditions that would allow the former court to block the enforcement of the judgment that had been declared enforceable. Such an interpretation would undermine the very principles on which that regulation is based.

The Court also held that the recognition of a situation of urgency in the case of a wrongful removal of the child would run counter to the aim of Regulation 2201/2003 to deter the wrongful removal or retention of children between Member States.[211] In order to punish the parent who wrongfully removed the child, and thereby make prevention of child abduction more effective, the Court ruled out the possibility for that parent to rely on Article 20.[212]

Furthermore, the Court observed that one of the fundamental rights of the child was the right, set out in Article 24(3) of the Charter, to maintain on a regular basis a personal relationship and direct contact with both parents and that Article 20 of the Regulation had to be interpreted in the light of that right.[213] So, quite surprisingly, instead of the Regulation being described as a limitation on the child's fundamental right to have one's best interest taken into account, the Court regarded Article 20 of the Regulation to be a restriction on the right to a personal relationship with both parents and the right to family life. Because the Court claimed that the right to have a regular personal contact with both parents 'merged' into that of respect for the best interest of the child, it did not have to treat the latter as a separate consideration. Moreover, the Court completely removed itself from the facts of the case before it and ignored the actual interest of Antonella and her wishes, further disregarding the duty to take into account the best interest of an individual child. The evidence for this is paragraphs 56 and 59 of the judgment. A wrongful removal of the child is presented as depriving the child of the possibility of maintaining a personal relationship with the other parent 'more often than not'. The Court also introduces a hierarchy between the right to a personal relationship with both parents and the right to have one's best interest taken into account. The latter may override the former only if it is 'of such importance that it takes priority',[214] to be assessed by the court with jurisdiction as to the substance, i.e., the Italian court.[215] In *Povse*,[216] the Court confirmed that the unlawful removal of a child should not, in

211 Ibid., para 48
212 Ibid., para 57.
213 Ibid., paras 54–55.
214 Ibid., para 59.
215 Ibid., para 60.
216 Case C-211/10 PPU *Doris Povse v Mauro Alpago* [2010] ECR I-6673.

principle, have the effect of transferring jurisdiction from the courts of the Member State where the child was habitually resident immediately before removal to the courts of the Member State to which the child was taken. This applied also where, following the abduction, the child has acquired a habitual residence in the latter Member State.[217]

Another avenue that has been tried by applicants in order to empower the enforcing court to refuse to order a child's return concerned the requirement that the judgment of another Member State's court be accompanied by a certificate confirming, inter alia, that the child had been given an opportunity to be heard.[218] In *Zarraga*,[219] the mother argued that the Spanish court's judgment against her should not be recognised because the child had not been heard and therefore that court should not have issued the required certificate. The Court of Justice held that granting the enforcing court the power to refuse the judgment's recognition on the ground that the certificate was incorrectly issued would undermine the effectiveness of the system set up by the Regulation and therefore could not be allowed.[220] The Court moreover exploited the fact that Article 24(1) of the Charter speaks only of the opportunity to be heard, and not the right to be heard, and that the child's freely expressed views should be taken into consideration solely 'in accordance with their age and maturity'. These formulations enabled the Court to rule that it was for the court that had to rule on the return of a child – i.e., the court with jurisdiction as to the substance – to assess whether such a hearing was appropriate.[221] The national court that failed to hear the child could therefore legitimately issue the required certificate. It followed that the only court that had the power to review compatibility of the judgment on the child's return with the Charter was the court of the state of origin and the enforcing court had no such competence.[222]

The Court's resistance to arguments of fundamental rights as a way of introducing exceptions to the formal rules of Regulation 2201/2003 is also visible in cases concerning rights other than those guaranteed by Article 24 of the Charter (rights of the child). *McB*[223] concerned a case arising in the context of Irish law under which the natural father of children did not have custody rights and had to apply to a court to have the rights granted. That meant that if the mother left Ireland with the children, the father had first to start separate proceedings to obtain custody rights. Yet, these proceedings could not be started if the mother had not been served the father's application. This was difficult if the mother was residing in another Member

217 Ibid., para 44.
218 Article 42 of the Regulation.
219 Case C-491/10 PPU *Joseba Andoni Aguirre Zarraga v Simone Pelz* [2010] ECR I-14247.
220 Ibid., para 54–55.
221 Ibid., para 64.
222 Ibid., para 69.
223 Case C-400/10 PPU *J. McB. v L. E.* [2010] ECR I-8965.

State. The enforcing court could not order the return of children to the father because he was unable to show that their removal breached his custody rights and was therefore 'wrongful', as required by the Regulation. The Irish Supreme Court asked the Court of Justice whether the Regulation interpreted in the light of the right to family life, as protected by Article 7 of the Charter of Fundamental Rights, precluded the rules of Irish law on paternal custody rights.

In this case, it was not clear what the consequences of precluding the Irish law would be. Should the enforcing court order the children's return to a father without formal custody rights? This would mean that the existence of custody rights and the wrongfulness of removal would no longer be the prerequisites of the Regulation's application. If it was the Irish court delivering a judgment for the father on the issue of return which was supposed to be bound in this context by Article 7 of the Charter, EU law would begin to have direct impact on the content of family law of a Member State, in contravention to the provisions of the Treaty on the EU's limited competence. Thus, the Court, unsurprisingly, did not review the compatibility of Irish law with the Charter. It was for the law of the Member State to determine the conditions under which the natural father acquired custody rights in respect of his child. At a more abstract level, the Irish law under which the natural father was not a parent who automatically possessed custody rights in respect of his child was held to be compatible with the right to family life because it did not affect its essence and was justified by the requirement of legal certainty and the need to protect the rights of the mother.[224]

4 Conclusion

The chapter considered the rich *acquis* of the EU falling within the AFSJ from the perspective of human rights. The discussion pointed to a number of concerns that arise with respect to EU measures adopted in the field of asylum and immigration, crime prevention and judicial cooperation in civil matters. Some of the identified human rights issues should be described as standard, such as those concerning the right to be heard, the right to an effective remedy and the right to data protection, and would arise also if the Member States had taken the action individually. Some other issues are, however, generated by the EU and its policies. The free movement of persons and the Schengen Agreement enable offenders to escape to another jurisdiction, or parents to leave with children over whom they do not have exclusive custody rights, more easily. This requires a response from the EU in the form of measures facilitating cooperation between authorities of the Member States aimed at ensuring effective prosecution and enforcement of criminal sanctions, or a quick return of a child to the parent with custody rights. The internal market

224 Ibid., para 57–59.

means more cross-border transactions and more interactions between parties from different Member States. This, on the other hand, requires a response in terms of jurisdictional rules, managing conflicts between different national procedural traditions. It is in asylum and immigration where the necessity to regulate centrally, at the EU level, is perhaps less obvious while the need for inter-State solidarity the greatest. It is also an area where human dignity and individual rights are most likely to be violated and where the EU acts as a *de facto* human rights organisation, ensuring that the Member States respect human rights of asylum-seekers and illegally staying third-country nationals. In this context, we may question whether the EU is doing enough, whether the legislative standards are sufficiently strict. As we have seen, the Court of Justice extended some of the explicit obligations of the Member States, interpreting the Directives in the light of EU fundamental rights, and in particular the Charter and the ECHR.

Measures taken as part of the judicial cooperation in criminal matters and in civil matters clash with human rights because their content frequently focuses on the successful achievement of practical goals. Judicial cooperation is most effective where national courts act on decisions taken by their counterparts in other EU jurisdictions without questioning their substance or the procedures employed in their adoption. This observation explains an almost irrebuttable presumption in EU law of mutual trust among the Member States' justice systems. The Court of Justice, as the *Melloni* judgment shows, considers mutual recognition of judicial decisions an aim in itself. This is why the best interest of the child does not trump the effective enforcement of a return decision. Or the goal of effective punishment justifies the duty to surrender a convicted individual even though he or she did not take part in the criminal proceedings in which the sentence giving rise to the arrest warrant was imposed. The Court's case law exhibits an extreme version of utilitarianism, which is incompatible with a corrective justice conception of human rights, underlying the ECHR and the Charter of Fundamental Rights. The Court abandons this approach in some cases; for example, where it accepts that a violation of the right to be heard or the right to an effective remedy may justify a refusal to recognise a judgment of another state's court in a commercial case. However, the choice as to where exceptions should be allowed is not entirely convincing, given the fact that so far the Court has not been prepared to accept them in the context of criminal proceedings or proceedings relating to the return of a child.

My objective in this chapter was to point to tensions that arise in the AFSJ and explain the ways in which they have been addressed by the Court of Justice. The Court is far from usurping a human rights jurisdiction for itself and the full potential of the Charter to infuse EU law in the AFSJ with content inspired by human rights has not yet been realised. Instead, the Court is often using the argument of effectiveness to resist arguments of human rights. With a few notable exceptions human rights seem to be protected in the AFSJ only insofar as they are recognised and codified in secondary law.

Part II

EU criminal law

5 The mutual recognition principle and EU criminal law

Inés Armada and Anne Weyembergh

1 Introduction

Three stages may be differentiated in the evolution of judicial cooperation in criminal matters in the EU.

The first stage corresponds to classic cooperation, mainly developed within the Council of Europe in the 1950s through multilateral agreements such as the 1957 Extradition Convention[1] or the Convention on Mutual Assistance in Criminal Matters of 20 April 1959 (hereafter the 1959 MLA Convention) and its protocols.[2] Strongly marked by sovereignty and the principle of territoriality, the cooperation mechanisms established by these conventions are generally slow and burdensome because of the diplomatic channels used to transmit requests, the broad grounds for refusal, the lack of specific time limits or the possibility left to State parties to formulate reservations or declarations.

The second stage started in the 1970s, with the Member States of the then European Communities reflecting on ways to improve the classic instruments of judicial cooperation.[3] The most representative instruments of this 'second wave' are the Convention Implementing the Schengen Agreement[4] (hereafter CISA) and a number of instruments concluded under the third pillar, notably the Convention of 10 March 1995 on simplified extradition procedure between the Member States of the European Union,[5] the Convention of 27 September 1996 relating to extradition between the Member States of the European Union[6] and the Convention on Mutual Assistance in Criminal

1 Council of Europe, European Convention on Extradition of 13 December 1957, Paris, ETS No. 024.

2 Council of Europe, European Convention on Mutual Assistance in Criminal Matters of 20 April 1959, Strasbourg, ETS No. 30. Two additional protocols were later adopted, in 1978, and 2001 (ETS No. 99 and ETS No. 182 respectively).

3 An example is the Agreement of 26 May 1989 between the Member States of the EC on the simplification and modernisation of methods of transmitting extradition requests, which had a limited impact.

4 OJ L 239, 22 September 2000, p. 1 See particularly Articles 48–53.

5 OJ C 78, 30 March 1995, p. 2.

6 OJ C 313, 23 October 1996, p. 11.

Matters between the Member States of the European Union[7] and its Protocol of 2001.[8] These brought about limited but tangible improvements, leading to faster, more flexible cooperation mechanisms. They introduced or developed more direct channels for transmitting requests, they operated a reduction of the grounds for refusal and they limited the possibilities of making reservations or declarations.

Since this improved model of judicial cooperation was considered insufficient to respond to the needs of an area without internal borders and to face challenges such as the development of serious transnational crime, the EU Member States decided to move to a third stage, namely to the principle of mutual recognition. During its presidency in 1998, the UK government proposed to 'import' the principle of mutual recognition into the field of criminal matters.[9] This principle was well-known in the EU. It played a key role in the field of judicial cooperation in civil and commercial matters, notably in the Brussels Convention of 27 September 1968. It also became the founding element upon which the internal market was built: in the Cassis de Dijon case[10] the ECJ established the 'equivalence' of national regulations, and in so doing, mutual recognition effectively neutralised the trade barriers resulting from the different national technical regulations and enabled free movement of goods within the Community.

The importance of the principle was confirmed at the Tampere European Council of October 1999, during which it was described as the 'cornerstone' of judicial cooperation both in the civil and criminal fields.[11] The principle was subsequently developed in a programme of measures adopted in 2000.[12] The Hague Programme[13] and the Stockholm Programme[14] confirmed its importance for the EU area of criminal justice. The entry into force of the Lisbon Treaty consecrated mutual recognition as the motor of EU integration in criminal matters.[15]

7 OJ C 197, 12 July 2000, p. 3 and OJ C 326, 21 November 2001, p. 1.

8 For an in depth analysis of the 2000 MLA Convention see E. Denza, 'The 2000 Convention on mutual assistance in criminal matters' (2003) 40 *Common Market Law Review* 1047.

9 Cardiff European Summit – Presidency Conclusions, 15 and 16 June 1998, SN 150/98, para 39. This transplant has been subject of criticism, see V. Mitsilegas, 'The constitutional implications of mutual recognition in criminal matters matters in the EU', (2006) 43 *Common Market Law Review* 1280.

10 ECJ, Case-120/78, *Rewe-Zentral AG c/ Bundesmonopolverwaltung für Branntwein*, judgment of 20 February 1979.

11 Tampere European Summit – Presidency Conclusions, 15 and 16 October 1999, SN 200/99, paras 33 and f.

12 OJ C 12, 15 January 2001, p. 10.

13 The Hague Programme, Presidency Conclusions, 4 and 5 November 2004, OJ C 53, 3 March 2005, p. 1.

14 The Stockholm Programme, Presidency Conclusions, 11 December 2009, OJ C 115, 4 May 2010, p. 1.

15 See in particular Articles 67(3) and 82(1) TFEU.

So far there are 11 instruments of mutual recognition, namely nine Framework Decisions adopted under the former third pillar of the TEU, and two Directives adopted under the Lisbon Treaty:

- Framework Decision of 13 June 2002 on the European Arrest Warrant and surrender procedures between the Member States;[16]
- Framework Decision 2003/577/ JHA of 22 July 2003 on the execution in the European Union of orders freezing property or evidence;[17]
- Framework Decision 2005/214/JAI of 24 February 2005 on the application of the principle of mutual recognition to financial penalties;[18]
- Framework Decision 2006/783/JHA of 6 October 2006 on the application of the principle of mutual recognition to confiscation orders;[19]
- Framework Decision 2008/675/JHA of 24 July 2008 on taking account of convictions in the Member States of the European Union in the course of new criminal proceedings;[20]
- Framework Decision 2008/947/JHA of 27 November 2008 on the application of the principle of mutual recognition to judgments and probation decisions with a view to the supervision of probation measures and alternative sanctions;[21]
- Framework Decision 2008/909/JHA of 27 November 2008 on the application of the principle of mutual recognition to judgments in criminal matters imposing custodial sentences or measures involving deprivation of liberty;[22]
- Framework Decision 2008/978/JHA of 18 December 2008 on the European Evidence Warrant for the purpose of obtaining objects, documents and data for use in proceedings in criminal matters;[23]
- Framework Decision 2009/829/JHA of 23 October 2009 on the application, between Member States of the European Union, of the principle of mutual recognition to decisions on supervision measures as an alternative to provisional detention;[24]
- Directive 2011/99/EU of 13 December 2011 on the European Protection Order;[25]
- Directive 2014/41/EU of 3 April 2014 regarding the European Investigation Order in criminal matters,[26] which replaces for Member

16 OJ L 190, 18 July 2002, p. 1.
17 OJ L 196, 2 August 2005, p. 45.
18 OJ L 76, 22 March 2005, p. 16.
19 OJ L 328, 24 November 2006, p. 59.
20 OJ L 220, 15 August 2008, p. 32.
21 OJ L 337, 16 December 2008, p. 102.
22 OJ L 327, 5 December 2008, p. 27.
23 OJ L 350, 30 December 2008, p. 72
24 OJ L 294, 11 December 2009, p. 20.
25 OJ L 338, 21 December 2011, p.2.
26 OJ L 130, 1 May 2014, pp. 1–36.

States bound by this Directive the provisions of Framework Decision 2003/577/JHA as regards freezing of evidence and the Framework Decision 2008/978/JHA on the European Evidence Warrant.

In order to have a complete picture of the mutual recognition principle in criminal matters, the case law of the ECJ must also be taken into consideration. Its rulings on the *ne bis in idem* principle represent, for instance, an important contribution to the implementation of the mutual recognition principle in criminal matters.[27] The same holds true with regard to the ECJ's case law on the EAW FD[28] or to the nascent case law on subsequent mutual recognition instruments, such as the financial penalties FD.[29]

This contribution does not intend to analyse in detail the 11 legislative instruments, nor all relevant rulings of the ECJ. It aims instead to highlight how mutual recognition contributes to the establishment of a true EU area of criminal justice.[30] With this purpose in view, Section 2 of this contribution identifies the most important cross-cutting features of the principle (I).

27 See ECJ, joined cases C-187/01 and C-385/01, *Hüseyin Gözütok and Klaus Brügge*, judgment of 11 February 2003; ECJ, Case C-469/03, *Filomeno Mario Miraglia*, judgment of 10 March 2005; ECJ, Case C-436/04, *Leopold Henri Van Esbroeck*, judgment of 9 March 2006; ECJ, Case C-150/05, *Jean Leon Van Straaten v Staat der Nederlanden and Republiek Italië*, judgment of 28 September 2006; ECJ, Case C-467/04, *Giuseppe Francesco Gasparini and Others*, judgment of 29 September 2006; ECJ, Case C-288/05, *Jürgen Kretzinger*, judgment of 18 July 2007; ECJ, Case C-367/05, *Norma Kraaijenbrink*, judgment of 18 July 2007; ECJ, Case C-297/07, *Klaus Bourquain*, judgment of 11 December 2008; ECJ, Case C-491/07, *Vladimir Turansky*, judgment of 22 December 2008; ECJ (GC), Case C-129/14 PPU, *Zoran Spasic*, judgment of 27 May 2014; ECJ, Case C-398/12, *M*, judgment of 5 June 2014.

28 ECJ (GC), Case C-303/05, *Advocaten voor de Wereld VZW v Leden van de Ministerraad*, judgment of 3 May 2007; ECJ (GC), Case C-66/08, *Szymon Kozlowski*, judgment of 17 July 2008; ECJ, Case C-296/08 PPU, *Ignacio Pedro Santesteban Goicoechea*, judgment of 12 August 2008; ECJ, Case C-388/08 PPU, *Leymann and Pustovarov*, judgment of 1 December 2008; ECJ (GC), Case C-123/08, *Dominic Wolzenburg*, judgment of 6 October 2009; ECJ, Case C-306/09, *IB*, judgment of 21 October 2010; ECJ (GC), Case C-261/09, *Gaetano Mantello*, judgment of 16 November 2010; ECJ, Case C-192/12 PPU, *Melvin West*, judgment of 28 June 2012; ECJ (GC), Case C-42/11, *Lopes Da Silva Jorge*, judgment of 5 September 2012; ECJ (GC), Case C-396/11, *Ciprian Vasile Radu*, judgment of 29 January 2013; ECJ (GC), Case C-399/11, *Stefano Melloni v Ministerio Fiscal*, judgment of 26 February 2013; ECJ, Case C-168/13 PPU, *Jeremy F. v Premier Ministre*, judgment of 30 May 2013; ECJ (GC), Case C-237/15 PPU, *Lanigan*, judgment of 16 July 2015.

29 ECJ (GC), Case C-60/12, *Marián Baláž*, judgment of 14 November 2013.

30 See in this regard, among others, D. Flore (with S. Bosly), *Droit Pénal Européen. Les Enjeux d'une Justice Pénale Européenne* (2nd edn, Larcier, 2014), p. 525; S.H. Satzger, *International and European Criminal Law* (Hart, Beck and Nomos, 2012), pp. 117f.; A. Suominen, *The Principle of Mutual Recognition in Cooperation in Criminal Matters: A Study of the Principle in Four Framework Decisions and in the Implementation Legislation in the Nordic Member States* (Intersentia, 2011), p. 112; G. de Kerchove and A. Weyembergh (eds.), *La Reconnaissance Mutuelle des Décisions Judiciaires Pénales dans l'Union Européenne* (Les éditions de l'université de Bruxelles 2001).

Section 3 analyses its first and last concretisations: the EAW FD and the EIO Directive (II).

2 Main changes in comparison with the previous cooperation models

Whereas previously judicial cooperation in criminal matters was marked by State sovereignty and the principle of national territoriality, with States retaining the power over what happens in their territory and enjoying considerable discretion as to whether or not to cooperate with the requesting authority, the introduction of the principle of mutual recognition represents a crucial change, in that decisions issued in other Member States of the EU must, in principle, be recognised and executed. This evolution is thus sensitive in terms of national sovereignty, and affects the principle of national territoriality. It is particularly representative of the notion of an EU *area* of criminal justice.

In this regard, the following definition of mutual recognition is enlightening:

> Mutual recognition is a principle that is widely understood as being based on the thought that while another state may not deal with a certain matter in the same or even a similar way as one's own state, the results will be such that they are *accepted as equivalent to decisions by one's own state. Mutual trust is an important element*, not only trust in the adequacy of one's partners rules, but also trust that these rules are correctly applied. Based on this idea of equivalence and the trust it is based on, the results the other state has reached are allowed to take effect in one's own sphere of legal influence. On this basis, a decision taken by an authority in one state could be accepted as such in another state, even though a comparable authority may not even exist in that state, or could not take such decisions, or would have taken an entirely different decision in a comparable case. Recognising a foreign decision in criminal matters could be understood as *giving it effect outside of the state* in which it has been rendered, be it by according it the legal effects foreseen for it by the foreign criminal law, or be it by taking it into account in order to make it have the effects foreseen by the criminal law of the recognising state.[31]

It shows that the philosophy underlying this new model of cooperation is a real difference with the previous stages of judicial cooperation (2.1). Other changes are to be mentioned as well (2.2).

31 Commission, Communication on mutual recognition of final decisions in criminal matters, COM(2000), 495 final, 26 July 2000 (emphasis added).

2.1 *The philosophy of the principle: mutual trust and reliance on the control performed in the issuing State*

Mutual recognition revolves around three elements, namely equivalence, mutual trust and extraterritoriality. The executing Member State receives a warrant/certificate/order coming from another Member State according to the laws of that State, and it must recognise it as if it had been issued in its own Member State, unless a ground for non-execution is resorted to. This implies, of course, granting judicial decisions an extraterritorial effect, since the decision taken in Member State A deploys its effects in Member State B. This is rendered possible thanks to mutual trust: the implementation of mutual recognition indeed presupposes that Member States have trust in each other's criminal justice systems, grounded in particular on their shared commitment to the principles of freedom, democracy, respect for human rights, fundamental freedoms and the rule of law.[32] These shared values justify and enable the free circulation of criminal decisions within the common area of criminal justice.

Mutual recognition implies a real effort towards as much automaticity as possible. Indeed, mutual recognition abolishes the *exequatur* procedure,[33] and thus the enforceability of a foreign decision no longer depends on it being 'transformed' into a national decision.[34] As a consequence, most controls should be performed in the issuing State and not in the executing State. This principle emerges from certain features of the mutual recognition instruments, such as the absence of a ground for refusal based on human rights[35] or the provision excluding the possibility of legal actions being brought against the decision at the origin of the cooperation request in the requested State. Trust is thus placed on the controls performed in the issuing State, which the executing State is deemed to consider equivalent to its own.

Mutual recognition must, however, not only strengthen cooperation between Member States, but also enhance judicial protection of individual rights and freedoms.[36] Therefore, accelerating and trusting the controls carried out in the issuing State must not run counter to other interests that also merit consideration. The position of the defence – and more generally the protection of human rights and the respect of individual guarantees – should not be sacrificed for the sake of more efficient cooperation. The challenge is thus to reconcile both concerns, and to find the right balance between them, i.e., limiting as much as possible double controls that would slow down

32 See Article 2 TEU.

33 J.A.E. Vervaele, 'European criminal law and general principles of Union law', in J.A.E. Vervaele (ed.), *European Evidence Warrant: Transnational Judicial Inquiries in the EU*, (Intersentia, 2005), p. 133.

34 As we shall see, this is questionable with regard to the EIO.

35 With the exception of the EIO Directive, which as we shall see does include such a ground in Article 11(1)(f).

36 Programme of measures to implement the principle of mutual recognition of decisions in criminal matters, p. 1. See also Tampere Conclusions, para 33.

the procedure, while avoiding at the same time blind confidence and 'de-responsibilisation' of the competent executing authorities.

In the quest for such difficult 'equilibrium', the case law of the ECJ is, of course, essential. In its decisions on *ne bis in idem*, and especially in its rulings interpreting Article 54 CISA,[37] the Court insisted on the importance of mutual trust.[38] This allowed the Court to give a broad interpretation of *ne bis in idem*, which is generally to the advantage of the suspect or accused. The recourse by the ECJ to trust has however sometimes been criticised by scholars. This was, for instance, the case in the *Mantello* decision, where the Court had to interpret *ne bis in idem* as a ground for refusal of a EAW.[39] Indeed, in spite of the *mandatory* nature of this ground for refusal, the Court excluded a second check of the *ne bis in idem* by the executing authority. This ruling, as well as others – such as those of *Radu* or *Melloni* – led some authors to denounce that the ECJ puts more emphasis on efficiency, simplification and acceleration of cooperation and less on the protection of human rights and individual guarantees.[40] In *Radu*, it avoided ruling on the legality of refusing the execution of an EAW on fundamental rights grounds,[41] but did state that the grounds for refusal included in the FD were exhaustive.[42] In *Melloni*, the Court gave prevalence to the EAW FD over Spanish constitutional law, which afforded a higher level of protection in case of *in absentia* decisions. However, the latter judgment was the logical consequence of the principle of primacy of EU law.[43] Moreover, in *Jeremy F.*,[44] the ECJ took a balanced approach, insisting on the importance of effective remedies and

37 On this topic, see A. Weyembergh and I. Armada, 'The principle of *ne bis in idem* in Europe's Area of Freedom, Security and Justice', in V. Mitsilegas, M. Bergström and T. Konstadinides (eds.), *Research Handbook on EU Criminal Law* (Edward Elgar, 2016) pp. 189–209.

38 See in particular ECJ, joined cases C-187/01 & C-385/01, *Hüseyin Gözütok and Klaus Brügge*, judgment of 11 February 2003, paras 32–33, ECJ, Case C-436/04, *Leopold Henri Van Esbroeck*, judgment of 9 March 2006, paras 29–32 and ECJ, Case C-261/09, *Gaetano Mantello*, judgment of 16 November 2010.

39 A. Weyembergh, 'Le principe *ne bis in idem:* pierre d'achoppement de l'espace pénal européen?', *Cahiers de Droit Européen* (2004) 337.

40 For a more detailed analysis of some relevant judgments, see A. Weyembergh and S. de Biolley, 'Chronique de jurisprudence consacrée à l'Espace de liberté, de sécurité et de justice II', *Cahiers de Droit Eeuropéen* 50 (2014) 427.

41 See by contrast the very interesting opinion of AG Sharpston in this case.

42 Para 36. At para 42, the ECJ acknowledged however that the executing State had to carry some degree of control before deciding upon execution of the EAW.

43 For a comment of this important judgment see J.A.E. Vervaele, *European Criminal Justice in the Post-Lisbon Area of Freedom, Security and Justice* (Quaderni Della Facoltà di Giurisprudenza Università degli Studi di Trento, 2014), available at http://eprints.biblio.unitn.it/4399/1/vervaele_european-criminal-justice_quaderni-n.5-2014.pdf (accessed May 2015), Chapter 7, particularly pp. 240ff. See also X. Groussot and I. Olsson, 'Clarifying or diluting the application of the EU Charter of Fundamental Rights? – the judgments in Åkerberg and Melloni' (2013) 2 *Lund Student EU Law Review* 7 and N. Lavranos, 'The ECJ's judgments in Melloni and Åkerberg Fransson: une ménage à trois difficulté', (2013) 4 *European Law Reporter* 133.

44 ECJ, Case C-168/13 PPU, *Jeremy F. v Premier Ministre*, judgment of 30 May 2013, para 50.

judicial control of the surrender procedure. It also underlined how respect of fundamental rights reinforces 'the high level of confidence between Member States and the principle of mutual recognition'.[45]

The case law of the ECtHR in relation to the EAW is also essential.[46] Regarding the reasoning and conclusion of two admissibility decisions, namely *Monedero Angora v Spain*[47] and *Stapleton v Ireland*,[48] it seems the ECtHR 'promotes' the mutual recognition underlying philosophy according to which most controls should be performed in the issuing State and not in the executing State.

2.2 *Other changes*

As seen in the introduction to this chapter, under the previous models, judicial cooperation was slow and burdensome. Mutual recognition brought about significant changes. The main ones concern terminology, simplification of formalities, 'judicialisation', acceleration of cooperation, reduction of grounds for refusal and rationalisation of applicable texts.

1 **Terminology:** A comparison of the terminology used in the traditional conventions of judicial cooperation with the wording of the mutual recognition instruments evidence the different rationales underlying those models of cooperation. The words 'requesting and requested States/authorities' have been replaced by 'issuing and executing States/authorities', 'extradition' by 'surrender', etc. Other representative examples may be referred to as well, such as the former following provision: 'The Contracting Parties *undertake to afford each other*, in accordance with the provisions of this Convention, *the widest measure of mutual assistance*'.[49] By contrast, mutual recognition instruments use quite a different wording, representative of its underlying philosophy: 'The competent authorities in the executing State *shall recognise a decision* [...] *without any further formality being required and shall forthwith take all the necessary measures for its execution*, unless the competent authority decides to invoke one of the grounds for non-recognition or non-execution provided for in Article'.[50]

45 Ibid., para 49.

46 See also, *inter alia*, ECtHR, 17 December 2013, *Černák v Slovakia*, Application no. 36997/08; or ECtHR, 28 October 2014, *Cavani v Hungary*, Application no. 5493/13.

47 ECtHR (admissibility decision), 7 October 2008, *Monedero Angora v Spain*, Application no. 41138/05.

48 ECtHR (admissibility decision), 4 May 2010, *Robert Stapleton v Ireland*, Application no. 56588/07.

49 Article 1(1) of the 1959 MLA Convention. See also Article 7(1) of the Council of Europe Convention on Laundering, Search, Seizure and Confiscation of the Proceeds from Crime of 8 November 1990, ETS No. 141, or Article 2(1) of the Council of Europe Convention on the Transfer of Sentenced Persons of 21 March 1983, ETS No. 112.

50 Article 3 of the financial penalties FD. See also Article 5(1) of the freezing FD or Article 11(1) of the EEW FD.

2 **Simplification of formalities:** Mutual recognition simplifies formalities, notably via the warrant[51]/order[52]/certificate[53] technique. These are standardised forms contained in the Annex of the respective instrument, which the executing authority must recognise with no further formality[54].
3 **'Judicialisation':** The procedure is further simplified through the granting of a prominent role to judicial authorities.[55] In principle, warrants/orders/certificates are to be directly exchanged between judicial authorities.[56] Cooperation therefore becomes a wholly judicial process. This aspect is, however, not innovative in relation to all fields of judicial cooperation: whereas it is new to extradition and one of the major innovations introduced by the EAW FD, the second generation of mutual legal assistance instruments had already introduced direct judicial contacts.[57]
4 **Acceleration of cooperation:** Mutual recognition significantly accelerates cooperation. Certain instruments provide for binding deadlines,[58] others provide indicative ones,[59] while others are less precise[60] or even silent[61] in this regard.
5 **Reduction of grounds for refusal:** Compared to traditional judicial cooperation, even in its improved version, mutual recognition implies a clear duty to provide cooperation, a limitation to the traditional requirement of double criminality,[62] and a significant reduction of the available grounds for refusal. This is a logical consequence of the change of philosophy and the will to establish a true AFSJ.

51 Used in the EAW (Article 8(1)) and the EEW (Article 6(1)) FDs.
52 Used in the EPO (Article 7) and the EIO Directives (Article 5(1)). The freezing and the confiscation FDs also refer to orders.
53 Used in the financial penalties (Article 4(1)), probation (Article 6(1)), custodial sentences (Article 4(1)), and the ESO (Article 10(1)), FDs.
54 They are first translated by the issuing authority into one of the official language(s) of the executing State.
55 In this regard, see A. Weyembergh, 'Transverse report on judicial control in cooperation in criminal matters: the evolution from traditional judicial cooperation to mutual recognition', in K. Ligeti (ed.), *Toward a Prosecutor for the European Union, Volume 1* (Hart Publishing, 2012) 945.
56 There are, however, still some exceptions. See, *inter alia*, Article 7(2) EAW FD, Article 8(2) EEW FD, Article 2(2) financial penalties FD, Article 3(2) confiscation orders FD, Article 4(2) EPO Directive, Article 7(3) EIO Directive or Article 4(2) freezing FD.
57 See for instance Article 6(1) of the 2000 MLA Convention.
58 Articles 17 and 23 respectively. This is the case of the EAW FD. The FDs on the EEW (Article 15), on custodial sentences (Article 12), on probation (Article 12), the ESO (Article 12) and the EIO Directive (Article 12) also provide for binding deadlines.
59 Article 5(3) freezing FD.
60 Article 17 confiscation FD, Article 9(1) EPO Directive.
61 Article 6 financial penalties FD.
62 Note that the requirement of double criminality was typical in extradition proceedings, not in MLA (except with regard to search and seizure). Its introduction in the EIO Directive, *albeit* in a restricted way, represents a step backwards in terms of efficient cooperation if compared to the former model.

6 **Rationalisation of applicable texts:** Lastly, mutual recognition entails a certain rationalisation of judicial cooperation instruments. Whereas before new instruments complemented pre-existing ones without replacing them, most mutual recognition instruments replace previous texts.[63]

3 The different faces of mutual recognition through two case studies: from the EAW to the EIO

Whereas *in abstracto* mutual recognition has certain common features, a closer look at the concrete instruments shows *in concreto* each instrument has its own particularities. Such variable geometry of mutual recognition[64] will be illustrated by resorting to two of its most important materialisations: the EAW and the EIO.

3.1 The EAW or the success story of the EU for criminal justice

3.1.1 The EAW – origins and features

The EAW FD corresponds to the third phase in the evolution of extradition within the EU. The first phase was governed by the application of the Council of Europe's 1957 Extradition Convention,[65] which was a classic judicial cooperation convention. An improved extradition regime was established via CISA and the 1995 and 1996 EU Extradition Conventions. The idea to further facilitate extradition was put forward[66] and made possible in the aftermath of the 9/11 attacks. Only eight days after the collapse of the World Trade Center, the European Commission presented its proposal for an EAW FD.[67] The JHA Council pushed for quick negotiations,[68] and an agreement

63 See A. Weyembergh, 'Reconnaissance mutuelle en matière pénale dans l'Union européenne', (2008) *Jurisclasseur, Europe Traité*, Fasc. 2720.

64 On the incoherences and variable geometry between mutual recognition instruments see A. Weyembergh, I. Armada and C. Brière, *Critical Assessment of the Existing European Arrest Warrant Framework Decision*, Research Paper at the request of the European Added Value Unit, European Parliament, January 2014, particularly pp. 60–62, available at www.europarl.europa.eu/RegData/etudes/etudes/join/2013/510979/IPOL-JOIN_ET%282013%29510979%28ANN01%29_EN.pdf (accessed May 2015).

65 Council of Europe, European Convention on Extradition, CETS No. 024, 13 December 1957.

66 Tampere European Summit, para 35.

67 Commission, Proposal for a Council Framework Decision on the European arrest warrant and the surrender procedures between Member States, COM(2001) 522 final. OJ C 332, 27 November 2001, pp. 305–319.

68 On the context of the adoption of the EAW FD, see A. Weyembergh, 'L'impact du 11 septembre sur l'équilibre sécurité/liberté dans l'espace pénal européen', in E. Bribosia and A. Weyembergh (eds.), *Lutte Contre le Terrorisme et Droits Fondamentaux* (Collection Droit et Justice, 2002), pp. 153f.

was reached in the Laeken European Council of 14–15 December 2001, barely three months after the proposal was put on the table. The Framework Decision was finally adopted on 13 June 2002, becoming the first instrument of mutual recognition in criminal matters.

In spite of the material act being the same[69] – that is, the transfer of a suspected or convicted person from one State to another – the EAW has been qualified as a revolution in extradition.[70] The FD no longer refers to requesting and requested States but to issuing and executing States, and speaks of surrender and not of extradition, which indeed reflects a change in mentality from the former system. The EAW undoubtedly brought about significant changes.

Notably, the EAW fully 'judicialised' the procedure.[71] As the Commission put it, 'the political phase inherent in the extradition procedure is abolished. Accordingly, the administrative redress phase following the political decision is also abolished.'[72] Replacing State-to-State relations with direct relations between judicial authorities meant the effectiveness and speed of extradition greatly improved.

The first instrument of mutual recognition moreover *simplified* the procedure by introducing the use of a warrant, included in the Annex. Indirectly, this limits the possibility of requesting additional information:[73] if the form is completed with care, no such request will be necessary (or even allowed).[74] The practice of systematically requesting additional information of the case has indeed been condemned by the Council as contrary to the principle of mutual recognition and a relic of the extradition procedure.[75] It somehow signals a lack of trust in the foreign counterpart, indicating that a double control is being carried out in the executing State.[76]

The EAW maintains a series of grounds for refusal, divided into two categories: the mandatory[77] and the optional.[78] However, in comparison with the

69 A. Klip, *European Criminal Law: An Integrative Approach* (2nd edn, Intersentia, 2012), pp. 411 and 412.

70 S. Bot, *Le Mandat d'Arrêt Européen* (Larcier, 2009), p. 194. For a more nuanced approach, see M. Plachta, 'European Arrest Warrant: revolution in extradition?' (2003) 11 *European Journal of Crime, Criminal Law and Criminal Justice* 178.

71 In a significant number of Member States, transmission of EAWs is, however, made preferentially via police channels or central authorities, or through judicial authorities other than those designated to deal with the case. See Council's Final Report on the fourth round of mutual evaluations, Doc. No. 8302/4/09, 28 May 2009, pp. 8 and 9.

72 See the Commission Explanatory Memorandum accompanying the proposal, p. 5.

73 See in this sense the *European Handbook on How to Issue a European Arrest Warrant*, Council document no. 8216/2/08 REV 2, p. 11. Ibid., p. 11.

74 On this point see Weyembergh et al., 'Critical assessment', particularly pp. 26–28.

75 Council of the EU, Final Report, pp. 20–21.

76 Some authors consider Article 15(2) as an implicit ground for refusal. See Suominen, *The Principle of Mutual Recognition*, p. 112.

77 Article 3 FD.

78 Article 4 FD.

former extradition instruments that often led to extradition being denied, the FD considerably restricted the grounds for refusal. For instance, those relating to nationality and double criminality were significantly reduced, which in certain Member States required important constitutional amendments.[79] A major change was indeed introduced through the listing of 32 categories of offences to which double criminality does not apply if punishable in the issuing Member State by a custodial sentence or a detention order for a maximum period of at least three years.[80] This list has given rise to much concern.[81] In *Advocaten voor de Wereld*,[82] the ECJ held, however, that Article 2(2) EAW FD as implemented in Belgium was consistent with the principle of legality. The Court relied in particular on the fact that the FD did not aim at harmonising the offences included in the list, but referred back to the law of the issuing State, which is committed to fundamental rights and fundamental legal principles, including the legality principle.[83]

The establishment of strict time limits is another non-negligible feature distinguishing the EAW from extradition. Article 17 FD fixes the deadline of ten days for taking the final decision on the execution of the EAW if the requested person has consented to the surrender, or otherwise a delay of 60 days after the arrest is provided, with an exceptional extension of 30 days being applicable in both cases. Article 23 EAW FD then sets a general ten-day time limit to surrender the person from the moment the final decision on the execution is taken. The 2011 Commission report referred to a one-year average waiting period under the extradition regime, which renders the time limits in the FD one of the provisions that have most contributed to the success of the EAW.[84]

Finally, it must be noted that the EAW FD replaced pre-existing extradition conventions between EU Member States.[85]

79 On this issue see V. Mitsilegas, *EU Criminal Law* (Hart Publishing, 2009), pp. 133–138, and the literature cited therein.

80 See Article 2(2) FD. The Commission's proposal had gone further and recital 14 referred to the absolute abolition of double criminality.

81 See for instance N. Keijzer, 'The double criminality requirement', in R. Blekxtoon and W. van Ballegooij (eds.), *Handbook on the European Arrest Warrant* (TMC Asser Press, 2005), pp. 137ff.

82 ECJ, *Advocaten voor de Wereld*. For a comment on this case see F. Geyer, 'Case note: European Arrest Warrant. Court of Justice of the European Communities' (2008) 4 *European Constitutional Law Review* 149.

83 Paras 52 and 53. This judgment has not managed to convince an important sector of academics; see for instance 'A manifesto on European criminal procedure law', *ZIS* 11/2013, p. 441, available at www.zis-online.com/dat/artikel/2013_11_777.pdf (accessed May 2015).

84 Report from the Commission to the European Parliament and the Council on the implementation since 2007 of the Council Framework Decision of 13 June 2002 on the European Arrest Warrant and the surrender procedures between Member States, COM(2011) 175 final of 11 April 2011, p. 3.

85 See Article 31 EAW FD.

3.1.2 *The critiques and downsides of the EAW*

In spite of the EAW being considered *the* success story and the flagship of the EU area of criminal justice, it has not escaped criticism.[86] The lack of an explicit fundamental rights ground for refusal has perhaps been the most commonly raised argument against the EAW.[87] References to fundamental rights in the final text of the FD are limited to Recital 12 and Article 1(3). This has been interpreted differently across the EU, with certain Member States respecting in practice the exact wording of the FD, and others introducing a general or more limited fundamental rights refusal ground.[88] As we have seen, so far the ECJ has avoided ruling on the legality of such a national ground for refusal in the light of EU law. The issue is of course delicate, since it is intrinsically linked to mutual trust, which, as we have seen, largely lies on the belief that respect of fundamental rights is a given among EU Member States.[89]

When it launched mutual recognition in 1998, the UK's objective was to use mutual recognition as an *alternative* to further harmonisation of national criminal legislations; however, it has been widely accepted that 'mutual trust is more likely to occur if legal systems are comparable to or at least easily understood by others'.[90] It is thus argued that, to work smoothly, mutual recognition requires a certain degree of approximation of the suspect and accused's procedural rights.[91] However, it was only in 2004 that the Commission finally put forward a proposal.[92] The latter encountered strong resistance within the Council, grounded on the disputed legal basis in the Treaty[93] and on the necessity and added value of EU action, given the protection already afforded by the ECHR.[94] The entry into force of the Lisbon Treaty and particularly

86 See, among others, Weyembergh et al., 'Critical Assessment', and the Manifesto.

87 See for instance B. Schünemann, 'Fortschritte und fehltritte in der strafrechtspflege der EU' 2004 *Goldtammer's Archiv für Strafrecht* 313; L. Marin, 'The European Arrest Warrant and domestic legal orders: tensions between mutual recognition and fundamental rights: the Italian case' (2008) 15 *Maastricht Journal of European and Comparative Law*.

88 See Weyembergh et al., 'Critical assessment', particularly pp. 8–9.

89 As the ECJ put it: 'the principle of mutual recognition on which the [EAW] system is based is itself founded on the mutual confidence between the Member States that their national legal systems are capable of providing equivalent and effective protection of the fundamental rights recognised at European Union level, particularly in the Charter', ECJ, *Jeremy F.*, para 50.

90 C. Rijken, 'Re-balancing security and justice: protection of fundamental rights in police and judicial cooperation in criminal matters' (2010) 47 *Common Market Law Review* 1473.

91 See in this sense E. Guild, 'Crime and the EU's constitutional future in an area of freedom, security and justice' (2004) 10 *European Law Journal* 218.

92 Proposal for a Council Framework Decision on certain procedural rights in criminal proceedings throughout the European Union, COM(2004) 328 final.

93 See Mitsilegas, 'The constitutional implications', pp. 1304–1307. See also R. Lööf, 'Shooting from the hip: proposed minimum rights in criminal proceedings throughout the EU' (2006) 12 *European Law Journal* 422.

94 M. Jimeno-Bulnes, 'Towards common standards on rights of suspected and accused persons in criminal proceedings in the EU?', CEPS Liberty and Security in Europe, February 2010, p. 5, available at http://aei.pitt.edu/15104/1/Jimeno%2DBulnes_on_rights_of_suspects.pdf

Article 82(2)(b) TFEU settled the question, and the Council adopted the Roadmap for strengthening procedural rights of suspected or accused persons in criminal proceedings.[95] At the time of writing, three of the procedural rights Directives listed have been adopted[96] and three others are on their way. Only time will tell if the adoption of these measures renders unnecessary the introduction or recourse by the executing authorities of a fundamental rights ground for refusal.[97] The role of the ECJ in articulating the EAW FD and the abovementioned Directives will, of course, be crucial.

The other major criticism raised against the EAW relates to proportionality,[98] which is closely linked to the question of equivalence. The problem of EAWs in relation to petty crimes[99] was brought up in the Commission's first EAW report,[100] and continued to be a problem in the Council Conclusions to the fourth round of mutual evaluations.[101] This problem is not only related to fundamental rights, but touches upon financial issues too, since the costs of executing an EAW are to be borne by the executing State.[102] One cannot question that abuse of the EAW mechanism for minor offences negatively impacts mutual trust, not only among practitioners but also in the eyes of the broader public.[103] To address these concerns, certain Member States such as

(accessed April 2015). For an analysis of what EU action can add to the protection afforded by the ECHR see A. Tinsley, 'Protecting criminal defence rights through EU law' (2013) 4 *NJECL* 467.

95 Council's Roadmap for strengthening procedural rights of suspected or accused persons in criminal proceedings, OJ C 295, 4 December 2009, p. 1.

96 Directive 2010/64/EU on the right to interpretation and translation in criminal proceedings, OJ L 280, 26 October 2010; Directive 2012/13/EU of 22 May 2012 on the right to information in criminal proceedings, OJ L 142, 1 June 2012, p. 1; Directive 2013/48/EU of 22 October 2013, on the right of access to a lawyer in criminal proceedings and in EAW proceedings, and on the right to have a third party informed upon deprivation of liberty and to communicate with third persons and with consular authorities while deprived of liberty, OJ L 294, 6 November 2013, p. 1. Two requests for a preliminary ruling are pending before the ECJ in relation to the first two Directives. A first case asks the Court to interpret Article 1(1) of the interpretation and translation Directive (Case C-25/15) while the other, which is a request for a preliminary ruling from the German Amtsgericht Laufen, asks the Court to interpret Articles 1(2), 2(1) and 8 of the interpretation and translation Directive as well as Articles 2, 3(1)(c), 6(1) and 6(3) of the right to information Directive (Case C-216/14).

97 On the influence these Directives are likely to have, see E. Smith, 'Running before we can walk? Mutual recognition at the expense of fair trials in Europe's Area of Freedom, Justice and Security' (2013) 1 *NJECL* 82.

98 E. Xanthopoulou, 'The quest for proportionality for European Arrest Warrant and fundamental rights protection in a mutual recognition environment' (2015) 6 *NJECL* 32.

99 This situation would fall under prospective proportionality, see on this point S. Haggenmüller, 'The principle of proportionality and the European Arrest Warrant', (2013) 3 *Oñati Socio-legal Series* 101.

100 Member States' comments to the Report from the 2005 Commission Evaluation Report, Council Doc. 11528/05, 2 September 2005, p. 70.

101 Council, Final Report, p. 15.

102 Article 30(1) FD.

103 See for instance the cases of Patrick Connor and Mikolaj Kowalski raised by Fair Trials International, 'The European Arrest Warrant – cases of injustice', p. 6, available for

the UK[104] have introduced an explicit ground for refusal in relation to proportionality, which runs counter to the principle of mutual recognition by introducing a double-check of proportionality.[105]

Making use of the possibility offered by Article 225 TFEU, on 27 February 2014 the European Parliament adopted a resolution requesting the Commission to submit, within a year, legislative proposals to address, *inter alia*, the problems of disproportionate EAWs and the lack of a fundamental rights ground for refusal in the EAW FD.[106] Viviane Reding's initial resistance to reform the EAW FD[107] was confirmed by the new Commission: 'the Commission does not consider that improving the European arrest warrant system requires a revision of the Framework Decision'.[108] In relation to the proportionality problem, the Commission has underlined 'the importance of the existing less intrusive alternatives to the EAW and is committed to continue work to improve the practical operation of the EAW, including updating and improving the European handbook on issuing an EAW'.[109] Whereas the European Parliament seems to have failed to promote a reform of the EAW FD, we will see that its co-decision powers in the negotiation of the EIO Directive have allowed it to introduce major changes to the principle of mutual recognition as we knew it back in 2002.

3.2 *The EIO – a new understanding of the principle of mutual recognition?*

3.2.1 *Introduction*

One can also distinguish three phases in the evolution of judicial cooperation for the purposes of obtaining evidence abroad. The first stage corresponds to the application of the Council of Europe's 1959 MLA Convention. This

download www.fairtrials.org/publications/european-arrest-warrant-cases-of-injustice (accessed April 2015).

104 See new section 21A of the Extradition Act 2003, entitled 'Person not convicted: human rights and proportionality'.

105 See Weyembergh et al., 'Critical assessment', particularly pp. 31–37.

106 European Parliament Resolution of 27 February 2014 with recommendations to the Commission on the review of the European Arrest Warrant (2013/2109(INL)).

107 She argued that it would be premature to reopen the European Arrest Warrant, that other EU laws such as the right to interpretation and translation and access to a lawyer provide a counterbalance to abuse and that abuses occur partly because not all Member States have transposed the complementary laws. EU Observer, 27 February 2014, available at https://euobserver.com/justice/123304 (accessed April 2015).

108 Answer given by Ms Jourová on behalf of the European Commission, Parliamentary questions, 9 February 2015, available at www.europarl.europa.eu/sides/getAllAnswers.do?reference=E-2014-010694&language=EN (accessed May 2015).

109 European Parliament Committee on Petitions, Petition No 1784/2013, 28 November 2014, p. 3, available at www.europarl.europa.eu/meetdocs/2014_2019/documents/peti/cm/1042/1042176/1042176en.pdf (accessed May 2015).

is a traditional MLA agreement in that it considers the obtaining of evidence abroad somehow a political issue: letters of request are exchanged between Ministries,[110] and the grounds for refusal are drafted in broad terms.[111] An improved cooperation regime was achieved with the CISA and the subsequent 2000 MLA Convention.[112] These conventions only supplemented the 1959 Convention,[113] but operated two major changes to its regime: direct judicial cooperation was introduced,[114] and the 2000 MLA Convention modified the regime of applicable law: Article 4(1) requires the Member State carrying out the investigative measure to 'comply with the formalities and procedures expressly indicated by the requesting Member State, unless otherwise provided in this Convention and provided that such formalities and procedures are not contrary to the fundamental principles of law in the requested Member State'.[115] The third stage of judicial cooperation relates to the application of mutual recognition in the field of evidence, and here two instruments must be mentioned: the freezing and the EEW FDs. Neither of these two instruments is considered a success. The former applies only to the freezing stage, and thus any subsequent transfer of evidence has to take place separately using MLA. As to the EEW, its scope of application is limited to already existing objects, documents or data, and thus no possibility exists to request the execution of an investigative measure under this instrument of mutual recognition.[116]

The EIO is the first instrument of mutual recognition adopted under the Lisbon Treaty in the field of evidence, without, however, making use of the possibility provided by Article 82(2)(a) TFEU to establish minimum rules in relation to mutual admissibility of evidence between Member States. Back in November 2009, the Commission issued a Green Paper on obtaining evidence in criminal matters from one Member State to another and securing its admissibility,[117] a first step to addressing the European Council's call on the Commission to propose a comprehensive system for obtaining evidence located in a different Member State on the basis of the principle of mutual recognition.[118] However, it was seven Member States, making use of the possibility afforded by Article 76(b) TFEU, that put forward the proposal for an EIO Directive in June 2010.[119] The text was thereafter negotiated

110 See Article 15(1) of the 1959 MLA Convention.

111 See Article 2(1) of the 1959 MLA Convention.

112 For an in depth analysis see E. Denza, 'The 2000 Convention on mutual assistance in criminal matters', (2003) 40 *Common Market Law Review* 1047.

113 See Article 48(1) CISA and Article 1(1)(a) 2000 MLA Convention.

114 See Article 53(1) CISA, and Article 6(1) 2000 MLA Convention.

115 E. Denza, 'The 2000 Convention', p. 1058.

116 For a deep analysis of this instrument see Vervaele, *European Evidence Warrant.*

117 COM(2009) 624 final.

118 Stockholm Programme, pp. 1–38, point 3.1.1.

119 Initiative of the Kingdom of Belgium, the Republic of Bulgaria, the Republic of Estonia, the Kingdom of Spain, the Republic of Austria, the Republic of Slovenia and the Kingdom

under the ordinary legislative procedure, so with the European Parliament co-legislating with the Council on equal footing. It was finally adopted on 3 April 2014, and its transposition is due by 22 May 2017.[120]

3.2.2 Differences with the EAW

When comparing the EAW and the EIO, certain differences must be stressed as a starting point. Mutual recognition is often divided into two categories: mutual recognition of pre-trial decisions and mutual recognition of post-trial decisions.[121] An EAW can be 'for the purposes of conducting a criminal prosecution or executing a custodial sentence or detention order';[122] thus either pre- or post-trial. By contrast, the EIO is in principle a pre-trial decision.[123] One of the differences between the two instruments is (partly) linked to this. For obvious reasons, it is virtually impossible to execute an EAW without the suspect becoming aware of it. By contrast, in many cases, the suspect will be unaware that an EIO has been issued and executed since the investigation phase of criminal proceedings tend to be secret. Consequently, the defence plays a more important role in the operation of the EAW than is expected to be the case in relation to the EIO, which in turn has an impact on issues such as the protection of human rights, particularly the rights of the defence, or the regime of legal remedies. This might explain a new feature of the EIO Directive in relation to executing authorities. According to Article 2(d), 'executing authority' means 'an authority having competence to recognise an EIO and ensure its execution in accordance with this Directive and the procedures applicable in a similar domestic case. Such procedures may require a court authorisation in the executing State where provided by its national law'.[124] This provision might, however, jeopardise the effective functioning of the Directive. Indeed, if the executing judge subjects its authorisation to compliance with national requirements, EIOs might not be executed on account of differences between national laws, i.e., a lack of equivalence, which is precisely what the mutual recognition principle seeks to avoid.

A second difference has perhaps more far-reaching consequences, and has to do with the kind of measure that each of the instruments seek to have

of Sweden for a Directive of the European Parliament and of the Council regarding the European Investigation Order in criminal matters, OJ C 165, 24 June 2010, pp. 22ff.

120 Article 36(1).

121 G. Vernimmen-Van Tiggelen and L. Surano, 'Analysis of the future of mutual recognition in criminal matters in the European Union – final report', study funded by the European Commission, IEE-ULB, ECLAN, 20 November 2008, p. 11.

122 Article 1(1).

123 Notwithstanding that an EIO can be issued during the trial phase, see Recital 25.

124 For a discussion of this provision see I. Armada, 'The European Investigation Order and the lack of European standards for gathering evidence: is a fundamental rights-based refusal the solution?' (2015) 6 *NJECL* 12.

executed abroad. The EAW is basically an order to arrest someone abroad, in order to have him/her surrendered. An arrest is an unequivocal act consisting of seizing (someone) by legal authority and taking him or her into custody.[125] The EIO Directive is by contrast meant to apply to all investigative measures[126] aimed at gathering evidence with the exception of joint investigation teams[127]. This means that an enormous variety of investigative measures can be ordered, ranging from questioning a witness to covert investigations.[128] As a consequence, one can distinguish various 'versions' of mutual recognition in the EIO depending on the degree of coerciveness of the investigative measure in question. For instance, more grounds for refusal are available where the investigative measures impinge on individual rights and liberties.

The diversity among the national procedural rules governing each investigative measure in the 26 Member States taking part in the Directive[129] is remarkable, and a source of problems.[130] National laws not only differ with regard to the conditions granting 'access' to a particular investigative measure – for example, the type of crime and degree of suspicion required by law to resort to surveillance measures – but also the way in which the investigative measure is executed will differ from one Member State to another. The practical application of the EAW has revealed how the first set of differences, i.e., those that arise at the issuing stage, can complicate the smooth operation of the FD. Proportionality is not necessarily a requirement for issuing an EAW in all Member States[131], or at least the proportionality thresholds differ across the EU, and thus problems arise in relation to EAWs issued for petty crimes. Similar problems could also arise in the context of the EIO, and specific mechanisms have been put in place to address the divergent national legal regimes governing access to the different investigative measures.

The main difference with the EAW regime has, however, to do with the fact that the way in which the investigative measure is *executed* differs from one Member State to another. Problems arising because of these differences

125 Oxford Dictionary.

126 That are not defined in the Directive, which has given rise to much criticism. See, for instance, C. Heard and D. Mansell, 'The European Investigation Order: changing the face of evidence-gathering in EU cross-border cases' (2011) 2 *NJECL*.

127 Recital 9 excludes also cross-border surveillance as referred to in CISA from the scope of application of the EIO Directive. However, there is no mention of it in Article 3, which only refers to joint investigation teams.

128 This has led some authors to conclude that applying mutual recognition to investigative measures was not possible. See J.R. Spencer, 'The Green Paper on obtaining evidence from one Member State to another and securing its admissibility: the reaction of one British lawyer' (2010) 9 *ZIS* 603.

129 Ireland and Denmark are not taking part in accordance with their respective Protocols. The UK has, however, opted in to this Directive.

130 For a thorough comparative study of Member States' legislations governing investigative measures see Ligeti, *Toward a Prosecutor.*

131 For instance in some of the Member States in which prosecutions are governed by the legality principle.

are a particularism of judicial cooperation in the field of evidence-gathering, since, as we have seen, an arrest, with slight differences, remains an arrest in all Member States.[132] Differences in national rules relating to the execution of investigative measures are problematic from the point of view of the admissibility of the evidence in the issuing State, but also from the point of view of human rights. The application of traditional MLA instruments had revealed that often evidence gathered in accordance with the rules of the requested State were then inadmissible because domestic procedural requirements had not been complied with. As a solution, and like the 2000 MLA Convention, Article 9(2) of the EIO Directive allows the issuing authorities to indicate the formalities and procedures they wish to be followed in the executing State. Besides this arrangement being potentially problematic from the point of view of the legality principle, particularly the foreseeability condition,[133] it is contrary to the logic of mutual recognition. Exporting national legal requirements indirectly implies that the foreign rules are not considered equivalent. Thus, mutual recognition in the EIO Directive applies only to the investigation order itself (i.e., the executing State trusts the issuing State), but not to the result arising from its execution (i.e., the issuing State does not trust the executing State).

3.2.3 Revising the philosophy of mutual recognition: alternative investigative measures and the fundamental rights ground for refusal

Put bluntly, mutual recognition consists in asserting the formal lawfulness of a national decision so it can 'travel' to another Member State.[134] As its wording suggests, mutual recognition entails that a decision taken by the issuing authority in accordance with its national law is *recognised* (as in a mirror) and executed in a different Member State. Article 9(1) contains the classic mutual recognition formula according to which 'the executing authority shall recognise an EIO [...] without any further formality being required, and ensure its execution'. Up to here, and notwithstanding the

132 It is interesting to note in connection to this that in spite of arrests being quite standardised, the EAW FD operated some sort of harmonisation of the execution of arrests conducted in EAW proceedings. For instance, Article 11 FD enumerates the rights of the requested person although it leaves the details to national law. No such approximation has taken place in relation to the execution of EIOs, and thus the EIO Directive limits itself to establishing a regime of applicable law.

133 See in this regard I. Armada, 'La reconnaissance mutuelle des décisions d´enquête nationales, repose-t-elle sur une protection adéquate des droits fondamentaux mis en cause par les mesures coercitives?' (Final Master's Dissertation, LL.M College of Europe, 2011–2012), available at www.academia.edu/6538237/La_reconnaissance_mutuelle_des_d%C3%A9cisions_d_enqu%C3%AAte_nationales_repose-t-elle_sur_une_protection_ad%C3%A9quate_des_droits_fondamentaux_mis_en_cause_par_les_mesures_coercitives (accessed May 2015).

134 S. Allegrezza, 'Critical remarks on the Green Paper on obtaining evidence in criminal matters from one Member State to another and securing its admissibility' (2010) 9 *ZIS* 572.

fact that Article 6 of the EIO Directive introduces the conditions for issuing an EIO – namely legality, proportionality and necessity – and entrusts their control to the issuing authority,[135] the EIO Directive is in line with the mutual recognition principle. Article 10(1) introduces, however, a major change by requiring the executing authority to resort to a different type of investigative measure – and thus not to recognise *stricto sensu* the foreign investigation order – in two situations:[136] (1) where the investigative measure indicated in the EIO does not exist and (2) where the investigative measure indicated in the EIO would not be available in a similar domestic case.[137]

It has been argued that this provision seeks to correct disproportionate investigation orders.[138] National laws restricting access to coercive/intrusive investigative measures act indeed as a guarantee that investigating authorities will only resort to such measures when they are necessary and proportionate. By allowing the executing authority to take its own law into account, the protective guarantees therein contained are applied to the issuing authority's decision. To ensure this 'shield' is used in practice, the issuing authority will have to provide sufficient information to the executing authority to allow it to assess whether the measure would (or would not) be available in a similar domestic case.[139] It appears that the executing authority is no longer required to trust, or at least not blindly, the proportionality assessment made by the issuing authority. If combined with the possible requirement of a national court order discussed above, it appears that the control of the proportionality condition is split between the two authorities involved.[140] This is a significant change compared to the EAW FD.

135 See para 2. An important novelty is introduced: the executing authority may consult the issuing authority if he/she believes those conditions are not met.

136 This provision does not apply to the 'non-coercive' investigative measure listed in Article 10(2).

137 According to Recital 10, availability refers to occasions where the indicated investigative measure exists under the law of the executing State but is only lawfully available in certain situations; for example, where the investigative measure can only be carried out for offences of a certain degree of seriousness, against persons for whom there is already a certain level of suspicion or with the consent of the person concerned. Article 10(3) moreover allows the executing authority to resort to an alternative investigative measure where a less intrusive one would achieve the same result.

138 According to some authors, it amounts to a hidden ground of refusal based on proportionality. See A. Mangiaracina, 'A new and controversial scenario in the gathering of evidence at the European level: the proposal for a Directive on the European Investigation Order' (2014) 10 *Utrecht Law Review* 127.

139 Recital 32 recalls this in relation to interception of telecommunications.

140 This division is, however, not reflected in the legal remedies regime. Like other instruments of mutual recognition, Article 14(2) of the EIO Directive recalls that the substantive reasons for issuing the EIO (among which proportionality) may be challenged only in the issuing State, without prejudice to the guarantees of fundamental rights in the executing State.

A similar situation arises in relation to fundamental rights. As we have seen, the EAW contained no express ground for refusal in this regard. The involvement of the European Parliament in the legislative process of the EIO Directive has meant a revolution: the EIO is the first instrument of judicial cooperation that expressly includes a ground for refusal based on fundamental rights. It is to be found in Article 11(1)(f), that reads: 'Without prejudice to Article 1(4), recognition or execution of an EIO may be refused in the executing State where: (f) there are substantial grounds to believe that the execution of the investigative measure indicated in the EIO would be incompatible with the executing State's obligations in accordance with Article 6 TEU and the Charter.'[141]

The wording of this ground for refusal seeks to strike a balance between mutual trust[142] and fundamental rights by establishing a rebuttable presumption of human rights compliance.[143] The executing authority may only refuse the execution of the EIO if there are *substantial grounds* to believe that the execution would lead to a fundamental rights' violation.[144] The balance is a very delicate one. If this ground were to lead to an automatic double-check of the issuing authority's decision, distrust would replace mutual trust and the principle of mutual recognition would be deprived of its very essence. Indeed, the broader the scrutiny of the original decision, the narrower the presumption of equivalent protection of fundamental rights inherent to mutual trust, and vice versa.[145] The extent to which the presumption operates will, however, largely depend on the national transposing laws and practice, and, of course, the ECJ's case law will be of utmost importance in this field. In any case, the introduction of this ground for refusal affects the division of tasks (and responsibilities) between cooperating States in relation to respect of fundamental rights.[146]

It must be noted that this ground for refusal will coexist with the advancements in the field of procedural rights. The three procedural rights Directives adopted so far will be relevant in the context of EIO proceedings, and consequently Recital 15 recalls that the EIO Directive should be implemented

141 On this topic, see Armada, 'The European Investigation Order', particularly pp. 22–29.

142 On the European institutions' view of mutual recognition as a principle of blind trust, see Marin, 'The European Arrest Warrant and domestic legal orders', pp. 481–483.

143 Recital 19 indeed reads: 'The creation of an area of freedom, security and justice within the Union is based on mutual confidence and a presumption of compliance by other Member States with Union law and, in particular, with fundamental rights. However, that presumption is rebuttable.'

144 Whose fundamental rights the ground for refusal seeks to protect is not determined in the Directive, which actually refers to the violation of the executing State's obligations and not to the violation of someone's fundamental rights. It seems that besides the suspect or accused, third parties could in principle also be covered by the ground for refusal.

145 Armada, 'The European Investigation Order'.

146 On this topic, see A.A.H. Van Hoek and M.J.J.P. Luchtman, 'Transnational cooperation in criminal matters and the safeguarding of human rights' (2005) 1 *Utrecht Law Review*.

taking them into account. However, the procedural rights Directives in force or on their way by no means cover all the procedural rights relevant to evidence-gathering.[147] With the exception of the Directive on the presumption of innocence currently under negotiation,[148] no initiative has been put forward to address the specific procedural rights that intervene in the field of evidence.[149] The practical application of the EIO Directive will most probably, as happened with the EAW, reveal the need to adopt complementary harmonising measures.[150] Again here, the role of the ECJ in articulating procedural rights and mutual recognition will be essential.

4 Conclusion: main challenges and prospects

This chapter has endeavoured to show that the principle of mutual recognition is undergoing important changes. Overall, the EIO Directive represents a move towards shared responsibility, with executing authorities being entrusted a role in relation to issues such as the protection of fundamental rights or proportionality. This change opens up a new set of questions, and might lead the ECJ and/or the ECtHR to adapt their case law to reflect this new division of labour and responsibilities between the two cooperating States. In this regard, the ECtHR's ruling in *Stojkovic v France and Belgium*[151] must be mentioned. The case concerned traditional MLA proceedings, but it reveals that the ECtHR is ready to hold the requesting and requested States jointly liable for an ECHR violation if the responsibility for it is shared (or blurred). It will be interesting to see how this line of case law develops in the future.

On a broader scale, the principle of mutual recognition faces numerous challenges.

First, mutual recognition is subject to a variable geometry, one with three different dimensions: the differences between national implementing laws, the inconsistency between instruments of mutual recognition and the uneven

147 Mangiaracina, 'A new and controversial scenario', p. 119.

148 Proposal for a Directive on the strengthening of certain aspects of the presumption of innocence and on the right to be present at trial in criminal proceedings, COM(2013) 821 final.

149 According to the Commission, 'fairness in handling evidence actually covers many rights and many aspects of the proceedings [... including,] *inter alia*, the right to silence, the right to have witnesses heard, the problem of anonymous witnesses, the right to disclosure of exculpatory evidence, how the presumption of innocence is to be understood (whether there are circumstances where the burden of proof may be reversed) and many other aspects of the law of evidence'; see Green Paper on procedural safeguards for suspects and defendants in criminal proceedings throughout the European Union, COM(2003)75 final, point 2.6.

150 C. Janssens, *The Principle of Mutual Recognition in EU Law* (Oxford University Press, 2013), p. 261.

151 ECtHR 27 October 2011, *Stojkovic v France and Belgium*, Application no. 25303/08. For a reflection of this judgment and the broader problem of a right to a fair trial in transnational proceedings see S. Gless, 'Transnational cooperation in criminal matters and the guarantee of a fair trial: approaches to a general principle', (2013) 9 *Utrecht Law Review*.

geographic application of the principle throughout the AFSJ. The concretisation of the principle and its practical application depend indeed to a large extent on the implementation carried out at national level. The experience of the EAW has revealed that such transposition is not always loyal to the European text.[152] While the entry into force of the Lisbon Treaty and the end of the transitional period now put bad implementations (and of course the lack of national implementation) at risk of infringement proceedings, one must not rule out the possibility that the national transposing laws of the EIO – and other future texts – are not in line with the Directive.[153] As with the EAW, this would lead to having as many EIOs as national implementing laws. The second aspect of this variable geometry relates to the inconsistencies and incoherence between the different instruments of mutual recognition. Such instruments share several features but they also present certain differences that are difficult to reconcile, such as the existence of a ground for refusal based on fundamental rights within the EIO Directive but not in the EAW FD.[154] Therefore, when reference is made to the principle of mutual recognition, one must keep in mind that this principle is not univocal. Lastly, the principle lacks a homogeneous scope of territorial application: for instance, the EAW applies in all Member States of the EU, while the EIO will not be applicable in Denmark or Ireland. This leads to a geographical fragmentation of the principle of mutual recognition, with the EIO replacing other MLA instruments only with regard to the Member States bound by the Directive.[155] This variable geometry puts at risk the completeness and coherence of the AFSJ.

152 See the successive Commission evaluation reports of the EAW FD: the first report dates back to 23 February 2005 (COM(2005) 63 and SEC (2005) 267). It was completed in January 2006 (COM(2006) 8 and SEC (2006) 79). A second report covering the implementation of the FD carried out between 2005 and June 2007 was issued in July 2007 (COM(2007) 407 and SEC (2007) 979). The last report was issued in April 2011 (COM(2011) 175 final and SEC (2011) 430 final). Among the doctrinal assessments, see for instance P. Albers, P. Beauvais, J-F. Bohnert, M. Böse, P. Langbroek, A. Renier and T. Wahl, *Towards a Common Evaluation Framework to Assess Mutual Trust in the Field of EU Judicial Cooperation in Criminal Matters*, final report, available at www.government.nl/documents/reports/2013/09/27/final-report-towards-a-common-evaluation-framework-to-assess-mutual-trust-in-the-field-of-eu-judicial-cooperation-in-criminal-matters.html (accessed May 2015); V. Mitsilegas, 'The Area of Freedom, Security and Justice from Amsterdam to Lisbon: challenges of implementation, constitutionality and fundamental rights, general report', in J. Laffranque (ed.), *The Area of Freedom, Security and Justice, Including Information Society Issues. Reports of the XXV FIDE Congress, Tallinn 2012* (Tartu University Press, 2012), pp. 21-142.

153 This is particularly true in relation to the complicated articulation of certain of its provisions. In this regard see Armada, 'The European Investigation Order', p. 17, footnote 49.

154 On this, see Weyembergh et al., 'Critical assessment', particularly pp. 60, 63ff.

155 See Article 34 of the EIO Directive on 'Relations to other legal instruments, agreements and arrangements'.

A second important challenge has to do with the relationship of the principle of mutual recognition and its accompanying measures. Among the latter, the determination of jurisdiction criterion is worth mentioning. In spite of the adoption of the Framework Decision 2009/948/JHA of 30 November 2009 on prevention and settlement of conflicts of exercise of jurisdiction in criminal proceedings, no real binding allocation of jurisdiction mechanism has been established so far. The articulation between mutual recognition and approximation of legislation, both substantive and procedural, is also crucial. The partial abolition of the dual criminality requirement facilitates and renders cooperation more effective. The debate on whether those offences should be subject to harmonising measures, however, remains open.[156] Besides the approximation of substantive criminal laws, Article 82(2) TFEU highlights the link between mutual recognition and the approximation of procedural rules. The adoption of the first three Directives on suspect and accused rights must be welcomed; their implementation will do much to rebalance the powers of prosecution and defence in transnational criminal proceedings. However, three nuances should be brought to this optimistic view. First, it must be stressed that these texts do not solve all fundamental rights issues that may arise in EAW proceedings.[157] Second, the adoption of new instruments of mutual recognition such as the EIO might require further *ex post* developments in this field. Third, the above-mentioned 'geographic' variable geometry will inevitably restrict any 'rebalance' of powers achieved with the adoption of flanking measures, at least with regard to Denmark.[158]

As to the prospects awaiting the principle of mutual recognition in the coming years, the end of the transitional period laid down in Article 10 of Protocol 36 to the EU Treaties must of course be underlined. From 1 December 2014, the Commission is empowered to bring infringement proceedings, and the ECJ enjoys full jurisdiction in the field of police and judicial cooperation in criminal matters. As a consequence, the ECJ is expected to have more ample opportunities to rule on the validity and interpretation of the instruments adopted, including, of course, those implementing the Tampere principle. Less is expected of the EU legislature in the field judging from the European Council's strategic guidelines of June 2014.[159] It is there stated that 'the overall priority now is to consistently transpose, effectively implement and consolidate the legal

156 See the Manifesto.

157 J.A.E Vervaele, 'The European Arrest Warrant and applicable standards of fundamental rights in the EU: ECJ judgment (Grand Chamber) C-399/11 of 26 February 2013' (2013) 6 *Review of European Administrative Law* 41.

158 A favourable result in the referendum due in Denmark before the end of this year with regard to its opt-out regime might, however, change things.

159 European Council – Presidency Conclusions, 26 and 27 June 2014, Doc. EUCO 79/14, OJ C 240, 24 July 2014, pp. 13–15, point 11.

instruments and policy measures in place'.[160] Indeed, no action is foreseen in direct relation to mutual recognition, although references are made to fundamental rights[161] and the promotion of mutual trust,[162] and a special call is made to 'continue efforts to strengthen the rights of accused and suspect persons in criminal proceedings'.[163] An interesting development might finally come from the setting up of the European Public Prosecutor's Office (EPPO),[164] since this EU body could become a new actor of mutual recognition. This would be the case, for instance, if the EPPO is given competence to cooperate with non-participating Member States. Such a situation would indeed result in an interesting combination of vertical and horizontal cooperation.

This chapter's focus was on mutual recognition in criminal matters. However, as underlined in the introduction, mutual recognition is also a cornerstone of other domains of EU integration, particularly of judicial cooperation in civil matters, where indeed mutual recognition has a long history and is – at least in some respects – more developed than in penal law. Keeping in mind the specificities and essential differences between civil and criminal matters, interesting comparative analysis and reflections can be made. For instance, ever since mutual recognition was launched in civil matters, the complementarity link between that principle and the definition of jurisdiction criteria was extremely narrow. Such a link is much looser, not to say neglected, in the criminal field. Another interesting difference relates to the kind of legislative instruments used: whereas mutual recognition in civil matters is developed via regulations, in the criminal field directives are used, which shows that mutual recognition in criminal matters is less mature but also more sensitive in terms of national sovereignty.

Interesting comparisons may also be made with other areas of the AFSJ where mutual recognition is used. Such is the case of the Directive 2001/40/EC of 28 May 2001 on the mutual recognition of decisions on the expulsion of third-country nationals[165] in the common immigration policy. A connection with the so-called Dublin System[166] is also clearly of interest. These instruments of the AFSJ are also based on mutual trust and some of the issues they raise are similar to the ones arising in criminal matters. An

160 Ibid., point 3.

161 Ibid., point 4.

162 Ibid., point 11.

163 Ibid.

164 Proposal for a Council Regulation on the establishment of the European Public Prosecutor's Office, COM(2013) 534 final, Brussels, 17 July 2013.

165 OJ L 149, 2 June 2001.

166 The last instrument in the field is: Regulation (EU) No 604/2013 of the European Parliament and of the Council of 26 June 2013 establishing the criteria and mechanisms for determining the Member State responsible for examining an application for international

example is the difficult balance to be struck between the efficiency of the cooperation mechanisms they establish on the one hand and the protection of human rights on the other. In this regard, every domain could learn from the others,[167] even if comparisons and analogies must be handled very carefully.

protection lodged in one of the Member States by a third-country national or a stateless person, OJ L 180, 29 June 2013, p. 31.

167 See, for instance, the lessons to be learned in the criminal field from the case law of the ECJ relating to the Dublin System (e.g., ECJ (GC) joined cases C-411/10 & C-493/10, *NS v Secretary of State for the Home Department* & *ME and Others*, judgment of 21 December 2011). See the references made by Advocate General Sharpston to this case law in her opinion of 18 October 2012 in the *Radu* case (para 76).

6 The European Arrest Warrant, constitutional rights and the changing legal thinking

Values once recognised lost in transition to the EU level?

Anneli Albi[*]

1 Introduction

The title of this chapter refers to an observation in an article by Ester Herlin-Karnell that in EU criminal law cooperation, 'important values once recognised within the nation state are lost in the transition to the European level' and, especially pre-Lisbon, 'in the pursuit of substantive changes at the EU level even basic concepts such as fair trial and legality, which traditionally are recognised in national criminal law, seem to be forgotten'.[1] Similar observations appear to be fairly widespread among scholars specialising in the field of criminal law.[2] In the EU constitutional law discourse, however, such concerns have overall been rare and with limited visibility, and – in the author's experience when presenting papers on this topic – often unheard of, evoking perplexed questions about whether one is Eurosceptic or advocating a 'return to the national'. The present contribution to the edited volume raises broader questions about the structure of the EU constitutional law discourse, which, it will be argued, for about a decade after the adoption of

* This chapter is part of the research project 'The Role and Future of National Constitutions in European and Global Governance', funded by European Research Council grant No. 284316. The views cannot be attributed to the European Research Council. I would like to thank Maria Fletcher, Ester Herlin-Karnell and Claudio Matera for their helpful comments on the article; any errors are solely those of the author.

1 E. Herlin-Karnell, 'The integrity of European criminal law co-operation: The nation state, the individual, and the Area of Freedom, Security and Justice', in F. Amtenbrink and P. Van Den Berg (eds.), *The Constitutional Integrity of the European Union* (Asser Press, 2010) pp. 238, 240.

2 See, for example, the concerns of 14 scholars in the 'Manifesto on the European criminal policy' (2009) 12 *Zeitschrift für Internationale Strafrechtsdogmatik*, 707, at p. 715, available online at www.crimpol.eu (accessed 8 September 2015); B. Schünemann, 'Alternative draft for a European criminal law and procedure' (2007) *Criminal Law Forum* 227; D.P.J. Walsh, 'The European Arrest Warrant in Ireland: surrendering our standards to a European criminal law area', in I.C. Bacik and L. Heffernan (eds.), *Criminal Law and Procedure: Current Issues and Emerging Trends* (First Law, 2009) 5.

the European Arrest Warrant (EAW) Framework Decision in 2002, broadly overlooked a significant erosion of classic constitutional safeguards for personal liberty.

The European Arrest Warrant system concerns the very heart of constitutionalism – the classic constitutional rights and safeguards applied in the process of depriving an individual of his or her personal liberty. National constitutions typically contain extensive and elaborate provisions, and often special chapters, to ensure *nulla poena sine lege*, the presumption of innocence, fair trial, access to judicial protection and defence rights. The most detailed in Europe is probably the Portuguese Constitution, where Articles 27 to 32 contain more than 30 provisions and safeguards under the headings 'Right to freedom and security', 'Remand in custody', 'Application of criminal law', 'Limits on sentences and security measures', 'Habeas corpus' and 'Safeguards in criminal procedure'. Such safeguards also tend to be extensive in the constitutions of countries that have had experience with authoritarian regimes with arbitrary exercise of power, especially in Germany, Italy and the new democracies of Central and Eastern Europe.

This chapter will document isolated and broadly overlooked concerns from judges, scholars, practising lawyers and NGOs in different Member States about a reduced level of protection in the EAW system for these classic, long-standing rights and rule of law safeguards. The study of such concerns was inspired by the media coverage of case studies by Fair Trials International on individuals caught up in foreign criminal systems, some of which will also be mentioned in this chapter. The chapter will argue that given the importance that scholarly expertise has traditionally played in the development and legitimisation of the EU legal order, the discourse has strengthened the legitimacy of and public confidence in the European Arrest Warrant by treating any dissenting national judges or authorities as deviants. But there is more at stake: the paper will argue, in the final sections, that the EAW and EU criminal law measures, along with the prevailing scholarly discourse, have reinforced a change from the more substantive, 'guarantistic' type of constitutionalism and the rule of law that prevails in the Member States, towards a thin, weak, procedural version of constitutionalism and the rule of law that prevails in the autonomous EU constitutional law, where the emphasis has primarily been on the rules of hierarchy and functioning of the EU legal order, with the keywords being supremacy, direct effect, uniformity, effectiveness, trust, loyal cooperation and correct implementation.

The arguments in this chapter are based on a longer, two-part article entitled 'Erosion of constitutional rights in EU law: A call for "substantive co-operative constitutionalism"'[3] (hereinafter 'Erosion of constitutional rights').

3 A. Albi, 'Erosion of constitutional rights in EU law: A call for "substantive co-operative constitutionalism"', Part 1 published in (2015) 9 *Vienna Journal of International Constitutional Law (ICL Journal)* 151, and Part 2 in (2015) 9 *Vienna Journal of International Constitutional Law (ICL Journal)* 291. The article is available open access in SSRN at http://ssrn.com/abstract=2746522.

In that article, I propounded the concept of 'substantive co-operative constitutionalism', which would seek to return to the values of classic constitutional law, such as constitutional safeguards for personal liberty and judicial protection. The chapter here will focus more specifically on how the EAW system could be recalibrated towards a greater responsiveness to classic substantive constitutional values. The chapter will additionally explore two broader implications of the above argument for the future development of the EU's Area of Freedom, Security and Justice (AFSJ). The first concerns the question whether in addition to changing the legal thinking and the mindset in the field of constitutional law, the autonomy of EU law may have changed the legal thinking and vocabulary in the field of criminal law. The second is a broader discussion about harmonisation and the balance between uniformity and diversity in the field of criminal law in Europe in the light of the literature on the epistemology of EU law.

2 The EU constitutional law discourse on the EAW judgments of constitutional courts: the focus on relinquishing sovereignty and compliance with *Pupino*

In the above-mentioned article 'Erosion of constitutional rights', I brought extensive examples, from a range of areas, of how the EU constitutional law discourse has come to assess national constitutional courts predominantly through the lens of whether the courts have been Euro-friendly and cooperative or Eurosceptic and parochial, depending on their perceived willingness or reluctance to relinquish the protection of the sovereign nation-state.[4] I retraced some of the reasons for this lens of assessment on the basis of the literature on the epistemology of EU law. The reasons include the tendency of the EU scholarship to portray the European as 'rational' and the national as 'irrational' and 'illogical';[5] the move from comparative constitutional law to autonomous, self-referential EU constitutional law where the discourse is conducted in English without reference to the domestic laws of the Member States beyond correct implementation;[6] and the discouragement of critical discussion in the historical evolution of EU law.[7]

To bring examples of the above frame of reference in the EU constitutional discourse in the field of the European Arrest Warrant, the judgments of the

4 See Albi, 'Erosion of constitutional rights', Part 1, supra note 3, sect I.

5 For a detailed account, see H. Schepel and R. Wesseling, 'The legal community: judges, lawyers, officials and clerks in the writing of Europe' (1997) 3 *European Law Journal* 186.

6 For a detailed account, see, for example: A. Vauchez, 'The transnational politics of judicialization: Van Gend en Loos and the making of the EU polity' (2009) 16 *European Law Journal* 1, at 20–21; Schepel and Wesseling, 'The legal community', supra note 5, p. 186; A. Kjaer, 'Theoretical aspects of legal translation in the EU: the paradoxical relationship between language, translation and the autonomy of EU law', in S. Sarcevic (ed.), *Language and Culture in EU Law: Multidisciplinary Perspectives* (Ashgate, 2015) 98.

7 For a detailed account, see Schepel and Wesseling, 'The legal community', supra note 5, p. 186.

national constitutional and supreme courts were predominantly assessed in the EU constitutional law discourse from the perspective of Euro-friendliness and to what extent the national courts took account of the European Court of Justice's *Pupino* ruling[8] (*Pupino* is one of the 'milestone' cases of EU constitutional law, where the communautaire reasoning and supranational principles of indirect effect, effectiveness and loyal cooperation were extended to the third pillar[9]). Other key frames of assessment of the constitutional courts' case law were to what extent the courts ensured loyal cooperation, the national courts' willingness to accept mutual trust and to relinquish sovereignty, and whether or not they annulled the national implementing law or found a way to interpret it in conformity with the Constitution.[10] The Czech Constitutional Court was typically found 'EU-friendly', while especially the German and Cypriot courts were widely described as 'reluctant' to yield sovereignty, not EU-friendly, parochial, undermining loyal cooperation, sending 'dark signals'[11] and going against the spirit of *Pupino*. For example, the commentary on the German EAW judgment in the most authoritative EU law journal, the *Common Market Law Review*, evaluates the judgment in the light of the '*Pupino* principle', on the basis of which the Court 'should have

8 Case C-105/03 *Pupino* [2005] ECR I-5285.

9 For a critical assessment of the the constitutional significance of *Pupino* for EU law, see E. Herlin-Karnell, 'In the wake of *Pupino*: *Advocaten voor der Wereld* and *dell'Orto*' (2007) 8 *German Law Journal* 1147.

10 Including the present writer, see A. Albi, 'Supremacy of EC law in the new Member States: bringing parliaments into the equation of "co-operative constitutionalism"' (2007) 3 *European Constitutional Law Review* 25. Among voluminous literature, see, for example: J. Komárek, 'European Constitutional Pluralism and the European Arrest Warrant: Contrapunctual Principles in Disharmony', Jean Monnet Working Paper No 10/05, www.jeanmonnetprogram.org (accessed 6 April 2006), subsequently published as 'European constitutionalism and the European Arrest Warrant: in search of the limits of "contrapunctual principles"' (2007) 44 *Common Market Law Review* 9; A. Hinajeros Parga, 'Bundesverfassungsgericht Decision of 18 July 2005 on the German European Arrest Warrant Law' (2006) 43 *Common Market Law Review* 583; S. Siegel, 'Courts and Compliance in the EU: the European Arrest Warrant in National Constitutional Courts', Jean Monnet Working Paper No 5/2008, www.jeanmonnetprogram.org (accessed 26 February 2010); E. Van Sliedregt, 'The European Arrest Warrant: extradition in transition' (2007) 3 *European Constitutional Law Review* 244; A. Łazowski, 'Constitutional tribunal on the surrender of Polish citizens under the European Arrest Warrant: decision of 27 April 2005' (2005) 1 *European Constitutional Law Review* 569, at 573ff; K. Kowalik-Bańczyk, 'Should we polish it up? The Polish constitutional tribunal and the idea of supremacy of EU law' (2005) 6 *German Law Journal* 1355; O. Pollicino, 'European Arrest Warrant and constitutional principles of the Member States: a case law-based outline in an attempt to strike the right balance between legal systems' (2009) 9 *German Law Journal* 1313; M. Fichera, 'The European Arrest Warrant and the sovereign state: a marriage of convenience?' (2009) *European Law Journal* 81; L. Marin, 'The European Arrest Warrant in the Italian Republic' (2008) 4 *European Constitutional Law Review* 268.

11 The wider reference to this phrase was sparked by its use in the dissenting opinion of Justice Lübbe-Wolff, Judgment of 18 July 2005, 2 BvR 2236/04, www.bverfg.de (accessed 5 March 2010), para 159.

done whatever was in its hand to ensure that … the EAW framework decision … was enforced and complied with'; the commentary finds that the Court should have chosen an '"EU-friendly" interpretation of the Constitution' and 'should have striven to enforce a reading of the EAW law which rendered it constitutional'.[12] One article, which came to be a particularly influential point of reference and has been widely cited in subsequent research,[13] assesses the EAW judgments of the Polish Constitutional Tribunal and the German Constitutional Court in the framework of the 'Contrapunctual Law' principles propounded by Miguel Poiares Maduro[14] and the 'Principle of Best Fit' put forward by Mattias Kumm,[15] two leading scholars who have applied the influential theories of constitutional pluralism to the resolution of conflicts by courts in practice. The article finds that the Polish Constitutional Tribunal, '[a]lthough … [it] probably could [have] escape[d] the constitutional conflict by interpreting the prohibition of extradition in a more EU-opened way […] acted in a much more pro-European way than its German counterpart', and mentions the 'parochialism' of the German Constitutional Court.[16] However, the article does additionally raise the question of limits to interpretation by courts, which is a theme that will be explored in Sections 5 and 6 of this chapter. Another article on the Polish Tribunal concludes that there are 'reasons for pessimism', first because the judgment will reinforce discussion on competence review at the expense of uniformity of EU law, and second, because the Tribunal's reasoning is 'based on fears' – of 'losing sovereignty, or not retaining "enough" of it'; additionally, there is a risk of individuals losing out on rights that are usually provided by EU acts because of the 'power show' by the Tribunal.[17] In articles on Italy, the early cases, where the courts had put fundamental rights (such as limits to pre-trial detention) first, are regarded as 'formalistic'; subsequent cases where the courts changed their stance are welcomed as more 'Europhile', as they avoided national 'particularism' and played along with the 'contrapunctual' principles.[18] European Commission officials, for their part, have described the EAW system as a 'success story'[19] or 'a success in operational terms', given the large number of persons extradited.[20]

12 Hinajeros Parga, 'Bundesverfassungsgericht Decision of 18 July 2005', supra note 10, pp. 587–588, 594–595.

13 Komárek, 'European Constitutional Pluralism', supra note 10.

14 M. Maduro, 'Contrapunctual law: Europe's constitutional pluralism in action', in N. Walker (ed.), *Sovereignty in Transition* (Hart Publishing, 2003) 501.

15 M. Kumm, 'The jurisprudence of constitutional conflict: constitutional supremacy in Europe before and after the Constitutional Treaty' (2005) 11 *European Law Journal* 262.

16 Komárek, 'European Constitutional Pluralism', supra note 10, pp. 5, 13, 26.

17 Kowalik-Bańczyk, 'Should we polish it up?', supra note 10, pp. 1365–1366.

18 Fichera, 'The European Arrest Warrant and the sovereign state', supra note 10, p. 94; Marin, 'The European Arrest Warrant in the Italian Republic', supra note 10, p. 269.

19 I. Pérignon and C. Daucé, 'The European Arrest Warrant: a growing success story' (2007) 8 *ERA Forum* 203.

20 Report from the Commission to the European Parliament and the Council of 11 April 2011 on the implementation since 2007 of the Council Framework Decision of 13 June 2002

In the above-mentioned article,[21] I invited the discourse to consider whether by virtue of the deeply embedded but somewhat simplistic focus on sovereignty and Euro-friendliness, along with a condescending approach towards the 'national', we are not inadvertently forgetting a whole set of other intrinsic values embodied by national constitutions and protected by constitutional courts, such as limiting public power to ensure the protection of the individual against arbitrary interference by the authorities, the protection of constitutional rights and civil liberties, the rule of law and separation of powers with due checks and balances, and judicial and constitutional review by courts to safeguard these values.

To this end, in the context of the EAW, it is significant that for about a decade after the adoption of the EAW in 2002, it went virtually unnoticed that the EAW system is in fact deeply flawed from the perspective of classic, substantive constitutional rights and safeguards. That the EAW has severe deficiencies gradually emerged from isolated concerns raised primarily by practitioners, NGOs and scholars specialising in the field of criminal law. However, for nearly a decade, such concerns had very limited visibility in the EU constitutional law discourse and were also broadly overlooked in the EU legislative process. Few EU law scholars looked at the actual rights involved, especially beyond the abolition of double criminality and the amendment of the ban on extradition. Those who did mainly specialise in the field of European criminal law,[22] having less visibility in the prevailing European constitutional law discourse. The editors of the present volume, specialising in the field of the AFSJ, have additionally pointed out that the concerns were mainly expressed by criminal lawyers and that lawyers specialising in EU criminal law were in fact also fairly uncritical.[23] Especially before the Lisbon Treaty – and beyond the above-mentioned focus on the cooperativeness of national courts – both the EU constitutional law discourse and the EU criminal law discourse were mostly preoccupied with the 'loyalty mantra' and the importance of exporting the EU supranational model to the third pillar, with

on the European Arrest Warrant and the surrender procedures between Member States (COM 2011 175 final – not published in the OJ), summarised at http://europa.eu/legislation_summaries/justice_freedom_security/judicial_cooperation_in_criminal_matters/l33167_en.htm.

21 Albi, 'Erosion of constitutional rights', Part 1, supra note 3, p. 156.

22 See, for example, an article written by lawyers representing Amnesty International and Justice, S. Alegre and M. Leaf, 'Judicial cooperation: a step too far too soon? Case study – the European Arrest Warrant' (2004) 10 *European Law Journal* 201. See also Herlin-Karnell, 'The integrity of European criminal law' supra note 1; Herlin-Karnell, 'In the wake of *Pupino*' supra note 9; V. Mitsilegas, 'The constitutional implications of mutual recognition in criminal matters in the EU' (2006) 43 *Common Market Law Review* 1309; S. Peers, 'Mutual recognition and criminal law in the European Union: has the Council got it wrong?' (2004) 41 *Common Market Law Review* 5. See also reports in E. Guild (ed.), *Constitutional Challenges to the European Arrest Warrant* (Wolf Legal Publishers, 2006).

23 I am particularly grateful to Ester Herlin-Karnell for this observation in her comments on this chapter.

consequent focus on the de-pillarisation and the extension of the jurisdiction of the European Court of Justice into this area.[24] As one scholar noted, '[w]hen discussing the concept of European criminal law, it is easy to gain the impression that in general it is the result of the tremendous success of the European project', even if 'from a historical perspective it is actually difficult to find a sensible meaning with regard to the "Europeanisation" of a criminal law which – inspired by the premises of the Enlightenment – is already European in so many senses'.[25]

What is striking about the whole process, and prompted the present writer's interest in pursuing research on the scholarly discourse in the field of the EAW, is that the isolated concerns were eventually brought to wider public attention as a result of the crucial role played by two UK non-governmental organisations, Fair Trials International (FTI) and Justice. With their persistent media and lobby campaign over several years, something that is not easy to mount given the language and distance barriers in Europe, the problems came to be more widely acknowledged. Indeed, a decade after the adoption of the EAW Framework Decision in 2002 and 80,000 arrest warrants later, EU institutions themselves are 'starting to wake up to lacking defence rights', as one media headline noted in 2010.[26] Following the Council's 2009 'Roadmap on procedural rights' under the Stockholm Programme,[27] the first three EU Directives were adopted: in 2010 to ensure the right to translation, in 2012 to ensure information on basic legal rights and in 2013 on the right of access to a lawyer (hereinafter the 'Roadmap Directives').[28] With the adoption of such measures still in progress, FTI has noted that 'the current system is in practice resulting in serious injustice'.[29]

With the curiosity sparked by FTI media articles on the rights affected in individual cases and the way these had changed my own thinking about the European Arrest Warrant system,[30] I carried out some preliminary research

24 The loyalty and depillarisation discourse is summarised by Herlin-Karnell, 'In the wake of *Pupino*', supra note 9, pp. 1148–1150.

25 Herlin-Karnell, 'The integrity of European criminal law', supra note 1, pp. 238–239 (references omitted).

26 C. Heard and D. Mansell, 'EU starting to wake up to lacking defence rights', *EU Observer*, 22 July 2010, www.euobserver.com.

27 2009/C 295/01.

28 Directive 2010/64/EU on the right to interpretation and translation in criminal proceedings, OJ EU, 26 October 2010, L 280/1; Directive 2012/13/EU on the right to information in criminal proceedings, OJ L 142/1, 1 June 2012; Directive 2013/48/EU on the right of access to a lawyer in criminal proceedings and in European Arrest Warrant proceedings, and on the right to have a third party informed upon deprivation of liberty and to communicate with third persons and with consular authorities while deprived of liberty, OJ EU 6 November 2013, L 294. For an overview of the relevant directives, see the contribution by V. Mitsilegas (Chapter 8) in this volume.

29 'European arrest warrant still "delivering injustice"', *EU Observer*, 22 July 2010, http://euobserver.com/22/30527.

30 For an earlier, more orthodox article addressing the European Arrest Warrant by this author, see Albi, 'Supremacy of EC law in the new Member States', supra note 10, pp. 25ff.

to explore to what extent similar concerns have been raised in other Member States beyond the UK. The results of this preliminary research were published in the above-mentioned 'Erosion of constitutional rights' article;[31] the next section here will summarise some of the more severe challenges to constitutional rights and rule of law safeguards. These preliminary results seem to indicate that fairly similar concerns have arisen in several Member States, showing the existence of more endemic problems. However, in general, the concerns have remained isolated, with little cross-border awareness, something that would seem to be in need of addressing in EU law and the EU law discourse in the future. The preliminary research prompted a subsequent, more systematic research project to explore how the adverse effects of the EAW (along with some other recent controversial EU measures) on constitutional rights have been addressed by the national courts and constitutional doctrine of the 28 Member States of the EU;[32] this research is at the time of writing in the final stages and will be outlined in Section 6 of this chapter.

3 Preliminary research results on concerns about the effects of the EAW on constitutional rights in different Member States

Based on the preliminary research results mentioned at the end of the previous section, it would appear that the adverse effects of the EAW system on a number of constitutional rights and safeguards have been raised in several Member States. The main concerns relate to the following: presumption of innocence in the context of the automaticity of extraditions without prior judicial review; the classic principle of *nullum crimen, nulla poena sine lege*; the compounded difficulties around fair trial in a foreign legal system, along with doubts about the suitability of transplanting mutual recognition from the single market to criminal law; *in absentia* judgments; and the broader questions regarding access to courts and the requirement of trust by courts in the context of mutual recognition. The subsequent sections will explore the concerns with regard to these rights and safeguards in greater detail.

3.1 The presumption of innocence, the right to judicial protection and the rule of law

The essence of the EAW system lies in rendering extradition speedy and automatic. The court that receives an extradition request from another Member State must automatically authorise extradition, with minimum formality and no consideration of evidence.

31 Albi, 'Erosion of constitutional rights', Parts 1 and 2, supra note 3, sections IV, V and IX.C.
32 See the research project mentioned in the opening footnote; the resulting national reports will be published in A. Albi and S. Bardutzky (eds.), *National Constitutions in European and Global Governance. Democracy, Rights, the Rule of Law* (Asser Press, 2017).

One of the few persons of authority to point out early on that such a rule has a perilous impact on the presumption of innocence, on the principle of the rule of law and on the principle of proportionality was Justice Broß in his dissenting opinion to the German Constitutional Court's EAW judgment.[33] He noted that the presumption of innocence protects the person from the disadvantages that are equivalent to a guilty verdict, where such disadvantages have not been preceded by proceedings where evidence of guilt has been provided in compliance with the code of procedure. He found that in the EAW system, which does not allow for examination of the circumstances pertaining to the alleged crime, the prosecuted persons are treated as guilty in the context of the extradition proceedings, which is contrary to the rule of law.

In Ireland, a similar point was made by Justice Peart of the High Court in the context of the right to a fair trial:

> If the applicant enjoys a Convention and a constitutional right to a trial of offences [...] that is a right which he is entitled to invoke and have protected on the first occasion in which it becomes relevant for argument, and that is not a matter to be postponed so that it can be ventilated at some date in future in another country, and after the respondent has been returned in custody to that place. There is, in my view, no meaningful distinction to be drawn between surrendering the respondent to the requesting state to face trial which would either be unfair or not within a reasonable time, and him actually facing trial.[34]

In Ireland, this decision, which was part of the earlier, more protective approach by the courts, was overturned on appeal by the Supreme Court, which placed a greater emphasis on mutual recognition and trust.[35] In Germany, the judgment of the Constitutional Court did mention the importance of the possibility of judicial review before a person is extradited to ensure effective judicial protection; however, the Court deemed this to be permissible only on limited grounds. Yet even this approach was strongly criticised in the literature for being Eurosceptic and as a sign of the Court's unwillingness to relinquish sovereignty.[36] One leading textbook refers to commentary according to which the German Constitutional Court's judgment has a 'parochial flavour';[37] this view has, in the experience of the

33 Judgment of 18 July 2005, 2 BvR 2236/04, available at www.bundesverfassungsgericht.de/SharedDocs/Entscheidungen/EN/2005/07/rs20050718_2bvr223604en.html (accessed 18 February 2016), paras 144–153.

34 *Minister for Justice v Stapleton* (2006) IEHC 43, citation completed from Walsh, 'The European Arrest Warrant in Ireland', supra note 2, p. 23 and A. Sanger, 'Force of circumstance: the European Arrest Warrant and human rights' (2010) 6 *Democracy and Security* 19 (references omitted).

35 Walsh, 'The European Arrest Warrant in Ireland', supra note 2, pp. 23, 26.

36 See articles in note 10 above.

37 D. Chalmers, G. Davies and G. Monti, *European Union Law* (2nd edn, Cambridge University Press, 2010), p. 601, citing Komárek, 'European Constitutional Pluralism', supra note 10, pp. 16–18.

present writer as a law lecturer, come to be widely adopted by students in their coursework.

Yet the very real need for judicial review before extradition, to ensure that there is a *prima facie* case to answer before a person is extradited, has been highlighted through a series of cases by the NGOs Fair Trials International, Liberty and Justice. They have in particular drawn attention to the case of Andrew Symeou,[38] a 19-year-old London student who was extradited to Greece in 2009 on manslaughter charges, without any opportunity to defend himself prior to extradition, despite compelling evidence of mistaken identity. As Symeou was not a Greek resident, he was not granted bail and he spent ten months in a maximum security prison, in what were described as 'appalling conditions', sharing a cockroach-infested, overcrowded cell with convicted murderers, and without understanding the language. After his eventual release on bail, he was still not allowed to leave Greece. He was finally acquitted by the Greek court in June 2011, after which he was able to enrol in a university course in London.

Yet this two-year ordeal could have readily been avoided if the EU rules had allowed for review of the compelling evidence of mistaken identity, which had been available at the outset, in a UK court. However, even where a person has committed an offence or a crime and is eventually found guilty, the absence of any possibility to contest the accusation or its aspects prior to extradition, and prolonged periods of detention in a foreign prison, place the extradited person under disproportionately onerous circumstances. Indeed, Judge Broß has noted that the presumption of innocence and the rule of law are violated 'by apodictically stating that all those who become part of criminal structures cannot fully rely on their citizenship providing them protection from extradition'.[39] It may be of interest to add that the German government in its submissions to this case in fact acknowledged a move from 'the nationally applicable requirements that result from the Basic Law's principle of the rule of law' to 'constitutional tradition that connects Europe and North America'.[40]

Some of the other individuals who, based on the classic national constitutional guarantees that will be explored in Section 5 of this chapter, should never have been caught up in extradition proceedings, include the British parents of five-year old brain tumour patient Ashya King, Dutch accountant Peter Tabbers, British secretary Tracey Molamphy and grandmother Deborah Dark, retired Bristol schoolteacher Jacek Jaskolski, Spanish osteopath José Vicent Piera Ripoll and car-wash attendant Oscar Sanchez, Estonian car service centre attendant Neeme Laurits and Albanian chef Edmond Arapi.[41]

38 Fair Trials International, www.fairtrials.net/cases/article/andrew_symeou (accessed 18 February 2016).

39 Judgment of 18 July 2005 (supra note 33) para 144.

40 Judgment of 18 July 2005 (supra note 33) para 39.

41 Most of the case studies are available at www.fairtrials.org (accessed 17 April 2015).

Officials have also noted 'a large volume of trivial extradition requests'; indeed, in the requests submitted to the UK, many offences have been so minor that under domestic law they would lead to a caution or no investigation at all, such as theft of a mobile phone and traffic offences.[42] As the EAW contains no filtering process, the above practice led the UK, in 2014, following a campaign by NGOs, to reintroduce a partial judicial review as regards a proportionality test prior to extradition (see Section 6 of this chapter).

3.2 Nullum crimen, nulla poena sine lege

The second central element of the EAW Framework Decision is that the rule of double criminality is abolished for 32 crimes, and thus a person must be extradited regardless of whether the activity is a crime under domestic law. This, however, means that each Member State must effectively accept the criminal laws of all other Member States of the EU, without a clear picture of what those laws might be.[43]

A Belgian association of lawyers, Advocaten voor de Wereld, raised the concern that the abolition of double criminality is incompatible with the principle of legality in criminal matters (*nullum crimen, nulla poena sine lege*). Under national constitutions, criminal legislation must satisfy the conditions of precision, clarity and predictability, allowing each person to know whether an act constitutes an offence. The Belgian Constitutional Court subsequently requested a preliminary ruling from the European Court of Justice on the legality of the European Arrest Warrant Framework Decision.[44]

The above concern was echoed in a more limited way by the German Constitutional Court,[45] which found that the issue of retroactive amendment of substantive criminal law would arise in those cases where an individual is extradited to another Member State for acts that do not have a significant connecting factor to that foreign country and that were not punishable in Germany when they were committed. The Court explained the threat to the rule of law as follows:

> The principle according to which an offence may only be punished if punishability was legally determined before the offence was committed is a special guarantee under the rule of law of the confidence in the reliability of the legal system, which is to provide clear orientation on what is

42 See A. Hirsch, 'Door thief, piglet rustler, pudding snatcher: British courts despair at extradition requests', *The Guardian*, 20 October 2008, www.theguardian.com/uk/2008/oct/20/immigration-extradition-poland-lithuania-law (accessed 4 March 2010); A. Wade, 'Extradited for "stealing" a mobile phone', *Times Online*, 13 August 2009, http://business.timesonline.co.uk/tol/business/law/article6792237.ece (accessed 13 August 2009).

43 Alegre and Leaf, 'Judicial cooperation', supra note 22, p. 208.

44 Case C-303/05 *Advocaten voor de Wereld* (2007) ECR I-3633.

45 Judgment of 18 July 2005, 2 BvR 2236/04 (supra note 33), para 99.

> punishable and what is not. Without such reliable orientation, individual freedom cannot develop: Whoever must expect an unpredictable retroactive amendment of criminal-law provisions will no longer be able to exercise his or her freedom of action with the necessary security and will lose his or her position as an autonomous individual in one of the areas that are most sensitive as concerns fundamental rights.

The legality of the abolition of dual criminality has also raised questions in Greece, Spain, Finland and Denmark;[46] Portuguese lawyers fear that 'it may foster a repressive "European criminal space"'.[47] In Italy, a report commissioned by the government expressed extensive concerns that the introduction of mutual recognition in the field of criminal law was incompatible with numerous constitutional rights, such as the rule of law and the principle of legality, which should ensure that crimes are determined in a predictable and specific way, and that any measure restricting personal freedom must be provided by a statutory law; additionally, such restrictive measures must be subject to a strict scrutiny of respect for constitutional fundamental rights carried out by the Constitutional Court.[48] On the basis of these concerns, the EAW Framework Decision was implemented with numerous additional guarantees. The European Commission has on several occasions pointed out that these guarantees do not completely comply with EU law. However, a constitutional scholar has found that even with the additional safeguards, the EAW system entails 'the first serious threat of disablement of the constitutional guarantees to the right of liberty'.[49]

One further issue that has provided grounds for concern is the wide, open-ended wording in the list of '32 types of offences'; it has been commented that these are merely 'types' and not well-defined offences (e.g. 'racism and xenophobia'), and that some offences are susceptible to politicisation.[50] The eminent scholar Christian Tomuschat has called the list of 'vague and indeterminate offences' a 'list of horrors' that went unnoticed by thousands of

46 See V. Mitsilegas, 'General report: the Area of Freedom, Security and Justice from Amsterdam to Lisbon. Challenges of implementation, constitutionality and fundamental rights', and country reports, in J. Laffranque (ed.), *Reports of the XXV FIDE Congress Tallinn 2012, Volume 3: The Area of Freedom, Security and Justice, Including Information Society Issues* (Tartu University Press, 2012).

47 A. Vitorino and R. Leandro Vasconcelos, 'Portugal', in Laffranque, *Reports of the XXV FIDE Congress Tallinn 2012, Volume 3*, supra note 46, p. 540.

48 See G. Martinico, B. Guastaferro and O. Pollicino, 'The Constitution of Italy: axiological continuity between the domestic and international levels of governance?', in Albi and Bardutzky, *National Constitutions in European and Global Governance*, supra note 32, Sect. 2.3.

49 C. Pinelli, 'La tutela multilivello dei diritti fondamentali nella prospettiva della giurisprudenza italiana. Una ricostruzione' in AA.VV., Scritti in Onore di Alessandro Pace, III (Editoriale Scientifica, 2012) 2399.

50 Sanger, 'Force of circumstance', supra note 34, pp. 21–22.

parliamentarians and staff at ministries of justice in Europe.[51] With a mention of 'naïve Euro-euphoria', Tomuschat outlines various other problematic aspects of the EAW and writes that '[n]ot everything that bears the label "European" is good for that sole reason'.[52] There have also been concerns about different penalties for the same crime in different Member States.

Despite the fact that the EAW system had prompted an unusually high number of constitutional courts and supreme courts to voice various concerns, the Grand Chamber of the European Court of Justice in *Advocaten voor de Wereld* upheld the legality of the European Arrest Warrant Framework Decision. The Court's reasoning was notably laconic; one commentator remarked that the Court 'refused to make any comment on much-contested issues' and made 'little effort to engage with the Court's national counterparts'.[53]

There is also a change underway – beyond EU criminal law – with regard to the broader rule, typically written in national constitutions, that obligations, interferences with rights, and especially administrative and penal fines, penalties and sanctions can only be imposed by a parliamentary statute. Such a rule is being abandoned as a result of pressures for speedy implementation of EU law.[54] For example, in Ireland, it was prohibited to introduce indictable offences by a governmental instrument; this rule was abolished in order to facilitate implementation of obligations necessitated by EU membership.[55]

3.3 Transplanting mutual recognition from the single market to deprivation of liberty: concerns about fair trial and the heightened likelihood of miscarriages of justice

Scholars specialising in criminal law have drawn attention to the unsuitability of transplanting the principle of mutual recognition from trade-related matters in the internal market to criminal law, as the logic of these two fields of regulation is entirely different.[56] Indeed, as was seen above, the EAW system entails severe consequences for individuals' personal liberty, which is rather different from mutual recognition of the alcohol content in blackcurrant liqueurs as in *Cassis de Dijon*, where the principle of mutual recognition was first established.[57]

51 C. Tomuschat, 'Inconsistencies: the German Federal Constitutional Court on the European Arrest Warrant' (2006) 2 *European Constitutional Law Review* 217.

52 Ibid., p. 214.

53 D. Sarmiento, 'European Union: the European Arrest Warrant and the quest for constitutional coherence' (2008) *ICON* 177.

54 See in more detail Albi, 'Erosion of constitutional rights', Part 2, supra note 3, p. 322.

55 See for relevant case law, G. Barrett, 'The evolving door to Europe: reflections on an eventful forty years of Article 29.4 of the Irish Constitution' (2013) *Irish Jurist* 132, at 154–155.

56 For a summary of the criticisms, see Mitsilegas, 'The constitutional implications of mutual recognition', supra note 22, p. 1280; Herlin-Karnell 'The integrity of European criminal law', supra note 1, pp. 237, 241, 245–246; Peers, 'Mutual recognition and criminal law in the European Union', supra note 22, pp. 5–36.

57 Case C-120/78 *Rewe-Zentral (Cassis de Dijon)* [1979] ECR 649. See also Herlin-Karnell 'The integrity of European criminal law', supra note 1, pp. 245–246.

In the early days of the EAW system, Judge Balík, who wrote a dissenting opinion to the EAW decision of the Czech Constitutional Court, expressed unease about the feasibility of defending oneself in a language other than one's mother tongue, and highlighted difficulties arising in the following hypothetical scenario.[58] A Czech citizen, who is innocent, is extradited to Greece, where he receives a visit from the '*δικηγορος*', presenting lengthy documentation written in Greek with the unfamiliar Greek alphabet. The Czech citizen has to communicate and defend himself via a poorly paid and disinterested interpreter, in English, which he does not speak well and with the meaning of any exchange inevitably getting lost in translation. He is unable to find, or in any event to afford, a Czech lawyer who is familiar with Greek criminal law. His family cannot afford the flights to visit him, and his marriage breaks apart. Given his absence from work, he also loses his job.

While the rest of the Court took what was widely applauded as an 'EU-friendly' approach and did not share this concern, such a scenario has sadly become all too common in practice. On the basis of numerous case studies identifying miscarriages of justice, FTI summarised the typical problems regarding fair trial that arise in EAW proceedings as follows:

> A single case often suffers multiple failures to respect basic rights, with for example the lack of access to a lawyer or legal aid being exacerbated by the lack of information on rights or on the prosecution case, or the lack of a quality interpreter or translations of important documents, or the inability of suspects to contact friends, family or consular officials as quickly as possible to help them avail themselves of these other basic measures quickly enough not to have their position irrevocably prejudiced.[59]

Although the above-mentioned Roadmap Directives[60] have since 2010 addressed some of these failures, they do not remove the intrinsic difficulties of defending oneself in a foreign legal system, a theme to which we will return in Sections 4 and 5 of this chapter.

It is notable that in the EU constitutional law literature, one of the key criticisms with regard to the EAW judgments of the German, Polish and Cypriot constitutional courts concerned their old-fashioned adherence to the idea of a bond between a citizen and the state. Yet the above developments make one wonder whether the discourse has perhaps been overly optimistic

58 Dissenting opinion by Judge Balík to Case No. Pl. ÚS 66/04, available at www.concourt.cz (accessed 17 April 2015). Some elements of the scenario have been changed or added by the author.

59 Memorandum submitted by Fair Trials International (FTI), Evidence submitted to the Justice Committee, www.publications.parliament.uk/pa/cm200910/cmselect/cmjust/162/162we04.htm (accessed 14 February 2012).

60 On the Roadmap Directives, see supra note 28.

about the capacities of EU citizenship, at least in the context of criminal law. One has to bear in mind that persons who are caught up in the Arrest Warrant system are typically not highly educated, multilingual, white-collar workers, who might find it easier to navigate in the system and challenge the authorities. Often they are, as one Estonian TV programme noted in a case to be explored at the end of this section, 'simple men from the countryside', who do not speak the language of the country to which they are extradited, or do not speak it well, and have only subsistence-level income. For them in particular, the 'journey into the unknown'[61] to defend themselves in an unfamiliar environment and in another language, without the support network available in their home country, makes the issue of a continued bond between the citizen and the state all too vital.

Indeed, the German Constitutional Court has explained the importance of the state's responsibility for its own citizens and why citizens ought not to be removed against their will from the legal system with which they are familiar. According to the Court, '[t]o the extent that they reside in the state territory, all citizens are supposed to be protected from the insecurities connected with being sentenced in a legal system that is unknown to them under circumstances that are inscrutable to them'.[62] The Court further noted that for the prosecuted person, 'transfer to another Member State's legal system, even though it has been brought closer by European integration [...] means discrimination under procedural law, which can consist in language obstacles, cultural differences and different procedural law and possibilities of defence'.[63]

One point that is in need of attention in relation to the miscarriages of justice in the EAW system is that the cases identified by FTI predominantly concern UK residents abroad;[64] no such proactive NGOs that might provide assistance and investigate any alleged failings exist in most other Member States. For example, Teresa Daniels, who was sentenced to ten years in prison in Spain in proceedings where no translation had been provided, was acquitted only after FTI looked into the case on appeal and discovered that the sentence had been based on an incorrect translation of the relevant documents.[65] It would seem important to research how many innocent persons might be caught up in foreign prisons from other, especially smaller Member States. The numbers may well be considerable, given that between 2005 and 2011 EU Member

61 Expression used by Mitsilegas, 'The constitutional implications of mutual recognition', supra note 22, p. 1309.

62 Judgment of 18 July 2005 (supra note 33) para 66.

63 Judgment of 18 July 2005 (supra note 33) para 86.

64 This is so despite the fact that FTI is not just for British nationals – it changed its name from Fair Trials Abroad to Fair Trials International – and a key part of their work is to build up a network of country experts. The author is grateful to Maria Fletcher for this clarification.

65 Fair Trials International, Submission to the EU Justice and Home Affairs Council Working Group, 9 July 2009, www.fairtrials.org/campaigns (accessed 4 March 2010), p. 6.

States issued a total of 78,785 EAW requests, with 19,841 requests leading to the effective surrender of the person.[66]

To bring one example from elsewhere, Neeme Laurits from Estonia was found innocent after having sat in a Finnish prison for nine months.[67] Despite having sent letters to numerous institutions asking for help because he was innocent, he received no assistance and his case was met with no interest whatsoever. The state bodies he approached referred to the obligation of mutual recognition and mutual trust of other Member States' legal systems, and the duty of loyal cooperation. It is difficult to avoid parallels with Franz Kafka's *The Trial*, which seems to have acquired a whole new contemporary European resonance. Indeed, a report written by officials from two Estonian ministries expresses considerable pride in the fact that Estonia extradites individuals faster than any other country, with the process taking only 8–10 days on average. Further, there are no specific fundamental rights grounds for refusal to execute an EAW and, as the procedure has 'worked out well', the officials see no need for further adoption of standards on the rights of defendants.[68] Mr Laurits, however, reminiscent of Czech Judge Balík's hypothetical scenario, lost his wife and his job in the process, and his health suffered considerably.

After Mr Laurits' case was highlighted in the media, an Estonian attorney, Kaido Pihlakas, drew attention to further individuals who had been extradited and had later been found innocent.[69] The attorney noted that extradition decisions are 'rubber-stamped' by judges. He called for granting a hearing to the accused prior to extradition, in order to avoid needless suffering by innocent persons. Had Mr Laurits been granted a hearing, his extradition would have been unlikely, as he had not visited Finland for five years and he had an alibi for the time of the alleged crime, having been on assignment in Germany and Sweden for his work. The attorney also noted that none of the innocent persons extradited have received compensation, although they and their relatives incurred not only significant legal costs but also costs related to their travel and stay in other Member States.

66 S. Carrera, E. Guild and N. Hernanz, 'Europe's Most Wanted? Recalibrating Trust in the European Arrest Warrant System', Centre for European Policy Studies Report No. 55 (March 2013) p. 4, www.ceps.be/system/files/SC_EG_and_NHontheEAWfinal.pdf (accessed 17 April 2015).

67 ETV programme 'Pealtnägija' ('Eyewitness'), summarised in R. Kagge, 'Narkoparuniks tembeldatud eestlane pisteti 9 kuuks Soome vanglasse' ('An Estonian who was labelled a drug baron thrown into a Finnish prison for 9 months'), *ERR*, 1 February 2012, http://uudised.err.ee/index.php?06244908 (accessed 17 February 2012).

68 J. Antonova, M. Mardla and I. Markus, 'Estonia' in Laffranque, *Reports of the XXV FIDE Congress Tallinn 2012, Volume 3*, supra note 46, p. 324.

69 'Advokaat: Eesti täidab Euroopa vahistamismäärusi liiga püüdlikult' ('An attorney: Estonia executes the European Arrest Warrant too eagerly'), *Postimees*, 29 February 2012, www.postimees.ee (accessed 17 April 2015).

In Finland, a range of strict human rights safeguards and preconditions were added to the rules on extradition at the expense of the 'maximal' implementation of the EAW.[70] However, the systemic problems nonetheless prompted the then president of the Finnish Supreme Court, Justice Pauliine Koskelo, to express her concerns as follows:

> On what basis and by what means is a judge expected to make a determination as to whether the person in question, if surrendered, would receive a trial within reasonable time and in accordance with the other relevant standards of a fair trial? The courts will normally have very little to rely on in order to be able to make any well-founded prognosis in this regard. In addition, there are tight time limits: the district court must reach a decision in these matters within 26 days. Appeals are directed straight to the Supreme Court which must take its decision within 20 days. The reality is that a Finnish judge, or any other national judge, has few practically viable means of reaching realistic and reliable conclusions as to whether or not the person whose surrender is requested can be expected to get a trial within reasonable time in another Member State. [...] [T]he tension that exists between the principle of mutual recognition and the concern for fundamental rights in general and procedural rights in particular is laid wide open. At the same time, it is obvious that this tension cannot be undone or properly resolved by shifting the problem down to judges to sort out.[71]

In a subsequent speech at the 2014 FIDE Congress, Justice Koskelo noted that based on the experience of Finnish courts, there has been a decline and a degradation of the rule of law in the European context, especially in areas of mutual recognition.[72] She suggested that there should be a mechanism to suspend mutual recognition in certain cases, to take the burden off individual judges. She also called for a greater focus on the outcomes of individual cases. Additionally, she noted that the most extensive level of protection ought to be provided, which may often be the protection granted under the national constitutions.

70 See T. Ojanen, 'The European Arrest Warrant in Finland: taking fundamental and human rights seriously' in Guild, *Constitutional Challenges to the European Arrest Warrant*, supra note 22, pp. 89ff.

71 Speech 'Justice in the EU – from the citizens' perspective', Stockholm (22–23 July 2009), on file with the author.

72 Additional comments by Justice Koskelo in the plenary discussion following her speech at the FIDE 2014 Congress in Copenhagen, in Plenary Session 'In the era of legal pluralism' on 31 May 2014. The main speech is available in U. Neergaard and J. Jacqueson (eds.), *Proceedings: Speeches from the XXVI FIDE Congress in Copenhagen*, Vol 4 (Copenhagen, 2014), www.fide2014.eu (accessed 13 March 2015).

3.4 Fair trial and in absentia *judgments*

Early on, FTI expressed further concern about cases where the offence had been committed a long time ago or the sentence had been issued *in absentia*.[73]

The EAW rules on *in absentia* judgments, as amended in 2009, prompted a preliminary ruling request by the Spanish Constitutional Court in *Melloni*.[74] In the past, the Spanish Constitutional Court had prohibited extradition to serve a severe sentence imposed in the absence of the requested person, where no possibility of a retrial was available, even where the person had been represented in the other Member State by a lawyer. In the Court's view, changing this practice would breach the constitutional right to a fair trial and the rights of defence in a way that affects human dignity. Article 24 of the Spanish Constitution provides that '[e]veryone has the right to obtain effective protection from judges and the courts in the exercise of his rights and legitimate interests, and in no case may there be a denial of defence'. The Court noted that in its case law:

> the right to participate in the oral procedure and to mount one's own defence forms part of the nucleus of the rights of defence which must be regarded as essential under Article 24 of the Constitution. In criminal proceedings, the right of the accused to be present at the hearing … enables a person to defend himself against an accusation. […] Only by means of physical presence at the trial can rejection of or acquiescence to the accusation be manifested, and the declaration by the accused can become part of his defence, witnesses can be questioned and examined, the defence conducted with specialised assistance from a lawyer can be coordinated and, finally, the right to the last word can be exercised …. The oral procedure … is the decisive moment at which … the merits of the prosecutorial contentions and the persuasiveness of the evidence produced by the prosecutor and the defence are discussed.

In the reference for a preliminary ruling, the Spanish Constitutional Court asked the Court of Justice whether Article 53 of the EU Charter of Fundamental Rights could be used to retain a higher level of protection than provided by the ECHR and by the EAW Framework Decision. The Spanish Constitutional Court noted that the protection of rights in EU law is autonomous, and that Articles 47 and 48 of the EU Charter of Fundamental Rights protect a fair, public hearing and the right to be defended and represented. The Constitutional Court referred to the Explanations to the Charter,[75] according to which Articles 47 and 48 are based upon Article 6

73 'UK grandmother "wanted" by France', *BBC News*, 26 July 2009, http://news.bbc.co.uk/1/hi/8169357.stm.

74 Case C-399/11 *Melloni* [2013] ECLI:EU:C:2013:107.

75 Explanations Relating to the Charter of Fundamental Rights (2007/C 303/02), 14 December 2007.

ECHR on fair trial. However, the key point to note here is that the ECHR only provides a minimum floor of protection, while the States may grant more extensive protection (Article 53 ECHR). Noting that the level of protection given by the Spanish Constitution is higher than the protection afforded by the ECHR and the EAW Framework Decision, the Spanish Constitutional Court asked whether it could invoke Article 53 of the Charter to provide a higher level of protection, should the Court of Justice declare Article 4a of the EAW Framework Decision (regarding trials at which the person did not appear in person) to be valid.

The Grand Chamber of the Court of Justice rejected both the validity challenge and the possibility to grant a higher standard of protection under the national constitution. The Court of Justice recalled the principle of primacy of EU law, including over national constitutions, and emphasised that:

> casting doubt on the uniformity of the standard of protection of fundamental rights as defined in [... the EAW] framework decision, would undermine the principles of mutual trust and recognition which that decision purports to uphold and would, therefore, compromise the efficacy of that framework decision.[76]

3.5 *Access to courts and the changing role of courts: towards trust, loyal cooperation and effectiveness?*

The European Arrest Warrant was also at the outset of more far-reaching changes to the right of access to courts, a right that has been of particular importance to the rule of law in the convergent principles of constitutional law in Europe, and one that has come to be explicitly recognised in national constitutions.[77]

It was seen that the right of access to courts has come under strain with the non-permissibility of judicial review in extradition cases in the domestic courts, bearing in mind the intrinsic challenges involved in defending oneself abroad. However, the use of mutual recognition instruments has been extended to a wide range of other areas. This has led a Czech scholar to note a wider 'shift of paradigm':

> The EU mutual recognition instruments, be it European arrest warrant, European evidence warrant, freezing order, confiscation order, mutual

76 Case C-399/11 *Melloni* [2013] ECLI:EU:C:2013:107, paras 59 and 63.

77 S. Galera, 'European legal tradition and the EU legal system: understandings and premises about the rule of law's requirements', in S. Galera (ed.), *Judicial Review: A Comparative Analysis Inside the European Legal System* (Council of Europe Publishing, 2010) 277, referring to E. Storskrubb and J. Ziller, 'Access to justice in European comparative law' in F. Francioni (ed.), *Access to Justice as a Human Right* (Oxford University Press, 2007) 180.

> recognition of financial penalties or sentencing judgments or probations, present great challenges for the legal systems of Member States [...]. One of the most significant challenges is the shift of paradigm, whereby executing authorities are supposed to recognise and execute foreign judgments and other judicial decisions (in case of financial penalties, the respective decisions might also come from administrative authorities) almost automatically, while trusting that underlying foreign procedures and decisions observed fundamental rights and fulfilled particularly fair trial requirements.[78]

The extension of the EU principle of mutual recognition to civil and commercial matters, along with the abolition of the *exequatur*, led an Estonian attorney to call for a public debate on access to judicial protection. The concerns were prompted by the case of Aivo Piirsoo, a truck driver who in 2009 suddenly discovered that his bank account was €430,000 in debt, with a further debt of €192,000 added by way of interest accrued. The Estonian customs authorities had automatically executed a customs tax request issued by the German authorities. Earning a meagre €700 a month and unable to contest the tax in Germany, the driver had little choice but to declare bankruptcy. The attorney in the case, Siim Roode, called for a parliamentary debate to highlight the need for Estonian authorities to provide assistance to their citizens.[79] He recalled that judicial protection must be accessible within a reasonable time and at a reasonable cost, and that the right to judicial protection must be exercisable in a manner that is not too onerous for the individual. The possibility to request judicial review of an act of a foreign authority in a foreign country does not meet these criteria, and is not within the reach of a natural person, i.e., an individual.[80]

The 'shift of paradigm' has a further element with a potentially far-reaching impact on classic constitutional values: the role of courts is increasingly shifting towards a framework of trust, loyal cooperation, and effectiveness in the context of EU law. Indeed, a recent Centre for European Policy Studies report compellingly shows why trust is not well placed in systems of criminal justice, which:

> are designed to operate on the basis of distrust among the actors. If judges and juries had mutual trust in the police, then there would be no need for a trial, the defendant would obviously be guilty because the police say so and the judge and the jury trust the police.[81]

78 M. Švarc, 'Czech Republic', in Laffranque, *Reports of the XXV FIDE Congress Tallinn 2012, Volume 3*, supra note 46, p. 269.

79 'Saksamaa nõuab eestlaselt miljoneid kroone' ('Germany demands millions of kroons from an Estonian'), *Postimees*, 4 November 2009, www.postimees.ee (accessed 17 April 2014).

80 Further comment by S. Roode on the case by e-mail of 6 February 2012, on file with the author.

81 Carrera et al., 'Europe's Most Wanted?', supra note 66, p. 20.

Discussion seems to be warranted on whether such changes are indispensable and to what extent it might be possible to reverse the process.

However, that no plans for change are underway was signalled by the Court of Justice's recent *Opinion 2/13* on the EU's accession to the ECHR, where the Court strongly reinforced the present approach. The Court of Justice rejected the possibility of EU accession to the ECHR partly on the grounds that as 'EU law imposes an obligation of mutual trust between those Member States, accession is liable to … undermine the autonomy of EU law'.[82] According to the Court:

> In so far as Article 53 of the ECHR essentially reserves the power of the Contracting Parties to lay down higher standards of protection of fundamental rights than those guaranteed by the ECHR, that provision should be coordinated with Article 53 of the Charter, as interpreted by the Court of Justice, so that the power granted to Member States by Article 53 of the ECHR is limited – with respect to the rights recognised by the Charter that correspond to those guaranteed by the ECHR – to that which is necessary to ensure that the level of protection provided for by the Charter and the primacy, unity and effectiveness of EU law are not compromised.[83]

4 Revisiting the adoption of the EAW Framework Decision: forsaking classic constitutional rights with 'almost total absence of political debate'?

The above sections seem to validate Ester Herlin-Karnell's concern, cited in the opening section of this chapter, that 'important values once recognised within the nation state' are 'lost' and 'forgotten' 'in the transition to the European level'.[84] A recent systematic analysis of reports on the national implementation of the EU measures also shows that '[t]he uncritical focus on security has [… led] to significant concerns regarding the impact of EU AFSJ law on the protection of fundamental rights'.[85]

With such far-reaching consequences for personal liberty, it is important to bear in mind that the introduction of the mutual recognition system in EU criminal law, as Fair Trials International noted, was marked by 'the lack of public engagement in the area of defence rights and the almost total absence of political debate on the subject'; '[t]he fundamental rights of citizens … received almost no attention'.[86] For a considerable time, extension of EU competence to this field had met objections from the Member States.

82 Opinion 2/13 of the Full Court, *Accession to the ECHR*, 18 December 2014, ECLI:EU:C:2014:2454, para 194.

83 Ibid., para 189.

84 Herlin-Karnell, 'The integrity of European criminal law', supra note 1, pp. 238, 240.

85 Mitsilegas, 'General report', supra note 46, p. 141.

86 Fair Trials International, 'Submission to the EU Justice and Home Affairs Council Working Group' 9 July 2009, www.fairtrials.org/campaigns (accessed 4 March 2010), p. 4. On the

However, the heightened concern about security in the aftermath of the 9/11 terrorist attacks offered an opportune moment to link criminal law and the fight against terrorism.[87] The European Arrest Warrant Framework Decision, the drafts of which had notably existed in the European Commission before 9/11, was rapidly pushed through.[88] Studies have documented the exertion of strong pressure by the European Commission, certain national governments and the media on the more hesitant Member States; indeed in Commissioner Vitorino's view, anyone opposing these measures behaved out of line, inappropriately and effectively supported terrorism indirectly by not closing the loopholes.[89] Even the European Parliament was only consulted at the time, with two members of the Committee on Citizens' Freedoms and Rights expressing concern about 'unprecedented pressure of time and totally inadequate preparations' and about 'such a hasty procedure as does not allow scope for anything approaching serious consideration of the proposal and a measured assessment of its particularly wide-ranging implications'.[90]

Thus it is important to bear in mind that a far-reaching measure of criminal law – the supremacy of which over the national constitutions has subsequently been consistently reaffirmed by the Court of Justice – was in fact adopted at a ministerial level by the EU Council. Yet 'it has, since the birth of the idea of separation of powers, been beyond doubt that the power to define criminal offences belongs to the core area … of the legislature'.[91] It might be worth adding a clarification – even if only for the sake of history – that while the European Arrest Warrant Framework Decision was predominantly associated with security, the above adoption process – with drafts of the measure having existed before – would seem to indicate that the EAW Framework Decision was primarily about seizing an opportune moment to expand EU competence to this new field. Regarding EU action in the field of criminal law more generally, scholars have questioned the presumed 'spillover' link between the open borders and the corresponding need for EU criminal policy; Fletcher and Lööf have developed a detailed analysis showing that the spillover argument, which the EU has traditionally used to justify expansion

need for democratic debate in this area, see also Mitsilegas, 'The constitutional implications of mutual recognition', supra note 22, p. 1309.

87 Sanger, 'Force of circumstance', supra note 34, pp. 27ff.

88 Kaunert's empirical interviews with European Commission officials confirm that the measures existed before; see C. Kaunert, '"Without the power of purse or sword": the European Arrest Warrant and the role of the Commission' (2007) 29 *Journal of European Integration* 387, cited in Sanger, 'Force of circumstance', supra note 34, p. 33.

89 Ibid., p. 32.

90 European Parliament Document A5-0397/2001 final (14 November 2001) cited in N. Keijzer, 'The European Arrest Warrant Framework Decision between past and future' in Guild, *Constitutional Challenges to the European Arrest Warrant*, supra note 22, p. 24.

91 Schünemann, 'Alternative draft for a European criminal law and procedure', supra note 2, p. 232.

of its competence, has tenuous empirical justification in the context of criminal law and that its use in this field is theoretically flawed.[92]

The manner in which the EAW was adopted needs wider awareness, and considerably more careful scrutiny is warranted with regard to other potential misuses of crisis situations to rush through questionable measures. While the Lisbon Treaty and the Stockholm Programme envisaged improvements in the area of defence rights, this work started more than eight years after the adoption of the EAW Framework Decision. Considerable and welcome focus has also been placed on improving the standards of defence rights in those Member States where they might be lacking, along with some notorious prison conditions,[93] in order to strengthen the system of mutual trust.

However, there has been very little attention on the intrinsic difficulties of defending oneself in a foreign legal system, which the above-mentioned Roadmap Directives alleviate to some extent but do not remove. Such intrinsic, compounded difficulties affecting personal liberty continue to make the *Cassis de Dijon*-style mutual recognition in the single market inherently unsuitable in the field of criminal law. Indeed, on the basis of a study of Irish EAW cases, Dermot Walsh has raised the question of whether the system of mutual recognition will 'contribute to miscarriages of justice which will be more difficult to detect and remedy'; he highlights a range of constitutional rights that have seen a reduced or even 'anaemic' level of protection, and finds that courts are taking 'a more purposive, and even a teleological, approach' to the application of criminal law legislation.[94] In the UK, there is concern that defendants and their defence rights may 'vanish down the cracks that exist between different national systems'.[95] The last two sections will explore how these questions could be addressed in the mindset of 'substantive co-operative constitutionalism'.

5 EAW and EU criminal law – reinforcing the thin, weak, procedural version of constitutionalism and the rule of law in the EU?

What is notable, and prompted the writing of this chapter, is that readers of EU constitutional law literature would have by and large been oblivious

92 M. Fletcher and R. Lööf with B. Gilmore, *EU Criminal Law and Justice* (Edward Elgar, 2008) pp. 22–31.

93 See especially the Roadmap Directives above in note 28, and the contribution by V. Mitsilegas to the present volume (Chapter 8). The question whether one or another Member State meets the same level of rights protection that applies in the issuing Member State, as well as the question of prison conditions, has also been one of the main questions in domestic litigation, see, for example, case law in Ireland in Walsh, 'The European Arrest Warrant in Ireland', supra note 2.

94 Walsh, 'The European Arrest Warrant in Ireland', supra note 2, see especially pp. 13, 22, 33.

95 Sanger, 'Force of circumstance', supra note 34, p. 25, citing J. Spencer, 'European criminal procedure: fantasy or a fact?' (2003) 4 *Archbold News* 5.

to the erosion of classic constitutional rights and safeguards for the rule of law discussed above. A similar concern about the discourse inspired a recent edited collection where leading, mainstream EU law scholars were invited to reflect on the 'EU's Justice Deficit'.[96] One of the editors notes that the approach to justice in the EU that enjoys the most popularity is that there is 'no problem with the current state of affairs, rehearsing twists and turns of ECJ case law uniquely and exclusively with the context of market integration in mind'; 'this approach is observable in the great majority of EU legal writing and also case law, driving – blindly – past the issues of justice and injustice'.[97]

In the field of the European Arrest Warrant, for example, for about a decade it would have been easy to get the impression that the main problem was that national courts were reluctant to relinquish sovereignty and failed to play along cooperatively in the contemporary, pluralist legal setting; examples were given in Section 2. Indeed, the EU constitutional discourse strengthened the legitimacy of, and public confidence in, the European Arrest Warrant, treating any dissenting judges or authorities as deviants or Eurosceptics. This is significant, given that scientific authority has been an essential element of the EU's political legitimacy[98] and there is an expectation that anyone wishing to authoritatively take part in EU debates should possess legal credentials and know-how.[99] Legal scholars have played an important role in the development of the notion of the Union as a juristic idea with its technical, autonomous and specific nature; EU law is studied and taught as 'a highly technical set of rules, a dense doctrinal thicket where only the ignorant or the foolish would "jump in"',[100] 'untouchable by outsiders not initiated into its special techniques'.[101]

If the way the discourse has handled constitutional rights and constitutional courts in the field of the European Arrest Warrant is indeed problematic, there would seem to be a need to recalibrate the discourse towards greater attention to the constitutional rights and values at stake. Against this background, I have elsewhere propounded the concept of 'substantive co-operative constitutionalism',[102] which seeks to remedy the shortcomings by inviting academic and judicial inquiry on several broader issues. The first central element of 'substantive co-operative constitutionalism' is that it seeks to move beyond

96 D. Kochenov, G. De Búrca and A. Williams (eds.), *Europe's Justice Deficit* (Hart Publishing, 2015).

97 D. Kochenov, 'The ought of justice' in Kochenov et al., *Europe's Justice Deficit*, supra note 96, p. 29.

98 For a detailed account, see, for example, Schepel and Wesseling, 'The legal community', supra note 5, pp. 165–188; J. Shaw, 'European Union legal studies in crisis? Towards a new dynamic' (1996) 16 *Oxford Journal of Legal Studies* 231; Vauchez, 'The transnational politics of judicialization', supra note 6, pp. 4 and 26ff.

99 Vauchez, 'The transnational politics of judicialization', supra note 6, pp. 4, 26.

100 F. Snyder, 'New directions in European community law' (1987) 14 *Journal of Law and Society* 167 (references omitted), cited in Shaw, 'European Union legal studies in crisis?', supra note 98, p. 234.

101 Shaw, 'European Union legal studies in crisis?', supra note 98, p. 235.

102 Albi, 'Erosion of constitutional rights', supra note 3.

the literature's focus on sovereignty, contest for power and the assessment of cooperativeness and Euro-friendliness as an aim in itself, towards a greater awareness of the constitutional rights and rule of law safeguards affected.

I have argued, with some concern, that the formal approaches to cooperation, along with changes in judicial behaviour, are part of a broader transition from what I would call 'the mindset of classic (continental) European constitutional law', which is more attuned to substantive constitutional guarantees, to 'the mindset of European Union constitutional law', which represents a more procedural, formal, foundational or thin type of constitutionalism.

The constitutions of the Member States adhere to a more substantive version of constitutionalism, both in terms of greater democratic legitimacy and accessible, responsive democratic participation, as well as in terms of the function of a constitution to protect the individual's rights and liberty, and provide for safeguards for the rule of law, the separation of powers, and judicial and constitutional review. For example, in Italy, the doctrine of 'guarantism' is used to denote the constitutional guarantees for individual liberty and for collective freedoms against potential arbitrary activity by public authorities, with a central role held by guarantees in the penal process for the prevention of arbitrariness in the exercise of political and judicial power, in particular in the context of emergency legislation.[103] While there are differences in the understanding of the concept of the rule of law, *Rechtsstaat* and *État de droit* in different European countries, there has been a general rejection in the national and classic comparative constitutional doctrine of the formalist, narrow version that denotes the principle of legality. European countries predominantly adhere to a material understanding of the rule of law, where requirements include the protection of individuals and guarantees for personal freedom and autonomy, legal certainty and lack of retroactivity, access to justice, the independence of judges, and other substantive rules.[104] The rule of law guarantees tend to be the most advanced and strictly protected by the constitutional courts in the countries that have experienced arbitrary exercise of power under an authoritarian past, especially Germany, Austria, Spain, Portugal, Italy and Greece; heightened guarantees for the rule of law and their vigorous protection by constitutional courts were also a distinctive and widely acclaimed part of the post-communist constitutional reforms in the new Member States from Central and Eastern Europe.[105] On the other hand, there are the countries that have historically had longstanding, well-functioning systems of government,

103 Martinico et al., 'The Constitution of Italy', supra note 48, Sect. 2.3.5.3.

104 I owe particular thanks to Hent Kalmo for his insights and discussion when developing the section on formal and material/substantive rule of law and constitutionalism, especially his 'Comparative report' (2010) (unpublished paper on file with the author), summarising extensive literature on the rule of law. See also R. Grote, 'Rule of law, Rechtsstaat and "Etat de Droit"', in C. Starck (ed.), *Constitutionalism, Universalism, and Democracy: A Comparative Analysis* (Nomos, 1999) 269.

105 For literature, see, for example, A. Albi, 'On secret legislation, blanket data recording, arrest warrants and property rights: questions on the rule of law and judicial review in the

with a high standard of rights protection, and where the texts of the constitutions have remained more flexible, evolutionary or political in nature, without any or with only weak classic constitutional review mechanisms. The constitutions of the UK, the Netherlands, Luxembourg and the Nordic countries could be placed in this category. The UK and the Netherlands broadly base the protection of rights on the ECHR; the UK's unwritten constitution is regarded as more 'pragmatic'[106] and is based on '[a]n enormous residue of discretion [...] per contra the *Rechtsstaat* ideal in Germany where the citizens' position is built on clearly defined rights which can only be interfered with through clearly defined legal norms'.[107] This difference may be important to bear in mind given the influence that British and Dutch scholars and law journals have had in shaping the research agendas in the English-language EU constitutional discourse, with one consequence being that the European discourse has generally come to focus on the protection of rights under the ECHR rather than under the national constitutions.[108] In the ECHR, the protection of rights in criminal trials is less detailed than typically in the post-authoritarian constitutions; the EU Charter of Fundamental Rights is in fact notably generic and laconic with regard to these rights.

By contrast, in the mindset of EU constitutional law, the emphasis has primarily been on the rules of hierarchy and functioning, especially in the relations between the polity and its constituent parts. The keywords of EU constitutional law are supremacy, direct effect, uniformity, effectiveness, autonomy, trust, coherence, loyal cooperation and correct implementation. The idea that the constitutionalisation of the (at the time) EC legal order consists of four judge-made doctrines – supremacy, direct effect, implied powers and human rights – has been attributed in particular to Joseph Weiler[109] and Eric Stein.[110] Both scholars equate constitutionalisation with the United States type of federalisation, i.e., creating a federal state-like structure for the relationship between the EC and the Member States, as a contrast to recourse to the methods traditionally applied in public international law.[111]

EU in the light of post-communist constitutions', in P. Popelier, C. Van De Heyning and P. Van Nuffel (eds.), *Human Rights Protection in the European Legal Order: The Interaction between the European and the National Courts* (Intersentia, 2011) 173.

106 Lord Neuberger, 'The British and Europe', Cambridge Freshfields Annual Law Lecture 2014 (12 February 2014), www.supremecourt.uk/docs/speech-140212.pdf (accessed 30 June 2015), para 26; P. Birkinshaw, *European Public Law: The Achievement and the Challenge* (2nd edn, Kluwer, 2014) 99.

107 Birkinshaw, *European Public Law*, supra note 106, p. 99.

108 For a detailed account on this and the preceding points as well as those that follow, see Albi, 'Erosion of constitutional rights', Part 2, supra note 3, Sect. VIII.

109 J.H.H. Weiler, 'The transformation of Europe' (1991) 100 *Yale Law Review* 2413.

110 E. Stein, 'Lawyers, judges, and the making of a transnational constitution' (1981) 75 *American Journal of International Law* 1.

111 For a similar observation, see M. Avbelj, 'Questioning EU constitutionalisms' (2008) 9 *German Law Journal* 4; M. Avbelj, *The Pitfalls of (Comparative) Constitutionalism for*

Another central element of EU constitutionalism has been 'the ordo-liberal project of a European economic constitution', guaranteeing economic freedoms and commitment to a 'system of undistorted competition' at the supranational level.[112] The introduction of EU citizenship and the EU Charter of Fundamental Rights raised hopes for a move from an economic to a more classic type of constitutionalism. However, after *Melloni* and *Opinion 2/13 on Accession to the ECHR*[113] it would seem that the Court of Justice primarily sees the Charter as a further instrument for ensuring the supremacy, autonomy, effectiveness and uniform application of EU law, while the standard of protection of national constitutional rights notably has to be lowered in cases of conflict. Regarding the concept of the rule of law, which is a key element of constitutionalism, an analysis by Dimitry Kochenov – developed before the recent improvements in *Kadi* in 2008 – shows that the idea of the rule of law at the EU level has been characterised 'by an extremely high level of formalism' and a 'de facto emptiness'.[114] He notes that scholars studying the functioning of the rule of law in the European Union legal context 'rarely go beyond a pure description of how the Community/Union legal system functions'; the Court of Justice has made limited use of it, having formulated its cornerstones primarily in terms of supremacy and direct effect, the idea of legality and procedural guarantees.[115]

One point that needs clarification is that there has been a powerfully perpetuated narrative about the EU granting rights directly to the individual. The literature in the field of EU law has traditionally focused on and acclaimed the various ways in which the European Court of Justice has developed the EU into an autonomous constitutional order and advanced free movement rights, economic freedoms, the rights of EU citizens, students and air passengers, and the rights relating to gender equality and non-discrimination on other grounds. These are important rights, which in very direct ways have enhanced individuals' quality of life and broadened their horizons. It is well-established that the European Court of Justice has typically gone to great lengths to create and expand the scope of such rights, by adopting a judicially activist stance, deploying teleological, purpose-oriented interpretation and the broad principle of effectiveness.

However, a limited number of scholars have expressed concern that beyond this narrative, the real picture has been rather disquieting. Stijn Smismans

European Integration, Eric Stein Working Paper No 1/2008, www.ericsteinpapers.cz (accessed 30 June 2015), pp. 9ff.

112 C. Joerges, 'Three transformations of Europe and the search for a way out of its crisis', in C. Joerges and C. Glinski (eds.), *The European Crisis and the Transformation of Transnational Governance: Authoritarian Managerialism versus Democratic Governance* (Hart Publishing, 2014) 27.

113 See Sections 3.4 and 3.5 of this paper.

114 D. Kochenov, 'The EU rule of law: cutting paths through confusion' (2009) 2 *Erasmus Law Review* 21.

115 Kochenov, 'The EU rule of law', supra note 114, pp. 22–24.

has noted more broadly the 'European Union's fundamental rights myth', which is a narrative that is based on non-rational elements and contains factual errors, but that is widely believed and acted upon.[116] For example, if one looks at the actual outcomes of judgments of the Court of Justice, it emerges that the protection of classic fundamental rights has by and large remained rhetorical, having been trumped by market freedoms or other aspects of EU policy until the *Omega* and *Schmidberger*[117] cases in 2003–2004, where priority was given to the right to human dignity and freedom of expression respectively. The low level of fundamental rights protection in the case law of the Court of Justice has been explored in greater detail elsewhere, with the conclusion that, by and large, the existing practice has been to routinely subordinate national constitutional rights to the expediencies of generic, vague objectives such as closer integration, cooperation, uniformity and effectiveness of EU law, the stability of the market and security.[118]

Indeed it is increasingly hard to avoid the impression, first pointed out by Jason Coppel and Aidan O'Neill in their classic 1992 article 'The European Court of Justice: taking rights seriously?', that in many cases the individual's rights seem to have been used in a somewhat instrumental way: these rights tend to be advanced primarily where this enables expansion of EU powers vis-à-vis the Member States.[119] The individual appears to have been quite ruthlessly neglected when his or her rights pose an obstacle to further integration. For example, while the European Commission and the Court of Justice have been vigilant and activist to ensure the protection of the rights of EU citizens, students and rights pertaining to gender equality, a Commission report laments that the human rights clauses in the legislation implementing the EAW in the Member States are 'disturbing',[120] as such clauses undermine the overriding goal of uniformity of EU law. The Court of Justice, as seen earlier, has, for example, rejected the Belgian concern about *nulla poena sine lege* and, in *Melloni*, emphasised the imperative of uniformity and effectiveness of EU law, which take priority over the Spanish ban on *in absentia* judgments.

A limited number of scholars have shared these concerns. In the context of the Area of Freedom, Security and Justice, Valsamis Mitsilegas has noted the 'slow emergence of the individual' in the system of enforced movement

116 S. Smismans, 'The European Union's fundamental rights myth' (2010) 48 *Journal of Common Market Studies* 45.

117 Case C36/02 *Omega* [2004] ECR I-9609 and Case C–112/00 *Schmidberger* [2003] ECR I-5659.

118 Albi, 'Erosion of constitutional rights', Part 2, supra note 3, Sect. VIII.D.

119 J. Coppel and A. O'Neill, 'The European Court of Justice: taking rights seriously?' (1992) 29 *Common Market Law Review* 670, at 692.

120 Report from the Commission based on Article 34 of the Council Framework Decision of 13 June 2002 on the European Arrest Warrant and the surrender procedures between Member States, COM(2005)63 final, Brussels, 23 February 2005, p. 5, cited in Mitsilegas, 'The constitutional implications of mutual recognition', supra note 22, p. 1293.

based upon the automatic transfer of individuals from one Member State to another; 'enforcement trumps', and the system of automaticity 'has a significant impact on the reconfiguration of the relationship between the individual and the State'.[121] A recent book by Cian Murphy argues that EU counterterrorism measures are weakening the rule of law and bypassing safeguards in favour of a system emphasising coercive control over individual autonomy.[122] Leonard Besselink has concluded from the *Melloni* ruling and extra-judicial statements by judges of the Court of Justice that:

> Once upon a time *Costa v ENEL* may have been about citizens' rights, but taken to its extreme 50 years later, it turns out to be about supremacy of EU law for which citizens' rights have to be set aside.[123]

Returning to the theme of a transition from the classic to the EU mindset of constitutional law, one should note that there is, on the one hand, a burgeoning volume of books and research papers on the constitutionalisation of various areas of EU law. Indeed, Matej Avbelj is among the few scholars who have observed that the EU constitutionalists attach 'the constitutional label ... everywhere'.[124] He finds that:

> The constitutional language has been used widely and fairly indiscriminately. Its tag has been attached to numerous elements of the European integration, ranging from the Treaty as a constitutional charter to the constitution of external relations and even to the constitutionalisation of comitology.[125]

Avbelj cautions that there is a need:

> to take a step back and ask a question that a great majority of proponents of EU constitutionalism in their sometimes overly enthusiastic constitutional enterprise surprisingly failed to address. Beyond constitutional nominalism, that is, beyond the pervasive constitutional labeling, what kind of constitutionalism are we actually talking about?[126]

121 V. Mitsilegas, 'The limits of mutual trust in Europe's Area of Freedom, Security and Justice: from automatic inter-state cooperation to the slow emergence of the individual' (2012) 31 *Yearbook of European Law* 319.

122 C. Murphy, *EU Counter-Terrorism Law: Pre-Emption and the Rule of Law* (Hart Publishing, 2012).

123 L. Besselink, 'The ECJ as the European "Supreme Court": setting aside citizens' rights for EU law supremacy', 18 August 2014, www.verfassungsblog.de/en/ecj-european-supreme-court-setting-aside-citizens-rights-eu-law-supremacy/#.VRPAD9i2-cw (accessed 1 July 2015); see also L. Besselink, 'The parameters of constitutional conflict after Melloni' (2014) 39 *European Law Review* 531.

124 Avbelj, 'Questioning EU constitutionalisms', supra note 111, p. 25.

125 Ibid., p. 2 (references omitted).

126 Ibid.

Indeed, a limited number of scholars have, by contrast, observed the 'erosion' of constitutionalism,[127] 'twilight of constitutionalism'[128] or 'the end of constitutionalism as we know it'[129] when writing about substantive standards of democracy and legitimacy in European and global governance. Some have additionally noted the emergence of a thin, weak, procedural version of the rule of law, judicial review and democratic control in the context of European and global economic cooperation, with reduced opportunities for citizens to challenge public decisions.[130] In the context of globalisation, Anne Peters has noted that besides positive effects, state constitutions have also been invisibly 'globalized' 'in a rather negative way' as regards the rule of law, social state, judicial review and some other key elements of the constitutions.[131] The issues explored in this article have led the author to share concerns about the erosion of constitutionalism and about a transition to a thin type of constitutionalism; the paper adds the concerns about erosion of constitutional rights and of further rule of law safeguards beyond judicial review, and about the changing legal thinking in the field of constitutional law, which have hitherto received virtually no attention. Besides important advances such as opening up the constitutions to European integration and the shared exercise of powers, there has thus also been an element of negative Europeanisation of constitutions. Additionally, as the expression 'European constitutional law' has, in the large volume of books and articles written in this field, predominantly come to denote EU constitutional law rather than comparative European constitutional law, there is an increasingly discernible tendency for the differences in the EU and the classic (continental) European concept of constitutionalism and of the rule of law, along with the relevant constitutional vocabulary, to become muddled. For example, there is a risk that what comes to be – and indeed already is – regarded as European rule of law is the more formalistic EU standard rather than the more substantive, 'guarantistic' national standard developed by constitutional and supreme courts under the influence of the Council of Europe, the Venice Commission and the ECtHR.[132]

127 D. Grimm, 'The achievement of constitutionalism and its prospects in a changed world', in P. Dobner and M. Loughlin (eds.), *The Twilight of Constitutionalism?* (Oxford University Press, 2010) 4.

128 P. Dobner and M. Loughlin, 'Introduction' in Dobner and Loughlin, *The Twilight of Constitutionalism?*, p. xi.

129 M-S. Kuo, 'The end of constitutionalism as we know it? Boundaries and the state of global constitutional (dis)ordering' (2010) 1 *Transnational Legal Theory* 329.

130 C. Harlow, 'Global administrative law: the quest for principles and values' (2006) 17 *European Journal of International Law* 195; S. Galera, 'The European contribution to an emerging global law' in Galera, *Judicial Review*, supra note 77, 302.

131 A. Peters, 'The globalization of state constitutions', in A. Nollkaemper and L. Nijman (eds.), *New Perspectives on the Divide Between National and International Law* (Oxford University Press, 2007) 254, at 273ff.

132 For this and the preceding points, see a more detailed account with references to literature Albi, 'Erosion of constitutional rights', Part 2, supra note 3, sect. VIII.

6 Towards 'substantive co-operative constitutionalism': implications for constitutional rights affected by the EAW system

In 'substantive co-operative constitutionalism', a conceptual approach that I developed more fully elsewhere,[133] scholars, courts and national and transnational institutions would explore how to develop European and global governance in a way that would seek to uphold and enhance the achieved standards of the classic, substantive, more 'guarantistic' and democratically responsive version of constitutionalism, including the individual's rights and rule of law safeguards, in a more proactive manner. Further elements of the concept of 'substantive co-operative constitutionalism' briefly include the following: (1) a return from the autonomous, self-referential approach in EU constitutional law to a greater awareness and use of comparative constitutional law; (2) a greater deference to, and accommodation of, the rule of law and constitutional safeguards built up by national constitutional and supreme courts, especially where the standard of protection is stricter; indeed, this is also allowed for under Article 53 of the EU Charter and would also be in line with the logic of other international human rights treaties, including the ECHR, which sets the minimum floor of protection; (3) a more proactive and probing role for constitutional and supreme courts to counter the risk of hollowing out the judicial function, along with a more robust communication with the Court of Justice; (4) a greater scope for protection of, and responsiveness by the EU to, constitutional rights, given the constraints of EU enforcement proceedings, fines and the imperatives of correct and speedy implementation; and, finally, (5) a call for greater critical scrutiny of the European Court of Justice, which, in contrast to the harsh language typically used with regard to national highest courts, has hitherto by and large been missing in the discourse.

In the context of the European Arrest Warrant, the adverse effects on constitutional rights raised in Sections 3 and 4 of this chapter – for example, on the presumption of innocence and the right to judicial review, on the principle of *nulla poena sine lege* and on the broader role of courts – would seem to be in need of attention in a more substantive approach to constitutionalism. In particular, as regards access to courts, there seems to be something inherently un-European about the requirement to send people thousands of miles away to foreign prisons under a near-automatic procedure, without prior judicial review. It was seen in Section 3.1 above that several judges in different Member States share this concern. Would it be outlandish to suggest restoring at least partial judicial review in the courts of the country of residence of the person affected, which are typically the most accessible and comprehensible to them? Perhaps not, since the UK introduced a proportionality

133 Albi, 'Erosion of constitutional rights', supra note 3, Part 2.

review in 2014,[134] and a recent House of Lords report calls for extradition to be made 'an instrument of last, rather than first, resort'.[135] Introduction of a proportionality review, as well as compensation for individuals affected, was also recommended in a comprehensive 2014 study commissioned by the European Parliament.[136] The European Parliament's study calls for revising the EAW, along with greater attention on the impact of the EAW on individuals' lives, even if the report cautions against regressing or departing from the principle of mutual recognition as such. However, in the cases of Mr Symeou and Mr Laurits reported in Section 3, a simple proportionality review would not have sufficed – questions of alibi and evidence obtained under duress also need to be considered. It is doubtful that individuals have implicitly agreed to give up rule of law safeguards for the sake of free movement.[137]

One commendable solution that in the present writer's view holds considerable promise to directly address the issues highlighted in this chapter is contained in the 'Alternative draft for a European criminal law and procedure', developed by 11 German criminal law professors led by Bernd Schünemann; the 'Alternative draft' propounds the 'most favoured treatment' and the Swiss model instead of mutual recognition.[138] As with the Swiss model, in relation to prosecution, the procedural law of the prosecuting country would apply. However, matters determining a citizen's freedom, including the irreparable consequences of extradition, pre-trial detention, incarceration, and the freezing or confiscation of assets should be governed by the law of the home state of the person enjoying the constitutional right.[139] The 'Alternative draft' also calls for the establishment at the EU level of an organisation called 'Eurodefensor', as a pendant to Eurojust, in order to provide assistance to defence lawyers in transborder cases.[140] The Eurodefensor would be financed by the EU, while the national bar or criminal defence associations would be responsible for the assistance.

The present writer would additionally recommend the introduction – within the Member States – of publicly funded institutions or non-governmental organisations that would monitor EAW cases and provide assistance to persons

134 Section 157 of the Anti-Social Behaviour, Crime and Policing Act 2014; for details see A. Young, P. Birkinshaw, V. Mitsilegas and T. Christou, 'United Kingdom' in Albi and Bardutzky, *National Constitutions in European and Global Governance*, supra note 32, Sect. 2.3.5.

135 House of Lords Select Committee on Extradition Law, 'Extradition: UK Law and Practice', 10 March 2015, www.publications.parliament.uk/pa/ld201415/ldselect/ldextradition/126/126.pdf (accessed 7 July 2015), p. 8.

136 European Parliamentary Research Service, 'Revising the European Arrest Warrant', March 2014, PE 510.979 www.europarl.europa.eu/committees/en/supporting-analyses-search.html (accessed 7 July 2015), for example, pp. 14, 20–27.

137 I am grateful to Hent Kalmo for this observation.

138 Schünemann, 'Alternative draft for a European criminal law and procedure', supra note 2, pp. 239ff.

139 Ibid., pp. 243–244.

140 Ibid., pp. 248ff.

caught up in transnational legal environment, including in cases under international extradition treaties. Among other issues raised in the earlier parts of the chapter, the Court of Justice's decision in *Melloni* to prioritise the uniformity and effectiveness of EU law over constitutional rights would also seem untenable; unlike harmonisation in the single market, it is not clear why uniformity is needed in the field of criminal law, especially at the cost of levelling down rights protection. For a substantive approach to constitutionalism, it is also of importance to place greater responsibility on EU institutions: the way a crisis situation was seized to expand EU powers into the field of criminal law (as retraced in Section 4 above) has resulted in structural damage that has set a new 'normal', which has proved difficult to remedy by national parliaments in the implementation process or by individual national and European courts in judicial proceedings.[141]

In the framework of an ongoing research project, I have sought to systematically bring together information from 28 Member States about national judgments and doctrine on some of the issues raised in this chapter, along with constitutional rights in other areas such as data retention and judicial review.[142] Some of the questions studied include: how were the concerns around the presumption of innocence and *nulla poena* accommodated; have there been calls at national level to restore some element of judicial review; and is there support for creating publicly funded or other organisations that would provide assistance to individuals caught up in foreign criminal proceedings, beyond standard consular assistance? It would seem that several Member States have had extensive debates on constitutional rights affected by the EAW, whereas many others have had no debate at all, focusing primarily on correct and speedy implementation; the national reports, along with a comparative synthesis, will be available in 2017.[143] It may well be that scholars overall do not share the concerns raised, and find that there has been no significant change in constitutional standards or in the type of constitutionalism, or that any potential change is justified in view of the considerable benefits of European integration. However, it seems important to have a considered discussion. This is especially so as there is the added risk of normalisation and ossification given the complexity of EU processes, the language and distance barriers, the absence of modalities of responsiveness to revise unanticipated or undesirable effects of EU law[144] and the difficulty of change, as well as a lack of understanding beyond specialist legal circles.

141 On the ways in which the EU may have set the 'new normal', see Albi, 'Erosion of constitutional rights', supra note 3, Part 1, Sect. VI, and Part 2, Sect. IX.D.

142 See the research project mentioned in the opening footnote; the resulting national reports will be published in Albi and Bardutzky, *National Constitutions in European and Global Governance*, supra note 32. Updates regarding the project are available at www.kent.ac.uk/roleofconstitutions (accessed 24 February 2016).

143 See the forthcoming book noted in the previous footnote.

144 On the lack of responsiveness, D. Chalmers, *Democratic Self-Government in Europe: Domestic Solutions to the EU Legitimacy Crisis*, Policy Network Paper (2013) www.policy-network.net/publications/4399/Democratic-Self-Government-in-Europe (accessed 1 July 2015), pp. 10ff.

7 The future development of the AFSJ: two broader observations regarding the changing legal thinking and the quest to harmonise criminal law

Beyond the impact of the EAW system on constitutional rights, it is hoped that the concerns raised in this chapter offer perhaps some good reasons to take a pause and consider the future direction of developing the EU's Area of Freedom, Security and Justice in a more balanced manner, especially with regard to two broader developments.

The first broader development that would seem to warrant attention is the following. In the above-mentioned paper, I argued – with examples from literature – that autonomous EU constitutional law is changing the mindset and vocabulary of classic comparative (continental) European constitutional law;[145] a summary was provided earlier in Section 5. In a similar way, it would seem to the present writer that there may also have been a change in the legal thinking in the field of criminal law. A good case in point seems to be the commentary on the *Pupino* case. As seen in Section 2, EU lawyers regard it as a milestone 'constitutional' case that extended indirect effect, effectiveness and loyal cooperation to the then third pillar. At the same time, lawyers specialising in the field of criminal law have pointed out that the case concerned the methods for taking the testimony of minors in criminal law proceedings; the question referred by the national court to the European Court of Justice was whether the prosecutor could rely on a framework decision that was not yet implemented in Italian law in order to allow minors to testify by alternative means (i.e., outside the courtroom in pre-trial proceedings).[146] Thus, while the mindset of classic criminal law – typically also protected at the level of national constitutions – proceeds from the principles of the rule of law, including maximum certainty in criminal law, clearly determined provisions and democratic legitimisation by parliamentary law,[147] EU constitutional law and EU criminal law would seem to represent quite a serious move away towards a paradigm of legal thinking based on indirect effect, effectiveness, teleological interpretation and trust. Furthermore, the legal measure to be interpreted in such a broad way in the *Pupino* case was a framework decision adopted at the ministerial level by the EU Council (with even the European Parliament having been only cursorily consulted at the time, as seen in Section 4). By way of another example, while 'trust has been the driving assumption in EU criminal law cooperation', Section 3.5 of this chapter recalled some of the reasons why trust has been regarded as

145 Albi, 'Erosion of constitutional rights', supra note 3 Part 2, Sect. VIII.

146 Herlin-Karnell, 'In the wake of *Pupino*', supra note 9, p. 1151.

147 See, for example, Herlin-Karnell, 'In the wake of *Pupino*', supra note 9, p. 1154; 'Manifesto on the European Criminal Policy', supra note 2, pp. 707ff; Schünemann, 'Alternative draft for a European criminal law and procedure', supra note 2, pp. 227ff.

wholly misplaced and even dangerous in classic criminal law.[148] As Berndt Schünemann has observed, 'the rule of law as well as the indispensable democratic fundamentals underlying the criminal law' were principles 'developed as early as during the period of Enlightenment, but have been disregarded in the prevailing discussion on EU criminal law'.[149] He continues: 'One must put one's illusions aside and acknowledge that, in the area of criminal justice, Europe is presently in the process of undermining much of the rule of law.'[150]

Furthermore, in the above-mentioned article, I argued that the autonomous EU constitutional law mindset seems to have become the new frame of reference, set point or baseline, against which national constitutional principles and rule of law safeguards, beyond areas where EU law increases standards, must be patiently explained and justified in dialogues with supranational courts and European scholarship, with little chance of success, as these are presumed to be idiosyncratic or parochial.[151] It might be interesting to consider whether a similar development with regard to a changing frame of reference might be emerging in the balance between autonomous EU criminal law and classic criminal law. Indeed I have come across a number of papers that seem to go to great lengths to explain why some key practices in EU law – while enhancing European integration – go against fundamental, settled, longstanding rules and 'important values once recognised within the nation state' and that in fact go back to the European Enlightenment tradition.[152] If there is indeed such a change in the criminal law mindset, it would need greater awareness, acknowledgement and scrutiny, also in terms of what type of research gets accepted for publication in leading, agenda-setting journals of EU law and of European and international constitutional law, as well as rewarded by research funding.[153] Not only lay audiences but

148 The quote is from Herlin-Karnell, 'The integrity of European criminal law', supra note 1, who also develops this point more fully. See also the accompanying text to note 81 above regarding the concerns about trust in the field of criminal law by Carrera, Guild and Hernanz.

149 Schünemann, 'Alternative draft for a European criminal law and procedure', supra note 2, p. 228.

150 Ibid., p. 229.

151 Albi, 'Erosion of constitutional rights', Part 2, supra note 3, Sect. VIII.

152 See, for example, Herlin-Karnell, 'The integrity of European criminal law', supra note 1; 'Manifesto on the European Criminal Policy', supra note 2; pp. 707ff; Schünemann, 'Alternative draft for a European criminal law and procedure', supra note 2 pp. 228ff.

153 Historical accounts have documented considerable investment by the European Commission in founding specialised EU law journals and university centres, with the aim of shifting EU studies away from a comparative analysis of national laws (which would aim to identify common principles) to the study of the 'specificity' of EU law, focusing on the relationships between EU law (and the CJEU) and national law (and courts) (see Vauchez, 'The transnational politics of judicialization', supra note 6, pp. 20–21). Notably the *European Law Journal* was established in 1995 to provide a forum for publishing critical, contextual or otherwise unconventional research in the field of EU law. Regarding EU funding, a report by Justice in 2009 notes: 'All Commission funded projects and Working Group reports have focused on the implementation of the Framework Decision' and there is, for example,

also legal communities assume that 'Europeanised criminal law' means higher standards. It is not only difficult but also requires a good dose of courage to put one's academic and professional credibility at risk to explain that 'Europeanised criminal law' has in fact become rather un-European and undermines long-established European values. In other areas of law, concern has been expressed that the 'self-referential European legal discourse [...] in a Europeanized legal language with no reference to the domestic laws of the Member States' is changing 'what people believe is real'.[154] Given this concern, as well as the changing judicial practice in national courts and the structural developments in the European law discourse that I have discussed elsewhere, will the legal community – 20 or 30 years from now – remember the stricter version of *nulla poena sine lege* and the reservation of law principles, which once upon a time were central elements of (continental) European constitutional law and European criminal law?[155]

The second broader development that warrants a pause for reflection concerns the prevailing view in the mainstream EU law discourse that sees the future in gradual harmonisation of substantive criminal law in Europe. Indeed, even among the scholars who acknowledge that the Area of Freedom, Security and Justice has predominantly been about security while neglecting justice, the prevailing view seems to be that the main obstacle to achieving justice is the reluctance of the Member States to transfer sovereignty in this field in favour of harmonising criminal law at the EU level. However, in the light of the concern expressed in this chapter that the EU constitutional discourse may have got this area wrong,[156] it is hoped that the discourse will lend a more sympathetic ear and give a more serious consideration to those who have highlighted reasons why criminal law remains best suited to state-level regulation.

Indeed, many criminal lawyers – often working within national systems and with less wider visibility in the mainstream European discourse – have pointed out that there are several profound and compelling reasons why

no extensive research in order to track the suspects. The Justice report also notes that while prosecutors and judges can cooperate through the European Judicial Network and police officers via Europol, 'resources must be made available with expediency' to establish a network of defence practitioners, the absence of which is 'a fundamental flaw in the EAW scheme'. Justice, 'The European Arrest Warrant Briefing and Suggested Amendments', September 2009, www.justice.org.uk (accessed 16 February 2010), paras 41, 47, 50, 51. In the European Commission's Horizon 2020 research funding programme, where academic research in this field would presumably fall under the heading 'Secure societies – protecting freedom and security of Europe and its citizens', the 'primary aims' are to enhance the resilience against disasters, 'to fight crime and terrorism', 'to improve border security' and 'to provide enhanced cyber-security'; on a cursory look, the present writer could not find a section about protection of fundamental rights; see http://ec.europa.eu/programmes/horizon2020/en/h2020-sections (accessed 11 September 2015).

154 Kjaer, 'Theoretical aspects of legal translation in the EU', supra note 6, pp. 98 and 105.

155 Albi, 'Erosion of constitutional rights', Part 2, supra note 3, p. 313.

156 For a similar concern with regard to EU institutions – that with regard to mutual recognition in EU criminal law, the 'Council got it wrong' – see Peers, 'Mutual recognition and criminal law in the European Union', supra note 22, pp. 5ff.

criminal law is an area that is best left for regulation by a community organised as a state. Such reasons include the fact that criminal law is closely linked to the value system, culture and morals of a community and to the question of what is regarded as dangerous conduct, as well as to general social policies.[157] There are the considerable differences, for example, between civil and common law traditions. Furthermore and crucially, criminal law is one of the areas of law with the most drastic consequences for the individual – with custodial sentences entailing 'the eradication of the citizen's social existence'[158] – and concerns the authorities' prerogative to punish, thus requiring clear and precise determination of powers, checks and balances, and safeguards.[159] By way of examples of different value systems in the Member States, the prison population in England and Wales is approximately 85,000 out of a population of 57 million and increasing, while prisoner numbers in Sweden have fallen to 4,500 out of a population of 9.5 million. The focus in Sweden is on prisoner rehabilitation and relatively short sentences, with the goal of getting the offenders 'back out into society in better shape than they were when they came in' and addressing the underlying problems such as drugs, alcohol and psychiatric problems.[160] Yet, in comparison with Poland, Britain takes a more lenient approach by not investigating conduct that in Poland would be classified as criminal offences.[161] Poland, however, along with other post-communist countries, places particular constitutional importance on the avoidance of teleological interpretation or *contra legem* interpretation, especially in criminal law, as such practices remind the judges and lawyers – and the present writer – of communist times; this has been a key area of difficulty with regard to EU law and the interpretation methods used by the Court of Justice.[162] Indeed as one Polish judge has noted: 'I don't like crossing the same river twice.'[163] These are but a limited number of examples of the cultural disparities that exist between the Member States.

157 For a summary of arguments and a case against a centralisation approach, see Herlin-Karnell 'The integrity of European criminal law', supra note 1, Sect. 1 and 5. See also Schünemann, 'Alternative draft for a European criminal law and procedure', supra note 2, pp. 229ff.

158 Schünemann, 'Alternative-project for a European criminal law and procedure', supra note 2, pp. 230ff.

159 Herlin-Karnell 'The integrity of European criminal law', supra note 1, Sect. 1 and 5; Schünemann, 'Alternative draft for a European criminal law and procedure', supra note 2, pp. 230ff.

160 E. James, 'Prison is not for punishment in Sweden: we get people into better shape', *The Guardian*, 26 November 2014, at www.theguardian.com/society/2014/nov/26/prison-sweden-not-punishment-nils-oberg (accessed on 7 September 2015).

161 See supra note 42 and the accompanying text.

162 U. Jaremba, *National Judges as EU Law Judges: The Polish Civil Law System* (Brill, 2014), Chapters 4 and 5, especially pp. 222, 232–233, 264, 270, 274, 276. For the background and reasons, see Albi, 'On secret legislation', supra note 105.

163 In an anonymous questionnaire, cited in Jaremba, *National Judges as EU Law Judges*, supra note 162, p. 222.

A further concern regarding approximation in the field of EU criminal law is that it may lead to increased repression. Indeed, the existing EU legislative measures harmonising different aspects of substantive criminal law have led an academic group of 14 criminal law professors from ten Member States to express concern, in their joint 'Manifesto on the European Criminal Policy', about 'alarming tendencies' with 'increasingly repressive acts'; they write that '[i]f the entailed risks are not acknowledged in time, we fear to be confronted with criminal laws that contradict our fundamental principles'.[164] These and other scholars have further pointed out that EU action in this field does not sit well with the principle of subsidiarity, which in criminal law is reflected in the minimalisation of criminalisation and using criminalisation as an *ultima ratio*.[165] It was also seen in Section 4 of this chapter that scholars find no empirical evidence for the spillover argument to justify extension of EU action into the field of criminal law. Overall, there would seem to be a strong case for leaving criminal law to the sphere of regulation of the Member States, rather than imposing an autonomous, top-down and hitherto repressively oriented EU criminal law that, furthermore, represents legal thinking that sits uneasily with classic values in the field of criminal law.

Given the focus of this chapter on the discourse and the epistemology of EU law, the discussion on whether criminal law should be harmonised at the EU level ultimately brings us to the central underlying tenet in the orthodox EU legal thinking – the 'integration-through-law' project. The eminent EU law scholar Christian Joerges sees the origin of the somewhat 'insensitive' drive towards 'ever-more-Europe' in '[t]he institutional framework of this project', which 'fosters the expansion of European law as an end in itself [, …] equating ever more law with ever more Europe and the promotion of the benefit of its citizens'.[166] Matej Avbelj is another scholar who has pointed out that the integration-through-law project has had 'a wide and strong impact on the epistemology of EU law',[167] in result of which the classic EU constitutional narrative has centred around '[h]armonisation, if not unification', where:

> all the differences and diversity existing in the integration were perceived as obstacles, originally to free trade and then to integration as such.

164 'Manifesto on the European Criminal Policy', supra note 2, at p. 715. On the repressive approach in EU criminal law, see also a note with references to literature in Herlin-Karnell, 'In the wake of *Pupino*', supra note 9, p. 1155, footnote 40.

165 E. Herlin-Karnell, 'Subsidiarity in the area of EU justice and home affairs – a lost cause' (2009) 15 *European Law Journal* 351; Herlin-Karnell 'The integrity of European criminal law', supra note 1, pp. 259–260; 'Manifesto on the European Criminal Policy', supra note 2, at pp. 707, 709; Schünemann, 'Alternative draft for a European criminal law and procedure', supra note 2, p. 229. See also Judge Broß' dissenting opinion in Judgment of 18 July 2005, 2 BvR 2236/04, supra note 33, para. 153.

166 Joerges, 'Three transformations', supra note 112, pp. 38–39.

167 For details, see Avbelj, 'The pitfalls', supra note 111, p. 15.

> They were expected to give way, albeit incrementally, to the supreme Community law requiring uncompromised uniformity of its application across all the Member States.[168]

In the context of EU criminal law, a plea that passing (increasingly repressive) legislation to answer every social problem should not be considered 'as a value in itself' has been put forward in the above-mentioned 'Manifesto on the European Criminal Policy'.[169]

Christian Joerges has over the years extensively drawn attention to the fact that EU law has a mandate to organise unity in diversity – with reference to the motto in the 2003 Constitutional Treaty – rather than centralising uniformity, given the very different political and economic philosophies in the Member States. In the above-mentioned paper 'Erosion of constitutional rights in EU law: a call for substantive co-operative constitutionalism', I argued in greater detail why the constitutional diversity model is better placed if we wish to retain a more classic, substantive version of constitutionalism. For the numerous reasons highlighted throughout this chapter, the field of criminal law and the EU's Area of Freedom, Security and Justice would seem to be a particularly strong case in point for substantive cooperative constitutionalism based on the diversity model.

However, the details would have to be worked out by those specialising in the field of (classic) criminal law. Indeed, many practical and commendable proposals already exist, such as the above-mentioned 'Manifesto on the European Criminal Policy' by an academic group of 14 criminal law professors, and the 'Alternative draft for a European criminal law and procedure' by 11 German criminal law professors led by Professor Berndt Schünemann from the University of Munich.[170] It is hoped that the EU discourse will in the future give such views a serious consideration, no longer dismissing them as manifestations of Euroscepticism, nationalism or old-fashioned, parochial protection of sovereignty.

168 As summarised by Avbelj, 'Questioning EU constitutionalisms', supra note 111, p. 8.
169 'Manifesto on the European Criminal Policy', supra note 2, p. 715.
170 Ibid., p. 707; Schünemann, 'Alternative draft for a European criminal law and procedure', supra note 2, p. 227.

7 The future of a European Public Prosecutor in the Area of Freedom, Security and Justice

Gerard Conway

1 Introduction

Article 86 TFEU creates a legal basis for the establishment of a European Public Prosecutor (EPP). It potentially represents a very far-reaching innovation in the structure of criminal justice in the Member States and represents the deepest potential encroachment on the core of State sovereignty. The EPP would have competence as a prosecutor in the courts of each of the Member States, representing for the first time the direct involvement of a Union agency as a party instigating proceedings in a national court under a criminal procedure with formal authority within a national criminal justice system relating to both investigation and prosecution. Much has been written in the literature on this topic, beginning with the *Corpus Juris* proposal of the 1990s.[1] To date, progress with an EPP has been notably slow compared to other areas of EU integration, reflecting exactly its sensitivity with regard to sovereignty. However, the logic of incrementalism, quite characteristic of the path of integration in many other spheres, can also be seen with regard to the EPP, and not just with regard to its relationship to Eurojust. The inclusion of a legal basis to extend its jurisdiction to serious crimes of a cross-border dimension is an example: the cross-border dimension element has great potential for the EPP to extend its jurisdiction to a wide variety of crimes. At the time of writing, the future of an EPP remains uncertain. The Commission has exercised its right of initiative and later maintained essentially intact its proposal, notwithstanding only the second use of the yellow-card subsidiarity procedure since the procedure's inclusion in the Lisbon Treaty.[2] This chapter

1 M. Delmas-Marty and J.A.E. Vervaele (eds.), *The Implementation of the Corpus Juris in the Member States: Volumes I–III* (Intersentia, 2000) (including the Guiding Principles of Corpus Juris 2000, Florence Draft).

2 The Commission made its proposal in 2013: European Commission, *Proposal for a Council Regulation on the Establishment of the European Public Prosecutor's Office*, Brussels, 17 July 2013, COM(2013) 534 final 2013/0255 (APP). The most recent version at the time of writing is that prepared by the Latvian presidency: Inter-institutional File 2013/0255 from the Presidency of Latvia to the Council, *Proposal for a Regulation on the Establishment of the European Public Prosecutor's Office*, Brussels, 12 June 2015, 9372/15.

focuses on the question of the structure and competence of an EPP in the context of the development of the concept of an EPP over time, in particular, focusing on: (1) the possible expansion of the jurisdiction of the EPP and (2) its relationship with national authorities. In addition, the question of accountability is addressed. Limitations of space mean that the important question of rights of the suspect can only be partially addressed. The term 'constitutionalisation' is sometimes overused in the context of the EU: the Treaties as interpreted by the Court of Justice have often been said to have constitutionalised the EU as a system, as if the conceptual framework of constitutionalisation almost by itself provides a legitimation of the process,[3] notwithstanding the increasingly contested institutional pathway of the EU. However, the frame of constitutionalisation as a basis for identifying normative concerns is very appropriate for an EPP: the development of an EPP would really give the EU a dimension of power that would transcend the core sovereignty of the Member States. Questions of competence and accountability, therefore, loom large.

The term 'AFSJ' is used to describe what used to be more commonly known as justice and home affairs (JHA), a term introduced at Maastricht to describe the then third pillar, which consisted of two aspects: (1) criminal justice cooperation and (2) cooperation in the area of visa, asylum and immigration. At the Treaty of Amsterdam, the second aspect of JHA – visa, asylum and immigration – was transferred to the first pillar. This meant that the term 'JHA' now covered the third pillar and an aspect of the first pillar. The term JHA has been superseded by AFSJ, although the term JHA is sometimes used still by the institutions. The AFSJ thus has a cross-cutting character. Its effect is to break down any tendency to isolate criminal justice from the internal market, thereby facilitating the idea that an EPP is closely connected with the internal market. This fits easily with the idea of an EPP having jurisdiction over financial crimes against the EU, but extension of its jurisdiction to serious crimes of a cross-border dimension shows the elasticity of the abstract terms 'freedom', 'security' and 'justice' and the ease with which the core idea of an internal market is transcended in favour of a broader conception of integration.

2 Background

The 2001 *Green Paper on Criminal-Law Protection of the Financial Interests of the Community and the Establishment of a European Prosecutor* is a central element of the backdrop to the provisions for an EPP in the Treaty of Lisbon.[4] In turn, the idea of an EPP had first publicly been developed by the

3 See, for example, G. Davies, 'Legislative control of the European Court of Justice' (2014) 51 *Common Market Law Review* 1579.

4 European Commission, *Green Paper on Criminal-Law Protection of the Financial Interests of the Community and the Establishment of a European Prosecutor*, COM(2001) 715 final, Brussels, 11 December 2001.

so-called *Corpus Juris* group of academics and practitioners in the 1990s in response to a request by the Commission,[5] with a model proposal in 1997, which was revised in 2000[6] (and which is an interesting example of the symbiotic relationship that can often exist between academia and institutional practice in the EU). The Treaty of Maastricht introduced criminal justice cooperation for the first time within the Community or Union, albeit at an intergovernmental level.

This *Corpus Juris* formed the basis for a *Commission Green Paper*,[7] which eventually led to Article 86 TFEU. Article 86 TFEU is largely based on Article III-274 of the Treaty establishing a Constitution for Europe[8]:

1 In order to combat crimes affecting the financial interests of the Union, the Council ... may establish a European Public Prosecutor's Office from Eurojust. The Council shall act unanimously after obtaining the consent of the European Parliament. ... if at least nine Member States wish to establish enhanced cooperation on the basis of the draft regulation concerned, they shall notify the European Parliament, the Council and the Commission accordingly....

2 The European Public Prosecutor's Office shall be responsible for investigating, prosecuting and bringing to judgment, where appropriate in liaison with Europol, the perpetrators of, and accomplices in, offences against the Union's financial interests.... It shall exercise the functions of prosecutor in the competent courts of the Member States in relation to such offences.

3 The regulations referred to in paragraph 1 shall determine the general rules applicable to the European Public Prosecutor's Office, ..., as well as those governing the admissibility of evidence, and the rules applicable to the judicial review of procedural measures taken by it in the performance of its functions.

4 The European Council may, at the same time or subsequently, adopt a decision amending paragraph 1 in order to extend the powers of the European Public Prosecutor's Office to include serious crime having a cross-border dimension ... The European Council shall act unanimously after obtaining the consent of the European Parliament and after consulting the Commission.

5 As Pujas notes, this can be seen in neo-functionalist terms as an example of the importance of the Commission as an agenda-setter: V. Pujas, 'The European Anti-Fraud Office (OLAF): a European policy to fight against economic and financial fraud?' (2003) 7 *Journal of European Public Policy* 778.

6 Delmas-Marty and Vervaele, op cit.

7 European Commission, *Green Paper on criminal law protection of the financial interests of the Community and the establishment of a European prosecutor*, COM(2001) 715 final, Brussels, 11 December 2001.

8 Treaty Establishing a Constitution for Europe, Brussels, 29 October 2004, CIG 87/2/04 REV 2.

Article 86 TFEU, for the most part, reproduces the text in the Treaty establishing a Constitution for Europe. One significant difference between the Treaty of Lisbon provisions and the Constitutional Treaty quoted above is the provision in Article 86(1)(3) TFEU enabling nine or more Member States to proceed with an EPP on the basis of enhanced cooperation.[9] The current state of negotiations indicates that an EPP could only be adopted under this latter provision, as a number of Member States, especially the UK, are not in favour of its creation.

A justification quite often given for considering an EPP has been stated to be 'a long held suspicion in Brussels that Member States fight fraud against their own national budgets with more alacrity than fraud against the European budget', although the actual extent of fraud on the Union budget is debatable due to a widely reported lack of reliable information.[10] The UK House of Lords European Select Committee has also noted the lack of dedicated national procedures for combating such fraud,[11] i.e., it is dealt with within existing national procedures for addressing fraud. Although the proposal for an EPP is motivated by a perception, especially among the EU institutions, that the Member States are less rigorous in pursuing fraud against the Union than against their own budget,[12] there is a lack of empirical data available on the matter in general[13] (and notwithstanding the codification of the principle of assimilation or equivalence in national sanctions for breaches of Union law[14]). The most comprehensive study to date has focused on the perception of national-level officials, which found a divergence between the perspective of national and supranational levels with the latter more likely to see a need for more EU involvement and adoption of an EPP.[15] In the

9 In the UK, ss. 2–5 of the European Union Act 2011 would require a referendum in the UK before it could agree to the UK accepting an EPP into UK law, although there are no indications the UK government wishes to opt-in to the proposed EPP.

10 B.J. Quirke, 'EU fraud: institutional and legal competence' (2009) 51(5) *Crime, Law and Social Change* 531, at p. 532. A pro-integration ideological outlook is also likely to have been influential (if not the most significant influence). See also W.A. Tupman, 'Supranational investigation after Amsterdam, the *Corpus Juris* and Agenda 2000' (1998) 7(2) *Information and Communications Technology Law Review* 85, at p. 87; U. Sieber, 'Euro-fraud: organised fraud against the financial interests of the European Union' (1998) 30(1) *Journal of Crime, Law and Social Change* 1, at p. 18; B.J. Quirke, 'Fraud against European public funds', (1999) 31(3) *Crime, Law and Social Change* 173, at p. 190; M. Zwiers, *The European Public Prosecutor's Office: Analysis of a Multilevel Criminal Justice System* (Intersentia, 2011), pp. 6–7.

11 House of Lords, *Prosecuting Fraud on the Community Finances: The Corpus Juris (with Evidence)*, (9th Report, Session 1998/1999), para 25.

12 Tupman, op cit., p. 87.

13 Quirke (2009), op cit., p. 532; H. Xanthaki, 'What is EU fraud? And can OLAF really combat it?' (2010) 17(1) *Journal of Financial Crime* 133, at pp. 133–140.

14 This was originally done in Article 209a ECT as introduced by the Treaty of Maastricht and is now contained in Article 325(2) TFEU.

15 See M.L. Wade, 'A European Public Prosecutor: potential and pitfalls' (2013) 59 *Crime, Law & Social Change* 439.

absence of clear evidence on the matter, it is difficult to establish that the subsidiarity and proportionality principles are being respected in the adoption of an EPP. Although the Court of Justice takes a very light touch approach to subsidiarity review, subsidiarity also has a political dimension in that the initial decision to proceed with an EPP is a political one that should be consistent with the constitutional values of the EU, including subsidiarity and proportionality. Subsidiarity requires that, in areas that do not fall within its exclusive competence, the Union shall act only if and insofar as the objectives of the proposed action cannot be sufficiently achieved by the Member States, either at central level or at regional and local level, but can rather, by reason of the scale or effects of the proposed action, be better achieved at Union level (Article 5(3) TEU). As the quote above indicates, the sense that there is a need for an EPP is based on a suspicion regarding lack of national enforcement, not on evidence of it. Proportionality requires that EU action does not go further than is necessary to achieve its objective (Article 5(4) TEU), which is relevant to the scope of power granted to an EPP over national enforcement authorities, which again depends on evidence of the current adequacy of national enforcement.

It is clear that the powers of the EPP go considerably beyond the common law tradition in this area. The EPP would have to combine the authority to 'investigate', 'prosecute', and 'bring to judgment'.[16] The legal basis certainly exists in Article 86 TFEU for the EPP to be assigned a full police arm, although it is also possible it would be given a supervisory role in relation to national police, as had been envisaged as a possibility under the *Corpus Juris* proposal.[17] In the current Commission proposal, the EPP can do either, i.e., the delegated EPP at national level may either undertake the investigation measures on his/her own or instruct the competent law enforcement authorities in the Member State where he/she is located (Article 18(1) of the Commission's proposed Regulation, see next section).

The reference to 'bringing to judgment' in Article 86(2) TFEU suggests complete responsibility of the EPP for the prosecution up to a verdict. Although there is a legal basis for EU rules of evidence in Article 86(3), it does not include an earlier radical proposal for 'free movement of evidence', i.e., the idea that evidence admissible in one Member State be automatically admissible in another Member State,[18] which would have dramatic implications for the much more restrictive common law rules of evidence.

The EPP is to be established 'from Eurojust',[19] which currently has a limited remit of facilitating, akin to a diplomatic agent, existing methods of

16 Article 86 TFEU.

17 See *Corpus Juris (Florence Draft)* in Delmas-Marty and Vervaele, op cit., Article 20; Green Paper, supra note 7, at 3.2.1.

18 Green Paper, supra note 7, at 6.3.4.

19 The phrase used in Article 8(1) TFEU. Council Decision establishing Eurojust 2002/187/JHA, 6 March 2002, OJ L 63 of 6 March 2002; Council Decision on the Strengthening of

criminal justice cooperation and coordination between EU Member States. The investigative power attributed to an EPP could also absorb the function of OLAF, a European Anti-Fraud Office that is a semi-autonomous element within the European Commission with responsibility for monitoring and investigating fraud on the Union budget.[20] Whether Eurojust would simply be transformed into an EPP or would be used to assist the formation of an EPP is an open question on the basis of the phrasing in Article 86(1). Whether it would be useful to continue Eurojust depends on several issues: would the EPP be established on the basis of enhanced cooperation involving not all Member States (if an EPP is established, it is very unlikely that all the Member States would initially participate, and the UK is unlikely to ever do so in the foreseeable future)? If an EPP is adopted by only some Member States, at least nine are needed, Eurojust would automatically remain for the non-participating Member States.[21]

3 The 2013 Commission proposal

3.1 The proposal

The Commission issued its proposal for an EPP, based on Article 86 TFEU, in the form of a draft Regulation in 2013.[22] The first paragraph of the accompanying explanatory memorandum of the Regulation itself provides a good summary of Commission thinking on the matter:

> Prosecuting offences against the EU budget is currently within the exclusive competence of Member States and no Union authority exists in this area. While their potential damage is very significant, these offences are not always investigated and prosecuted by the relevant national authorities, as law enforcement resources are limited. As a result, national law enforcement efforts remain often fragmented in this area and the cross-border dimension of these offences usually escapes the attention of the authorities.[23]

For critics of the proposal, this logic may slide too easily from the observation that fraud on the budget of the EU is not being fully prosecuted to the conclusion that an EPP is the most suitable solution. In the context of the

Eurojust amending Decision to establish Eurojust 2009/426/JHA, 4 June 2009, OJ L 138 of 4 June 2009.

20 See S. White, 'EU anti-fraud enforcement: overcoming obstacles' (2010) 17(1) *Journal of Financial Crime* 81.

21 The European Commission accompanied its 2013 proposed Regulation on an EPP with a proposed Regulation to reform Eurojust: ***Proposal for a Regulation of the European Parliament and of the Council on the European Union Agency for Criminal Justice Cooperation* (Eurojust)**, Brussels, 17 July 2013, COM/2013/0535 final – 2013/0256 (COD).

22 European Commission, supra note 2.

23 Ibid, p. 2.

financial crisis, it is easier to justify more determined EU action concerning fraud against what are now more limited resources. The comments observe that because national resources are limited, the offences are not always investigated. Nonetheless, resources of an EPP would not be unlimited either. An additional point made in the quote above, although the comment links it to limited resources rather than to a coordination problem, is that law enforcement against fraud on the EU budget remains fragmented. However, the memorandum immediately moves on to observe that the current levels of information exchange and coordination are not sufficient to achieve this, despite the intensified efforts of Union bodies, such as Eurojust, Europol and the European Anti-Fraud Office (OLAF). The memorandum continues that Eurojust and Europol have a general mandate to facilitate exchange of information and coordinate national criminal investigations and prosecutions, but lack the power to carry out acts of investigation or prosecution themselves, and that OLAF has a mandate to investigate fraud and illegal activities affecting the EU, but its powers are limited to administrative investigations, with the result that action against fraud may currently not be considered as effective, equivalent and deterrent as required under the Treaty. On this basis, the memorandum concludes that the Union not only has the competence under Article 86 TFEU, but also the obligation to act. It further notes that Article 325 TFEU *requires* so from a legal perspective, but taking into account the specific Union rules that apply in this field, the Union is also best placed to protect its own financial interests, including via the prosecution of offences against these interests.[24]

Article 325 TFEU is the provision specifically on fraud, setting out in general a responsibility to effectively tackle fraud and to do so in an equivalent way to combating fraud at national level:

1 The Union and the Member States shall counter fraud and any other illegal activities affecting the financial interests of the Union through measures to be taken in accordance with this Article, which shall act as a deterrent and be such as to afford effective protection in the Member States, and in all the Union's institutions, bodies, offices and agencies.
2 Member States shall take the same measures to counter fraud affecting the financial interests of the Union as they take to counter fraud affecting their own financial interests.
3 Without prejudice to other provisions of the Treaties, the Member States shall coordinate their action aimed at protecting the financial interests of the Union against fraud. To this end they shall organise, together with the Commission, close and regular cooperation between the competent authorities.

24 Ibid.

> 4 The European Parliament and the Council, acting in accordance with the ordinary legislative procedure, after consulting the Court of Auditors, shall adopt the necessary …

On the face of it, this provision does not require the introduction of an EPP if the Member States are combatting fraud both (1) effectively and (2) in a way equivalent to the combatting of fraud at national level. Thus, the Commission position is that the current approach is neither effective nor satisfies equivalence. In terms of the justification of the Commission proposal regarding subsidiarity and proportionality, one challenge that the proposal needs to meet is that less involved or less intrusive regulation at EU level, through a more intergovernmental approach based on an enhancement of existing coordination, could not attain a level of effectiveness and equivalence. On subsidiarity, the Commission summarises its reasoning as follows:

> In accordance with the subsidiarity principle, this objective can only be achieved at Union level by reason of its scale and effects. As stated above, the present situation, in which the prosecution of offences against the Union's financial interests is exclusively in the hands of the authorities of the Member States is not satisfactory and does not sufficiently achieve the objective of fighting effectively against offences affecting the Union budget.[25]

The Commission describes the model it proposes as a decentralised, integrated office, relying on national judicial systems, which its Impact Assessment concluded offered the most benefits and generates the lowest costs.[26]

The main elements of the Commission's proposed Regulation are:

- Exclusive competence for an EPP to try in the courts of the Member States crimes against the financial interest (but not other cross-border crimes) of the EU (Article 11(4)).
- In the event of a conflict between the Regulation and national law, national law would prevail (Article 11(3)).
- EPP jurisdiction over ancillary offences, offences connected with crimes against the financial interests of the EU where the latter are the preponderant offences on the same facts (Article 13).
- Investigative measures to be undertaken by the EPP itself or it could direct national authorities to do so (Article 18(1)), but coercive powers would be carried out by national authorities (Article 18(6)) subject to national judicial control.

25 Ibid, p. 4.

26 Ibid.; European Commission Staff Working Document, *Impact Assessment Accompanying the Proposal for a Council Regulation on the establishment of the European Public Prosecutor's Office*, Brussels, 17 July 2013 SWD(2013) 274 final.

- Judicial review of the validity of acts of the EPP to take place at national level without recourse to the jurisdiction of the Court of Justice of the EU, but preliminary rulings to the Court of Justice could be made under Article 267 TFEU (Recital 38).
- European Delegated Prosecutors (EDPs) would be established at national level, subject to direction of the EPP (Articles 6, 18(4)).[27]

Article 11(4) on exclusive competence is of especial importance. It can be compared to the doctrine of pre-emption in external relations developed by the Court of Justice: once the EU develops a competence, national competence is prevented.[28] In the context of an EPP, it would mean that once an EPP has competence regarding a matter, national competence is excluded unless the facts disclose offences that are preponderantly subject to national law. As discussed further below, this may become complex where both national interests and EU interests are at stake, which the latest version of the Regulation, at the time of writing, addresses in somewhat more detail (see Section 4.5 below).

On proportionality, the Commission stated that key features of the proposal, such as the choice of the law that applies to investigative measures, the figure of Delegated Prosecutors, the decentralised character of the European Public Prosecutor's Office and the system of judicial review, were designed in order not to go beyond what was necessary to achieve the main objectives of the proposal.[29]

3.2 *The proposal in context – models of an EPP*

Although Article 86 TFEU provides for an EPP to operate within each national procedure, various models of an EPP are possible and remain undetermined by Article 86 TFEU and would be open to the Member States to adopt through amending the Commission proposal. Several models have been proposed in academic literature, with a typology of models possible to envisage. Unsurprisingly in light of the development of criminal justice cooperation, in the EU, these models can be mapped on an axis ranging from a more intergovernmental or horizontal method to a more supranational or vertical approach.[30] At the intergovernmental end of the spectrum, it is possible to even base an EPP on Article 85 TFEU, dealing with Eurojust.[31] On this model, Eurojust would be developed to the fullest extent on the

27 The present contribution, due to limitations of space, does not consider the detail of the proposal concerning appointment and dismissal of an EPP, for example.

28 Case 22/70, *Commission v Council (Re European Road Transport Agreement)* (1971) ECR 263 *(ERTA)*.

29 Ibid.

30 Varying terminology is found in the literature.

31 S. White and N. Dorn, 'Towards a decentralised European Public Prosecutor's Office' (2012) 89 *Amicus Curiae* 2, at pp. 3–4. See also K. Ligeti and M. Simonato, 'The European

basis of Article 85 TFEU, involving an enhancement of national cooperation, and could be renamed an EPP, but would essentially be a cooperative entity without enforcement power in national systems. At the supranational end of the spectrum, a very vertical model would provide for an EPP to operate within national systems through delegated EPPs, but independently of national prosecutors, as opposed to national prosecutors being designated with a second hat of being a delegated EPP, as well as exercising national prosecution power. The Commission proposal provides that an EPP could either direct national authorities in investigation and prosecution or do so itself and seems to leave open the question of whether an EPP would be an independent entity at national level or would become a part of the functions of national prosecution authorities, who would be designated as delegated EPPs. Article 10(1) of the Commission proposal provides that the European Delegated Prosecutors (the national-level appointees) shall be appointed by the European Public Prosecutor from a list of at least three candidates, who comply with the requirements set out in paragraph 2, submitted by the Member State(s) concerned. This indicates that an EPP would not automatically be head of national prosecution service, but this is not ruled out, and the relationship of delegated EPPs with national prosecution authorities is not really addressed. Article 10(2) confirms the possibility of an integrated national prosecutor and delegated EPP, in stating that Member States shall appoint the European Delegated Prosecutor as a prosecutor under national law, *if at the time of his/her appointment as a European Delegated Prosecutor, he/she did not have this status already*. The Commission proposal states in Article 6(5) that *when a delegated EPP acts within their mandate under the draft Regulation*, they shall be fully independent from the national prosecution bodies and have no obligations with regard to them, again leaving open the possibility that a national prosecution official could wear two hats, albeit having to act independently when exercising the powers of a delegated EPP. The advantages of a more integrated model would be greater coordination and less inter-institutional rivalry at national level. A further variation would be for a collegial model at supranational level: an EPP would make collective decisions as a college, with delegated EPPs voting on decisions, which is not what the Commission proposal envisages (providing in Article 6(5) that delegated EPPs will act under the instructions of an EPP).[32]

As discussed below in Section 4.5, one of the main changes made to the Commission proposal during the legislative process to date has been to replace the Commission's unitary, hierarchical model with a much more collegiate model.

Public Prosecutor's Office: towards a truly European prosecution service?' (2013) 4(1) *New Journal of European Criminal Law* 7, at p. 11.

32 Ligeti and Simonato, op cit., pp. 13–14, who associate a collegial model with minimal approach.

4 Reaction to the Commission proposal

4.1 The reaction of national parliaments – subsidiarity concerns and the yellow-card procedure

The Commission's proposed regulation on an EPP triggered the first major use of the new yellow-card procedure introduced by the Treaty of Lisbon, under which one-third of national parliaments can trigger a review of a proposed legislation (before it is formally presented to the European Parliament and the Council in the legislative process). It was triggered in October 2013 submissions by the parliaments of the following Member States: Austria, Belgium, Croatia, Cyprus, Czech Republic, Finland, France, Germany, Hungary, Ireland, Italy, Lithuania, Malta, the Netherlands, Poland, Portugal, Romania, Slovakia, Slovenia, Spain, Sweden and the United Kingdom, which included 13 reasoned opinions from parliaments, sometimes with two opinions from the same Member State.[33] Taken as a whole, several subsidiarity concerns can be identified across the submissions of Member State parliaments, who invoked (for the second time since its adoption[34]) the yellow-card procedure introduced by the Lisbon Treaty:

- The Commission has not demonstrated enough data to prove the insufficiency of Member State action.
- The Commission has not adequately considered the possibility of enhancing the use of existing mechanisms, especially in light of the quite recent new Decision of Eurojust.
- The Commission's proposal goes too far in according exclusive competence to an EPP and that supporting or complementary competence would be sufficient.
- The competence of an EPP, especially as regards ancillary competences and exclusive instructions, needs to be further specified.
- The Commission's proposal would be best reformulated along a more collegiate, less supranational, model.
- The Commission's proposal generally does not pay adequate attention to the impact of the proposal on national constitutional and/or procedural law, including in the list of investigative powers in Article 26 of the draft Regulation.
- The appointment of delegated prosecutors requires clarification.

33 See the IPEX website: www.ipex.eu/IPEXL-WEB/dossier/document/COM20130534.do.

34 For a fuller discussion, see, for example, G. Conway, 'Article 69 TFEU', in Centre for International Legal Studies, *Smith & Herzog on the Law of the European Union* (19th edn, Lexis-Nexis, 2015).

- The admissibility of evidence needs to be more fully addressed (somewhat surprisingly, this point was not emphasised much by common law jurisdictions, perhaps because both common law jurisdictions, the UK and Ireland, raised more fundamental objections to the proposal overall).[35]
- The risk of resources being diverted from national priorities.[36]

Only a few national parliaments also referred to the accompanying Eurojust proposal in any detail, but several pointed out the possibility of considering more fully alternatives to the Commission model of an EPP. Overall, parliaments did not tend to rank or weigh their concerns, although some noted constitutional objections at national level; for example, concerning the independence of the public prosecutor. More of a sense of the weight of concerns can be gathered from an interparliamentary declaration jointly made on behalf of a number of parliaments in 2014, discussed further below in Section 4.4.

4.2 Opinion of Committee of the Regions

The Committee of the Regions[37] welcomed the proposal as providing the EU with comparable resources to national institutions for combatting fraud against the EU and contributing to systematic prosecution of fraud.[38] It had no fundamental subsidiarity-related objections to giving a European Public Prosecutor's Office the power to prosecute offences against the Union, despite the impact this will have on national sovereignty in one of the most sensitive areas.[39] However, it pointed out that in its Communication, the Commission did not adequately consider the subnational dimension when assessing the sufficiency of Member State action, whereas the principle of subsidiarity as enshrined in Article 5(3) of the Treaty on European Union differentiates between the central, regional and local levels[40] and suggested amending the structure so as to allow at least one national or regional prosecutor at the seat of the EPP.[41] It stressed that the financial interests of the Union must be protected in all Member States without exception, which was why a supranational framework and institution

35 The House of Lords, op cit., referred to it briefly at para 14.

36 See, for example, ibid.

37 Opinion of the Committee of the Regions: The Establishment of the European Public Prosecutor's Office (105th Plenary Session, 30–31 January 2014), OJ C 126, 26 April 2014, p. 37. The Committee of the Regions was one of the EU bodies to whom the Commission proposal was addressed. The Committee of the Regions is appointed as a consultative body to advise the EU institutions on regional cross-border issues: Article 13 TEU and Articles 305–307 TFEU.

38 Opinion of the Committee of the Regions, op cit., paras 2 and 3.

39 Ibid., para 7.

40 Ibid., para 10.

41 Ibid., para 16.

can provide added value in comparison with national law enforcement,[42] thereby indicating that in its view there existed variations or exceptions in enforcement at national level that an EPP could better address than could a refinement or development of existing mechanisms. However, the Committee did not cite any specific national weaknesses. Further, on subsidiarity, it recommended that the responsibilities of the EPP be limited in order to take into account the subsidiarity-related concerns that have been raised and that the criminal offences that are to fall within the remit of the European Public Prosecutor's Office be defined in an annex to the proposal for the sake of legal and procedural clarity, which will need to be ensured precisely and unequivocally.[43] An important recommendation that the Committee made related to the proposal for exclusive responsibility or competence of an EPP, which it considered would go too far, and instead suggested that the Member States and the European Public Prosecutor's Office be given concurrent responsibility, while at the same time making it possible for the European Public Prosecutor's Office to take over investigations (evocation) if national prosecutors are already investigating and it turns out that the financial interests of the Union are at stake[44] (see further below). A further aspect of competence concerns human rights. In this regard, the Committee proposed that, in addition to the EU Charter of Fundamental Rights, the Member States would also be bound by their own fundamental rights and by the European Convention on Human Rights (ECHR) when implementing the Regulation, to the extent that this involved applying their own national law.[45] Nonetheless, given that an EPP could take over any investigation with an EU dimension, the scope for the application of national constitutional guarantees seems to be limited, since it seems an EPP would not be bound by these guarantees insofar as they were inconsistent with EU law, at least any obligation to do this by the EPP is not made explicit in the Committee's opinion. The Committee noted that intrusive investigative powers of an EPP should be defined[46] and that the issue of enforcement had not been addressed in the proposal and indicated a need for rules on this matter,[47] while also suggesting that in mixed cases involving both the interests of the EU and Member States, a transaction (or settlement) could only be entered into by an EPP with the consent of the Member State concerned.[48]

Overall, the Committee is supportive of the Commission proposal. It pays more attention to the subsidiarity concerns of national parliaments, but the

42 Ibid., para 11.
43 Ibid., paras 20–21.
44 Ibid., para 23.
45 Ibid., para 26.
46 Ibid., para 31.
47 Ibid., para 32.
48 Ibid., para 34.

amendments it proposes to address this are modest and likely would not significantly detract from the powers of an EPP as the Commission has envisaged (as discussed further below).

4.3 *Response of the Commission to national parliaments*

The Commission issued, in some respects, quite a brief response, not replying very specifically or in detail to the objections raised by national parliaments.[49] The review by the Commission was triggered in October 2013 and the Commission responded shortly after in November 2013. For example, concerning the argument from the UK House of Commons (among others) that the proposal was insufficiently justified and tended to conflate the elements of the subsidiarity test (whether, first, the proposed action could be sufficiently achieved by the Member States acting on their own and, second, whether the action can be better achieved at Union level, by reason of scale and effects by the EU), the Commission responded as follows:

> The subsidiarity test involves two closely interrelated questions: first, whether the proposed action can or cannot be sufficiently achieved by the Member States acting on their own; and second, whether the action can be, by reason of its scale or effects, better achieved at Union level. Both steps are connected, as the insufficiency of Member State action will often lead to a finding that Union action will better achieve the proposed policy objective. The text of Article 5(3) TEU makes the connection clear ('but can rather') and the Court of Justice of the European Union has often carried out one single analysis of the two questions, implicitly recognising a certain margin of discretion to the Union institutions.[50]

On the issue of whether existing or alternative mechanisms could be used to achieve the same objective of combatting, the Commission was somewhat more elaborate. It observed that 'objective and clear statistical information shows that the Treaty objective of an effective, deterrent and equivalent level of protection is not achieved in general', in particular referring to reports from OLAF. It did not, however, reply specifically to the concern raised by the Cypriot parliament, for example, that data were limited in nature and did not demonstrate the comparative efficiency of different alternative approaches to that proposed by the Commission.[51]

49 European Commission, *Communication on the Review of the Proposal for a Council regulation on the Establishment of the European Public Prosecutor's Office with Regard to the Principle of Subsidiarity, in accordance with Protocol No. 2*, COM(2013) 851 final.

50 Ibid., p. 4 (references omitted).

51 See Reasoned Opinion submitted by the House of Representatives of the Republic of Cyprus with regard to the Commission's proposal for a Council Regulation on the establishment of the European Public Prosecutor's Office, COM(2013) 534.

On the added value that an EPP would bring (a key issue raised by national parliaments as insufficiently addressed by the Commission), the Commission identified six elements in favour of its proposal. However, it did not seek to rejustify them in light of the objections raised by national parliaments other than noting that the proposal seeks: the strengthening of procedural safeguards; the establishment of a common, Union-level prosecution policy, preventing forum-shopping by perpetrators; the likelihood of greater detention and more effective coordination; a reduction in the time spent on mutual legal assistance; greater ease of admissibility of evidence; and pooling of expertise.[52]

On the possibility of a more collegial structure, the Commission considered that this was not a subsidiarity issue, since it was about a different way of dealing with the matter at Union level, rather than not dealing with it at Union level and instead doing so at national level. On this basis, it seems the Commission does not consider proportionality an aspect of subsidiarity,[53] which is surprising given that the relevant Treaty Protocol addresses both subsidiarity and proportionality. However, the Commission went on to state that a fully-fledged collegial structure could hamper the efficiency of an EPP, rendering its decision-making less efficient.[54]

On exclusive competences, the Commission repeated its earlier approach that the need to grant the European Public Prosecutor's Office exclusive competence for all crimes affecting the financial interests of the Union, including non-cross-border cases, arises out of the nature of the crimes in question, which have an intrinsic Union dimension. It rejected the view of the National Assembly of Hungary[55] that Article 86 TFEU did not provide for exclusive competence, by noting that that fact did not mean secondary legislation could not establish exclusive competence.[56] On ancillary competences, the Commission noted that a rule of preponderance, based on the relevant facts relating more to national offences than an offence against the EU, could result in prosecutions being dealt with at national level (rather than EU level) and that the principle of *ne bis in idem* would mean parallel proceedings could not be allowed once a final decision had been taken in one case relevant.[57] However, this presupposes an *in concreto* application of *ne bis in idem*, as opposed to an *in abstracto* application, and the Commission did not note the significance of the distinction. An *in abstracto* application of *ne bis in idem* only prevents prosecution of the same offences, it does not

52 European Commission, supra note 49, pp. 9–10.

53 Ibid., p. 10.

54 Ibid.

55 Reasoned Opinion of the Parliament of Hungary of 21 October 2013 in accordance with Act No. XXXVI of 2012 on the Hungarian National Assembly and Resolution No. 46/1994 (IX. 30).

56 European Commission, supra note 37, p. 11.

57 Ibid., 12.

prevent several different charges relating to the same facts from being tried successively; for example, the forgery of financial documents could be subject to charges relating to the act of forgery itself as well as any consequential misappropriation of monies.

Overall, the response of the Commission to national parliaments was essentially formalistic and minimal. In some respects, concerns were not specifically or substantively addressed, especially concerning the comparative merits of the Commission proposal over less intrusive alternatives, as discussed in the next section.

4.4 *Common declaration of the inter-parliamentary exchange*

The minimalistic approach of the Commission is reflected in the outcome of a meeting of 21 chambers of 17 parliaments at the invitation of the Commission, which took place in September 2014 at the French National Assembly. In the communiqué published after the meeting, it was noted that the Commission had confirmed its original proposal following the yellow-card and that a number of parliaments were not entirely satisfied with this.[58] The two main concerns of France were the avoidance of a hierarchical relationship between an EPP and national prosecutors and the protection of personal property of suspects. The communiqué summarised the debate and the positions of the parties as follows:

> It emerged from the debate that the majority of Member States accepted the principle of a European prosecutor but that they had objections to certain of the specific points in the Commission proposal. Concrete or specific examples: (1) the European prosecutor should take the form of a college (Hungary, Greece, Croatia, France and Lithuania), (2) the European prosecutor should be chosen by the European parliament (Germany), (3) the competences of the European prosecutor should be clearly defined (Germany, Luxembourg, and Lithuania) and (4) the competence of a European prosecutor should not threaten fundamental rights (Germany, Croatia and France). Given that national parliaments should be able to play their role in European debate, it was pleaded – by Mme Margehm (Belgium – Chamber) – that national parliaments would together deliver a strong message to the European Commission. Only the representatives of the Netherlands and of the United Kingdom considered that a European prosecutor was superfluous.[59]

58 La Cellule d'Analyse Européenne de l'Assemblée Nationale de France, *Réunion Interparliamentaire Sur Le Parquet Européen et La Protection de Données à Caractère Personnel – Rapport*, 17 September 2014, pp. 2–3.

59 Ibid., p.2 (author's translation from the original French).

The meeting resulted in a common declaration signed by representatives of all the Chambers except the House of Representatives of the Netherlands, the House of Commons of the United Kingdom, and the Riksdag of Sweden.

The key point in the common declaration was the belief that the EPP should have a collegial structure. It was also noted that judicial review, rules on the admissibility of evidence and limitation/prescription periods still needed to be regulated. This is fully reflected in the latest draft of the EP Regulation prepared by the Latvian presidency of the Council and published in June 2015.

4.5 *Amendments in the legislative process*

The Latvian presidency published a proposed Regulation for an EPP in June 2015,[60] which it noted was the product of intense work on the first five chapters of the Commission's proposal.[61] This document represents a comprehensive framework for an EPP and the key change it represents from the original Commission proposals is an innovative, fully collegial structure for an EPP, with several layers of authority and of checks and balances built into it. First, the document provides it is to apply only to offences against the financial interests of the EU (Articles 4, 17), so the possibility for broader jurisdiction over serious cross-border crimes is not included. On the central question from a sovereignty point of view, the document proposes a right of pre-emption (which it calls 'evocation') for an EPP (Article 21a), but supplements this with a more sovereignty-sensitive position in the case of ancillary offences, i.e., in cases where the facts disclose offences against both the EU and offences contrary to national law (Article 18). The European prosecutor has a right to take over a prosecution, i.e., to evoke, under Article 21a, except where the primary offences disclosed by evidence relate to national law (if there is disagreement on the latter, the issue is to be settled by the national authorities under Article 8). The proposed structure is notable for its novelty and attempt to balance supranational and national concerns. The structure is fourfold: a coordinating role for a Chief European Prosecutor and two deputies, operational decision-making by a system of Chambers consisting of three members, supervision of national investigation and prosecution by European prosecutors appointed from national systems, and actual conduct of investigation and prosecution by delegated European prosecutors appointed from and operating within the national prosecution/ system (Articles 7–12). Under Article 8, the College is to consist of the Chief European Prosecutor and European prosecutors, is to decide by simple majority and is to have responsibility for strategic direction, general oversight

60 Inter-institutional File 2013/0255, *Proposal for a Regulation on the Establishment of the European Public Prosecutor's Office*, Brussels, 12 June 2015 (OR. en), 9372/15.

61 Ibid., p. 1.

of individual cases (but not operational decisions), and the adoption of the Internal Rules of Procedure (to be adopted by two-thirds majority under Article 16(2)). The Chief Delegated European Prosecutors will inform a Chamber of the existence of facts possibly disclosing an offence against the financial resources of the EU for a decision whether to proceed with investigation and/or prosecution (Article 20), which should minimise the need to invoke the Article 21a right of evocation. When the Chamber orders that proceedings are to begin, the European delegated prosecutor at national level, who may be an official appointed specifically to this function or may also exercise national prosecution responsibilities, will carry out the investigation and prosecution where appropriate (Article 12), under supervision of the European prosecutor (Article 11). In certain, exceptional cases, the European prosecutor may undertake the investigation himself/herself, in the interests of efficiency given the seriousness of the offence, the involvement of a member of the EU institutions or the inability of the European delegated prosecutor to carry it out (Article 23(4)). Investigation and prosecution at national level by delegated European prosecutors shall entail the same powers as exist in these areas under national law, either exercised by the delegated European prosecutor or by national authorities acting under direction of the former (Articles 23, 25), while Article 26 specifies certain powers they will have in serious cases (involving a possibility of four years or more in prison), which generally already exist in national law: search, production of documents, freezing of assets and future financial transactions and interception of electronic communications. In exceptional cases, the European prosecutor may give instructions to the European delegated prosecutor and carry out investigation/prosecution whenever necessary for an efficient or coherent handling of the case or in the interests of justice (Article 11(2)). This is quite a broad basis for a European prosecutor to direct the delegated European prosecutor and if not circumscribed by practice or more fully specified in later drafting might undermine the vision of responsibilities between the two functions, and the same applies to the use of Article 23(4). The points raised in the common declaration above are addressed except for limitation periods: judicial review is left subject to two alternative approaches to be determined later in the drafting process, either to take place entirely under national law or before the ECJ regarding procedural matters, but without prejudice to Article 267 TFEU (Article 33); and evidence gathered is to be automatically admissible irrespective of national rules if decided by the national court (Article 30). Regarding areas where there are clear differences between the common law and civil law traditions, provision for automatic admissibility of evidence in Article 30 is clearly contrary to the much more restrictive common law approach to admissibility of evidence, while pre-trial detention is to be governed by national law under Article 26b.

Some ambiguity possibly exists regarding the hierarchical relationship between EU law and national law. While the Regulation is stated to prevail where both it and national law are applicable, specific provisions make national law determinative in certain situations, chiefly regarding ancillary offences under Article 8.

If an EPP Regulation is adopted, then the draft presented by Latvia is perhaps as sensitive to national sovereignty in most respects as could be expected (apart perhaps from the provision on automatic admissibility of evidence). However, the preliminary reference procedure under Article 267 will presumably apply, and this leaves open the possibility of an expansive approach by the CJEU to the powers of the European prosecutor based on considerations of effectiveness and uniformity at the level of Treaty interpretation under Article 86, which could minimise the autonomy of the European delegated prosecutor and the scope for national competence regarding ancillary offences.

5 The EPP in context: AFSJ with or without an EPP

5.1 General comments on the AFSJ

The AFSJ can be conceptualised very broadly as covering the realisation of the internal market principles of free movement, along with associated concerns as to individual rights. It is perhaps best to see it more specifically as concerning the security and law-enforcement aspects of free movement, including the question of individual rights, connoted by the term 'freedom'. The EPP is the most important aspect of the AFSJ to date in the sense of having the most profound impact in national legal systems, involving as it would for the first time an EU-level institution acting as a party, and a primary party at that, with in the criminal procedure of Member States (although Commission powers regarding competition law, which can be quite intrusive, might be analogised here to some extent). It would involve the most intrusive use of national law in the enforcement of EU law, i.e., criminal sanctions. This is quite unique among transnational legal institutions and illustrates well that the EU crosses into national sovereignty in a way that can be compared to a federal or confederal system.

5.2 Constitutional concerns

5.2.1 Legitimacy of supranational criminal law[62]

The EPP proposal has clearly far-reaching implications for the legal systems of the Member States in what is generally acknowledged to be the sovereignty-sensitive area of criminal law and procedure. In a quite subtly worded formula, the Opinion of the Committee of the Regions notes that

62 E. Herlin-Karnell, *The Constitutional Dimension of European Criminal Law* (Hart Publishing, 2012).

it 'underlines that the Member States would also be bound by their own fundamental rights and by the European Convention on Human Rights (ECHR) when implementing the Regulation, *to the extent that this involved applying their own national law*'.[63] The last proviso might give the impression that national law may still have a determinative effect in some way, but does not address the extent to which this is so. As noted above, the scope of the Commission proposal, in the context of the potential application by the Court of Justice of its standard meta-teleological reasoning, and by analogy with case law on pre-emption and exclusivity in external relations law, could make great in-roads into the criminal law and procedure of Member States. Thus, in the process of adopting an EPP, Member States need to reflect on the connection between the rationale of criminal punishment and State sovereignty, rather than employing the more functional logic of an internal market based on a desire for quickly facilitating investigation and prosecution without adequate attention to normative principles of national criminal law.[64] Except with regard to mutual admissibility of evidence, the latest draft of the Regulation is more sensitive to national sovereignty as well as to procedural safeguards (the latter set out in Article 32, facilitated by a range of very recent EU instruments).

5.2.2 Defining competences and models of the structure of an EPP

If an EPP proposal is ever formally adopted, a key issue affecting its operation will be interpretation of its competences by the CJEU. There are two primary jurisdictional or competence issues here. First, what threshold of impact on EU finances is needed in order for fraud to be considered fraud against the EU budget, as opposed to fraud against national budgets? Where money is allocated directly by the EU (e.g., through structural funds, although how these are spent is largely for the discretion of the Member States), there is a clear connection with the EU. However, when the EU is assisting or supplementing Member State initiatives, it may be harder to determine what is the preponderant interest at stake. Based on the pattern of EU case law, the Court tends to assert competence when there is any potential impact at EU or cross-border level (e.g., the *Dassonville* formula[65] in the context of free movement whereby any actual or potential Union dimension is enough to engage internal market competence). The Court has not yet developed any clear *de minimis* doctrine in the area of free movement (although there are some indications in case law of this at times), and while the Court has adopted an appreciable impact on cross-border competition as a threshold

63 Opinion of the Committee of the Regions, op cit., para 26, emphasis added.
64 See generally, Herlin-Karnell, op cit., passim.
65 Case 8/74, *Procureur du Roi v Benoît and Gustave Dassonville* (1974) ECR 837.

for EU competition law,[66] this has not been applied systematically in that context either.

A similar issue arises, but in a more amplified way, in the context of the possible extension of the competence of an EPP to crimes with a cross-border dimension. This has the potential for a very great extension of EPP jurisdiction if a similar approach as found in the *Dassonville* line of case law were followed, whereby any cross-border dimension was enough to engage Union competence. The famous *Dassonville* formula engages free movement rights or rules whenever a national trading rule is 'capable of hindering, directly or indirectly, actually or potentially, intra-Community trade'. What will matter here is the threshold rendering a crime within EPP jurisdiction; if the *Dassonville* formula was applied by analogy, very many criminal offences would be brought within the jurisdiction of an EPP. Article 86 TFEU does adopt a threshold of 'serious crime', which should exclude the hugely expansive approach in *Dassonville*, but this is still a broad category and could potentially cover any offences other than summary or petty offences. Organised crime, drug dealing, the supply of unlawful weapons, terrorism and many of the crimes listed in existing EU instruments as having an EU dimension (e.g., the list of 32 in the EAW for which double criminality is not needed) could encroach very significantly on national competences.

As noted above, the Committee of the Regions proposed that an EPP be given concurrent responsibility, while at the same time making it possible for the EPP to take over investigations (evocation) if national prosecutors are already investigating and it turns out that the financial interests of the Union are at stake,[67] a point addressed in detail in the Council as discussed above in Section 4.5. Although this proposal has the appearance of limiting the competence of an EPP, the effect would not be that different to exclusive competence for an EPP, it would simply (possibly) affect the timing of the competence of an EPP: a national-level investigation against fraud could commence, whereupon it could be taken over automatically by an EPP if there was an EU dimension. This proposal would operate very similarly to the notion of shared competences introduced by the Lisbon Treaty, whereby once the EU exercises competence, the Member States lose theirs (and an analogy could also be drawn with the doctrine of parallelism in external relations). However, unlike in the case of shared competences under Article 4 TFEU, the 'loss' of national competence here would be by decision of an EU-level supranational body (at least according to the model of an EPP proposed by the Commission, which the Committee of the Regions largely agrees with), rather than the collective decision of Member State representatives and the European Parliament. Further, it is not clear from the proposal

66 Case C-376/98, *Germany v Parliament and Council* (2000) ECR I-8419 ('*Tobacco Advertising*').

67 Opinion of the Committee of the Regions, op cit., para 23.

how it would be possible to distinguish clearly between fraud against national budgets and fraud against the EU budget and how an allocation of competence could be worked out in a scenario on the boundaries of EU and national competence. For example, funding at national level may involve a mix of EU and national financial resources. This could give rise to parallel procedures: it is not obvious why either one or the other should automatically have priority.

A key feature of the current proposal that the Commission identifies as catering to subsidiarity concerns, and which does represent a serious reserve of existing competence to the Member States, is that an EPP would operate within existing national criminal procedures.[68] Thus, an EPP would use standard national methods of investigation and prosecution procedures. There have been some convergences in these as a result of EU law, chiefly through the European Arrest Warrant[69] and European Investigation Order[70] to date, but very significant national differences remain. Harmonisation of these procedures is begun by Article 26 of the Commission proposal, which lists a very extensive set of powers that an EPP could exercise, including search and seizure of premises and property, interception of communications, and surveillance, but not arrest. Further, in the context of the incremental or constructivist logic of EU competence generally, and the push towards uniform standards, it is not difficult to imagine future proposals seeking to harmonise national procedures in the interests of uniform treatment of crime, one of the main reasons given for the adoption of the EPP in the first place.

5.2.3 *Rights of the suspect*

Rights of the suspects have not been addressed in any depth in the Commission's EPP proposal, a point largely remedied, as noted above, in Article 32 of the draft published in June 2015 by the Latvian presidency. The EPP is intended to be embedded in national criminal procedural systems, which already have established regimes of rights of the suspect. Given the acceptance by the EU Member States of the ECHR on national law and the (perhaps) imminent accession of the EU to the ECHR, it might be thought that a consensus exists as to the basic rights of suspects. However, in some respects at least, the ECHR in this context really does represent minimum standards. Criminal procedural regimes vary quite markedly from the common law to the civil law traditions, perhaps most obviously in the scope of entitlement to jury trial, associated rules concerning the admissibility of evidence and the permissibility of investigative detention. In this context, the common law can be seen as more rights-focused, i.e., the balance between the enforcement powers of

68 The EPP will not replace Eurojust, which will continue in its current role regarding all offences other than those against the financial interests of the EU.
69 OJ L 190 18/07/2002 p. 1.
70 OJ L 130 1.5.2014 p. 1.

criminal justice institutions and the rights of the suspects is more clearly titled toward the latter in the common law: in serious cases, there is a right to a jury trial (although there is some use of jury trials in civil law Member States), while in all trials quite strict rules governing what evidence can be admitted (e.g., character evidence is usually not admissible until the sentencing stage) and investigative detention (i.e., detention prior to a decision to charge with specific offences) is generally prohibited. At present, cooperation in these matters, i.e., mutual legal assistance, is regulated by the European Arrest Warrant and the European Investigation Order, the implementation of which has been arranged so as to satisfy common law concerns regarding investigative detention,[71] while existing practice in extradition and MLA and now the EAW allows transfer or surrender of suspects from a common law jurisdiction to a civil law one where there may be no jury trial. An EPP would be acting primarily within the national law of one Member State, rather than in the context of MLA. If criminal justice cooperation develops at EU level in favour of more harmonisation and convergence, or MLA becomes especially prevalent in the context of an EPP (e.g., regarding complex cases with a cross-border dimension, which seems quite likely), pressure may be placed on the common law tradition to accept features such as greater use of investigative detention. It is not difficult to envisage arguments being made that the treatment of suspects regarding offences against the EU budget (and perhaps later regarding serious cross-border offences) varies from one Member State to another and that equality before the law requires greater harmonisation, and this is certainly something that could be developed through judicial activism by the CJEU. However, it might be that the mutual recognition principle would prevail here as it has prevailed in the context of free movement of goods, to favour continued diversity of national traditions, rather than harmonisation of procedures. It seems unlikely that common law jurisdiction would change current practice and surrender suspects for investigative detention. The *Corpus Juris* proposal envisaged a Judge of Freedoms being created, with the specific function of ensuring the rights of the suspect in the context of an EPP,[72] a proposal not included in the current draft.

5.2.4 *Accountability and a separation of powers in the criminal justice process*

Although not typically an aspect considered under the heading of rights of the suspect,[73] the configuration of powers in a criminal justice system, and

71 See, for example, in Ireland, the European Arrest Warrant Act 2003, s. 11(3).

72 Article 25 of the *Corpus Juris* and in its Article 27 on national appeals.

73 The issue has been the subject of fairly sparse academic commentary, see generally, for example, D.A. Daugherty, 'The separation of powers and abuses in prosecutorial discretion' (1988) 79(3) *Journal of Criminal Law & Criminology*; R.E. Barkow, 'Separation of powers and the criminal law' (2006) 58(4) *Stanford Law Review* 989.

specifically the division of powers between criminal justice institutions, can have a very important practical impact on respect for suspects' rights and on addressing abuses or problems in criminal law enforcement. A separation of powers is emerging as a defining characteristic of common law criminal procedures: there is quite a clear division of responsibility between the police (investigation), the prosecutor (prosecution at trial) and the court (supervision of the trial process subject to the adversarial principle whereby the judge is a neutral umpire and may be sitting with a jury responsible for fact-finding). The advantage of a separation of powers is that bias or corruption is made less likely or less harmful, with more checks and balances. Bias and corruption are not eliminated but are made less likely because they would require more personnel from different institutions to collude. In contrast, with a centralised model characteristic of some civil law jurisdictions, the dominant role of the prosecutor is less subject to an independent police investigation and the balancing effect of a neutral judge and jury. Article 86 TFEU would represent a change in common law jurisdictions. This is not without current precedent, as, for example, in the UK, the Serious Fraud Office both investigates and prosecutes in the context of a more regulatory-style approach to law enforcement in this sphere in which rights of the suspect tend to be less prominent. It is worth noting that the collegial model of an EPP contained in the latest draft of the Regulation reflects a careful and novel balancing of authority within the institution itself between the different levels of authority – delegated European prosecutor, European prosecutors, Chambers and the Chief European Prosecutor and the College.

6 Conclusion

The adoption of an EPP has rightly been described as 'potentially revolutionary'.[74] Various models of an EPP are possible, ranging from a more intergovernmental and collegial approach (even based on Article 85 TFEU) to a more supranational or vertical model based on Article 86 TFEU. Further, an EPP could be independent of national prosecutors or be a second task assigned to existing national prosecution institutions. The latest version of the Regulation at the time of writing marks an important development towards a collegial model. An EPP would involve for the first time the active involvement of an EU institution in national criminal procedure, bringing a supranational criminal competence into the heart of national criminal justice systems with the implications of supremacy and pre-emption of overlapping national competence. This will especially be the case if its jurisdiction is gradually extended to include serious crimes with a cross-border dimension. It is unlikely that an EPP will be adopted on a Union-wide basis; certainly the current UK government has indicated

74 Wade, op cit., p. 440.

clear opposition to any proposal for an EPP. Of decisive importance for the impact of an EPP in national criminal procedure will be its relationship with national authorities: will the logic of supremacy and pre-emption of national competences apply? The Treaty is silent on the issue, which is addressed in the draft Regulation, and much will depend on how the CJEU chooses to interpret the Treaty and whether it extends its pro-integration teleology to this area. In conjunction with the possible extension of an EPP jurisdiction to crimes of a serious cross-border dimension, the scope for long-term displacement of national criminal procedure and national jurisdiction by EU-wide criminal jurisdiction is considerable.

8 Legislating for human rights after Lisbon

The transformative effect of EU measures on the rights of the individual in criminal procedure

Valsamis Mitsilegas

1 Introduction

The entry into force of the Treaty of Lisbon has opened the door to the adoption of European Union human rights law in the field of criminal procedure. Article 82(2) TFEU confers upon the Union express competence to adopt legislation on the rights of individuals in criminal procedure. The conferral of such competence is functional: it exists to the extent that it is necessary to facilitate the operation of mutual recognition in criminal matters. The extent of EU competence is further circumscribed to address national sensitivities on the potential impact of EU harmonisation on national law: the EU has competence to legislate in the field only in the form of Directives; the EU legislators can only adopt minimum rules; and it is stated expressly that such minimum rules must take into account the differences between the legal traditions and systems of Member States. On the basis of Article 82(2) TFEU, a number of measures on the rights of the individual in criminal procedure have been adopted. These are, thus far, a Directive on the right to interpretation and translation;[1] a Directive on the right to information;[2] and a Directive on the right of access to a lawyer.[3] The Commission has also published a Green Paper on the application of EU criminal justice legislation in the field of detention[4] and has tabled, in November 2013, a number of draft Directives on legal aid,[5] procedural safeguards for children[6] and the

1 Directive 2010/64/EU on the right to interpretation and translation in criminal proceedings, OJ L280, 26 October 2010, p. 1.
2 Directive 2012/13/EU on the right to information in criminal proceedings, OJ L142, 1 June 2012, p. 1.
3 Directive 2013/48/EU on the right of access to a lawyer in criminal proceedings and in European Arrest Warrant proceedings, and on the right to have a third party informed upon deprivation of liberty and to communicate with third persons and with consular authorities while deprived of liberty, OJ L294, 6 November 2013, p. 1.
4 COM(2011) 327 final, Brussels, 14 June 2011.
5 COM(2013) 824 final, Brussels, 27 November 2013.
6 COM(2013) 822 final, Brussels, 27 November 2013.

presumption of innocence.[7] These proposals have been accompanied by Commission Recommendations on the right to legal aid[8] and on procedural safeguards for vulnerable persons.[9]

The aim of this chapter is to demonstrate that, notwithstanding the Treaty legal basis limitations and national concerns regarding an adverse impact of EU law on the diversity and integrity of national criminal justice systems, EU legislation on the rights of the individual in criminal procedure will have a transformative effect for the protection of human rights in Europe's area of criminal justice. EU legislative intervention in the field will ensure widening the scope and raising the level of protection of human rights in criminal procedure across the EU; ensure effective enforcement and monitoring of the implementation of these rights at national level; overcome obstacles to the protection of rights arising from divergences in protection at national level; and address the issue of variable geometry in the protection of human rights in Europe's area of criminal justice. This chapter will address each of these points in turn, and synthesise the transformative effect of EU law on the rights of the individual in criminal procedure in its concluding part.

2 Widening the scope and raising the level of protection of procedural rights

Although the Lisbon Treaty has conferred upon the EU competence to legislate in the form of minimum rules, a careful reading of all Directives adopted thus far reveals that the scope and level of protection envisaged in EU law is considerable. With regard to the scope of application, it is important to note that, notwithstanding the link with mutual recognition that the legal basis to these instruments (Article 82(2) TFEU) entails, all adopted measures apply not only in cross-border cases involving the operation of the European Arrest Warrant system, but also in purely domestic cases.[10] This is an important development, as the implementation of the EU procedural rights measures in domestic law will have to cover all cases in the field of domestic criminal procedure that fall within the scope of the Directives. As Caeiro has noted, the Directives have created an autonomous, self-designed project for the protection of individual rights in criminal proceedings before the authorities of Member States.[11] In this manner, it can be argued that the

7 COM(2013) 821 final, Brussels, 27 November 2013.

8 OJ C 378/11, 24 December 2013.

9 OJ C 378/8, 24 December 2013.

10 Directive on the right to interpretation and translation: Article 1(1); Directive on the right to information: Article 1; Directive on access to a lawyer: Article 1.

11 P. Caeiro, 'Introduction (or: every criminal procedure starts with a Bill of Rights)', in P. Caeiro, *The European Union Agenda on Procedural Safeguards for Suspects or Accused Persons: The 'Second Wave' and its Predictable Impact on Portuguese Law* (Instituto Juridico, Faculdade de Direito, Universidade de Coimbra, 2015) 13, at p. 17.

necessity requirement of Article 82(2) TFEU has in practice been viewed from the perspective of the individual and not solely of the State or of the authorities that are called upon to apply inter-State cooperation.[12] As regards cross-border cases, it is worth noting that the Directive on access to a lawyer extends the applicability of this right not only to the executing,[13] but also to the issuing Member State.[14] However, in a provision reflecting the case law of the Court of Justice on the requirement of speed regarding the operation of the European Arrest Warrant,[15] the Directive places the right of access to a lawyer in European Arrest Warrant cases under strict time limits: the right of a requested person to appoint a lawyer in the issuing Member State is without prejudice to the time limits set out in the European Arrest Warrant Framework Decision or the obligation on the executing judicial authority to decide, within those time limits and the conditions defined under that Framework Decision, whether the person is to be surrendered.[16] All three adopted Directives trigger the rights enshrined therein at an early stage and they apply the rights up to the point of finality of the criminal process: rights are applicable from the time that suspects or accused persons are made aware by the competent authorities of a Member State, by official notification or

12 V. Mitsilegas, 'The limits of mutual trust in Europe's Area of Freedom, Security and Justice: from automatic inter-state cooperation to the slow emergence of the individual', (2012) 31 *Yearbook of European Law 2012* 319.

13 Article 10(1): Member States shall ensure that a requested person has the right of access to a lawyer in the executing Member State upon arrest pursuant to the European arrest warrant. 2. With regard to the content of the right of access to a lawyer in the executing Member State, requested persons shall have the following rights in that Member State: (a) the right of access to a lawyer in such time and in such a manner as to allow the requested persons to exercise their rights effectively and in any event without undue delay from deprivation of liberty; (b) the right to meet and communicate with the lawyer representing them; (c) the right for their lawyer to be present and, in accordance with procedures in national law, participate during a hearing of a requested person by the executing judicial authority. Where a lawyer participates during the hearing this shall be noted using the recording procedure in accordance with the law of the Member State concerned. 3. The rights provided for in Articles 4, 5, 6, 7, 9, and, where a temporary derogation under Article 5(3) is applied, in Article 8, shall apply, mutatis mutandis, to European arrest warrant proceedings in the executing Member State.

14 According to Article 10(4), the competent authority in the executing Member State shall, without undue delay after deprivation of liberty, inform requested persons that they have the right to appoint a lawyer in the issuing Member State. The role of that lawyer in the issuing Member State is to assist the lawyer in the executing Member State by providing that lawyer with information and advice with a view to the effective exercise of the rights of requested persons under Framework Decision 2002/584/JHA. Article 10(5) continues by stating that where requested persons wish to exercise the right to appoint a lawyer in the issuing Member State and do not already have such a lawyer, the competent authority in the executing Member State shall promptly inform the competent authority in the issuing Member State. The competent authority of that Member State must, without undue delay, provide the requested persons with information to facilitate them in appointing a lawyer there.

15 Case C-168/13 PPU, *Jeremy F.*, judgment of 30 May 2013, para 65.

16 Article 10(6).

otherwise, that they are suspected or accused of having committed a criminal offence until the conclusion of the proceedings, which is understood to mean the final determination of the question whether they have committed the offence, including, where applicable, sentencing and the resolution of any appeal.[17] EU law thus establishes a broad temporal scope of application of procedural rights.[18]

The EU Directives on procedural rights in criminal proceedings have translated, expanded and clarified rights enshrined in the ECHR – in particular in Articles 5 and 6 – and in the EU Charter of Fundamental Rights, in particular in Articles 47 and 48.[19] The Directives themselves include provisions to address the key question of the relationship between general ECHR and Charter human rights norms with the specific provisions of EU secondary law on procedural rights. As regards the ECHR, it has been acknowledged from the outset that its provisions constitute the starting point and the benchmark against which the legality and legitimacy of EU secondary legislation on procedural rights should be judged. In the development of EU secondary legislation, every effort has been made from the outset[20] and throughout negotiations to ensure compliance with the ECHR by seeking the opinion of the Council of Europe on draft proposals.[21] Moreover, the Preambles to the adopted EU Directives include extensive references to their relationship with the ECHR. It is noted in particular that the right to interpretation and translation for those who do not speak or understand the language of the proceedings is enshrined in Article 6 of the ECHR, as interpreted in the case law of the European Court of Human Rights and that the Directive on the right to interpretation and translation facilitates the application of that right in practice.[22] The Preamble to the Directive on the right to information states that Article 5 ECHR enshrines the right to liberty and security of person, adding that any restrictions on that right

17 Directive on the right to interpretation and translation, Article 1(2). Directive on the right to information, Article 2(1). Directive on access to a lawyer, Article 2(1).

18 See also in the context of the Directive on the right to interpretation and translation the remarks of AG Bot in his Opinion on Case C-216/4, *Criminal Proceedings against Gavril Covaci*, 7 May 2015, para 51; and in the context of the Directive on the right to information, the same Opinion, para 100.

19 The EU Charter of Fundamental Rights includes a general provision on the right to a fair trial (Article 47) and a specific provision guaranteeing respect for the rights of the defence of anyone who has been charged (Article 48(2)).

20 Roadmap Resolution: point 5: The Council will act in full cooperation with the European Parliament, in accordance with the applicable rules, and will duly collaborate with the Council of Europe.

21 Opinion of the Secretariat on the Commission's proposal for a Directive of the European Parliament and of the Council on 'the right to access to a lawyer in criminal proceedings and on the right to communicate upon arrest', Strasbourg, 9 November 2011; Opinion of the Secretariat on the Commission's proposal for a Directive of the European Parliament and of the Council on 'the right to information in criminal proceedings', Strasbourg, 8 December 2010.

22 Preamble, recital 14.

must not exceed those permitted in accordance with Article 5 ECHR and inferred from the case law of the European Court of Human Rights.[23] The same provision makes reference to Article 6 of the Charter. The Directive on the right of access to a lawyer, on the other hand, while continuing to refer to the ECHR, contains more detailed provisions and arguably demonstrates a greater emphasis on rights as enshrined in the Charter. It is stated that the conditions in which suspects or accused persons are deprived of liberty should fully respect the standards set out in the ECHR, in the Charter and in the case law of the Court of Justice of the European Union and of the European Court of Human Rights.[24] Moreover, the Preamble adopts a holistic approach to rights on the basis of the Charter stating that the Directive upholds and should be implemented in accordance with the fundamental rights and principles recognised by the Charter, including the prohibition of torture and inhuman and degrading treatment, the right to liberty and security, respect for private and family life, the right to the integrity of the person, the rights of the child, integration of persons with disabilities, the right to an effective remedy and the right to a fair trial, the presumption of innocence and the rights of the defence.[25] Both the ECHR and the Charter constitute benchmarks for the provisions of the access to a lawyer Directive: the level of protection should never fall below the standards provided by the ECHR or the Charter as interpreted in the case law of the Court of Justice and of the European Court of Human Rights.[26]

The Preambles to all Directives adopted thus far state that their provisions that correspond to rights guaranteed by the ECHR should be interpreted and implemented consistently with those rights, as interpreted in the relevant case law of the European Court of Human Rights.[27] However, this wording leaves open the possibility of a higher level of protection for provisions that do not correspond to ECHR rights. Moreover, the possibility of offering a higher level of protection is further enshrined in the text of the Directives via the introduction of non-regression clauses, affirming that nothing in the Directives must be construed as limiting or derogating from any of the rights and procedural safeguards that are ensured under the Charter, the ECHR or other relevant provisions of international law or the law of any Member State that provides a higher level of protection.[28] This is in particular the case in situations not explicitly dealt with by EU law.[29] The non-regression clauses

23 Preamble, recital 6.
24 Preamble, recital 29.
25 Preamble, recital 52.
26 Preamble, recital 54.
27 Directive on the right to interpretation and translation, recital 33 (referring also to the Charter and the interpretation by the CJEU); Directive on the right to information, recital 42; Directive on access to a lawyer, recital 53.
28 Directive on the right to interpretation and translation, Article 8; Directive on the right to information, Article 10; Directive on access to a lawyer, Article 14.
29 Directive on the right to interpretation and translation, recital 32; Directive on the right to information, recital 40.

confirm that the Court's case law in *Melloni* does not apply here:[30] national law that provides a high level of protection of procedural rights will apply, even if the level of protection is higher than that provided by EU (in any case minimum) standards. The *Melloni* principles of unity, primacy and effectiveness of EU law take second place here, in particular as regards ensuring the operational effectiveness of the European Arrest Warrant system. As the Preamble to the access to a lawyer Directive states expressly, a higher level of protection by Member States should not constitute an obstacle to the mutual recognition of judicial decisions that those minimum rules are designed to facilitate.[31] On the contrary, it is clear that a higher level of human rights protection would rather facilitate – and not hinder – mutual recognition.

3 Ensuring the enforcement and effective implementation of rights in Member States

The EU Directives on the rights of the individual in criminal procedure will have a significantly positive impact on the protection of fundamental rights in domestic systems of criminal procedure. The Directives translate, clarify and at times go beyond the standards enshrined by the ECHR and the European Court of Human Rights.[32] The standards established therein apply not only to cross-border, but also to domestic cases. And although the aim of the Directives has been to establish minimum standards, in essence they have introduced a series of binding norms that are designed to ensure the respect of human rights and that must be interpreted broadly in order for their practical effectiveness to be ensured.[33] There are four main ways in which the Directives on procedural rights in criminal procedure will enhance the protection of fundamental rights in EU Member States. First of all, a number of key provisions conferring rights in the Directives have direct effect. This means that, in a system of decentralised enforcement of EU law, individuals can evoke and claim rights directly before their national courts if the EU Directives have not been implemented or have been inadequately implemented. Direct effect means in practice that a suspect or accused person can derive a number of key rights – such as the right to an interpreter or the right of access to a lawyer – directly from EU law if national legislation has not made appropriate provision in conformity with EU law. Second, this avenue

30 Case C-399/11, *Melloni*, judgment of 26 February 2013.

31 Preamble, recital 54.

32 For instance, in an important move towards enhancing human rights protection, the Directive on the right to access to a lawyer clarifies and strengthens the impact of the Strasbourg ruling in the case of *Salduz* on national law, by narrowing the national margin of appreciation in implementing the access to a lawyer obligations and in particular by expressly extending the application of the right of access to a lawyer in cases where no deprivation of liberty is involved.

33 Opinion of AG Bot, Case C-216/4, *Criminal Proceedings against Gavril Covaci*, 7 May 2015, paras 32–33, 74.

of decentralised enforcement is coupled with the high level of centralised enforcement of EU criminal law that has been 'normalised' after the entry into force of the Lisbon Treaty. The European Commission now has full powers to monitor the implementation of these Directives by Member States and has the power to introduce infringement proceedings before the Court of Justice when it considers that the Directives have not been implemented adequately. In view of the Court's approach regarding the applicability of the Charter, which will be examined below, and the broad objectives of the procedural rights Directives, the scope of the Commission's monitoring exercises is broader than to check merely the provision of national legislation adopted to specifically implement the EU Directives in question. The Commission is also entitled to monitor national criminal procedure systems more broadly to ensure that effective implementation has taken place, as well as to ensure that rights are applied in practice and not only in the books. Third, and aligned to the point above, national criminal procedural law must be applied and interpreted in compliance and conformity with the Directives. The procedural standards set out in the Directives will have an impact on a wide range of acts under national criminal procedure.[34] Fourth, the implementation of the Directives must take place in compliance with the Charter of Fundamental Rights (Charter). The Charter will apply not only to national legislation that specifically implements the EU Directives on procedural rights, but also to all other elements of domestic criminal procedure that have a connection with EU law on procedural rights in criminal proceedings. In the case of *Fransson*,[35] the Court of Justice adopted a broad interpretation of the application of the Charter, including in cases where national legislation does not implement expressly or directly an EU criminal law instrument. Following *Fransson*, the Court of Justice ruled in *Siragusa*[36] that the concept of 'implementing Union law', as referred to in Article 51 of the Charter, requires a certain degree of connection above and beyond the matters covered being closely related or one of those matters having an indirect impact on the other.[37] In the case of the Directives on procedural rights, there are a number of elements in domestic criminal procedures that, although not implementing specifically the Directives, meet this degree of connection required by the Court's case law and thus trigger the applicability of the Charter. This view is reinforced by the Court's finding in *Siragusa* that it is important to consider the objective of protecting fundamental rights in EU law, which is to ensure that those rights are not infringed in areas of EU activity, whether through action at EU level or through the implementation of EU law by the Member States.[38]

34 See Opinion of AG Bot above, in particular paras 105–106.
35 Case C-617/10, *Åklagaren v Hans Åkerberg Fransson*, judgment of 26 February 2013.
36 Case C-206/13, *Siragusa*, judgment of 6 March 2014.
37 Para 24.
38 Para 31.

4 Addressing gaps in protection stemming from national diversity – the role of autonomous concepts

One of the key challenges in reaching agreement on EU standards on procedural rights in criminal proceedings has been to accommodate Member States' concerns with regard to the potentially adverse impact of EU law in the field on the diversity of national criminal justice systems. Faced with the diversity of national criminal justice systems,[39] negotiations on the specific EU Directives on procedural rights after Lisbon have proven to be complex, notwithstanding the limited ambition to introduce minimum standards based on the ECHR and leaving – via the introduction of non-regression clauses – Member States free to maintain or introduce higher standards of protection. The price of reaching agreement has been the adoption of a number of provisions (especially as regards the access to a lawyer Directive) that have been the outcome of comparative law exercises and of criminal policy compromises, with the Directives containing a number of exceptions and lengthy Preambular provisions.[40] In spite of all these efforts, the existing EU Directives on procedural rights – even in their minimum standards form – will have a profound impact on national criminal justice systems. They will have an impact because, as Advocate General Bot has noted, the minimum standards character of EU law in the field does not mean that this is not equally binding as other standards of EU law – on the contrary, minimum standards must be interpreted broadly, to ensure the effectiveness of EU law in a field that is marked by considerable diversity between national legal systems.[41] Moreover, the Court will attempt to address the existence of national legal diversity in the field by developing autonomous concepts in the field of criminal procedure. The Court of Justice has developed autonomous concepts in order to ensure the uniform and independent interpretation of EU law, in cases where the latter does not refer expressly to national law as a tool for interpretation of the relevant EU law provisions. Autonomous concepts have been developed by the Court on the basis of a teleological and contextual interpretation, as well as on the basis of the need to ensure equality across the EU legal order.[42]

This approach is directly applicable to a number of provisions in EU criminal law, including the EU Directives on procedural rights in criminal proceedings.[43] The need to agree on common EU minimum standards in the

39 For an overview of different national systems of criminal procedure in the investigative context, see, inter alia, E. Cape, J. Hodgson, T. Prakken and T. Spronken (eds.), *Suspects in Europe: Procedural Rights at the Investigation Stage of the Criminal Process in the EU* (Intersentia, 2007).

40 For an analysis, see S. Cras, 'The Directive on the right of access to a lawyer in criminal proceedings and in European Arrest Warrant proceedings' (2014) 1 *EUCRIM* 32.

41 AG Bot, paras 32–33.

42 See, inter alia, Case C-195/06 *Oesterreichischer Rundfunk*.

43 V. Mitsilegas, 'Managing legal diversity in Europe's area of criminal justice: the role of autonomous concepts' in R. Colson and S. Field (eds.), *EU Criminal Justice and the Challenges*

field while respecting national legal diversity has led to the inclusion, in all three Directives adopted thus far, of general and broad terminology that remains undefined in the EU instruments and that is not to be defined in accordance with national law. This choice renders considerable the potential of the future development of autonomous concepts by the Court of Justice as a key mechanism to flesh out the meaning of these terms. Key concepts that have the potential to be defined as autonomous concern both the determination of the scope and the applicability of the defence rights Directives, as well as the interpretation of the content of the rights granted. With regard to the *scope* of the Directives, it is noteworthy that the terms 'suspect', 'accused' and 'criminal proceedings' are not defined in the text. Treating these concepts as autonomous EU law concepts is key to ensuring the effectiveness of the measures and achieving equality and the key objective of establishing a level playing field of protection across Europe. Autonomous concepts will also have an influence on the interpretation of further specific provisions on the applicability of the Directives. The Directives limit access to a lawyer[44] and to an interpreter[45] to proceedings before courts having jurisdiction in criminal matters. However, this limitation must be interpreted consistently with the ruling of the Court of Justice in *Baláž*,[46] in which the Court has adopted a broad definition of the concept of a 'court having jurisdiction in criminal matters' as an autonomous concept of EU law. Notwithstanding detailed provisions in the Directives, aspects of the temporal scope of the Directive, including the precise time when rights become applicable or cease to become applicable, may be interpreted autonomously by the Court of Justice to create a level playing field across the EU.[47]

Autonomous concepts will also be key in defining the *content* of the rights of suspects and accused persons. All three Directives oblige Member States to ensure that rights are granted 'promptly'[48] 'without undue delay',[49]

of Legal Diversity: Towards A Socio-Legal Approach to EU Criminal Policy (Cambridge University Press, forthcoming).

44 Article 2(4) and recitals 16 and 17.

45 Article 1(3).

46 C-60/12, *Baláž*, judgment of 14 November 2013.

47 As seen above, the Directive on access to a lawyer applies to suspects or accused persons in criminal proceedings from the time when they are made aware that they are suspected or accused of having committed a criminal offence until the conclusion of the proceedings, which is understood to mean the final determination of the question whether the suspect or accused person has committed the offence, including, where applicable, sentencing and the resolution of any appeal (Article 2(1)). For a similar wording, see Article 2(1) of the Directive on the right to information and Article 1(2) of the Directive on the right to interpretation and translation.

48 Key rights in the right to information Directive including the right to information about rights (Article 3(1)), the right to information about the accusation and relevant changes in such information (Article 6 paragraphs (1) and (4) respectively) and the provision of the Letter of Rights (Article 4(1)).

49 See with regard to the Directive on access to a lawyer in particular: the right to access to a lawyer (Article 3(2)); the right to communicate with third persons and with consular

'without delay',[50] 'in due time'[51] or 'within a reasonable period of time.'[52] The Court will be called to interpret these concepts autonomously, as they are not defined further in the Directives nor are they defined by reference to national law. Treating these concepts as autonomous will give flesh to the rights enshrined in the Directives. The same will potentially occur in the Court defining other key concepts inherent in the content of the rights provided by EU law, including what constitutes access to 'essential' documents for the purposes of the right to information[53] and right to translation,[54] what constitutes interpretation and translation 'of sufficient quality to safeguard the fairness of the proceedings' for the purposes of the said Directive,[55] and what is the meaning of the right of access to a lawyer 'in such time and in such a manner so as to allow the persons concerned to exercise their rights of defence practically and effectively.'[56] The treatment of these concepts as autonomous will significantly influence criminal law and practice in EU Member States, in particular in view of the fact that the Directives apply not only to cross-border, but also to purely domestic cases. By superimposing a Union meaning of key domestic law concepts, autonomous concepts become a mechanism of enforcement of EU law, which has significant impact on domestic criminal justice systems and legal cultures, in changing both perceptions and practice in national criminal justice systems.[57]

authorities (Articles 6(1) and 7(1) respectively); the obligation to inform a person deprived of liberty in the execution of a European Arrest Warrant that they have the right to appoint a lawyer in the issuing Member State (Article 10(4)).

50 The right to interpretation (Article 2(1) of the Directive on the right to interpretation and translation).

51 See the Directive on the right to information on the right of access to the materials of the case (Article 7(3)).

52 The right to translation (Article 3(1) of the Directive on the right to interpretation and translation).

53 According to Article 7(1) of the right to information Directive, Member States must ensure access to documents related to the specific case in the possession of the competent authorities, which are essential to challenging effectively, in accordance with national law, the lawfulness of the arrest or detention.

54 Article 3(1) of the Directive on the right to interpretation and translation grants a right to translation of essential documents: Member States must ensure that suspected or accused persons who do not understand the language of the criminal proceedings concerned are, within a reasonable period of time, provided with a written translation of all documents that are essential to ensure that they are able to exercise their right of defence and to safeguard the fairness of the proceedings.

55 Articles 2(8) and 3(9) respectively.

56 Article 3(1).

57 On the concept of legal culture as one encompassing these elements see D. Nelken, 'Using legal culture: purposes and problems', in D. Nelken (ed.), *Using Legal Culture* (Wildy, Simmonds and Hill, 2012) 1. On a view of legal culture as embracing the participants' experience, see R. Cotterrell, 'Comparative law and legal culture', in M. Reimann and R. Zimmermann (eds.), *The Oxford Handbook of Comparative Law* (Oxford University Press, 2008) 709.

5 Addressing fragmented human rights protection in Europe's area of criminal justice – achieving coherence

National concerns over the impact of EU harmonisation in the field of criminal procedure after Lisbon have led to a number of questions regarding the coherence of the EU legal framework on the protection of fundamental rights in particular when viewed within the broader framework of its place in the EU system of mutual recognition of judicial decisions in criminal matters. These questions are exemplified by the position of the United Kingdom after the entry into force of the Treaty of Lisbon. The United Kingdom has negotiated an extension of its 'opt-out' Protocol after Lisbon to also apply to criminal justice measures adopted under Title V TFEU post-Lisbon.[58] On the basis of this protocol, the United Kingdom has chosen to opt in to the Directives on the right to translation and interpretation and the right to information, but to opt out of the key Directive on the right to access to a lawyer in criminal proceedings as the latter was deemed to be too disruptive for the UK criminal justice system.[59] At the same time, the end of the five-year transitional period from the entry into force of the Lisbon Treaty set out in another Protocol on Transitional Provisions annexed to the Lisbon Treaty[60] saw the United Kingdom opt out of all the EU pre-Lisbon third-pillar *acquis*, but opt back in to a list of 35 measures. These include the majority of the mutual recognition measures, and most significantly the Framework Decision on the European Arrest Warrant. The selective participation of the United Kingdom in this context is problematic not only from the perspective of the protection of fundamental rights, but also from the perspective of the coherence of EU law.[61] The legal basis for the Directive on access to a lawyer (as with the other Directives implementing the Stockholm Roadmap) is Article 82(2) TFEU. This provision grants for the first time express competence to the European Union to legislate on aspects of criminal procedure (including explicitly the rights of the defence) where necessary to facilitate the operation of the principle of mutual recognition in criminal matters. The legality of post-Lisbon legislation on defence rights, including the Directive on access to a lawyer, is thus inextricably linked with the effective operation of mutual recognition in criminal matters, including of the Framework Decision on the European

58 Protocol No. 21 on the position of the United Kingdom and Ireland in respect of the Area of Freedom, Security and Justice.

59 House of Lords European Union Committee, *The European Union's Policy on Criminal Procedure*, 30th Report, session 2010–12, HL paper 288, paragraph 99.

60 Protocol 36 on 'Transitional provisions concerning acts adopted on the basis of Titles V and VI of the former version of the TEU prior the entry into force of the Treaty of Lisbon'.

61 V. Mitsilegas, S. Carrera and K. Eisele, 'The end of the transitional period for police and criminal justice measures adopted before the Lisbon Treaty: who monitors trust in the European Justice Area?' (2014) 74 *CEPS Paper in Liberty and Security in Europe*.

Arrest Warrant. This link is confirmed in the Preamble of the Directive on access to a lawyer itself,[62] which states that:

> Mutual recognition of decisions in criminal matters can operate effectively only in a spirit of trust in which not only judicial authorities, but all actors in the criminal process consider decisions of the judicial authorities of other Member States as equivalent to their own, implying not only trust in the adequacy of other Member States' rules, but also trust that those rules are correctly applied. Strengthening mutual trust requires detailed rules on the protection of the procedural rights and guarantees arising from the Charter, the ECHR and the ICCPR. It also requires, by means of this Directive and by means of other measures, further development within the Union of the minimum standards set out in the Charter and in the ECHR.[63]

The non-participation of the United Kingdom in measures on procedural rights, including the Directive on access to a lawyer, undermines the effective operation of the Framework Decision on the European Arrest Warrant as far as the UK is concerned. There is a direct causal link under EU constitutional law between the adoption of EU defence rights measures under Article 82(2) TFEU and the effective operation of mutual recognition in criminal matters. The non-participation of the UK in such measures poses fundamental challenges with regard to compliance by the UK with the fundamental rights obligations incumbent upon EU Member States participating in the system of mutual recognition in criminal matters. The UK's non-participation also challenges the coherence of EU criminal law in an integrated Area of Freedom, Security and Justice where EU criminal law measures are increasingly interconnected. It could be argued that from a black letter perspective, the current position of the United Kingdom is tenable: after all, under the Lisbon Treaty the UK can opt in to (or opt out from) any post-Lisbon legislative proposal in the field of criminal justice on a case-by-case basis (and has decided not to participate in the access to a lawyer Directive). On the other hand, the day after the end of the transitional period of Protocol 36 will see the agreed participation of the UK in a list of enforcement measures including the Framework Decision on the European Arrest Warrant. However, this argument runs counter to a more teleological approach that respects fully the objectives and the integrated nature of the Area of Freedom, Security and Justice. There are important precedents by the Court of Justice in that respect in cases involving UK requests to participate in measures related to border controls. A key ruling in

62 OJ L294, 6 November 2013, p. 1.

63 Recital 6. The Preamble continues as follows: 'Common minimum rules should lead to increased confidence in the criminal justice systems of all Member States, which, in turn, should lead to a more efficient judicial cooperation in a climate of mutual trust and to the promotion of a fundamental rights culture in the Union' (recital 8).

this context concerns the UK request to participate in a third-pillar Decision (Decision 2008/633) authorising access to the Visa Information System by law enforcement authorities.[64] The Decision is a third-pillar measure (and at the time the Treaties did not include a Protocol extending the UK's opt-out arrangements to the third pillar). In applying for annulment of Decision 2008/633, the United Kingdom submitted that that decision does not constitute a development of provisions of the Schengen *acquis* in which the United Kingdom did not take part, but a police cooperation measure, as is also apparent from the Council's choice of legal basis.[65] The Court, however, ruled against UK participation in the Decision. According to the Court, when classifying a measure as falling within an area of the Schengen *acquis*, and the need – where that *acquis* evolves – to maintain that coherence, must be taken into account.[66] The Court added that the cooperation established by Decision 2008/633 could not, from both a functional and a practical point of view, exist independently of the VIS, which falls, like Decision 2004/512 and the VIS Regulation on which the VIS is based, within the scope of the Schengen *acquis* concerning the common visa policy.[67] The Court adopted a teleological and contextual approach focusing on the coherence of the Schengen *acquis*, following largely precedents in earlier rulings excluding the UK participation in the *Frontex* and biometrics Regulations.[68] The Court's rulings are also applicable with regard to the UK participation in EU criminal law measures. The legality of the adoption of procedural rights measures under Article 82(2) TFEU is inextricably linked with the effective operation of mutual recognition measures. In fact, as the Treaty is currently worded, defence rights measures under Article 82(2) TFEU cannot exist independently of measures on mutual recognition, including the Framework Decision on the European Arrest Warrant. Participating in the enforcement measures but not in the measures granting rights in order to facilitate judicial cooperation challenges the coherence of Europe's area of criminal justice and is contrary to EU law.

6 Conclusion: the transformative effect of legislating for human rights in Europe's area of criminal justice

The entry into force of the Treaty of Lisbon has enabled the European Union to innovate and legislate for the protection of human rights by fleshing out in detail key procedural rights in criminal proceedings in secondary EU law. EU legislative intervention will have a transformative effect for the development

64 Case C-482/08, *United Kingdom v Council*, judgment of 26 October 2010.
65 Para 30.
66 Para 48.
67 Para 54.
68 Case C-77/05, *United Kingdom v Council*, judgment of 18 December 2007 (*Frontex*), para 55. Case C-137/05, *United Kingdom v Council*, judgment of 18 December 2007 (biometrics).

of Europe's area of criminal justice. It signals a paradigm shift from a system focused primarily – if not solely – on promoting the interests of the state and of law enforcement under rules of quasi-automatic mutual recognition to a system where the rights of individuals affected by such rules are brought into the fore, protected by and enforced in EU law. It also extends the scope of human rights protection. The Directives adopted thus far go beyond the strict requirements of the Article 82(2) TFEU legal basis (which links harmonisation in the field of criminal procedure with the effective operation of mutual recognition) in applying not only to cross-border, but also to purely domestic cases. In this manner, national criminal procedural law – to the extent that it implements the Directives – must be applied in conformity with EU law. This means that national rules of criminal procedure must be applied in conformity with EU secondary human rights law (the Directives on procedural safeguards) as well as with EU constitutional human rights law (the Charter). The Court's case law on the applicability of the Charter indicates that the latter is applicable not only in cases where national law implements specifically EU law, but also to cases where national law has a connection with EU law. These findings are applicable to a wide range of national provisions on criminal procedure, which are closely linked with the achievement of the objectives and the effective implementation of the EU Directives on procedural rights. In addition to these avenues of protection, the normalisation of large aspects of EU criminal law after Lisbon mean that secondary EU law on procedural rights enjoys the enhanced supranational enforcement mechanisms of EU law. At the level of decentralised enforcement, affected individuals can claim direct effect before national courts. At the level of centralised enforcement, the Commission now has full powers to monitor the effectiveness of the implementation of the procedural rights Directives in Member States and take action before the Court of Justice if such implementation is unsatisfactory. The scope of the Commission's monitoring exercises is broader than to merely check the provision of national legislation adopted to implement specifically the EU Directives in question. The Commission must also monitor national criminal procedure systems more broadly to ensure that effective implementation has taken place, as well as to monitor compliance on the ground in addition to compliance on paper. Legislating for human rights at EU level further addresses gaps in protection arising from the diversity of national rules by creating a level playing field of protection across the EU. The Court's case law on managing diversity (via the development of autonomous concepts in EU law), stressing the coherence of EU law (via setting limits to the choices of states with opt-out privileges with regard to participation in integrated measures in the Area of Freedom, Security and Justice), and ensuring the effective applicability of fundamental rights provides clear guiding principles in this context. The adoption of further measures on the rights of the individual in criminal proceedings will expand further and consolidate the protection of human rights in Europe's area of criminal justice.

Part III

Border controls, immigration, asylum and AFSJ paradigms

9 Frontex and the European system of border guards

The future of European border management

Jorrit J. Rijpma

1 Introduction

The Regulation establishing the European Agency for the Management of Operational Cooperation at the External Borders of the Member States of the European Union (Frontex) was adopted in 2004.[1] Since 2005, Frontex has been operating from its headquarters in Warsaw, Poland. In December 2014, Fabrice Leggeri succeeded the Agency's first executive director, Ilkka Laitinen.

Over the past decade, the Agency has developed into a key actor in the management of the external borders of the Schengen area. Its tasks and resources have expanded in line with the consistent call for a reinforcement of the external borders of the European Union at political level. In 2015 the Agency's budget amounted to more than €114 million with a staff of 317.[2] Its founding regulation was amended twice, once in 2007 and then again in 2011, providing for new tasks and instruments. New legislation supplementing the existing Schengen borders *acquis* has likewise added to its tasks. It may be expected that the Agency will play an important role in a future 'integrated management system for the external borders' for which the Lisbon Treaty provided an explicit legal basis in article 77(2)(d) of the Treaty on the Functioning of the European Union (TFEU).

Although the Agency was deliberately set up as a body with a degree of autonomy that should shield it from political influence, it has had to operate in a very political environment.[3] It has received fierce criticism either

1 Council Regulation (EC) No 2007/2004 of 26 October 2004 establishing a European Agency for the Management of Operational Cooperation at the External Borders of the Member States of the European Union [2004] OJ L 349/1 ('Frontex Regulation').

2 Frontex budgets are available at http://frontex.europa.eu/about-frontex/governance-documents (live on 1 July 2015). The Agency started with a budget of almost €6.3 million and 57 staff; in 2010 its budget had reached over €92.8 million with a staff of 281.

3 J. Rijpma, 'Hybrid Agencification in the Area of Freedom, Security and Justice and its Inherent Tensions: The Case of Frontex', in M Busuioc, M. Groenleer and J. Trondal (eds.), *The Agency Phenomenon in the European Union: Emergence, Institutionalisation and Everyday Decision-Making* (Manchester University Press, 2012); A. Neal, 'Securitization and Risk at the EU Border: The Origins of Frontex' (2009) 47 *Journal of Common Market Studies* 333;

for reinforcing the proverbial 'Fortress Europe' or for not doing enough to protect it. While its founding Regulation paid little to no attention to the human rights dimension of border management, the respect for fundamental rights has moved high up the Agency's agenda, first in practice and later by means of legislative amendment. However, questions remain as regards the precise division of responsibilities between Frontex and the Member States that cooperate under its auspices, as also the European Ombudsman has pointed out.

This chapter will argue that the development of Frontex and a future European System of Border Guards (ESBG) shows a strong need to think more deeply about multilevel policing in the Area of Freedom, Security and Justice (AFSJ) and the constitutional implications of a further Europeanisation of executive powers in this field. This is first and foremost necessary in order to be able to guarantee the respect for fundamental rights within the AFSJ, but also because it has consequences for the nature of European integration.

2 Frontex's expanding role

In line with the principle that the Member States remain ultimately responsible for their national security, each Schengen country remains in charge of guarding its respective stretch of the external border.[4] The Schengen Borders Code, which contains common rules for controls at the external borders, does not provide much detail on border surveillance and leaves the national organisation of border management in the hands of the Member States.[5] Because border control is, however, in the interest of the Schengen area as a whole, its external border is only as strong as its weakest link.[6] Member States are required to deploy 'appropriate staff and resources' to ensure 'an efficient, high and uniform level of control at their external borders'. This means that some of them may face a disproportionate burden due to the length of their borders or their geographical location on migratory routes into the EU.[7]

S. Carrera, *The EU Border Management Strategy: Frontex and the Challenges of Irregular Immigration in the Canary Islands*, CEPS Working Document No. 261 (2007), www.ceps.eu/publications/eu-border-management-strategy-frontex-and-challenges-irregular-immigration-canary (live on 1 July 2015).

4 Article 4(2) Treaty on European Union (TEU), Article 72 TFEU, Recital 4, Frontex Regulation.

5 Regulation (EC) No 562/2006 of 15 March 2006 establishing a Community Code on the rules governing the movement of persons across borders (Schengen Borders Code) [2006] OJ L105/1. On the basis of Article 12(5), the Commission may adopt delegated acts concerning additional measures on border surveillance. See also Regulation (EU) No 656/2014 of 15 May 2014 establishing rules for the surveillance of the external sea borders in the context of operational cooperation coordinated by [Frontex] [2014] OJ L189/93.

6 Recital 6, Schengen Borders Code.

7 Article 14, Schengen Borders Code.

Article 16 of the Schengen Borders Code provides that Member States shall assist each other and maintain 'close and constant cooperation' for an effective implementation of border control. Frontex was established both as a solidarity instrument, as well as a means of promoting a more efficient and integrated approach to border management, reinforcing the overall control of the external borders.

The creation of a regulatory agency confirmed the supranationalisation of the powers over borders in the Treaty of Amsterdam, by moving away from earlier, more intergovernmental coordinating and cooperation initiatives within the Council towards an independent body funded from the EU budget.[8] At the same time, the choice for a regulatory agency reflected the intergovernmental origins of this cooperation, placing the agency at the centre of a network of national border guard authorities and endowing it with tasks aimed to support the Member States rather than the European Commission.[9] The establishment of a regulatory agency that only has supporting and coordinating tasks was also much more modest than the Commission's ideas on the creation of a 'European Corps of Border Guards', which, although it would not replace national border guards authorities, would consist of staff having 'the full prerogatives of public authority needed to perform these functions, irrespective of their nationality and their place of deployment'.[10]

The Agency's tasks are listed in Article 2(1) of the Frontex Regulation. These have been amended by regulation in 2007 and 2011, and have been supplemented by subsequent legislative measures, most importantly the External Borders Fund and its successor, the Schengen Governance Package and the Regulation setting up Eurosur.[11]

Frontex is an agency with a dual character.[12] On the one hand, it fulfils the role of a classic EU regulatory agency, assisting in the implementation of a common policy through the provision of technical and informational support, such as the drawing up of risk analyses, following up on technical research and developing common training programmes. These tasks, however, are at least in part carried out as a function of Frontex's second role, that of an operational agency endowed with the power to coordinate joint operational activity between Member States' national border guards. Here Frontex resembles more its counterparts in the field of criminal justice, Europol and Eurojust, which also coordinate cooperation between national law enforcement authorities.[13] Much like Europol and Eurojust, but unlike the proposed

8 Rijpma (n. 3), 89 and Neal (n. 3).

9 Ibid.

10 Commission, 'Towards Integrated Management of the External Borders of the Member States of the European Union' (Communication) COM(2002) 233 final, 22.

11 Discussed in detail below.

12 Rijpma (n. 3).

13 Council Decision 2009/371/JHA of 6 April 2009 establishing the European Police Office (Europol) [2009] OJ L 121/37 and Council Decision 2002/187/JHA of 28 February

European Public Prosecutor, Frontex does not have any executive powers and Frontex staff cannot be equated with national border guards.[14]

Subsequent legislative amendments have done two things. On the one hand, they have reinforced Frontex's 'regulatory' role, supporting not only the Member States, but also the Commission. At the same time, they have strengthened the Agency's operational role, slowly but steadily pushing it into the direction originally envisaged by the Commission in its 2002 Communication.

2.1 The 2007 and 2011 amendments

In 2007, amid the continued arrival of boat people across the Mediterranean and on the Canary Islands, the EU legislator adopted the first amendments to the Frontex Regulation, which introduced a rapid response mechanism for situations of 'urgent and exceptional pressure', characterised by the arrival of large numbers of third-country nationals trying to cross the external borders illegally.[15] It provided for emergency response teams consisting of national border guards that could be drawn from a pool of national border guards who would be selected and trained for that purpose. In principle, Member States would be under an obligation to make the border guards listed in the pool available, as such creating an embryonic European Corps of Border Guards consisting of national border guards at the immediate disposal of the Agency.

Importantly, the 2007 Regulation for the first time defined the powers and tasks of national border guards ('guest officers') deployed in the context of rapid border intervention or joint operations. Guest officers dispose of all powers necessary to perform the tasks under the Schengen Borders Code.[16] They are allowed to carry their service weapons, when authorised by the host Member State's law and use force under the command of the officers of the host Member State.[17] The 2007 Regulation further allowed Frontex to acquire its own technical equipment.[18]

2002 setting up Eurojust with a view to reinforcing the fight against serious crime [2002] OJ L 63/1.

14 Commission, 'Proposal for a Council Regulation on the Establishment of the European Public Prosecutor's Office' COM(2013) 534 final.

15 Chapter I, Regulation (EC) No 863/2007 of 11 July 2007 establishing a mechanism for the creation of Rapid Border Intervention Teams and amending Council Regulation (EC) No 2007/2004 as regards that mechanism and regulating the tasks and powers of guest officers [2007] L 199/30 ('2007 Regulation').

16 Article 10(1), Frontex Regulation.

17 Article 10(5) and (6), Frontex Regulation.

18 Article 7, Frontex Regulation. However, contrary to popular belief, Frontex does not possess vehicles, ships or aircraft acquired on the basis of this article. Such assets are instead made available by the Member States. However, Frontex has in 2013 procured 'aerial surveillance services', which includes the use of aerial means: Frontex, Annual Information on the Commitments of the Member States to the European Border Guard Teams and the

In 2011, following an external evaluation of the agency, yet another Regulation strengthened Frontex's operational tasks even more.[19] The Rapid Border Intervention Teams (RABITs) were rebaptised as European Border Guard Teams (EBGTs), which could now be deployed also in normal joint operations.[20] Like the RABITs, the EBGTs are drawn from a pre-established list of national border guards.[21] Importantly, the 2011 Regulation introduced the possibility for national border guards that are seconded to the Agency to be included in the EBGT pool, reinforcing the character of this pool as a nascent European Corps of Border Guards.[22] The 2011 Regulation formalised the position of coordinating officer, the member of Frontex staff that is responsible for the on-the-ground coordination of joint operational activity.[23] It also allowed the Agency to independently finance operations.[24]

Finally, the 2011 Regulation reinforced the external powers of the Agency. From the outset, the Agency's tasks have included the facilitation of operational cooperation between Member States and third countries.[25] For that purpose, it may conclude working arrangements on the management of operational cooperation with the authorities of third countries, generally the authorities responsible for border management in those countries.[26] New was the possibility for the Agency to send liaison officers to third countries and to independently launch and finance technical assistance projects in third countries.[27] Member States 'may' in the conclusion of bilateral agreement with third countries include provisions on the role of the Agency and the powers of guest officers in the context of joint operations, which should be read as an encouragement to do so.[28]

Technical Equipment Pool (Report 2014), 18, www.statewatch.org/news/2014/mar/eu-frontex-rep-ep-msd.pdf (accessed 1 May 2015).

19 COWI, External evaluation of the European Agency for the Management of Operational Cooperation at the External Borders of the Member States of the European Union (Final Report January 2009), www.statewatch.org/news/2009/may/frontex-eval-report-2009.pdf (accessed 1 May 2015); Regulation (EU) No 1168/2011 of 25 October 2011 amending Council Regulation (EC) No 2007/2004 [...] [2011] OJ L301/1 ('2011 Regulation').

20 Article 3b, Frontex Regulation.

21 Ibid.

22 Article 3b(3), Frontex Regulation.

23 Article 8g, Frontex Regulation.

24 Article 3(4), Frontex Regulation.

25 Article 14(1), Frontex Regulation.

26 See A. Ott, E. Vos and F. Coman-Kund, 'European Agencies on the Global Scene: EU and International Law Perspectives', in M. Everson, C. Monda and E. Vos (eds), *European Agencies in between Institutions and Member States* (Wolters Kluwer, 2014), 109ff.

27 Article 14(3) and (5), Frontex Regulation. So far no Frontex liaison officers have been posted. Interestingly, the Commission's European Agenda on Migration only refers to the posting of national liaison officers under Council Regulation (EC) No 377/2004 [2007] OJ L 64/1: Commission, 'A European Agenda on Migration' (Communication) COM(2015) 240 final, 8.

28 This article confirms existing practice, see, for instance, the agreement between Spain and Cape Verde: Acuerdo entre España y Cabo Verde sobre vigilancia conjunta de los espacios marítimos bajo soberaníay jurisdicción de Cabo Verde, *BOE* No 136, 5 June 2009, 47545.

2.2 *The European Border Surveillance System*

In October 2013, in the aftermath of yet another deadly incident off the coast of Lampedusa, the European legislator adopted the Regulation for the establishment of a European Border Surveillance System (Eurosur).[29] Eurosur should allow for a near-real-time information exchange on the situation at the external borders and was intended to improve situational awareness with a threefold purpose: to prevent irregular migration, fight organised crime and contribute to the rescue of life at sea.[30]

More than a technological system, Eurosur is an organisational model, in which Frontex takes centre-stage.[31] The Eurosur Regulation has strengthened Frontex's role in risk analysis, making it the central hub in a system of information exchange between national border guard authorities. The Agency is responsible for the functioning of the system and uses its own information, as well as the input from the national contact points to draw up a European situational picture, as well as a 'Common Pre-Frontier Intelligence Picture'.[32] On the basis of the situational pictures, the Agency attributes impact levels (low, medium and high) to the external land and sea border sections.[33] Depending on the impact level, Member States are required to adjust their 'reaction capability' accordingly, where needed with the assistance of Frontex.[34]

Despite the fact that the Eurosur Regulation explicitly excludes from its scope the legal or administrative measures taken in response to criminal activities, it has allowed Frontex to branch out its activities to criminal law, collecting and exchanging information related to cross-border crime.[35] This seems in line with the objective of integrated border management and with the merging of the pillar system by the Lisbon Treaty there seems to be no legal obstacle to this.[36] Still, it is remarkable that the Member States and Frontex actively support this expansion of the Agency's remit, while remaining opposed to the inclusion of organising and coordinating search and rescue activities in its tasks.[37]

29 Regulation (EU) No 1052/2013 of 22 October 2013 establishing the European Border Surveillance System (Eurosur) [2013] L 295/11 ('Eurosur Regulation').
30 Article 2(1), Eurosur Regulation.
31 J. Rijpma and M. Vermeulen, 'EUROSUR: Saving Lives or Building Borders?' (2015) 24 *European Security* 1.
32 Articles 7, 10 and 11, Eurosur Regulation.
33 Article 15, Eurosur Regulation.
34 Article 16, Eurosur Regulation.
35 Articles 2(3) and 18(2)(a), Eurosur Regulation.
36 See Section 4 below.
37 See, for instance, the statement added by the Council to the Eurosur Regulation emphasising that 'search and rescue at sea is a competence of the Member States'. See also *The Guardian*, 22 April 2015, 'EU borders Chief Says Saving Migrants' Lives "Shouldn't Be Priority" for Patrols', www.theguardian.com/world/2015/apr/22/eu-borders-chief-says-saving-migrants-lives-cannot-be-priority-for-patrols (accessed 8 July 2015).

2.3 The European Borders Fund

The European Borders Fund (EBF) was set up in 2007 as part of the Solidarity and Management of Migration Flows Framework Programme.[38] An overhaul of funding in the AFSJ resulted in the creation of two new funds in 2014: the Asylum, Migration and Integration Fund and the Internal Security Fund. As part of the latter, the Instrument for Financial Support for External Borders and Visa (ISF-Borders) was adopted, replacing the EBF.[39] As was the case under the EBF, Frontex plays an important regulatory role in supporting the Commission in the allocation of funds to the Member States.

Financing under the Fund is provided as a basic amount allocated to the Member States at the start of the Programme, with a flexible amount to be added halfway through the run-time of the programme.[40] The flexible amount per Member State is allocated on the basis of the type of border (land, sea, air), the length and the threat level for each external border section of the Member States (land and sea) or the number of passengers and persons refused (air). That threat level is determined by the Commission in accordance with Frontex's risk analysis report and in consultation with the Agency.[41]

On the basis of a policy dialogue between senior officials of the Commission and the Member State, Member States must submit their draft multi-annual programme to the Commission.[42] The Commission must consult Frontex on these programmes, in particular on proposed activities that finance operating support.[43] Member States are allowed to use up to 40 per cent of the allocated funds to support their public authorities such as border guards or visa services.[44] The input by Frontex should ensure the actions by the Member States complement rather than overlap with the Agency's activities.

2.4 The Schengen Governance Package

The national programmes under the IFS-Borders may be adjusted not only in line with Frontex's risk analyses, but also as a result of the Commission's Schengen Evaluation Reports, which scrutinise the implementation of the

38 Decision No 574/2007/EC of 23 May 2007 establishing the External Borders Fund for the period 2007 to 2013 as part of the General programme 'Solidarity and Management of Migration Flows' [2007] OJ L 144/22 ('EBF').

39 Regulation (EU) No 515/2014 of 16 April 2014 establishing, as part of the Internal Security Fund, the instrument for financial support for external borders and visa and repealing Decision No 574/2007/EC ('ISF-Borders').

40 Article 6, ISF-Borders, see also Commission, 'Proposal for a Regulation establishing, as part of the Internal Security Fund, the instrument for financial support for external borders and visa' COM(2011) 750 final, 8.

41 Article 8, ISF-Borders.

42 Article 9, ISF-Borders.

43 Article 9(4), ISF-Borders.

44 Article 10, ISF-Borders.

Schengen *acquis* by the Member States. It is the task of the Commission and Frontex 'to address the findings and implement the recommendations' of these reports. Priority is to be given to tackling deficiencies identified in Member States' management of their external borders.[45]

Originally Schengen evaluations were carried out by the Schengen Evaluation Committee, a Council Working Party made up of Member States' representatives reporting to the Council.[46] It can be seen as a clear remnant of the intergovernmental origins of the Schengen cooperation. The system was criticised for lacking consistency and effectiveness.[47] As early as 2008, the Commission hinted at Frontex's involvement in the evaluation process for its 'independent status, its expertise on external border control and surveillance and its activities on training and risk analysis'.[48]

It was the concern over a lack of control over the external borders and a political row at the height of the Arab Spring over the granting of temporary residence permits by Italy that resulted in the Commission's proposal for the so-called Schengen Governance Package.[49] The package consisted of a Communication and two proposals for regulations; one strengthening the supervisory mechanism, transferring powers of supervision to the Commission and one amending the Schengen Borders Code as regards the rules on temporarily reinstating checks at the internal borders.[50]

In the legislative process, the Council significantly limited the supranational elements of the proposals, in particular the Commission's say over the reinstatement of checks at the internal borders.[51] Under Article 26 of the amended Schengen Borders Code, the Council may now recommend

45 Article 12, ISF-Borders.

46 The Schengen Evaluation Committee was originally set up by the Decision of the Schengen Executive Committee of 16 September 1998 setting up a Standing Committee on the evaluation and implementation of Schengen (SCH/ Com-ex (98) 26 def.).

47 G. Callovi, *Securing External Frontiers in a Union of 25*, Migration Policy Institute, Policy Brief No. 5 (2004).

48 Commission, 'Report on the evaluation and future development of the FRONTEX Agency' COM(2008) 67 final, 8.

49 J. Rijpma, 'Institutions and Agencies: Government and Governance after Lisbon' in D. Acosta Arcarazo and C. Murphy (eds.), *EU Security and Justice Law after Lisbon and Stockholm* (Hart Publishing, 2014), 54, 60ff.

50 Commission, 'Schengen Governance – Strengthening the area without internal border controls' (Communication) COM(2011) 561 final; Commission, 'Proposal for a regulation amending Regulation (EC) 562/2006 in order to provide for common rules on the temporary reintroduction of border control at internal borders in exceptional circumstances' COM(2011) 560; Commission, 'Proposal for a regulation on the establishment of an evaluation and monitoring mechanism to verify the application of the Schengen *acquis*' COM(2011) 559 final.

51 Regulation (EU) No 1051/2013 of 22 October 2013 amending Regulation (EC) No 562/2006 in order to provide for common rules on the temporary reintroduction of border control at internal borders in exceptional circumstances [2013] OJ L 295/1.

the reintroduction of border controls 'where exceptional circumstances put the overall functioning of the area without internal border control at risk'. In these situations, the Commission, before making a proposal for a Council Recommendation, may ask Member States, Frontex and other EU agencies such as Europol for more information and conduct on-site visits with their experts.[52]

The Council did replace the Schengen Evaluation Committee with oversight by the European Commission.[53] In view of the full supranationalisation of the AFSJ by the Treaty of Lisbon, it seems logical to endow the Commission rather than the Council with this task. Although border management is only part of the Schengen *acquis*, it still is interesting that the power to assess Member States' compliance with the rules on border management was not given to Frontex, considering that its establishment as an autonomous agency could in part be explained by the Member States' reluctance to confer powers in this field on the Commission.[54]

The Agency was nonetheless given an important supporting role. Frontex produces yearly risk analyses that include recommendations as regards the priorities for both announced and unannounced inspections.[55] Evaluation reports of inspections are drawn up under the joint responsibility of the Commission and national experts. They are adopted by the Commission under comitology.[56] Frontex may be invited to on-site visits and may be asked for its input on the standard questionnaire, but it does not – at least not under this Regulation – play a role in the formulation of recommendations and their follow-up.[57] However, as was noted earlier, under the ISF-Borders, it is to address the findings from the report together with the Commission in the context of the adjustment of national programmes under the instrument.[58] Moreover, where serious deficiencies are reported, the Commission may, on the basis of the amended Schengen Borders Code, recommend that the Member State in question requests deployment of a Rapid Intervention Team or sends its strategic plans, including information on the deployment of personnel and equipment, for an opinion to Frontex.[59]

52 Article 26a, ibid.

53 Council Regulation (EU) No 1053/2013 of 7 October 2013 establishing an evaluation and monitoring mechanism to verify the application of the Schengen *acquis* and repealing the Decision of the Executive Committee of 16 September 1998 setting up a Standing Committee on the evaluation and implementation of Schengen [2013] OJ L 295/27.

54 Rijpma (n. 3), 89.

55 Article 7, Council Regulation (EU) No 1053/2013.

56 Article 14, ibid.

57 Articles 9(1) and 10(5), ibid.

58 Article 12, ISF-Borders.

59 Article 19a(3), Schengen Borders Code.

2.5 *The development of the Schengen borders* acquis

From the above overview of different tasks that have been added to the Agency's mandate since its establishment in 2004, it becomes clear that although Frontex plays a key role in the management of the external borders, it operates within – and in support of – a broader institutional and regulatory framework. That regulatory framework, the Schengen borders *acquis*, has significantly expanded over the past decade. Two observations can be made in this regard.

First, the Commission appears to have strengthened its grip over the management of the external borders, which can be interpreted as a reflection of the mainstreaming of this policy area in post-Lisbon law. If one considers Frontex under the principal-agent theory, this means that, at least as far as its regulatory tasks are concerned, it increasingly acts as an agent for the Commission rather than the Member States. This is different for the operational side of its mandate. Here, there are two possible views. Either one considers the delegation of powers to Frontex still as a Europeanisation of powers previously held by the Member States, which through their representation in the Agency's management board continue to exercise important oversight, or one considers the Agency more as an agent for the Council, which coordinates the overall operational coordination in the AFSJ through the Committee for Internal Security (COSI), established on the basis of Article 71 TFEU.[60] It thus seems that despite its formal autonomy, Frontex is really serving two masters at the same time: (the Member States represented in) the Council and the Commission.

Second is the increased importance of the related concepts of solidarity and trust. Frontex was not only set up as an instrument to contribute to more evenly share the burden of managing the external border, it was also to foster trust between Member States, some of which no longer had external land borders and therefore had to rely on the management of the external borders by other Member States, as well as their border management authorities, who were expected to work together more closely in order to develop a common approach to border management and share the burden of managing the external border.[61]

It was only in the Commission's 2002 Communication on the external borders that explicit reference was made to the disparate burden upon Member States of the management of the external borders.[62] Until then, the argument had been largely absent both in the discussions on the internal market as well as the Schengen cooperation. Interestingly, financial burden-sharing

60 Council Decision 2010/131/EU of 25 February 2010 on setting up the Standing Committee on operational cooperation on internal security [2010] OJ L52/50.

61 S. Stetter, 'Regulating Migration: Authority Delegation in Justice and Home Affairs' (2000) 7 *Journal of European Public Policy* 80, 83.

62 COM(2002) 233 (n. 10), 24.

was to precede and be supplemented by operational burden-sharing in the form of a European Corps of Border Guards.[63] Yet, it was not until 2006 that a significant migratory pressure on the Mediterranean Member States created a 'sufficient critical mass' in the Council for the adoption of the EBF, the first financial burden-sharing mechanism.[64] Numerous European Council Conclusions, including the multi-annual policy programmes for the AFSJ, have underscored the importance of solidarity.[65] The Lisbon Treaty included an explicit reference to the principle of solidarity in the field of migration, asylum and borders, stating that these policies shall be 'governed by the principle of solidarity and fair sharing of responsibility, including its financial implications'.[66] In practice, both financial and operational solidarity have been reinforced, yet the actual sharing of responsibility for irregular migrants and asylum-seekers remains highly problematic.[67]

Closely linked to this is the need for Member States to be able to trust each other that the management of the external borders is carried out in accordance with common standards and procedures. Frontex is to play an important role here by fostering a common culture of border management through the development of a common core curriculum, joint training and joint operational activity. Already in 2002 the Commission underscored mutual confidence between the Member States as one of the major needs for the EU's external borders policy.[68] Yet, in a way, the reinforced Schengen evaluation mechanism and the possibility to reinstate checks at the internal borders in case of serious deficiencies are a sign of distrust rather than trust.

More generally, a lack of trust in Member States' legal and political systems can jeopardise the functioning of the Schengen system and the development of an integrated system for the management of the external borders. This is,

63 Ibid., 19.

64 J. Monar, 'Justice and Home Affairs', in U. Sedelmeier and A. Young (eds.), *JCMS Annual Review of the European Union in 2007* (Blackwell, 2008), 109, 113.

65 See for a recent example the European Council Statement on the Special Meeting of the European Council on Migration and Asylum of 23 April 2015, www.consilium.europa.eu/en/press/press-releases/2015/04/23-special-euco-statement (accessed 8 July 2015).

66 Article 67(2) TFEU and Article 80 TFEU.

67 As regards asylum-seekers, the principles laid down in the Dublin Regulation remain valid also under its recast, namely that in most cases the country of first illegal entry or request for asylum is responsible for the claim: Article 3, Regulation (EU) No 604/2013 of 26 June 2013 establishing the criteria and mechanisms for determining the Member State responsible for examining an application for international protection lodged in one of the Member States by a third-country national or a stateless person (recast). Initiatives for voluntary resettlement have not proven successful and the reactions to the Commission's most recent proposal for an EU-wide resettlement scheme do not bode well for the future: COM(2015) 240 final (n. 27), 5. See also European Parliament, 'The implementation of Article 80 TFEU on the principle of solidarity and fair sharing of responsibility, including its financial implications, between the Member States in the field of border checks, asylum and immigration' (Study), PE 453.167, 2011.

68 COM(2002) 233 final (n. 10), 5.

for instance, evidenced by the continuing opposition in the Council against the lifting of internal border controls with Romania and Bulgaria, despite the fact that they have fulfilled all technical requirements. But also in the AFSJ as a whole, based on mutual confidence and a presumption of compliance with fundamental rights, systemic deficiencies can put at risk the functioning of common rules. This was, for instance, the case with Greece in the context of the Common European Asylum System.[69]

3 Guarding the guards: fundamental rights protection

The ongoing reinforcement of Frontex's powers beg the question of the Agency's accountability, in particular for possible violations of fundamental rights in the context of its operational activities. Border management, like other policing tasks, remains an area in which human rights violations may occur, in particular when force is used or when access is denied to people that have justified protection claims. From the very start, the Agency has been the subject of fierce criticism for alleged human rights violations at the EU's external border.[70] To some extent, Frontex came to symbolise the EU's migration and asylum policy at large, as well as questionable practices of national border guards for which, however, as an agency, it could not take responsibility. Nonetheless, more specific criticism could also be targeted at the Agency itself. Questions were raised as regards the transfer of intercepted migrants to Italian ships during a joint operation, who were subsequently returned to Libya; a practice later condemned by the European Court of Human Rights.[71] The participation of RABIT-teams at the Greek–Turkish border was said to have indirectly contributed to the detention of irregular migrants under inhumane and degrading conditions.[72]

The initial Frontex Regulation did not contain a reference to the respect for fundamental rights other than an obligatory recital stating that the Regulation respects fundamental rights, which is a general obligation under EU law.[73] The European Parliament, in particular the LIBE Committee, came to play a critical role in monitoring the Agency's activities. In October 2008, the Parliament used its budgetary prerogative to freeze part of a €30 million increase in the EU's subsidy to the Agency in order to force it to

69 Joined Cases C-411/10 and C-493, *NS and ME* (ECLI:EU:C:2011:865), para 106.

70 Giving rise to websites such as: www.frontexit.org and www.frontexplode.eu (last accessed 8 July 2015).

71 Human Rights Watch, 'Pushed Back, Pushed Around: Italy's Forced Return of Boat Migrants and Asylum Seekers, Libya's Mistreatment of Migrants and Asylum Seekers' (Report, 2009), www.hrw.org/reports/2009/09/21/pushed-back-pushed-around (accessed 1 May 2015). *Hirsi Jamaa and others v Italy* Application No. 27765/09 (ECHR, 23 February 2012).

72 Human Rights Watch, 'The EU's Dirty Hands: Frontex Involvement in Ill-Treatment of Migrant Detainees in Greece' (Report, 2011), www.hrw.org/reports/2011/09/21/eu-s-dirty-hands (accessed 1 May 2015).

73 Recital 22, Frontex Regulation.

improve its 'accountability and effectiveness'.[74] In subsequent amendments to the Frontex Regulation, the Parliament – by then co-legislator in this field – consistently emphasised the importance of fundamental rights protection and enhanced accountability mechanisms.

However, the real problem was, and remains to this day, the uncertainty regarding the division of responsibility for fundamental rights violations in the context of joint operational activity among the participating Member States, but in particular also between Frontex (or rather the EU) and the participating Member States.[75] Frontex and the European Commission have consistently maintained that this responsibility lies exclusively with the Member States, either the host Member State or the home Member States of the guest officers. According to that view, the Agency's coordinating activities do not trigger responsibility as they do not involve the taking of legal decisions, nor does the Agency exercise control over the participating Member States' border guard authorities. The 2007 Regulation, which provided that guest officers could be held civilly and criminally liable for misconduct under the rules of the host Member State, seems to confirm that any redress for fundamental rights violations is to be had at Member State level.[76]

Concerns over the respect for fundamental rights during joint operations, as well as compliance with international refugee law and the international law of the sea became particularly pressing in the context of joint operations at the southern maritime borders and the continuing loss of life of people trying to cross to Europe over the Atlantic and Mediterranean. Here, three separate yet related issues can be distinguished. First, the extent to which the EU can be held responsible for violations of human rights in the context of joint operational activity. Second, the question whether the EU has competence in matters of search and rescue and the extent to which Frontex's mandate allows it to engage in search and rescue activities. Third, the lack of a common approach to search and rescue and refugee protection in the context of joint operational activity at sea. Only as regards the latter, a Regulation amending the Schengen Borders Code has brought some degree of harmonisation.[77] It is, however, still contested whether Frontex's mandate allows it to set up joint operations aimed at search and rescue, rather than leaving search and rescue to be dealt with by the Member States under the legal framework of public international law, whenever such a situation arises in the context

74 House of Lords Select Committee on the EU, 'Frontex: the EU external borders agency' (HL Paper 60, Session 2007–08, 9th Report, 2008), 28. See European Parliament, Resolution of 13 December 2007 on the draft general budget of the European Union for the financial year 2008 as modified by the Council (P6_TA(2007)0616).

75 The EU has international legal personality (Article 47 TEU). For the purpose of responsibility under international law, Frontex's staff acts as organs of the EU.

76 Articles 10b and 10c, Frontex Regulation.

77 Regulation (EU) No 656/2014 (n. 5).

of joint border patrols.[78] Also, the more general question remains regarding the extent of the EU's responsibility for fundamental rights violations in the course of joint operational activity.

Nonetheless, Frontex's approach to fundamental rights and its public discourse have significantly evolved since its establishment. Although at no point has responsibility been accepted for potential fundamental rights violations, the Agency has increasingly reaffirmed its commitment to full respect for fundamental rights in all of its activities.[79] In part this was a response to external pressure, such as from the European Parliament. In part it evidences an increasing awareness within the Agency, in which the influx of staff with a background outside national border guard authorities may have played a role.

Frontex thus started a process of mainstreaming human rights in its activities. It concluded a working arrangement with UNHCR (2008), as well as the EU Fundamental Rights Agency (2010), discussions started in Brussels on guidelines for operations at sea, fundamental rights were included in the Common Core Curriculum for border guards and the Agency's training activities and a fundamental rights clause was included in the operational plans of its joint operations and pilot projects.[80] All of these helped to raise awareness of fundamental rights not only within the Agency, but importantly also within its network of national border guard authorities.[81]

The next step was made with the development of a more structured and generalised approach to fundamental rights with the adoption of the Frontex Fundamental Rights Strategy, the Fundamental Rights Action Plan and the Code of Conduct for all persons engaged in Frontex-coordinated activities, which were all endorsed by the Management Board.[82] It is difficult to

78 See J. Rijpma, 'The Patrolling of the European Union's External Maritime Border: Preventing the Rule of Law from Getting Lost at Sea', in A. Del Vecchio (ed.) *International Law of the Sea: Current Trends and Controversial Issues* (Eleven Publishing, 2013). See also n. 37.

79 This shows, for instance, in the increasing attention paid to fundamental rights in the Agency's annual reports. References to fundamental rights were absent until 2008. Annual reports are available at http://frontex.europa.eu/about-frontex/governance-documents (accessed 1 May 2015).

80 P. Slominski, 'The Power of Legal Norms in the EU's External Border Control' (2013) 51 *International Migration* 41, 44.

81 J. Rijpma, 'Frontex: Successful Blame Shifting of the Member States?' (Analysis of the Real Instituto Elcano, No 69, 2010), 5, www.realinstitutoelcano.org/wps/portal/web/rielcano_en/contenido?WCM_GLOBAL_CONTEXT=/elcano/Elcano_in/Zonas_in/ARI69-2010#.VVstLmdxmUk (accessed 1 May 2014). See also S. Horii, 'It is About More Than Just Training: The Effect of Frontex Border Guard Training' (2012) 31 *Refugee Survey Quarterly* 158, 170. She does note that the outcome of this training is difficult to measure, ibid., 175.

82 The Fundamental Rights Strategy was 'endorsed' by the Management Boards on 31 March 2011: http://frontex.europa.eu/assets/Publications/General/Frontex_Fundamental_Rights_Strategy.pdf (accessed 8 July 2015). The Code of Conduct was adopted by the executive director, Decision No 24/2011 of 21 March 2011, http://frontex.europa.eu/assets/Publications/General/Frontex_Code_of_Conduct.pdf (accessed 8 July 2015).

determine the precise legal status of these documents. The most accurate classification would be that of soft-law, of governance documents, with which the Agency is essentially binding itself. Even so, these documents contribute again to the awareness of fundamental rights in the Agency's activities. They also improve public accountability of the Agency, as its actions can be judged against its own standards.

The final step in the juridification of these fundamental rights obligations was made by the EU legislator. After it had proven impossible to adopt binding guidelines for joint operations at sea, the Council adopted an implementing decision to the Schengen Borders Code in 2010, which was, however, annulled by the European Court of Justice (ECJ) for being *ultra vires.*[83] Its effects were nonetheless upheld until the adoption of the Regulation on the matter in 2014.[84]

Meanwhile, the 2011 Regulation, as a result of amendments proposed by the European Parliament, imposed even stronger monitoring, reporting and transparency requirements on the Agency. The Frontex Regulation now explicitly mandates compliance with the Charter of Fundamental Rights, relevant international law, such as the Geneva Refugee Convention and fundamental rights.[85] In fact, fundamental rights are mentioned throughout the Regulation as regards the Agency's joint operational activities, including return, data, training, as well as its relations with third countries.

The amended Regulation also refers to the Code of Conduct, reaffirming that it applies to all persons participating in the Agency's activities, so not only Frontex staff, but also national border guards.[86] Even so, it is difficult to see how the Agency could enforce respect for this Code given its lack of command and control over participating officers. In fact, there is a separate obligation spelled out for guest officers to respect fundamental rights in Article 3b(4), and the obligation on Member States to provide for appropriate disciplinary measures or other measures in accordance with *national law* in case of human rights violations in Article 3(1a). The Code of Conduct is attached to the Operational Plan, which was formalised by the 2011 Regulation as well, although here again, the legal status of the plan under EU law seems unclear.[87]

83 Council Decision of 26 April 2010 supplementing the Schengen Borders Code as regards the surveillance of the sea external borders in the context of operational cooperation coordinated by [Frontex] [2011] OJ L 111/20; Case C-355/10 *European Parliament v Commission and Council* (ECLI:EU:C:2012:516).

84 Regulation (EU) No 656/2014 (n. 5).

85 Article 2(2), Frontex Regulation.

86 See also the separate obligation to adopt a Code of Conduct for Return in Article 9(1a), Frontex Regulation. Available at http://frontex.europa.eu/assets/Publications/General/Code_of_Conduct_for_Joint_Return_Operations.pdf (accessed 8 July 2015).

87 Article 3a(1), Frontex Regulation. One could argue that the operational plan is an implementing act adopted by an Agency on the basis of the Frontex Regulation, but since it is

The 2011 Regulation obliged the Agency to adopt and develop its Fundamental Rights Strategy and to ensure an 'effective mechanism to monitor respect for Fundamental Rights'.[88] It furthermore provided for a Consultative Forum to be set up in which the UNHCR, the European Asylum Support Office (EASO) and the Fundamental Rights Agency (FRA) would be represented, as well as 'other relevant governmental and non-governmental organisations'.[89] The Forum is to be consulted on the Fundamental Rights Strategy, the Code of Conduct and the Common Core Curricula. It must produce an annual report and is to be given access to all information concerning respect for fundamental rights.

In addition to the setting up of the Consultative Forum, the amended regulation mandated the appointment by the Management Board of a Fundamental Rights Officer (FRO), who is independent and reports to both the Management Board and the Consultative Forum on a regular basis.[90] The FRO's observations form an integral part of the evaluation of joint operational activity.[91] Like the Consultative Forum, the FRO is to be given access to all information concerning respect for fundamental rights.

Finally, and probably the strongest obligation imposed on the Agency, more specifically on its executive director, is the duty to suspend or terminate an operation in case of fundamental rights violations that are of a serious nature and are likely to persist.[92] Although the obligation is clear, its formulation implies a high threshold and a large margin of appreciation, raising doubts as to its effectiveness.

In view of the extensive amendments made to the Frontex Regulation and the widespread concerns as regards the respect for fundamental rights during Frontex-coordinated activity, the Ombudsman started an own initiative inquiry to see how Frontex would implement these obligations.[93] The report provides for an interesting read on how the Agency is making a serious effort to integrate fundamental rights in all its activities and on the implementation of the 2011 Regulation. Two important conclusions can be drawn from the Ombudsman's observations.

drafted by the executive director and agreed by all participating Member States and all adaptations require the agreement of the host Member States it is doubtful whether it can really be considered an act of the Agency.

88 Article 26a(1), Frontex Regulation.

89 Article 26a(2), Frontex Regulation. See Management Board Decision No 12/2012 of 23 May on the Composition of the Consultative Forum. The current representation includes inter alia: Amnesty International, Caritas Europa and the European Council on Refugees and Exiles (ECRE).

90 Article 26a(3), Frontex Regulation. This post has been held by Ms Inmaculada Arnaez Fernandez since 27 September 2012.

91 Article 3(3), Frontex Regulation.

92 Article 3(1a), ibid.

93 Decision of the European Ombudsman closing own-initiative inquiry OI/5/2012/BEH-MHZ concerning the European Agency for the Management of Operational

First, even under the regime of the 2011 Regulation, there is no mechanism for individual redress. In reply to questions by the Ombudsman whether the Fundamental Rights Officer would be able to receive complaints from individuals, Frontex repeated its well-known position that only Member State authorities perform activities that may affect individuals' rights and hence it is the Member States that should be addressed rather than Frontex.[94] It did point at internal procedures, including its incident reporting system, but emphasised that it has no power to force a Member State to follow-up on such reports.[95]

Second, as Frontex itself acknowledged, gaps remain as regards the clarification of responsibilities between the numerous different actors. The Agency declared its intention 'to bring more clarity, at practitioner's level, within the limits of its mandate'.[96] It seems difficult, however, to envisage a practical solution to complex questions of public international and EU law.[97] This would support the conclusion of Aas and Gundhus that Frontex's concern with human rights at least in part consists of 'the mobilization of emotional responses of compassion and the urge to assist practically thereby takes precedence over formal structures of rights and legal obligations'.[98]

In the absence of a transfer of independent enforcement powers to the Agency, it remains difficult to construe the legal responsibility of the EU. Such transfer could be envisaged as part of the development of a European System of Border Guards, although the question remains whether the current constitutional set up of the EU would allow for such a legal system, especially in the absence of a system for effective judicial review.

4 Towards a European System of Border Guards

The Lisbon Treaty introduced a new Article 77(2)(d) TFEU providing the EU with a legal basis for the 'gradual introduction of an integrated management system for the external borders'. Prior to the inclusion of this

Cooperation at the External Borders of the Member States of the European Union (Frontex), www.ombudsman.europa.eu/en/cases/decision.faces/en/52477/html.bookmark#hl9 (accessed 8 July 2015), point 4.

94 Ibid., point 22.

95 Ibid., point 100.

96 Ibid., point 93.

97 Some research is being done, see for instance: R. Mungianu, *The Principle of Non-refoulement in the European Union's Border Control Joint Operations: On the Interpretation and Application of the Principle of Non-refoulement by Frontex* (PhD thesis, Copenhagen University, 2013) and M. Fink, 'A "Blind Spot" in the Framework of International Responsibility? Third Party Responsibility for Human Rights Violations: The Case of Frontex', in T. Gammeltoft-Hansen and J. Vedsted-Hansen (eds.), *Human Rights and the Dark Side of Globalisation: Transnational Law Enforcement* (2015) at http://papers.ssrn.com/sol3/papers.cfm?abstract_id=2591126 (accessed 1 May 2015).

98 K. Aas and H. Gundhus, 'Policing Humanitarian Borderlands: Frontex, Human Rights and the Precariousness of Life' (2014) 54 *British Journal of Criminology* 1, 13.

article measures such as the Schengen Borders Code (SBC) and Frontex had been adopted on the legal basis for rules on standards and procedures for crossing the external borders, former Article 62(2)(a) EC, and the provision on administrative cooperation in the AFSJ, Article 66 EC.[99]

Article 77 TFEU is a very broadly formulated legal basis, raising questions as to the extent of powers that may be carried over to the EU level on the basis of this Article. It also remains unclear what exactly is to be understood by what is ultimately to be achieved under this power, namely 'an integrated management system for the external borders'. The Commission's 2002 Communication 'Towards Integrated Management of the External Borders' identified five elements to a common policy: a common corpus of legislation, a common coordination and operational cooperation mechanism, common integrated risk analysis, staff trained in a European dimension and interoperational equipment and burden-sharing between the Member States *in the run up to the establishment of a European Corps of Border Guards.*[100]

A common policy on the external borders would also seem to include the broad notion of integrated border management (IBM) that was adopted by the Council in its IBM Strategy of 2006. That strategy included inter-agency cooperation between all law enforcement authorities at the border (border guards, customs, police) and a four-tier access/control model covering measures in the Schengen area itself, at the external borders, in neighbouring countries and beyond.[101] Intra-service, inter-agency and international cooperation are considered the three key elements of IBM.[102] The importance of IBM was confirmed by the Commission in its 2008 Communication on the next steps in border management.[103] It advocated the multiplication and diversification of border controls, in particular through the use of modern technology. The 2014 Strategic Guidelines of the European Council for the future development of the AFSJ reaffirm this focus on 'modernising' IBM.[104]

The 2008 Communication no longer referred to a European Corps of Border Guards and there was altogether less focus on the institutional side

99 Now Articles 77(2)(b) TFEU and 74 TFEU.

100 COM(2002) 233 final (n. 10), 12, emphasis added.

101 JHA Council, Council Conclusions on Integrated Border Management (Brussels, 4–5 December 2006).

102 See also the definition of IBM in Commission, 'EU Guidelines for Integrated Border Management in European Commission External Cooperation, European Commission' (2010), http://capacity4dev.ec.europa.eu/ibm-eap/document/1-guidelines-integrated-border-management-european-commission-external-cooperation-european#sthash.veslRARI.dpuf (accessed 8 July 2015).

103 Although defining this notion in rather enigmatic terms: 'combining control mechanisms and the use of tools based on the flows of persons towards and into the EU': Commission, 'Preparing the next steps in border management in the European Union' (Communication) COM(2008) 69 final, 3.

104 European Council, Conclusions of 26–27 June 2014 (European Council Document EUCO 79/14), 4.

of border management. Frontex was explicitly referred to as the operational dimension of IBM, but it was the European Borders Fund that was qualified as the Union's solidarity instrument.[105] Still, the long-term development of European border management and the future of Frontex was explicitly considered in the Stockholm Agenda, the multi-annual policy for the period 2009–2014, the 2011 amendment to its founding Regulation and the 2014 Strategic Guidelines.[106] All called for further study into the feasibility of setting up a European System of Border Guards (ESBG). This would presumably form part of an integrated management system for the external borders and include Frontex, considering that establishment of an ESBG was explicitly linked to the long-term development of the Agency.

From the point of view of its operational powers, one could in theory envisage roughly three different roles for the Agency:

1 The status quo, in which the Agency exists alongside national border guard authorities and its powers remain limited to the coordination of cooperation between national authorities.
2 The Agency and its staff are given genuine executive powers, *complementing* the activities of national border guard forces. Here three different options could be distinguished:
    a The Agency employs genuine European border guards, endowed with executive powers under EU law, which act, however, under command and control of the Member State hosting joint operational activity.
    b The Agency is given command and control over national border guards in the context of joint operational activity.
    c A combination of (a) and (b) under which the Agency is given command and control over European border guards endowed with executive powers under EU law.
3 A centralised European Corps of Border Guards *replacing* national border guard authorities.

The study commissioned by the European Commission on the feasibility of an ESBG adopted a similar approach, distinguishing between (1) an optimal use of existing instruments, (2) a 'participation option' and (3) a full integration option.[107] The participation option would entail an extended

105 COM(2008) 69 final (n. 103), 2.
106 European Council, 'The Stockholm Programme: An Open and Secure Europe Serving and Protecting Citizens' (Conclusions) (2009) OJ C 115/1, 26; Article 33(2)(a), Frontex Regulation, European Council Conclusions (n. 104), 4.
107 Unisys, 'Study on the feasibility of the creation of a European System of Border Guards to control the external borders of the Union (ESBG) (2014)', http://ec.europa.eu/dgs/home-affairs/what-we-do/policies/borders-and-visas/border-crossing/docs/20141016_home_esbg_frp_001_esbg_final_report_3_00_en.pdf (accessed 8 July 2014).

role for seconded national officers acting under the command and control of the Agency at so-called 'hot spots', stretches of the external borders facing 'urgent and exceptional' migratory pressure.[108]

The full integration option would entail the setting up of a permanent structure for the daily management of Schengen borders.[109] The study suggests that such a structure consist of national border guards acting under the command and control of a new EU body, the Committee on Schengen Border Management (CSBM). In a somewhat creative use of the institutional toolbox, this 'body' would be set up as a comitology committee – a committee of Member State experts normally set up to oversee the Commission's use of implementing powers delegated to the Commission – and presumably established under the secondary legislation setting up the ESBG.[110] The executive director of Frontex, as well as a newly appointed European Border Corps commander-in-chief would attend the weekly meetings. An independent evaluator would assess the work carried out by both the EBC and the Frontex Agency, which would continue supporting the executive role. The study did not elaborate on how this independent evaluator would be appointed and what its relation to the EU institutions and Frontex would be.

The question is whether the current Treaties provide a sufficiently clear legal basis for either option, that is the partial or full conferral of executive powers in border management on EU officials. Article 77(2)(d) TFEU on face value seems to allow for the conferral of executive power to the EU level, albeit under the terms of its cautious formulation ('gradual'). This reading seems to be confirmed by the European Convention's Final Report of Working Group 10 on the AFSJ, which explicitly referred to the possibility of the establishment in the long-term of a common European border guard unit, with the specific limitation that this unit would operate *in conjunction with national border control services*.[111] The fact that competences in the AFSJ are shared does not in itself have to be an impediment, as these competences may become exclusive through the EU's use of its powers (pre-emption).[112]

Still, there appear to be two important constitutional obstacles to the transfer of genuine executive powers on European border guards. The first is the recognition in the EU Treaties that the Member States are ultimately responsible for their own internal security as expressed in Article 4(2) TEU and Article 72 TFEU.[113] This point was already raised at the time

108 Ibid., 24.
109 Ibid., 28.
110 Article 291(3) and Regulation (EU) No 182/2011 of 16 February 2011 laying down the rules and general principles concerning mechanisms for control by Member States of the Commission's exercise of implementing powers (2011) OJ L55/291.
111 European Convention, 'Final Report of Working Group X on Freedom, Security and Justice' (CONV 426/02), 17.
112 Articles 2(2) and 4(2) TFEU. Unisys (n. 107), 8.
113 See also R. Mungianu, 'Frontex: Towards a Common Policy on External Border Control' (2013) 15 *European Journal of Migration and Law* 359, 370.

of the introduction of the so-called 'mandatory solidarity' under the 2007 Regulation providing for the obligation to make available national border guards for the RABITs.[114] It explains that this obligation is qualified, and allows a Member State not to deny a request for deployment of its national border guards when 'faced with an exceptional situation substantially affecting the discharge of national tasks'.[115] Finally, Article 73 TFEU reserves to the Member States the power 'to organize forms of administrative cooperation aimed at the safeguarding of national security'.

A comparison with Europol may also be useful. Unlike Article 77(2)(d), Article 88 specifically provides for the establishment of this Agency, yet its powers have been expressly limited.[116] First, no operational activity can take place within the territory of a Member State without that country's explicit consent. Second, coercive measures remain the exclusive responsibility of the competent national authorities. Similarly, with Eurojust, the Treaty explicitly states in Article 85(2) TFEU that formal acts of judicial procedure shall be carried out by the competent national officials. It seems difficult to understand why limits on the powers of Union agencies in the field of judicial and police cooperation should be greater than in the case of external border management.

If one accepts that similar limits should apply to Frontex, its current legal framework already stretches these by conferring executive powers to guest officers in the framework of joint operations. Nonetheless, these powers may only be exercised under supervision of the host Member State and within the boundaries of its national laws.[117] However, to allow guest officers, or even EU officials, to operate without prior authorisation from the home Member State and without a final say over their actions would disregard the division of powers between the EU and the Member States under the current Treaty framework.

The second argument against the conferral of executive powers in external border management to an EU body would be based upon the ECJ's Meroni-doctrine, which limits the conferral of discretionary powers to bodies other than the EU institutions.[118] It could be argued that where there is a transfer of powers held by the Member States directly to the EU level, there is no question of delegation and hence the question becomes one of conferral and the extent of powers provided for under the legal basis in question.[119]

114 Council Document 8456/07.

115 Article 3(b)(2), Frontex Regulation. It is submitted that in the assessment thereof the Member States have a considerable discretion.

116 Article 88(3) TFEU.

117 Article 10, Frontex Regulation.

118 Case 9/56 *Meroni* [1957] ECR 11 at 147–149 and Case 10/56 *Meroni* [1958] ECR 53 at 169–171.

119 Renaud Dehousse, *Misfits: EU Law and the Misfits of European Governance*, Jean Monnet Working Paper 2 (2002), 12, www.jeanmonnetprogram.org/archive/papers/02/020201.html (accessed 1 May 2014). See also Advocate General Jääskinen in his opinion in Case C-270/12 *UK v European Parliament and Council* (ESMA) (ECLI:EU:C:2013:562), para 6.

While the TFEU explicitly provides for the establishment of Europol, Eurojust and a European Public Prosecutor, Article 77(2)(d) TFEU only provides the legal basis for a 'system' for the integrated management of the external borders. Nonetheless, in the ENISA case, the Court confirmed the practice of the Commission to use the substantive legal Treaty basis, to set up an institutional structure in support of the regulatory framework adopted on that legal basis.[120]

In a challenge to the legality of the Regulation setting up the European Securities and Markets Authority (ESMA), the ECJ did look at the establishment of this regulatory body through the lens of delegation, even if also here powers were conferred from the Member States to the EU level.[121] It held that the conferral of implementing powers to agencies by the EU legislator was implicitly sanctioned by the Treaty. It did not fall under, nor was it limited by the rules on the delegation of implementing powers under Article 291 TFEU.[122]

The Court confirmed its Meroni doctrine, repeating that powers conferred upon agencies must be precisely delineated and amenable to judicial review in the light of the objectives established by the delegating authority.[123] It was, however, very lenient in the application of these conditions to the ESMA, essentially discarding the UK's arguments as to the subjective nature of the ESMA's tasks. It argued that the Authority's founding Regulation allows it to address threats to the financial markets only where no competent national authority has acted or where one or more of those authorities has done so inadequately.[124] The Court furthermore emphasised that the ESMA has to examine a significant number of factors detailed in its founding Regulation and that it is only allowed to adopt two kinds of measures that are of a temporary nature.[125] Finally, it stated that the ESMA's discretion was further circumscribed by consultation requirements and the Commission's power to adopt delegated acts specifying criteria and factors to be taken into account by the ESMA.[126]

In the words of one commentator, the ECJ in the ESMA case 'refrained from identifying meaningful constitutional boundaries on the establishment of "operational support" mechanisms' under Article 114 TFEU.[127] It is tempting to apply the reasoning of the Court under Article 114 TFEU by analogy to operational support mechanisms under Article 77(2)(d) TFEU.

120 Case C-217/04 *UK v European Parliament and Council* [2006] ECR I-3771 (ECLI:EU:C:2006:279), paras 44–45.
121 Case C-270/12 *UK v European Parliament and Council* ('ESMA') (ECLI:EU:C:2014:18).
122 Ibid., paras 77–87.
123 Ibid., 41 and 53.
124 Ibid., 46.
125 Ibid., 47–49.
126 Ibid., 50–51.
127 P. van Cleynenbreugel, '*Meroni* Circumvented? Article 114 TFEU and EU Regulatory Agencies' (2011) 21 *Maastricht Journal of European and Comparative Law*, 87.

It is, however, submitted that there is a fundamental difference between the regulatory powers of an agency in the internal market and operational policing powers in the AFSJ. While the Lisbon Treaty provided for a framework for the delegation of regulatory powers – even if only implicitly when it comes to agencies – operational powers were explicitly left to the Member States, with mere coordinating powers being conferred on the COSI.[128] Policing powers, which may include powers of coercion and the use of force, are factual rather than legal and involve a level of discretion that is difficult to regulate. In this different policy context, the limitations from the Meroni doctrine will much more readily impose themselves, even when applied leniently as was done in the ESMA case.

Border control consists of both border checks and border surveillance. It could be argued that a decision on entry and exit could qualify as an implementing decision of a Union body, limited to either a positive or negative decision, based on the specific criteria provided for in the Schengen Borders Code and subject to judicial review under Article 263 TFEU. The question is whether the EU's judicial system would be capable of coping with this inevitable increase in caseload as a result of appeals against refusal of entry.[129] A full transfer of powers would in any case be difficult in view of the Court's emphasis on the subsidiary nature of the ESMA's powers in the ESMA case.

Judicial review would not be available for purely factual actions during border checks and surveillance, although the possibility of an action for damages would be open in case these would not be in line with the rules of the Schengen Borders Code or infringe fundamental rights as protected in the Charter of Fundamental Rights. A transfer of these operational powers would require extensive regulation of conduct during border checks and border surveillance. For the time being, there are only very limited rules on surveillance and it has to be questioned to what extent the discretion involved in these activities can be effectively circumscribed in legislation.[130] It must therefore be argued that under the current Treaty rules, the establishment of an autonomous EU border guard authority is not possible. Having said that, a genuine transfer of executive power to an EU body would, in case of violations of fundamental rights, place the responsibility for such violations squarely with the EU and from that point of view would bring clarity to the legal twilight within which Frontex currently operates.

128 Article 71 TFEU. See also the European Convention (n. 111), 3 emphasising the separation of legislative and operational tasks in the AFSJ.

129 Article 13, Schengen Borders Code.

130 Note that the Commission in its Agenda on Migration expressed its intention to consolidate the 'patchwork of sectorial documents and instruments' into a – presumably non-legislative – Union standard for border management by 2016, COM(2015) 240 final (n. 27), 11.

5 Conclusion

Frontex has developed as an important actor within the nascent EU's Integrated Management System for the External Borders. Its powers have been consistently adapted and expanded, resulting in the steady movement towards a more autonomous 'European Corps of Border Guards' as originally envisaged by the European Commission. This shows also in the emphasis that is put on operational cooperation in the discussion on the future of EU border management. The feasibility study for an ESBG in its most far-reaching scenario envisages the creation of a parallel structure alongside Frontex, integrating national border guard authorities and effectively ignoring the existence of the COSI, provided for in the TFEU itself.

However, various reports, including the Study itself, show a reluctance on the side of the Member States for further integration on an operational level that goes beyond technical and operational assistance. At the same time, they actively support in particular the more regulatory tasks of the Agency, such as risk analysis and common training.[131] In fact, much progress towards an ESBG could be made already by reinforcing the regulatory tasks of Frontex, allowing for a reinforcement of its intelligence-gathering role and a further centralisation of training, as well as the purchase of interoperable equipment. Developing the Agency's regulatory role would do justice to the institutional set-up of the European Union and the division of competences between the EU and its Member States in the Treaties. It could make an important contribution to a more integrated and efficient management of the borders without unnecessary duplication or undue centralisation. Importantly, this could be done within the current Treaty framework, as it must be argued that the continued expansion of Frontex's powers and tasks is reaching its constitutional limits.

The current Treaty framework neither allows for the transfer of executive law enforcement powers to the exclusion of the Member States, nor for the conferral of such discretionary power without procedures for judicial review and a detailed legislative framework circumscribing it. At the same time, paradoxically, anything other than a full transfer of executive law enforcement powers to the EU would only exuberate the existing uncertainty as regards the responsibility for possible violations of fundamental rights in the joint operational activity, raising questions of a constitutional nature of its own.

This problem is not exclusive to Frontex, but applies to multilevel law enforcement cooperation in the AFSJ in general. Border management has always been at the forefront of cooperation in law enforcement, being among the first policing powers to have been supranationalised by the Amsterdam Treaty. As such, the experience in this field may inform the development of

131 Unisys (n. 107), 18; Horii (n. 81), 170. See also S. Wolff and A. Schout, 'Frontex as Agency: More of the Same?' (2013) 14 *Perspectives on European Politics and Society* 305, 318.

other Union agencies in the AFSJ. Although the constitutional limits to an expansion of the powers of Europol and Eurojust have been more clearly specified in the TFEU, their coordinating powers equally raise questions as regards the responsibility for fundamental rights violations in the context of joint operational activity.

Outside the realm of law enforcement cooperation, a possible conferral of binding administrative powers on the European Asylum Support Office (EASO) in the context of the Common European Asylum System would raise questions in terms of judicial review, similar to those identified above in the case of a centralised European border authority. The current proposal for a European Public Prosecutor's Office recognises that a transfer of genuine law enforcement powers to the EU level requires a decentralisation of judicial protection. This, however, implies a fundamental rethinking of the centralised system of judicial review of measures adopted by the EU institutions or agencies.

Frontex and the EU's border policy exemplify that, with the advent of the AFSJ, an ever-closer Union is not exclusively made through law. Increasingly, the Union is joining the Member States as an internal security actor, constructing the institutional infrastructure that allows it to play that role. As it stands, the EU's constitutional framework seems, however, ill-fit to accommodate the EU's ambitions for the AFSJ, without fundamentally changing the nature of the European project, ignoring the limits imposed by the Treaties or risking to lose sight of its commitment to fundamental rights.

Bibliography

Aas, K. and Gundhus, H., 'Policing Humanitarian Borderlands: Frontex, Human Rights and the Precariousness of Life' (2014) 54 *British Journal of Criminology* 1

Callovi, G., *Securing External Frontiers in a Union of 25*, Migration Policy Institute, Policy Brief No. 5 (2004)

Carrera, S., *The EU Border Management Strategy: Frontex and the Challenges of Irregular Immigration in the Canary Islands*, CEPS Working Document No. 261 (2007), www.ceps.eu/publications/eu-border-management-strategy-frontex-and-challenges-irregular-immigration-canary (accessed 1 May 2015)

Dehousse, R., *Misfits: EU Law and the Misfits of European Governance*, Jean Monnet Working Paper 2 (2002), www.jeanmonnetprogram.org/archive/papers/02/020201.html (accessed 1 May 2014)

Fink, M., 'A "Blind Spot" in the Framework of International Responsibility? Third Party Responsibility for Human Rights Violations: The Case of Frontex', in T. Gammeltoft-Hansen and J. Vedsted-Hansen (eds.), *Human Rights and the Dark Side of Globalisation: Transnational Law Enforcement* (2015), http://papers.ssrn.com/sol3/papers.cfm?abstract_id=2591126 (accessed 1 May 2015)

Horii, S., 'It is About More Than Just Training: The Effect of Frontex Border Guard Training' (2012) 31 *Refugee Survey Quarterly* 158

House of Lords Select Committee on the EU, *Frontex: The EU External Borders Agency*, HL Paper 60, Session 2007–08, 9th Report (2008)

Human Rights Watch, 'Pushed Back, Pushed Around: Italy's Forced Return of Boat Migrants and Asylum Seekers, Libya's Mistreatment of Migrants and Asylum Seekers' (Report, 2009), www.hrw.org/reports/2009/09/21/pushed-back-pushed-around (accessed 1 May 2015)
Human Rights Watch, 'The EU's Dirty Hands: Frontex Involvement in Ill-Treatment of Migrant Detainees in Greece' (Report, 2011), www.hrw.org/reports/2011/09/21/eu-s-dirty-hands (accessed 1 May 2015)
Monar, J., 'Justice and Home Affairs', in U. Sedelmeier and A. Young (eds.), *JCMS Annual Review of the European Union in 2007* (Blackwell, 2008) 109
Mungianu, R., 'Frontex: Towards a Common Policy on External Border Control' (2013) 15 *European Journal of Migration and Law* 359
Mungianu, R., *The Principle of Non-refoulement in the European Union's Border Control Joint Operations: On the Interpretation and Application of the Principle of Non-refoulement by Frontex* (PhD thesis, Copenhagen University, 2013)
Neal, A., 'Securitization and Risk at the EU Border: The Origins of Frontex' (2009) 47 *Journal of Common Market Studies* 333
Ott, A., Vos, E. and Coman-Kund, F., 'European Agencies on the Global Scene: EU and International Law Perspectives', in M. Everson, C. Monda and E. Vos (eds.), *European Agencies in Between Institutions and Member States* (Wolters Kluwer, 2014) 87
Rijpma, J., 'Frontex: Successful Blame Shifting of the Member States?' (Analysis of the Real Instituto Elcano, No 69, 2010), www.realinstitutoelcano.org/wps/portal/web/rielcano_en/contenido?WCM_GLOBAL_CONTEXT=/elcano/Elcano_in/Zonas_in/ARI69-2010#.VVstLmdxmUk (accessed 1 May 2014)
Rijpma, J., 'Hybrid Agencification in the Area of Freedom, Security and Justice and its Inherent Tensions: The case of Frontex', in M. Busuioc, M. Groenleer and J. Trondal (eds.), *The Agency Phenomenon in the European Union: Emergence, Institutionalisation and Everyday Decision-Making* (Manchester University Press, 2012) 84
Rijpma, J., 'The Patrolling of the European Union's External Maritime Border: Preventing the Rule of Law from Getting Lost at Sea' in A. Del Vecchio (ed.), *International Law of the Sea: Current Trends and Controversial Issues* (Eleven Publishing, 2013) 77
Rijpma, J., 'Institutions and Agencies: Government and Governance after Lisbon', in D. Acosta Arcarazo and C. Murphy (eds.), *EU Security and Justice Law after Lisbon and Stockholm* (Hart Publishing, 2014) 54
Rijpma, J. and Vermeulen, M., 'EUROSUR: Saving Lives or Building Borders?' (2015) 24 *European Security* 454
Slominski, P., 'The Power of Legal Norms in the EU's External Border Control' (2013) 51 *International Migration* 41
Stetter, S., 'Regulating Migration: Authority Delegation in Justice and Home Affairs' (2000) 7 *Journal of European Public Policy* 80
van Cleynenbreugel, P., 'Meroni Circumvented? Article 114 TFEU and EU Regulatory Agencies' (2011) 21 *Maastricht Journal of European and Comparative Law* 64
Wolff, J. and Schout, A., 'Frontex as Agency: More of the Same?' (2013) 14 *Perspectives on European Politics and Society* 305

Legislation, proposals for legislation, Treaties and other legal texts

Acuerdo entre España y Cabo Verde sobre vigilancia conjunta de los espacios marítimos bajo soberaníay jurisdicción de Cabo Verde, BOE No 136, 5 June 2009, 47545
Commission, 'Proposal for a Council Regulation on the establishment of the European Public Prosecutor's Office' COM(2013) 534 final
Commission, 'Proposal for a regulation amending Regulation (EC) 562/2006 in order to provide for common rules on the temporary reintroduction of border control at internal borders in exceptional circumstances' COM(2011) 560
Commission, 'Proposal for a Regulation establishing, as part of the Internal Security Fund, the instrument for financial support for external borders and visa' COM(2011) 750 final
Commission, 'Proposal for a regulation on the establishment of an evaluation and monitoring mechanism to verify the application of the Schengen acquis' COM(2011) 559 final
Commission, 'Report on the evaluation and future development of the Frontex Agency' COM(2008) 67 final
Committee of 16 September 1998 setting up a Standing Committee on the evaluation and implementation of Schengen [2013] OJ L 295/27
Council Decision 2002/187/JHA of 28 February 2002 setting up Eurojust with a view to reinforcing the fight against serious crime [2002] OJ L 63/1
Council Decision 2009/371/JHA of 6 April 2009 establishing the European Police Office (Europol) [2009] OJ L 121/37
Council Decision 2010/131/EU of 25 February 2010 on setting up the Standing Committee on operational cooperation on internal security [2010] OJ L52/50
Council Decision of 26 April 2010 supplementing the Schengen Borders Code as regards the surveillance of the sea external borders in the context of operational cooperation coordinated by [Frontex] [2011] OJ L 111/20
Council Regulation (EC) No 2007/2004 of 26 October 2004 establishing a European Agency for the Management of Operational Cooperation at the External Borders of the Member States of the European Union [2004] OJ L 349/1
Council Regulation (EU) No 1053/2013 of 7 October 2013 establishing an evaluation and monitoring mechanism to verify the application of the Schengen acquis and repealing the Decision of the Executive
Decision of the Executive Committee of 16 September 1998 setting up a Standing Committee on the evaluation and implementation of Schengen (SCH/ Com-ex (98) 26 def.)
Decision No 574/2007/EC of 23 May 2007 establishing the External Borders Fund for the period 2007 to 2013 as part of the General programme 'Solidarity and Management of Migration Flows' [2007] OJ L 144/22 ('EBF')
Regulation (EC) No 562/2006 of 15 March 2006 establishing a Community Code on the rules governing the movement of persons across borders (Schengen Borders Code) [2006] OJ L105/1
Regulation (EC) No 863/2007 of 11 July 2007 establishing a mechanism for the creation of Rapid Border Intervention Teams and amending Council Regulation (EC) No 2007/2004 as regards that mechanism and regulating the tasks and powers of guest officers [2007] L 199/30 ('2007 Regulation')

Regulation (EU) No 1168/2011 of 25 October 2011 amending Council Regulation (EC) No 2007/2004 establishing a European Agency for the Management of Operational Cooperation at the External Borders of the Member States of the European Union [2011] OJ L301/1 ('2011 Regulation')

Regulation (EU) No 182/2011 of 16 February 2011 laying down the rules and general principles concerning mechanisms for control by Member States of the Commission's exercise of implementing powers (2011) OJ L55/291

Regulation (EU) No 604/2013 of 26 June 2013 establishing the criteria and mechanisms for determining the Member State responsible for examining an application for international protection lodged in one of the Member States by a third-country national or a stateless person (recast) ('Dublin III Regulation')

Regulation (EU) No 1051/2013 of 22 October 2013 amending Regulation (EC) No 562/2006 in order to provide for common rules on the temporary reintroduction of border control at internal borders in exceptional circumstances [2013] OJ L 295/1

Regulation (EU) No 1052/2013 of 22 October 2013 establishing the European Border Surveillance System (Eurosur) [2013] L 295/11 ('Eurosur Regulation')

Regulation (EU) No 515/2014 of 16 April 2014 establishing, as part of the Internal Security Fund, the instrument for financial support for external borders and visa and repealing Decision No 574/2007/EC ('IFS-Borders') Regulation (EU) No 656/2014 of 15 May 2014 establishing rules for the surveillance of the external sea borders in the context of operational cooperation coordinated by [Frontex] [2014] OJ L189/93

Policy documents and reports

Commission, 'Towards Integrated Management of the External Borders of the Member States of the European Union' (Communication) COM(2002) 233 final

Commission, 'Preparing the next steps in border management in the European Union' (Communication) COM(2008) 69 final

Commission, 'EU Guidelines for Integrated Border Management in European Commission External Cooperation, European Commission' (2010), http://capacity4dev.ec.europa.eu/ibm-eap/document/1-guidelines-integrated-border-management-european-commission-external-cooperation-european#sthash.veslRARI.dpuf (accessed 1 May 2015)

Commission, 'Schengen Governance – Strengthening the Area Without Internal Border Controls' (Communication) COM(2011) 561 final

Commission, 'A European Agenda on Migration' (Communication) COM(2015) 240 final

European Convention, 'Final Report of Working Group X on Freedom, Security and Justice (CONV 426/02)

European Council, 'The Stockholm Programme: An Open and Secure Europe Serving and Protecting Citizens' (Conclusions) (2009) OJ C 115/1, 26

European Council, Conclusions of 26–27 June 2014 (European Council Document EUCO 79/14)

European Council, 'Statement on the Special Meeting of the European Council on Migration and Asylum' (23 April 2015), www.consilium.europa.eu/en/press/press-releases/2015/04/23-special-euco-statement (accessed 1 May 2015)

European Parliament, Resolution of 13 December 2007 on the draft general budget of the European Union for the financial year 2008 as modified by the Council (P6_TA(2007)0616)
European Parliament, 'The implementation of Article 80 TFEU on the principle of solidarity and fair sharing of responsibility, including its financial implications, between the Member States in the field of border checks, asylum and immigration' (Study), PE 453.167, 2011
House of Lords Select Committee on the EU, 'FRONTEX: the EU external borders agency' (HL Paper 60, Session 2007–08, 9th Report, 2008)
Human Rights Watch, 'Pushed Back, Pushed Around: Italy's Forced Return of Boat Migrants and Asylum Seekers, Libya's Mistreatment of Migrants and Asylum Seekers' (Report, 2009) www.hrw.org/reports/2009/09/21/pushed-back-pushed-around (accessed 1 May 2015)
Human Rights Watch, 'The EU's Dirty Hands: Frontex Involvement in Ill-Treatment of Migrant Detainees in Greece' (Report, 2011) www.hrw.org/reports/2011/09/21/eu-s-dirty-hands (accessed 1 May 2015)
JHA Council, Council Conclusions on Integrated Border Management (Brussels, 4–5 December 2006)
Unisys, 'Study on the feasibility of the creation of a European System of Border Guards to control the external borders of the Union (ESBG) (2014)', http://ec.europa.eu/dgs/home-affairs/what-we-do/policies/borders-and-visas/border-crossing/docs/20141016_home_esbg_frp_001_esbg_final_report_3_00_en.pdf (accessed 1 May 2014)

Case law

Case 9/56 *Meroni* [1957] ECR 11 at 147–149 and Case 10/56 *Meroni* [1958] ECR 53 at 169–171.
Case C-217/04 *UK v European Parliament and Council* ("ENISA") [2006] ECR I-3771 (ECLI:EU:C:2006:279)
Case C-270/12 *UK v European Parliament and Council* ("ESMA") (ECLI:EU:C:2014:18)
Case C-355/10 *European Parliament v Commission and Council* (ECLI:EU:C:2012:516)
Joined Cases C-411/10 and C-493, *N.S. and M.E.* (ECLI:EU:C:2011:865)
Hirsi Jamaa and others v Italy Application No. 27765/09 (ECHR, 23 February 2012)

10 The rule of life

Family reunification in EU mobility and migration laws

Dora Kostakopoulou and Ariadna Ripoll Servent

1 Introduction

Institutions are created in order to regulate social life and to aid human activity. Their existence is the product of sociopolitical activity and the main purpose underpinning their creation and maintenance is to enhance human life as suffused in social relations. Accordingly, norms are 'in politics', but are also a reflection of rules of life. They represent a vision of things from above but at their centre lays an intelligible plan to facilitate human flourishing, that is, to serve human beings in their relations. One such rule of life is the founding of a family and the protection of the family unit.

As Article 16(3) of the Universal Declaration on Human Rights states, 'the family is the natural and fundamental group unit of sociality and is entitled to protection by society and the state'. The entitlement to protection stems from the simple fact that individuals can only flourish by experiencing the love, care, protection and warmth that close, familial, relations emit. The continuity of this experience contributes to human beings' well-being. When continuity is disrupted by other contingencies, including border crossings and one's settlement in another state, relations are under strain as personal and family lives become disentangled. The reunification of the family ends the disjunction and preserves the integrity of familial relations.

Although almost all international law instruments recognise these facts, the family reunification of migrant workers with their spouses and dependent children has not been recognised as a right in international law. Notwithstanding their positive obligations to facilitate family reunification, states enjoy a level of discretion in this area – a certain margin of appreciation, owing to their sovereign jurisdiction in migration and refugee matters.[1]

1 Compare Article 44(2) of the *International Convention on Migrant Workers*. The ECtHR has ruled that the obligations imposed on states by Article 8 ECHR do not extend to a general obligation to respect the choice by married couples of the country of matrimonial residence so as to require them to grant entry to the non-national spouse for settlement; *Abdulaziz v United Kingdom* (1985) 7 EHRR 471 at para 68; *Rodrigues Da Silva Hoogkamer v The Netherlands* (2007) 44 EHRR 34 at para 39; *Y v Russia* (2008) 51 EHRR 21 at para 103.

In contrast, European Union law recognises a concrete and fully-fledged right to family reunification that all EU national migrant workers in the past, and now EU citizens, have. Since the early days of European integration, family unification was deemed to be an important aid to intra-Community mobility and necessary for the integration of the worker and his family into the host Member State. It has also been a manifestation of his/her equal treatment in relation to nationals of that state. The term 'family' was defined in the Council Regulation 1612/68 (Article 10(1)), which implemented the right to free movement for workers established by the Rome Treaty in 1957. It consisted of a worker's spouse, their descendants who are under the age of 21 or are dependants and dependent relatives in the ascending line of the worker and his spouse.[2] Directive 2004/38, which repealed Articles 10 and 11 of the Council Regulation 1612/68, broadened the definition of 'family member' by including registered partners – if the legislation of the host Member State treats registered partnership as equivalent to marriage and in accordance with the conditions laid down in national law – and their descendants and dependent direct relatives in the ascending line.[3] It also provides for the facilitated entry of Union citizens' other dependant family members or members of their household or recipients of personal care by the Union citizen (Article 3(a) of the Directive). In addition, Article 3(b) recommends that Member States facilitate the entry of Union citizens' cohabitees.

By establishing a European Union fundamental right law to family reunification, the Court of Justice of the European Union has limited the Member States' sovereign prerogatives in the field of migration law and has tamed nationalist narratives. The right to family reunification has also been extended to third-country nationals (TCNs) residing legally in the European Union following the adoption of Directive 2003/86.[4] But whereas 'communitarian egalitarianism' has characterised the European Union's law and policy towards the family reunification of EU citizens, the family reunification of TCNs has been governed by a rival policy belief system; namely, by what may be termed 'restrictive collectivism'.

In this chapter, we examine the regulation of family reunification in EU internal mobility law, on the one hand (Section 2), and EU migration law (Section 3), on the other, and contrast the policy priority of facilitating intra-EU mobility and recognising the reality of family life with those of migration control and of ensuring national cohesion. We make a case for rethinking the restrictive family reunification rules applying to EU migration law and for the coherent application of the normative standards pertaining to the right to family reunion without differentiation on the basis of the sponsor's

2 European Council Regulation 1612/68 *on Free Movement of Workers* OJ Special Edition 475, OJ L257/2.

3 Council Directive 2003/86/EC of 22 September 2003 *on the Right to Family Reunification* [2003] OJ L251/12.

4 Ibid.

nationality. If families are treated differently on the basis of contingent characteristics, such as the nationality of the sponsor, and differences are drawn on the basis of spouses' geographical location, then a legal order's normative commitment to respect for family life is not deep enough. One cannot separate the same from its other except by abandoning the norm altogether. In principle, all family units should be treated alike and the continuity of family life and experience is equally valuable to all human beings so as to command protection.

2 From value commitment to contention

The Court of Justice of the European Union has been proactive and uncompromising in establishing a Community law fundamental right to family reunification. Since the early days of European integration, family unification was deemed to be an important aid to intra-Community mobility and necessary for 'the integration of the worker and his family into the host MS without any difference in treatment in relation to nationals of that state'.[5] Third-country national spouses of initially Community workers, Community nationals in the early 1990s and of Union citizens following the entry into force of the Treaty on European Union on 1 November 1993, have not fallen within the regulatory realm of, often restrictive, national migration laws, but have enjoyed derived rights as members of the worker's family. In addition, the EU's normative commitment in this domain has been enhanced by the fact that the Court of Justice of the EU has not hesitated to pronounce respect for family life (Article 8 ECHR) an integral part of the general principles of Community law. In *Commission v Germany*, the requirement of German law that made the issuing of residence permits to family members of Community workers on the fact that they live in appropriate accommodation for the duration of their stay in the host Member State, and not only at the time of their move into a dwelling, was found to contravene Article 10(3) of Council Reg. 1612/68.[6]

In the new millennium, aided by the institutional architecture of the partial formal basis of Article 6(2) TEU, which stated that the Union 'shall respect fundamental rights, as guaranteed by the European Convention for the Protection of Human Rights and Fundamental Freedoms signed in Rome on 4 November 1950 and as they result from the constitutional traditions common to the MS, as general principles of Community law' and the Charter of Fundamental Rights (Article 7), which was proclaimed in Nice on 7 December 2000,[7] and being attuned to the debate about possible accession to the ECHR by the EU, the Court elevated the fundamental right of

5 Case 249/86 *Commission v Germany* (re housing of migrant workers) [1989] ECR 1263, paras 10, 11.
6 Ibid.
7 [2000] OJ C364/1.

respect for family life at the expense of national migration laws. In *Carpenter*, it ruled that a derivative right of residence can be implied from the right to provide services (formerly Article 49 EC), thereby overriding restrictive national immigration rules.[8] The Court's attribution of normative priority to respect for family life has been reiterated in subsequent rulings, such as *MRAX*, *Baumbast*, *Commission v Spain*, *Jia*, *Eind*, culminating in *Metock and Others*,[9] where the Court outlawed national legislation making the right of residence of third-country national family members of EU citizens subject to prior lawful residence in another MS.[10] Notwithstanding the controversy associated with the latter ruling in Denmark, the UK and elsewhere, the Court progressively sought to reduce barriers to the family reunification of EU citizens erected by restrictive national migration regimes. In the case of *Reyes*, for instance, the Court ruled that a third-country national descendant, who is dependent on a Union citizen receiving a steady income, does not have to show that she tried unsuccessfully to find employment in the state of origin in order to obtain a residence permit in Sweden where her mother, an EU national, lived.[11] To impose such a requirement on a dependant family member would contravene the letter (Article 23) and the spirit of Directive 2004/38. And in the Cases C-456/12 *O and B* and C-457/12 *S and G*, the Court held that TCN family members of EU citizens enjoy derived rights of residence when Union citizens return to the Member State of origin following a period of residence in another Member State (*O and B*) as well as when they are travelling to another Member State as frontier workers (*S and G*).[12]

The Court's normative commitment to family reunion has been anchored on what may be termed 'communitarian egalitarianism'. EU citizens and their lifeworlds need to be protected so as to be able to lead full and dignified lives. Pursuing this fundamental policy belief system with respect to EU citizens has not always been easy. This was not only due to intergovernmental reactions. It was also due to the fact that the Court had to tread carefully around what

8 Case C-60/00 *M. Carpenter*, Judgment of the Court of 11 July 2002. See G. Barret, 'Family Matters: European Community Law and Third Country Family Members' (2003) 40 *Common Market Law Review* 369, 406.

9 Case C-459/99 *MRAX*, Judgment of the Court of 25 July 2002; Case C-413/99 *Baumbast and R v Secretary of State for the Home Department* [2002] ECR I-7091; C-157/03 *Commission v Spain* [2005] ECR I-2911; C-1/05 *Jia v Migrationsverket* [2007] ECR I-1; Case C-291/05 *Eind*, Judgment of the Court of 11 December 2007; Case C-127/08, *Metock and Others*, Judgment of the Court of 25 July 2008. See also the Commission's 5th Report on Citizenship of the Union that mentions the need to interpret the right to free movement in the light of fundamental rights, including the right to respect for family life, and the principle of proportionality; COM(2008) 85 Final, 15 February 2008.

10 D.S. Martinsen, 'Judicial Policy-Making and Europeanization: The Proportionality of National Control and Administrative Discretion' (2011) 18(7) *Journal of European Public Policy* 956.

11 Case C-423/12 *Flora May Reyes v Migrationsverket*, Judgment of the Court, 16 January 2014.

12 Judgment of the Court (Grand Chamber), 12 March 2014.

has been termed 'wholly internal situations' that are governed by national law because they do not involve cross-border activity in order to trigger the application of European Union law. Such cases involved the family reunion of Union citizens who had never exercised their free movement rights and thus did not fall within the scope of the Citizenship Directive (2004/38).[13] Although sedentary Union citizens could not invoke the free movement provisions of EU law, the Court could not ignore their plight at the end of the first decade of the new millennium as shown in the triptychon of *Zambrano*,[14] *McCarthy*[15] and *Dereci*[16] cases. Ruiz Zambrano was a Colombian national who had been residing in Belgium without a residence permit following the rejection of his asylum application but could not be deported to his country of origin, Colombia, owing to *non-refoulement* reasons. His wife gave birth to two children, Diego and Jessica, both Belgian nationals and EU citizens as the father failed to register the births with the Colombian embassy. Although Mr Zambrano and his wife could not leave Belgium and were denied work and residence permits, he nevertheless had taken up full-time employment for five years in order to support his family and contributed to the tax and social security burden of the Belgian commonwealth. But when, following his redundancy, he challenged the authorities' refusal to recognise his entitlement to unemployment benefit, he and his family faced the prospect of expulsion from Belgium and thus from the European Union. The Court ruled that Mr Zambrano was entitled to remain and work in Belgium without a work permit as the parent of EU citizen children who would have to leave the territory of the Union if their father did not have the right to live and work in Belgium. Advocate General Sharpston highlighted the importance of fundamental rights in the light of the legally binding Charter of Fundamental Rights,[17] but the Court premised its decision on EU citizenship rather than on fundamental rights. As the Court stated:

> Article 20 TFEU precludes national measures which have the effect of depriving citizens of the Union of the genuine enjoyment of the substance of the rights conferred by virtue of their status as citizens of the Union. A refusal to grant a right of residence to a third country national

13 Directive 2004/38 of 29 April 2004 [2004] OJ L158/77.

14 Case C-34/09 *Ruiz Zambrano v Office National de l'Emploi (ONEM)* [2011] ECR I-0000.

15 Case C-434/09 *Shirley McCarthy v Secretary of State for the Home Department* [2011] ECR I-03375.

16 Case C-256/11 *Dereci, Heiml, Kokollari, Maduike and Stevic v Bundesministerium fur Inneres*, Judgment of the Court, 15 November 2011.

17 Case C-54/09, Opinion delivered on 30 September 2010. Notably, AG Sharpston had also stated that 'Article 18 TFEU should be interpreted as prohibiting reverse discrimination caused by the interaction between Article 21 TFEU and national law that entails a violation of a fundamental right protected by EU law, where at least equivalent protection is not available under national law' (point 144).

with dependent minor children in the Member State where those children are nationals and reside [...] has such an effect.[18]

The refusal to grant a right to residence to the parents of the children would thus result in the children's departure from 'the territory of the Union' and the deprivation of the opportunity to exercise their EU citizenship rights.

But, in *McCarthy*, the Court could not sidestep national migration rules since Mrs McCarthy had never exercised her free movement rights. She was a dual national of British and Irish nationality and wished to secure a right of residence for her spouse, a Jamaican national, by invoking her newly acquired Irish nationality. The Court distinguished this case from *Zambrano* in that the restrictive UK migration provisions did not have the effect of necessitating Mrs McCarthy's departure from the territory of the Union (para 50) and thus not resulting in the deprivation of the genuine enjoyment of her rights or impeding the exercising of her freedom to move and reside freely within the territory of the MS under Article 21 TFEU (para 49). Similarly, in *Dereci and Others* the Court ruled that third-country national family members of EU citizens (the latter were Austrian nationals) who had never exercised their right to free movement and did not rely on their spouses for their subsistence fell within the ambit of the internal situation doctrine. As both the Family Reunification Directive (Article 3(3) 2003/86) and the Citizenship Directive (Dir. 2004/38) did not apply, the Court was reluctant to extend the ambit of EU citizenship protection since the Austrian measures would not lead to the forced departure of the Austrian nationals from not only the territory of a MS but also the territory of the Union (para 66) thereby compromising or undermining the effectiveness of EU citizenship (para 67). Whether the Austrian measures had this effect was a matter for the referring court to verify (para 74), but, if they did not, the issues at hand would have to be addressed with reference to the protection of fundamental rights and the right to respect for private and family life (Article 7 of the EUCFR and 8(1) of ECHR), which would lead to the grant of a right of residence. It concluded that it was a matter for the referring court to establish whether the situation was covered by Union law (which would have been the case if Austria implemented EU law), thus necessitating the application of the Charter, or, if it was not covered, then Article 8(1) of the ECHR would be applicable. The Court (Grand Chamber) thus circumscribed the novelty of

18 *Ruiz Zambrano* at para 43. For commentary, see also C. Lenaerts, '"Civis Europeaus Sum": From the Cross-Border Link to the Status of Citizen of the Union' (2011) 2 *Online Journal of Free Movement of Workers Within the EU* 12; D. Kochenov, 'A Real European Citizenship: The Court of Justice Opening a New Chapter in the Development of the Union in Europe' (2012) 18(1) *Columbia Journal of European Law* 55–109; M. Hailbronner and S.I. Sanchez, 'The European Court of Justice and Citizenship of the European Union: New Developments Towards a Truly Fundamental Status' (2011) 5 *International Criminal Law and Justice* 498.

Zambrano and at the same time refrained from 'clarifying the substance of rights' doctrine as well as from commenting on the possible links between Article 20 and 21 TFEU and fundamental rights.[19]

Subsequently, in *O, S and L*[20] the Court reflected on the applicability of the Zambrano doctrine to the cases of reconstituted families where the step-parent of an EU citizen child has no parental or financial responsibility over him or her. In *O and S*, a Ghanaian national, who had been married to a Finnish national with whom she had a child of Finnish nationality and had sole custody of the child before and after her divorce, remarried a third-country national (an Ivory Coast national), O, and had another child with him. When O applied for a residence permit, his application was refused on the ground that he did not have sufficient means of subsistence. The same refusal of a residence permit took place in *L*, where an Algerian national, married another Algerian national following her divorce from a Finnish national with whom she had a child of Finnish nationality who was under her sole custody. Although it was suggested that the denial of resident permits to the step-fathers would not result in the forced departure of the children from the territory of the EU[21] and the Court left this matter to the national court, it urged the latter to examine 'all the circumstances of the case'[22] and to note that what would compel the child's departure would be the relationship of 'legal, financial or emotional dependence'.[23] If, on the other hand, the Zambrano doctrine could not apply, under the Family Reunification Directive (2003/86),[24] the third-country national mothers could be viewed to be 'sponsors' of their third-country national husbands within the meaning of Article 2(c) of the Directive and the Member States have 'precise positive obligations with corresponding clearly defined individual rights ... to authorise the family reunification of certain members of the sponsor's family, without being left a margin of appreciation'.[25] Their decision must also comply

19 The association of fundamental rights and Union citizenship was discussed more explicitly in *Yoshikazu Iida v Stadt Ulm*, Judgment of the Court of 12 November 2012. For the proposal of linking the substance of rights doctrine of Union citizenship with fundamental rights, thereby enabling EU citizens to activate a 'reverse Solange' situation and rebut the presumption that MS comply with fundamental rights by relying on Article 20 TFEU before national courts and the Court, see A. Von Bogdandy, M. Kottmann, C. Antpohler, J. Dickschen, S. Hentri and M. Smrkolj, 'Reverse Solange: Protecting the Essence of Fundamental Rights against EU Member States' (2012) 49 *Common Market Law Review* 489.

20 Joined Cases C-356/11 and C-357/11 *O, S and L* (ECJ, 6 December 2012).

21 Joined Cases C-356/11 and C-357/11 *O, S v Maahanmuuttovirasto and Maahanmuuttovirasto v L*, Opinion of AG Bot delivered on 27 September 2012, points 44–46. The Advocate General stressed that such decision would be 'freely' taken by the mother for a reason linked to the preservation of family life.

22 Ibid. [53].

23 Ibid. [56] and AG Bot's Opinion (n. 21) point 44.

24 Council Directive 2003/86/EC of 22 September 2003 on the Right to Family Reunification [2003] OJ L251/12.

25 *O, S and L* (n. 20) [70].

with the *Chakroun* ruling on the meaning of the requirement on the possession of 'stable and regular resources' by the sponsor under Article 7(1)(c) of the Family Reunification Directive[26] and with the Charter of Fundamental Rights. In particular, Article 7 on the right to respect family life must be read in conjunction with the obligation to take into account the best interests of the child recognised in Article 24(2) and his or her interest to maintain a personal relationship with both parents on a regular basis under Article 24(3). As the Court stated:

> The Member States must not only interpret their national law in a manner consistent with European Union law but also make sure that they do not rely on an interpretation of an instrument of secondary legislation which would be in conflict with the fundamental rights protected by the legal order of the European Union.[27]

The above-mentioned judgments reveal the Court's attempts to strike a balance between national regulatory competences and the evolving dynamics of Community law and EU citizenship while preserving the EU's value commitment to respect for family life. Its rulings may unavoidably lead to differentiated results and somewhat inconsistent action. But, at the same time, they draw attention to the need for more comprehensive solutions to intra-EU family migration issues in the future. Calls to preserve the normative integrity of family reunification are bound to increase given the fact that the EU Charter of Fundamental Rights has been upgraded to a constitutional guarantee. And this upgrading calls into question the dependence of effective family reunification on the mobility status of Union citizens. Both Carlier[28] and Groenendijk[29] have pointed out that the Commission's proposed draft directive on family reunification (Dir. 2003/86) included the provision that sedentary Union citizens should be governed by the rules of Community law relating to free movement for the purposes of family reunification. Since the latter is a necessary condition for leading a stable and healthy life, another institutional solution might be the future activation of the so-called 'elastic clause' of Article 25 TFEU resulting in a new explicit template of respect for family life stating: 'The European Union and the Member States shall respect the right of family reunification for all Union citizens.'[30]

26 Case C-578/08 *Chakroun v Minister van Buitenlandse Zaken* [2010] ECR I-1839.

27 *O, S and L* (n. 20) [78].

28 J-Y. Carlier, 'La Libre Circulation des Personnes dans et vers l'Union Européenne' (2013) *Journal de Droit Europeen* 103.

29 K. Groenendijk, 'Reverse Discrimination, Family Reunification and Union Citizens of Immigrant Origin', in E. Guild, C. Gortazar-Rotaeche and D. Kostakopoulou (eds.), *The Reconceptualisation of EU Citizenship* (Brill/Nijhoff, 2014) 169.

30 D. Kostakopoulou, 'Co-creating EU Citizenship: Institutional Process and Crescive Norms' (2013) 15 *The Cambridge Yearbook of European Legal Studies* 255, at p. 276.

Critics might argue here that the present environment in Europe is not conducive for enlightened and liberal migration reforms in this domain and in the Area of Freedom, Security and Justice, in general. The ethical embedding of family reunification will not transcend certain Member States' rival policy belief in migration restriction and interest in electoral victories. For the time being, it seems that the European Convention of Human Rights (Article 8) could provide a solution, if the Charter of Fundamental Rights were not applicable. And although the context of justification for the recognition of a right to family reunification for EU citizens remains unchanging – that is, human welfare becomes undermined without the care, support and warmth of the loved ones – at present, mobility status serves to categorise EU citizens into privileged and less privileged classes. Communitarian egalitarianism therefore coexists with prioritarianism.

3 Between migration control and rights

Whereas communitarian egalitarianism has characterised the European Union's law and policy towards the family reunification of EU citizens, the family reunification of third-country nationals (TCNs) has been governed by a rival policy belief system; namely, by restrictive collectivism. This is mainly due to the fact that the Member States had competence over this area under the diluted intergovernmentalist framework of the justice and home affairs pillar (the so-called third pillar) of the Treaty on European Union (1993) and thus their policies were characterised by restriction, tight controls on border crossings and the depiction of family migration as an obstacle to societal integration. One should not forget that family migration presents one of the biggest challenges to liberal states: on the one hand, fundamental rights norms make it difficult to deny or stop the reunion of family members; on the other hand, there are fewer and fewer possibilities to enter EU territory by legal means. As a result, family reunification has become one of the main channels to get to the EU and, therefore, challenges the policy goals of many governments, which have sought to curb down and 'manage' migration by choosing who enters and resides on their territory.[31] In 2006, family migration made for 62 per cent of Portugal migration flows, 59 per cent for France, 47 per cent in the Netherlands, 40 per cent in Austria and Italy, 23 per cent in Germany and 18 per cent in Denmark.[32] In 2012, these numbers were down in almost all countries, but still migration continued. France and Portugal remained among the highest ones (with 38 and 37 per cent respectively), followed by Italy (32 per cent). The Netherlands were down to 20 per cent, similar to Austria (15 per cent) and Germany (14 per cent).

31 C. Boswell and A. Geddes, *Migration and Mobility in the European Union* (Palgrave MacMillan, 2011), pp. 103 et seq.

32 OECD, *International Migration Outlook 2008* (OECD Publishing, 2008), http://dx.doi.org/10.1787/migr_outlook-2008-en.

Denmark reached very low figures, with only 8 per cent of migrants coming through the family reunification route.[33] The UK has maintained a relatively low proportion of migrants coming through family reunification (18 per cent in 2006, 12 per cent in 2012).

Following the partial communitarisation of the justice and home affairs pillar and the establishment of a new Migration Title at Amsterdam (1999), the European Council at Tampere identified four key elements for the development of a common migration policy between 1999 and 2004; namely, (1) partnership with the countries of origin; (2) a common European asylum policy; (3) the fair treatment of TCNs; and (4) the fair management of migration flows.[34] The Tampere's commitment to policy priority (3) – that is, the fair treatment of resident TCNs and the development of a vigorous integration policy by granting long-term resident TCNs rights and obligations comparable to EU citizens – created the preconditions for greater symmetry in the treatment of Union citizens and their family members and of resident TCNs. A visible manifestation of the emerging symmetry was the Commission's proposed directive on family reunification (1999),[35] which sought to harmonise national legislations in this area by granting the right to family reunification to all TCNs – including refugees under the Geneva Convention of 1951 and persons enjoying temporary protection, who resided lawfully in a Member State and held a residence permit for at least a year regardless of the purpose of their residence. It also covered Union citizens who had not exercised their right to free movement whose situation had hitherto been subject solely to national rules, as we argued above. The Commission's proposals did not meet the Member States' approval and were adjusted in order to fit with national migration rules. Accordingly, the final draft included provisions on integration conditions and measures: Article 7(2) of the Family Reunification Directive states that 'Member States may require third country nationals to comply with integration measures in accordance with national law'. These could take place before or following the entry into the host Member State. The former policy is known as pre-departure integration or integration abroad. Although this provision was not among the contested provisions in *European Parliament v Council*,[36] the Court, nevertheless, noted the obligations that the Member States have under Article 8 ECHR and invited national courts to use the preliminary ruling reference procedure if they faced interpretational difficulties.

33 OECD, *International Migration Outlook 2014* (OECD Publishing, 2014), http://dx.doi.org/10.1787/migr_outlook-2014-en.

34 *Tampere Presidency Conclusions*, European Council 15–16 October 1999, SN 200/99 Brussels.

35 COM(1999) 638 final CNS 1999/0258, Amended Commission Proposal COM(2000) 624 final.

36 Case C-540/03, 27 June 2006, [2006] ECR I-5769.

According to the Family Reunification Directive, the sponsor – that is, the TCN lawfully residing in a Member State and applying, or whose family members apply, for family reunification – must have a resident permit of at least one year's validity and reasonable prospects for obtaining permanent residence there. And they must be 21 years of age, able to provide adequate accommodation for their family, be covered by health insurance and must have sufficient stable and regular resources to sustain themselves and all family members. Unlike the definition of family members pertaining to EU citizens, Article 4 of the Directive confines family reunification to the nuclear family of the TCN: the spouse and natural or adopted children who are unmarried and minors. First-degree relatives in the ascending line, adult unmarried children and cohabitees do not have a right to family reunification: they fall within the category of eligible family members and are thus subject to the Member States' discretion. In all cases, the Member States may request the sponsor to meet a two-year residence requirement prior to applying for family reunification. This requirement does not apply to refugees (Article 12(2) of the Directive). A similar derogation exists for TCN researchers under Directive 2005/71,[37] who do not enjoy a right to family reunification but have the expectation that a MS will facilitate their family reunion,[38] and highly skilled migrants under Directive 2009/50[39] who enjoy the most favourable rules on family reunification, such as the prohibition of the application of 'integration-abroad' measures (Article 15(2)), a decision on family reunification within six months (Article 15(4)) and immediate access of family members to the labour market of the host state.[40] Public order, public security and public health concerns can constitute grounds for the rejection of an application for family reunion, according to the Family Reunification Directive.

In the years that followed the adoption of the Family Reunification Directive, the Commission broadly maintained its rights-based approach: '[It] is a necessary way of making a success of the integration of third country nationals residing lawfully in the [Member State]. The presence of family members makes for greater stability and deepens the roots of these people since they are enabled to lead a normal family life.'[41] The Communication on *Immigration, Integration and Employment*[42] thus explicitly stated that 'even though the role of the family varies from one culture to the other, it generally plays a central role in the integration process as it represents a fixed point of reference for

37 Directive 2005/71/EC *on a specific procedure for admitting third-country national researchers for the purpose of scientific research* [2005] OJ L 289/15.

38 Recital 18 of the Preamble to the Directive.

39 Directive 2009/50/EC *on the conditions of entry and residence of third country nationals for the purposes of highly qualified employment* [2009] OJ L155/17, 18 June 2009.

40 For an excellent discussion, see A. Wiesbrock, *Legal Migration to the European Union: Ten Years After Tampere* (Wolf Publishers, 2009), pp. 225 et seq.

41 COM(99) 638 final, 3.

42 COM(2003) 336 final, 3 June 2003.

immigrants in the host country. Family reunification with the nuclear family is a key tool in this respect'.[43] And the 2007 Communication, entitled 'Towards a Common Immigration Policy', emphasised the fact that 'integration policy should therefore be seen as a continuum, running from entry through to settlement and to social and economic inclusion'.[44] Following the 2007 Communication and the European Council's meetings in December 2007 and spring 2008,[45] which underlined the need for the development of a comprehensive European migration policy, the Commission issued a new Communication on *A Common Immigration Policy in Europe: Principles, Actions and Tools.*[46] The latter outlined ten common principles upon which a future common immigration policy would have to be based, which were grouped under three main strands of European policies, namely, prosperity, solidarity and security. Each of these principles was accompanied by actions. The third section of the Communication called for a common strategy on immigration governance and the development of new tools to strengthen the monitoring and evaluation of the implementation of these principles:

> The positive potential of immigration can only be realized if integration into host societies is successful. This requires an approach that does not only look at the benefit for the host society but takes also account of the interests of the immigrants: Europe is, and shall continue to be, a welcoming environment for those who have been granted the right to stay, be they labour immigrants, family members, students or persons in need of international protection.[47]

Interestingly, the Communication also mentioned the assessment of 'the implementation and the need for modification of the Council Directive 2003/86/EC on the right to family reunification'.[48] It reiterated the latter in its Communication 'on an Area of Freedom, Security and Justice serving the citizen', which aimed to influence the adoption of the new multi-annual programme, the so-called Stockholm Programme, which was adopted in December 2009.[49] The Communication called for the development of a dynamic immigration policy based on 'respect for fundamental rights and human dignity'.[50]

43 Ibid., at p. 25. It echoed the 1999 Communication: '[It] is a necessary way of making a success of the integration of third country nationals residing lawfully in the MS. The presence of family members makes for greater stability and deepens the roots of these people since they are enabled to lead a normal family life'; COM(99) 638 final, 3.
44 COM(2007) 780 final, at p. 8.
45 Presidency Conclusions, Brussels 13/14 March 2008, point 14.
46 COM(2008) 359 final, 17 June 2008.
47 Ibid., at p. 3.
48 Ibid., at p. 8.
49 COM(2009) 262/4, 10 June 2009, Brussels.
50 Ibid., at p. 34.

Notwithstanding the Commission's normative response to the family reunification of TCNs,[51] the Member States continued to pursue their restrictive policies and subject applicant spouses to integration tests, which became de-territorialised. Certain Member States, such as the Netherlands, which pioneered this policy in 2005,[52] the UK, Denmark and Germany, for instance, required spouses to meet linguistic requirements and/or pass civic orientation tests abroad in order to gain authorisation of their entry to the country. This requirement cannot but interfere with the normative structure of the right to respect for family life (Article 8 ECHR) since failure in an exam or a test would preclude the grant of a temporary entry visa to the spouse of a sponsor. The European Committee of Social Rights shares the view that such integration requirements 'constitute a restriction likely to deprive the obligation laid down in Article 19(6) of the European Social Charter, which guarantees the right to family reunion, of its substance and is consequently not in conformity with the Charter'.[53]

The Court of Justice of the EU did not have an opportunity to rule on the compatibility of 'integration abroad' or pre-entry tests with the Family Reunification Directive (Article 7(2) of Dir. 2003/86) until recently. The first case, which reached the Court of Justice of the EU in 2011, *Imran*, was withdrawn before the Court ruled on the matter because the Dutch government gave a visa to the sponsor's spouse.[54] However, Block and Bonjour noted that the Commission issued a statement declaring the Dutch 'integration abroad' tests incompatible with the Directive, which – despite its non-binding effects – did have some informal influence on German national courts.[55] More recently, the president of the Court ordered *Ayalti*, which was a request for a preliminary ruling from the Verwaltungsgericht Berlin, to be removed from the register.[56] On 9 July 2015, the Court considered a preliminary ruling reference from the Dutch Council of State of 1 April 2013 on whether the term 'integration conditions' contained in Article 7(2) of the Family Reunification Directive allows national authorities to impose linguistic and civic integration testing before granting a TCN family member permission for entry and residence.[57] The District Court in The Hague

51 Compare, D. Thym, 'EU Migration Policy and its Constitutional Rationale: A Cosmopolitan Outlook' (2013) 50 *Common Market Law Review* 709.

52 The Act (*Wet inburgering in het buitenland*) was adopted on 22 December 2005 and entered into force on 15 March 2006.

53 ECSR, Conclusions 2011, General Introduction, January 2012, statement of interpretation on Article 19(6).

54 Case C-155/11 PPU *Imran* of 10 June 2011.

55 L. Block and S. Bonjour, 'Fortress Europe or Europe of Rights? The Europeanisation of Family Migration Policies in France, Germany and the Netherlands' (2013) 15(2) *European Journal of Migration and Law* 203.

56 Case C-513/12 *Aslihan Nazli Ayalti v Federal Republic of Germany* of 13 November 2012. The case closed by an Order of the President of the Court of 15 March 2013.

57 Case C-153/14 *Minister van Buitenlandse Zaken v K and A*, Judgment of the Court of 9 July 2015.

(Rechtbank's-Gravenhage) had ruled that it was contrary to the Family Reunification Directive to require that both K, an Azerbaijani national who had health problems, and A, a Nigerian national who suffered from psychological problems, satisfy civic integration requirements abroad before being allowed to reunite with their spouses in the Netherlands. The Dutch Minister for Foreign Affairs appealed against this decision and the Council of State sought the Court's guidance on the meaning of Article 7(2) of the Directive. The Court ruled that since family reunification is the general rule, the first subparagraph of 7(2) of Directive 2003/86 must be interpreted strictly (para 50). The Member States should not use this provision in order to undermine the objective and effectiveness of the Directive (para 50 et seq.). The Court also noted that the principle of proportionality requires that, in addition to attention being paid to specific individual circumstances, any conditions relating to civic integration testing and any associated costs imposed by national authorities must not make family reunification impossible or excessively difficult (paras 63–71). It was made clear that 'integration measures' 'must be aimed not at filtering those persons who will be able to exercise their right to family reunification, but at facilitating the integration of such persons within the Member States' (para 57).

On the other hand, national courts have ruled that integration abroad tests are not a disproportionate interference with family life and are thus justified.[58] This reasoning is based on the belief that such measures prepare spouses for integration at a very early stage and increase their employability. However, the conditionality attached to them makes such arguments debatable. Hardly anybody would dispute the fact that facilitating one's employability and settlement are legitimate social interests, thereby meeting the suitability test required by the principle of proportionality. But it is doubtful whether the tests of necessity and adequacy or reasonableness (proportionality *stricto sensu*) that proportionality entails are met. This is because the above-mentioned legitimate objectives could be achieved by less restrictive means; that is, by providing opportunities for language class attendance on arrival and/or participation in targeted training programmes designed to equip spouses with the skills and knowledge required in order to exercise specific professions. Being essentially admission requirements, integrations tests abroad serve as a device of migration control.

One notices the clear juxtaposition of two rival policy beliefs; on the one hand, in the EU legal framework governing the free movement of EU citizens, family reunification is a right that is associated with, and enhances, the right to cross-border mobility, whereas, with respect to TCNs, restrictive collectivism subsumes respect for family life to political expedience, migration

58 England and Wales High Court, *Chapti and Others v Secretary of State for the Home Department*, Judgment of 16 December 2011 [2011] EWHC 3370 (Admin); German Constitutional Court, Case 2 BvR 1413/10, 25 March 2011.

control and to vague notions of integration, on the other.[59] In EU free movement law, integration has always been firmly situated within the host Member State and has been intimately connected with processes of equalisation so that an EU citizen becomes part of the fabric of the host society. In EU migration law, on the other hand, integration-testing is more about controlling, testing, restricting mobility and less about 'integration'. It is not based on a sustainable theory of integration or on how community building works.[60] Instead, it is based on a number of problematic assumptions, such as that integration can be objectively determined, can be measured and can be captured once and for all by a paper and pen exercise and thus the award of a passing score. Interestingly, in the first case on integration requirements for third-country nationals under the Long-term Residence Directive (2003/109), while the Court ruled that the Dutch requirement to attend a civic integration course did not contravene the Directive, it also observed that the level of knowledge required, the level of registration fees, the accessibility of the courses and the material to be studied and other 'specific individual circumstances' might undermine the aims of the Directive and thus deprive it of its effectiveness.[61]

Perhaps a clear manifestation of the tensions surrounding the coexistence of the two rival policy beliefs can be seen in *Dogan v Germany*.[62] The case concerned the refusal of family reunion to the spouse of a Turkish national company director on the ground that she was illiterate and her written German was not satisfactory. Although the referring court in Berlin raised two questions about the compatibility of the national rule with the 1970 Protocol to the EC-Turkey Association Agreement that prohibits the introduction of new restrictions on establishment or the provision of services (Article 41(1)), on the one hand, and with Article 7(2)(1) of the Family Reunification Directive, on the other, the Court confined its reasoning to the former question, which it addressed by activating EU mobility law's normative commitment to family reunion. In the Court's view, the national immigration rule constituted a restriction upon the enjoyment of the right of establishment exercised by Mr Dogan since it made family reunion 'difficult or impossible', thereby in effect prompting Mr Dogan to choose between his activity in Germany and his family life in Turkey. In brief, it made family reunion more difficult and thus violated Article 41(1) of the Protocol (the standstill clause). It is the simple act of living that we all enjoy that has prompted, and prompts, the Court to

59 D. Kostakopoulou, 'The Anatomy of Civic Integration' (2010) 73(6) *Modern Law Review* 933.

60 See D. Kostakopoulou, 'Liberalism and Societal Integration: In Defence of Reciprocity and Constructive Pluralism' (2014) 43(2) *Netherlands Journal of Legal Philosophy* 127; D. Kostakopoulou, *The Future Governance of Citizenship* (Cambridge: Cambridge University Press, 2008).

61 Case C-579/13 *P and S v Commissie Sociale Zekerheid Breda, College van Burgemeester en Wetouders van de gemeente Amstelveen*, Judgment of the Court, 4 June 2015.

62 Case C-138/13 *Dogan v Germany*, Judgment of the Court of 29 August 2014.

overcome the contradictions imposed by restrictive national migration rules and practices and to sediment a pro-family normative commitment. By so doing, it simply makes dignified and wholesome human living go on.

4 Conclusion

The discussion in this chapter has provided an overview of the norms underpinning the evolution of EU family reunification laws. It revealed the discrepancies between a norm of 'communitarian egalitarianism' – deriving from the original principles of Community law based on freedom of movement – and a conflicting norm of 'restrictive collectivism' based on traditional understandings of sovereignty and migration controls. These two norms continue to coexist both at the EU and national level and are most visible when they reach the arena of judicial politics. It is, therefore, often left to courts to decide where the borders between these two norms lie. As we have seen, as soon as 'communitarian egalitarianism' has left its natural domain of freedom of movement, it had been put to the test. We have now a three-tier system with EU citizens that exercise (or would be deprived from exercising) their right to move freely across the Union benefiting from more rights and easier conditions to reunite their family, while 'sedentary' EU citizens and long-term resident third-country nationals have to face more stringent tests to benefit from their right to family life and are often left at the Member States' discretion.

If one looks back at the EU Charter of Fundamental Rights, it underlines that '*everyone* has the right to respect for his or her private and family life, home and communications' (Article 7, emphasis added) and includes also the right to marry and found a family – although in accordance with national laws (Article 9). Therefore, the Charter enters into conflict with this highly fragmented regime that now differentiates between the right to family reunification of mobile EU citizens, static EU citizens and third-country nationals. For that reason, we consider the present situation as 'constitutionally unsustainable' in the light of the Charter and a potential source of judicial conflict in the coming years. In a way, the decision on the case *K & A* (see above) is a first step in bringing closer together the message of the Charter and the practices of Member States by clarifying the hierarchy of principles in family reunification law. It remains to be seen whether this decision will lead to a new jurisprudence or whether national courts will prefer to provide a more nuanced interpretation of 'proportionality' when striking a balance between the right to family reunification and the 'social interests' of integrating third-country nationals in member states' societies and markets.

On this basis, although European and national courts have allowed citizens and third-country nationals to test the strength of these two principles, we cannot yet speak of a full and generalised recognition of respect for family life as a fundamental right in the European Union. Certainly, the existing rules have served to, at least, lock in some minimum standards and prevented further attempts to restrict migrants' rights.[63] However, if we review again the numbers of family migrants showed above, we can see a generalised trend downwards in the proportion of people coming through family reunification. In most Member States, the application of the Family Reunification Directive has halved the proportion of permanent migrants that come through the family channel. This means that, generally, Member States have used the Directive to introduce and legitimise further restrictions in their national laws. Indeed, Member States have been reluctant to reopen the Directive and in order to address its manifold weaknesses the Commission has had to content itself with producing another Communication to provide some guidance for its correct implementation.[64] In the current political and social climate, there does not seem to be a favourable context to review family reunification and to bring these different categories of people to the same standards.

63 S. Bonjour and M. Vink, 'When Europeanization Backfires: The Normalization of European Migration Politics' (2013) 48(4) *Acta Politica* 389.

64 COM(2014) 210 final, 3 April 2014, Communication on guidance for application of Directive 2003/86/EC on the right to family reunification.

11 The Common European Asylum System

Where did it all go wrong?

Cathryn Costello and Minos Mouzourakis[*]

1 Introduction

The Common European Asylum System (CEAS) is neither truly common nor a system.[1] This chapter outlines the content of the legal measures that fall under the CEAS, and its structural problems. It is set against the backdrop of the arrival in 2015 of refugees and migrants to EU Member States dubbed variously the 'refugee crisis', 'migration crisis' or even the 'Mediterranean crisis'. Evidently, a defining feature was an increase in the numbers of people arriving by sea.[2] Those arriving were mainly refugees with international protection needs, fleeing Syria, Iraq and Afghanistan (making up 90 per cent of arrivals).[3] The main entry route in 2015 became the sea route from Turkey to Greece. As Fargues argues, talk of 'mixed flows' of refugees and migrants became increasingly inapt in this context.[4]

The situation where refugees are compelled to have recourse to dangerous means of travel if they wish to seek asylum in Europe is nothing new, but rather the culmination of years of policies aimed at deterring and deflecting refugees.[5] The mode of arrival was a significant part of why events unfurled as a crisis. Large numbers of people arriving on small boats to small islands induced a humanitarian crisis. The movement of refugees defied the logic

* The authors thank Maria Fletcher and Ester Herlin-Karnell for most helpful comments.

1 For a similar observation, see V. Chetail, 'The Common European Asylum System: bric-à-brac or system?', in P. de Bruycker and F. Maiani (eds.), *Reforming the Common European Asylum System: The New European Refugee Law* (Martinus Nijhoff, 2016).

2 While 59,421 persons arrived by sea in 2013 and 216,054 in 2014, the year 2015 saw as many as 1,015,078 arrivals in the Mediterranean: UNHCR, *Refugees/Migrants Emergency Response: Mediterranean*.

3 UNHCR (n. 2).

4 P. Fargues, '2015 – the year we mistook refugees for invaders', MPC Policy Brief 2015/12.

5 A. Grahl-Madsen, 'Identifying the world's refugees' (1983) 467 *Annals of the American Academy of Political and Social Science* 11; T. Gammeltoft-Hansen, *Access to Asylum: International Refugee Law and the Globalization of Migration Control* (Cambridge University Press, 2011); M. den Heijer, *Europe and Extraterritorial Asylum* (Bloomsbury, 2012); V. Moreno-Lax, *Facilitating Access to Protection, (Discarding) Offshore Processing* (Red Cross, 2016).

of the Dublin System,[6] but this instrument has always been more ruse than reality – refugees in Europe have always tended to claim asylum and have their claims examined in states that were not technically responsible under the Dublin criteria.[7] So on that too, we find continuities rather than change.

What did change in 2015 were the responses of European states: some characterised arrivals as posing a threat, and set about using their borders and criminal laws to deflect and deter. Most did nothing in terms of providing asylum – out of the 28 Member States of the European Union, the majority had no significant increase in the number of people seeking protection on their territory. They are free-riders on the protection offered by others, in particular by Germany, Sweden, Austria, Italy and France. These five Member States together account for more than 75 per cent of all first-time applicants in the EU-28 in 2015.[8]

The language of crisis has become pervasive, but it is worth recalling that '2015' began with a different crisis: deaths at sea on the Central Mediterranean route. While deaths of those travelling irregularly from Libya to Italy are nothing new, on 18 April 2015, when 800 people died in a single incident off the Libyan coast, a new set of responses emerged, focusing on combatting smuggling in particular.[9] The dangers of that crossing have increased with instability in Libya and the ruthlessness of smugglers there. It is now the world's most lethal maritime crossing,[10] although for many who use it, the ordeals on their previous land journeys (including for some across the Sahara) may eclipse its horrors.[11] At the EU level, the first responses focused on the Central Mediterranean, with the focus on combatting smuggling as a means to stem arrivals. Military operation 'EUNAVFOR MED', later renamed 'Sophia', was launched in May 2015, with the aim of 'contributing to the disruption of the business model of human smuggling and trafficking networks in the Southern Central Mediterranean'.[12] Later in

6 Regulation (EU) No 604/2013 of the European Parliament and of the Council of 26 June 2013 establishing the criteria and mechanisms for determining the Member State responsible for examining an application for international protection lodged in one of the Member States by a third-country national or stateless person (recast) [2013] OJ L180/31.

7 F. Maiani and V. Vevstad, *Reflection Note on the Evaluation of the Dublin System and the Dublin III Proposal* (2009) European Parliament, PE410.690; ECRE, *Dublin II Regulation: Lives on Hold* (ECRE, 2013).

8 Eurostat, *Asylum and First Time Applicants Annual Aggregated Data*, migr_asyappctza. While Hungary received 177,135 applications that year, the overwhelming majority of cases were closed due to the asylum-seekers' departure from the country.

9 For a response at the time, see C. Costello and M. Giuffre, ' "Tragedy" and responsibility in the Mediterranean', *Open Democracy*, 27 April 2015, https://goo.gl/wBP53V (accessed 30 May 2016).

10 Fargues reports that from 2000 to 2015, there were 26,018 deaths for 1.2 million persons. This amounts to a 2 per cent chance of dying: Fargues (n. 4).

11 P. Kingsley, *The New Odyssey: The Story of Europe's Refugee Crisis* (Faber, 2016).

12 Council Decision (CFSP) 2015/778 of 18 May 2015 on a European Union military operation in the Southern Central Mediterranean (EUNAFVOR MED) [2015] OJ L122/31, Article 1.

2015, another route opened up, much safer and shorter, from Turkey to the Greek islands.

Lest the impression be given that the world's refugees are all making their way to Europe *en masse*, it should be emphasised that most remain in the regions of origin. Of the more than 4 million Syrian refugees, over 90 per cent are in four countries – Lebanon, Jordan, Turkey and Iraq.[13] This reflects the global pattern – 86 per cent of the world's refugees are in poor countries.[14] In terms of arrivals in Europe, while the refugee arrivals of 2015 were routinely characterised as 'unprecedented', that is not accurate. A UNHCR statement that there were 'more displaced persons (65 million) than at any other time since the aftermath of World War II' was widely misconstrued.[15] The UNHCR figure encompasses 40 million internally displaced persons, and 20 million refugees, most of whom are not in Europe. Yet the evocation of a crisis in numbers in Europe pervaded. For comparison, it should be recalled that by December 1995 (the signing of the Dayton Peace Agreement) there were an estimated 1.3 million Bosnian IDPs and 2.5 million refugees displaced in the sub-region, and some 700,000 refugees in Western Europe.[16]

This chapter aims to understand the legal context for this 'crisis'. In Section 2, we begin by sketching the legal contents of the CEAS, providing a chronological account of their development. While many important aspects of process, status and rights both during and after recognition or rejection as a refugee[17] have been harmonised, as asylum processes remain national, many divergences in outcomes and treatment of refugees persist. In Section 3, we identify the main structural shortcomings, namely (1) the lack of legal access routes to the EU to claim asylum; (2) tensions between legal duties at borders (such as *non-refoulement*, the prohibition on collective expulsion and other human rights obligations) and political discourse and framings of the nature of 'effective border controls'; and (3) the pathologies of the Dublin System.[18] This section explains how the fissures in the CEAS became fractures and schisms in 2015, when the EU was faced with large numbers of protection-seekers, predominantly arriving irregularly in Greece. The CEAS, as currently designed, makes responsibility-sharing less likely, exacerbating the crisis for those seeking protection. Section 4 examines the legal responses

13 UNHCR, *Syria Regional Refugee Emergency Response.*

14 UNHCR, *World at War: Global Trends, Forced Displacement in 2014* (NHCR, 2015).

15 UNHCR, *Global Trends: Forced Displacement in 2015* (UNHCR, 2016), 5.

16 UNHCR, *The State of the World's Refugees, Fifty Years of Humanitarian Action* (Oxford University Press, 2000), 219.

17 EU law reflects the 1951 Convention definition of the refugee and creates a 'subsidiary protection' status for others in need of international protection. For ease, both categories are referred to as 'refugees' here, with 'Convention refugee' and 'subsidiary protection beneficiary' used only when the context demands differentiation.

18 The 'Dublin System' is used to refer to the latest iteration of the Dublin Regulation and the EURODAC Regulation. Regulations (EU) No 604/2013 and 603/2013 of the European Parliament and of the Council of 26 June 2013 [2013] OJ L180/1.

adopted thus far to deal with the 'crisis'. These include (1) a range of unilateral measures, some legal, some blatantly illegal under EU and international law; (2) various attempts to respond to the 'crisis' at the EU level on an ad hoc basis, including EU relocation, resettlement and the EU–Turkey 'deal'; and (3) in May 2016, a package of proposals for harmonisation and centralisation of the CEAS.[19] Our concluding observation is that as yet the EU has not addressed the structural problems identified in Section 3.

2 The development of the CEAS

2.1 The prelude

While the Treaty of Amsterdam is the watershed for formal law-making competence in asylum,[20] the EU's role in asylum predates that formal legal competence. Like other issues deemed matters of internal security, European informal intergovernmental cooperation shaped what came later, notably by creating the basic legal frameworks of the Schengen[21] and Dublin Conventions.[22] Schengen, it will be recalled, began in the mid-1980s with just five States (Germany, France, the Netherlands, Belgium and Luxembourg), gradually expanding to include the EU Member States (bar the UK, Ireland and Denmark) and being integrated into the EU Treaties by the Treaty of Amsterdam. As well as these formal conventions, there was also considerable horizontal policy-sharing across Western European States on asylum. For instance, European States developed safe country concepts individually, shared them horizontally, and then they made their way into the pre-Amsterdam non-binding asylum *acquis*.[23] As will be seen in the next section, introducing formal law-making competence on asylum incorporated many of the logics of the earlier period.

19 European Commission, *Proposal for [a recast Dublin Regulation]*, COM(2016) 270, 4 May 2016; *Proposal for [a recast Eurodac Regulation]*, COM(2016) 272, 4 May 2016; *Proposal for a Regulation of the European Parliament and of the Council on a European Union Agency on Asylum*, COM(2016) 271, 4 May 2016. For a discussion, see S. Peers, 'The orbanisation of EU asylum law: the latest EU asylum proposals' (2016) *EU Law Analysis* 6 May 2016.

20 For a collection of essays examining the early legal measures, see C. Harlow and E. Guild, *Implementing Amsterdam: Immigration and Asylum Rights in EC Law* (Hart Publishing, 2001).

21 Convention implementing the Schengen Agreement of 14 June 1985 [2000] OJ L239/19.

22 Convention determining the State responsible for examining an asylum application lodged in one of the Member States of the European Communities – Dublin Convention [1997] OJ C254/1.

23 See C. Costello, 'The Asylum Procedures Directive and the proliferation of safe country practices: deterrence, deflection and the dismantling of international protection' (2005) 7 *European Journal of Migration and Law* 35.

2.2 *The Treaty framework*

The Treaty of Amsterdam set out the parameters for EU law-making. For the first five years, binding measures on asylum were to be adopted by unanimity in the Council, setting 'minimum standards'. Asylum policy forms part of the Area of Freedom, Security and Justice (AFSJ), with asylum and immigration policies portrayed as subservient to internal mobility for 'citizens', as set out in Article 3(2) of the Treaty on European Union (TEU):

> The Union shall offer its citizens an area of freedom, security and justice without internal frontiers, in which the free movement of persons is ensured in conjunction with appropriate measures with respect to external border controls, asylum, immigration and the prevention and combating of crime.

The AFSJ is thus an offering for EU citizens. There is an ambiguity about who should benefit from free movement – it seems to suggest all 'persons', provided there are 'appropriate' external border controls and measures on asylum and immigration. But another reading would confine internal free movement to 'citizens'. This reflects the oddity that is the AFSJ – it may be seen as an inert set of platitudes to capture the incoherent status quo, or mined for its constitutionally transformative potential.[24] One enduring legacy of this 'flanking measures' framing is the placing apart of asylum-seekers and refugees, with their immobility being seen as necessary to maintain the AFSJ.[25]

The position of refugees is apparently safeguarded by the strong endorsement of the UN Convention on the Status of Refugees 1951 ('the Refugee Convention' or 'CSR') in both the EU Treaties and the EU Charter of Fundamental Rights ('the Charter' or 'EUCFR'). The former provides that the EU's policy on asylum 'shall be in accordance with [CSR]' and the Court of Justice of the European Union (CJEU) repeats that the CSR is 'the cornerstone of the international legal regime for the protection of refugees.'[26] The Charter enshrines the right to asylum, albeit with a somewhat ambiguous formulation, being a right to asylum, 'in accordance with the [CSR]'. The legal implications of Article 18 EUCFR have yet to be fully clarified.[27]

24 C. Costello, *The Human Rights of Migrants and Refugees in European Law* (Oxford University Press, 2016), Chapter 1 'Destination Europe'.

25 See further E. Guild, 'The Europeanisation of Europe's asylum policy' (2006) 18 *International Journal of Refugee Law* 630, 634–635.

26 Case C-604/12 *HN* [2014] OJ C202/6, para 27, citing *X, Y & Z*, para 39 and the case law cited.

27 M.T. Gil-Bazo, 'The Charter of Fundamental Rights of the European Union and the right to be granted asylum in the Union's law' (2008) 27(3) *Refugee Survey Quarterly* 33; M. Garlick, 'International protection in court: the asylum jurisprudence of the Court of Justice of the EU and UNHCR' (2015) 34(1) *Refugee Survey Quarterly* 107.

The legal endorsement of the Refugee Convention in EU law may give the appearance that all its aspects have a place in EU law. However, the CJEU has taken a different view. In 2014 in *Qurbani*,[28] it declined to interpret Article 31 CSR. This Article requires State parties not to penalise refugees for illegal entry or stay, subject to certain conditions, and is a crucial part of the refugee regime.[29] The Court held that this provision had no basis in EU law.[30] At one point, EU accession to the Refugee Convention was on the political agenda,[31] but that seems no longer to be the case.

The Treaty does not introduce the CEAS – that came at the Tampere European Council.[32] The CEAS is, according to the Council Conclusions, to be based on the full and inclusive application of the Geneva Convention. Tampere, informed by Article 63 TEC, envisaged various stages of harmonisation, from allocation criteria, to common standards on reception, procedures, and status.[33] It emphasised that the CEAS would come to include 'a common asylum procedure and a uniform status for those who are granted asylum valid throughout the Union'. The idea of asylum valid throughout the Union now appears in the TFEU,[34] but has yet to emerge. In spite of

28 Case C-481/13 *Qurbani* [2014] OJ C31/24.

29 G. Noll, 'Article 31 (Refugees Unlawfully in the Country of Refuge)', in A. Zimmermann (ed.), *The 1951 Convention Relating to the Status of the Refugees and its 1967 Protocol: A Commentary* (Oxford University Press, 2011) 1243; G.S. Goodwin-Gill, 'Article 31 of the 1951 Convention Relating to the Status of Refugees: Non-Penalization, Detention, and Protection', in E. Feller, V. Turk and F. Nicholson (eds.), *Refugee Protection in International Law: UNHCR's Global Consultations on International Protection* (Cambridge University Press, 2003) 185.

30 Y. Holiday, 'Penalising refugees: when should the CJEU have jurisdiction to interpret Article 31 of the Refugee Convention?' (2014) *EU Law Analysis* 19 July 2014.

31 European Council, *Stockholm Programme: An Open and Secure Europe Serving and Protecting Citizens* [2010] OJ C115/1, 6.2.1.

32 Council of the European Union, *Tampere European Council 15 and 16 October 2009: Presidency Conclusions.*

33 Article 63 TEC laid out the measures on asylum to be adopted at EU level, namely:
(a) criteria and mechanisms for determining which Member State is responsible for considering an application for asylum submitted by a national of a third country in one of the Member States,
(b) minimum standards on the reception of asylum seekers in Member States,
(c) minimum standards with respect to the qualification of nationals of third countries as refugees,
(d) minimum standards on procedures in Member States for granting or withdrawing refugee status;
(2) measures on refugees and displaced persons within the following areas:
(a) minimum standards for giving temporary protection to displaced persons from third countries who cannot return to their country of origin and for persons who otherwise need international protection,
(b) promoting a balance of effort between Member States in receiving and bearing the consequences of receiving refugees and displaced persons.

34 Article 78(2)(a) TFEU.

all the harmonisation of process and rights, the status of refugees remains national in scope.

2.3 *Dublin*

The first binding measure to be adopted in the EU context was the Dublin Convention, which predates the Treaty of Amsterdam and the CEAS. Originally adopted by European States intergovernmentally in 1990 (and entering into force in 1997), it institutionalises a system for allocation of responsibility of asylum claims across its State parties.[35] These currently include the EU Member States with Norway, Iceland, Switzerland and Liechtenstein. Its original apparent rationales were to clarify the responsible State and institute a 'one-shot' rule for asylum claims. It also appears to permit safe third country (STC) practices, allowing transfers elsewhere if they are deemed 'safe',[36] a matter later regulated in significant detail in the Procedures Directive (PD) and Recast PD.[37] Since the Convention, there have been two further iterations of Dublin in the form of Regulations, and a further revision is currently under contemplation.[38] In spite of these revisitations, the basic allocation criteria have remained largely the same. In order of priority and somewhat simplified, the State responsible is the one where:

- a family member of an unaccompanied minor is legally present,[39] or if there is no such State, where the unaccompanied minor makes her most recent application;[40]
- a family member has been recognised as a refugee or has an outstanding asylum application[41] (note the narrow definition of family under the Dublin II Regulation has been broadened by the Dublin III Regulation[42]);

35 Convention determining the State responsible for examining applications for asylum lodged in one of the Member States of the European Communities – Dublin Convention [1997] OJ C254/1.

36 Article 3(5) Dublin Convention.

37 Council Directive 2005/85/EC of 1 December 2005 on minimum standards on procedures in Member States for granting and withdrawing refugee status [2005] OJ L326/13; Directive 2013/32/EU of the European Parliament and of the Council of 26 June 2013 on common procedures for granting and withdrawing international protection (recast) [2013] OJ L180/60.

38 European Commission, *Proposal for [Dublin Regulation] (recast)*, COM(2016) 270, 4 May 2016. See also footnote 18.

39 Article 8(1)–(3) Dublin III Regulation.

40 Article 8(4) Dublin III Regulation, as interpreted by the CJEU in Case C-648/11 *MA v Secretary of State for the Home Department* [2013] 3 *Common Market Law Review* 49. Note that a proposal by the Commission clarifying this provision was currently under negotiation: European Commission, COM(2014) 382. This will be withdrawn in light of the Commission proposal to recast the Dublin III Regulation.

41 Articles 9–11 Dublin III Regulation.

42 Article 2(h) Dublin III Regulation now includes a new definition of 'relative', distinct from that of 'family members' under Article 2(g).

- a visa or residence permit has been issued;[43]
- the first irregular external border crossing took place;[44]
- visa requirements have been waived for the particular applicant;[45]
- the application was first lodged.[46]

As discussed below, asylum-seekers are rarely issued visas or residence permits, even if they have family members in the EU. Under those circumstances, asylum-seekers are usually irregular entrants, meaning the State whose external border is crossed irregularly is usually responsible under the Dublin System. However, that is rarely the case in practice, as Dublin has become one of the structural problems of the CEAS, as discussed in the next section. Notably, while it allocates responsibility, it undermines equitable responsibility-sharing. Indeed, Article 63(3)(b) TEC required measures 'to promote a balance of effort between Member States in receiving and bearing the consequences of receiving refugees and displaced persons'. That notion has been fortified, with strong duties of solidarity in the Treaty of Lisbon.[47]

2.4 *Dormant or defunct? Temporary protection in Europe*

The Treaty of Amsterdam (1997) was adopted when the embers of the Balkan Wars were still glowing. The end of the Cold War saw not only new opportunities for international governance and cooperation, but also new nationalisms, conflicts and instabilities. Asylum in Europe became a flashpoint in two respects: refugees fled the Balkan conflicts in large numbers, and European states (in particular Germany) offered temporary protection. And asylum, as it had developed in the Cold War as an offer of permanent settlement to those fleeing communist regimes, seemed less viable to governments. As those seeking protection became more diverse, so too did the viability of return. Simultaneously in the 1990s, UNHCR characterised repatriation as a viable 'solution' at the end of wars or when regimes changed.

The European practices of temporary protection in the 1990s were legally ambiguous, in particular their relationship to the Refugee Convention (CSR).[48] As Durieux explains, scholars since the mid-1980s, argued that a customary norm of temporary refuge existed, protecting 'refugees' defined more broadly than under the CSR.[49] European states' reactions to those

43 Article 12 Dublin III Regulation.
44 Article 13 Dublin III Regulation.
45 Article 14 Dublin III Regulation.
46 Article 3(") Dublin III Regulation.
47 Article 80 TFEU. See D Vanheule et al., *The Implementation of Article 80 TFEU* (2011) European Parliament, PE453.167.
48 J-F. Durieux, 'Temporary protection: hovering at the edges of refugee law' (2014) 45 *Netherlands Yearbook of International Law* 221.
49 Goodwin-Gill (n. 28); D. Perluss and J. Fitzpatrick Hartman, 'Temporary refuge: emergence of a customary norm' (1986) 26 *Virginia Journal of International Law* 551.

fleeing the violent break-up of Yugoslavia constituted 'a watershed in the formalization of temporary protection'.[50] Of those those who fled to Western Europe, the distribution was as follows: Germany 345,000; Austria 80,000; Sweden 57,000; Switzerland 25,000; Netherlands 24,000; Denmark 20,000; France 15,000; United Kingdom 13,000; Other 37,000; 9,000 refugees; total 616,000.[51] For countries such as the United Kingdom, the number of asylum claims made in 2015 is far lower than its peak – 100,000 people claimed asylum in 2002, while in 2015, the total was only around 25,000.[52]

The backdrop of temporary protection practices is important to understand the first legal measure to which the EU turned when it gained formal legislative competence over asylum; the Temporary Protection Directive (TPD). The European Commission explicitly acknowledged the Kosovar experience as influencing its Proposal in October 2000, which was eventually adopted in July 2001.[53] The TPD aims to clarify many legal questions about temporary protection. It envisages that in times of 'mass influx', the EU would put in place cooperative mechanisms not only to offer protection, but also, by separate agreement, to distribute displaced persons unable to return to their country of origin[54] in a spirit of solidarity.[55] It applies in instances of 'mass influx' defined as 'a large number of displaced persons, who come from a specific country or geographical area, whether their arrival in the Community was spontaneous or aided'.[56] For Durieux, 'solidarity' is lacking in the TPD, as the only 'measures promoting a balance of efforts between Member States' mentioned in the text are of a procedural character, or rely on a pre-existing common fund, the European Refugee Fund.[57] However, evidently, the Directive presupposes cooperation and a collective response, not least as this is required in order to trigger the application of the Directive. The process requires a Commission proposal (which may be requested by a Member State) and a Council decision adopted by a qualified majority.[58]

The Directive has lain dormant since. The Commission and some EU governments seem to have considered it fleetingly in 2015, and concluded that it was ill-fitting for the current circumstances. The rationales for this inaction

50 J.-F. Durieux and A. Hurwitz, 'How many is too many? African and European legal responses to mass influxes of refugees' (2004) 47 *German Yearbook of International Law* 105 at 138.

51 See OECD, 'Is this humanitarian migration crisis different?' Migration Policy Debates No. 7, September 2015, www.oecd.org/migration/Is-this-refugee-crisis-different.pdf.

52 EU Council Directive 2001/55/EC on minimum standards for giving temporary protection in the event of a mass influx of displaced persons and on measures promoting a balance of efforts between Member States in receiving such persons and bearing the consequences thereof, 20 July 2001 (TPD).

53 Ibid.

54 Article 2(a) TPD.

55 Article 25 TPD.

56 Article 2(d) TPD.

57 Chapter VI TPD.

58 Article 5 TPD.

have not been clearly or publicly articulated. Speculating somewhat, it seems for some that the TPD was considered ill-fitting because of the nature of arrivals: not a single influx from a particular conflict with a clear end in sight, but large numbers from different countries, often experiencing related but distinct sources of instability. Using the TPD would simply mean deeming all arrivals to benefit from protection, but that seemed inapt in the circumstances. For others, the objection was not the scope of beneficiaries, but rather the rights package included – in particular family reunion from the outset. Setting up the irregular arrivals with a clear offer of EU protection was seen by others as likely to induce further arrivals. European governments seem to invoke the 'pull factors' rationale as a kneejerk – no matter how strong the drivers of displacement (the 'push factors'), it is imagined that those fleeing are highly responsive to policy changes in their potential countries of asylum. These various rationales are not clearly articulated in any EU policy statement, or even discussion document. Arrivals continued in 2015, with international protection on offer for many, but only after the territory of a country of asylum was reached. While there have been some academic calls for the Directive to be used, politically it remains dormant, if not defunct.[59]

2.5 Asylum policy harmonisation

Aside from the Temporary Protection Directive, the CEAS encompasses directives harmonising 'qualification' as an international protection beneficiary, the reception conditions that should be provided to applicants while their claims are being examined, and the procedures applicable to these processes. The studies on the implementation of the first-phase instruments showed quite varied impacts and approaches.[60]

Those Directives have been 'recast' a second time recently, making them more elaborate. The recasting process involved was subject to the normal legislative procedure, so the European Parliament succeeded in raising standards

59 M. Ineli-Ciger, 'Has the Temporary Protection Directive become obsolete? An examination of the Directive and its lack of implementation in view of the recent asylum crisis in the Mediterranean', in C. Bauloz, M. Ineli-Ciger, S. Singer and V. Stayanova (eds.), *Seeking Asylum in the European Union: Selected Protection Issues Raised by the Second Phase of the Common Asylum System* (Brill/ Martinus Nijhoff Publishers, 2015) 225; M. Ineli-Ciger, 'The missing piece in the European agenda on migration: the Temporary Protection Directive' (2015) *EU Law Analysis*, 8 July 2015, http://goo.gl/kYqMdd (accessed 30 May 2016).

60 K. Zwaan (ed.), *The Qualification Directive: Central Themes, Problem Issues, and Implementation in Selected Member States* (Wolf Legal Publishers, 2007); United Nations High Commissioner for Refugees, *Asylum in the European Union: A Study on the Implementation of the Qualification Directive* (UNHCR, 2007) 13; European Council on Refugees and Exiles, *The Impact of the Qualification Directive on International Protection* (ECRE, 2008); United Nations High Commissioner for Refugees, *Improving Asylum Procedures Comparative Analysis and Recommendations for Law and Practice: A UNHCR research project on the application of key provisions of the Asylum Procedures Directive in selected Member States* (UNHCR, 2010).

somewhat, but the reform process overall was piecemeal. The recast Directives remain minimum standards, in that Member States are permitted to maintain higher domestic standards. Although the Treaty of Lisbon envisages 'common' standards on asylum,[61] the enacted Directives each contain a clause allowing Member States to impose higher standards.[62] In addition, they leave considerable leeway for policy variation across a range of important practical matters.

2.5.1 *Who is entitled to international protection?*

The EU's Qualification Directive (QD), the 2004 Original and later 2011 Recast form, clarifies that EU states offer 'international protection' to refugees (within the sense of the CSR) and subsidiary protection (SP).[63] SP under the QD protects those at risk of three forms of 'serious harm' namely the death penalty or execution; torture, inhuman and degrading treatment 'in the country of origin'; or some 'individual risks' from 'indiscriminate violence'.

The first three CJEU cases on the QD concerned the limits of refugee protection; the temporal limits of cessation (*Abdulla*[64]); the personal limits as regards Palestine refugees under Article 1D (*Bolbol*,[65] later followed by *El Kott*[66]); and exclusion under Article 1F (*B & D*[67]). Several cases have now addressed the central issue in refugee law; that is, the meaning of persecution. *Y & Z*[68] addressed religious persecution, while *X, Y & Z*[69] addressed

61 Article 78(2) Treaty on the Functioning of the European Union.

62 Article 5 RPD; Article 4 RPD; Article 3 RQD.

63 Council Directive 2004/83/EC of 29 April 2004 and Directive 2011/95/EU of the European Parliament and of the Council of 13 December 2011 on standards for the qualification of third-country nationals or stateless persons as beneficiaries of international protection, for a uniform status for refugees or for persons eligible for subsidiary protection, and for the content of the protection granted (recast) (RQD) [2011] OJ L337/9, Article 2(a) QD. On the implementation of the Original QD, see UNHCR QD Study; European Commission, *Report on the Application of Directive 2004/83/EC* COM(2010) 314; United Nations High Commissioner for Refugees, *Safe at Last? Law and Practice in Selected EU Member States with Respect to Asylum-Seekers Fleeing Indiscriminate Violence* (UNHCR, 2011).

64 Joined Cases C-175/08, C-176/08, C-178/08 and C-179/08 *Aydin Salahadin Abdulla and others* [2010] ECR I-1493. See R. Errera, 'Cessation and assessment of new circumstances: a comment on *Abdulla*, CJEU, 2 March 2010' (2011) 23 *International Journal of Refugee Law* 521.

65 Case C-31/09 *Bolbol* [2010] ECR I-5539.

66 Case C-364/11 *El Kott* [2013] OJ C 46/8.

67 Joined Cases C-57/09 and C-101/09 *Germany v B & D* [2010] ECR I-10979. See further G. Gilbert, 'Exclusion under the Qualification Directive and the German Reference' (2009), paper presented at the IARLJ Conference, Berlin, 19–20 October 2009.

68 Joined Cases C-71/11 and C-99/11 *Germany v Y & Z* [2013] 1 *Common Market Law Review* 5.

69 Joined Cases C-199/12, C-200/12 and C-201/12 *X, Y & Z v Minister voor Immigratie en Asiel* [2014] OJ C9/8. See further S. Chelvan, 'Case comment: *X, Y & Z v Minister voor Immigratie en Asiel*: a missed opportunity or a new dawn?' (2013) 5 *Chambers Newsletter*;

persecution on grounds of sexual orientation, and *Shepherd* dealt with conscientious objectors and military service.[70] There are now two CJEU cases on the interactions between refugee status and SP (*MM* and *HN*[71]), while two dealt with the scope of SP: *Elgafaji*,[72] and *Diakité*.[73] The European Court of Human Rights (ECtHR) case law played a decisive role in informing the EU definition of SP in the QD. In some respects, the QD simply codifies the Strasbourg case law, in particular in its Article 15(b) on torture, inhuman and degrading treatment. However, it appears that EU SP status is narrower than the ECHR protections.[74]

Differences in rights between refugees and subsidiary protection beneficiaries have been reduced in EU law, as is evident from the QD to the Recast QD. However, some differences remain at the EU level. Notably, only Convention refugees are entitled to family reunion under the EU's Family Reunification Directive, not subsidiary protection beneficiaries.[75] A recent trend is that some Member States appear to be reducing the rights of subsidiary protection beneficiaries.[76] And new limits on family reunion rights are also being introduced.[77]

2.5.2 *Reception conditions*

The Reception Conditions Directive (RCD)[78] deals with living conditions and rights while asylum claims are processed. It regulates 'reception', which encompasses questions as diverse as detention, free movement, documentation, access to the labour market, vocational training and the treatment of 'vulnerable persons', including unaccompanied minors.

There have only been three rulings on the RCD. The first, *Arslan*,[79] is really about detention under the Returns Directive, but also clarifies the scope of detention provisions under the RCD. The second, *Cimade & GISTI*,[80]

M. Mouzourakis, 'Case Comment: *X, Y & Z v Minister voor Immigratie en Asiel*' (*Rights in Exile*, 1 December 2013).

70 Case C-472/13 *Shepherd v Germany* [2015] WLR (D) 88.

71 Case C-277/11 *MM* [2013] OJ C26/9.

72 C-465/07 *Elgafaji v Saatssecreteris van Justitie* 17 February 2009 [2009] ECR I-921.

73 Case C-285/12 *Diakité* [2014] OJ C93/6.

74 Case C-542/13 *M'Bodj* [2014] ECR I-0000, 18 December 2014.

75 Council Directive 2003/86/EC of 22 September 2003 on the right to family reunification [2003] OJ L251/12. Three EU Member States (Denmark, Ireland and the UK) are not bound by this Directive.

76 See among others Sweden, http://goo.gl/wJY26X; Austria, http://goo.gl/F71Usm; Germany, http://goo.gl/w47YtK; Denmark, http://goo.gl/4Idpfw (accessed 30 May 2016).

77 This is the case for SP beneficiaries in Sweden (Ibid).

78 Council Directive 2003/9/EC of 27 January 2003 laying down minimum standards for the reception of asylum-seekers [2003] OJ L31/18.

79 Case C-534/11 *Arslan*, 30 May 2013.

80 Case C-179/11 *Cimade & GISTI*, 27 September 2012.

clarified that the reception conditions due to asylum-seekers also applied to those subject to Dublin procedures (contrary to the French practice at that time). The third, *Saciri*,[81] concerned the grant of reception conditions in the form of financial allowances. The Court emphasised that such allowances must be made available from arrival, and be sufficient to ensure a dignified standard of living and adequate for the health of applicants and capable of ensuring their subsistence, enabling them in particular to find housing, having regard, if necessary, to the preservation of the interests of persons having specific needs, pursuant to Article 17. The ruling is significant in particular for its emphasis on human dignity and family unity. While the RCD only expressly deals with the matter of family unity if the Member State provides accommodation, the CJEU confirmed that financial allowances also had to be such as to enable families to live together.

Remarkably, the first ruling on the detention provisions came in *JN*.[82] The CJEU's interpretation seems to provide some useful guidance on the Directive, but is unhelpful on the broader questions about the right to liberty. It seems to conflate the right to liberty under the EU Charter and ECHR, by holding that the detention of an asylum-seeker on public order grounds is permissible under human rights law insofar as it pursues a legitimate objective and is necessary and proportionate. The ruling appears to omit the scrutiny of detention against the circumscribed grounds of Article 5 ECHR altogether. As the Charter requires EU human rights standards to be at least as protective as the ECHR, that aspect of the ruling may have to be revisited.

2.5.3 Asylum procedures

Procedural harmonisation predates the CEAS by decades. Indeed, as mentioned, the earliest informal European horizontal policy transfer concerned procedural matters – or perhaps better put, tools to manage asylum processes and responsibilities, notably safe country notions, both safe third country (STC) and safe country of origin (SCO). After the process of horizontal policy transfer, non-binding EU resolutions were adopted in 1992 on three asylum matters – STC, SCO and unfounded applications.[83] This also set up an enduring policy frame, whereby claiming asylum was assumed to be liable to 'abuse' by economic migrants. And procedural matters, more typically in the EU system of decentralised administration left to the domestic level, became highly regulated, politicised and contested in EU law.

81 Case C-79/13 *Saciri*, 27 February 2014.

82 Case C-601/15 PPU *JN v Staatssecretaris van Veiligheid en Justitie*, 15 February 2016.

83 Council of the European Union, Resolution on a Harmonized Approach to Questions Concerning Host Third Countries; Resolution on Manifestly Unfounded Applications for Asylum; Conclusions on Countries in which there is Generally no risk of persecution (London, 30 November–1 December 1992).

When the EU turned to formal procedural harmonisation, the Directive on this topic proved the most difficult to agree, and resulted in a loose set of stipulations, and great leeway for procedural restriction. So much so that UNHCR and asylum advocates made an unprecedented call for the PD to be abandoned.[84] The Recast PD contains many improvements over its predecessor, in part by integrating principles espoused in the case law of the ECtHR.[85] Somewhat surprisingly, in contrast, the general principles of EU law and the EU rights to fair procedures and effective judicial protection, have not driven significant changes in this domain.[86] With some notable exceptions, asylum procedures have remained highly fragmented and stratified across the EU, with different procedures used for different types of claims and claimants. EU fundamental rights principles have had some significant impact, notably the *A, B & C* case in rooting out some evidential practices that were deemed to violate human dignity and privacy.[87] However, the procedural landscape remains highly fragmented.

2.5.4 *Conclusion on the success and contents of the CEAS*

The above sketch of the CEAS provides a sense of its complexity. Some matters are regulated in great detail, while others are left to national discretion. In some ways, the degree of harmonisation is surprising, particularly of procedures, as these are not usually regulated at the EU level. No doubt the process of legislative harmonisation has been rights-protective in some respects. Most significant of all is perhaps the creation of a formal status for subsidiary protection beneficiaries, which was a significant move for those who previously may have benefitted from *non-refoulement*, but no formal status.[88] Yet, undoubtedly, some elements of the first phase of the CEAS fell below international minimum standards, such as the rules on 'internal

84 ECRE et al., *Call for Withdrawal of the Asylum Procedures Directive* (22 March 2004).

85 C. Costello and E. Hancox, 'The Recast Asylum Procedures Directive: caught between the stereotypes of the abusive asylum-seeker and the vulnerable refugee', in V. Chetail, P. De Bruycker and F. Maiani (eds.), *Reforming the Common European Asylum System: The New European Refugee Law* (Martinus Nijhoff, 2016).

86 One of the authors had earlier anticipated a significant role for the general principles. C. Costello, 'The Asylum Procedures Directive in legal context: equivocal standards meet general principles', in A. Baldaccini, E. Guild and H. Toner (eds.), *Whose Freedom, Security and Justice? EU Immigration and Asylum Law After 1999* (Hart Publishing, 2007) 151.

87 Joined Cases C-148/13, C-149/13 and C-150/13 *A, B & C v Staatssecretaris van Veiligheid en Justitie*, 2 December 2014. The CJEU interpreted Article 4 QD (on evidential assessment in asylum) in light of Articles 1, 3 and 7 of the Charter, such as to preclude recourse to undignified and invasive forms of questioning and testing in establishing sexual orientation and identity.

88 J. McAdam, 'The European Union Qualification Directive: the creation of a subsidiary protection regime' (2005) 17 *International Journal of Refugee Law* 461 McAdam notes, however, that SP under the QD is much narrower than complementary protection under international law.

flight',[89] and introducing the notion of non-state actors of protection.[90] The approach to 'particular social group' in the original QD suggested an overly restrictive approach.[91] However, the second phase is somewhat better on these issues, and some progressive developments in refugee law have been made.[92]

Along with this mixed assessment of the substance, it must be asked whether the CEAS meets its stated aims. One predominant rationale for harmonising legislation is to avoid 'secondary movements' of asylum-seekers by creating a level playing field.[93] However, in reality, not only do the outcomes of asylum processes still vary greatly for claimants from the same countries seeking protection at the same time, but so too do the living conditions and prospects for family reunion. For instance, the Recast RCD requires Member States, at a minimum, to allow asylum-seekers to work after nine months' stay, if decisions on their claims still have not been made. In practice, some Member States allow asylum-seekers to work after shorter periods (Spain, Sweden and Greece on arrival, Italy after two months, Germany after three months).[94] The UK has not opted in to the Recast Directive, so keeps a one-year bar on labour market access, and shockingly Ireland, which did not opt into the RCD at all, never allows asylum-seekers access to the labour market, in spite of prolonged asylum procedures. The result is that the lived experience of claiming asylum varies greatly across the EU.

Furthermore, we question the underlying premise of this policy rationale. The linkage with 'secondary movements' presupposes that asylum-seekers choose destinations based on the conditions there. Even if that premise were empirically well-founded (which it is not, or at least is only a very small part of the explanation),[95] the asylum Directives are not likely to institute a true level playing field. Indeed, it is doubtful whether that is ever achievable through legislation alone, when implementation and national institutional divergence

89 See, for example, ECRE et al., *Actors of Protection and the Internal Protection Alternative* (ECRE, 2014).

90 See Original QD and RQD.

91 See Original QD and RQD; and C. Querton, 'The interpretation of the convention ground of "Membership of a Particular Social Group" in the context of gender-related claims for asylum: a critical analysis of the Tribunal's approach in the UK', Refugee Law Initiative Working Paper No. 3 (January 2012).

92 For a comprehensive assessment of the Recast Directives, see V. Chetail, P. De Bruycker and F. Maiani (eds.), *Reforming the Common European Asylum System: The New European Refugee Law* (Martinus Nijhoff, 2016).

93 On the aim of limiting secondary movements, see Recital 7 of the Original PD; Recital 6 PD; Recital 8 RCD.

94 See further AIDA, *Common Asylum System at a Turning Point: Refugees Caught in Europe's Solidarity Crisis* (2015) Annual Report 2014/2015.

95 H. Crawley, 'Chance or choice? Understanding why asylum seekers come to the UK' (Refugee Council, January 2010), 17, citing E. Thielemann, 'Does policy matter? On Governments' attempts to control unwanted migration' (2003), IIIS Discussion Paper No. 9, 32 and E. Neumayer, 'Asylum destination choice: what makes some Western European countries more attractive than others?' (2004) 5(2) *EU Politics* 155.

remain so pervasive. It is for this reason we suggest that the CEAS is not truly common. National authorities grant national status according to established practices in the main. A refugee's chance of recognition as such depends on where she claims asylum, as do her living conditions and time period spent in the limbo of asylum-seeking. Even once her claim is recognised, her status is national. As discussed below, there is no positive mutual recognition of asylum decisions, and unless she waits for EU long-term residence status or waits for naturalisation, she is effectively confined to a single Member State.

3 Structural deficiencies of the CEAS

The legal instruments that make up the CEAS are complex and elaborate, as the preceding section has illustrated. However, on top of these complexities (which in turn undermine its claim to be common), as an ostensible system, the CEAS is structurally flawed. By structural flaw, we mean regulatory features that undermine the basic aims of the purported system, and lead to perverse effects and incentives for all the actors in the regime – States, the EU and asylum-seekers and potential asylum-seekers. These structural flaws are such as to undermine any claim to constituting a system, in the sense of an interlocking set of mutually reinforcing policies. There are three main structural flaws. The first is the lack of legal and safe access to asylum in Europe, the second related flaw is the ambiguities around 'effective border controls', and third is Dublin and the perverse incentives it creates.

3.1 Lack of legal and safe access to asylum in Europe

The CEAS formally begins on the territory or on the territorial waters[96] of a Member State. However, to get there, asylum-seekers must travel. Asylum-seekers potentially encounter EU law in their home countries, or countries of transit or first asylum. If they approach the embassy of a Schengen State, that country's visa system is partly governed by EU law. If someone who is likely to claim asylum applies for a temporary visa (and temporary visas are all the system provides), that is in effect grounds for refusal. This phenomenon has been illustrated by the EU's Fundamental Rights Agency (FRA),[97] and investigated more thoroughly by Czaika and de Haas.[98] Not by accident but by design, those with protection needs are often prevented from getting visas. Most need them: exceptionally, those from the Western Balkans who come to the EU to claim asylum do not, and find their claims rejected. So the refugees with perhaps the strongest contemporary protection needs face legal barriers that others do not.

96 Article 3 RPD.

97 FRA, *Legal Entry Channels to the EU for Persons in Need of International Protection*, 02/2015.

98 M. Czaika and H. de Haas, 'The effect of visa policies on international migration dynamics' IMI Working Paper 89, April 2014.

While politicians often insist that a sharp distinction between refugees and 'economic migrants' must be maintained, external border controls draw no such distinction. Visa requirements and processes are crude, and in effect exclude anyone who would claim asylum. Indeed, in reality, those in need of international protection face barriers that other travellers do not. As currently operated, visa policies combine with carriers' sanctions to prevent refugees from boarding regular planes and ferries to enter the EU.[99] The carrier sanctions regime privatises border controls, and means that those without their papers in order will not be able to board regular ferries and planes to fly to their destinations to claim asylum.

This means that irregular journeys must involve clandestine means of transport, and hence the role of smugglers. The feasibility of getting smuggled across a land border depends on the nature of the border crossings, terrain and fortifications. Greece and Turkey share a land border that has been fortified, as do Turkey and Bulgaria. In 2015, there were many credible reports of shootings by Bulgarian border guards at the latter border,[100] and of the Turkish authorities impeding access to the Greek–Turkish land border. The causes of the exodus by sea thus become apparent, with more than 800,000 people making the short dinghy crossing, allegedly paying smugglers more than €1,000 each. The crisis of 2015 began with deaths at sea on the Central Mediterranean route. Libya to Italy is one of the deadliest smuggling routes in the world, with overcrowded boats being launched that are often simply too overloaded to make it to their destination. Maritime search and rescue has become a normalised part of the process. While their political masters envisage that their role undermines the smugglers' 'business model',[101] in reality, search and rescue has a more complex relation with smuggling.[102]

The option of opening up orderly departure programmes, creating humanitarian visa programmes, or protected entry procedures has long been urged. A 2002 study notes that '[d]isorderly movement is presently the main avenue to safety in the EU, and human smugglers act as important facilitators'.[103] The study explained that:

99 S. Scholten, *The Privatisation of Immigration Control through Carrier Sanctions* (Brill, 2014).

100 Human Rights Watch, 'Universal periodic review submission: Bulgaria' (September 2014); Human Rights Watch, 'Bulgaria: pushbacks, abuse at borders' (20 January 2016). See also generally, report by Nils Muiznieks following his visit to Bulgaria, Strasbourg 22 June 2015, CommDH(2015) 12.

101 This is the language used in the documents concerning the EU mission in the Central Mediterranean, EUNAVFOR MED: Council Decision (CFSP) 2015/778 of 18 May 2015 on a European Union military operation in the Southern Central Mediterranean (EUNAFVOR MED) [2015] OJ L122/31.

102 EEAS, *EUNAFVOR MED Operation Sophia: Six Monthly Report* (February 2016) WikiLeaks, available at https://wikileaks.org/eu-military-refugees.

103 G. Noll, J. Fagerlund and F. Liebaut, 'Study on the feasibility of processing asylum claims outside the EU against the background of the Common European Asylum System and the

> Provided they are well-crafted, Protected Entry Procedures could drain parts of the market for human smuggling, attract bona fide refugees who presently opt for the smuggling services and thereby decrease the total number of disorderly arrivals and partially eliminate the problem of returning the rejected caseload. An obvious security advantage for states is to know in advance who wishes to enter their territory. In addition, important synergies with integration and labour immigration policies can be created.[104]

All this advice fell on deaf ears. Indeed, the European states such as Switzerland and Spain that ran such procedures have tended to retract them, leaving a growing demand for protection, and no regular means to access it. Why did so many people come to Europe in 2015? At least part of the answer seems to be the opening up of a new, relatively inexpensive smuggling route.[105] Still dangerous and expensive, but nothing like as hazardous or deadly as other routes.

3.1.1 Visas – duties at embassies

The EU Visa Code[106] has a provision allowing for humanitarian visas to be processed. On one view, there is a legal obligation to do so.[107] The European Parliament supports this move.[108] There are many good examples of humanitarian visa practice, both contemporary[109] and historical.[110]

Under some circumstances, embassy officials are currently obliged to take into account the human rights of those who apply for visas.[111] Current conceptions of the scope of human rights obligations turn on the concept of 'jurisdiction', understood as the exercise of effective control over persons or territory. For instance, at least when consular officials exercise effective

goal of a common asylum procedure', study carried out by the Danish Centre for Human Rights on behalf of the European Commission (Directorate General for Justice and Home Affairs, 2002), 3, 252.

104 Ibid, 3.

105 G. Abdul-Ahad, 'Some tips for the long-distance traveller' (2015) 37(19) *London Review of Books* 39.

106 Regulation (EC) No 810/2009 of the European Parliament and of the Council of 13 July 2009 establishing a Community Code on Visas (Visa Code) [2009] OJ L243/1.

107 U. Iben-Jensen, 'Humanitarian visas: option or obligation?' (2014) European Parliament, PE509.986.

108 European Parliament, 'MEPs want EU embassies and consulates to grant asylum seekers humanitarian visas' (16 March 2016).

109 See, for example, M. Calegari and R. Baeninger, 'From Syria to Brazil' (2016) 51 *Forced Migration Review* 96.

110 Shutzpass in RWI, http://rwi.lu.se/app/uploads/2016/04/Humanitarian-Visas-policy-brief.pdf.

111 K. Ogg, 'Protection closer to home? A legal case for claiming asylum at embassies and consulates' (2014) 33 *Refugee Survey Quarterly* 81.

control over persons, ECHR obligations become applicable.[112] However, such scenarios are exceptional.

More typically, visa processing is not only extraterritorial, but completely de-territorialised. States contract out much of the process to private corporations, and the process is generally handled predominantly online, often requiring high up-front charges for visa processing, with no appeal rights. The cyber-border is often an effective barrier, as are fees. Hence in 2015 a Belgian citizens' initiative 'Un Visa, Une Vie' began, and has crowdfunded visa applications for family members of refugees in Belgium.[113] The need for such support illustrates the practical barrier visa processes embody, even for those with a strong right to enter, such as the family members of recognised refugees.

3.2 Borders – the obligations of border states

As legal routes are virtually non-existent, refugees come irregularly, and for the reasons explained above, often by boat. Most of us criss-cross borders at great heights, and encounter official controls at airports, whether at counties of departure or arrival. As discussed, most refugees seeking protection in Europe do not have this option. Of course, some fleeing conflict simply cross Europe's land borders unhindered. It appears that the majority of Ukrainians arriving in Poland were granted stay without applying for asylum, triggering any crisis or dying on the way.[114] In contrast, those arriving in Greece tended to use a dangerous sea route. It is worth pausing to consider why the Greek–Turkish and Greek–Bulgarian land borders were not also places where refugees could seek entry to the EU. This is, of course, in need of empirical investigation, but it appears that fortifications of land borders through physical obstacles and – often violent – policing has effectively barred persons from attempting to enter.[115] More recent border closures further afield, discussed below, have had similar effects.

When refugees arrive irregularly, it is important to clarify the legal duties at physical borders. Legal and political framings are in tension here. Letting refugees in when they arrive at borders (at least in order to carry out a proper assessment of protection needs), in particular when they arrive irregularly, is evidently a legal obligation. However, it is simultaneously framed politically as a failure of border controls. As Macklin has put it, 'every asylum seeker

112 *R (B & Others) v. SSFCA* [2005] QB 643.

113 See www.facebook.com/Syrieunvisaunevie.

114 M. Szczepnaik and E. Tylec, 'Ukrainian asylum seekers and a Polish immigration paradox' (2016) 51 *Forced Migration Review* 71.

115 On unlawful killings by Bulgarian border guards, see Human Rights Watch, 'Bulgaria: pushbacks, abuse at borders' (20 January 2016). Note also a subsequent gift of patrol vehicles by the UK Government to Bulgaria: House of Lords, 'Gifting of Land Rovers to the government of Bulgaria: written statement' HLWS566, 4 March 2016.

who reaches the frontier of a State Party simultaneously embodies that State's international protection obligation under the Refugee Convention, and the failure of that State's border control apparatus to prevent the asylum-seeker's arrival'.[116]

The legal obligations at physical borders are set out in the Schengen Borders Code (SBC)[117] and they reflect the position in international human rights and refugee law that non-admission at the frontier may amount to *refoulement*. While some states and authorities contest that view, it is the better interpretation of the CSR, and indeed the customary norm of *non-refoulement*.[118] This means that some examination of protection needs must take place if people are not to be admitted. Moreover, the ECtHR has clarified that the prohibition on collective expulsion requires an individualised assessment before expulsion.[119]

At the political level, much of the discussion of border states' failures is highly ambiguous. If border control were effective, would it mean simply registering all arrivals (and thereby becoming legally responsible under the Dublin System for all but those with close family elsewhere in Europe) or does it mean turning refugees away without due process? The latter would evidently not be legal. The dilemma for border states is induced by Dublin. If they comply with duties to register, verify identity and the rest, their asylum systems would be under immense strain in situations of mass influx.

In the absence of safe and legal travel routes for refugees, search and rescue obligations have come under scrutiny. In the maritime context, search and rescue duties only require that those rescued are disembarked in a place of safety.[120] In the context of the Central Mediterranean, that currently precludes returns to Libya (as does international human rights and refugee law).[121]

116 A. Macklin, 'A safe country to emulate? Canada and the European Refugee', in H. Lambert, J. McAdam and M. Fullerton (eds.), *The Global Reach of European Refugee Law* (Cambridge University Press, 2013) 100.

117 Regulation (EU) No 2016/399 of the European Parliament and of the Council of 9 March 2016 on a Union code on the rules governing the movement of persons across borders (Schengen Borders Code) [2016] OJ L77/1.

118 E. Lauterpacht and D. Bethlehem, 'The scope and content of the principle of non-refoulement', in E. Feller, V. Türk and F. Nicholson (eds.), *Refugee Protection in International Law: UNHCR's Global Consultations On International Protection* (Cambridge University Press, 2003) 87.

119 *Khlaifia and Others v Italy*, Application no. 16483/12; *N.D. v Spain and NT v Spain*, Application nos. 8675/15 and 8697/15; *Hirsi Jamaa and Others v Italy*, Application no. 27765/09.

120 United Nations Convention on the Law of the Sea, 10 December 1982; Regulation (EU) No 656/2014 of the European Parliament and of the Council of 15 May 2014 establishing the rules for surveillance of the external sea borders in the context of operational cooperation coordinated by [Frontex] [2014] OJ L189/93.

121 *Hirsi Jamaa and others v Italy*, App. No. 27765/09 [GC] (23 February 2012).

3.3 Dublin as structural problem

In the absence of legal routes to claim asylum, refugees and migrants normally arrive in the EU irregularly, which at present means by sea in Italy and Greece. Under these circumstances, those States would normally be responsible for the asylum claims under Dublin, unless the family criteria prevail. In practice, these family criteria are poorly implemented, and accordingly responsibility remains with the State of arrival.[122]

A cursory glance at asylum statistics shows that relatively few people claim asylum in their countries of arrival: of those arriving in Italy in 2015, slightly over 50 per cent claimed asylum there, while less than 2 per cent claimed in Greece. It was ever thus – as Maiani and Vevstad showed in 2009, 'responsibility ultimately lies, in the vast majority of cases, with the State where the application was first filed'[123] rendering the system 'unworkable and dysfunctional'.[124] This is a result of both Member State and asylum-seekers' evasive strategies. The forms of State evasion and avoidance of Dublin are many and varied, but selective fingerprinting of arrivals is now well-established. Asylum-seekers too often simply avoid the authorities in States of first arrival, and seek to move on in a clandestine manner. They do so to avoid illegal detention and degrading living conditions in many instances. In 2015, that onward movement was facilitated by Greece and Italy, in an overt manner.[125] They were not the only EU Member States to 'wave through' refugees in order to encourage them to claim asylum in Germany or Sweden.[126]

Nonetheless, Dublin does have teeth: since 2000 it has been complemented by the EURODAC system, which means Member States are obliged to fingerprint asylum-seekers on arrival. It seems this obligation is enforced highly selectively. For some asylum-seekers, it means their journey through Dublin States leaves a trace, and they are often made aware if they move on from one State, they risk later detention and deportation back to their country of arrival or transit. It is difficult to assess the impact of 'Dublin' as a mechanism to deter such movements, but as most asylum-seekers do move on, it seems reasonable to infer that it fails to deter onward movement in many cases. Of those who do move on, only a small minority get caught up in Dublin return proceedings.

122 ECRE, (n. 7); ICF, *Evaluation of the Implementation of the Dublin III Regulation* (March 2016).

123 Maiani and Vevstad (n. 7).

124 Ibid., 2. See also European Asylum Support Office (EASO), *Annual Report on the Situation of Asylum in the European Union 2013*, 30: 'Dublin transfers were made in the case of only about 3% of those making an asylum claim in the EU.'

125 See, for example, AIDA, 'Greece: ferry for refugees to leave the Aegean islands', 21 August 2015, http://goo.gl/KijpOa.

126 On the 'wave through' approach across the Western Balkan route, involving Hungary, Croatia and Slovenia, see, for example, ECRE, Western Balkan News Briefs series.

But there are a misfortunate few who do get caught up in Dublin proceedings. A State may request the first State to 'take back' the asylum-seeker. Such requests are made in about 15 per cent of cases,[127] although the pattern varies considerably. If such requests are made, state practice in responding to these requests is also variable: over the years, some have accepted back the person but not examined the asylum claim. For instance, for a time, Greece operated a law that suspended the examination of claims of Dublin returnees, leaving people in limbo.[128] Currently Hungary is liable to eject Dublin returnees to Serbia, under a quasi-automatic STC rule. The legislation adopted in 2015 provides that in parallel with an inadmissibility decision, the authorities also expel the asylum-seeker and impose a ban on re-entry. Shockingly, the CJEU recently held (in an urgent preliminary ruling) that there is no obligation on Hungary to inform the returning State that this is a likely outcome of the transfer.[129]

Even in instances when transfers back do happen and the asylum claim is examined in the responsible State, the transfer is highly consequential. Even if the applicant is recognised as a refugee or subsidiary protection beneficiary, that status is national in scope. There is no duty of mutual recognition of positive determinations (although the European Parliament has recently endorsed such a move); in other words, recognition as a refugee or subsidiary protection beneficiary still leaves the refugee confined to one Member State.[130] It is only after five years that this status takes on a transnational character with EU free movement rights, since the Long Term Residents Directive (LTRD) now includes beneficiaries of international protection.[131] However, *rejection* of an asylum claim *does* have consequences beyond the particular deciding state, and the rejected asylum-seeker is effectively prevented by Dublin from posing another asylum claim in the EU. So for an asylum-seeker with strong reasons to claim asylum in one country or another due to pre-existing connections there, the transfer back may isolate her from the sorts of social networks that could have supported her integration.

Perhaps most egregiously, in spite of two rounds of legislative harmonisation, outcomes in asylum determinations have not converged across the EU. For decades, Dublin has been decried as unfair for this reason. The chances

127 Percentages range from 11 per cent to 17 per cent in the period 2008–2014: ICF, *Evaluation of the Dublin III Regulation* (December 2015), 6. While figures relate to the total number of claims rather than those potentially within the scope of the Dublin System, it is worth recalling that more than 99 per cent of persons arriving in Greece in 2015 moved onwards; these would thus fall within the remit of Dublin.

128 P. Papadimitriou and G. Papageorgiou, 'The new Dubliners: implementation of Council Regulation 343/2003 by the Greek authorities' (2006) 18 *Journal of Refugee Studies* 299.

129 Case C695/15 PPU *Mirza*, 17 March 2016.

130 Admittedly, the CSR does provide some rights to onward movement, but these are couched in tentative terms. See further, J.C. Hathaway, *The Law of Refugee Status* (Butterworths, 1991) 840–874.

131 Directive 2011/51/EU of the European Parliament and of the Council of 11 May 2011 amending Council Directive 2003/109/EC to extend its scope to beneficiaries of international protection [2011] OJ L132/1.

of recognition as a refugee for those fleeing Iraq, Afghanistan, Eritrea and even Syria, at various points in time have varied enormously. There is now an extensive and literature on this phenomenon.[132]

Evidently, if Dublin worked properly, in the sense that it were fully implemented by states, it would break down. Greece would have had more than 900,000 asylum claims to examine in 2015 alone, and it is difficult to see how that would be sustainable. The forms of state evasion and avoidance of Dublin are many and varied, but selective fingerprinting of arrivals is now well-established. Asylum-seekers too engage in various evasion strategies. Dublin encourages clandestinity, refusing to be fingerprinted or mutilating fingertips. Some wait out the Dublin time periods often in dire circumstances, unable to access proper reception conditions.[133] Empirical studies of Dublin at work demonstrate the 'Lives on Hold' phenomenon[134]. While Dublin is meant to ensure a swift allocation of responsibility, instead it creates clandestinity and protracted procedures.

Resisting Dublin returns has also entailed recourse to the judiciary, and latterly human rights bodies.[135] Those seeking to resist return have invoked their human rights, in particular under the ECHR. The voluminous Dublin case law, including both hundreds if not thousands of Rule 39 orders, and several high-profile Grand Chamber rulings, have over the years clarified that the sending state must make a limited but important human rights assessment: return is prohibited if there are substantial grounds to believe there is a real risk of treatment contrary to Article 3 ECHR. (Presumably a risk of Article 2 or 4 breach would also be grounds to prohibit a Dublin transfer, or a 'flagrant breach' of another right.)[136]

It the landmark ruling of *MSS v Belgium and Greece*,[137] the ECtHR held that not only were detention conditions in Greece likely to violate Article 3 ECHR, but so too were the degrading living conditions. That conclusion was based on the legally constructed 'vulnerability' of asylum-seekers,

132 See ECRE, *Five Years on Europe is still Ignoring its Responsibilities towards Iraqi Refugees* (2008) AD1/03/2008/ext/ADC. The rates concern first instance decisions. See further M. Sperl, 'Fortress Europe and the Iraqi "intruders": Iraqi asylum-seekers and the EU, 2003–2007' (2007) UNHCR Working Paper No 144, 6. A 2011 UNHCR study examined the treatment of Iraqi, Somali and Afghan asylum-seekers, finding significant divergences in the treatment of all three. See UNHCR, *Safe at Last?* (n. 62).

133 This practice was successfully challenged by French NGOs in *Cimade & GISTI* (n. 79).

134 ECRE et al., *Dublin II Regulation: Lives on Hold* (February 2013), www.refworld.org/docid/513ef9632.html

135 UN Human Rights Committee, *Communication 2360/2014*, 4 September 2015, halting a Dublin transfer from Denmark to Italy.

136 In *Tarakhel v Switzerland*, Application no. 29217/12, the applicants sought to argue that for transfers across the Council of Europe, the 'flagrant breach' standard was inappropriate for breaches of the right to family life, but this aspect of the claim was not examined and it was determined under Article 3 ECHR: C. Costello and M. Mouzourakis, 'Reflections on reading *Tarakhel*: is "how bad is bad enough" good enough?' (2014) 10 *Asiel en Migrantenrecht* 404, 406.

137 (2011) 53 EHRR 2.

which created a positive duty on states to ensure their living conditions (the acknowledgment of this obligation was manifest in the RCD). In the wake of *MSS*, litigation continued, notably for the first time before the CJEU. In its *NS & ME* ruling, the CJEU largely followed Strasbourg's lead in *MSS*. However, it emphasised more strongly (if somewhat ambiguously) that Dublin institutionalised mutual recognition across the EU, which was a cornerstone of the CEAS. And so it stated that suspension of transfer was obligatory if the transferring Member State authorities cannot be unaware that systemic deficiencies amount to substantial grounds for believing that there is a real risk of treatment contrary to Article 4 of the Charter (Article 3 ECHR).[138]

Since then, further national and supranational litigation has ensued. Courts have been confronted with cases concerning reception standards in Italy and Bulgaria, and procedural protections in Hungary, among others. The CJEU has given several rulings on the procedural dimensions of Dublin, and on the question of unaccompanied minors. For the latter category, it has obliged Member States to take charge of cases rather than transfer elsewhere, in order to deal with claims swiftly.[139]

In *Tarakhel v Switzerland*, the ECtHR's Grand Chamber set out requirements on returns to Italy, emphasising the need for individual assessment and assurances in light of the individuals' particular vulnerability. That ruling entailed a shift in the conceptualisation of 'vulnerability' – from the structural-legal vulnerability of all asylum-seekers in *MSS* to the embodied vulnerability of the children, women and only some men.[140] Subsequent rulings have illustrated the pitfalls of the embodied vulnerability approach, with men being viewed as better able to withstand harsh treatment.

At the time of writing, a new litigation front on Dublin returns to Hungary is opening up.[141] Those recently returned find themselves either detained or returned to Serbia. The existing Strasbourg rulings would suggest that returns should be prohibited as legislation introduced by Hungary in 2015 makes returns to Serbia quasi-automatic.

138 *NS & ME*, para 94. See also para 106 where this test is stated as a requirement of Article 4 of the Charter.

139 *MA*, para 55.

140 The phrase 'embodied vulnerability' comes from M. Finemann, *The Vulnerable Subject: Anchoring Equality in the Human Condition* (Princeton University Press, 2013) and feminist legal theory. In this context, we simply use it to differentiate between the approach in *MSS*, where vulnerability was a legally structured feature of asylum-seeker, to the more embodied personal notion of vulnerability in later cases.

141 In recent months, Dublin transfers to Hungary have been halted by domestic courts in France, Germany, Austria, the Netherlands, Switzerland, Sweden, Finland, Denmark and Norway. See ECRE, *Case Law Fact Sheet: Prevention of Dublin Transfers to Hungary* (ECRE, 2016).

4 Responses appraised

This part examines the legal responses adopted thus far to deal with the 'crisis'. These include (1) a range of unilateral measures, some legal, some blatantly illegal under EU and international law; (2) various attempts to respond to the 'crisis' at the EU level on an ad hoc basis, including EU relocation, resettlement and the EU–Turkey 'deal'; and (3) in May 2016, a package of proposals for harmonisation and centralisation of the CEAS. Notably, none of these responses deals head-on with the structural flaws identified above.

4.1 Unilateral measures

The numbers of arrivals, concentrated in particular on the Greek islands, entailed a humanitarian crisis for those arriving. The route involved a short but dangerous journey, and often jettisoning all but the scantest belongings. Arriving with nothing, a humanitarian response with food, shelter, water and sanitation facilities was needed, but not forthcoming. The humanitarian crisis was acute – those arriving walked across the islands, bought their own tents, and found makeshift accommodation wherever they could.[142] Facing large numbers of arrivals on small islands, the Greek authorities managed to ensure passage to the Greek mainland and a perfunctory registration.[143]

As Greece could not offer effective protection, people moved onward by land, leaving the EU and re-entering it. For a time, this meant Hungary was another country experiencing large numbers of arrivals. The Hungarian authorities sought to deflect arrivals by constructing a fence, engaging in highly truncated mock asylum procedures (of doubtful legality under EU law) while allowing only a few to enter border-crossing points, and legislating to criminalise irregular entry for all others, in defiance of Article 31 CSR. At the time of writing, more than 2,500 people have been prosecuted for crimes related to illegal entry. Of the cases that have come to trial, over 98 per cent have led to convictions.[144]

The Hungarian response has been at the sharp end, but other states have also reinstituted internal border controls. Eight Member States used their Schengen option to temporarily reintroduce internal border controls,[145] and

142 The International Rescue Committee notes that although the Greek government has created temporary housing sites, many do not meet accepted humanitarian standards: see www.rescue.org/country/greece#what-are-the-main-humanitarian-challenges-in-greece. MSF states: 'The reception conditions in Greece and in Italy are still completely inadequate to provide adequate care and support to refugees and migrants': see MSF, 'EU migration crisis update – June 2016' (17 June 2016), www.msf.org/en/article/20160617-eu-migration-crisis-update-june-2016. See also C. Costello, 'Welcome to the European Union: notes from Lesbos', Open Democracy (9 September 2015), www.opendemocracy.net/can-europe-make-it/cathryn-costello/welcome-to-european-union-notes-from-lesbos.

143 European Commission, 'Commission adopts Schengen evaluation report on Greece', 2 February 2016.

144 Hungarian Helsinki Committee, Twitter, 20 April 2016.

145 European Commission, *Back to Schengen: A Roadmap*, COM(2016) 120, 4 March 2016, 9.

the threat of suspending Greece's Schengen membership is under active discussion.[146]

The option to reinstitute internal border controls was introduced in 2011. Thousands of people arrived in Italy, fleeing the Arab Spring, and moved on to France. Consequently, in a foreshadowing of the events of 2015, a border control dispute between France and Italy arose. The result was the adoption of a provision in the SBC allowing for temporary introduction of checks at internal borders. In 2015 and 2016, these closures proliferated – the Franco–Italian dispute resurfaced, controls were officially reintroduced by Hungary, Germany, Austria, Slovenia, Denmark, Sweden, Norway and Belgium.[147]

While for some, this signalled that Schengen was under threat, others took a more sanguine view.[148] Yet, the irregular arrivals of 2015 simply rendered obvious the absurdities of an unworkable Dublin in an AFSJ. Nonetheless, the parameters of the political debate pitted 'effective external border controls' or losing Schengen.[149] In this context, Greece became the weak link, and its actions were scrutinised as a potentially serious deficiency in the control of Schengen borders.[150] The Commission may propose a temporary suspension of Greece's participation in Schengen if a plethora of recommendations are not met.[151] While there is scope for such suspension, we note that it depends on a finding that the offending state has 'serious deficiencies' in the application of Schengen rules, and it is unclear how Greece could have acted otherwise in the context of the mass influx of 2015.

At the same time, critical closures of 'external' Schengen borders, leading to the containment of refugees in countries of first arrival, have been endorsed in parallel to discussions on the road back to Schengen. The 'wave-through approach' followed by states along the Balkan route until late 2015 was initially restricted to specific nationalities at the Greek–Macedonian border in November, only to be completely abandoned in February 2016. The ostensibly unilateral closure of Macedonia's frontiers has, however, been spearheaded by a regional coalition of EU Member States (Austria, Slovenia, Croatia) and non-EU countries (Macedonia, Serbia),[152] yet appeared to be rubberstamped by the EU, despite the palpable risk of a humanitarian disaster unfolding in Greece.[153]

146 See, for example, European Commission, *Assessment of Greece's Action Plan to Remedy the Serious Deficiencies in the 2015 Evaluation on the Application of the Schengen Acquis*, COM(2016) 220, 12 April 2016.

147 European Commission (n. 143).

148 E. Guild et al., 'What is happening to the Schengen Borders?' (2015) CEPS Paper in Liberty in Security No 86 / December 2015.

149 European Council, *Conclusions 18/19 February 2016*, EUCO 1/16.

150 European Commission, 'Commission adopts Schengen evaluation report on Greece', 2 February 2016.

151 Ibid.

152 Joint Statement of the Heads of Police Services from the meeting held in Zagreb, Croatia on 18 February 2016, http://goo.gl/hDzxYo (accessed 30 May 2016).

153 European Commission (n. 143), 8.

Other unilateral measures include rights reduction, diminution of family reunification rights discussed above, as well as procedural restrictions.[154]

4.2 *EU ad hoc responses: hotspots, relocation and the EU–Turkey deal*

To turn the tide of the 'crisis' and the 'disorderly' mode of arrivals in Europe, the EU envisaged the establishment of boosted asylum and border control systems at the outer edges of its territory through what became known as the 'hotspot' approach.[155] Hotspots were envisaged on various points along the Italian and Greek coasts, where the field presence of different agencies – Frontex, EASO, Europol and possibly Eurojust – would ensure orderly management of migration flows. Within those sites, the newly arrived would be screened and undergo an assessment of protection needs, which would determine whether they should travel onwards to Europe or be returned.

In response to those who had already arrived in Italy and Greece (as well as Hungary initially), an emergency relocation mechanism was proposed as a partial and temporary derogation to the Dublin System.[156] While this is portrayed as benefitting those 'frontline' states, its true value lay in distributing asylum-seekers across the entire EU, using a distribution key, rather than letting 'self-relocation' to Germany and Sweden continue. That key used objective criteria to decide the proportion of asylum-seekers with strong claims that would be sent to each Member State.[157] The distribution key was based on that used internally in Germany to distribute asylum-seekers across the *Länder*. Strikingly, there was no provision for asylum-seekers' say in their relocation.

Only certain nationalities were eligible – those deemed to be in 'clear need of international protection'. The rationale for only providing relocation opportunities to those who are likely to be recognised as refugees is not difficult to fathom, but of course, given that conditions in Greece remain inhuman and degrading for many,[158] creating a system that ignores the protection

154 On the expansion of accelerated procedures and SCO, see among others Germany, http://goo.gl/Z697uQ; Netherlands, http://goo.gl/D3PSnK (accessed 30 May 2016).

155 European Commission, *Explanatory Note on the 'Hotspot' Approach*, July 2015, http://bit.ly/1N46jcT, 12 (accessed 30 May 2016).

156 Council Decisions (EU) 2015/1523 of 14 September 2015 and 2015/1601 of 22 September 2015 establishing provisional measures in the area of international protection for the benefit of Italy and Greece [2015] OJ L239/146 and L248/80.

157 The distribution key is based on two major factors: (1) a Member's State's population size (40 per cent); and (2) its total GDP (40 per cent). Two 'corrective factors' are also 'applied inversely': 'the number of the asylum applications received and resettlement places already offered in the past 5 years (10%) and the unemployment rate (10%)'. See European Commission, 'Fact sheet: first measures under the European Agenda on Migration: questions and answers' (27 May 2015), http://europa.eu/rapid/press-release_MEMO-15-5038_en.htm.

158 See, for example,. ECRE and ICJ, *Fifth Joint Submission to the Council of Europe Committee of Ministers on the execution of MSS v Belgium and Greece* (March 2016).

needs of others is dubious. Moreover, the proxy for identifying 'clear need' is the past recognition rates of those of the same nationality across the EU. A threshold of 75 per cent past recognition rate has been set. The most recent report on relocation identifies the eligible nationalities as Burundi, Central African Republic, Eritrea, Costa Rica, and Saint Vincent and the Grenadines. When the Council Decisions were adopted, the nationalities eligible for relocation were Syria, Iraq and Eritrea. At the first update (Q3-2015), the nationalities eligible for relocation were: Bahrain, Central African Republic, Eritrea, Iraq, Syria, Swaziland and Yemen.[159]

As relocation is not working properly yet, with only 1,441 persons relocated out of a rather modest target of 106,000,[160] the effects of this discrimination are not as extensive as they would otherwise be. But the usage of past recognition rates is dubious, particularly when situations in origin countries are volatile, and those fleeing may be women and/or belong to ethnic, religious or other minority groups, where their country of origin is only part of a complex set of risk factors for persecution or serious harm. Notably, recognition rates for Afghans are not high enough to make them eligible for relocation, although many fleeing are from ethnic minorities. Taking nationality alone as the baseline is clearly a particularly crude method, and leaves many with strong protection claims out.

The sluggish implementation of relocation is mainly due to slow response in destination countries, which have submitted insufficient or no relocation pledges at all, hesitated to accept persons with particular vulnerabilities (contra the priority afforded to those by the Council Decisions), and have delayed procedures or even rejected relocation requests for no legitimate reason.[161] At the same time, the relocation scheme paradoxically hinges on asylum-seekers' successful access to an asylum procedure widely acknowledged as dysfunctional in Greece. The registration of an asylum claim, a prerequisite for eligibility for relocation, is a highly onerous hurdle to overcome in various European countries; in Greece, an insurmountable one.[162] Without effective means of lodging an application, those who should in theory be relocated from Greece to other countries – a large proportion of the 53,000 currently stranded in the country[163] – have no legal way out. Also currently stranded in Greece are many family members, including unaccompanied children, of people who are refugees or asylum-seekers elsewhere in the EU. Again, their

159 European Commission, *Second Report on Relocation and Resettlement*, COM(2016) 222, 12 April 2016.

160 European Commission, *Member States' Support to Emergency Relocation Mechanism*, data as of 4 May 2016.

161 European Commission, *First Report on Relocation and Resettlement*, COM(2016) 165, 16 March 2016.

162 Beyond Greece, examples can be drawn from France or Austria: AIDA, 'France: Authorities under court order to register asylum applications' (25 April 2016).

163 Greek Ministry of Interior, *Summary Statement of Refugee Flows*, data as of 4 May 2016.

right to be reunified is clear, but there are huge practical impediments for them to access their rights.[164]

On the other hand, for those seeking entry into the EU, there are many ways to 'disrupt the smugglers' business model' by reducing demand for irregular journeys. Some find not a whisper on the political agenda, such as suspending or moderating carrier sanctions or organising humanitarian evacuation. Instead, resettlement has modestly appeared on the EU agenda. The European Commission made a Recommendation for a European resettlement scheme, which was met by a pledge of 22,504 persons by the Council.[165] One concern at present is that EU resettlement pledges are being recycled in the international system, with no overall increase in protection for refugees. That is because the resettlement scheme does not clarify whether the pledges made by EU Member States are additional to resettlement commitments they have already made, and does not appear to have led to meaningful results in 2015.[166]

More importantly, resettlement appears as a component of the 'EU–Turkey deal'. The EU has offered to resettle Syrian refugees from Turkey on a one for one basis in exchange for Turkey's acceptance of Syrian deportees from Greece. This time it is clear that these resettlement places are not additional to those committed earlier: the EU will use the remaining pledges from its July 2015 resettlement scheme, as well as the unused pledges under the emergency relocation scheme (54,000), to resettle a maximum of 70,800 persons from Turkey under the one for one arrangement.[167]

In practical terms, the scope of legal avenues is minimal. Policy initiatives to offer resettlement are superimposed to existing commitments or trade-off with intra-EU relocation arrangements, while a voluntary humanitarian admission programme proposed in December 2015[168] is only to be activated once irregular arrivals from Turkey have come to an end.

In practice, 'hotspots' have become sites of coercion, including illegal detention of children and families.[169] States were encouraged to use coercive means – detention or even force – to identify and fingerprint entrants

164 See, for example, ECRE & AIRE Centre, *With Greece: Recommendations for Refugee Protection* (ECRE, July 2016), 19 et seq.

165 Council of the European Union, *Justice and Home Affairs Council 20 July 2015*, http://goo.gl/l56LN5 (accessed 30 May 2016).

166 A total of 8,155 persons were resettled by the EU Member States, while as many as 12 countries (Bulgaria, Czech Republic, Spain, Greece, Estonia, Croatia, Malta, Poland, Romania, Slovenia, Slovakia, Cyprus) made no resettlements: Eurostat, *Resettled Persons Annual Data*, migr_asyresa.

167 European Commission, *First Report on the Progress Made in the Implementation of the EU–Turkey Statement*, COM(2016) 231, 20 April 2016, 7.

168 Commission Recommendation C(2015) 9490 of 15 December 2015 for a voluntary humanitarian admission scheme with Turkey.

169 OHCHR, 'UN Special Rapporteur on the Human Rights of Migrants concludes his follow up visit to Greece' (16 May 2016), http://goo.gl/7XpS0z (accessed 30 May 2016).

in EURODAC,[170] while the operation of 'hotspots' was clouded in legal ambiguity.[171]

As most people who arrived in Greece moved onwards to seek protection in Germany, Sweden and elsewhere in Western Europe, there was huge political pressure to suppress irregular departures from Turkey. Following an EU–Turkey Action Plan in late November 2015 to financially support Turkey in exchange for deterring refugees from leaving its shores,[172] an EU–Turkey Statement announced on 18 March 2016 that '[a]ll new irregular migrants crossing from Turkey into Greek islands as from 20 March 2016 will be returned to Turkey'.[173] In exchange, Turkey was promised some resettlement of Syrian refugees (with 2.7 million on its territory), substantial financial assistance, visa liberalisation for Turkish nationals wishing to travel to the EU and the opening of EU accession talks.

This so-called 'deal' is informal. It has been suggested that if it were an international treaty, the EU has breached the EU Treaties by adopting it without involving the European Parliament and following Treaty-based processes.[174] The EU Council treats it rather as a mere political statement. The legality of returning people seeking refuge from the Greek islands to Turkey depends on Turkey being 'safe' in a legal sense, which means complying with the conditions for STC (or possibly first country of asylum) in the RPD.[175] There is a pre-existing readmission agreement between the EU and Turkey, but a legal decision is needed to make its provisions on returns of third-country nationals effective.

Shortly after their establishment, the Greek 'hotspots' were fully repurposed to serve as return centres for the implementation of the 'EU–Turkey deal', with the assistance of a broad variety of EU countries' experts, ranging from asylum officers and judges to interpreters and border guards.[176] Asylum-seekers entering Greece often face truncated procedures in inhumane detention conditions,[177] leading to summary rejections of their claims

170 Council of the European Union, *Implementation of the Eurodac Regulation as Regards the Obligation to Take Fingerprints*, 11013/15 ASIM 60 EURODAC 8, 17 July 2015.

171 Hotspots to date lack legal basis in Italy, while their status as Reception and Identification Centres was only clarified in Greece by Law 4375/2016, adopted in April 2016.

172 European Council, *Meeting of Heads of State or Government with Turkey: EU–Turkey Statement*, 29 November 2015, http://goo.gl/H7FiDH (accessed 30 May 2016).

173 European Council, *EU–Turkey Statement*, 18 March 2016, http://goo.gl/ymaOAJ (accessed 30 May 2016).

174 M. den Heijer and T. Spijkerboer, 'Is the EU–Turkey refugee and migration deal a treaty?' (2016) *EU Law Analysis Blog*, 7 April 2016.

175 E. Roman et al., 'Why Turkey is not a "safe country"' (February 2016) Statewatch; D. Thym, 'Why the EU–Turkey deal is legal and a step in the right direction' (2016) *Verfassungsblog*, 9 March 2016.

176 See European Commission, *Operational Implementation of the EU–Turkey Agreement*, http://goo.gl/p7UYJ0 (accessed 30 May 2016).

177 See, for example, Human Rights Watch, 'Greece: asylum seekers locked up' (14 April 2016); Amnesty International, 'Greece: refugees detained in dire conditions amid rush to implement EU–Turkey deal' (7 April 2016).

as inadmissible through a highly contestable application of the STC concept. It seems that some negative decisions of the Greek Asylum Service are a mere rubberstamp on assumption that Turkey is safe, as determined by EASO officials.[178] Of course, there is ample evidence of the country's human rights violations against refugees and the lack of possibilities to obtain protection in accordance with the Refugee Convention.[179] Many aspects of the 'deal' are legally dubious, but its lynchpin is the assumption that Turkey meets the EU standards to be a STC (or perhaps 'first country of asylum'). While legal scholars debated this question, the preponderance of opinion was that the claim of Turkey's legal safety would be difficult to sustain.[180]

For a time, the Greek Appeals Committees held that Greece was not safe, and so they refused to permit returns under the 'deal'.[181] However, Greece introduced a new law on 16 June 2016 to reform the composition of Greek Appeals Committees.[182] It remains to be seen how this legal question will ultimately be resolved, but this aspect of the 'deal' is fraying.

Overall, the closure of the Greek–Turkish 'route' is also framed as a means to 'break the business model of smugglers'. Yet it purports to end irregular migration without addressing the key demand for smuggling, stemming from the ever-absent legal channels of accessing the CEAS. Be they routes to lawfully enter the EU or to move within it, alternatives for refugees remain nearly illusory.

4.3 Third time's the charm? The next harmonisation of the CEAS

The foundational flaws of the CEAS would have hopefully been the target of the EU's reflections on fundamental reforms. Yet the third phase of harmonisation, currently in the form of fresh or forthcoming proposals by the Commission,[183] seems all but designed to remedy those pitfalls. Leaving

178 See, for example, Kollect News, 'Λέσβος: Άρνηση παροχής ασύλου σε πρόσφυγα με αιτιολογία η Τουρκία είναι ασφαλής χώρα' (16 April 2016). In English, 'Lesvos: Refusal to grant asylum to refugee on grounds of Turkey being a safe country' (16 April 2016) (translation second author's own).

179 See, for example, Amnesty International, 'Turkey: illegal mass returns of Syrian refugees expose fatal flaws in EU–Turkey deal' (1 April 2016); AIDA, Country Report Turkey: First Update, December 2015.

180 Thym (n. 173). Cf. S. Peers and E. Roman, 'The EU, Turkey and the Refugee Crisis: what could possibly go wrong?' EU law analysis, 5 February 2016, http://eulawanalysis.blogspot.ie/2016/02/the-eu-turkey-and-refugee-crisis-what.html.

181 See, for example, Greece – Appeals Committee PD 114/2010, Decision 05/133782, 17 May 2016.

182 See ECRE & AIRE Centre (n. 162), 12.

183 European Commission, *Towards a Reform of the Common European Asylum System and Enhancing Legal Avenues to Europe*, COM(2016) 197, 6 April 2016.

its previous path unchallenged,[184] the new Dublin Regulation – a fourth attempt at allocating responsibility among EU countries – not only leaves the responsibility principles intact, but risks exacerbating the undue emphasis placed on the criterion of irregular entry by removing its temporal limitation. Though a 'corrective fairness mechanism' is introduced to Dublin as a way of remedying disproportionate pressure on a particular Member State, deflection and buy-out options take precedence over distribution of responsibility.

The promise of a more 'robust'[185] Dublin System builds on a future CEAS of greater harmonisation between national asylum systems. The widely discretionary provisions of the PD and QD would become mandatory rules under an Asylum Procedures Regulation and a Qualification Regulation, to be tabled in July 2016. These proposals would not, however, approximate laws with the aim of raising standards. On the contrary, deflective and restrictive rules are harmonised Europe-wide: STC, SCO, accelerated procedures and the internal protection alternative are the most vivid examples. Coercion and sanction of refugee mobility across the EU, framed as 'absconding', are the hallmark of the new era. Rather than being abandoned as ill-fitted and ineffective, they are strengthened as ostensible deterrents of clandestinity.

If it has all gone wrong, why then are we drifting further away from better responses? Crisis may generate new thinking and 'never again' reflection of past failures. We have yet to see this at the EU level.

Bibliography

Abdul-Ahad, G., 'Some tips for the long-distance traveller' (2015) 37 *London Review of Books* 39

Amnesty International, 'Turkey: illegal mass returns of Syrian refugees expose fatal flaws in EU–Turkey deal' (1 April 2016)

Amnesty International, 'Greece: refugees detained in dire conditions amid rush to implement EU–Turkey deal' (7 April 2016)

Asylkoordination Osterreich, Diakonie, Volkshilfe, SOS Mitmensch and Integrationshaus, *Stellungnahme Agenda Asyl: Zum Bundesgesetz, mit dem das Asylgesetz geandert wird* (November 2015)

Asylum Information Database, *Common Asylum System at a Turning Point: Refugees Caught in Europe's Solidarity Crisis* (September 2015) Annual Report 2014/2015

Asylum Information Database, 'Country report Turkey: first update' (December 2015)

Asylum Information Database, 'Netherlands: the expanding list of safe countries of origin' (24 February 2016)

184 On the relevance of 'path dependence' in the Dublin System, see M. Mouzourakis, 'We need to talk about Dublin: responsibility under the Dublin System as a blockage to asylum-burden sharing in the EU' (2014) RSC Working Paper 105.

185 European Commission, 'Towards a sustainable and fair Common European Asylum System', IP/16/1620, 4 May 2016.

Asylum Information Database, 'Germany: accelerated procedure and other restrictions enter into force' (17 March 2016)

Asylum Information Database, 'France: authorities under court order to register asylum applications' (25 April 2016)

Chelvan, S., 'Case comment: *X, Y & Z v Minister voor Immigratie en Asiel*: a missed opportunity or a new dawn?' (2013) 5 *Chambers Newsletter*

Costello, C., 'The Asylum Procedures Directive and the proliferation of safe country practices: deterrence, deflection and the dismantling of international protection' (2005) 7 *European Journal of Migration and Law* 35

Costello, C., 'The Asylum Procedures Directive in legal context: equivocal standards meet general principles', in A. Baldaccini, E. Guild and H. Toner (eds.), *Whose Freedom, Security and Justice? EU Immigration and Asylum Law after 1999* (Hart Publishing, 2007)

Costello, C., *The Human Rights of Migrants and Refugees in European Law* (Oxford University Press, 2016)

Costello, C. and Hancox, E., 'The recast Asylum Procedures Directive: caught between the stereotypes of the abusive asylum-seeker and the vulnerable refugee', in V. Chetail, P. De Bruycker and F. Maiani (eds.), *Reforming the Common European Asylum System: The New European Refugee Law* (Martinus Nijhoff, 2016)

Costello, C. and Mouzourakis, M., 'Reflections on reading *Tarakhel*: Is "how bad is bad enough" good enough?' (2014) 10 *Asiel en Migrantenrecht* 404

Council of Europe, *Report by Nils Muiznieks following his visit to Bulgaria*, Strasbourg 22 June 2015, CommDH(2015) 12

Council of the European Union, *Implementation of the Eurodac Regulation as Regards the Obligation to Take Fingerprints*, 11013/15 ASIM 60 EURODAC 8, 17 July 2015

Council of the European Union, *Justice and Home Affairs Council 20 July 2015*, http://goo.gl/l56LN5

Czaika, M. and de Haas, H., 'The effectiveness of immigration policies' (2013) 39 *Population and Development Review* 47

Czaika, M. and de Haas, H., 'The effect of visa policies on international migration dynamics', International Migration Initiative Working Paper 89 (April 2014)

Dearden, L., 'Denmark refugee law: concern over "inhumane" family reunification delays that could cause more deaths' (2016) *The Independent* 27 January

den Heijer, M., *Europe and Extraterritorial Asylum* (Bloomsbury, 2012)

den Heijer, M. and Spijkerboer, T., 'Is the EU–Turkey refugee and migration deal a treaty?' (2016) EU Law Analysis Blog, 7 April 2016

den Heijer, M., Rijpma, J. and Spijkerboer, T., 'Coercion, prohibition and great expectations: The continuing failure of the Common European Asylum System' (2016) *Common Market Law Review*

Eaton, J., 'The internal protection alternative under European Union law: examining the Recast Qualification Directive' (2012) 24 *International Journal of Refugee Law* 765

Errera, R., 'Cessation and assessment of new circumstances: a comment on *Abdulla*, CJEU, 2 March 2010' (2011) 23 *International Journal of Refugee Law* 521

European Commission, *Report on the Application of Directive 2004/83/EC*, COM(2010) 314, 16 June 2010

European Commission, *Proposal for a Regulation of the European Parliament and of the Council Amending Regulation (EU) No 604/2013 as Regards Determining*

the Member State Responsible for Examining the Application for International Protection of Unaccompanied Minors with no Family Member, Sibling Or Relative Legally Present in a Member State, COM(2014) 382, 26 June 2014
European Commission, *Explanatory Note on the 'Hotspot' Approach* (July 2015), http://bit.ly/1N46jcT
European Commission, *Proposal for a Regulation Establishing an EU Common List of Safe Countries of Origin for the Purposes of Directive 2013/32/EU of the European Parliament and of the Council on Common Procedures for Granting and Withdrawing International Protection, and Amending Directive 2013/32/EU*, COM(2015) 452 final, 9 September 2015
European Commission, 'Commission adopts Schengen evaluation report on Greece' (2 February 2016)
European Commission, *Back to Schengen: A Roadmap*, COM(2016) 120, 4 March 2016
European Commission, *First Report on Relocation and Resettlement*, COM(2016) 165, 16 March 2016.
European Commission, *Assessment of Greece's Action Plan to Remedy the Serious Deficiencies in the 2015 Evaluation on the Application of the Schengen Acquis*, COM(2016) 220, 12 April 2016
European Commission, *Second Report on Relocation and Resettlement*, COM(2016) 222, 12 April 2016
European Commission, *First Report on the Progress Made in the Implementation of the EU–Turkey Statement*, COM(2016) 231, 20 April 2016
European Commission, *Operational Implementation of the EU–Turkey Agreement*, available at: http://goo.gl/p7UYJ0
European Commission, *Member States' Support to Emergency Relocation Mechanism*, accessed 4 May 2016
European Commission, *Proposal for a Regulation of the European Parliament and of the Council Establishing the Criteria and Mechanisms for Determining the Member State Responsible for Examining an Application for International Protection Lodged in One of the Member States by a Third-Country National or Stateless Person (Recast)*, COM(2016) 270, 4 May 2016
European Commission, *Proposal for a Regulation of the European Parliament and of the Council on the Establishment of 'Eurodac' (Recast)*, COM(2016) 272, 4 May 2016
European Commission, *Proposal for a Regulation of the European Parliament and of the Council on a European Union Agency on Asylum*, COM(2016) 271, 4 May 2016
European Council, *Stockholm Programme: An Open and Secure Europe Serving and Protecting Citizens* [2010] OJ C115/1
European Council, *Meeting of Heads of State or Government with Turkey: EU–Turkey Statement* (29 November 2015), http://goo.gl/H7FiDH
European Council, *Conclusions 18/19 February 2016*, EUCO 1/16
European Council, *EU–Turkey Statement* (18 March 2016), http://goo.gl/ymaOAJ
European Council on Refugees and Exiles, *The Impact of the Qualification Directive on International Protection* (ECRE, 2008)
European Council on Refugees and Exiles, *Five Years on Europe is Still Ignoring its Responsibilities Towards Iraqi Refugees* (2008) AD1/03/2008/ext/ADC

European Council on Refugees and Exiles, *Case Law Fact Sheet: Prevention of Dublin Transfers to Hungary* (ECRE, 2016)

European Council on Refugees and Exiles, Amnesty International, Human Rights Watch, Caritas Europa, Churches Commission for Migrants in Europe, International Lesbian and Gay Association Europe, Médecins Sans Frontières, Pax Christi International and Save the Children, *Call for Withdrawal of the Asylum Procedures Directive* (22 March 2004)

European Council on Refugees and Exiles, Asylum Aid, Hungarian Helsinki Committee and Dutch Refugee Council, *Actors of Protection and the Internal Protection Alternative* (ECRE, 2014)

European Council on Refugees and Exiles and International Commission of Jurists, *Fifth Joint Submission to the Council of Europe Committee of Ministers on the execution of MSS v Belgium and Greece* (ICJ March 2016)

European Parliament, 'MEPs want EU embassies and consulates to grant asylum seekers humanitarian visas' (16 March 2016)

Eurostat, *Asylum and First Time Applicants Annual Aggregated Data*, migr_asyappctza

Eurostat, *Resettled Persons Annual Data*, migr_asyresa

Fargues, P., '2015 – the year we mistook refugees for invaders', Migration Policy Centre Policy Brief 2015/12

Finemann, M., *The Vulnerable Subject: Anchoring Equality in the Human Condition* (Princeton University Press, 2013)

Fundamental Rights Agency, *Legal Entry Channels to the EU for Persons in Need of International Protection*, 02/2015

Gammeltoft-Hansen, T., *Access to Asylum: International Refugee Law and the Globalization of Migration Control* (Cambridge University Press, 2011)

Garlick, M., 'International protection in court: the asylum jurisprudence of the Court of Justice of the EU and UNHCR' (2015) 34 *Refugee Survey Quarterly* 107

Government of Sweden, 'Proposal to temporarily restrict the possibility of being granted a residence permit in Sweden' (8 April 2016), http://goo.gl/QT9lzq

Grahl-Madsen, A., 'Identifying the world's refugees' (1983) 467 *Annals of the American Academy of Political and Social Science* 11

Guild, E., 'The Europeanisation of Europe's asylum policy' (2006) 18 *International Journal of Refugee Law* 630

Guild, E., Brouwer, E., Groenendijk, K. and Carrera, S., 'What is happening to the Schengen Borders?' (2015) Centre for European Policy Studies Paper in Liberty in Security No 86 / December 2015

Hamlin, R., *Let Me Be a Refugee: Administrative Justice and the Politics of Asylum in the United States, Canada and Australia* (Oxford University Press, 2014)

Hathaway, J.C., *The Law of Refugee Status* (Butterworths, 1991)

House of Lords, 'Gifting of Land Rovers to the Government of Bulgaria: Written Statement' HLWS566, 4 March 2016

Human Rights Watch, 'Universal Periodic Review Submission: Bulgaria' (September 2014)

Human Rights Watch, 'Bulgaria: Pushbacks, Abuse at Borders' (20 January 2016)

Human Rights Watch, 'Greece: Asylum Seekers Locked Up' (14 April 2016)

Hungarian Helsinki Committee, Twitter 20 April 2016

Iben-Jensen, U., 'Humanitarian Visas: Option or Obligation?' (2014) European Parliament, PE509.986

ICF International, *Evaluation of the Dublin III Regulation* (European Commission, December 2015)

Ineli-Ciger, M., 'The missing piece in the European agenda on migration: the Temporary Protection Directive' (2015) *EU Law Analysis Blog*, 8 July

International Organisation for Migration, *Fatal Journeys: Tracking Lives Lost During Migration* (IOM, 2014)

Jesuit Refugee Service, 'The EU–Turkey deal analysis and considerations' (Jesuit Refugee Service Europe Policy Discussion Paper, 29 April 2016)

Joint Statement of the Heads of Police Services from the meeting held in Zagreb, Croatia on 18 February 2016, available at: http://goo.gl/hDzxYo

Kingsley, P., *The New Odyssey: The Story of Europe's Refugee Crisis* (Faber, 2016)

Klug, A., 'Regional developments: Europe', in A. Zimmermann (ed.), *The 1951 Convention Relating to the Status of Refugees and its 1967 Protocol: A Commentary* (Oxford University Press, 2011)

Kollect News, 'Λέσβος: Άρνηση παροχής ασύλου σε πρόσφυγα με αιτιολογία η Τουρκία είναι ασφαλής χώρα' (16 April 2016)

Macklin, A., 'A safe country to emulate? Canada and the European refugee', in H. Lambert, J. McAdam and M. Fullerton (eds.), *The Global Reach of European Refugee Law* (Cambridge University Press, 2013)

Maiani, F. and Vevstad, V., *Reflection Note on the Evaluation of the Dublin System and the Dublin III Proposal* (2009) European Parliament, PE 410.690

Ministry of Interior of the Hellenic Republic, *Summary Statement of Refugee Flows* (4 May 2016)

Moreno-Lax, V., *Facilitating Access to Protection, (Discarding) Offshore Processing* (Red Cross, 2016)

Mouzourakis, M., 'Case Comment: *X, Y & Z v Minister voor Immigratie en Asiel*' (*Rights in Exile,* 1 December 2013)

Mouzourakis, M., 'We need to talk about Dublin: responsibility under the Dublin System as a blockage to asylum-burden sharing in the EU' (2014) RSC Working Paper 105

Nascimbene, B. and Di Pascale, A., 'The "Arab Spring" and the extraordinary influx of people who arrived in North Italy from North Africa' (2011) 13 *European Journal of Migration Law* 346

Office of the United Nations High Commissioner for Human Rights, *Recommended Principles and Guidelines on Human Rights at International Borders* (OHCHR, March 2015)

Papadimitriou, P. and Papageorgiou, G., 'The new Dubliners: implementation of Council Regulation 343/2003 by the Greek authorities' (2006) 18 *Journal of Refugee Studies* 299

Peers, S. and Roman, E., 'The EU, Turkey and the refugee crisis: what could possibly go wrong?' (2016) *EU Law Analysis Blog*, 5 February 2016

Scholten, S., *The Privatisation of Immigration Control through Carrier Sanctions* (Brill, 2014)

Sperl, M., 'Fortress Europe and the Iraqi "intruders": Iraqi asylum-seekers and the EU, 2003–2007' (2007) UNHCR Working Paper No. 144

Spijkerboer, T., *Europe's Refugee Crisis: A Perfect Storm* (2016) Border Criminologies, https://goo.gl/L5ocgd

Szczepnaik, M. and Tylec, E., 'Ukrainian asylum seekers and a Polish immigration paradox' (2016) 51 *Forced Migration Review* 71

Trauner, F., 'Asylum policy: the EU's "crises" and the looming policy regime failure' (2016) 38:3 *Journal of European Integration* 311

United Nations High Commissioner for Refugees, *Asylum in the European Union: A Study on the Implementation of the Qualification Directive* (UNHCR, 2007)

United Nations High Commissioner for Refugees, *Improving Asylum Procedures Comparative Analysis and Recommendations for Law and Practice: A UNHCR Research Project on the Application of Key Provisions of the Asylum Procedures Directive in Selected Member States* (UNHCR, 2010).

United Nations High Commissioner for Refugees, *Safe at Last? Law and Practice in Selected EU Member States with Respect to Asylum-Seekers Fleeing Indiscriminate Violence* (UNHCR, 2011)

United Nations High Commissioner for Refugees, *World at War: Global Trends, Forced Displacement in 2014* (UNHCR, 2015)

United Nations High Commissioner for Refugees, *Refugees/Migrants Emergency Response: Mediterranean*, accessed 4 May 2016

United Nations High Commissioner for Refugees, *Syria Regional Refugee Emergency Response*, accessed 4 May 2016

Velluti, S., *Reforming the Common European Asylum System – Legislative Developments and Judicial Activism of the European Courts* (Springer, 2014)

Walsh, J., 'Is temporary protection the answer to Europe's refugee crisis?' (2015) 19 *The Researcher* 31

EEAS, *EUNAFVOR MED Operation Sophia: Six Monthly Report* (February 2016) WikiLeaks, https://wikileaks.org/eu-military-refugees

Zwaan, K. (ed.), *The Qualification Directive: Central Themes, Problem Issues, and Implementation in Selected Member States* (Wolf Legal Publishers, 2007)

Part IV

Civil law cooperation

12 Civil justice

Constitutional and regulatory issues revisited

Eva Storskrubb

1 Introduction

It is an exciting prospect and daunting challenge to contribute to this volume. The particular point in time of the progression of the Area of Freedom, Security and Justice (AFSJ) is significant. We are at a crossroads, driving from the end of the long tunnel of the Stockholm Programme[1] and turning towards a new landscape of unnamed and streamlined guidelines.[2] At this junction, my task is to comment on and analyse the constitutional perspectives, the governance perspectives and regulatory challenges of civil justice as a particular policy area of the AFSJ.[3] It is also a particular pleasure to

1 The five-year programme of the European Council for the development of the AFSJ: 'The Stockholm Programme: an open and secure Europe serving and protecting citizens', OJ C 115, 4 May 2010, p 1.

2 No new detailed policy programme setting out priorities and the direction for the development of the AFSJ has been agreed and declared by the European Council for the period following the end of the five-year Stockholm Programme, supra note 1 (i.e., for 2015 and onwards). This is in contrast to practice that had been established by the European Council for the first 15 years of development of the AFSJ; starting with the Tampere Conclusions in 1999 (Council Conclusions No 200/1/99, www.europarl.europa.eu/summits/tam_en.htm (accessed 25 May 2016)) and the Hague Programme in 2004 (OJ C 53, 3 March 2005, p. 1). However, under Article 68 of the Treaty on the Functioning of the European Union (TFEU) the European Council is obliged to define the strategic guidelines for the legislative and operational planning of the AFSJ. Thus, the European Council has set out comparatively brief and general strategic guidelines, EUCO 79/14, 2 June 2014, for the current five years.

3 I use the term 'civil justice' as a diminutive term for the policy area within the AFSJ provided for in Articles 67(4) and 81 TFEU, called 'judicial cooperation in civil matters' originally introduced in the AFSJ context in the Treaty of Amsterdam in 1999, see Section 2.1 in this chapter. Neither the traditional legal concepts of private international law nor international civil procedure encompass the full breadth of the policy area. In its broadest sense, the policy area includes procedural cooperation, specific procedures and choice of law measures for cross-border civil and commercial matters as well as specifically for certain family law matters and overarching measures such as networks and online tools. It has even at times been held by the institutions to encompass certain projects of substantive private law. See E. Storskrubb, 'Civil justice: the contested nature of the scope of EU legislation', in F. Trauner and A. Ripoll Servent (eds.), *Policy Change in the Area of Freedom Security and Justice* (Routledge, 2014) 198.

contribute to this volume because the emerging literature on the AFSJ often neglects civil justice and focuses on immigration and security aspects of the AFSJ.[4] Fruitful and important comparisons can, however, arguably be made, for example, between the civil and criminal justice cooperation in the AFSJ. Thus, it is to be hoped that this chapter and volume will provide a useful platform or starting point for such endeavours.

Many of the constitutional aspects of civil justice as a policy area appear at first glance to remain stable at this junction; for example, structural issues relating to the role of the EU institutions and the legislative methods to be used for the policy area appear settled.[5] The question that this chapter seeks to address is whether this stability is true or a mere illusion. It is pertinent to ask whether certain constitutional conundrums and regulatory issues identified already nearly a decade ago have been resolved or whether they remain relevant. In addition, it is necessary to identify whether new issues or pressures have arisen.

A traditional and basic constitutional issue is that of the competence of the EU to legislate within the field. I have, in the past, identified a central constitutional conundrum for civil justice in the tension between the Treaty limits imposed on the competence of the EU in the field and the dynamism of the policy area, a tension that has led to a clash of opposing forces.[6] This conundrum relates intimately to the issue of whether integration of civil procedural law is considered politically, practically and theoretically feasible, or rather, how far is the EU prepared to go in relation to civil procedural harmonisation. The identified problem and tension will be dealt with in detail in Section 2. The issue will be revisited and examined critically in light of subsequent and recent developments. Thus, both the traditional cross-border struggle (Section 2.2) as well as the challenge of sector-specific development (Section 2.3) formally outside the AFSJ framework will be discussed.

Commentators have also in the past identified other regulatory issues such as a lack of coherence, fragmentation and ad hoc harmonisation, and thus called for reflection on an overall and coherent regulatory strategy for civil justice.[7]

4 Exceptions naturally exist; for example, Trauner and Ripoll Servent, supra note 3, and V. Mitsilegas, 'The limits of mutual trust in Europe's Area of Freedom, Security and Justice: from automatic inter-state cooperation to the slow emergence of the individual' (2012) 31 *Yearbook of European Law* 337.

5 The main framework for the policy area was set in the Treaty of Amsterdam, with some significant amendments in the Treaty of Nice and more fine-tuned changes in the Lisbon Treaty the most important being the added jurisdiction and role of the Court of Justice. See, inter alia, E. Storskrubb, 'Civil justice: a newcomer and an unstoppable wave?' in P. Craig and G. de Búrca (eds.), *The Evolution of EU Law* (2nd edn, Oxford University Press, 2011) 302; G-R. de Groot and J-J. Kuipers, 'The new provisions on private international law in the Treaty of Lisbon' (2008) *MJL* 1.

6 E. Storskrubb, *Civil Procedure and EU Law: A Policy Area Uncovered* (Oxford University Press, 2008) pp. 272ff.

7 M. Tulibacka, 'Europeanization of civil procedures: in search of a coherent approach' (2009) *Common Market Law Review* 1533; Storskrubb, supra note 6, pp. 305–307 and note 5, pp. 318–321.

In part, these tensions stem from or are intertwined with the competence issue and with the debate on potential harmonisation of civil procedure. For example, sector-specific or fragmented procedural development may be the result of a lack of coherence in regulatory strategy or a way to practically deal with and even circumvent unresolved competence issues. In part, the identified issues relate to the broader and general EU regulatory debate on governance and integration strategies. In such a debate, the principles of subsidiarity and proportionality as well as alternative governance modes to legislation may also play a role. These observations will also now be revisited in light of recent developments as well critically examined in the light of the new political realities including the new European Council guidelines for the AFSJ (Sections 2.4 and 3).

A further development that has slowly crept into the constitutional and regulatory dialogue on civil justice is its interaction with fundamental procedural rights. Underlying the fundamental rights question and intertwined with the deeper regulatory choices and structures is the question of mutual trust. Mutual trust as an adjunct to mutual recognition has become the new political 'panacea' for the AFSJ, often used as an ostensible solution where difficult divergences emerge between the Member States. Precisely because these situations often evidence important differences and potential lacunae, they occasion a renewed harmonisation debate and, by connection, interact with the competence issue raised above. One of the many consequences of the difficulties demonstrated with mutual trust is a new debate on the need for minimum or common standards in civil procedure. In Section 3, such future perspectives and reflections will be dealt with. The debate on mutual trust in the civil justice field provides one example of an issue that can be compared and contrasted with the ongoing debates in the criminal justice as well as in the immigration and asylum fields of the AFSJ.[8]

Thus, a tentative hypothesis is that the scene is not as stable as it may seem and that there may even be old and new pressures that will impact on the future development of civil justice as well as on the AFSJ as a whole that will be dealt with in the concluding reflections (Section 4).

2 The remit of EU legislative competence

2.1 Background

The evolution and creation of civil justice as a policy field of the EU and the history of its legal basis from the original Treaty of Rome to the present has been related elsewhere and will not be expounded upon in full detail here.[9]

8 See the contributions by Albi (Chapter 6) and Costello and Mouzourakis (Chapter 11) in this volume as well as E. Brouwer and D. Gerard (eds.), *Mapping Mutual Trust: Understanding and Informing the Role of Mutual Trust in EU Law*, EUI Working Paper MWP13/2016.

9 See, inter alia, P-E. Partsch, *Le Droit International Privé Européе. De Rome à Nice* (Larcier, 2003); Storskrubb, supra note 6, pp. 33–46 ; de Groot and Kuipers, supra note 5, pp. 109–114.

However, some of the basic events and facts are necessary to recount in the following for the ensuing analysis. The Treaty of Amsterdam, which came into force in 1999, contained the first separate legal basis for civil justice with a detailed list of themes for measures to be adopted. The Treaty of Amsterdam also set the development of civil justice with the broader AFSJ project. Subsequent to Amsterdam, a wealth of measures were enacted in civil justice; including both generic measures as well as measures specifically in the family law field. These measures include traditional measures of international procedural law, such as measures on jurisdiction, enforcement, service, taking of evidence and choice of law. In addition, they include innovative or novel measures of international judicial cooperation dealing with, among other mediation, small claims and account preservation orders as well as overarching measures such as networks and e-justice support platforms. Some of these measures introduce minimum procedural standards for cross-border litigation, while others create parallel supranational procedures for cross-border claims.[10]

Civil justice competence was in the Amsterdam Treaty specifically restricted in Article 65 of the EC Treaty. Civil justice measures were thus limited to 'matters having cross-border implications' and 'insofar as necessary for the proper functioning of the internal market'. The formulations of the restrictions in competence were only changed slightly at Lisbon in Article 81 of the Treaty on the Functioning of the European Union (TFEU). The cross-border limitation was retained whereas the internal market limitation was subtly broadened to 'particularly when necessary'. This means that one can say that the competence was expanded and the second restriction was *de facto* turned from a limitation to an impetus.[11] This slight extension of the competence has not yet had any identifiable practical implications.[12] In contrast, the cross-border limitation that has remained unchanged since Amsterdam has been central to the civil justice competence debate. One can even say that it has been the focal point in the battle against incursion of the EU into national procedural autonomy.[13]

10 See Storskrubb, supra note 3, pp. 198, 201–204 for a list of the measures and a brief discussion of their evolution. Some commentators consider that there are different generations of evolution in the measures, see, inter alia, B. Hess, 'The state of the Civil Justice Union' in B. Hess, M. Bergström and E. Storskrubb (eds.), *EU Civil Justice: Current Issues and Future Outlook, Swedish Studies in European Law, Vol. 7* (Hart Publishing, 2016) 2; C. Crifó, 'Civil procedure in the European order: an overview of the latest developments' in D. Dwyer (ed.), *The Civil Procedure Rules: Ten Years On* (Oxford University Press, 2009) 359. See Sections 2.4 and 3 in this chapter for further discussion.

11 Storskrubb, supra note 6, p. 306.

12 See I. Benöhr, 'Consumer dispute resolution after the Lisbon Treaty: collective actions and alternative procedures' (2013) 36 *Journal of Consumer Policy* 95, the absence of the 'market-objective' requirement may come to affect envisaged measures.

13 Storskrubb, supra note 3, p. 205.

In parallel with the cross-border issue, another development has come to challenge national procedural autonomy and highlight the difficult regulatory choices in relation to civil justice and procedural harmonisation, namely sector-specific EU legislation with procedural rules. This development may, in practice, come to overtake the cross-border issue and may even come to make it in some respects redundant. It is nevertheless important to first deal with and understand the cross-border issue as well as the forces and actors involved in the struggle. From the events surrounding this fundamental constitutional issue that forms a central part of the past of civil justice, we can better understand the future regulatory issues and challenges of the policy area. The cross-border issue and the challenge of sector-specific procedural regulation will be separately dealt with below (Sections 2.2 and 2.3) before some conclusions are drawn in relation to the remit of EU action in the civil justice field (Section 2.4).

2.2 *The cross-border struggle*

2.2.1 *Institutional positions established*

The competence debate and struggle that has been waged between the EU institutions, has been concerned with whether the scope of EU civil justice should be defined in a restrictive or expansive way, specifically how 'matters having cross-border implications' should be interpreted. The Commission has argued for a broad interpretation. The Member States in the Council have acted as gatekeepers, working for a narrow interpretation of the competence in comparison to the Commission's interpretation and striving to strictly limit any legislation to cross-border matters. The first legislative proposal that caused these controversies was the legal aid Directive.[14] The Commission argued that it would be inconsistent and discriminatory if Member States provide better support mechanisms for cross-border disputes than purely domestic disputes. The proposed Directive contained rules 'to facilitate the compatibility of national laws [applicable] in all civil proceedings'.[15] Later, the same issue arose in relation to the proposals regarding the mediation Directive, the European order for payment procedure Regulation and the small claims Regulation.[16] In relation to the mediation Directive, the Commission argued

14 Council Directive 2002/8/EC of 27 January 2003 to improve access to justice in cross-border disputes by establishing minimum common rules relating to legal aid for such disputes, OJ L 26, 31 January 2003, p. 41.

15 COM(2002) 13 final, 18 January 2002, p. 3.

16 Directive 2008/52/EC of the European Parliament and of the Council of 21 May 2008 on certain aspects of mediation in civil and commercial matters, OJ L 136, 24 May 2008, p. 3; Regulation (EC) No 1896/2006 of the European Parliament and of the Council of 12 December 2006 creating a European order for payment procedure, OJ L 399, 30 December 2006, p. 1; and Regulation (EC) No 861/2007 of the European Parliament and of the Council of 11 July 2007 establishing a European Small Claims Procedure, OJ L 199, 31 July 2007, pp. 1–22. The latter two Regulations have been amended by Regulation

that it would be discriminatory only to promote mediation of cross-border disputes.[17] In relation to the order for payment Regulation, the Commission advocated a broad interpretation of 'cross-border implications' and wanted to include within the scope of the Regulations even ostensibly domestic disputes; for example, two parties domiciled in the same jurisdiction but there is a potential future cross-border effect, such as subsequent enforcement against assets in another jurisdiction.[18] It also proposed to include domestic litigation, for example, if the provision of two different regulatory regimes, the domestic and supranational, would create discrimination among litigants; for instance, a claimant would want to bring a simplified European small claims procedure against two defendants where one is domiciled locally and one is domiciled in another Member State.[19]

The Member States in the Council did not accept such broad interpretations of 'cross-border implications' and it is clear from the Council documents, or other accounts of the Council's position that are available, that they have not accepted an interpretation that would potentially cover domestic litigation.[20] The European Parliament[21] has so far ultimately supported the Council in this respect, but it appears mainly in order to reach a compromise. The rapporteur of Parliament for the order for payment Regulation specifically acknowledged the difficulties experienced in the Council owing to the reluctance of many Member States to accept the use of the proposed Regulations in non-cross-border cases.[22] Thus, the European Parliament sought to allow these concerns to be taken into account without ruling out a different solution in the future. In relation to the mediation Directive, the European Parliament also recognised the problem and proposed stricter wording on the scope of application, in tandem, however, emphasising that the Member States should be encouraged to also apply the provision of the Directive to internal matters and that the Directive should not limit rules on national law.[23]

In the latest Regulation to be enacted in the civil justice field, the Regulation on the European account preservation order,[24] we can see that

(EU) 2015/2421 amending Regulation (EC) No 861/2007 establishing a European Small Claims Procedure and Regulation (EC) No 1896/2006 creating a European order for payment procedure [2015] OJ L341/1.

17 COM(2004) 718 final, 22 October 2004, p. 5.

18 COM(2004) 173 final, 19 March 2004, pp. 7f.

19 COM(2005) 87 final, 9 February 2005, pp. 5f.

20 Press release of the Council Meeting for Justice and Home Affairs 5731/10, 2005.

21 Note that the European Parliament did not have legislative power in relation to civil justice measures until the Nice Treaty entered into force in 2003. Prior to that point in time, the European Parliament was only consulted as a deviation from the ordinary legislative procedure. For further analysis see sources in supra note 5.

22 A6-240/2005, 18 July 2005, p. 17.

23 A6-74/2007, 22 March 2007, pp. 12 and 22.

24 Regulation (EU) No 655/2014 of the European Parliament and of the Council of 15 May 2014 establishing a European Account Preservation Order procedure to facilitate cross-border debt recovery in civil and commercial matters, OJ L 189, 27 June 2014, p. 59.

the same institutional dynamic is repeated, albeit in a more limited manner, since the proposal of the Commission was explicitly aimed at addressing difficulties in cross-border debt collection and a definition of 'cross-border' was included in the original proposal. However, the definition of cross-border proposed by the Commission was worded in a negative manner, such that all instances that did *not* fall within the definition were considered cross-border matters.[25] The Member States in the Council stressed that the Regulation should apply to cross-border cases only and considered that a positive definition of what constitutes a cross-border case in the particular context was necessary and gave preliminary parameters for such a definition.[26] The European Parliament again agreed with the Council that a clear definition was important and would not accept the proposal of the Commission, its Committee specifically proposing 'that the criteria which define the cross-border dimension of the matter be tightened up by reversing the presumption'.[27] This shows that the underlying issue was that the Commission's definition was too broadly or too loosely worded. The final version of the Regulation's wording of the definition of 'cross-border' follows the wording that was included in the Parliament's amendment proposal.[28] This means that the more strict view and stringent interpretation of cross-border of the Council and the Parliament prevailed.

Finally, it is notable that most recently the Commission proposed a broadening of the scope of the cross-border definition in the amendment to the small claims Regulation.[29] The original Regulation applied only to disputes where at least one of the parties was domiciled or habitually resident in a Member State other than the Member State in which the claim was lodged. However, the Commission noted that disputes involving parties domiciled in the same Member State but that have a cross-border element could not benefit from the small claims procedure and were left outside the scope of the Regulation. The Commission mentioned as examples, inter alia, where the place of performance of the contract is in another Member State or where the enforcement of the judgment is to take place in another Member State. Thus, the Commission proposed to extend the application and definition of cross-border.[30] It is notable that the Commission's approach was more moderate than the ones mentioned above when the cross-border struggle arose. The Commission appeared to realise that a very broad interpretation, which *de facto* could extend the

25 COM(2011) final 445, 25 July 2011, p. 16, see also pp. 1 and 4f.

26 Summary of Council Meeting 6 December 2013, www.europarl.europa.eu/oeil/popups/summary.do?id=1327531&t=e&l=en (accessed 25 May 2016).

27 A7-227/2013, p. 65.

28 See Article 3.

29 COM(2013) 794. See also C. Oro Martinez, 'The Small Claims Regulation: on the way to an improved European procedure?' in B. Hess, M. Bergström and E, Storskrubb (eds.), *EU Civil Justice: Current Issues and Future Outlook, Swedish Studies in European Law, Vol 7* (Hart Publishing, 2016) 129.

30 Ibid., p. 6.

application to domestic cases, would not be acceptable to the Member States. However, the Commission's proposed new definition of 'cross-border' was worded in a negative manner, noting when the Regulation would not apply, and listed a number of criteria linked to only a single Member State.[31] Some of these criteria could be uncertain at the point of filing of a claim (e.g., potential future enforcement) and some were vague (e.g., the place where the facts on which the claim is based arose). These criteria would be very difficult for a claimant without legal representation to understand and for a small claims court to review in an efficient manner. Thus, there were question marks regarding how the Commission's definition would work in practice. The Council and the Parliament unsurprisingly rejected a broadening of the cross-border scope and the original wording in Article 3 of the Regulation has been retained unchanged.[32]

2.2.2 Collective redress

The process in relation to potential collective redress legislation at the EU level is particularly relevant and interesting with respect to competence and the cross-border issue. The latest consultation of the Commission was launched in 2011 with the title *Towards a Coherent European Approach to Collective Redress.*[33] The Commission acknowledged that several crucial and primary regulatory or institutional issues needed to be addressed, noting that careful consideration should be given as to whether EU action would give added value.[34] Various stakeholders and contributors to the consultation also emphasised several regulatory concerns, among these the cross-border issue. In its report, the European Parliament called on the Commission to examine thoroughly the appropriate legal basis (i.e., competence) for any measures in the field. The European Parliament also considered that horizontal action at the EU level would be most beneficial in cross-border cases where the rights that have been infringed are based on EU legislation.[35] The rapporteur of the Parliament noted in his explanatory statement that several Member States are critical of any potential EU legislative proposal and that the rejection of EU action in the field by the governments of the Member States must be 'taken seriously'.[36] The rapporteur specifically referred to the responses to the consultation of the French and German governments.[37] The Council

31 Ibid., p. 16, Article 2.2.

32 See Council Document 15841/14 (24.11.2014) p. 2 and Parliament Report A8-0140/2015, pp. 10f.

33 SEC(2011) 173 final, 4 February 2011; this consultation had been preceded by diverse sector specific policy documents and consultations at the EU level on collective redress starting around 2008 see, inter alia, http://ec.europa.eu/consumers/archive/redress_cons/collective_redress_en.htm (accessed 25 February 2015).

34 Ibid., pp. 6f.

35 A7-12/2012, 12.1.2012, pp. 6f.

36 Ibid., p. 11.

37 Ibid., p. 11 and note 2.

does not formally respond to Green Papers. However, several Member State governments responded individually to the consultation, being entitled to do so voluntarily.[38] The overwhelming majority of the Member State governments that responded to the consultation had regulatory concerns at the prospect of action at the EU level in relation to collective redress and many raised issues linked to the legal basis and competence or to national procedural autonomy, both explicitly and implicitly referring to the cross-border issue.[39]

Subsequent to the completion of the consultation process the Commission has not put forward a legislative proposal for regulating collective redress at the EU level. In the summer of 2013, it instead published two soft-law measures: a Communication, *Towards a European Horizontal Framework for Collective Redress*[40] and a Recommendation, *Common Principles for Injunctive and Compensatory Collective Redress Mechanisms in the Member States Concerning Violations of Rights Granted under Union Law*.[41] The Recommendation sets out a 24-month deadline by which the Member States 'should' implement its specific principles into their national systems.[42] In addition, the Recommendation states that the Commission will assess the implementation and practical experience within four years and assess whether further measures of consolidation on collective redress are needed.[43] The Recommendation does not appear to be limited to cross-border matters. The fact that it, in paragraphs 17 and 18, specifically addresses certain issues that only arise in cross-border cases gives a strong indication that the Recommendation is not intended to be limited to such cases. In the Communication, the Commission notes the concerns raised by the European Parliament in the consultation process and also mentions briefly the 'strong scepticism' of some Member States.[44] While identifying these regulatory concerns, the Commission nonetheless proceeded to outline what it considered to be the main substantive issues of collective redress to be addressed in the Recommendation.

The scope of EU action, the legal basis and the competence for action are not addressed specifically in the Communication, although the Commission does note the need to respect the different legal traditions and systems of the Member States by making reference to Article 67(1) TFEU.[45] However, at the beginning of the Communication, when outlining its objectives, the

38 All responses are available at http://ec.europa.eu/dgs/health_consumer/dgs_consultations/ca/replies_collective_redress_consultation_en.htm (accessed 25 February 2015).

39 Ibid. See, inter alia, the responses of the governments or specific ministries of Italy, Greece, Denmark, Sweden, France and Poland, available online.

40 COM(2013) 401, 11 June 2013.

41 C(2013) 3539, 11 June 2013; OJ L 210, 26 July 2013, p. 60.

42 Ibid., para 38.

43 Ibid., para 41.

44 COM(2013) 401, 11 June 2013, pp. 6 and 8f.

45 Ibid., p. 3.

Commission states that a party should be able to obtain collective redress in cross-border cases and in cases where rights infringed have been conferred upon it by EU law.[46] These latter cases are not defined but are clearly aimed at *domestic* cases in the traditional international procedural law or private international law sense, such as cases between parties domiciled in the same Member State with no connecting factor to other states. In its broadest interpretation, the latter types of cases might include rights based on any type of EU legislative measure, including Directives, in the fields of consumer law, employment, intellectual property law and product liability law, to mention but a few. This shows that at least at this soft-law level, the Commission has a much broader aim for EU influence in the procedural regulation of collective redress than the consistently strict approach of the Council that has been supported by the Parliament. On the one hand, it is not surprising that the Commission pushes for a much broader civil justice vision, because it has done so several times before as outlined above. On the other hand, it is surprising that it does, given the very public and clear regulatory (including competence) concerns voiced by parties representing the two legislative decision-makers, the Council and the European Parliament. Because the Commission did not put forward a legislative proposal but chose to publish the Recommendation and the Communication, there is no formal process by which the Council and European Parliament can impact on their content. From the perspective of institutional and even democratic legitimacy, this is unwelcome. It is also unfortunate that the difficult constitutional and regulatory issues were not tested and finally resolved between the institutions. The Commission will earliest in 2017 revert to whether it considers further action necessary, including potentially 'hard' legislation.[47]

2.3 *The challenge of sector-specific legislation*

2.3.1 *Introduction*

A parallel and related debate to the above-mentioned competence debate concerns the role of sector-specific EU legislation in civil or commercial law.[48] It is not a new phenomenon that sector-specific legislative instruments include private international law or even procedural rules. However, traditionally, these rules have been fairly limited in scope and in impact in practice when looked at from a broader procedural perspective. Such rules were often only an ancillary part of sector-specific initiatives that focused on harmonisation of substantive rules.[49] However, broadly since the Treaty of Amsterdam created civil justice as a policy area within the AFSJ, we

46 Ibid., p. 2.

47 Storskrubb, supra note 3, p. 211.

48 See, inter alia, Tulibacka, supra note 7, pp. 1546–1533.

49 See, inter alia, H. Duintjer Tebbens, 'Les règles de conflit contenues dans les instruments de droit dérivé', in A. Fuchs, H. Muir Watt and E. Pataut (eds.), *Les Conflits de Lois et le Système*

have seen a surge of sector-specific initiatives with procedural rules as their focus. Below, such recent developments in the areas of consumer, IP and competition law will be touched upon. These are all significant policy areas within the core of substantive and harmonised EU law intended to support the internal market. When procedural issues are raised and procedural rules are enacted within these mainstream areas of EU substantive civil law, it is a trend or a development with a certain dynamism that cannot be ignored. The impact of such a development on civil justice and its interaction with civil justice forms one of the most crucial constitutional and regulatory issues of the policy area today.

2.3.2 *Developments in the consumer sector*

The sector in which procedural issues have for a long time been raised at the EU level is the field of consumer protection.[50] The Directive on injunctions for the protection of consumer interests that establishes a procedure for seeking an injunction in another Member State is the first example in this respect.[51] This Directive that solely regulates a procedural issue, albeit a limited and specific one, was enacted already in 1998. However, it is limited to facilitating cross-border consumer claims. More recently, the EU focus has been on improving consumer redress mechanisms and on procedural means to further facilitate consumers' access to justice on a broader scale. There have been two strands to the efforts in this respect. The first strand relates to collective redress. Many of the consultations and studies published as well as other policy efforts taken in relation to collective redress at the EU level before 2011 were done with a consumer policy focus.[52] However, no sector-specific legislative measures were adopted. Instead, the latest collective redress consultation resulted in the above-mentioned horizontal soft-law measures (the Recommendation and the Communication) that are intended

Juridique Communautaire (Dalloz, 2004) 102, in relation to choice of law rules. See further T. Andersson, 'Approximation of procedural law in Europe' in M. Storme (ed.), *Procedural Laws in Europe: Towards Harmonisation* (Maklu, 2003) 56; M. Dougan, 'The vicissitudes of life at the coalface: remedies and procedures to enforcing Union law before national courts', in P. Craig and G. de Búrca (eds.), *Evolution of European Law* (2nd edn, Oxford University Press, 2011) 435, in relation to procedural rules and remedies.

50 See, inter alia, COM(93) 576 final, Green Paper on Access of Consumers to Justice and the Settlement of Consumer Disputes in the Internal Market; and COM(96) 13 final, 14 February 1996, Action Plan on Access of Consumers to Justice and the Settlement of Consumer Disputes in the Internal Market.

51 Directive 98/27/EC of the European Parliament and of the Council of 19 May 1998 on injunctions for the protection of consumers' interests OJ L 166, 11 June 1998, p. 51. The Directive has been amended several times and has therefore been replaced by Directive 2009/22/EC of the European Parliament and of the Council of 23 April 2009 on injunctions for the protection of consumers' interests (Codified version), OJ L 110, 1 May 2009, p. 30.

52 See information of the Commission available online, supra note 33.

to be general and apply to all civil matters rather than be sector-specific to consumer law.

The second strand relates to alternative dispute resolution (ADR). The Commission had already, in 1998 and 2001, adopted two recommendations to promote consumer ADR.[53] In addition, several substantive Directives on various types of consumer services encourage the Member States to establish ADR schemes or require that such schemes are put in place.[54] Two networks have also been set up by the Commission to facilitate consumer access to ADR.[55] Thus, several measures were in place that structurally supported the use of ADR in consumer disputes (mainly related to cross-border disputes).[56] Subsequently, in 2007, the mediation Directive was enacted within the auspices of civil justice and the AFSJ.[57] It regulates certain aspects of mediation generically for cross-border disputes. It encourages the promotion and quality of mediation and aims at clarifying the interplay between the mediation process and judicial proceedings by establishing common rule on key aspects of procedure, such as the effects of mediation on limitation and prescription periods as well as the confidentiality of mediation.[58] The mediation Directive was enacted following a consultation process raising a number of regulatory

53 Recommendation 98/257/EC on the principles applicable to bodies responsible for the out-of-court settlement of consumer disputes (OJ L 115, 17 April 1998, p. 31) that relates to consumer ADR schemes that either propose or impose a solution to resolve a dispute. Recommendation 2001/310/EC on the principles for out-of-court bodies involved in the consensual resolution of consumer disputes (OJ L 109, 19 April 2001, p. 56) relates to so-called 'facilitative' ADR where a third party assists the parties in finding a solution by common consent.

54 See the Commission consultation paper 2011 on the use of ADR as a means to resolve disputes related to commercial transactions and practices in the EU, http://ec.europa.eu/dgs/health_food-safety/dgs_consultations/ca/docs/adr_consultation_paper_18012011_en.pdf (accessed 23 March 2015), para 13; for example, the consumer credit Directive (Directive 2008/48/EC, OJ L 133, 22 May 2008, p. 66) and the E-commerce Directive (Directive 2000/31/EC, OJ L 178, 17 July 2000, p. 1).

55 Fin-Net for national ADR schemes that handle cross-border disputes between consumers and financial services providers and the European Consumer Centre Network directs consumers to an appropriate ADR scheme in another Member State. See http://ec.europa.eu/finance/fin-net/index_en.htm and http://ec.europa.eu/consumers/solving_consumer_disputes/non-judicial_redress/ecc-net/index_en.htm (accessed 23 March 2015). See also I. Benöhr, 'Alternative dispute resolution for consumers in the financial services sector: a comparative perspective', *SIEPS European Policy Analysis* 6/2013.

56 See I. Benöhr, 'Alternative dispute resolution in the EU' in C. Hodges, I. Benöhr and N. Creutzfeldt-Banda (eds.), *Consumer ADR in the EU* (Hart Publishing, 2012).

57 The Directive had been preceded by a Green Paper consultation process, COM(2002) 196 final, 19 April 2002. The Commission also supported the Code of Conduct for Mediators that was elaborated subsequent to the Green Paper as a generic ADR self-regulatory measure among and with stakeholders and published in 2004, see http://ec.europa.eu/civiljustice/adr/adr_ec_code_conduct_en.htm (accessed 22 March 2015).

58 Directive 2008/52/EC of the European Parliament and of the Council of 21 May 2008 on certain aspects of mediation in civil and commercial matters (OJ L 136, 24 May 2008, p. 3), Articles 1, 4, 7 and 8.

questions including the appropriate level to regulate ADR. The resulting Directive was seen as a 'light-touch' approach specifically only regulating certain issues and allowing mediation schemes to develop organically in the Member States.[59] The Directive was nevertheless the first generic ADR legislative instrument at the EU level and had its transposition deadline in 2011.[60]

The same year that the mediation Directive was to be transposed, and at a time when the domestic rules based on its implementation were only starting to be applied in domestic proceedings, the Commission launched further and new initiatives for specific ADR measures to be taken in the consumer field.[61] These sector-specific initiatives resulted in what are commonly called the Directive on consumer ADR[62] and the Regulation on consumer ODR[63] (ODR being the abbreviation used for online dispute resolution). In its Impact Assessment preceding these measures, the Commission observed that the current status of ADR in the EU has shortcomings that hinder effectiveness, in particular: gaps in ADR coverage, low awareness and varied quality of ADR schemes.[64] It noted that insufficient and fragmented development of ADR in the EU did not fulfil the requirements of the internal market and that a well-functioning system of domestic ADR is necessary for the development of efficient and effective ADR for cross-border disputes.[65] In addition, the limited amount of schemes for ADR in relation to e-commerce consumer transactions needed to be addressed according to the Commission.[66] The Directive on consumer ADR provides for a more far-reaching framework than the mediation Directive. It obliges the Member States to ensure that consumers have access to ADR for consumer disputes involving a trader established in the EU and a consumer resident in the EU (thus encompassing

59 Storskrubb, supra note 6, pp. 194f.

60 Not all Member States had transposed the Directive in time and the Commission commenced legal proceedings by sending letters of formal notice to nine in July 2011. Three of them (Finland, Slovakia and the United Kingdom) subsequently notified the Commission of their national measures while the other six (Cyprus, the Czech Republic, Spain, France, Luxembourg and the Netherlands) received a reasoned opinion for failing to do so. For additional information see C. Besso, 'Implementation of the EU Directive N. 52/ 2008: a comparative survey', www.mediation-in-europe.eu (accessed 25 May 2016).

61 COM(2011) 793 final, 29 November 2011, Proposal for a Directive on alternative dispute resolution for consumer disputes and amending Regulation (EC) No 2006/2004 and Directive 2009/22/EC (Directive on consumer ADR); and COM(2011) 794 final, 29 November 2011, Proposal for a Regulation on online dispute resolution for consumer disputes (Regulation on consumer ODR).

62 Directive 2013/11/EU of the European Parliament and of the Council of 21 May 2013 on alternative dispute resolution for consumer disputes, OJ L 165, 18 June 2013, p. 63.

63 Regulation (EU) No 524/2013 of the European Parliament and of the Council of 21 May 2013 on online dispute resolution for consumer disputes, OJ L 165, 18 June 2013, p. 1.

64 SEC(2011) 1409 final, 29 November 2011, Executive Summary of the Impact Assessment, p. 4, and SEC(2011) 1408, 29 November 2011, Impact Assessment, pp. 23–27.

65 SEC(2011) 1409 final, 29 November 2011, p. 5.

66 Ibid., p. 4.

both domestic and cross-border disputes). Such procedures must be accessible online and available at a nominal fee for the consumers.[67] In addition, both ADR entities and traders are under an obligation to provide information regarding ADR to consumers.[68] The Directive also sets out certain minimum standards for the ADR procedure and requirements of expertise and impartiality on the person in charge of the ADR process.[69] To ensure effectiveness, the outcome of the ADR procedure should according to the Directive be resolved within 90 days.[70] Finally, there are provisions regarding cooperation between the ADR entities and their cooperation with national authorities as well as rules on assistance for consumers in cross-border matters.[71]

The ODR Regulation provides for a multilingual and user-friendly online platform to be set up by the Commission that would constitute an interactive website.[72] The platform is intended to be a single entry-point for consumers (and under certain circumstances, traders) to submit their complaints for out-of-court resolution of their disputes concerning online consumer transactions. The platform will transmit complaints to the relevant local ADR entity in a Member State.[73] The Regulation is thus linked to the ADR Directive that obliges the Member States to ensure that such local entities exist and the national consumer ADR procedures fulfil the requirements set out in the Directive.[74] The platform will also provide a free electronic case management tool to enable the entities to handle the matters entirely online should they so wish. The Regulation also supports the online handling of the disputes in that it specifically prohibits the ADR entities from requiring the physical presence of the parties or their representatives in dealing with the matter unless the parties agree.[75] The Regulation finally provides for a network comprised of domestic contact points that have various duties of support, facilitation and information.[76]

Although neither the Directive nor the Regulation impose ADR as a mandatory procedure, they are clearly intended to provide support for ADR and facilitate ADR resolution of consumer disputes. The deadline for the transposition of the Directive on ADR was in July 2015 and the Regulation on ODR became applicable from January 2016.[77] Thus, much of the impact and effect of these measures is yet to be seen. However, commentators already provide divergent analyses of the results. Some strongly support consumer ADR and

67 Directive on consumer ADR, supra note 62, Articles 5 and 8.
68 Ibid., Articles 7 and 13.
69 Ibid., Articles 6 and 9.
70 Ibid., Article 8(e).
71 Ibid., Articles 14, 16 and 17.
72 Regulation on consumer ODR, supra note 61, Article 5(1).
73 Ibid., Articles 5(2) and 9(6).
74 Ibid., inter alia, Articles 1, 7, 10(a).
75 Ibid., Articles 1(d), 10(d) and 10(b).
76 Ibid., Article 7.
77 Ibid., Article 22 and Directive on consumer ADR, supra note 61, Article 25.

emphasise its benefits for these specific types of consumer claims (low value and often multiple in nature dealing with a simple legal issue)[78], others question both the ethos behind the promotion of ADR as a law-enforcement tool and the schemes themselves, which, it is argued, provide a mixed and incomplete approach.[79] From a civil justice perspective, there are several issues that arise.[80] For present purposes, is notable that both the Directive and the Regulation are not limited to cross-border matters and that they provide a framework for much deeper integration in ADR specifically in the consumer field rather than the mediation Directive that applies to civil and commercial matters generically or horizontally.[81] It is also notable that what the Commission considers to be the general 'insufficient and fragmented development of ADR in the EU', including apparently the mediation Directive in this development, is an argument for deeper integration in one specific sector. However, this is in stark contrast to the chosen regulatory strategy, i.e., the 'light touch' adopted for the mediation Directive to allow organic development or mediation at the local level. It is further notable that the Commission argues that a well-functioning system of domestic ADR is necessary for the development of efficient and effective ADR for cross-border disputes.

2.3.3 Developments in the intellectual property sector

Another sector that has focused on procedural issues is that of intellectual property (IP). The first IP measure dealing with procedural law was enacted in 2004 and known as the 'enforcement Directive'.[82] The use of the word 'enforcement' is interesting because it is not used to mean enforcement of

78 See C. Hodges, I. Benöhr and N. Creutzfeldt-Banda, 'Consumer-to-business dispute resolution: the power of CADR' (2012) 13 *ERA Forum* 199, summarising the main findings of a study conducted by the same authors and published as C. Hodges, I. Benöhr and N. Creutzfeldt-Banda, *Consumer ADR in Europe* (Hart Publishing, 2010); and Benöhr, supra note 55, pp. 10–13.

79 See G. Wagner, 'Private law enforcement through ADR: wonder drug or snake oil?' (2014) 51 *Common Market Law Review* 165; J. Davies, 'ADR/ODR: too much optimism in the promotion of cross-border trade?' in B. Hess, M. Bergström and E. Storskrubb (eds.), *EU Civil Justice – Current Issues and Future Outlook, Swedish Studies in European Law, Vol 7* (Hart Publishing, 2016) 55.

80 See, inter alia, Hess, supra note 10, noting that the balance between dispute resolution provided by courts and other bodies as well as the fundamental procedural guarantees of the consumers are issues that have not been sufficiently discussed. For some tentative observations see E. Storskrubb, 'Alternative dispute resolution in the EU: regulatory challenges' (2016) 24 *European Review of Private Law*, pp. 25–31.

81 The specific consumer measures are intended to be without prejudice to the mediation Directive and for cross-border matters where the consumer ADR procedure is specifically dealt with in mediation procedure they will be mutually applicable. See Directive on consumer ADR, supra note 61, recital 19, and Regulation on consumer ODR, supra note 61, recital 12.

82 Directive 2004/48/EC of the European Parliament and of the Council of 29 April 2004 on the enforcement of intellectual property rights, OJ L 157, 30 April 2004, p. 45. (Note corrigenda OJ L 195, 2 June 2004, p. 16, and OJ L 204, 4 August 2007, p. 27.)

judgments or execution rules in relation thereto, but in the broader, more general sense of realisation of rights.[83] The recitals to the Directive note that it is not intended to deal with judicial cooperation (i.e., issues that fall under civil justice such as jurisdiction or recognition and enforcement of judgments), nor is it intended to affect substantive IP rights. However, the Directive provides for the approximation of 'measures, procedures and remedies' in relation to, inter alia, injunctions, provisional measures and access to information and evidence.[84] These 'measures, procedures and remedies'[85] regulate distinct and fundamental procedural matters such as: standing, standard of proof, disclosure and obtention of evidence from the counterparty as well as from third parties, various types of interim and injunctive relief both to preserve evidence and to support substantive rights and litigation costs.[86] In addition, the Directive regulates the type of available relief or remedies, in addition to the previously mentioned provisions on interim and injunctive remedies.[87] Member States were obliged to transpose the Directive and ensure that the procedures outlined are available in litigation concerning all the IP rights provided in EU law and in national law regardless of whether the disputes are of a domestic or cross-border nature.[88]

The Directive has come under criticism and scrutiny in relation to its remedies and disclosure provisions, in particular for the difficult balancing that is often necessary in practice between these rights and the rights of third parties in relation to fundamental rights of data protection and privacy.[89] The Commission has also noted that the Directive has encountered challenges in relation to protection of IP infringements on the internet.[90] The provisions of the Directive have also led to divergent interpretations, implementations and practices in the Member States. Therefore, further clarification in the form of more detailed provisions has been envisaged by the Commission.[91] However, so far, no amendment has been proposed. Instead, a European Observatory has been set up to provide information and support networks and meetings among relevant stakeholders.[92] In addition, the Commission has conducted a follow-up online consultation on the efficiency of proceedings and

83 G. Wagner, 'Harmonisation of civil procedure: policy perspectives', in X. Kramer and C.H. van Rhee (eds.), *Civil Litigation in a Globalising World* (T.M.C. Asser Press, 2012) 102.
84 Enforcement Directive, supra note 82, recitals 7–24.
85 Ibid., see, inter alia, Articles 2(1) and 3(1).
86 Ibid., Articles 4–9, 11, 14.
87 Ibid., Articles 10 and 13. See also Wagner, supra note 83, pp. 103–106, for a brief description of the procedural rules.
88 Ibid., Articles 2 and 20. The transposition date was 29 April 2006.
89 See, inter alia, I. Baraliug, S. Depreeuw and S. Gutwirth, 'Copyright enforcement in the digital age: a post-ACTA view on the balancing of fundamental rights' (2012) 1 *International Journal of Law and Information Technology* 95. See also COM(2010) 779, 22 October 2010, pp. 7f.
90 COM(2010) 779 final, 22 December 2010, p. 4.
91 Ibid., p. 4.
92 Regulation (EU) No 386/2012 of 19 April 2012 on entrusting the Office of Harmonization in the Internal Market with tasks related to the enforcement of intellectual property rights, including the assembling of public and private sector representatives as a European

accessibility of measures for the civil enforcement of IP rights.[93] This consultation dealt with specific issues arising from the application of the enforcement Directive such as the practice in relation to injunctions but also with overarching and structural procedural issues such as ADR, fast-track proceedings, small claims procedures, specialisation of courts, length of proceedings, costs of proceedings and overall use of litigation versus refraining from litigation.[94]

The consultation was followed in 2014 by a Communication of the Commission, *Towards a Renewed Consensus on the Enforcement of Intellectual Property Rights: An EU Action Plan*, which has been welcomed by the Council.[95] In relation to procedure, the main point of the Action Plan is Action 4, in which the term 'redress' is now used rather than 'enforcement'. The Commission notes that in addition to the already available measures – such as the enforcement Directive for IP rights and the various generic civil justice measures such as the small claims Regulation – it will consider whether further action is needed in the future to improve 'civil redress procedures'.[96] It further notes that the high costs and the complexity of litigation often dissuades potential litigants and rights-holders, and it focuses in particular on the position of innovative SMEs. The already pending proposal of the Commission to amend the generic small claims regulation and the EU Justice Scoreboards that are general civil justice measures are mentioned as measures already taken that will improve the efficiency of the justice systems of the Member States, and thus by implication also the efficiency of cases dealing with IP rights.[97] In its conclusions on the Action Plan, the Council has stressed the importance of accessible and cost-efficient judicial systems.[98]

Aside from these developments that are relevant for IP rights, a specific development has taken place in the context of one IP right, namely patent law. Agreement was reached in 2011 among 25 Member States to pursue

Observatory on Infringement of Intellectual Property Rights, OJ L 129, 16 May 2012, p. 1. See https://oami.europa.eu/ohimportal/en/web/observatory/home (accessed 25 March 2015).

93 See information on the consultation and the questionnaire at http://ec.europa.eu/internal_market/consultations/2012/intellectual-property-rights_en.htm and http://ec.europa.eu/internal_market/consultations/docs/2012/intellectual-property-rights/questionnaire_en.pdf (accessed 25 March 2015).

94 Ibid. See also responses at http://ec.europa.eu/internal_market/consultations/docs/2012/intellectual-property-rights/summary-of-responses_en.pdf (accessed 25 May 2016).

95 COM(2014) 392 final, 1 July 2014, p. 7. See also Council conclusions 15321/14 of 10 November 2014.

96 Ibid., p. 7. In Action Point 5, a more focused procedure-related action is proposed as the Commission proposes to launch a consultation on best practices in relation to financing schemes that can assist SMEs to protect their rights, such as litigation insurance.

97 Ibid., p. 7.

98 Conclusions, supra note 95, p. 4. In 2015 a further consultation was launched on the functioning of the enforcement Directive and in the online environment, see http://ec.europa.eu/growth/tools-databases/newsroom/cf/itemdetail.cfm?item_id=8580 (accessed 21 September 2016).

enhanced cooperation in relation to the unitary patent protection package. This package includes two EU Regulations intended to create a unitary patent that has uniform protection in the 25 Member States that are participating in the scheme.[99] The future system is arguably an improvement of the current system that requires national validation in each Member State where the patent applicant wants protection.[100] The project has a long and fraught history and there have been challenges to its legality that were recently dismissed.[101] From a procedural perspective, the project is nevertheless remarkable because as part of the package, the participating Member States have entered into an international agreement to set up the Unified Patent Court.[102] This court is not yet operational, but the intention is to create a supranational court (with first instance and appeal levels) to deal with disputes relating to European patents and European patents with unitary effect.[103]

The aim of this specialised court is to provide a single jurisdiction and for parties to avoid multiple litigations in several Member States, which has been a necessary feature in many cases under the current system.[104] The agreement

99 Regulation (EU) No 1257 /2012 of 17 December 2012 implementing enhanced cooperation in the area of the creation of unitary patent protection (OJ L 361, 31 December 2012, p. 1) and Regulation (EU) No 1260/2012 of 17 December 2012 implementing enhanced cooperation in the area of the creation of unitary patent protection with regard to the applicable translation arrangements (OJ L 361, 31 December 2012, p. 89).

100 At the time of writing the system has not yet become operational. The Regulations, supra note 99, entered into force on 20 January 2013. However, they will only apply from the date of entry into force of the Agreement on a Unified Patent Court, see note 103.

101 For a brief history and critique of the use of enhanced cooperation see M. Lamping, 'Enhanced cooperation – a proper approach to market integration in the field of unitary patent protection?' (2011) 8 *International Review of Intellectual Property and Competition* 900. Spain and Italy first brought actions for annulment concerning the EU Regulation to adopt enhanced cooperation in the field of intellectual property that were dismissed, see C-274/11 and C-295/11. Spain thereafter brought two actions for annulment before the CJEU C-146/13 and C-147/13 against the Regulations themselves. Both actions were dismissed on 5 May 2015. Note that earlier the Council had asked the CJEU for an opinion on the proposed patent litigation system and its compatibility with the EU Treaties. CJEU Opinion 1/09 found that the draft agreement was not compatible with the Treaties and occasioned changes to the agreement.

102 Agreement on a Unified Patent Court (OJ C 175, 20 June 2013, p.1).

103 Ibid., Article 1. For a brief explanation of difference between the patents see http://ec.europa.eu/growth/industry/intellectual-property/industrial-property/patent/faqs/index_en.htm (accessed 25 May 2016). Note that the Court of First Instance of the Unified Patent Court will have a central division as well as local and regional divisions. The central division will be seated in Paris, with sections in London and Munich. Every Contracting Member State may set up a local division or together with one or more other Contracting Member States a regional division of the Court of First Instance (several regional divisions have been set up). The Court of Appeal of the Unified Patent Court will have its seat in Luxembourg. The Registry will be set up at the seat of the Court of Appeal. In addition a patent mediation and arbitration centre with seats in Ljubljana and Lisbon and a training framework for judges with facilities in Budapest shall be established. See also Article 89 in relation to entry into force, at present the requisite ratifications have not been notified.

104 See S. Luginbuehl, *European Patent Law: Towards a Uniform Interpretation* (Edward Elgar Publishing, 2011).

on the court stipulates some basic features of the proceedings to be heard before the court, inter alia, in relation to the public nature of the proceeding, representation, phases of the procedure, evidence, language and costs.[105] The agreement also provides that the court shall have rules of procedure that will be adopted by the Administrative Committee of the court based on broad consultations among stakeholders.[106] A full body of procedural rules has been adopted.[107] These rules encompass matters normally included in a civil procedure code, such as rules on what should be included in the statement of claim and statement of defence, service, rights and obligations of the parties, time periods, rules on case management and the phases of the proceedings (three phases: written procedure, interim procedure, oral procedure), security for costs, evidence including orders for production of evidence, as well as rules on costs and a separate procedure for a costs decision.[108] The first judges are also in the process of being trained.[109] There is thus for the first time a supranational court to which the parties will be able to turn with their claims related to patent rights under a set of procedural rules that will be agreed by and are in that sense common to 25 Member States. These common procedural rules will be ones that the parties must use for the relevant types of patent claims – there will be no domestic procedure for these claims – and the Unified Patent Court will be able to refer questions for preliminary referral directly to the Court of Justice of the European Union (CJEU).[110]

2.3.4 *Developments in the competition law field*

Finally, in the field of competition law, so-called private enforcement – for example, civil claims and litigation based on breaches of competition law – have become a common feature in the EU in the past decade since the CJEU confirmed that Articles 101 and 102 can form the basis for a claim for compensation by anybody that has suffered such harm[111] and the Commission's promotion of private enforcement.[112] As for all claims based on rights derived from EU law heard before national courts, the procedural rules applicable in

105 Agreement, supra note 102, Part III Organizational and Procedural Provisions, Chapters I–III.

106 Ibid., Article 41.

107 The 18th draft was adopted in October 2015 www.unified-patent-court.org/sites/default/files/UPC-Rules-of-Procedure.pdf (accessed 21 September 2016).

108 Ibid.

109 See www.unified-patent-court.org/news (accessed 30 March 2015).

110 Agreement, supra note 102.

111 The seminal cases being C-453 *Courage* EU:C:1974:25 and joined cases C-295/04-C-298/04 *Manfredi* EU:C2006:461. See also, inter alia, P. Komninos, 'New prospects for private enforcement of EC competition law: *Courage* v. *Crehan* and the Community right to damages' (2002) 39 *Common Market Law Review* 447.

112 COM(2005) 672 final, 19 December 2005, Green Paper Damages Actions for Breach of the EC Antitrust Rules and COM(2008) 165 final, 2 April 2008, White Paper on Damages Actions for Breach of the EC Antitrust Rules. The Commission has published

such cases are the domestic ones, qualified by the principles of equivalence and effectiveness as developed by the CJEU.[113] However, the Commission has argued that the differing procedural rules affect the competitive advantage of companies operating in different Member States and create a disincentive to enforcement of rights in some Member States. Therefore, the differences also may affect the internal market. In addition, large-scale infringements of competition law often have a cross-border element.[114] Hence, to ensure a level playing field for all actors and to increase legal certainty, the Commission subsequent to consultation proposed a Directive to specifically regulate certain issues in relation to such actions for damages.[115] The so-called damages Directive is to be transposed by 27 December 2016 and deals with specific issues of procedure, such as disclosure of evidence, limitation periods, effects of consensual settlement, burden and standard of proof as well as issues of remedies and liabilities.[116] There has been an extensive debate on these rules already prior to their transposition in relation to their desirability as well as content.[117] The rules are to apply when there is an infringement of Articles 101 or 102 TFEU or of national competition law. However, national competition law is defined in a limited manner to encompass cases in which national competition provisions are to be applied in parallel to the EU provisions in

Communication on quantifying harm in actions for damages based on breaches of Article 101 or 102 of the Treaty on the Functioning of the EU, C(2013) 3440, 11 June 2013.

113 Case 33/76 *Rewe-Zentralfinanz eG and Rewe-Zentral AG v Lanswitschaftskammer für das Saarland* EU:C:1976:188 and subsequent cases. This case law has occasioned a rich plethora of writing, see, inter alia, M. Dougan, *National Remedies Before the Court of Justice, Issues of Harmonisation and Differentiation* (Hart Publishing, 2004) and supra note 49, as well as J. Engström, *The Europeanisation of Remedies and Procedures through Judge-made Law: Can a Trojan Horse Achieve Effectiveness?* (PhD thesis EUI, 2009). Note that most of the case law has developed in the context of administrative or public law but the importance for the private law field has been perceived as increasing; see Storskrubb, supra note 6, pp. 16–17.

114 Directive 2014/104/EU of 26 November 2014 on certain rules governing actions for damage under national law for infringements of the competition law provisions of the Member States of the European Union (OJ L 349, 5 December 2014, p. 1), recitals 7–9.

115 COM(2013) 404 final, 11 June 2013, proposal for a Directive on certain rules governing actions for damages under national law for infringements of the competition law provisions of the Member States and of the European Union, see in particular pp. 4–5, 8–10. The preceding consultation phase included a Green Paper and a White Paper, see supra note 112, as well as external studies commissioned by the Commission.

116 Directive, supra note 114, see, for example, Articles 5–8 on disclosure that include rules on evidence in the files of a competition authority and rules on penalties for breach of disclosure rules and obligations; Article 10 on limitation periods; and Articles 18–19 on effects of consensual settlement. See also Articles 3, 9, 11–15 and 17 that regulate the right to full compensation, the effect of a decision of a national competition authority, joint and several liability, passing-on overcharge, indirect purchasers, claims from different levels of a supply chain and quantification of harm. These Articles interrelate issues of standing, burden and standard of proof as well as the availability and level of remedies.

117 See, inter alia, C. Hodges, 'Competition enforcement, regulation and civil justice: what is the case?' (2006) 43 *Common Market Law Review* 1381.

the same case.[118] Thus, its rules, including those on procedural matters, will not apply to purely domestic cases. Nevertheless, there is a risk or potential of a 'spillover' effect of the procedural choices made in the Directive on the purely domestic level. In a critical examination of the rules in relation to many procedural institutions such as burden of proof, it has been observed that the rules shift the balance of arms between claimants and defendants in comparison to what would be the original balance in civil proceedings.[119] Thus, particular sector-specific policy choices influence the elaboration of supranational procedural rules. How such sector-specific choices will interact with overall procedural goals and principles is an important concern, for example, in the context of fundamental procedural rights.

Finally, it should be noted that in the consultation on private enforcement of competition law, the prospect of collective redress mechanisms was also raised.[120] Once the decision was taken to deal with collective redress in a horizontal manner rather than separately on a sector-by-sector basis, no specific rules have been included on collective redress in the damages Directive. However, the Recommendation and Communication on collective redress (see Section 2.2.2 above) were published by the Commission on the same day as the damages Directive and the Commission perceives collective redress as particularly important for consumers harmed by antitrust violations.[121]

2.4 *Constitutional incoherence*

2.4.1 *Two contrasting approaches*

From the analysis of the cross-border struggle in Section 2.2, it is clear that the Member States in the Council have wanted to keep the development of the policy area of civil justice limited to cross-border procedures and have never agreed to an expansive interpretation of the legal basis, i.e., to an expansive interpretation of the legislative competence in relation to generic procedural cooperation. The 'cross-border' limitation has even been called the 'vigorously defended' 'wall of exceptionalism' around the policy area and against its expansion.[122] A broad and too expansive interpretation of 'cross-border implications' could ultimately form grounds for an action for

118 Directive, supra note 114, Articles 1 and 2(1)–(2).

119 See Hodges, supra note 117.

120 See Green Paper, supra note 112. See also Study commissioned by the European Parliament, www.europarl.europa.eu/document/activities/cont/201206/20120613ATT46782/20120613ATT46782EN.pdf (accessed 25 May 2016).

121 European Commission, Competition Policy Brief, 11 January 2015, p. 4, http://ec.europa.eu/competition/publications/cpb/2015/001_en.pdf (accessed 25 May 2016).

122 C. Crifò, '"Trusted with a muzzle and enfranchised with a clog": The British approach to European civil procedure', in B. Hess, M. Bergström and E. Storskrubb (eds.), *EU Civil Justice: Current Issues and Future Outlook, Swedish Studies in European Law, Vol 7* (Hart Publishing, 2016) 94.

annulment before the CJEU for breaching the attribution of competence as defined in the treaties.[123] No actions for annulment have been brought against any of the generic civil justice measures to date. Rather, the Council has emphasised and protected the limitations in the Article 81 TFEU legal basis at the stage of the legislative process with support from the European Parliament as evidenced by the numerous examples related above. The example of collective redress is a different but also instructive example, since there has only been a consultation process that was not subsequently followed by a legislative process. The Member State responses in the consultation process publicly evidenced the concerns of some of them in relation to protecting the legal basis and the importance of respecting the national procedural systems.

The continued cross-border limitation in respect of generic measures can be contrasted with the situation in relation to the sector-specific arena (discussed in Section 2.3), where there has been dramatic procedural development in recent years. The impact of much of this development is yet to been seen, since many of the new procedural rules briefly presented above are not yet applicable. But it is clear that there are now several significant sector-specific sets of EU rules that regulate procedural issues, some also applicable in a domestic – i.e., in a non-cross-border – context. In addition, the consultation process in the IP sector described above demonstrates that full-blown and essential procedural issues – including costs of proceedings, efficiency of proceedings and proportional procedural rules such as procedural tracks – are being debated within a sector-specific setting in a much more holistic and concrete manner than so far undertaken in the generic civil justice context. In addition, the measures do not simply provide for new sets of rules but they also introduce considerable structural changes and mechanisms such as online platforms for litigants in the consumer field or the Unified Patent Court system in the IP field. This dynamic and broad development cannot be ignored.

This development is possible due to the link of the relevant sectors to the creation of the internal market. Thus, the legal bases under which the measures have been adopted have been the specific substantive legal basis of the chosen sector or the general legal basis for the establishment and functioning of the internal market.[124] These legal bases contain no cross-border limitation but are purpose-based to ensure and achieve the goals of the EU in a specific sector and in the internal market. It might be questioned whether it is acceptable or logical that the general internal market legal basis in Article 114 can be used for procedural harmonisation in this manner when Article 81 specifically mentions that measures under it can be taken to eliminate 'obstacles to the proper functioning of civil proceedings, if necessary by promoting the

123 Ibid., noting the comments of the UK House of Commons European Scrutiny Committee in relation to the first proposal of the Commission for a small claims Regulation.

124 See Articles 103, 114 and 146 TFEU. See also Study, supra note 120, pp. 55–63, for a discussion on the choice of legal basis.

compatibility of the rules on civil procedure' and 'when necessary for the proper functioning of the internal market' but only when there are 'cross-border implications'. If there is no sector-specific legal basis, using the general internal market legal basis of Article 114 may be a circumvention of the procedural legal basis in Article 81 and its relevant limitations that exclude procedural harmonisation also for domestic matters.

However, there have been no actions for annulment against any of these sector-specific procedural measures alleging incorrect legal basis.[125] The Member States thus appear to accept that the EU has competence to regulate procedural matters on a sector-specific basis for both cross-border and domestic matters. The result of this difference between generic civil procedural regulation and sector-specific procedural regulation is a constitutional incoherence. This incoherence has become more pronounced due to the recent sector-specific developments. These developments are so significant that it leads one to wonder whether the cross-border issue has been overtaken by these events and become redundant. It has not yet become redundant but its reach becomes circumscribed by the sector-specific development because for certain types of civil procedural matters there is a broader mandate to legislate at the EU level. The more such types are identified and regulated at the EU level, the more the cross-border limitation loses its impact and thus becomes redundant, at least from a constitutional competence perspective. One cannot help but wonder whether all Member State regulators and legislators in the justice field are fully aware of the Janus-faced reality that is being created.[126] This constitutional incoherence raises several questions that will be dealt with below. One of these is whether the difference in development relates to the fact that the more limited strand has developed under the aegis of the AFSJ and the other more expansive strand has developed in the context of the market-driven realities of the internal market.

2.4.2 Procedural harmonisation or not?

Linked to the strict constitutional question on competence is an underlying tension between a restrictive and an expansive political vision of EU civil justice, with the Commission at least historically arguing more for the latter vision. The opposing visions relate to how far procedural harmonisation in Europe is considered practically feasible and politically desirable. A debate specifically on the feasibility and desirability of such harmonisation took

125 Against the unitary patent Regulations in the intellectual property field there have been actions for annulment on other grounds, supra note 101.

126 See though the UK Government's Report, *Review of the Balance of Competences between the United Kingdom and the European Union: Civil Judicial Cooperation*, February 2014, paras 2.10–2.14, www.gov.uk/government/uploads/system/uploads/attachment_data/file/279228/civil-judicial-cooperation-report-review-of-balance-of-competences.pdf (accessed 25 May 2016).

place among the academic community in Europe close to two decades ago, subsequent to the Storme Report on harmonisation of civil procedure.[127] The perspectives put forward in that debate are still highly relevant and a fleeting analysis can lead us to think that there has been no resolution of these issues and that we still find ourselves at the same starting point. A more searching analysis nevertheless leads me to conclude that we have come some distance from that point and that we now find ourselves at a new juncture. We already have a wealth of generic civil justice measures enacted. These measures are much broader than the purely private international law or even international procedural law in its traditional sense. Although these may be limited to the cross-border realm, many of the reforms of the enacted Regulations demonstrate incremental pressures towards deeper integration. When reports are compiled on the application of civil justice measures in the Member States that evidence divergent interpretations, there often arises an ostensible need to provide for more uniform solutions, more detailed rules and additional mutual minimum standards of procedural protection.[128] In addition, some of the later civil justice measures such as the small claims, payment order and account preservation order Regulations create discrete, alternative and independent supranational procedures.[129] Thus, we are already invariably dealing with some form of harmonisation, albeit limited so far. In addition, we have the parallel and more recent development of sector-specific rules. This development has been called a ‘new approach’ to procedural harmonisation.[130] Another commentator has called it ‘vertical harmonization’.[131] These sector-specific measures show that the Member States are willing to proceed with procedural harmonisation in some instances

127 M. Storme (ed.), *Approximation of Judiciary Law in the European Union* (Nijhoff, 1994). For an overview of the subsequent debate see Storskrubb, supra note 6, pp. 21–25. A few of the voices in the debate include: P.H. Lindblom, ‘Harmony of the legal spheres: a Swedish view on the construction of a unified European procedural law’ (1997) 5 *ERPRIVL* 11; T. Andersson, ‘Approximation of procedural law in Europe’, in M. Storme (ed.), *Procedural Laws in Europe: Towards Harmonisation* (Antwerpen, 2003) 55; J. Niemi-Kiesiläinen, ‘International cooperation and approximation of laws in the field of civil procedure’ in V. Heiskanen and K. Kulovesi (eds.), *Function and Future of European Law* (Publications of the Faculty of Law, University of Helsinki, 1999) 249; P. Biavati, ‘Is flexibility a way to the harmonization of civil procedural law in Europe?’ in F. Carpi and M. Lupoi (eds.), *Essays on Transnational and Comparative Civil Procedure* (Giappichelli, 2001) pp. 85–104.

128 See, inter alia, COM(2013) 858 final, 4 December 2013, Report on the application of Regulation (EC) No 1393/2007 on the service in the Member States of judicial and extra-judicial documents in civil and commercial matters, pp. 6, 11 and 13–14; and COM(2013) 795 final, 19 November 2013, Report on the application of Regulation (EC) No 861/2007 establishing a European Small Claims Procedure, p. 10.

129 X. Kramer, ‘Harmonisation of civil procedure: interaction with private international law’ in X. Kramer and C.H. van Rhee (eds.), *Civil Litigation in a Globalising World* (T.M.C. Asser Press, 2012) 127.

130 B. Hess, ‘Procedural harmonisation in a European context’ in X. Kramer and C.H. van Rhee (eds.), *Civil Litigation in a Globalising World* (T.M.C. Asser Press, 2012) 164.

131 Wagner, supra note 83, p. 101.

under the guise of effective enforcement of EU law and rights based on EU law.[132]

The persistent reluctance of the Member States in the Council against a broad interpretation of the cross-border limitation and against a deeper procedural harmonisation at least on a generic level must, nonetheless, be acknowledged. It demonstrates that justice matters under the AFSJ, including civil justice, are sovereignty-sensitive. Procedural systems are deeply ingrained in the society and its fundamental legal structures. Procedural reforms that have been undertaken and are ongoing in the Member States demonstrate that quests for efficiency and proportionality are finely tuned and that the effect of any reform needs to be carefully considered as to how it impacts on the justice system as a whole. If the underlying structural features of the Member States' procedural systems differ – for example, in relation to the organisation of the relevant actors (inter alia, courts, bailiffs and the bar) – is it at all possible to harmonise? Will any supranational harmonisation attempts harm the carefully created balances of a justice system behind which feature broader societal goals and visions; for example, in relation to costs or litigiousness?[133] Are we able to say that we have such a mutual vision in Europe or should a political will concerning that understanding and vision first be clearly uniform before any harmonisation is attempted? The basic principle of national procedural autonomy as consistently confirmed by the CJEU[134] has supported an impression that procedural law still falls within the competence and remit of the Member States. This perception does not give the full picture, since the CJEU has qualified the principle with the principles of equivalence and effectiveness and many commentators find it misleading to refer to the 'autonomy' of the Member States.[135] It is nonetheless clear that there needs to be a political will of the Member States in order for any broader attempts to move forward in procedural harmonisation. It is also apparent that a mutual vision on justice may be necessary if any such project is to succeed.

2.4.3 *The need for a regulatory strategy*

Notwithstanding the strict competence issue, it is apparent from the above review and analysis that there is a discrepancy between the sector-specific development including a willingness of the Member States to proceed with procedural harmonisation in certain fields of the internal market and the strict approach of the Member States in relation to the civil justice competence in the AFSJ. The strict cross-border logic upheld for civil justice may at first appear to be less politically justified if such measures are proposed in

132 See Hess, supra note 130, pp. 164–165.
133 Hodges, supra note 117, pp. 1398–1401, 1404 and 1406.
134 See supra note 113.
135 Storskrubb, supra note 6, pp. 19–20, and the sources mentioned therein.

substantive policy fields linked to the internal market. The broader regulatory question that nevertheless immediately arises is why the strict cross-border limitation is upheld for some types of procedures but not for others. There may be valid arguments for a fragmented or partial approach; testing different or new (procedural) rules in a limited setting before full-scale change is not an uncommon feature of legislative reform. However, in the EU context, the sector-specific developments are clearly disparate and there does not appear to be any coordination between procedural projects or any overall regulatory vision or model. From the perspective of domestic procedural systems, many of which have generally applicable rules for most civil disputes, such a fragmented approach seems to be problematic both on a practical and principled level. In addition, in a domestic setting, if specific procedural rules are developed for specific types of cases, there is often a careful systematic analysis of the benefits of such an approach and consideration of how such a specific procedure relates to the general rules on civil proceedings. Significantly, the so-far fragmented approach in the EU creates the risk that overarching procedural principles are neglected when procedural regulation in one sector is proposed.[136] In addition, a too-narrow sector-specific focus and a multitude of different measures may create unnecessary regulatory complexity that may impact on user-friendliness and legal certainty, as well as create a risk of conflicts between different procedural rules. Furthermore, many of the measures interact, rely upon and refer to national procedural rules, which augments fragmentation and creates challenges of implementation.[137]

In addition, the dividing line between generic civil justice and the sector-specific development in the EU is inevitably not a clear one on the regulatory level. Commentators refer to one of these strands of procedural regulation to justify action in the other,[138] as does the Commission, examples of which were related above in relation to regulation of ADR and IP strategy. The history on collective redress also in a concrete manner demonstrates that the strands may interact and impact on one another. It was the sector-specific pressures and debates in both the consumer and the competition sectors on the desirability of regulating collective redress at an EU level that preceded and ultimately resulted in the latest generic consultation on collective redress. If these strands of development start to coalesce, there is more than ever a need for a regulatory strategy that would encompass both strands. It seems to me that the lesson from the civil justice context noted above – i.e., that there is a need to be sensitive to the relationship between procedural development and reform at the domestic level and any EU development – must also be

136 See, for example, Benöhr, supra note 55, p. 13, and the Commission's Impact Assessment SEC(2011) 1409 final, 29 November 2011, p. 5.

137 Crifó, supra note 10.

138 Wagner, supra note 83, pp. 110; M.E. Storme, 'Harmonisation of civil procedure and the interaction with substantive private law', X. Kramer and C.H. van Rhee (eds.), *Civil Litigation in a Globalising World* (T.M.C. Asser Press, 2012) 152.

relevant for the sector-specific procedural strand. Inversely, the discussion started in the sector-specific IP context on procedural efficiency and adequate and proportional procedural rules should be relevant and highlighted more broadly also in the context of civil justice.

Ultimately, it appears less beneficial to differentiate between strands and to deal with procedural developments discretely and in a void. So far, an overall roadmap and systematic approach has been lacking to coordinate these developments.[139] Coordination and coherence have been advocated by many commentators as important for further improvement and this plea remains salient today.[140] In addition an overall regulatory strategy should be debated and crafted on all levels; a formidable and significant challenge. Such a strategy should, however, be more than a systematic and coherent legislative approach. It would also include an active debate on whether there is a sufficient mutual vision on justice; on how far procedural harmonisation is desirable and feasible today; on the level of governance including what issues remain better left to the Member States to regulate; and on what types of legislative or other measures are the best ones to progress civil justice in Europe today.[141] It may be that a continued incremental approach with coordination is the best way forward, but this should be a conscious regulatory choice. In such a debate, the further regulatory perspectives dealt with in Section 3 should also be taken into account.

3 Further regulatory perspectives

3.1 Subsidiarity and governance

The constitutional perspective on civil justice can no longer be one of simply harmonisation or not, of competence or not. The consultation process on collective redress showed that other constitutional and regulatory issues such as subsidiarity and proportionality are intertwined with the competence issue. Several Member States stated that the principles of subsidiarity and proportionality must be respected; some noted that any measures must not go beyond what is strictly necessary and preferably only relate to minimum standards while others noted that there must be respect for the national procedural traditions of the Member States.[142] The consultation process showed that there is a need to be sensitive to the relationship

139 Hess, supra note 10.

140 See, inter alia, Tulibacka and Storskrubb, supra note 7; Hess, supra note 10; X. Kramer, 'Procedure matters: construction and deconstructivism in European civil procedure' (2013) 33 *Erasmus Law Lectures* 24.

141 Crifó, supra note 10, notes that the Storme Report advocated a Directive as the appropriate type of instrument.

142 See, inter alia, the responses of Italy, France, Greece, Poland, Latvia, Denmark and Sweden available at supra note 38.

between procedural development and reform at the domestic level and EU development. Even if there is legislative competence in the strict sense with respect to procedural matters, this does not mean that it is always desirable to exercise it. The cross-border issue as well as the other regulatory challenges emerging from the deepening of civil justice over the past years show that the institutions must grapple with the question of whether to and how best to exercise competence.

At the current juncture, parallel and general developments in the EU underline the complexity and political sensitivity of the regulatory matrix. The principles of subsidiarity and proportionality have gained structural and political importance with the increased scrutiny provisions and role of the national parliaments in this respect in the Lisbon Treaty.[143] Subsequent practice has shown that justice issues may trigger broad subsidiarity concerns.[144] In addition, the new guidelines of the European Council for the AFSJ are more general than before and the first subsequent annual work programme of the Commission outlines a slimmer legislative agenda emphasising that the EU should focus on 'big economic and social challenges' and interfere less on issues where the Member States are 'better equipped to give the right response at a national and regional level'.[145] This does not mean that there will be no development in civil justice in the coming years or that subsidiarity concerns will always have a significant impact on any future measures.[146] However, it demonstrates that there is at the very least more lip-service paid to regulatory concerns in general and more overt awareness of them. Also, thanks to the subsidiarity 'watchdog' mechanism, an additional actor in the form of national parliaments may come to impact more directly on the EU development of civil justice.

In connection with subsidiarity and proportionality, a more searching and active approach to governance in the justice field may be valuable. This would include such questions as which stakeholders are involved in the consultation processes? Are dialogues on best practices, networks and training a better way of achieving measures, mutual trust and harmonisation or are they a necessary complementary tool? The role of measures to support legislative measures should be further considered[147] and the actors in the civil justice arena should not be forgotten. It is still not clear that all the actors in

143 Articles 5 and 12 TEU and Protocol (No 1) to the TEU and the TFEU.

144 So far subsidiarity concerns have formally only been raised in the criminal justice field in relation to the proposal for a Regulation on the establishment of a European Public Prosecutor's Office, see, inter alia, COM(2014) 506 final, 5 August 2014, Annual Report 2013 on Subsidiarity and Proportionality, pp. 8–10.

145 COM(2014) 910 final, 16 December 2014, p. 2.

146 However, the initial justice focus of the Commission appears to not have a strong civil justice element, see ibid., pp. 9–10.

147 See H. Hartnell, 'EUstitia: institutionalising justice in the European Union' (2002) *Northwestern Journal of International Law and Business* 65; Storskrubb, supra note 6, pp. 233–255, in relation to the use of networks and other structures to support civil justice.

all Member States are even aware of the measures that have been enacted so far.[148] Addressing the information deficit should improve usage and implementation as well as subsequently enable a deeper and empirically based discussion on next steps.

3.2 *Mutual trust and common procedural standards*

Many of the policy documents on civil justice and in particular the Stockholm Programme refer to 'mutual trust'. It was even stated in the Stockholm Programme that '[e]nsuring trust and finding new ways to increase reliance on, and mutual understanding between, the different legal systems in the Member State will be one of the main challenges for the future'.[149] In addition, the unnamed guidelines that provide the current overriding political impetus also refer to mutual trust and state that 'mutual trust in one another's justice systems should be further enhanced'.[150] The discussion on mutual trust has arisen in the AFSJ and particularly in the civil justice context in connection with the so-called abolition of *exequatur*, i.e., in the debate on whether and how far we can remove certification procedures and safeguards in cross-border recognition of judgments.[151] Mutual trust has thus been propagated as a necessary adjunct to mutual recognition of judgments and the ever-closer judicial cooperation across borders. However, it is significant to note that the Member States were not prepared to remove safeguards or grounds for refusal in the recent reform and recast of the Brussels I Regulation.[152] It is also notable that mutual trust appears most difficult and sensitive in respect of the guarantee of fundamental rights and potential breaches thereof.[153] The first difficult cases heard by the CJEU in the AFSJ context on mutual recognition, including civil justice cases, show that mutual

148 See, inter alia, Report, supra note 126, paras 3.46–3.47.

149 Supra note 1, p. 5. On the emergence of mutual trust as a concept in civil justice see E. Storskrubb, 'Mutual trust and the limits of abolishing *exequatur*' in E. Brouwer and D. Gerard (eds.), *Mapping Mutual Trust: Understanding and Informing the Role of Mutual Trust in EU Law*, EUI Working Paper MWP x/2016, pp. 19–26. See also M. Weller, 'Mutual trust: in search of the future of European Union private international law' (2015) *Journal of Private International Law*.

150 Supra note 2, p. 5.

151 See, inter alia, M. Requejo Isidro, 'On the abolition of the *exequatur*', and M. Linton, 'Abolition of *exequatur*, all in the name of mutual trust', both in B. Hess, M. Bergström and E. Storskrubb (eds.), *EU Civil Justice: Current Issues and Future Outlook, Swedish Studies in European Law, Vol 7* (Hart Publishing, 2016). See also X. Kramer, 'Cross-border enforcement and the Brussels I-bis Regulation: towards and new balance between mutual trust and national control over fundamental rights' (2013) *Netherlands International Law Review* 343.

152 See Kramer, supra note 151, pp. 367–370 for a review of the new enforcement provisions and the balance between the rights of the creditor and debtor.

153 Ibid., pp. 364–367. See also Requejo Isidro and Linton, supra note 151, which both discuss the difficult cases that have arisen in the family law context.

trust and the upholding of fundamental rights is often presumed.[154] This blind trust, also called the 'systematic approach' to mutual trust, is premised on the assumption that all Member States are capable of providing effective protection of fundamental rights on an institutional level.[155]

Arguably, this presumption should be rebuttable and mutual trust should instead be linked to actual and true protection of fundamental rights in the singular case; otherwise the system can quickly serve to feed distrust instead of trust.[156] These brief observations serve to underline that mutual trust should not simply be presumed in the EU and cannot be a panacea that solves the difficult questions in the AFSJ. Mutual trust can logically not be imposed in a top-down manner, nor be created by force. It is nevertheless logical that mutual trust and a mutual vision as mentioned above are important for any future harmonisation. It is also possible that harmonisation is seen as a complement to and tool for achieving or supporting mutual recognition and mutual trust.[157] Thus, even the sovereignty-sensitive policy areas of the AFSJ may come under harmonisation pressures. Harmonisation or approximation may be more desirable to Member States once they come to realise that mutual recognition in itself entails a significant loss of sovereignty and reconfigures it.[158]

The Commission has also stated that mutual trust requires mutual minimum standards and an understanding of the different legal (procedural) traditions in Europe. Under the Stockholm Programme, the Commission thus envisaged a consultation process on minimum standards for civil procedure.[159] No such consultation took place towards the end of the period of the Stockholm Programme and the new political climate of limited guidelines for the AFSJ with a streamlined Commission agenda perhaps make it less likely that such a project will progress quickly. However, this may not in itself be a negative

154 Ibid. See also Mitsilegas, supra note 4. See, however, M. Moraru, in E. Brouwer and D. Gerard (eds), *Mapping Mutual Trust: Understanding and Informing the Role of Mutual Trust in EU Law*, EUI Working Paper MWP13/2016 on the strategies of national courts.

155 Mitsilegas, supra note 4, pp. 353–355. See also Opinion 2/13, ECLI:EU:C:2014:2454, para 191–192; K. Lenaerts, 'The principle of mutual recognition in the Area of Freedom, Security and Justice', http://1exagu1grkmq3k572418odoooym.wpengine.netdna-cdn.com/wp-content/uploads/2015/02/The-Principle-of-Mutual-Recognition-in-the-area-of-Freedom-Security-and-Justice.pdf.

156 Mitsilegas, supra note 4, pp. 355–359; V. Mitsilegas, 'Conceptualising mutual trust in European criminal law: the evolving relationship between legal pluralism and rights-based justice in the European Union', in E. Brouwer and D. Gerard (eds.), *Mapping Mutual Trust: Understanding and Informing the Role of Mutual Trust in EU Law*, EUI Working Paper MWP13/2016. See aslo the most recent case law, joined Cases C-404/15 and C-659/15 PPU *Aranyosi* and *Căldăraru* ECLI:EU:C:2016:198.

157 See E. Storskrubb, 'Mutual recognition as a governance strategy for civil justice?' in B. Hess, M. Bergström and E. Storskrubb (eds.), *EU Civil Justice: Current Issues and Future Outlook, Swedish Studies in European Law, Vol 7* (Hart Publishing, 2016) 315.

158 Ibid.

159 COM(2010)171 final, Action Plan Implementing the Stockholm Programme, pp. 22f.

matter. A top-down led project to develop an understanding of the procedural systems and traditions may not be the only way forward. It is notable that several commentators in the civil justice field have also called for renewed work on the future of civil justice in Europe at this juncture.[160] In the words of Kramer: 'What is the overall architectural plan for European Civil Procedure? Where do we want to go?'[161] and in the words of Hess 'what shall be achieved, what should be avoided, which improvements are necessary?'.[162] The collaborative research project between the European Law Institute (ELI) and UNIDROIT on European Principles of Civil Procedure[163] that commenced in 2014, may be an example of a 'soft governance' project that can provide the platform for a debate among experts, practitioners and users across Europe to truly identify best practices and a solid basis for future reform. The European Parliament's Legal Affairs Committee decided in the spring of 2015 to prepare its own report on the project and has started its own debate on the need for minimum or common standards in civil procedure.[164] Also, the Commission in June 2015 published a call for a study on national procedural laws and practices.[165] Thus, there are several levels of study and debate in progress that can hopefully contribute to the debate on a broader regulatory strategy and indeed the need for common procedural rules in Europe.

3.3 *Efficient justice systems*

Finally, fairly recently the EU has become an actor in the broader justice field. Since 2013, the Commission has published annual so-called Justice Scoreboards.[166] These comprise data collected by the Council of Europe and its European Commission for the Efficiency of Justice (CEPEJ) as well as information published by the World Bank, the World Economic Forum and the World Justice Project on the functioning of the justice systems in the Member States.[167] For the two latest Justice Scoreboards, the Commission

160 See Hess, supra note 130, pp. 171f, for a recent call for debate.

161 Kramer, supra note 140, pp. 26–28.

162 Hess, supra note 10.

163 See project description at www.europeanlawinstitute.eu/projects/current-projects-contd/article/from-transnational-principles-to-european-rules-of-civil-procedure/?tx_ttnews%5BbackPid%5D=137874&cHash=30981e5bc9618fbff47b45f915463642 (accessed on 25 May 2016).

164 See information on hearing before the European Parliament Legal Affairs Committee on 15 June 2015, www.europarl.europa.eu/committees/en/juri/events-hearings.html?id=20150615CHE00181 (accessed on 25 May 2016).

165 See http://ec.europa.eu/justice/newsroom/contracts/2015_s_104-188196_en.htm(accessed on 25 May 2016).

166 COM(2013) 160 final, COM(2014) 155 final, COM(2015) 116 final and COM(2016)199 final.

167 COM(2013) 160, p. 3. See in particular the website of the Commission on the Evaluation of Justice of the Council of Europe CEPJ, www.coe.int/t/dghl/cooperation/cepej/evaluation/default_en.asp (accessed on 26 June 2015).

has collected information in cooperation with the various European Judicial Networks and conducted its own pilot studies.[168] The Commission has also set up a group of contact persons on national justice systems including two contact points per Member State to provide information on best practices and on the effectiveness of the national judicial systems.[169] The Justice Scoreboards provide information on the length of proceedings, the case clearance rates and the number of pending cases in Member State courts in civil and administrative matters. They also focus on the monitoring and evaluation of courts: the ICT systems in courts, ADR possibilities and training of judges, as well as the perceived independence of the justice systems. For the first Scoreboard, the Commission organised a high-level conference of stakeholders for joint reflection. As such, this kind of information-gathering appears important and useful for the further work of the EU in civil justice, to gain more insight into the realities of the national procedural systems, thereby also strengthening mutual trust.

It is apparent that the Scoreboards help the Commission to make country-specific recommendations for reform in discussion and dialogue with the Member States. They also form the basis for Council recommendations and for allocations of support for Member State efforts to improve their justice systems via the EU Structural and Investment Funds.[170] These EU efforts to support Member States to improve their domestic justice systems are justified in the Scoreboard by stating that effective justice systems support investment and sustainable growth as well as provide stability for the business environment. Further, the effectiveness of the domestic justice systems is, according to the Commission, essential for the internal market.[171] Thus, the internal market and a drive towards efficiency also emerge as important factors behind the Scoreboard project. However, the constitutional mandate of the EU to engage with and have an impact upon the justice systems of particular Member States, in a potentially significant manner, appears unclear based on the analysis above (Section 2). Equally, can the beneficiaries of this support, the Member States, also legitimately maintain a strict view on the cross-border limitation on the remit of EU action? Is it logical to accept that the EU has an impact on or makes recommendations for a domestic justice system but not to accept harmonisation of procedural rules?

It will be interesting to gauge in the future what impact this support will have on justice in Europe. As the Commission has noted, many Member States are in the process of enacting reforms or instituting changes to

168 See COM(2014) 155, pp. 3 and 27. The networks include the European Network of the Council of the Judiciaries; the Network of the Presidents of the Supreme Judicial Court of the EU and the Association of the Councils of the State and Supreme Administrative Jurisdictions as well as other association of legal practitioners.

169 COM(2015) 116, p. 4.

170 COM(2014) 155 p. 6; COM(2015) 116 p. 4.

171 See, inter alia, COM(2013) 160, pp. 1–2.

modernise their justice systems.[172] How potential dialogue or structural support within the Justice Scoreboard project can impact on the substance of these reforms remains undocumented. It would be desirable that there is further transparency in relation to such impact.[173] There is a possibility that such dialogue will constitute one step in forming a mutual vision in the EU of how an efficient justice system is built, even though the Commission, of course, has stated that the project should respect the different legal traditions of the Member States. If that is the case, the Justice Scoreboards may even have nigh revolutionary potential. As noted above, to simply harmonise rules may not be enough or indeed the relevant first step if the procedural systems and structures remain diverse and if the vision of justice is idiosyncratic.

4 Concluding reflections

Based on the review in this chapter, it is apparent that 'civil justice' in the EU is an evolving and dynamic concept. I have hitherto used the term 'civil justice' to denote the generic procedural regulation under Article 81 TFEU with the context of the AFSJ.[174] However, based on the views presented above in Sections 2.4 and 3, this development should not be isolated from the sector-specific development or from the other ongoing developments, such as Justice Scoreboards. Thus, 'civil justice' is a living landscape and might in a broader sense be considered to encompass all developments that *de facto* impact on civil procedure. Based on the analysis of this chapter, it is also apparent that EU 'civil justice' is still in its infancy and although we have progressed from its embryonic beginnings, we have not reached its mature or grown-up form.[175] The development so far can be called constitutionally incoherent, and the reality is fragmented and complex for relevant actors such as national judges and national courts. Furthermore, several strands of procedural development now taking place in the EU point to deeper integration or potential harmonisation, be it the context of civil justice, sector-specific measures or the potential 'soft' impact. And researchers and various EU institutions have begun to really engage in a debate on future common procedural rules in Europe. At this junction and juncture, the EU suddenly appears to have an excellent vantage point and an opportunity to seriously embark upon a regulatory debate encompassing all strands. Stand

172 COM(2015) 116, p. 3; COM(2016) 199, p. 3.

173 For analysis in relation to the limits of data of the Scoreboards and transparency issues, see A. Dori, *The EU Justice Scoreboard: Judicial Evaluation as a New Governance Tool*, MPILux Working Paper Series 2 (2015), pp. 24–28; E. Storskrubb, 'Några tankar om hur EU-rättens tentakler genomtränger processrätten' (forthcoming).

174 See supra note 3.

175 See X. Kramer, 'European procedures on debt collection: nothing or noting? Experiences and future prospects', in B. Hess, M. Bergström and E. Storskrubb (eds.), *EU Civil Justice: Current Issues and Future Outlook, Swedish Studies in European Law, Vol 7* (Hart Publishing, 2016) 120 and Crifò, supra note 122.

back, look at the full panoply and find the most appropriate regulatory strategy to go forward. Otherwise there is a risk that the development will remain disparate, without direction and not be supported.

That there are competing pressures behind civil justice is partly an old phenomenon but it appears now in new guise or with renewed force, i.e., competition between the quest for efficiency, the quest for mutual trust and the need for safeguarding fundamental procedural rights.[176] These alternative pressures are also evident in that procedural development in the EU is partly taking place under the aegis of the AFSJ and partly under the banner of the internal market as demonstrated above. In addition, in the financial crisis some policy documents referred to 'justice for growth', thus clearly combining civil justice to market efficiency.[177] Nevertheless, since Lisbon, the EU has had a new constitutional setting in light of which the balance between these pressures and how they are resolved needs to be critically reviewed. Efficiency can arguably not be the sole driver behind mutual trust and mutual recognition when fundamental rights are at stake. Thus, some regulatory choices taken may need to be revisited in order for blind trust to be replaced with binding trust. The protection of fundamental procedural rights must be the paramount driver of a justice system and behind procedural rules, even when these are enacted to support the internal market.

When we hopefully strive forward with more purpose towards coherence and increased regulatory awareness and debate in civil justice, another facet to be remembered is that of the justice system as a whole. Both the domestic justice systems and, at the EU level, the AFSJ consist of different parts that can, for example, be characterised as civil, criminal and administrative. Developments in one part of a justice system may impact on or provide a useful example for another part of the system. Therefore, there should be more overlapping debates and more coordination at the EU level where relevant. This chapter has hopefully highlighted some challenges that may be compared and contrasted to, for example, criminal justice cooperation in the EU.

Finally, this chapter calls for a regulatory debate and strategy. The justice community at large has its own responsibility to engage in the process and in the debate at the different levels available to it. Let's grasp the nettle!

176 Storskrubb, supra note 6, pp. 278–284.
177 Hess, supra note 10.

13 Multiple faces of mutual recognition

Unity and diversity in regulating enforcement of judgments in the European Union

Vesna Lazić

1 Introduction

The area of private law was largely omitted from the 1957 Treaty on the European Economic Community (Treaty of Rome), whose major objective was the establishment of a common internal market. Yet, the harmonisation of private law rules appeared useful. In order to enhance the process of creating a common market where a free movement of goods, services, persons and capital was to be ensured, efforts have been made to harmonise substantive and private international law rules on the Community level. On the basis of Article 220 EEC Treaty,[1] a number of legal instruments were adopted in the area of private international law, in particular the 1968 Brussels Convention on Jurisdiction and the Enforcement of Judgments in Civil and Commercial Matters[2] and the 1980 Rome Convention on the Law Applicable to Contractual Obligations.[3]

Divergences in legal regulation of civil law matters among the Member States, as well as difficulties in their unification and approximation, further increased the relevance of unifying private international law issues on the EC level. Under the 1992 Treaty of Maastricht 'judicial cooperation' was put in the so-called 'third pillar' of the EU's architecture. Within that framework, a number of conventions were negotiated,[4] but none of them came into force

1 Several of the issues mentioned in Article 220 EEC Treaty are relevant for cross-border aspects of private law, such as the enjoyment and protection of rights under the same conditions as accorded to own nationals of the Member State, the mutual recognition of companies or firms and the retention of legal personality in the event of transfer of seat from one country to another, and the simplification of formalities concerning the reciprocal recognition and enforcement of judgments of courts or tribunals or of arbitration awards.

2 1968 Brussels Convention on Jurisdiction and the Enforcement of Judgments in Civil and Commercial Matters of 27 September 1968, OJ L 299, 31 December 1972, pp. 32–42.

3 Convention on the Law Applicable to Contractual Obligations of 19 June 1980, OJ L 266, 9 October 1980, pp. 1–19.

4 See, for example, the Convention on the Service in the Member States of the European Union of Judicial and Extrajudicial Documents in Civil or Commercial Matters of 26 May 1997

by the time another amendment of the EU Treaties entered into force in 1999. Indeed, the Treaty of Amsterdam not only conferred powers on the EU to adopt legislation on issues of jurisdiction, mutual recognition and enforcement of judgments rendered by the courts in the EU Member States, but it also conferred powers to address questions of conflict of laws and, more generally, judicial cooperation in civil matters. Article 81 TFEU presents the current legal basis for unifying certain aspects of international civil procedure and, more generally, of private international law on the EU level.

In pursuing the objective of maintaining and developing an Area of Freedom, Security and Justice, the EU legislator has undertaken significant action in unifying rules of private international law. A major part of the unification in that area of law concerns international civil procedure. The EU legislator attaches particular importance to the principle of mutual recognition and free circulation of judgments rendered by courts in the Member States. Within the AFSJ context, this principle was first endorsed at the European Council Meeting at Tampere on 15 and 16 October 1999 and is now enshrined in the Treaty on the Functioning of the EU. With a view to achieving it, the Council and the Commission have adopted a number of legislative acts that unify not only the conditions for mutual recognition of judgments, but also rules on international jurisdiction, as well as certain aspects of civil procedure. Besides, various legal instruments have been adopted with the purpose of generally enhancing judicial cooperation[5] and access to justice. These include legislative acts, the purpose of which is to facilitate the use of out-of-court dispute settlement mechanisms.[6]

In regulating private international law aspects in civil and commercial matters, there is a diversity of approaches, as well as a disparity of legal instruments. Thus, some of the unified rules cover a wide range of 'civil and

and the Convention on Jurisdiction and the Recognition and Enforcement of Judgments in Matrimonial Matters of 28 May 1998 (Brussels II Convention) and the Protocol on its interpretation by the Court of Justice (OJ C 221 of 16 July 1998).

5 See, for example, Council Regulation (EC) No 1206/2001 of 28 May 2001 on cooperation between the courts of the Member States in the taking of evidence in civil or commercial matters; Regulation (EC) No 1393/2007 of the European Parliament and of the Council of 13 November 2007 on the service in the Member States of judicial and extrajudicial documents in civil or commercial matters (service of documents), and repealing Council Regulation (EC) No 1348/2000. On the perception of ADR as a mechanism to enhance the internal market, see M. Stürner, 'ADR and Adjudication by State Courts: Competitors or Complements?', GPR 3/2014, Sellier European Law Publisher, p. 122.

6 See, for example, Directive 2008/52/EC of the European Parliament and of the Council of 21 May 2008 on certain aspects of mediation in civil and commercial matters; Directive 2013/11/EU of the European Parliament and of the Council of 21 May 2013 on the alternative dispute resolution for consumer disputes and amending Regulation (EC) No 2006/2004 and Directive 2009/22/EC; Regulation (EU) No 524/2013 of the European Parliament and of the Council of 21 May 2013 on online dispute resolution for consumer disputes and amending Regulation (EC) No 2006/2004 and Directive 2009/22/EC.

commercial' matters,[7] whereas others focus on one[8] or a rather a limited number of subject-matters in the area of private law.[9] Thereby, some of them – and particularly those recently adopted – unify all private international law issues,[10] whereas others include only unification of rules on certain aspects of civil procedure and the enforcement of judgments.[11] Just a few legal instruments deal only with the applicable law.[12] Yet the largest number of legislative

7 See, for example, Council Regulation (EC) No 44/2001 of 22 December 2000 on jurisdiction and the recognition and enforcement of judgments in civil and commercial matters (hereinafter: Regulation Brussels I) as revised in Regulation (EU) No 1215/2012 of the European Parliament and of the Council of 12 December 2012 on jurisdiction and the recognition and enforcement of judgments in civil and commercial matters (recast), OJ L 351, as amended by Regulation No 542/2014, which applies on litigations commenced on and after 10 January 2015 (hereinafter: Regulation Brussels Ibis or Regulation 1215/2012).

8 See, for example, Council Regulation (EC) No 4/2009 of 18 December 2008 on jurisdiction, applicable law, recognition and enforcement of decisions and cooperation in matters relating to maintenance obligations (protocol does not apply in the UK) (hereinafter: Maintenance Regulation); Regulation (EU) No 650/2012 of the European Parliament and of the Council of 4 July 2012 on jurisdiction, applicable law, recognition and enforcement of decisions and acceptance and enforcement of authentic instruments in matters of succession and on the creation of a European Certificate of Succession (OJ L 201 of 27 July 2012) – in force as of 17 August 2014 (does not apply in Denmark and UK) (hereinafter: Regulation on Wills and Succession).

9 Council Regulation (EC) No 2201/2003 of 27 November 2003 concerning jurisdiction and the recognition and enforcement of judgments in matrimonial matters and the matters of parental responsibility, repealing Regulation (EC) No 1347/2000 (hereinafter: Regulation Brussels IIa or Brussels IIbis).

10 See, for example, Maintenance Regulation and Regulation on Wills and Succession.

11 See, for example, Regulation (EC) No 861/2007 of the European Parliament and of the Council of 11 July 2007 establishing a European Small Claims Procedure as amended in Regulation (EU) 2015/2421 of the European Parliament and of the Council of 16 December 2015 amending Regulation (EC) No 861/2007 establishing a European Small Claims Procedure and Regulation (EC) No 1896/2006 creating a European order for payment procedure OJ of 24 December 2015, OJ L 341 of 24 December 2015, p. 1, which will apply as from 14 July 2017 (hereinafter: Regulation on Small Claims Procedure); Regulation (EC) No 1896/2006 of the European Parliament and of the Council of 12 December 2006 creating a European order for payment procedure, OJ L 399, 30 December 2006, pp. 1–32 as amended in Regulation (EU) 2015/2421 of the European Parliament and of the Council of 16 December 2015 amending Regulation (EC) No 861/2007 establishing a European Small Claims Procedure and Regulation (EC) No 1896/2006 creating a European order for payment procedure OJ of 24 December 2015, OJ L 341 of 24 December 2015, p. 1, which will apply as from 14 July 2017 (hereinafter: Regulation on European Payment Order).

12 There are only three private international law instruments of the EU legislator that regulate exclusively conflict of law rules: Regulation (EC) No 864/2007 of the European Parliament and of the Council of 11 July 2007 on the law applicable to non-contractual obligations (hereinafter: Regulation Rome II), Regulation (EC) No 593/2008 of the European Parliament and of the Council of 17 June 2008 on the law applicable to contractual obligations (hereinafter: Regulation Rome I) and Council Regulation (EU) No 1259/2010 of 20 December 2010 implementing enhanced cooperation in the area of the law applicable to divorce and legal separation (hereinafter: Rome III).

acts limits its scope to issues of jurisdiction and recognition and/or enforcement of decisions.[13]

Such diversity in unifying private international law issues in combination with insufficiently precise definitions of the scope of application may cause difficulties for national courts that are seised to apply such legal instruments. Particularly challenging may prove an attempt to draw the lines of the substantive scope of application among various unified private international law rules. Case law of the CJEU concerning the scope of application of the Insolvency Regulation and other legal sources, in particular the regime of Brussels I or Brussels Ibis, is illustrative.[14] The cause of the difficulty may be found in the fact that the Insolvency Regulation only provides for the rule on jurisdiction to open insolvency proceedings, but does not define the extent of jurisdiction of that court. The recently revised Insolvency Regulation[15] attempts to remedy this shortcoming by clarifying the scope of jurisdiction of the courts opening insolvency proceedings.[16]

This chapter will focus specifically on the different approaches employed by the EU legislator when unifying the rules in the area of the enforcement and recognition of judgments. It examines whether such diversity in legal regulation is justified (Section 2) and how it reflects on the level of legal protection for certain parties in different legal instruments (Section 3). With respect to the latter point, the different regimes under the Regulation Brussels I and Brussels Ibis, Regulations European Enforcement Order,[17] European Payment Order[18] and Small Claims Procedure are analysed. Thereafter some conclusions are drawn and the possibilities for achieving a greater degree of uniformity are considered (Section 4).

13 Regulations Brussels I and Brussels Ibis; Regulation Brussels IIbis.

14 See, for example, Case C-292/08 *German Graphics Graphische Maschinen* [2009] ECR I-08421 and Case C-157/13 *Nickel & Goeldner Spedition* judgment of 4 September 2014.

15 Regulation EU 2015/848 of the European Parliament and of the Council of 20 May 2015 on insolvency proceedings (recast) OJ L 141/19 (hereinafter: Insolvency Regulation Recast)

16 Article 6 paragraph 1 and recital 35 of the Insolvency Regulation Recast. It is yet to be seen whether the revised text would successfully deal with the problem. However, the wording 'action which derives directly from the insolvency proceedings and is closely linked with them, such as avoidance actions' is too broad and insufficiently precise, and as such is likely to cause difficulties in application. Regrettably the chance was missed to more clearly define the scope of jurisdiction of the court where insolvency proceedings are opened.

17 Regulation (EC) No 805/2004 of the European Parliament and of the Council of 21 April 2004 creating a European Enforcement Order for uncontested claims, OJ L 143, 30 April 2004, pp. 5–39 (hereinafter: Regulation European Enforcement Order).

18 Regulation (EC) No 1896/2006 of the European Parliament and of the Council of 12 December 2006 creating a European order for payment procedure, OJ L 399, 30 December 2006, pp. 1–32 (Regulation European Payment Order).

2 Unifying the rules on recognition and enforcement of decisions rendered by the courts of the EU Member States

2.1 General remarks

Mutual recognition has been and remains the ordering principle and the incentive for the unification of private international law rules of the Member States. It was the underlying idea of the 1968 Brussels Convention, the first legal instrument that unified certain rules of private international law in the European Community. The Convention was the result of efforts to ensure a free circulation of judgments rendered by courts of the Member States, sometimes referred to as 'fifth freedom'. Since the Treaty of Amsterdam, mutual recognition and the related concept of 'mutual trust' has squarely underpinned legislative actions in unifying and simplifying the conditions for the enforcement of judgments. Thus, when revising the Regulation Brussels I,[19] the Commission justified its suggestion to abolish the *exequatur* by referring to the mature level of trust among Member States.

In some EU legal measures, rules on recognition and enforcement are unified together with the rules on jurisdiction.[20] On the other hand, there are a number of regulations that do not specifically unify the rules on jurisdiction, but instead regulate the questions of the enforcement of judgments, either exclusively or in combination with the unification of other rules of civil procedure. The underlying purpose is to create conditions for enforcement without '*exequatur*' either by providing for the so-called minimum standards that have to be fulfilled[21] or by unifying the rules for conduct of proceedings.[22]

Yet, in pursuing the principle of mutual recognition, no uniform approach has been employed when drafting various regulatory schemes. In some legal instruments, a declaration of enforceability (*exequatur*) in the country of enforcement is required to enforce a judgment rendered by the court of another EU Member State (see Section 2.2). In others, especially those recently enacted or revised, no *exequatur* is necessary (see Section 2.3). However, although the *exequatur* in all of them is formally abolished, the possibilities to oppose the enforcement differ substantially across the various legal instruments. The present chapter discusses how such diversity of approaches may result in differences in legal protection of the so-called 'weaker parties' (Section 3).

19 Council Regulation (EC) No 44/2001 of 22 December 2000 on jurisdiction and the recognition and enforcement of judgments in civil and commercial matters, OJ 2001 L 12 (hereinafter: Regulation Brussels I).

20 This is so in Regulation Brussels I, Regulation Brussels Ibis, Regulation Brussels IIbis, Maintenance Regulation, Regulation on Wills and Succession and Insolvency Regulation Recast.

21 This is provided under the Regulation European Enforcement Order.

22 For example, the Regulation on European Payment Order and Regulation on European Small Claims Procedure.

2.2 *Enforcement regimes in legislative instruments requiring* exequatur

Enforcement is still subject to *exequatur* under a number of legal instruments, such as the Brussels I[23] and the Regulation on Wills and Succession.[24] The same holds true under the Regulation Brussels IIbis in some cases of recognition of divorces and the enforcement of decisions relating to parental responsibility.[25] Judgments in cases of maintenance are enforced according to the Regulation 4/2009,[26] in which the *exequatur* is abolished. However, as the United Kingdom and Denmark[27] have not adhered to the Hague Protocol on the applicable law,[28] maintenance judgments in and from these two Member States are enforceable under the rules contained in Section 2, which are formulated along the lines of the Regulation Brussels I.

Legal instruments requiring *exequatur* maintain a comparable regime for the recognition and enforcement of judgments rendered by the courts of EU Member States. As to recognition arising as a preliminary or incidental issue, no special procedure is required. If the recognition has been requested in litigation pending before a court of a Member State, the court before which the litigation is pending will decide on an incidental question of recognition whereby no special procedure applies. In other words, if the outcome of the main proceeding depends on determining an issue with respect to which a judgment has already been rendered in another Member State, the court in front of which the litigation is pending will decide on the incidental question

23 Council Regulation (EC) No 44/2001 of 22 December 2000 on jurisdiction and the recognition and enforcement of judgments in civil and commercial matters, OJ 2001 L 12 (all Member States, including Denmark).

24 Regulation (EU) No 650/2012 of the European Parliament and of the Council of 4 July 2012 on jurisdiction, applicable law, recognition and enforcement of decisions and acceptance and enforcement of authentic instruments in matters of succession and on the creation of a European Certificate of Succession, OJ 2012 L 20 (Denmark and the United Kingdom are not bound by it).

25 Council Regulation (EC) No 2201/2003 of 27 November 2003 concerning jurisdiction and recognition and enforcement of judgments in matrimonial matters and the matters of parental responsibility, repealing Regulation (EC) No 1347/2000, OJ 2003 L 338. The provisions on the enforcement requiring *exequatur* relate to judgments on divorce and parental responsibility. However, this enforcement regime does not cover decisions relating to the right to contact, and orders for return of a child rendered by the court of the habitual residence of the child before wrongful removal or retention. These decisions are enforced under the special regime provided for in Chapter 4 of the Regulation.

26 Council Regulation (EC) No 4/2009 of 18 December 2008 on jurisdiction, applicable law, recognition and enforcement of decisions and cooperation in matters relating to maintenance obligations.

27 In accordance with Article 3(2) of the Agreement of 19 October 2005 between the European Community and the Kingdom of Denmark on jurisdiction and the recognition and enforcement of judgments in civil and commercial matters, concluded by Council Decision 2006/325/EC. Denmark has already, by letter of 14 January 2009, notified the Commission of its decision to implement the content of Maintenance Regulation to the extent that it amends Regulation Brussels I.

28 Hague Protocol of 23 November 2007 on the Law Applicable to Maintenance Obligations.

of recognition of that judgment.[29] However, such decision will be binding only in the proceeding for the purposes of which the decision on the recognition is brought.

If the recognition is requested as a principal issue, then the procedure for the enforcement is applicable. A judgment or other decision of the court or other authority in a Member State may be enforced in another Member State after obtaining a declaration of enforceability.[30] In principle, such a declaration is given automatically with no possibility of raising an objection to it or invoking grounds for refusal of the enforcement at this stage. Only after the declaration has been issued may the debtor oppose the enforcement by invoking, usually, a rather limited number of grounds; public policy, violations of due process and the existence of irreconcilable judgments. Only exceptionally may the judgment be refused enforcement when the rules on jurisdiction of the Regulation are violated.[31] Save upon the grounds expressly mentioned,[32] the jurisdiction of the court of a Member State of origin may not be reviewed. The test of public policy may not be applied to the rules relating to jurisdiction.[33]

Moreover, in the view of the CJEU, the grounds for refusal of enforcement must be interpreted restrictively 'inasmuch as it constitutes an obstacle to the attainment of one of the fundamental objectives' of a particular legal instrument.[34] This is especially so as far as the public policy exception is concerned under the enforcement regime of the Regulation Brussels I. The judgment in *Renault/Maxicar*[35] illustrates this point well. In the decision rendered by a French court, the defendant was found guilty of forgery for having manufactured and marketed body parts for Renault vehicles and a declaration of enforceability was requested in Italy on the basis of the 1968 Brussels Convention. The defendant opposed the enforcement in Italy on the basis that it was irreconcilable with a decision given in a dispute between the same parties in Italy and was contrary to public policy in economic matters. The latter allegation concerned a possible violation of EU competition rules. The CJEU emphasised that the public policy exception had to be interpreted

29 Article 33 para 3, Regulation Brussels I.

30 Under Regulation Brussels I, it is the procedure provided in Articles 41 and 42. The provisions relevant for procedure for obtaining *exequatur*, jurisdiction and procedure after the declaration has been obtained are contained in Articles 38–52.

31 See, for example, Article 35 Regulation Brussels I, according to which the recognition and enforcement may be refused if the rules on exclusive jurisdiction are violated, as well as the jurisdictional rules relating to certain 'weaker parties', such as consumers and insured or insurance policy-holder.

32 See, for example, Article 45 para 1(e) Regulation Brussels Ibis.

33 Article 45 para 3 Regulation Brussels Ibis.

34 See C-38/98, *Renault v Maxicar and Formento* [2000] ECR I-2973, para 26. See also, C-414/92 *Solo Kleinmotoren* [1994] ECR I-2237, para 20, and Case C-7/98 *Krombach* [2000] ECR I-1935, para 21.

35 *Renault/Maxicar*.

restrictively and could be relied upon only in exceptional cases.[36] In the view of the CJEU 'a discrepancy between the legal rule applied by the court of the State of origin and that which would have been applied by the court of the State in which the enforcement is sought had it been seised of the dispute, cannot qualify as a ground for refusal of the enforcement' and 'the court of the State in which enforcement is sought cannot review the accuracy of the findings of law or fact made by the court of the State of origin'.[37] The fact that a court in a Member State of enforcement considers that the court misapplied national or EU law cannot be a valid reason to refuse the enforcement,[38] as long as an error in law does not constitute 'a manifest breach of rule of law regarded as essential in the legal order of the State in which enforcement is sought'.[39] The CJEU concluded that:

> a judgment of a court or tribunal of a Contracting State recognizing the existence of an intellectual property right in body parts for cars, and conferring on the holder of that right protection by enabling him to prevent third parties trading in another Contracting State from manufacturing, selling, transporting, importing or exporting in that Contracting State such body parts, cannot be considered to be contrary to public policy.

Lack of reasoning on the merits in a judgment given in the default of appearance may be a violation of public policy only if 'that judgment is a manifest and disproportionate breach of the defendant's right to a fair trial referred to in the second paragraph of Article 47 of the Charter, on account of the impossibility of bringing an appropriate and effective appeal against it'.[40]

It may be concluded that the legal instruments requiring for *exequatur* provide for a rather limited number of reasons for which the enforcement may be refused. In addition to that, the grounds must be interpreted restrictively so that the denial of enforcement occurs rather exceptionally.

2.3 Enforcement regimes in which exequatur *is abolished*

Whereas the grounds and procedure are rather similar in the legal instruments requiring *exequatur*, there is no uniform system of enforcement in those legislative acts where it is unnecessary to obtain a declaration of enforceability. In the latter scenario, formal proceedings for attaining enforcement are abolished so that a foreign judgment automatically has

36 Ibid., para 26. See also, C-145/86 *Hoffmann v Krieg* [1988] ECR 645, para 21; C-78/95 *Hendrikman and Feyen v Magenta Druck Sc Verlag* [1996] ECR 1-4943, para 23.

37 *Renault/Maxicar*, para 29. See also *Krombach*, para 36.

38 *Renault/Maxicar*, para 33.

39 Ibid.

40 C-619/10 *Trade Agency Ltd v Seramico Investments Ltd* judgment of 6 September 2012.

legal effects on the territory of the enforcing state.[41] This framework reflects the idea of mutual trust among Member States and the presumption that a foreign judgment should be enforced as if it was issued by the courts of the state where the enforcement is sought. However, this underlying idea of enhancing a level of mutual trust is not implemented and materialised in all EU private international law instruments in the same manner. Instead, there are different regimes of enforcement as well as diversity of grounds for which the enforcement may be refused among these Regulations.

Thus, in some legal acts no *exequatur* is required, but a party against whom the enforcement is sought still has the right to oppose the enforcement on certain grounds. This is particularly so under the 1214/2012 Regulation/ Regulation Brussels Ibis, where the party has the right to oppose the enforcement on almost the same grounds as under the Regulation Brussels I. The difference is in the procedure in which these grounds may be invoked. Thus, under the Regulation Brussels I, it was in appellate proceedings against the declaration of enforceability obtained in the enforcement procedure initiated by a party seeking enforcement. In contrast to that, under the Regulation Brussels Ibis, a party opposing the enforcement may initiate proceedings in which the reasons for refusing the enforcement may be invoked. The grounds or reasons justifying denial of enforcement are almost identical under both legal acts. The only difference is that the violation of the jurisdictional grounds in employment contracts are now expressly indicated among the reasons to oppose the enforcement under Article 45 of the Regulation Brussels Ibis. All other grounds are the same as those contained in Articles 34 and 35 of the Regulation Brussels I.[42]

Similarly, no *exequatur* is required under the Insolvency Regulation. A decision opening insolvency proceedings, as well as decisions brought by the same court in matters closely related to insolvency proceedings are recognised in other Member States whereby no special procedure is required. However, the recognition of such decisions may be refused if the recognition would be contrary to public policy in the Member State where the enforcement is sought.

Furthermore, Regulations on European Enforcement Order (EEO), Small Claims Procedure (ESCP) and European Payment Order (EPO) require no *exequatur* for the enforcement of the decisions rendered under conditions provided in these legal instruments. The enforcement may be refused only if there is an earlier irreconcilable judgment rendered in the Member State

41 See provision of Articles 1 and 5 of the Regulation European Enforcement Order, Articles 1 and 20 of the Regulation on Small Claims Procedure; Articles 1 and 19 of the Regulation European Payment Order indicating that the *exequatur* is abolished. The same holds true with respect to the Brussels Ibis, Maintenance Regulation and the recognition of decisions under Articles 41 and 42 of the Regulation Brussels IIbis.

42 The procedure for the refusal of enforcement is provided in Subsection 2 of Section 3 and Section 4.

of enforcement or rendered abroad but that fulfils the conditions for the enforcement. No other reasons may be invoked against the enforcement, not even the public policy exception. A rather similar regime of enforcement applies with respect to judgments under the Maintenance Regulation[43] for judgments rendered in those Member States that have ratified the 2007 Hague Protocol;[44] all EU Member States except Denmark and the United Kingdom. The latter has declared itself to be bound by the Maintenance Regulation, but has not ratified the 2007 Hague Protocol on the applicable law. Accordingly, judgments concerning maintenance obligations rendered in the United Kingdom will be enforceable in other EU Member States under the enforcement regime analysed in Section 2.2, which is comparable to the regime under Regulation Brussels I.[45]

Finally, the most favourable regime of enforcement is provided under Articles 41 and 42 of the Regulation Brussels IIbis on the return of child orders under Article 11(8) and on the access rights with virtually no possibility to oppose the enforcement. The only possibility exists under Article 47(2) when there is a subsequent enforceable conflicting decision rendered by the courts in the Member State of origin.[46]

3 Different standards in protecting interests of 'weaker parties' in EU private international law (PIL) instruments[47]

The EU legislator has been pursuing efforts to minimise the unequal bargaining position of parties in commercial legal relationships not only by harmonising substantive law of Member States, but also by unifying procedural and private international law rules. In essence, harmonised substantive law rules ensure that certain rights obtained in commercial legal transactions by dominant parties remain unenforceable against a 'weaker party', whereas from the point of view of procedural law, rules on jurisdiction are adjusted so as to protect the position of a weaker party in legal proceedings. Such protections had been incorporated in the 1968 Brussels Convention and were maintained in

43 Supra note 26.

44 Supra note 28.

45 Denmark is generally not bound by the Regulations on the civil procedure and more generally on private international law. The only exceptions are the Regulation Brussels I and the Service Regulation that became applicable on the basis of international conventions concluded between the European Union and Denmark. As already explained, supra note 24, Denmark submitted its declaration to be bound by certain provisions of the Maintenance Regulation that amend the Regulation Brussels I.

46 Clearly it must be a decision of the court in the Member State of origin and not of the court in the Member State where the enforcement is sought. See, Case C-211/10 PPU *Povse v Alpago* [2010] ECR I-6673, para 78.

47 This is partly based on research presented in an earlier publication: V. Lazić, 'Procedural justice for weaker parties in cross-border litigation under the EU Regulatory Scheme' (2014) 10 *Utrecht Law Review* 100.

the Regulation Brussels I. The legal framework under both legal instruments was adapted so as to ensure that any advantage presumed or achieved by a contracting party with a dominant bargaining position was to remain without legal entitlement and effect. Most importantly, it ensured that the procedural position of 'weak parties' was protected and that a violation of jurisdictional rules was sanctioned by a refusal to enforce a judgment rendered in such proceedings. A 'weaker party' in the EU private international law rules in civil and commercial matters refers to consumers, employees and insurance policy-holders or other beneficiaries under insurance contracts.[48]

The rules intended to protect the procedural position of 'weaker' parties under the Brussels I regime can be summarised as follows:

1 A weaker party – a policy-holder, the insured or a beneficiary, consumer or employee – has a choice to bring proceedings against the other party to a contract either in the court of the Member State in which that other party is domiciled or in another forum that is more convenient to a weaker party (most likely in the country of its own domicile) or that is otherwise closely related to dispute.
2 Conversely, proceedings may be brought against a weaker party to the contract only in the courts of the Member State in which a 'weaker' party is domiciled.
3 Forum selection clauses in these disputes have limited binding effect against a 'weaker' party. In other words, they may be successfully invoked against a weaker party only if the conditions provided in the relevant provisions of the Regulation are met.
4 Violation of the protective rules on jurisdiction presents the reason to refuse the enforcement of judgment rendered under Article 35 of the Regulation Brussels I and Article 45 Brussels Ibis. The latter provision is adjusted so as to expressly include judgments in employment disputes.

Interpretation of the rules on jurisdiction by the CJEU illustrates that the CJEU is inclined to maximise the protection of weaker parties. The legal reasoning in the relevant case law indicates that the CJEU gives prevalence to the higher degree of protection for consumers over the interests of commercial parties.[49]

48 The present contribution does not address other legal instruments harmonising or unifying substantive rules of private law aimed at protecting a party with a weaker bargaining position in certain legal relationships, such as agency and distributorship agreements.

49 See, for example, Case C-144/09 *Peter Pammer v Reederei Karl Schlüter GmbH & Co KG* [2010] ECR I-12527. Some authors have expressed their criticism of the 'high level of protection' given to consumers by this judgment. See C. Bisping, 'Mandatorily protected: the consumer in the European conflict of laws' (2014) 22 *European Review of Private Law* 513; D.J.B. Svantesson, '*Pammer* and *Hotel Alpenhof*: CJEU decision creates further uncertainty about when e-business "direct activities" to a consumer's state under the *Brussels I Regulation*' (2011) 27 *Computer Law & Security Review* 298. A number of subsequent CJEU judgments confirm the trend in ensuring the protection of consumers. See, for

Moreover, the idea of protecting the procedural position of 'weak' parties has been maintained and further developed in the Regulation Brussels Ibis. Most importantly, even though the *exequatur* is abolished under the revised Regulation, the grounds on which a party may apply for a refusal of recognition and enforcement have been retained in Article 45 and almost fully reflect the list of reasons provided in Articles 34 and 35 of the Regulation Brussels I. Just as under previous regulatory schemes, a violation of protective jurisdictional rules in disputes involving 'weak' parties presents one such ground justifying refusal of enforcement. The revised Regulation widens the list by expressly including disputes arising from individual contracts of employment. Such an expansion of the protective rules will be briefly outlined in Section 3.1.

However, in some other legal instruments, no such high degree of protection is provided with respect to procedural position of weaker parties, especially consumers. This holds true not only as far as issues of jurisdiction or other aspects of civil procedure are concerned, but also with respect to the regulatory regime for enforcement of judgments. Thus, the policy considerations and legal regulation aiming at the protection of procedural position of weaker parties in the Brussels I regime is not reflected in the same manner in the European Enforcement Order for uncontested claims,[50] European Order for Payment Procedure[51] and the Regulation on a European Small Claims Procedure.[52] Diversity in the level of protection in these legal sources will be addressed in Section 3.2.

3.1 Procedural position of 'weaker' parties under the Brussels I regime

The revised Brussel Ibis Regulation introduces a number of amendments that further enhance the degree of protection for weaker parties. Thus, the scope

example, Case C-190/11, *Daniela Mühlleitner v Ahmad Yusufi, Wadat Yusufi* judgment of 6 September 2012; Case C-218/12 *Lokman Emrek v Vlado Sabranovic* judgment of 17 October 2013.

50 Regulation (EC) No 805/2004 of the European Parliament and of the Council of 21 April 2004 creating a European Enforcement Order for uncontested claims, OJ L 143, 30 April 2004, pp. 5–39.

51 Regulation (EC) No 1896/2006 of the European Parliament and of the Council of 12 December 2006 creating a European order for payment procedure, OJ L 399, 30 December 2006, pp. 1–32.

52 Regulation (EC) No 861/2007 of the European Parliament and of the Council of 11 July 2007 establishing a European Small Claims Procedure, OJ L 199, 31 July 2007, pp. 1–22. The latter is currently the subject of revision – Proposal for a Regulation of the European Parliament and of the Council amending Regulation (EC) No 861/2007 of the European Parliament and of the Council of 11 July 2007 establishing a European Small Claims Procedure and Regulation (EC) No 1896/2006 of the European Parliament and of the Council of 12 December 2006 creating a European order for payment procedure of 19 November 2013, COM(2013) 794 final, 2003/0403(COD). The Commission's proposal suggests introducing some modifications, such as widening its scope, extending the definition of cross-border cases and improving the use of information technology.

of application *ratione personae* in disputes involving weaker parties has been expanded so as to enable certain categories of 'weaker' parties domiciled in the EU to rely on the protective procedural rules regardless of the domicile of the other party.[53] Consequently, a court in a Member State may establish its jurisdiction on the basis of the jurisdictional rules of the Brussels Ibis Regulation in all disputes involving a consumer or an employee regardless of the domicile of the other party. The provision of Article 6(1) refers only to consumer (Article 1(1)) and labour disputes (Article 21(2)), but there is no reference to insurance contracts. Consequently, these rules relating to insurance contracts only apply if a defendant is domiciled in an EU Member State.[54] The relevant provisions on jurisdiction in Article 18[55] relating to consumer contracts (Article 16 of the Brussels I Regulation) and Article 21[56] relating to contracts of employment (Article 19 of the Brussels I Regulation) have been adjusted so as to reflect the changes introduced to the territorial scope of application in Article 6 of the Recast.

Accordingly, the new regulatory scheme further enhances the protection of consumers and employees. In particular, such 'weaker parties' may rely on the rules on international jurisdiction in disputes against professionals and employees domiciled outside the European Union. On the other hand, the Regulation continues to apply only to claims against consumers and

53 The provision of Article 6(1) of the Recast Regulation (the current Article 4 of the Brussels I Regulation) reads as follows: '1. If the defendant is not domiciled in a Member State, the jurisdiction of the courts of each Member State shall, subject to Articles 18(1), 21(2) and Articles 24 and 25, be determined by the law of that Member State.'

54 For more particulars on the territorial scope of application of the Recast Regulation, see V. Lazić, 'Enhancing the efficiency of dispute settlement clauses in the European Union', in N. Bodiroga-Vukobrat et al. (eds.), *Legal Culture in Transition: Supranational and International Law Before National Courts* (Europaisches und Internationales Wirtschaftsrecht, 2013) 184.

55 Article 18, Regulation 1215/2012 reads as follows (emphasis added):

1 A consumer may bring proceedings against the other party to a contract either in the courts of the Member State in which that party is domiciled or, *regardless of the domicile of the other party*, in the courts for the place where the consumer is domiciled.

2 Proceedings may be brought against a consumer by the other party to the contract only in the courts of the Member State in which the consumer is domiciled.

3 This Article shall not affect the right to bring a counter-claim in the court in which, in accordance with this Section, the original claim is pending.

56 Article 21(1) of Regulation 1215/2012 reads as follows (emphasis added):

1 An employer domiciled in a Member State may be sued:
   (a) In the courts of the Member State in which he is domiciled; or
   (b) In another Member State:
      (i) in the courts for the place where or from where the employee habitually carries out his work or in the courts for the last place where he did so, or
      (ii) if the employee does not or did not habitually carry out his work in any one country, in the courts for the place where the business which engaged the employee is or was situated.

2 *An employer not domiciled in a Member State may be sued in a court of a Member State in accordance with point (b) of paragraph 1.*

employees domiciled in the EU Member States. Such a conclusion follows from the fact that Article 6 refers only to Article 18 paragraph 1[57] and Article 21 paragraph 2 respectively.

In addition to that, the Regulation Brussels Ibis introduces a number of new provisions in order to either ensure a greater degree of protection for weaker parties or to clarify the existing regulatory scheme aimed at the protection of such parties. First of all, there is an amendment to the provision on the tacit prorogation of jurisdiction. It has been amended so as to better accommodate the interests of 'weaker' parties. Under the current regime of Brussels I, if a defendant enters an appearance, a court in an EU Member State in principle does not examine *ex officio* whether or not it has jurisdiction under the Regulation. The exception is an obligation to examine whether a court in another state has exclusive jurisdiction. This follows from the text of Article 24 of Brussels I, which relates to tacit prorogation,[58] as well as from Article 25.[59] The newly introduced provision in Article 26(2) of the Regulation Brussels Ibis improves the positions of weaker parties. It imposes the obligation on the court seised to inform a 'weaker' party defendant of the right to contest the jurisdiction and of the consequences of entering or not entering an appearance. Such additional protection for a weaker party is to be met with approval.[60]

The present author in an earlier publication[61] expressed the view that a failure of the seised court to warn a weaker party of its right would present a reason to refuse the recognition or enforcement under Article 45 of the Regulation Brussels Ibis.[62] Thereby a somewhat lessened degree of protection triggered by the reasoning of the CJEU in the *Bilas* judgment has been remedied.[63] Otherwise, inserting paragraph 2 in Article 26 would have been

57 Article 18(1) determines jurisdiction when a professional is the defendant, see the text supra note 51.

58 Article 24 of Regulation 44/2001 reads as follows:

> Apart from jurisdiction derived from other provisions of this Regulation, a court of a Member State before which a defendant enters an appearance shall have jurisdiction. This rule shall not apply where appearance was entered to contest the jurisdiction, or where another court has exclusive jurisdiction by virtue of Article 22.

59 Where a court of a Member State is seised of a claim which is principally concerned with a matter over which the courts of another Member State have exclusive jurisdiction by virtue of Article 22, it shall declare of its own motion that it has no jurisdiction.

60 See also, P. Hays, 'Notes on the European Union's Brussels-I "recast" regulation: an American perspective' (2013) 1 *The European Legal Forum* 4; V. Lazić, 'The revised *Lis pendens* rule in the Brussels Jurisdiction Regulation' (2013) 2 *Review of European Law* 12.

61 Lazić, supra note 47, pp. 100–117.

62 Contra A.-L. Calvo Caravaca and J. Carrascosa Gonzalez in U. Magnus and P. Mankowski (eds.), *Brussels Ibis Regulation* (Sellier, 2015), p. 682, para 35, referring to Nuyts, 'La refonte du règlement Bruxelles I', RCDIP 2013, 1, 60. The authors, however, give no reason or argumentation in support of such a view.

63 Case C-111/09 *ČPP Vienna Insurance Group v Michal Bilas* [2010] ECR I-04545, where the Court held that 'Article 24 [...] must be interpreted as meaning that the court seised,

meaningless, if a failure to apply the rule introduced was to be left with no consequence or sanction. It would be rather strange indeed if the mandatory language in the new provision could simply be ignored by national courts without thereby affecting the enforceability of the judgment rendered. Additionally, the new provision in Article 26(2) renders moot the discussion in the literature on whether the reasoning in this judgment applies to all 'weaker' parties under the Regulation Brussels I, including consumers. A minority view rightly questioned the appropriateness of 'automatic' application of this reasoning in consumer cases,[64] as it would be incompatible with the relevant case law on the interpretation of other sources of EU law, such as the Consumer Directive. Namely, the CJEU on various occasions held that that the courts were to examine *ex officio* whether a dispute settlement clause, including forum-selection clauses, had to be considered as unfair contractual terms.[65] In any case, the provision introduced in Article 26(2) of the Regulation Brussels Ibis offers a useful clarification on the application and interpretation of the rules on tacit prorogation in 'weaker' party disputes.

There are a number of other amendments in the Regulation that may have bearing on the procedural rules applicable to weaker parties. They are not discussed in greater detail here as they do not reduce or diminish the level of protection. Thus, the revised general rule on prorogation of jurisdiction may to some extent affect the protective procedural rules, but the special provisions applicable to weaker parties have remained unchanged. A reversed priority in the *lis pendens* rule has virtually no impact on the position of weaker parties, since the application of the new rule is excluded when weaker parties

where the rules in Section 3 of Chapter II of that regulation were not complied with, must declare itself to have jurisdiction where the defendant enters an appearance and does not contest that court's jurisdiction, since entering an appearance in that way amounts to a tacit prorogation of jurisdiction'.

64 U. Magnus and P. Mankowski (eds.), *Brussels I Regulation* (Sellier, 2012), pp. 390–391.

65 See, for example, Case C-243/08 *Pannon GSM Zrt.* of 4 June 2009 [2009] ECR I-04713. See also joined cases C-240/98 to C-244/98 *Océano Grupo Editorial and Salvat Editores* [2000] ECR I-04941, paras 21–24. For the debate on the case law of the CJEU and whether the CJEU in interpreting these Directives overemphasises consumer interests, see V. Trstenjak and F. Beysen, 'European consumer protection law: *curia semper dabit remedium?*' (2011) 48 *Common Market Law Review* 95. The same line of reasoning may be applied with regard to arbitration agreements. In Article 3(3) of the Directive reference is made to the Annex, which provides for an indicative and non-exhaustive list of the terms that may be regarded as unfair. The Annex expressly refers to arbitration agreements as follows: '(q) excluding or hindering the consumer's right to take legal action or exercise any other legal remedy, particularly by requiring the consumer to take disputes exclusively to arbitration not covered by legal provisions, unduly restricting the evidence available to him or imposing on him a burden of proof which, according to the applicable law, should lie with another party to the contract.' On the interpretation of the Directive with respect to arbitration clauses in consumer contracts, see Case C-40/08 *Asturcom Telecomunicaciones SL* [2009] ECR I-09579 and Case C-168/05 *Elisa María Mostaza Claro v Centro Móvil Milenium SL* [2006] ECR I-10421. See also, in Case C-342/13 *Katalin Sebestyén v Zsolt Csaba Kővári, OTP Bank, OTP Faktoring Követeléskezelő Zrt, Raiffeisen Bank Zrt* judgment of 3 April 2014.

are claimants. In other words, when a weaker party initiates proceedings in 'violation of a forum-selection-clause', the rule on the priority in favour of a 'chosen court' does not apply. Thereby the revised Regulation pursues the same underlying purposes and policy considerations of the previous regulatory scheme.[66]

Moreover, the procedural position of weaker parties is further enhanced. In principle, when deciding on the recognition and enforcement of a judgment rendered by a court of an EU Member State, the courts are not permitted to examine whether or not jurisdiction was properly ascertained. Yet, in exceptional circumstances it is possible to review a decision as to jurisdiction even though such a possibility is very much restricted.[67] As mentioned previously, a violation of protective procedural rules is sanctioned at the enforcement stage so that courts in other Member States may refuse to give effect to judgments rendered. The list of reasons justifying such a denial of enforcement provided in Article 45 is expanded by adding judgments in labour disputes. Thus, regardless of the fact that the *exequatur* is abolished under the Regulation Brussels Ibis, a compliance with the protective procedural rules in weaker parties' disputes has remained ensured.

3.2 *Procedural position of weaker parties in other EU legal instruments unifying procedural and enforcement rules in civil and commercial matters*

Within the context of enhancing the principle of mutual recognition, the European Union enacted certain legal instruments the purpose of which is to facilitate free circulation of judgments within EU. They all abolish *exequatur* and provide for the possibility to refuse enforcement in only very exceptional circumstances. The idea is based on the mutual trust among EU Member States and their judicial systems. Thereby some legal sources merely provide certain minimum standards that have to be complied with so that judgments can be enforced in other Member States under the rules and conditions provided in the Regulation. It is so under the European Enforcement Order. The other two – the European Order for Payment Procedure and the Regulation on a European Small Claims Procedure – go a step further and unify the rules of procedure to be applied by national courts, as well as the conditions for the enforcement. These legal instruments do not reflect the same considerations and concerns with respect to weaker parties as the regulatory scheme under the Brussels Regulation.

In principle, neither of three instruments regulates specifically issues of jurisdiction. Yet, jurisdictional grounds under Regulation 44/2001 have been expressly referred to in some other EU private international law instruments.

66 For more particulars, see Lazić, supra note 47, p. 113.
67 A. Leyton and H. Mercer, *European Civil Practice*, 2004, para 26.086.

In other words, in these legal sources a jurisdictional rule in certain weaker party disputes must be respected in order to enable a court of the country of origin to certify its judgment for 'free circulation' within the European Union – i.e., to enable recognition or enforcement where no *exequatur* is required. Thus, certain rules of Regulation 44/2001 must be respected if a judgment is to be certified as a 'European Enforcement Order'. According to Article 6(b) of this Regulation, a judgment must be rendered in compliance with jurisdictional rules for insurance contracts and exclusive jurisdiction provided in the Brussels Regulation. Besides, a judgment can be certified as a 'European Enforcement Order' if it is rendered against a consumer only by the court in the EU Member State of the consumer's domicile, unless the consumer has expressly agreed to a claim by admission, by means of settlement or in an authentic instrument within the meaning of Article 3(1)(a) and (d) respectively.

Also, certain rules of Regulation 44/2001 have also been referred to in Article 6 of the European Order for Payment Procedure. In Article 6(1), it provides that for the purposes of its application, 'jurisdiction shall be determined in accordance with the relevant rules of Community law, in particular Regulation (EC) No 44/2001'. Additionally, in Article 6(2), it specifically provides that the consumer may be sued only in the courts of its domicile. With respect to determining domicile, reference is made to Article 59 of Regulation Brussels Ibis. If these requirements regarding jurisdiction are not met, an application for a European Order for Payment Procedure shall not be granted as is expressly provided in Article 11(a).

However, in the Regulation on a European Small Claims Procedure, there is no reference whatsoever to a 'weaker' party or a 'consumer'.[68] Thus, in contrast to the European Enforcement Order and the European Payment Order, under the Regulation on a European Small Claims Procedure, a court in an EU Member State of origin is not required to observe protective rules on jurisdiction. Yet, a judgment rendered in accordance with the procedure regulated therein is enforceable without the need to obtain *exequatur*, i.e., declaration of enforceability in the Member State of enforcement. The conditions for the recognition and enforcement of judgments are similar to those falling under the European Enforcement Order and the European Payment Order.

Finally, even in the legal sources that do refer to the jurisdictional rules of the Regulation Brussels I, respect for jurisdictional rules intended to protect the procedural position of a weaker party incorporated in the Brussels Ibis Regulation is not ensured in the same manner and to the same extent. In

68 Regulation on Small Claim Procedure has recently been revised by Regulation (EU) 2015/2421 of the European Parliament and of the Council of 16 December 2015 amending Regulation (EC) No 861/2007 establishing a European Small Claims Procedure and Regulation (EC) No 1896/2006 creating a European order for payment procedure OJ of 24 December 2015, OJ L 341 of 24 December 2015, p. 1, which will apply as from 14 July 2017.

other words, even under these legal sources, where the rules on jurisdiction in cases involving weaker parties are referred to and the court in the Member State of origin is required to respect them, a possible failure of the court in the country of origin to respect those rules may not be sanctioned by refusing the recognition or enforcement in another EU Member State. Namely, the reasons to deny the enforcement are reduced to the irreconcilability of judgments provided that this objection could not have been raised in the proceedings in the Member State where the judgment was brought.

Clearly such an enforcement regime deviates from the enhanced protection of procedural position of weaker parties under the Regulation Brussels Ibis. The reasons for such a discrepancy among the various legal instruments within the European Union are not easily discernible. Obviously the emphasis is on the procedure in a Member State where the proceedings are carried out. Thus, there is a presumption and trust among Member States that the court in the country of origin would apply EU sources correctly and issue judgments only when the conditions provided therein are fulfilled, including the requirement that jurisdiction is properly established in certain cases involving weaker parties. Yet it is not easily explained why the EU legislator opted for different paths and for a distinct degree of control in the Member State of the enforcement. It is often argued that identifying minimum standards and unifying the rules of procedure to be followed in the Member State of origin remove the need for control in the Member State of enforcement. However, it is difficult to explain how unification of such aspects can impact on the correctness of a decision to assume jurisdiction. In that context of mutual trust regarding application of the rules on jurisdiction, there is no difference between the Brussels I regime and other two legal sources. Yet decisions on jurisdiction in cases involving weaker parties can be 'controlled' in a Member State of the enforcement under the former, but not under the latter two legal regimes.

The present author had hoped the EU legislator would take the opportunity when revising the Regulation on a European Small Claims Procedure to bring about changes in that respect. This is especially so bearing in mind that the revised Regulation increased the value of the amount in dispute up to €5,000[69] for the purpose of the application of the Regulation. Regrettably, the revised Regulation does not introduce any special provision for a 'weaker party' or a 'consumer', and only refers to consumers in the recital on the basis of a previous report of the Commission.[70] Just like the previous Regulation 861/2007, Regulation 2015/2421 does not contain provisions

69 European Commission in its Proposal suggested increasing the value of the amount in dispute up to €5,000 or €10,000.

70 Commission's report of 19 November 2013 on the application of Regulation (EC) No 861/2007. See recital (3) of Regulation (EU) 2015/2421 where it is stated that '[c]onsumers should be able to use the opportunities afforded by the internal market to the fullest extent, and their confidence should not be limited by the lack of effective legal remedies for disputes

on jurisdiction or any special provision concerning consumers.[71] Obviously, the protection of weaker parties is not incorporated, in the same or a similar manner, in the different instruments regulating certain aspects of international civil procedure.

4 Conclusion

In pursing the principle of mutual recognition and enhancing a free circulation of decisions, the European Union legislator uses different paths and develops diverse regimes of enforcement of judgments. A lack of uniformity in that respect can sometimes be justified by reasons of diversity of subject-matters or differences in substantive scope of application among various private international law instruments. It seems, however, more difficult to find explanation and legal reasoning for a diversity of approaches in those sources that regulate private international law issues with respect to similar subject-matters. Even though the substantive scope of application is not entirely identical in the Regulation Brussels Ibis, European Enforcement Order, European Payment Order and Regulation on Small Claims Procedure, they all deal with civil and commercial matters. Thereby the scope is defined in a rather similar manner and the subject-matters, albeit not identical, are substantially similar and to a large extent overlapping.

Although *exequatur* is abolished in all four legal sources, the enforcement regime under the Brussels Ibis Regulation substantially differs from the legal framework and reasons for refusal under the other three legal instruments. It is true that setting common minimum procedural standards, as well as the unification of certain aspects of civil procedure in itself diminishes the need for control, or implies a lesser degree of control, at the enforcement stage. Unification of such rules, however, cannot necessarily ensure compliance with certain jurisdictional rules, including those that are meant to protect the position of weaker parties. While the Regulation Brussels Ibis enhances the level of protection and maintains the system of control, the compliance with protective rules at the enforcement stage, no such controlling mechanism is provided under the European Enforcement Order and European Payment Order. Namely, the latter instruments do refer to protective provisions on jurisdiction with respect to consumers, but provide for no 'controlling' mechanism at the enforcement stage that would ensure that these jurisdictional rules been respected by the court in the Member State where the judgment was rendered. In other words, a violation of any jurisdictional ground by a court in a Member State does not present a reason to

in which there is a cross-border element' and that '[t]he improvements to the European Small Claims Procedure proposed in this Regulation aim to provide consumers with a means of effective redress, and thus contribute to the practical enforcement of their rights.'

71 A reference to the Regulation Brussels I and Brussels Ibis respectively is contained in Article 3 paragraph 2 for the purposes of determining 'domicile' of a party.

refuse the recognition and enforcement of that judgment in another Member State under the two legal instruments. This is in apparent contrast to the enforcement under the Brussels I regime with respect to judgments rendered in disputes involving consumers.

Moreover, the Regulation on the Small Claims Procedure does not even mention or refer to the protective jurisdictional rules. This is in apparent contrast to the European Payment Order and European Enforcement Order where compliance with certain rules on jurisdiction is at least a condition for certifying that judgments are directly enforceable. It is regrettable that in the Regulation on Small Claims no 'protection rules' are found for consumers, especially bearing in mind that their involvement in this type of proceeding is likely to occur rather frequently.

In general, a higher level of consistency and coherence in pursuing underlying principles and policy considerations should be achieved in unifying various aspects of private international law on the European Union level. When looking for best ways and practices to achieve this aim, a choice between unification in the form of a 'EU PIL Code' and 'separate legal instruments' is not necessarily decisive. Far more important seems to be an appropriate assessment of priorities, finding a proper balance of underlying policies and enhancing cooperation and coordination in law-making process. In other words, a clear formulation of aims, policies and means of achieving them combined with closer cooperation among various expert groups engaged in drafting rules in different subject-matters in the area of private law would enhance the consistency and coherence in unifying private international law rules.

As to the objective of pursuing the principle of mutual recognition and free circulation of judgments within the European Union, a general trend towards excluding or minimising control at the stage of enforcement and reasons for refusing enforcement is to be expected. Yet it seems appropriate to retain a certain degree of control at the stage of enforcement so as to leave the possibility for courts in the Member State of enforcement to refuse giving effect to judgments that violate fundamental rights, basic notions of justice and underlying policies.[72]

72 Relevant case law of the CJEU illustrates serious shortcomings of the enforcement regime under Articles 41 and 42 of the Regulation Brussels Ibis, which provides for almost unconditional enforcement of return orders and decision on contacts with a child. For more particulars, see, 'Family private international law issues before the European Court of Human Rights – lessons to be learned from *Povse v Austria* in revising the Brussels IIa Regulation and its relevance for future abolition of *exequatur* in the European Union', in C. Paulussen, T. Takacs, V. Lazić and B. Rompuy (eds.), *Fundamental Rights in International and European Law – Public and Private Law Perspectives* (Asser Press/Springer, 2016) 161. It is to be hoped that alteration of this enforcement regime will be a top priority in a future revision of this Regulation.

Part V

External dimension and impact

14 An external dimension of the AFSJ?

Some reflections on the nature and scope of the externalisation of the AFSJ domains

Claudio Matera

1 Introduction

As preceding chapters have shown, developing the European Union (EU) as an Area of Freedom, Security and Justice (AFSJ) challenges the European integration process on a number of levels, from the institutional one, to the societal one. More specifically, it can be said that the establishment of the AFSJ directly challenges a number of *constitutional foundations*[1] of the EU legal order such as the distribution of competences between the EU and its Member States and the vertical relationship between public authority and the rights and liberties of individuals. In spite of its prominent position within the Treaties, as the first objective mentioned in Article 3 TEU, and the fast pace at which AFSJ policies have been developed in the past 16 years,[2] the AFSJ as an objective of the integration process appears to be still in the making: not only there are numerous difficulties in implementing the different measures adopted,[3] but also the specific choices made in relation to certain policies have triggered a number of disputes and raised many doubts on their legality.[4]

1 The CJEU has referred to the constitutional foundations of the EU legal order on a number of occasions and, in particular, in *Opinion 1/91* (European Economic Area), [1991] ECR I-6079 and in Joined Cases C-402/05 P and C-415/05 P *Kadi and Al Barakaat*, 8 September 2008 ECR I-6351. For an academic insight on the meaning of the expression and its use by the Court, see M. Dony, *Droit de l'Union Européenne*, ULB, 2012, p. 242; N. Lavranos, 'Revisiting Article 307 EC: The Untouchable Core of Fundamental European Constitutional Law Values and Principles', in F. Fontanelli, G. Martinico and P. Carrozza (eds.), *Shaping the Rule of Law Through Dialogue*, Europa Law Publishing, 2009, pp. 119–146; N. Lavranos, 'Protecting European Law from International Law' (2010) 15 *European Foreign Affairs Review* 265.

2 Of course, I acknowledge that cooperation in 'justice and home affairs' officially began with the entry into force of the Maastricht Treaty in 1993.

3 Taking EU asylum law as an example, suffice to mention here the recent wave of infringement proceedings initiated by the Commission; see European Commission Press release of 23 September 2015: http://europa.eu/rapid/press-release_IP-15-5699_en.htm.

4 Numerous examples can be made. In relation to the difficulties linked to implementation, the most prominent example pertains the relocation of asylum-seekers on the basis of Decision 22 September 2015; in relation to legitimacy issues, I can refer to the disputes on human rights protection standards in the context of the transfer system of the Dublin Regulation or in the

To date, the AFSJ project remains a controversial, if not contested, development of the EU integration process not only in relation to the factual premise used to justify its development, but also in relation to the regulatory choices adopted by the institutions.[5] Yet, three factors seem to have played a major role in influencing the development of the AFSJ: the continuous revision Treaty process, the dominance of the executives and the perception that the AFSJ should be developed to address unspecified security threats that resulted from the establishment of the internal market. The first factor that must be considered is the semi-permanent Treaty reform process that, since the entry into force of the Maastricht Treaty, has characterised the recent evolution of the European integration process.[6] In some 20 years since the entry into force of that Treaty, the EU has undergone three main Treaty changes, temporary regimes and smaller revisions were introduced, and a radical constitutional reform was abandoned at photo-finish. This semi-permanent revision process has disadvantaged the sedimentation and integration of norms. This, of course, weakens legal certainty and interferes, at least potentially, with the independent role of the Court of Justice of the European Union (CJEU), since the Court has been called to interpret and apply Treaty provisions while, simultaneously, political and institutional actors were discussing and/or revising such rules.[7] These considerations are particularly relevant for the AFSJ because both the institutional and the material dimensions were affected by the different reforms of the Treaties.[8]

The second factor to take into account when analysing the development of the EU *qua* AFSJ is the role that national governments have played in the development of this policy. Contrary to the integration process that

context of the application of the European Arrest Warrant. See, inter alia, the contributions by Peers (Chapter 2), Albi (Chapter 6) and Leczykiewicz (Chapter 4) in this collection.

5 Many authors in this book discuss this issue. For an earlier analysis see D. Kostakopoulou, 'The Area of Freedom, Security and Justice and the European Union's Constitutional Dialogue', in C. Barnard, (ed.), *The Fundamental of EU Law Revisited: Assessing the Impact of the Constitutional Debate*, Oxford University Press, 2007, pp. 153–191 and, more recently H. Labayle, *Refonder l'Espace de Liberté, Sécurité et Justice à la Lumière de l'Arrêt van Gend en Loos?* http://curia.europa.eu/jcms/upload/docs/application/pdf/2013-12/qd30136442ac_002.pdf.

6 B. de Witte, 'The Closest Thing to a Constitutional Conversation in Europe: The Semi Permanent Treaty Revision Process', in P. Beaumont, C. Lyons and N. Walker (eds.), *Convergence and Divergence in European Public Law*, Hart Publishing, 2002, pp. 39–57.

7 An analysis of the relationship between the treaty reform process and the case law of the CJEU in the past 20 years goes beyond the scope of this contribution. As first example of how the CJEU is called upon to assess the impact of the treaty reform process on the AFSJ see case C-363/14, *European Parliament v Council*, 10 September 2015. As an example of how the case law of the CJEU has affected the treaty reform process suffice here to mention the impact that the Kadi judgment of 2008 has had on the Treaty provisions concerning the regime of restrictive measures ex Article 215 TFEU.

8 For an overview of the evolution of the AFSJ Project see the contribution of S. Peers in this volume.

characterised the internal market project where the Commission played the leading role in shaping the overall strategy as well as in promoting and enforcing legislation, the development of the AFSJ has been led and controlled by the executives.[9] The special role of the executives in the AFSJ goes beyond the emergency breaks that national governments have according to Articles 82(3) and 83(3) TFEU; and it equally goes beyond the last remaining vestiges of pre-Lisbon unanimity such as in the case of Article 81(3) TFEU. Rather, the special role of the executives in the AFSJ is best represented by the role that the European Council has secured for itself over the past years in this field.[10] Indeed, the European Council has exercised its leading role within the AFSJ as the driving institution that identifies priorities and promotes the adoption of specific legislative measures. Since the Tampere meeting of 1999, the European Council has designed the evolution of the AFSJ by the means of detailed quinquennial plans and even though the tradition has been abjured with the adoption of the succinct 2014 guidelines,[11] the leading position of this institution has been codified by the Lisbon Treaty in Article 68 TFEU, with the result that the European Council's role and leadership in the AFSJ is firmly anchored to a primary law provision. This is because Article 68 TFEU clearly confers to this institution the task of 'defining the strategic guidelines for legislative and operational planning of the AFSJ'.[12] As a consequence of this, the heads of state and heads of governments have the power to shape the AFSJ, with the result that this field of EU competence is particularly influenced by (national) political agendas. At the same time, however, the guiding role of the European Council has not managed to contribute positively to the coherence of AFSJ initiatives and, in the specific field of the external AFSJ, the prominent role

9 It should be added that until December 2014 the CJEU was prevented from receiving infringement proceedings in various AFSJ fields. See S. Peers, 'Finally "Fit for Purpose"? The Treaty of Lisbon and the End of the Third Pillar Legal Order' (2008) 27 *Yearbook of European Law* 47.

10 For an analysis of the constitutional shortcomings of the pre-Lisbon AFSJ architecture and the impact of the new one see S. Peers, 'Finally "Fit For Purpose"?', supra note 9; S. Peers, 'Justice and Home Affairs Law Since the Treaty of Lisbon: A Fairy-Tale Ending?' in D. Acosta Arcazo and C.C. Murphy (eds.), *EU Security and Justice Law After Lisbon and Stockholm*, Hart Publishing, 2014, pp. 17–37; S Peers, 'Mission Accomplished? EU Justice and Home Affairs Law After the Treaty of Lisbon' (2011) 48 *Common Market Law Review* 661.

11 See the European Council conclusions of 27 June 2014, EUCO 79/14, and the specific guidelines for justice and home affairs, www.consilium.europa.eu/en/policies/strategic-guidelines-jha (accessed May 2016).

12 Article 68 TFEU affirms that 'The European Council shall define the strategic guidelines for legislative and operational planning within the area of freedom, security and justice'. For an analysis of the role of this institution in the external AFSJ, see S. Poli, 'The Institutional Setting and the Legal Toolkit', in M. Cremona, J. Monar and S. Poli (eds.), *The External Dimension of the European Union's Area of Freedom, Security and Justice*, Peter Lang, 2011, pp. 26–32.

of the European Council leaves less room for other institutions such as the European External Action Service or the Commission to fulfil their tasks with the necessary functional autonomy.[13]

The third factor is related to the political perception according to which the creation of an area without internal borders made the EU's public space vulnerable to security threats. In one way, this perception is part of the rationale for the development of the AFSJ itself: the development of the AFSJ has been explained with the assumption that the creation of the internal market and the abolition of internal border controls required compensatory measures to tighten external borders and develop new means of internal surveillance.[14] Even though no clear, objective data was used to support this narrative and orientation, the development of the AFSJ has been characterised by an abundance of procedural and security measures, often to the detriment of civil liberties and fundamental rights of citizens and third-country nationals.[15]

At the same time, it is also true that soon after the creation of the AFSJ in 1999, the terrorist attacks of 9/11, Madrid, London and, more recently, Paris and Brussels objectively called for the EU to act and adopt measures in the fields of police cooperation and criminal law. However, the emergence of international terrorism as a direct security threat for the EU also meant that the AFSJ project could not solely address internal security issues, but had to undertake an international dimension. While the existence of external security threats was not at the centre of the AFSJ project at the time of the Tampere conclusions of 1999, it can be argued that external security threats later became driving factors for integration in the AFSJ domains.

More specifically, it can be said that external driving factors have influenced the development of the AFSJ in three main ways. First, these external driving factors have pushed the EU to proactively act internally in various policy fields of the AFSJ, with a focus on measures connected to the maintenance of public order and public security such as the European Arrest Warrant and

13 For an analysis of the relationships between the different institutional actors involved in the external AFSJ, see M. Gatti, 'The Role of the European External Action Service in The External Dimension of the Area of Freedom, Security and Justice', in C. Flaesch-Mougin and L.S. Rossi (eds.), *La Dimension Extérieure de l'Espace de Liberté, Sécurité et Justice après le Traité de Lisbonne*, Bruylant, 2013, pp. 171–193; J. Monar, 'The External Dimension of the EU's Area of Freedom, Security and Justice. Progress, Potential and Limitations after the Treaty of Lisbon' (2012) 1 *SIEPS*.

14 D. Kostakopoulou, 'The Area of Freedom, Security and Justice and the European Union's Constitutional Dialogue', in C. Barnard, (ed.), *The Fundamental of EU Law Revisited: Assessing the Impact of the Constitutional Debate*, Oxford University Press, 2007, pp. 153–191, at p. 171.

15 See the contributions by Leczykiewicz (Chapter 4), Albi (Chapter 6), Mitsilegas (Chapter 8) and Peers (Chapter 2) in this volume.

the Framework Decision on terrorism.[16] Second, the impact of external security threats influenced the development of the AFSJ's external dimension because, as Jörg Monar has argued, the security challenges faced by the EU that come from the outside 'have in common the fact that the EU's capacity to respond effectively to them depends crucially on cooperation with third countries'.[17] Third, the concern for external security threats has affected the development of AFSJ law with the result that, as Violeta Moreno Lax has observed in relation to EU migration and asylum law, 'third-country nationals (including refugees) have been conceptualized as a threat to market integration requiring measures of exception and control'.[18]

While the existence of external driving factors has had a major impact on the development of the whole AFSJ project and its externalisation, it is not yet clear what exactly this externalisation entails. Partly the difficulty is linked to the fact that also internally it is still difficult to identify an overall AFSJ objective.[19] In this respect, Marise Cremona has argued that this is because the AFSJ comprises numerous, heterogeneous policies.[20] At the same time, because the Treaties' objectives explicitly link internal and external security in Article 3(5) TEU, the internal–external nexus blurs the distinction between internal and external AFSJ objectives. Furthermore, the numerous and ambitious policy documents adopted by the European Council over the years have also contributed to making such distinctions fuzzy.

With a view to clarify the scope of the external AFSJ, this chapter is structured as follows. First, this contribution will look at the evolution of this AFSJ dimension and the legal implications and challenges thereof (Section 2). Second, the contribution will analyse some of the key actualisations of the external AFSJ in order to evaluate how this dimension of the AFSJ has been reconciled with the complex rules governing the distribution of competences in EU external relations (Section 3).

16 Council Framework Decision of 13 June 2002 on the European Arrest Warrant and the surrender procedures between Member States – Statements made by certain Member States on the adoption of the Framework Decision, OJ L 190, 18 July 2002, p.1 and Council Framework Decision of 13 June 2002 on combating terrorism, OJ L 164, 22 June 2002, pp. 3–7.

17 Monar, 'The External Dimension of the EU's Area of Freedom, Security and Justice', supra note 13.

18 V. Moreno Lax, 'Life After Lisbon: EU Asylum Policy as a Factor of Migration Control', in D. Acosta Arcarazo and C. Murphy (eds.), *EU Security and Justice Law: After Lisbon and Stockholm*, Hart Publishing, 2014, p. 165.

19 See N. Walker, 'In Search of the Area of Freedom, Security and Justice: A Constitutional Odyssey', in N. Walker (ed.), *Europe's Area of Freedom Security and Justice*, Academy of European Law/EUI, 2004, pp. 5–7; M. Cremona, 'EU External Action in the JHA Domain. A Legal Perspective', in M. Cremona, J. Monar and S. Poli (eds.), *The External Dimension of the European Union's Area of Freedom, Security and Justice*, Peter Lang, 2011, pp. 81–82. For an alternative view see R.A. Wessel, L. Marin and C. Matera, 'The External Dimension of the EU'S Area of Freedom, Security and Justice', in C. Eckes and T. Konstadinides (eds.), *Crime within the Area of Freedom, Security and Justice: A European Public Order*, Cambridge University Press, 2011, pp. 272–300.

20 M. Cremona, 'EU External Action in the JHA Domain', supra note 19, pp. 81–82.

2 An external dimension of the AFSJ?

In the introductory section of this chapter, it was argued that the externalisation of the AFSJ project emerged as a reaction to a number of driving factors, especially the rise of international terrorism. Since 9/11, more driving factors of the external AFSJ have emerged; for instance, the Arab Spring and the civil war in Syria. Yet, almost 17 years since the Tampere conclusions of 1999, it is still difficult to define, *in concreto*, what is meant by the expression 'external dimension of the AFSJ'. This section will analyse the evolution of this specific parcel of the AFSJ project and will assess its evolution against the backdrop of the EU legal system. In doing so, this section will try to clarify what should be understood with the expression 'external dimension of the AFSJ' and highlight where its shortcomings reside.

2.1 Tous pour un et un pour tous*: the AFSJ policy programmes and the development of the external AFSJ*

One of the characterising features of the development of the EU *qua* AFSJ is the role of the European Council. As was argued in the previous section, this institution has an outstanding mandate to mould the AFSJ and consequentially its external projection. This section analyses the different policy programmes developed by the European Council in the past 17 years of AFSJ integration.

The first milestone in the construction of the (external) AFSJ was posed at the summit of the European Council in Tampere in 1999. In the conclusions of that summit, not only did the European Council adopt the first AFSJ programme, but also included a special section on the development of the external projection of this policy. More specifically, the Tampere conclusions identified two main characteristics of the external AFSJ. First, it was held that 'all competences and instruments at the disposal of the Union, and in particular, in external relations must be used in an integrated and consistent way to build the area of freedom, security and justice'.[21] With this first statement, the European Council indicated that the AFSJ was not simply substituting the justice and home affairs pillar. Rather, the AFSJ was presented as a new goal of the European integration process and it emphasised that in order to achieve this goal, the EU had to contribute with all its powers and instruments (including the external ones) to achieve it. Second, the Tampere conclusions went as far as affirming that AFSJ concerns had to be integrated '*in the definition* and implementation of other Union policies and activities'.[22] This, of course, went beyond the mere integration of AFSJ-related clauses in other policies and went as far as affirming that AFSJ matters should *redefine* and *influence* the implementation of other EU policies. However, it was

21 Paragraph 59 of the Tampere Conclusions.
22 Ibid., second sentence, emphasis added.

very clear already at that time that the holistic manner in which the external AFSJ was presented required a deeper reflection: not only in relation to the identification of objectives and priorities, but also in relation to institutional matters such as working methods within and between institutions.[23]

The second milestone on the development of the external dimension of the AFSJ was a document setting priorities objectives and measures to implement the Tampere remit. This document adopted by the European Council at the Feira meeting of 2000 provided institutional actors with a first comprehensive framework on the basis of which the external AFSJ had to be developed. The Feira document combined constitutional and institutional questions with policy priorities and was divided into three sections: one on the relationship between the AFSJ and EU external relations, one on policy priorities and one on instruments. However, while the Tampere conclusions affirmed that EU competences and instruments, *including* external relations, had to contribute to the establishment of the AFSJ, the Feira document changed the paradigm: here the document is built on the premise that the AFSJ is a policy with an external projection and, consequentially, AFSJ objectives must be integrated in the numerous instruments of EU external action. This appears as a crucial factor: back in Tampere, the externalisation of the AFSJ was not really on the table; rather, the European Council concluded that as a new policy and new objective of the integration process, the AFSJ needed the complementary support of other EU policies and instruments, including external relations. Therefore, the externalisation of the AFSJ had only an instrumental role for the establishment of the AFSJ. With the Feira document, on the other hand, the EU put forward a stronger external role for the AFSJ: rather than envisaging mechanisms and priorities through which external relations instruments of the EU could contribute to the attainment of the AFSJ, the document changed the paradigm and presented the external dimension of the AFSJ as a *sub*-policy of the AFSJ itself.

According to this new vision, the AFSJ was made a transversal driving component of EU external relations.[24] The subtle paradigm shift that occurred at Feira was later confirmed in subsequent policy programmes beyond the context of AFSJ-specific policy documents. The best example of this is still represented by the European Security Strategy (ESS).[25] Adopted in 2003, the document held that collective (regional) security was facing new threats such as organised crime and terrorism, two fields in relation to which EU competences are anchored to the AFSJ project.[26] Therefore, in order to face these

23 Tampere Conclusions, paragraph 62.

24 'European Union Priorities and Policy Objectives for External Relations in the Field of Justice and Home Affairs', Doc. No. 7653/00 of 6 June 2000, Section 2(A).

25 'A Secure Europe in a Better World' European Security Strategy, 12 December 2003, in www.consilium.europa.eu/uedocs/cmsUpload/78367.pdf.

26 For an analysis of the challenges linked to combining AFSJ and CFSP actions see P. Koutrakos, 'The External Dimension of the AFSJ and Other EU External Policies: An Osmotic Relationship', in M. Cremona, J. Monar and S. Poli (eds.), *The External Dimension*

new security threats, the European Council called for a better coordination between external action based on the TFEU Treaty and external action based on the Common Foreign and Security Policy (CFSP) and the Common Security and Defence Policy (CSDP). The ambivalent, if not ambiguous, scope of the external projection of the AFSJ was then confirmed in The Hague Programme, which indicated the different instances in which the EU should make use of its external powers to externalise the AFSJ project.[27]

In relation to the external projection of the AFSJ, The Hague Programme was built on the basis of the Feira one and confirmed the following guidelines. First, The Hague Programme made clear that the external projection of the AFSJ had to be anchored to existing internal policies of the EU. This was probably introduced as a parameter of legitimacy for external action in a field such as the AFSJ in which only a couple of provisions conferred express external powers to the Union; yet, it could be argued that, from a systematic perspective, this concern was covered by the doctrine of implied powers and that it did not innovate the existing *acquis* in the field. Second, The Hague Programme made clear that the external dimension of the AFSJ had to bring an added value to the action of the Member States. Obviously, also in this case the parameter in question did not necessarily bring anything new, since the principle of subsidiarity also applies to the AFSJ. Possibly, the European Council wished to emphasise that Member States considered action by the EU as a complement to theirs.[28] Third, The Hague Programme held that the external dimension of the AFSJ had to contribute to the broader objectives of EU external action as codified in Article 3(5) TEU. And this last aspect acquired momentum with the adoption of the Commission Communication of October 2005, in which a renewed strategy for the externalisation of the AFSJ was spelled out.[29]

The significance of the 2005 Strategy resides in the fact that the externalisation of the AFSJ is pushed further away from internal AFSJ objectives. As a result of this, the external AFSJ once more emerged as a sub-policy of EU

of the European Union's Area of Freedom Security and Justice, Peter Lang, 2011; C. Matera, 'The European Union Area of Freedom, Security and Justice and the Fight Against New Security Threats: New Trends and Old Constitutional Challenges', in M. Arcari and L. Balmond (eds.), *Global Governance and the Challenges of Collective Security*, Editoriale Scientifica, 2012, pp. 69–87.

27 The Hague Programme: Strengthening Freedom, Security and Justice in the European Union, Council document 16054/04, 13, December 2004.

28 Today, the subsidiarity principle in relation to the external AFSJ has to be interpreted alongside with Declaration 36 to the Treaties: Declaration on Article 218 of the Treaty on the Functioning of the European Union concerning the negotiation and conclusion of international agreements by Member States relating to the Area of Freedom, Security and Justice. The Conference confirms that Member States may negotiate and conclude agreements with third countries or international organisations in the areas covered by Chapters 3, 4 and 5 of Title V of Part Three insofar as such agreements comply with Union law.

29 Communication from the Commission – a strategy on the external dimension of the area of freedom, security and justice, COM(2005) 491 final, Council Document 14366/3/05.

external action. The fact that the 2005 Strategy went beyond the initial idea according to which internal AFSJ objectives required the support of external policies can be inferred from the wide types of objectives envisaged by the document. For instance, the document refers to a number of capacity-building types of activities such as addressing the root causes of migration, supporting the transformation of weak or non-existent law enforcement institutions and the need to support legal certainty.[30] The role of the EU as a promoter of good practices and European standards in justice and home affairs shows that the externalisation of the AFSJ is coined as a capacity-building policy that is firmly rooted in the broader promotion of the rule of law ex Articles 2 and 21 TEU. And this becomes even clearer in Section IV of the document, in which five specific issues are identified and addressed.

Indeed, in Section IV of the Strategy, the Commission describes a policy that appears closer to the objectives of Article 21 TEU than to the objectives at the heart of the AFSJ project and now codified in Articles 3(2) TEU and 67 TFEU: the promotion of international human rights standards in third countries, strengthening the rule of law and good governance, improving third countries' capacity for migration management and refugee protection, providing support to third countries for institution-building and implementation of international instruments in the fight against international terrorism and supporting the development of institutional capacity in the fight against organised crime. At the same time, the document did include certain AFSJ-proper aspects to the external strategy. Thus, for instance, the document does pay attention to law enforcement cooperation as well as judicial cooperation instruments with third countries, but the document places much more emphasis on the former elements than on the latter ones.

The strong foreign policy accent attached to the type of activities and priorities set out in the 2005 documents were later confirmed in the Stockholm Programme for the AFSJ adopted at the end of 2009. Also in this case, the policy programme adopted by the European Council focused on the relationship between foreign policy and justice and home affairs matters. Thus, while the document confirms the need to integrate AFSJ matters into other (external) policies of the EU, the thematic priorities identified focus on capacity-building measures and addressed only marginally law enforcement and judicial cooperation.[31] In addition, the Stockholm Programme introduced two new ideas: first, it held that the externalisation of the AFSJ should include synergies with the CFSP and the CSDP;[32] second, it held that the externalisation of the AFSJ should include also the activities of the specialised AFSJ agencies: Europol, Eurojust, Frontex and the European Asylum

30 See sections II, III.

31 See Section 7.2 of the Stockholm Programme, OJ C 115/15 May 2010.

32 See Sections 4.3.1 and 7.1 of the Stockholm Programme, OJ C 115/15 May 2010.

Support Office (EASO).[33] In this respect, it can be said that, from a policy perspective, the Stockholm Programme completes the evolution of the externalisation of the AFSJ: by taking stock of the evolution occurred since the adoption of the Tampere conclusions in 1999 the Stockholm Programme extended the spectrum of the external AFSJ to the role of agencies and the admixture of AFSJ actions with CSDP initiatives.[34]

The last key policy document on the AFSJ was expected to be adopted during the Italian presidency of the council in the last semester of 2014, but for the first time since the Tampere conclusions, a different approach was followed. The meeting of the European Council at the end of June 2014 had a charged agenda: the heads of state and government of the Member States were called upon to put forward the name of the new president of the European Commission and had to decide on a number of strategic issues such as a roadmap on economic growth, discuss the Ukrainian crisis and sign the association agreements (AAs) with Moldova, Ukraine and Georgia under the umbrella of the European Neighbourhood Policy (ENP). In this political context, the European Council opted to follow the same format as the Tampere agenda: defining the AFSJ strategy within the document adopted at the end of the meeting. Because of this decision, the document is less detailed than the Stockholm and the Hague programmes and merely confirms three elements that had been addressed already in the past: first, that the answers to many of the challenges of the AFSJ reside in the establishment of cooperation with third countries; secondly, the European Council recognised that the EU should promote human rights and data protection while developing the AFSJ and its external dimension and, thirdly, the European Council emphasised the importance of assisting countries of origin and transit to strengthen their migration and border management capacity.[35]

This overview of the key policy documents on the external dimension of the AFSJ shows that the externalisation of the AFSJ has acquired a dichotomous nature. While the externalisation of the AFSJ appeared as a mere complement to the establishment of the Area at the time of the Tampere programme, the EU has turned the externalisation of the AFSJ as a facet of EU external relations or, to put it more clearly, as a sub-policy of EU external action. With this in mind, it is possible to distinguish actions envisaged to complement and support the development and consolidation of the EU *qua* AFSJ, such as the conclusion of agreements on visas, border controls, and mutual legal assistance, from other actions that are supposed to help partner countries in

33 See F. Trauner, *New Kids on the CFSP Block: The JHA Agencies*, European Institute for Security Studies, Brussels, 2016, www.iss.europa.eu/uploads/media/Brief_7_JHA_agencies.pdf; J. Santos Vara, 'The External Activities of AFSJ Agencies: The Weakness of Democratic and Judicial Controls' (2015) 20(1) *European Foreign Affairs Review* 118.

34 See also Council Doc. 15562/11, 'Strengthening Ties between CSDP and FSJ' of 17 October 2011 and the latest report by the European External Action Service Document 'Strengthening Ties between CSDP and FSJ: Road Map Implementation', Doc. 02230/13, 14 November 2013.

35 European Council, Conclusions 26/27 June 2014, EUCO 79/14.

consolidating *their* internal policies and legislation in AFSJ-related matters such as the administration of justice or the regulatory response to global security threats such as international terrorism.

While the two aspects may coexist in specific contexts such as the European Neighbourhood Policy (ENP) or the Stabilisation and Association Process (SAP), practice reveals that in the majority of agreements concluded, the second element is the dominant one. In fact, the EU cooperates on issues contributing to the development of the internal AFSJ only with selected countries, either by reason of their geographical location (ENP and SAP countries), or by reason of their strategic importance (USA).[36] From an analytical perspective, it appears preferable to keep this distinction in mind and further elaborate on the very notion of the 'external dimension of the AFSJ'. More specifically, it is submitted here that because of the different policies covered by the AFSJ, one the one hand, and because of the plurality of objectives pursued by the integration of justice and home affairs matters in EU external relations, on the other, it is preferable to speak of 'the external *dimensions* of the AFSJ'.[37]

A second element that emerges from the analysis above and that is equally important relates to the institutional implications of the choices made by the European Council. Indeed, by promoting the integration of the AFSJ within other external policies, the European Council calls for improving the working synergies of the different actors involved. However, while the documents make reference to the principle of coherence, the different strategic documents fail to address minutely how the different dimensions of the (external) AFSJ should be developed in a coherent manner. The impression here is that the EU has not yet managed to do so, with the result that the external dimensions of the AFSJ appear to be at odds with the requirements of Article 21(3) TEU.[38]

All in all, the holistic approach used by the European Council to develop the external dimensions of the AFSJ is not convincing. First, it is not convincing because the design does not pay sufficient attention to the sector-specific objectives of the different fields of the AFSJ and the different external instruments available to the EU; second, it is not convincing because it does not pay sufficient attention to the institutional dimension of such process. From a conceptual perspective, the picture that emerges does not convince also in relation to another crucial aspect; the third main finding of this section.

36 In relation to the first aspect see M. Dony (ed.), *La dimension Externe de l'Espace de Libérté Sécurité et Justice au Lendemain de Lisbonne et de Stockholm: un Bilan à Mi-parcours*, Editions de l'Université Libre de Bruxelles, 2012. See the contribution by Fletcher and Herlin-Karnell (Chapter 16) in this volume.

37 See Section 3 in this chapter.

38 J. Monar, 'The EU's Growing External Role in the AFSJ Domain: Factors, Framework and Forms of Action' (2013) 1 *Cambridge Review of International Affairs* 12; M. Gatti, 'The Role of the European External Action Service in the External Dimension of the Area of Freedom, Security and Justice', in C. Flaesch-Mougin and L.S. Rossi (eds.), *La Dimension Extérieure de l'Espace de Liberté, Sécurité et Justice après le Traité de Lisbonne*, Bruylant, 2013, pp. 171–193. See Section 3 in this chapter.

Because the different fields of the AFSJ affect the vertical relationship between public authority and the rights and liberties of individuals in a plurality of ways, also the externalisation of the AFSJ project should make sure that human rights and civil liberties are not negatively affected whenever the EU concludes agreements with third countries or international organisations. However, the different programmatic documents marginalise this dimension: instead of building cooperation with third countries and international organisations around a reasonable balance between the public interest to security against the rights and liberties of individuals, the different actions envisaged by the programmes focus on maximising the first aspect to the detriment of the second.[39] Yet, this is probably one of the biggest challenges for the externalisation of the AFSJ, as the recent 'deal' with Turkey has revealed.[40] The combined reading of Articles 2 and 21(1) TEU demands that EU external action must be guided by the universality and inviolability of human rights, the rule of law, democracy and solidarity; however, since the *Kadi* saga the EU has not yet come to terms with the implications of Article 21 TEU.[41] Since the CJEU delivered its landmark ruling in *Kadi*, a number of AFSJ external activities have raised doubts over their legitimacy.[42]

The controversial elements that were identified in relation to the policy ambitions on the external dimensions of the AFSJ acquire particular significance if those documents are further contextualised within the framework of EU constitutional law and, in particular, EU external relations law. Therefore, the next section will analyse the main traits of the policy programmes against the backdrop of the Treaties and the existing *acquis* in EU external relations law.

2.2 *Putting the cart in front of the horses: the legal challenges of developing an external dimension of the AFSJ*

In international affairs, the EU 'must always give precedence to considerations of competence over considerations of effectiveness'.[43] This means also that, in relation to the externalisation of the AFSJ, considerations of competence must precede ambitions and goals. In the light of this observation, it appears

39 See in comparison Article 21(1) TEU and paragraph 7.2 of the Stockholm Programme. See the contributions of Poli (Chapter 15) and Fletcher and Herlin-Karnell (Chapter 16) in this volume.
40 For a short analysis of this 'deal' see above. The EU–Turkey deal can be retrieved here: www.consilium.europa.eu/en/press/press-releases/2016/03/18-eu-turkey-statement. See the contribution by Costello and Mouzourakis (Chapter 11) in this volume.
41 Joined Cases C-402/05 P and C-415/05 P *Kadi and Al Barakaat*, supra note 1.
42 A burgeoning legal literature has developed throughout the years. See the contributions of Fletcher and Herlin-Karnell (Chapter 16) and Poli (Chapter 15) in this volume. See also C. Matera and R.A. Wessel, 'Context or Content? A CFSP or AFSJ Legal Basis for EU International Agreements' (2014) 47(3) *Revista de Derecho Comunitario Europeo* 1047; E. Papastavridis, '"Fortress Europe" and Frontex: Within or Without International Law?' (2010) 79 *NJIL* 75; V. Mitsilegas, *EU Criminal Law*, Hart Publishing, 2009, pp. 291–319.
43 G. de Baere, *Constitutional Principles of EU External Relations*, Oxford University Press, 2008, p. 10.

crucial to analyse the extent to which the ambitious policy plans analysed in the previous section are compatible with the constitutional specificities of the EU legal system and the provisions on the AFSJ. To date, the sole comprehensive attempt of the institutions to address this question is the 2005 Commission Communication 'A Strategy on the External Dimension of the Area of Freedom, Security and Justice'.[44] Section VI of the Strategy provides a list of the 'policy instruments' at the disposal of the EU to act internationally in AFSJ matters. However, this document does not discuss the *legal* challenges linked to the implementation of the Strategy and does not indicate how internal and external objectives linked to the AFSJ and to other external policies are to be combined in a manner consistent with the principle of conferral and the choice of the appropriate legal basis.

Moreover, the document and the list of 'policy instruments' provided in Section VI of the Strategy can also be criticised from a policy perspective. This is because in its 11 points about 'policy instruments', the Commission disorderly combined *policies* such as the ENP in point (3) with *instruments* such as bilateral agreements in point (1) or with international *partners* in point (10) of the document. The result of this is a *confounded* and *confused*[45] list, deprived of any analytical significance since policies, instruments and partners are mixed up, with the obvious result that some entries of the list such as the broad category of 'bilateral agreements' absorb, from a legal perspective, all the other categories except for the reference to 'international organisations' in point (10), since in this context the EU often (but not exclusively) works in multilateral contexts.[46] Similarly, the reference to 'monitoring' in point (11) – where the Commission clearly intended to refer to soft-law implementation and supervision mechanisms – is applicable to all the categories, but surely has no autonomous significance. The second criticism is that the list of Section VI on policy instruments of the Strategy does not have an accompanying narrative, with the result that it is not clear how the Commission envisaged the external dimension of the AFSJ to function. Eleven years since that document was adopted, the European Council and the Commission still have not clarified these points. For instance, neither the Stockholm Programme of 2010[47] nor the Strategic Guidelines of 2014 for legislative and operational planning of AFSJ policies in the period 2015–2020 address the above-mentioned challenges.[48] Indeed, the predominant concern of the institutions has been to integrate thematic and geographic priorities of different EU policies so as to comprise them into one external

44 COM(2005) 491 final of 12 October 2005.

45 Both words originate from Latin: *cum-fundere*, to mingle together.

46 For example, when the EU concluded the UNTOC Convention. See Council Decision of 29 April 2004 on the conclusion, on behalf of the European Community, of the United Nations Convention Against Transnational Organised Crime; OJ L261 of 6 August 2004, p. 69.

47 The Stockholm Programme: An Open and Secure Europe: Serving and Protecting Citizens, Section 7.1, OJ C115/1 4 May 2010.

48 European Council, Conclusions, 26/27 June 2014, EUCO 79/14, Brussels, 27 June 2014.

policy or one external instrument. This was made clear, once more, in a paragraph of the European Council Conclusions of June 2014, where it is held that to maximise the role of the EU as a global actor, it is necessary to ensure 'consistency between member states' and EU foreign policy goals and [to improve] coordination and coherence between the main fields of EU external action, such as trade, energy, justice and home affairs, development and economic policies'.[49]

The observations that precede suggest that the European Council and the Commission have placed the cart in front of the horses. Instead of developing a strategy on the externalisation of the AFSJ by distinguishing complementary external actions to build the internal AFSJ from other external policies and/or instruments in relation to which AFSJ elements could be integrated, the internal–external AFSJ nexus is never explained and instruments and policies are simply mixed together.[50] However, it is submitted that such distinction is not only possible, but necessary. *Necessary*, because the EU is founded on the principle of conferral and on its corollary on the choice of the proper legal basis to adopt measures. As a result of the principle of conferral, action by the EU must always be construed in connection to a specific legal basis and this duty must be based on objective criteria amenable to judicial review.[51] This necessity, however, seems at odds with the holistic approach used by the European Council and the Commission in promoting the integration of the AFSJ into the various external activities of the EU because it may be impossible to combine different legal bases for the purpose of concluding an international agreement; for example, if the EU wishes to integrate AFSJ objectives with CFSP and CSDP ones.[52]

Therefore, in order to combine policy ambitions within the existing legal framework, it is necessary to clarify the relationship between AFSJ objectives with the different external instruments available in the Treaties. And in this respect, it must be emphasised that it is *possible* to clarify such relationship on the basis of the existing *acquis* on EU external relations law, as the next section will argue.

49 Ibid., p. 20.

50 Suffice to mention the laconic third paragraph of section 7 of the Stockholm Programme: 'As reiterated by the 2008 European Security Strategy report, internal and external security are inseparable. Addressing threats even far away from our continent is essential to protecting Europe and its citizens', Stockholm Programme, OJ C115 4 May 2010, p. 33.

51 See Case 45/86, *Commission v Council* (Generalised Tariff Preference) [1987] ECR 1493, Case C-300/89 *Commission v Council* (Titanium Dioxide) and, more recently, C-658/11 *European Parliament v Council* (Mauritius Agreement).

52 See in relation to restrictive measures case C-130/10, *European Parliament v Council*, Judgment 19 July 2012, paragraphs 36, 42–44, ECLI:EU:C:2012:472.

3 The external dimensions of the AFSJ: policy, practice and disputes

3.1 The AFSJ and EU external relations law

In order to clarify the nature and scope of powers available to the EU to externalise the AFSJ project, it is necessary to analyse the different AFSJ provisions of the TFEU. This is necessary for two main reasons. First, it is necessary in order to ascertain whether express external competences exist in the AFSJ field or whether the external dimensions of the AFSJ must be linked to the doctrine of implied powers now codified in Article 216(1) TFEU. Second, it is necessary in order to ascertain if, in the absence of express external AFSJ competences, external AFSJ objectives may be attained in the framework of specific external policies of the EU such as the Development Cooperation Policy (Article 208 TFEU). Lastly, this is also necessary to assess whether the decision-making procedures applicable in the AFSJ fields internally and externally can be combined with those applicable to other policies for the purpose of concluding an international agreement.

First, it should be borne in mind that the policies and the specific provisions of the AFSJ are largely inward-looking and mainly aim at safeguarding 'freedom', 'security' and 'justice' within the EU.[53] Thus, the majority of AFSJ provisions aim at creating common or uniform rules among the Member States so as to facilitate and foster cooperation between national authorities. This is the case of Articles 81–89 TFEU on judicial cooperation in civil matters, judicial cooperation in criminal matters and police cooperation: the interpretation of the different provisions shows that the focus of the AFSJ project is on creating regulatory measures to facilitate cooperation among Member States.[54] Therefore, in relation to all these domains, the external dimension of the AFSJ should be understood as a complementary tool available to attain the objectives of Articles 3(2) TEU and 67 TFEU. As a result of this, the expression 'external dimension of the AFSJ' should cover all those external activities that are *directly* related to internal developments. In this regard, three main examples come to mind: the conclusion of the Lugano Convention on jurisdiction and the recognition and enforcement of judgments in civil and commercial matters,[55] the conclusion of the Mutual Legal Assistance agreements with the USA and Japan,[56] the

53 These are the three public goods at the centre of the AFSJ project. See A. Gibbs, *Constitutional Life and Europe's Area of Freedom, Security and Justice*, Routledge, 2011.

54 See, for instance, Article 81 (2) TFEU, 82 (1) TFEU, 85(1) TFEU and 87 (2) TFEU. There is also a strong link with the subsidiarity principle, especially in the peculiar context of EU cooperation in criminal law. See E. Herlin-Karnell, 'Subsidiarity in the Area of EU Justice and Home Affairs Law: A Lost Cause?' (2009) 15(3) *European Law Journal* 351.

55 OJ L339, 21 December 2007, p. 3.

56 Agreement on mutual legal assistance between the European Union and the United States of America, OJ L181 19 July 2003, p.34 and Agreement between the European Union and Japan on mutual legal assistance in criminal matters, OJ L39 12 February 2010, p.20.

extradition agreement with the USA and, finally, the operational agreements concluded by Europol and Eurojust.[57]

In relation to policies on border checks, asylum and immigration, a *similar* conclusion can probably be drawn. Although Article 79(3) TFEU contains the only express external competence of the whole AFSJ in relation to the conclusion of readmission agreements, Article 79 TFEU on migration mainly aims at conferring to the EU the necessary powers to approximate national laws for the purpose of developing a common immigration policy. Similarly, Article 78 TFEU on the development of a common asylum policy predominantly aims at conferring to the EU the powers to create uniform asylum laws and only incidentally refers to partnership and cooperation with third countries for the purpose of managing inflows of people applying for asylum or subsidiary protection.[58] Lastly, while the mandate conferred to the EU on border controls predominantly aims at internal initiatives such as ensuring the absence of internal border controls, the different tasks attributed to the EU such as regulating the checks at the external borders of the EU and the gradual introduction of an integrated border management system appear to be 'open provisions', i.e., provisions that inherently have an external projection.[59]

This short overview suggests that the AFSJ project is mostly internally oriented and is composed of mostly 'internal provisions', i.e., provisions 'specifically focused on matters which are in principle confined within the four walls of the [EU] legal order'.[60] Bearing in mind the evolution of the AFSJ project since the entry into force of the Maastricht Treaty, it is not surprising that the different AFSJ provisions focus on the creation of common rules among the Member States. What is certain, is that the different AFSJ provisions are not related to objectives such as the promotion of 'the rule of law

57 The agreements are not published on the official journal but can be retrieved on the websites of the respective agencies. For a recent critical analysis, see J. Santos Vara, 'The External Activities of AFSJ Agencies: The Weakness of Democratic and Judicial Controls' (2015) 20(1) *European Foreign Affairs Review* 118.

58 Article 78(2)(g) TFEU. There is, however, no unanimous interpretation of this provision in the academic debate: some consider this provision an express external competence, others consider this an internal competence only. See M. Cremona, supra note 20; P. García Andrade, 'Initiatives of EU Member States in Managing Mixed Flows in the Mediterranean and the EU Distribution of Competences', in C. Matera and A. Taylor (eds.), *The Common European Asylum System and Human Rights: Enhancing Protection in Times of Emergencies*, CLEER Working Papers Series, 7/2014; G. de Baere, 'The Basics of EU External Relations Law: An Overview of the Post-Lisbon Constitutional Framework for Developing the External Dimensions of EU Asylum and Migration Policy', in M. Maes, M-C. Foblets and P. De Bruycker (eds.), *External Dimension of European Migration Law and Policy/ Dimensions Externes du Droit et de la Politique d'Immigration et d'Asile de l'UE*, Bruylant, 2011, p. 168.

59 A. Dashwood, 'The Attribution of External Relations Competence', in A. Dashwood and C. Hillion (eds.), *The General Law of E.C. External Relations*, Sweet & Maxwell, 2000, p. 131.

60 Ibid. For a recent reference to this concept see also the opinion of AG Kokott in case C-263/14 *European Parliament v Council*, paragraph 58.

and human rights, good governance, fight against corruption, the civil law dimension, promote security and stability and create a safe and solid environment for business, trade and investment'[61] in third countries; nor the AFSJ provisions seem directly related to the development of 'capacities of prevention and answers to major technological and natural catastrophes as well as to meet threats from terrorists'.[62] As a matter of fact, the treaties have ad hoc provisions for these matters in the fields of external relations such as Development Cooperation (Articles 208–211 TFEU); economic, financial and technical cooperation with third countries (Article 212 TFEU); humanitarian aid (Article 214 TFEU); and the CFSP in the TEU. Contrary to what the European Council has been advocating over the years, these last instruments alone provide the correct legal basis to conduct external relations in the fields mentioned above; not AFSJ provisions.

Moreover, this short overview also suggests that the external projection of the AFSJ needs to be developed on the basis of the doctrine of implied powers. With the entry into force of the Lisbon Treaty, Article 216 TFEU has codified the doctrine of implied powers developed by the CJEU.[63] As it has been noted by de Baere, the doctrine of implied powers 'can be inferred from the broader principle of effectiveness'.[64] On the basis of this, it is assumed that, by means of a teleological reasoning, the EU Treaties must be intended as conferring to the Union the necessary powers to achieve the envisaged objectives, including the power to conclude international agreements.[65] Furthermore, in Opinion 2/94, the CJEU held that: 'whenever [Union] law has created for the institutions of the Community powers within its internal system for the purpose of attaining a specific objective, the Community is empowered to enter into the international commitments necessary for attainment of that objective even in the absence of an express provision to that effect'.[66] Therefore, the doctrine of implied powers is closely linked to the principle of *effet utile* and EU external action is legitimised only to the extent that a given external agreement is instrumental to the attainment of the objective(s) set in a given Treaty provision. However, this does not mean that the EU is competent to act internationally with regard to every single policy for which it has internal legislative competence.[67] In fact, the use of the doctrine of implied powers is justified only to the extent that the external agreement envisaged is directly related to an internal objective and one

61 Section 7, Stockholm Programme, OJ C 115, 4 May 2010.

62 Ibid.

63 Case 22/70 *Commission v Council* (ERTA) [1971] ECR 263, paras 15,16,19.

64 De Baere, *Constitutional Principles of EU External Relations*, supra note 43

65 Ibid.

66 *Opinion 2/94* Accession by the Communities to the Convention for the Protection of Human Rights and Fundamental Freedoms [1996] ECR I-1759, para 25.

67 *Opinion 1/94* Competence of the Community to conclude international agreements concerning services and the protection of intellectual property [1994] ECR I-5267, paragraph 81 and *Opinion 2/94*, supranote.

or more provision(s) of the TFEU. Conversely, foreign policy objectives ex Article 3(5) TEU cannot be used to legitimise the conclusion of any agreement unless one or more of the conditions set out in Article 216 TFEU are fulfilled.[68] This, however, does not necessarily mean that EU external action is restricted to the scope of Article 216 TEFU: the unspecified purpose of Article 37 TEU may well be considered in this sense as a residual, general, external power of the EU that needs to be anchored solely to one or more tenets of Article 21 TEU. Yet, also in the latter case, the legitimate conclusion of an agreement on the basis of Article 37 TEU is limited by the non-affectation clause of Article 40 TEU.[69]

It emerges from the foregoing that the policy ambitions on the external dimensions of the AFSJ need to be contextualised within the existing legal framework regulating the AFSJ and the one regulating EU external relations. In the next section, a few recent initiatives will be analysed so as to indicate where the challenges reside in practice.[70]

3.2 Redefining the external dimensions of the AFSJ: practice and case law

In the introductory remarks of this contribution, it was argued that a number of factors such as the role of the executives and the emergence of (new) security threats have pushed for the externalisation of the AFSJ project. Against this backdrop, Section 2 argued that the policy programmes and ambitions of the European Council and of the Commission were disconnected from the EU legal framework inasmuch as those documents were not paying attention to a number of principles and rules regulating EU external relations on the one hand and the scope of ASFJ powers on the other. This final part of the chapter will look at whether recent developments confirm the discrepancies previously identified.

3.2.1 The relationship between the CFSP and the AFSJ

The first issue to analyse pertains the relationship between the AFSJ and the CFSP. In Section 2 it was argued that the ambitious plans to combine AFSJ policies and objectives with CFSP and CSDP ones has been at the centre of

68 This can be inferred from *Opinion 2/94*, 28/3/1996, ECLI:EU:C:1996:140.

69 In relation to the significance of Article 40 TEU see, inter alia, P. van Elsuwege, 'EU External Action After the Collapse of the Pillar Structure: In Search of a New Balance Between Delimitation and Consistency' (2010) 47 *Common Market Law Review* 987; S. Blockmans and M. Spernbauer, 'Legal Obstacles to Comprehensive EU External Security Action' (2013) 18 *European Affairs Review* 7; Matera and Wessel, 'Context or Content?' supra note 42.

70 See Case C-377/12, *Commission v Council*, Judgment 11 June 2014, ECLI:EU:C:2014:1903, on the relationship between the external dimension of the AFSJ and the Development Cooperation Policy and Case C-658/11 *European Parliament v Council*, Judgment 24 June 2014, ECLI:EU:C:2014:2025.

numerous initiatives. However, this ambition needs to be analysed on the basis of two major constraints: the different decision-making procedures existing in the TEU and the TFEU on the one side, and the ambiguous meaning of the non-affectation clause codified in Article 40 TEU. While it is undeniable that the EU faces transnational security threats that relate to both the CFSP and the AFSJ, such as transnational organised crime and international terrorism, it is equally certain that the rules on the choice of the proper legal basis and the existing differences between external action under the CFSP and external action anchored to the TFEU make it very difficult to combine legal bases for the purpose of concluding an international agreement.[71] This specific problem was brought in front of the CJEU by the European Parliament in relation to the conclusion of a number of agreements on the basis of Article 37 TEU for the transfer of arrested pirates in the framework of Operation Atalanta.[72]

Operation Atalanta is the first EU naval operation and it was launched in 2008 with the objective of contributing to the deterrence, prevention and repression of acts of piracy and armed robbery off the Somali coast.[73] Parallel to securing the waters of the Gulf of Aden, Joint Action 2008/851/CFSP introduced a regime for the purpose of prosecuting the (suspected) pirates arrested during the mission.[74] To implement this mandate, the EU chose to outsource the prosecution of suspected pirates to third countries and has concluded a number of agreements on the basis of Article 37 TEU. However, because of the *content* of these agreements,[75] the European Parliament argued that such agreements should integrate, inter alia, the relevant AFSJ legal bases on judicial cooperation in criminal matters, with the result that the Parliament would be involved in their conclusion.

On 24 June 2014, the CJEU rejected the pleas of the European Parliament and upheld the choice of the Council. The decision of the Court and the opinion of AG Bot suggest that the policy context at the heart of an agreement justifies the choice of one given legal basis against another. For the purposes of our analysis, this decision suggests that whenever the EU has to conclude an international agreement that is embedded within a specific foreign policy context, the EU can act on the basis of Article 37 TEU alone and does not have to take into consideration whether other EU policies anchored to the

71 The academic debate on this matter has not yet provided for a generally accepted answer. In relation to the specific combination of a CFSP legal basis and a TFEU one, see references at note 69 above.

72 C-263/14 *European Parliament v Council*, pending and C-658/11 *European Parliament v Council*, Judgment 24 June 2014, ECLI:EU:C:2014:2025.

73 Council Decision 2008/918/CFSP, in OJ L 330/19, 9 December 2008. For a recent analysis of the different ways the EU is involved to fight piracy in Somalia, see P. Ehrart, 'The EU, the Somalia Challenge, and Counter-piracy: Towards a Comprehensive Approach?' (2012) *European Foreign Affairs Review* 261.

74 Article 12 of Joint Action 2008/851/CFSP.

75 Matera and Wessel, 'Context or Content?' supra note 42.

TFEU are also connected. In this case, because the transfer agreements were concluded within the *context* of a CSDP operation, the fact that the *content* of the agreement related to AFSJ matters was not relevant to determine the appropriate legal basis. In a way, this choice is consistent with the reasoning used by the Court in the case revolving on restrictive measures: C-130/10 *European Parliament v Council.* Also on that occasion, the CJEU used the link to the international dimension on the fight against terrorism to confirm the use of Article 215 TFEU against the use of Article 75 TFEU.

In can be inferred from the existing case law on the relationship between the external dimension of the AFSJ and external action under the CFSP context that the Court supports the choices made by the Council against the arguments of the European Parliament.[76] Possibly, the decisions are influenced by the fuzziness of Article 40 TEU, but they do confirm that the provisions of the AFSJ are 'internal provisions' and that the institutions should prefer other forms of external powers to conclude agreements that are not directly related to the internal AFSJ objectives.[77] Yet, another recent decision of the CJEU seems to support the idea according to which express external instruments and policies can pursue and regulate AFSJ-related matters independently from AFSJ considerations.

3.2.2 The relationship of the external AFSJ with Development Cooperation

The second context in relation to which the policy programmes of the European Council are at odds with the EU legal system concerns the integration of AFSJ elements in mainstream EU external policies anchored to the TFEU. Once again also in this context, the main challenges relate to the choice of the proper legal basis for the conclusion of an international agreement. While EU external policies such as the European Neighbourhood Policy and other forms of association can be linked to AFSJ objectives under the broad umbrella of Article 217 TFEU on association agreements, the relationship between AFSJ objectives and other external policies may appear more challenging. This is the case, for example, of the relationship between EU Development Policy (Article 208 TFEU) and the external projection of the AFSJ.

In May 2012, the Council adopted Decision 2012/272/EU[78] on the signing, on behalf of the Union, of a Framework Agreement on Partnership and Cooperation between the EU and its Member States on one part and

76 The pleas brought forward by the EP in C-263/14 *European Parliament v Council*, pending, C-658/11 *European Parliament v Council*, Judgment 24 June 2014, ECLI:EU:C:2014:2025, and in relation to restrictive measures, see case C-130/10, *European Parliament v Council*, Judgment 19 July 2012, paras 36, 42–44, ECLI:EU:C:2012:472.

77 This seems to be the opinion of AG Kokott. See her opinion in case C-263/14 *European Parliament v Council*, delivered on 28 October 2015, paragraphs 60–69.

78 OJ 25 May 2012 L134/3.

the Republic of the Philippines on the other. Similarly to other Partnership and Cooperation Agreements (PCAs) concluded by the EU,[79] the EU–Philippines PCA[80] covers a wide range of dossiers: from economic and development cooperation, to trade and investment; from general political dialogue to justice and security matters, including migration. Because of the wide scope of the EU–Philippines agreement, the Council decided that the development and trade legal bases needed to be supported by sector-specific additions. As a result of this, the EU–Philippines Agreement was concluded on the basis of the following provisions: Article 79(3), readmission agreements; Articles 91 and 100, transport policy; Article 191(4), environmental policy; and Articles 207, Common Commercial Policy (CCP), and 209, Development Cooperation, in conjunction with Article 218(5), negotiation and conclusion of international agreements, TFEU. On the other side, the Commission considered this choice wrong since, according to this institution, there was no need to supplement the Development Cooperation and CCP legal bases. The Commission eventually attacked the decision of the Council ex Article 263 TFEU and on the basis of a single plea in law alleging that the Council infringed Treaty rules and established case law pertaining to the choice of the proper legal basis.

In case C-377/12 *Commission v Council*,[81] and similarly to what the CJEU had declared in *Portugal v Council*, the CJEU adhered to a broad notion of the EU's development policy. Indeed also in this case the Court affirmed that Development Cooperation pursues a wide spectrum of objectives including those 'referred to in Article 21(2) TEU, such as the objective, set out in Article 21(2)(d) TEU, of fostering the sustainable economic, social and environmental development of developing countries with the primary aim of eradicating poverty'.[82] This is an interesting point because by bridging Article 21 TEU with Article 211 TFEU, the CJEU uses a comprehensive approach to interpret EU external relations provisions so as to reflect the post-Lisbon unity of the legal order; however, and similar to what has emerged in relation to the use of Article 21 TEU to define the scope of powers attributed to the EU *qua* CFSP/CSDP, the broad scope of the provisions used by the CJEU are ill-fitted to satisfy the test concerning the identification of *objective factors* to support the choice of a determined legal basis for the purpose of concluding an agreement. Thus, also in this context, the Court gives preference to broad notions of general policies over sector-specific considerations;

79 See, for instance, the PCAs with Tajikistan OJ 29 December 2009 L350/1 or the one with Iraq 31 July 2012 L204/18.

80 For the text of the Agreement, see Brussels, 18 December 2013 COM(2013) 925 final.

81 C-377/12, *Commission v Council*, Judgment 11 June 2014. For a commentary see M. Broberg and R. Holdgaard, 'Demarcating the Union's Development and Cooperation Policy after Lisbon: *Commission v Council* (Philippines PCFA)' (2015) 52 *Common Market Law Review* 547.

82 Paragraph 37 of Case C-377/12, *Commission v Council*, Judgment 11 June 2014, nyr.

with this technique, the Court manages to solve disputes without entering into the details of a case and facilitates the absorption of sector-specific legal bases against generalist ones.

With specific regard to the topic of this contribution, it can be inferred by this decision of the CJEU that the court is willing to consider as falling under the broad umbrella of Development Cooperation even provisions that identify *in concreto* specific commitments between the parties: this was the case of Article 26(3) of the EU–Philippines Agreement because it identified a number of specific commitments on the readmission of irregular migrants between the contracting parties.[83] Therefore, also in the case of Development Cooperation, the application of EU external relations law downscales the scope of application of AFSJ provisions for the purpose of concluding international agreements if AFSJ objectives can be pursued on the basis of other external policies of the EU.

Taking into consideration the existing case law on the relationship between the AFSJ and other external relations instruments and policies, it could be argued that the objective of integrating the AFSJ with other external policies of the EU has been confirmed by the CJEU. However, the reality is more nuanced than this. Indeed, with its decisions in relation to the fight against piracy and the transfer of arrested pirates analysed above and the decision on the conclusion of the EU–Philippines Partnership and Cooperation Agreement, the CJEU suggests that AFSJ matters can be absorbed by generalist external policies of the EU with the result that the expression 'external dimension of the AFSJ', from a strict legal perspective, should be used to describe only those agreements that the EU concludes solely on the basis of an AFSJ provision, such as the ones analysed in the next section of this chapter.

83 Article 26 (3) of the EU–Philippines Agreement reads as follows: 'Within the framework of cooperation in this area and without prejudice to the need to protect victims of human trafficking, the Parties further agree that: a) The Philippines shall admit back any of its nationals as defined under paragraph 2, point e) of this Article present in the territory of a Member State upon request by the latter, without undue delay once nationality has been established and due process in the Member State carried out. b) Each Member State shall readmit any of its nationals as defined under paragraph 2, point e) of this Article present in the territory of the Philippines upon request by the latter, without undue delay once nationality has been established and due process in the Philippines carried out. c) The Member States and the Philippines will provide their nationals with required documents for such purposes. Any request for admission or readmission shall be transmitted by the requesting state to the competent authority of the requested state. Where the person concerned does not possess any appropriate identity documents or other proof of his/her nationality, the competent diplomatic or consular representation concerned shall be immediately requested by the Philippines or Member State to ascertain his/her nationality, if needed by means of an interview; and once ascertained to be a national of the Philippines or Member State, appropriate documents shall be issued by the competent Philippine or Member State authorities.'

3.2.3 The external dimension of the AFSJ: between coordination and soft law

The third context this chapter looks into is the one that directly concerns the use of internal AFSJ powers to conclude international agreements. One striking characteristic of the AFSJ is the peculiar tension existing between the national and the EU level. This to say that in addition to the vertical tensions existing over the attribution and scope of EU competences, in the fields of the AFSJ another factor comes into play: national sovereignty and its link to the exercise of sovereign prerogatives over the maintenance of public order and public security. True, the treaties acknowledge the existence of these reserved domains in Articles 4(2) TEU and 72 TFEU, but it is undeniable that each time the EU exercises its competences internally and externally, this factor comes into play, as the recent tensions over the management of the migration crisis show. However, the EU has managed to find, in respect of a number of AFSJ policies, a good balance between the exercise of external AFSJ competences with national prerogatives.

The first example is represented by the EU–USA extradition and mutual legal assistance agreements.[84] The EU–USA agreements can be considered as umbrella agreements. This means that the agreements concluded by the EU do not preclude the conclusion of bilateral Member State–USA agreements; rather, the EU–USA agreements constitute a benchmark for the conclusion of bilateral agreements between Member States and the USA: Article 18 of the Extradition Agreement and Article 14 of the Mutual Legal Assistance condition the legitimacy of bilateral agreements to the consistency of those agreements with the main EU–USA one.[85] This shows that the externalisation of the AFSJ is leading the EU to new methods of conducting external relations, a method that goes beyond the shared *versus* exclusive competence dichotomy, in order to combine integration with sovereign prerogatives and national policies.

Similar systems have also been developed in the fields of border checks and judicial cooperation in civil law. In the case of external borders checks, under the Schengen Code adopted in 2006,[86] the Regulation foresees explicitly a new type of external action for the Union and its Member States that we could call 'regulated external competence'. Article 16 of the Schengen Code establishes a special regime for 'local border traffic' and holds that rules in derogation to the Schengen Code are allowed in relation to small and local border traffic at the external borders of the Member States. By way of implementing that provision, Regulation 1931/2006 on Local Border Traffic was adopted with the objective of (1) establishing the derogatory regime of local border traffic and (2) setting the rules that Member States

84 V. Mitsilegas, 'The New EU–USA Cooperation on Extradition, Mutual Legal Assistance and the Exchange of Police Data' (2003) 8(4) *European Foreign Affairs Review* 515.

85 OJ L181, 19 July 2003, p. 34; L 181, 19 July 2003, p. 27.

86 Regulation 562/2006, of 15 March 2006; OJ of 13 April 2006, L105, p.1.

have to follow if they intend to conclude such type of agreements with a third country, including an obligation to notify the Commission, prior to its conclusion, the text of the envisaged agreement in order for the Commission to check the compatibility with the founding Regulation. Moreover, also in the fields of judicial cooperation in civil matters and private international law in general, the EU has developed new forms of external delegated powers whereby the EU entitles and authorises Member States to conclude international conventions.[87]

At the same time, where the EU does not manage to conclude bilateral agreements on AFSJ matters, the externalisation of the AFSJ takes the form of soft law initiatives.[88] For instance, soft law cooperation takes the form of mobility partnerships. Mobility partnerships are considered to be an instrument, a tool, at the disposal of the EU in order to implement the four pillars of the EU's Global Approach to Migration and Mobility (GAMM). According to the 2011 Communication of the Commission, the four pillars are: (1) organising and facilitating legal migration and mobility; (2) preventing and reducing irregular migration and trafficking in human beings; (3) promoting international protection and enhancing the external dimension of asylum policy; and (4) maximising the development impact of migration and mobility.[89] With these objectives or pillars in mind, Mobility Partnerships are positioned as a cushion between Association Agreements or other traditional frameworks of cooperation and implementation such as the Action Plans used in the framework of the ENP. Their specific advantage is that, as soft law instruments, the participation of the Member States is on a voluntary basis, allowing each EU country to decide whether to cooperate with a given third country on the basis of specific and selected topics related to migration.

However, recent developments in the fields of EU asylum law appear to be more controversial than the examples thus far considered in this section.[90] At the time of sending this contribution to press, the EU closed a deal with Turkey in order to cooperate with the latter country on the management of the Syrian refugee crisis. At the moment, the Commission is keeping an online European Agenda on Migration where it is possible to accede the

87 It is impossible to go into the details of this aspect here. For an analysis of the external dimension of judicial cooperation in civil matters, see M. Cremona, 'External Relations and External Competence of the European Union: The Emergence of an Integrated Policy', in P. Craig and G. de Búrca (eds.), *The Evolution of EU Law*, Oxford University Press, 2011, pp. 217–268.

88 See P. García Andrade, 'La Dimension Externe de la Politique Migratoire de l'Union Europeenne: un Bilan au Rravers de ses Instruments', in M. Dony (ed.), *La Dimension Externe de l'Espace de Libérté Sécurité et Justice au Lendemain de Lisbonne et de Stockholm: un Bilan à Mi-parcours*, Editions de l'Université Libre de Bruxelles, 2012.

89 Commission Communication 'The Global Approach to Migration and Mobility', COM(2011) 743 final, 18 November 2011.

90 See contribution by Costello and Mouzourakis (Chapter 11) in this volume.

different initiatives taken since May 2015.[91] On top of internal measures such as the internal relocation system that bypasses the Dublin transfer system so as to help Italy and Greece to cope with the migratory pressure,[92] and measures to financially support Regional Protection Plans and the new Regional Development and Protection Programmes, the biggest policy achievement was the negotiation of a 'deal' with Turkey.[93]

Indeed, on 18 March 2016, the EU concluded a deal with Turkey to manage the influx of asylum-seekers coming via Turkey to Greece. The deal – which was not negotiated under the terms of Article 218 TFEU and, therefore, appears to fall outside the scope of any provisions of the Treaties – is built under nine action points, of which four are worth mentioning here: (1) all new irregular migrants arriving to Greece from Turkey are to be returned to Turkey, but will be given the opportunity to seek protection under EU rules; (2) for every irregular migrant that is not entitled to receive protection in Greece and is returned to Turkey, another Syrian refugee will be resettled from Turkey to a Member State on the basis of a voluntary resettlement scheme; (3) Turkey will take any necessary measure [sic] to prevent new sea or land routes for illegal migration; (4) once the irregular crossing stops, a voluntary humanitarian admission scheme will be adopted.[94] At the same time, the deal also comes with a counterpart, or incentive, for Turkey: visa liberalisation with participating Member States, further financial aid to implement the deal, an unspecified upgrade of the custom union with the EU and a commitment to re-energise the accession process.[95]

The EU–Turkey deal epitomises the fact that the EU has tried to bypass the decision-making process regulated by the Treaties to act internationally in the field of asylum. First, it opted for soft-law instruments anchored to existing financial instruments such as the European Refugee Fund (ERF) and the Asylum, Migration and Integration Fund (AMIF);[96] second, for the purpose of striking a deal with Turkey the EU bypassed the Treaties and opted for the conclusion of an uncharted pact. At the time of closing this chapter, the deal with Turkey – which undoubtedly is an international agreement from a material perspective because it codifies obligations and rights between

91 COM(2015) 240 final, 13 May 2015, http://ec.europa.eu/dgs/home-affairs/what-we-do/policies/european-agenda-migration/background-information/index_en.htm.

92 Council Decision (EU) 2015/1601 of 22 September 2015 establishing provisional measures in the area of international protection for the benefit of Italy and Greece, OJ L 248/80 24 September 2015.

93 The precursor of the deal of March 2016 was a summit at the end of 2015, 'Meeting of the EU heads of state or government with Turkey', 29 November 2015, www.consilium.europa.eu/en/meetings/international-summit/2015/11/29.

94 EU Turkey statement, 18 March 2016, www.consilium.europa.eu/en/press/press-releases/2016/03/18-eu-turkey-statement.

95 Ibid.

96 http://ec.europa.eu/dgs/home-affairs/financing/fundings/migration-asylum-borders/index_en.htm.

the two parties,[97] appears as a striking violation of all decision-making procedures and hence the rule of law principle enshrined in the Treaties. Two main questions remain open: why wasn't the urgent procedure of Article 218 TFEU used? And why didn't the Council use the powers it has under the CFSP to address the crisis and conclude a first political agreement on the basis of Article 37 TEU? Furthermore, and from a substantive perspective, the deal does not provide for convincing mechanisms dedicated to effectively protect the rights of asylum-seekers and migrants but merely refers to the fact that Turkey will apply EU standards and that Turkey is a safe third country to which asylum-seekers can be returned with no risks for the *non-refoulement* principle. Clearly, further analysis of this uncharted pact will tell if the above-mentioned concerns are justified.

4 Conclusions

This chapter wished to analyse the manner in which the external projection of the AFSJ has been developed over the past 16 years. First, I argued that the European Council has promoted the externalisation of the AFSJ in a plurality of ways and with a view to attain a number of objectives. However, what was presented as a complementary field of EU action in order to develop and consolidate the EU as an internal Area of Freedom, Security and Justice quickly evolved into something bigger. At the same time, it was also argued that the different policy programmes have called for the integration of AFSJ elements into different external policy fields from the CFSP to the Development Cooperation Policy of the EU. Considering the broad policy spectrum covered by the policy programmes on the AFSJ and the even broader geographical spectrum covered, it was also argued that the external projection of the AFSJ as an instrument to strengthen the internal development of this policy was not at the core of the Brussels agenda.

This chapter also sought to address the relationship between the development of the external AFSJ within the policy programmes adopted by the European Council against the constitutional framework of the EU legal system. In the introduction, it was argued that the development of the AFSJ project was heavily influenced by a number of factors such as Treaty reforms, the dominance of the executives and the emergence of a number of (transnational) security threats. In Section 2, it was argued that the different policy programmes adopted between 1999 and 2014 paid no attention to the principle of conferral and its relationship with the *acquis* on EU external relations. As a result of this, while the European Council called for the integration of AFSJ objectives in a holistic manner, the same institution did not consider and address the challenges linked to such ambitions. In a legal system in

97 I refer to the broad definition of international agreement proposed by J. Klabbers, *The Concept of Treaty in International Law*, Kluwer Law International, 1995, p. 249.

which the legitimisation of an act depends on the choice of the appropriate legal basis, it is surprising that such a question was never addressed in a comprehensive manner. As a result of this, the externalisation of the AFSJ has been at the centre of a number of disputes pertaining the choice of the correct legal basis in relation to a wide array of external policies: from agreements concluded under the CFSP umbrella to agreements concluded under the Development Cooperation Policy.

The last part of this chapter analysed the questions raised in the previous section against the backdrop of existing agreements and decisions of the CJEU. From this last section, it emerged that the expression 'external dimension of the AFSJ' only covers those agreements concluded by the EU on the basis of AFSJ provisions, whereas other instruments of external action have been deemed appropriate tools to address other AFSJ-related aspects. More specifically, it can be inferred that whenever EU action contains CFSP and AFSJ elements, the former external policy absorbs AFSJ elements. However, this seems problematic if such agreements directly affect the rights and liberties of individuals because under the CFSP, the European Parliament does not take part in the decision-making process and the Court of Justice has a very limited jurisdiction. At the same time, the broad scope given to specific external policies such as the Development Cooperation Policy of the EU in the case of the readmission clauses inserted in the EU–Philippines agreement confirms that the external dimension of the AFSJ is concerned solely with the conclusion of agreements related to enforcement and operational cooperation between the EU and third countries. Lastly, the analysis of some of the key agreements concluded by the EU in the AFSJ fields show that the EU is capable of innovating the way it develops its external relations with the conclusion of umbrella agreements and with the adoption of legislative measures conferring external powers to Member States.

Finally, this chapter may also tell us something about the development of the AFSJ project. First, it suggests that the adoption of strategic policy documents to build the AFSJ has not proven to bring coherence and consistency to the policy and that in spite of all the documents adopted, the AFSJ project still lacks a clear objective. In this respect, the recent external developments in migration and asylum law show that the EU is only capable of reacting to crises, rather than preventing them. Moreover, the use of unspecified soft law instruments to address complex policies such as asylum and migration suggests that the AFSJ project, in spite of the ambitions of the European Council, increases the fragmentation of EU external action.

The development of the external dimensions of the AFSJ also tells us that very often EU external action has been developed at the edges of EU constitutional rules. Whether it relates to the division of tasks between institutions or the vertical distribution of competences between the EU and Member States, the development of the external AFSJ contributes to making this field of the EU integration process a challenging one. Lastly, another point of concern is the lack of consideration that the external dimensions of the AFSJ seem to have in relation to the rights of individuals. This is particularly evident when the EU concludes agreements that directly affect the rights of individuals within a framework such as the CFSP/CSDP, in which basic democratic and judicial instances are expressly excluded or when the EU concludes 'uncharted deals' with third countries over the faith of asylum-seekers. Further developments and research will tell us whether such approaches are sustainable in a system that should be governed by the core elements of modern constitutionalism.

References

Blockmans, S. and Spernbauer, M., 'Legal Obstacles to Comprehensive EU External Security Action' (2013) 18 *European Affairs Review* 7

Broberg, M. and Holdgaard, R., 'Demarcating the Union's Development and Cooperation Policy after Lisbon: *Commission v Council* (Philippines PCFA)' (2015) 52 *Common Market Law Review* 547

Cremona, M., 'EU External Action in the JHA Domain: A Legal Perspective', in M. Cremona, J. Monar and S. Poli (eds.), *The External Dimension of the European Union's Area of Freedom, Security and Justice*, Peter Lang, College of Europe Studies, Bruxelles, 2011, pp.81–82

Dashwood, A., 'The Attribution of External Relations Competence', in A. Dashwood and C. Hillion (eds.), *The General Law of E.C. External Relations*, Sweet & Maxwell, 2000

de Baere, G., *Constitutional Principles of EU External Relations*, Oxford University Press, 2008

de Baere, G., 'The Basics of EU External Relations Law: An Overview of the Post-Lisbon Constitutional Framework for Developing the External Dimensions of EU Asylum and Migration Policy', in M. Maes, M.-C. Foblets and P. De Bruycker (eds.), *External Dimension of European Migration Law and Policy/Dimensions Externes du Droit et de la Politique d'Immigration et d'Asile de l'UE*, Bruylant, 2011

de Witte, B., 'The Closest Thing to a Constitutional Conversation in Europe: the Semi Permanent Treaty Revision Process', in P. Beaumont, C. Lyons and N. Walker (eds.), *Convergence and Divergence in European Public Law*, Hart, 2002, pp. 39–57

Dony, M., *Droit de l'Union Européenne*, ULB, 2012

Dony, M. (ed.), *La Dimension Externe de l'Espace de Libérté Sécurité et Justice au Lendemain de Lisbonne et de Stockholm: un Bilan à Mi-parcours*, Editions de l'Université Libre de Bruxelles, 2012

Ehrart, H.G. and Petretto, K., 'The EU, the Somalia Challenge, and Counter-piracy: Towards a Comprehensive Approach?' (2012) *European Foreign Affairs Review* 261

García Andrade, P., 'Initiatives of EU Member States in Managing Mixed Flows in the Mediterranean and the EU Distribution of Competences', in C. Matera and A. Taylor (eds.), *The Common European Asylum System and Human Rights: Enhancing Protection in Times of Emergencies*, CLEER Working Papers Series, 7/2014

Gatti, M., 'The Role of the European External Action Service in The External Dimension of the Area of Freedom, Security and Justice', in C. Flaesch-Mougin and L.S. Rossi (eds.), *La Dimension Extérieure de l'Espace de Liberté, Sécurité et Justice après le Traité de Lisbonne*, Bruylant, 2013, pp.171–193

Gibbs, A., *Constitutional Life and Europe's Area of Freedom, Security and Justice*, Routledge, 2011

Herlin-Karnell, E., 'Subsidiarity in the Area of EU Justice and Home Affairs Law: A Lost Cause?' (2009) 15(3) *European Law Journal* 351

Klabbers, J., 'The Concept of Treaty in International Law' (1995) *Kluwer Law International* 249

Kostakopoulou, D., 'The Area of Freedom, Security and Justice and the European Union's Constitutional Dialogue', in C. Barnard (ed.), *The Fundamental of EU Law Revisited: Assessing the Impact of the Constitutional Debate*, Oxford University Press, 2007, pp. 153–191

Koutrakos, P., 'The External Dimension of the AFSJ and Other EU External Policies: An Osmotic Relationship', in M. Cremona, J. Monar and S. Poli (eds.), *The External Dimension of the European Union's Area of Freedom, Security and Justice*, Peter Lang, 2011

Labayle, H., *Refonder l'Espace de Liberté, Sécurité et Justice à la Lumière de l'Arrêt van Gend en Loos?* http://curia.europa.eu/jcms/upload/docs/application/pdf/2013-12/qd30136442ac_002.pdf

Lavranos, N., 'Revisiting Article 307 EC: The Untouchable Core of Fundamental European Constitutional Law Values and Principles', in F. Fontanelli, G. Martinico and P. Carrozza (eds.), *Shaping the Rule of Law Through Dialogue*, Europa Law Publishing, 2009, pp.119–146

Lavranos, N., 'Protecting European Law from International Law' (2010) 15 *European Affairs Review* 265

Matera, C., 'The European Union Area of Freedom, Security and Justice and the Fight Against New Security Threats: New Trends and Old Constitutional Challenges', in M. Arcari and L. Balmond (eds.), *Global Governance and The Challenges of Collective Security*, Editoriale Scientifica, 2012, pp. 69–87

Matera, C. and Wessel, R.A., 'Context or Content? A CFSP or AFSJ Legal Basis for EU International Agreements' (2014) 47(3) *Revista de Derecho Comunitario Europeo* 1047

Mitsilegas, V., 'The New EU–USA Cooperation on Extradition, Mutual Legal Assistance and the Exchange of Police Data' (2003) 8(4) *European Foreign Affairs Review* 515

Mitsilegas, V., *EU Criminal Law*, Hart Publishing, 2009

Monar, J., 'The External Dimension of the EU's Area of Freedom, Security and Justice. Progress, potential and imitations after the Treaty of Lisbon' (2012) 1 *SIEPS*

Monar, J., 'The EU's Growing External Role in the AFSJ Domain: Factors, Framework and Forms of Action' (2013) 1 *Cambridge Review of International Affairs*

Moreno Lax, V., 'Life After Lisbon: EU Asylum Policy as a Factor of Migration Control', in D. Acosta Arcarazo and C. Murphy (eds.), *EU Security and Justice Law: After Lisbon and Stockholm*, Hart Publishing, 2014, p. 165

Papastavridis, E., '"Fortress Europe" and Frontex: Within or Without International Law?' (2010) 79 *NJIL* 75

Peers, S., 'Finally Fit For Purpose? The Treaty of Lisbon and the End of the Third Pillar Legal Order' (2008) 27 *Yearbook of European Law* 47

Peers, S., 'Mission Accomplished? EU Justice and Home Affairs Law After the Treaty of Lisbon' (2011) 48 *Common Market Law Review* 661

Peers, S., 'Justice and Home Affairs Law Since the Treaty of Lisbon: A Fairy-Tale Ending?' in D. Acosta Arcarazo and C. Murphy (eds.), *EU Security and Justice Law After Lisbon and Stockholm*, Hart Publishing, 2014, pp. 17–37

Poli, S., 'The Institutional Setting and the Legal Toolkit', in M. Cremona, J. Monar and S. Poli (eds.), *The External Dimension of the European Union's Area of Freedom, Security and Justice*, Peter Lang, 2011

Santos Vara, J., 'The External Activities of AFSJ Agencies: The Weakness of Democratic and Judicial Controls' (2015) 20(1) *European Foreign Affairs Review* 118

Trauner, F., *New Kids on the CFSP Block: The JHA Agencies*, European Institute for Security Studies, Brussels (2016) www.iss.europa.eu/uploads/media/Brief_7_JHA_agencies.pdf

van Elsuwege, P., 'EU External Action After the Collapse of the Pillar Structure: in Search of a New Balance Between Delimitation and Consistency' (2010) 47 *Common Market Law Review* 987

Walker, N., 'In Search of the Area of Freedom, Security and Justice: A Constitutional Odyssey', in N. Walker (ed.), *Europe's Area of Freedom Security and Justice*, Academy of European Law/EUI, 2004

Wessel, R.A., Marin, L. and Matera, C., 'The External Dimension of the EU's Area of Freedom, Security and Justice', in C. Eckes and T. Konstadinides (eds.), *Crime within the Area of Freedom, Security and Justice: A European Public Order*, Cambridge University Press, 2011, pp. 272–300

15 The EU anti-terrorism policy in its external AFSJ dimension

Democratic accountability and human rights protection in the post-Lisbon Treaty era

Sara Poli

1 Introduction

The EU counters terrorism in its relations with the outer world both in the context of the Area of Freedom Security and Justice (AFSJ) and the Common Foreign and Security Policy (CFSP). In these areas before the Lisbon Treaty entered into force, executive powers dominated the decision-making process. The European Parliament was excluded both from the decision-making process leading to conclusion of international agreements in the former third pillar and from the CFSP. The role of the Court of Justice of the European Union (CJEU) was limited in the AFSJ.[1] The Treaty change of 2009 enhanced the democratic oversight over the approval of EU international agreements and broadened the competence of the Court in the context of the CFSP. Under Article 275 TFEU, second paragraph, the legality of decisions providing for restrictive measures against natural or legal persons adopted by the Council on the basis of the CFSP is subject to judicial review.[2]

The aim of this chapter is to examine how the Parliament and the Court of Justice have influenced the EU external counterterrorism policies in the light of their newly empowered status. In particular, the chapter asks if they have been capable of adequately securing the protection of human rights,

1 The research at the basis of this chapter is carried out in the context of the activities of the Jean Monnet Chair, financed by the Lifelong Learning Programme (2013–2016) and is in most of its part updated to May 2015. The CJEU's role was even more limited in the domain of the Common Foreign and Security Policy.

2 Before the Lisbon Treaty, the CJEU did not have the competence to examine the legality of CFSP measures. Nonetheless, in the *Kadi* case of 2008, the Court could examine the legality of Community measures (based on Articles 60 EC, 301 EC and 308 EC Treaty) enacted to achieve the CFSP objectives of the EU Treaty. The Court was dissatisfied with the use of Community Treaty provisions, such as Article 352 TFEU (former Article 308) to pursue CFSP objectives. See joined cases C-402/05 P and C-415/05 P, *Kadi* and *Al Barakaat v Council and Commission*, ECLI:EU:C:2008:461, paras 197–204. The position of the Court was taken into consideration in the revision of the Lisbon Treaty, which introduces Article 275 TFEU, second paragraph.

given that the atmosphere in Europe has turned as 'single-minded' about the defeat of terrorism as has the US after 9/11.[3]

In order to address this, it is necessary to sketch out the legal framework. Section 2 of this chapter maps out the legal bases justifying EU counterterrorism action in its international dimension. The description of the Treaty provisions will be complemented by a short overview of the practice to see if the EU has mainstreamed cooperation to fight terrorism in all its external relations. Section 3 focuses on the decision-making process and, in particular, on the strengthening of democratic accountability in the negotiation and conclusion of international agreements designed to prevent and pursue terrorist activities and other forms of crime. The way the Parliament has exercised its new powers in practice will be illustrated. Section 4 considers whether the weakening of intergovernmentalism in the external dimension of the AFSJ has resulted in the fortification of the substantive human rights standards, taking the Parliament's fight to strengthen the right to data protection for European citizens as a test case. Shifting attention from the Parliament to the Court of Justice, Section 5 explores whether the EU has been able to defend its values when implementing the United Nations Security Council (UNSC) resolutions, designed to tackle the financing of terrorism. In an area in which democratic accountability is conspicuously absent, it is contended that the Court of Justice has injected important antidotes to protect the due process rights of persons listed by the UNSC resolutions. Indeed, the *Kadi* line of case law[4] on restrictive measures against individuals is exemplary of the high degree of autonomy in providing legal safeguards in circumstances where the protection afforded in the international context is not satisfactory.

2 EU competence and instruments to tackle terrorism in the EU external relations

Terrorism is a global threat that concerns EU security and, at the same time, that of Member States. While the latter have the primary responsibility in adopting counterterrorism measures, the EU enjoys certain powers. For example, in order to achieve a high level of (*internal*) security (Article 67(3) TFEU), action can be taken to define minimum rules as far as criminal offences for serious forms of crimes, including terrorism (Article 88 TFUE). In its relations with the wider world, the EU has the task of contributing to security (Article 3 TEU) and to strengthening it (Article 21(2)(c) TEU). International terrorism is certainly a threat to the EU security and, more broadly, to that of the international community. Whenever a counterterrorism

3 This expression is borrowed from C. Warbrick, 'The European Response to Terrorism in an Age of Human Rights', (2004) 5 *EJIL* 995.

4 See Section 5 of this chapter.

initiative has to be taken, the EU may act either in the framework of the AFSJ or the CFSP.

In principle, the EU may act to achieve the objective of preventing and combating terrorism, under Article 75 TFEU, located in the context of the AFSJ.[5] More precisely, legislative measures may be enacted to set out a framework for administrative measures with regard to capital movements and payments, such as the freezing of funds, financial assets or economic gains belonging to, or owned or held by, natural or legal persons, groups or non-State entities. Yet, in practice, this provision, granting full legislative powers to the Parliament, has never been used by the EU. In Case C-130/10, the Court of Justice has detailed the reasons to prefer Article 215(2) TFEU as the legal foundation of these acts, when they implement a UNSC Resolution.[6] This provision enables the EU to enact measures against natural or legal persons and groups or non-State entities to implement a CFSP decision on a joint proposal from the High Representative and the Commission. The Parliament is merely informed.[7] Despite the lack of any reference to terrorism, the Court considers that Article 215(2) is better suited than Article 75 TFEU to justify measures directed to addressees implicated in acts of terrorism, having regard to their activities globally and to the international dimension of the threat they pose.[8] The Court has boosted the CFSP dimension of the counterterrorism and has underplayed the link between the financing of terrorism and the EU's internal security, which is implicitly made by Article 75 read in conjunction with Article 67 TFEU. The implication of the judgment is that Article 75 should be used to fight home-grown terrorists, although this has not happened so far.[9] From an institutional perspective, this

5 Outside the AFSJ, a further relevant provision of the TFEU, explicitly mentioning terrorism, is Article 222 TFEU. The latter is related to the internal rather than the external dimension of EU counterterrorism, since it makes it possible for the EU and its Member States to act jointly in a spirit of solidarity if a Member State is the object of, inter alia, a terrorist attack. The Union may act to prevent the terrorist threat in the territory of the Member States, to protect democratic institutions and the civilian population from any terrorist attack; and to assist a Member State in its territory, at the request of its political authorities, in the event of a terrorist attack. The so-called 'solidarity clause' has not been implemented yet.

6 C-130/10, *European Parliament v Council of the European Union*, ECLI:EU:C:2012:472.

7 See European Parliament recommendation to the Council of 2 February 2012 on a consistent policy towards regimes against which the EU applies restrictive measures, when their leaders exercise their personal and commercial interests within EU borders (2011/2187(INI)).

8 'Given that terrorism constitutes a threat to peace and international security, the object of actions undertaken by the Union in the sphere of the CFSP, and the measures taken in order to give effect to that policy in the Union's external actions, in particular, restrictive measures for the purpose of Article 215(2) TFEU, can be to combat terrorism.' Case C-130/10, *Parliament v Council*, supra note 6, para 63.

9 P. Van Elsuwege, 'The Interface between the Area of Freedom, Security and Justice and the Common Foreign and Security Policy of the European Union: Legal Constraints to Political Objectives', in R.H. Holzacker and P. Luif (eds.), *Freedom, Security and Justice in the European Union: Internal and External Dimensions of Increased Cooperation after the Lisbon Treaty* (Springer, 2014), pp. 132–133.

means that the Parliament is excluded from the decision-making process of restrictive measures.

Turning to the CFSP, Article 24(1) TEU and Article 2(4) TFEU provide that the Union's competence in CFSP matters 'shall cover … all questions relating to the Union's security'. The only explicit mention of terrorism is made in the context of Common Security and Defence Policy (CSDP). After the Lisbon Treaty, Article 43(1) TEU confers on the Union the competence to use civilian and military means to carry out various tasks that contribute to the fight against terrorism and support third countries in combating terrorism in their territories. EU action in this field, which is addressed to unstable countries unable to counter terrorist activities, has been quite modest to date. Two CSDP missions designed to enhance the capacity of third countries to fight against terrorism have been authorised. The first is the 'EUCAP Sahel Niger' mission to support capacity-building of the Nigerian security actors to fight terrorism and organised crime.[10] The second is 'EUTM Mali',[11] which purports to provide 'in the South of Mali, military and training advice to the Malian Armed Forces … in order to contribute to the restoration of their military capacity with a view to enabling them to conduct military operations aiming at restoring Malian territorial integrity and reducing the threat posed by terrorist groups'.[12] In Mali, the EU supports the work of the United Nations stabilisation mission MINUSMA.

As noted by Hillion: 'The formulation of Article 43(1) TEU cannot be understood as mainstreaming the fight against terrorism into CSDP tasks, in the sense of obliging the EU institutions systematically to consider this aspect in setting up CSDP missions. Instead the formulation of Article 43 TEU makes it plain that this is a possibility which EU decision-makers may decide to take up, or not.'[13] The use of the CSDP seems somehow exceptional. In Mali, Niger and other Sahel countries, the roots of terrorism lie in the fragility of the concerned States, the insufficient operational and strategic capacities to control the territory, to ensure human security, to prevent and to respond to the various security threats, and to enforce the law (conduct investigations, trials, etc.).[14] In addition, '[t]he available resources

10 Decision no. 2012/392/CFSP of 16 July 2012 on the European Union CSDP mission in Niger (EUCAP Sahel Niger), OJ 2012, L 187/48.

11 Council Decision no. 2013/34/CFSP of 17 January 2013 on a European Union military mission to contribute to the training of the Malian Armed Forces (EUTM Mali), OJ 2013, L 14/19.

12 Article 1.

13 C. Hillion, 'Fighting Terrorism through the Common Foreign and Security Policy', in I. Govaere and S. Poli (eds.), *EU Management of Global Emergencies: Legal Framework for Combating Threats and Crises* (Brill Nijhoff, 2014), p. 77.

14 See Strategy for Security and Development in the Sahel, www.eeas.europa.eu/africa/docs/sahel_strategy_en.pdf (accessed 30 May 2016), p. 3.

are insufficiently used to target terrorism and illegal activities'.[15] Therefore, other non-military instruments in the context of the development cooperation seemed to be favoured by the EU.[16] However, after the *Charlie Hebdo* terrorist attack, the announcement was made that '[c]ounter-terrorism may be mainstreamed fully into EU foreign policy'.[17] This may imply a wider use of CSDP missions with a counterterrorism purpose.

The EU has also concluded a number of bilateral international agreements to fight serious international crime and terrorism relying on the provisions of judicial cooperation in criminal matters. Articles 82(1)(d) and 87(2)(a) TFEU were used in the latest version of the so-called 'PNR agreements'[18] with Australia, Canada and the US, involving the transfer of Passenger Name Record (PNR) booking data by air carriers to custom authorities of the concerned third countries. A first wave of Treaties were finalised in 2004 (with the US)[19] and 2006 (with Canada),[20] in the framework of the first pillar, after the Commission found that the transfer of passengers information to third countries' authorities ensured adequate personal data protection. However, the 2004 PNR agreement was successfully challenged by the Parliament before the Court;[21] one of the grounds was that its legal basis, lying in the first pillar, was inappropriate.[22] Unfortunately, it was a pyrrhic victory for the Parliament. The implication of the ruling was that the agreement had to be renegotiated in the framework of the third pillar in which there were no standards as far as data protection was concerned.[23] In 2006, an interim agreement was

15 Ibid.

16 See infra.

17 Foreign Affairs Council meeting, document no. 6044/15, 9 February 2015, p. 7.

18 These agreements are based on the processing and transfer of data held by private entities to border and custom authorities of third countries.

19 Council Decision 2004/496/EC of 17 May 2004 on the conclusion of an Agreement between the European Community and the United States of America on the processing and transfer of PNR data by Air Carriers to the US Department of Homeland Security, Bureau of Customs and Border Protection, OJ 2004, L 183/83.

20 See Agreement between Canada and the European Community on the transfer and processing of Passenger Name Record data, OJ 2006, L 82/15. By contrast with the EU–US PNR Treaty of 2004, this agreement was not challenged before the Court since it did not raise data protection concerns. V. Mitsilegas, *EU Criminal Law* (Hart Publishing, 2009), p. 304.

21 See C-317/04 and 318/04, *Parliament v Council*, ECLI:EU:C:2006:346.

22 The background of this challenge was that the Parliament found the US data protection standards were inadequate with respect to the European ones.

23 The only existing instrument on data protection was Directive 95/46/EC of the European Parliament and of the Council of 24 October 1995 on the protection of individuals with regard to the processing of personal data and on the free movement of such data. This piece of legislation did not apply to activities falling outside the scope of Community law. The first act addressing data protection standards in the context of cooperation in criminal matters was the Framework Decision 2008/977/JHA of 27 November 2008 on the protection of

concluded and was followed by a second one in 2007. In addition, the text 'clearly and consistently steer[ed] away from all European basic data protection principles'.[24] As hinted above, in the post-Lisbon era, the first generation of agreements were then replaced by new ones with Australia (2012),[25] the US (2012)[26] and Canada (2014).[27] The content of these Treaties reflects a higher standard of data protection, as we shall see later.[28]

Beyond the PNR agreement, a second example of a treaty with the US, which is based on the provisions of the AFSJ, is that on the Terrorist Finance Tracking Programme (TFTP).[29] The legal foundations of the Council decision are Articles 87(2)(a) and 88(2) TFEU, in conjunction with Article 218(5) TFEU. The TFTP is aimed at collecting information on financial transactions in order to cut the financing of terrorist activities. The TFTP is the first EU Treaty that was rejected by the Parliament, shortly after the entry into force of the Lisbon Treaty.[30] As with the PNR agreements, these negotiations were fraught with data protection concerns. So, although cooperation with the US, Australia and Canada on terrorism is intense and advanced,[31] it has certainly not been plain sailing.

personal data processed in the framework of police and judicial cooperation in criminal matters, OJ 2008, L 350/60.

24 For a full account of these concerns see V. Papakonstantinou and P. De Hert, 'The PNR Agreement and Transatlantic Anti-terrorism Co-operation: No Firm Human Rights Framework on either Side of the Atlantic', (2009) 46 *Common Market Law Review* 913.

25 See Agreement between the European Union and Australia on the processing and transfer of Passenger Name Record (PNR) data by air carriers to the Australian Customs and Border Protection Service, OJ 2012, L 186/4.

26 See the Agreement between the United States of America and the European Union on the use and transfer of PNRs to the United States Department of Homeland Security, published in OJ 2012, L 215/5.

27 See the Agreement between Canada and the European Union on the transfer and processing of PNR data signed on 25 June 2014. The agreement is not yet in force, pending an opinion of the CJEU on the compatibility of the envisaged agreement with the Treaty, under Article 218(11). See Section 3 of this chapter.

28 See Section 3 of this chapter.

29 Agreement between the European Union and the United States of America on the processing and transfer of Financial Messaging Data from the European Union to the United States for purposes of the Terrorist Finance Tracking Program, OJ 2010, L 8/11.

30 See infra.

31 This is witnessed by the number of international agreements and by the quality of the cooperation (legally binding agreement versus mere joint political declarations). The scope of the cooperation is also broad; it includes exchange of information in the context of police cooperation. The US was the first third country to sign a cooperation agreement with Europol in December 2001. Australia and Canada also signed similar agreements with Europol in 2007 and 2005. Further agreements concluded in the framework of the third-pillar provisions of the EU Treaty before the Lisbon Treaty are the Agreement on mutual legal assistance between the European Union and the United States of America (OJ 2003, L 181/34) and the Agreement on extradition between the European Union and the United States of America (OJ 2003, L 181/27). Both agreements supplement

Cooperation on combating terrorism is not framed in legally binding terms with other key international actors, such as Japan (2001),[32] India (2010),[33] Pakistan (2012)[34] and Russia (2014).[35] Indeed, most of these initiatives have been criticised at practitioner level since they have failed to yield concrete results.[36] The EU–Japan declaration is a particularly loose form of cooperation, merely *encouraging* cooperation in multilateral fora, early finalisation of the UN Comprehensive Convention against international terrorism and a commitment to assist post-Afghanistan. Other declarations are more detailed in describing the spectrum of the cooperation.[37] In addition, the possibility to upgrade the cooperation into full international agreements, including exchange of information (Russia) or mutual legal assistance and extradition (India), is left open but there is no timeline for this objective to be achieved.

As a result of the European Council's call to incorporate the fight against terrorism into all aspects of the Union's external relations (June 2002), the EU has indeed mainstreamed cooperation on counterterrorism in the framework of single external policies (such as the enlargement and European Neighbourhood and Development Cooperation Policies). After 2004, the EU envisages counterterrorism cooperation in all bilateral agreements with candidate countries[38] as well as in the action plans

existing bilateral agreements (Article 3). The former Treaty, inter alia, lays down the terms of the cooperation in case a request concerns counterterrorism. Under Article 4(4)(b), the Member States must as a minimum cooperate with the US 'in the identification of accounts associated with terrorist activity and the laundering of proceeds generated from a comprehensive range of serious criminal activities, punishable under the laws of both the requesting and requested States'.

32 See EU–Japan Joint declaration, 8 December 2001.

33 See EU–India Joint declaration on international terrorism, 10 December 2010.

34 See EU–Pakistan strategic dialogue, 5 June 2012.

35 See Joint EU–Russia statement on combatting terrorism, 28 January 2014.

36 J. Argomaniz, *The EU and Counter-Terrorism: Politics, Polity and Policies After 9/11* (Routledge, 2011), p. 94.

37 For example, in the Declaration with Russia, emphasis is placed on the strengthening of cooperation in countering terrorist financing activities, as well as legal cooperation, in particular in extradition and legal assistance on criminal cases, including identification, arrest, confiscation and return of property acquired through terrorist activities. In the declaration with India, the parties envisage to coordinate efforts against terrorists and terrorist groups so as to deny them safe haven and freedom of travel in accordance with international law. They also encourage more efficient controls on issuance of identity and travel documents to prevent movement of terrorists and terrorist groups across national borders.

38 The parties' cooperation concerns the financing of terrorism and money-laundering. In these areas, the EU encourages the partners to adopt the standards of the Financial Action Task Force. In addition, the parties agree to implement UNSC 1373 (2001) and to exchange information on terrorist groups. See Articles 82 and 87 of the EU stabilisation and association agreement with Montenegro, OJ 2010, L 108/3. The content of these provisions is replicated in other agreements of this kind.

with neighbouring countries[39] and other third countries[40] or groups of States.[41]

Cooperation in the area of counterterrorism is also included in the association agreements with Eastern European countries such as Georgia, Moldova and Ukraine. The cooperation envisaged with Georgia is the most far-reaching one. The EU extends its internal *acquis* on the criminalisation of terrorist offences to the Party concerned.[42] This country agrees to cooperate in the framework of the UN and the Council of Europe in order to exchange information on terrorist groups (with due respect to privacy and data protection). Further exchanges concern best practices in addressing and countering radicalisation and recruitment and as regards the protection of human rights in the fight against terrorism, in particular in relation to criminal justice proceedings.[43] Turning to the association agreement with Ukraine, this act envisages the cooperation between the Parties on counterterrorism action but, by contrast with that of Georgia, it does not cover the cooperation on the best practices in relation to terrorism and human rights.[44] It should be noted that in none of these three agreements is the cooperation on counterterrorism considered an essential element of the agreements.[45] Therefore, a breach of the clause may not lead to the suspension of the agreement.

39 In this context, cooperation on terrorism and broad forms of crime is a common feature in all ENP Action Plans and this cooperation has been progressively framed in legally binding terms. Cooperation in these areas features in all association agreements concluded with Southern neighbours and negotiated after 2005.

40 Such as Tajikistan and Iraq. For a more detailed analysis of counterterrorism clauses, see C. Matera, 'The Development of an External Dimension of the EU Counter-terrorism Policy: A Framework for an Analysis', in C. Matera and E. Herlin-Karnell, *The External Dimension of the EU Counter Terrorism Policy*, CLEER Working papers no. 2014/2, p. 22. The EU has also included counterterrorism clauses in the EU framework agreement with the Republic of Korea (Council Decision of 10 May 2010 on the signing, on behalf of the European Union, and provisional application of the Framework Agreement between the European Union and its Member States, on the one part, and the Republic of Korea, on the other part (2013/40/EU), OJ 2013, L 20/2). Article 7 refers to the Parties' cooperation in the prevention and suppression of terrorist acts in the context of the UN and to the sharing and exchange of practices and information, including in the area of protection of human rights in the fight against terrorism.

41 See Article 16 of the Agreement establishing an Association between the European Union and its Member States, on the one hand, and Central America (2012), OJ 2012, L 346/3. This is the first bi-regional agreement signed after the entry into force of the Lisbon Treaty.

42 Georgia is required to ensure the criminalisation of terrorist offences, in line with the definition contained in the Council Framework Decision 2008/919/JHA of 28 November 2008 amending Framework Decision 2002/475/JHA on combating terrorism. See Article 20 of the association agreement between the EU and the European Atomic Energy Community and its Member States, of the one part, and Georgia, of the other part, OJ 2014, L 261/13.

43 This form of cooperation is also envisaged in the association agreement between the EU and the European Atomic Energy Community and its Member States, of the one part, and Moldova of the other part (Article 19), OJ 2014, L 260/4.

44 Association agreement between the EU and its Member States of the one part, and Ukraine, of the other part, OJ 2014, L 161/3.

45 Respect for the democratic principles, human rights and fundamental freedoms and countering the proliferation of weapons of mass destruction are considered to be essential elements of these agreements (see Article 2 of the association agreement with Moldova).

The EU also assists third countries in strengthening their capacity to fight terrorism. Providing assistance is a way to implement the Union's strategy to 'increase its involvement in the efforts of the international community to prevent and stabilise regional conflicts and promote good governance and the rule of law'.[46] The Instrument for Stability, established by Regulation (EC) No. 1717/2006, revised in 2014,[47] is 'the only instrument specifically designed to address pure counter-terrorism (civilian) needs, including at national and regional levels'.[48] It sets out to assist developing countries[49] in addressing global and trans-regional threats to peace, international security and stability, such as terrorism, organised crime, all forms of illegal trafficking, as well as emerging threats such as cybercrime by strengthening the capacity of law enforcement and judicial and civil authorities involved in fighting these sources of threats (Article 5(2)(a)). Assistance is given to individual countries or countries of the same region or regional international organisations.[50] Supporting measures that are prioritised include:

> the development and strengthening of counter-terrorism legislation, the implementation and practice of financial law, of customs law and of immigration law, the development of law-enforcement procedures which are aligned with the highest international standards and which comply with international law, the strengthening of democratic control and institutional oversight mechanisms, and the prevention of violent radicalism.[51]

Unlike the 2006 Regulation, the new one dedicates a self-standing provision (Article 10) to 'human rights', thus showing a special attention toward this issue in its external counterterrorism strategy. The Commission shall develop operational guidance to ensure that human rights[52] are taken into consideration in the design and implementation of the supporting measures to counter terrorism. This institution undertakes to carefully monitor that the mentioned measures are implemented in line with human rights obligations.[53] However, nowhere in the Regulation are the consequences of a

46 See the European Council Declaration on combating terrorism, 25 March 2004.

47 Regulation (EU) 230/2014 of the European Parliament and of the Council of 11 March 2014 establishing an instrument contributing to stability and peace, OJ 2014, L77/1.

48 European Commission, *Addressing Conflict Prevention, Peace-Building and Security Issues Under External Cooperation Instruments*, guidance note, p. 14. Counterterrorism assistance is excluded under both the European Development Fund and the Development Cooperation Instrument. Ibid., p. 13.

49 The Regulation is based on Articles 209 and 212 TFEU. The use of the latter implies that countries other than developing countries are entitled to benefit from EU financial support.

50 Article 5(3)(a).

51 Article 5(3)(c).

52 In particular, as regards the prevention of torture and other cruel, inhuman or degrading treatment and respect for due process, including the presumption of innocence, the right to a fair trial and the right of defence (Article 10(2)).

53 Article 10(3).

failure to comply with the Commission's guidelines spelled out. For example, it is not specified whether the breach of human rights counterterrorism action of assisted countries could lead to a suspension of financial assistance.

It should be noted that the cooperation on counterterrorism is a 'principled one'. The Commission emphasises that when developing cooperation with third countries on counterterrorism, the EU demands respect of 'human rights law, international humanitarian and refugee law, free and fair judicial proceedings, as well as the protection of personal and private data. In its human rights dialogues with third countries, the EU already raises violations of human rights committed under the guise of counter terrorism activities'.[54] Probably, the EU acts through quiet diplomacy, since there do not seem to be any situations in which counterterrorism action of a third country, disrespecting human rights, was publicly brought to the attention of the international community by the EU executives.[55] While the EU Charter applies to all EU measures countering terrorism, including international agreements, by contrast, it does not apply to counterterrorism action taken at national level. Indeed, the EU competence in this field has constitutional limits. Under Article 4(2) of the TEU, 'the Union shall respect the equality of Member States [...] as well as their national identities [...] It shall respect their essential state functions, including [...] safeguarding national security.' In addition, under Article 72 TFEU, maintenance of law and order and the safeguarding of internal security remain Member States' prerogatives. Although the Court of Justice has widely interpreted Article 51(2) in the *Fransson* case,[56] it would be very difficult for the Court to demand that Member States respect the Charter when acting to protect the national security from a terrorist threat. Indeed, such an action would lie outside the scope of EU law. This means that where Member States, in the name of national security, carry out counterterrorism activities that breach human rights standards, the EU's safeguards are not applicable, *qua* EU law. However, it should be noted there is tension

54 Joint Communication to the European Parliament and the Council, *Human Rights and Democracy at the Heart of the EU External Action: Toward a More Effective Approach*, COM(2011) 886 final, 12 December 2011, p. 13.

55 By contrast, the Parliament has raised the human rights concerns of the US practices in countering terrorism on more than one occasion. In its view, 'the EU must consistently raise with strategic partners all examples of non-compliant counter-terrorism measures and seek accountability for violations both within and outside the EU'. See European Parliament Resolution of 18 April 2012 on the Annual Report on Human Rights in the World and the European Union's policy on the matter, including implications for the EU's strategic human rights policy (2011/2185(INI)), para 152). For example, the Parliament has urged President Obama to honour its promise to close the Guantánamo Bay detention facility and has emphasised that normal criminal trials under civilian jurisdiction are the best way to resolve the status of Guantánamo detainees. See European Parliament Resolution of 23 May 2013 on Guantánamo: hunger strike by prisoners (2013/2654(RSP)), P7_TA(2013)0231, para 9.

56 C-617/10 *Åklagaren v Hans Åkerberg Fransson*, ECLI:EU:C:2013:105.

at EU level as to the scope of national security, as we shall see in the next section.

3 The strengthening of democratic oversight and problems of secrecy

Before the Lisbon Treaty, the EU cooperation with third countries in the area of criminal and police cooperation was based on third-pillar provisions of the Treaty (i.e., Article 38 TEU). This meant that the Parliament was not even consulted when international agreements in this area were concluded. In a resolution of 2007, the European Parliament complained about the lack of democratic accountability in the external dimension of the AFSJ and advocated a number of changes to be introduced. The first request concerned the consultation of the Parliament in respect of 'third-pillar' agreements, especially those affecting the fundamental rights of Union citizens and the main aspects of judicial and police cooperation with third countries or international organisations. The second recommendation was to keep the Parliament regularly informed of the negotiations on agreements dealing with the AFSJ and to make sure that Parliament's views were duly taken into consideration.[57] The Lisbon Treaty and an inter-institutional agreement between the Parliament and the Commission of 2010[58] have partially addressed the democratic deficit.

Under Article 218(6)(v) TFEU, the Parliament has to express its consent to all agreements that concern matters subject to the ordinary legislative procedure or to a procedure where its consent is required. In addition, under Article 218(10) TFEU, the Parliament must be kept fully informed during all stages of the negotiation and conclusion of the agreement. The interinstitutional agreement mentioned above includes the obligation of the latter to forward the former with all relevant information that it provides to the Council. In addition, the Commission is bound to take due account of Parliament's comments.[59] It should be noted that informal cooperation between the EU and third countries is not subject to the requirements of Article 218(10) and of the inter-institutional agreements and therefore is not well-received by the Parliament.[60]

57 Parliament Resolution of 21 June 2007 on an Area of Freedom, Security and Justice: Strategy on the external dimension, Action plan implementing the Hague Programme (2006/2111(INI)), OJ 2008, C 146/354, points 1 and 2.

58 Framework agreement on relations between the European Parliament and the European Commission, OJ 2010, L 304/47.

59 Annex III, points 3 and 5. For additional comments on the scope of the Parliament's rights see C. Eckes, 'How the European Parliament's Participation in International Relations Affects the Deep Tissue of the EU's Power Structures' (2014) Jean Monnet Working Paper, 12/14, pp. 6–7.

60 European Parliament Resolution of 11 November 2010 on the global approach to transfers of passenger name record (PNR) data to third countries, and on the recommendations

Not only the letter of legal process but also practice confirms the prominent role of the Parliament. In December 2009, the Parliament rejected the EU–US agreement with the US on the TFTP[61] on data protection grounds,[62] using for the first time its power of consent. This is notable because the negotiations took place just prior to the entry into force of Lisbon on 1 December 2009 and therefore technically EP consent was not required. The Commission was forced to renegotiate the agreement. In July 2010, finally, the Parliament approved the text on account of the strengthened level of data protection.

The TFTP saga also led to an important and welcome ruling that narrowly construed the scope of one of the exceptions to the principle of access to documents and, more broadly, reinforced the principle of transparency in EU external relations. A member of the Parliament had asked the Council to have access to the opinion of the Council legal service on the choice of the legal basis of the envisaged agreement. Only partial access was authorised by the Council. The latter's decision was challenged before the General Court (GC) by Ms In'tVeld. The protection of the EU public interest as regards the EU's international relations was the exception invoked by the defendant as the ground to refuse full access to this document. The GC,[63] which partially upheld the action, considered that the Council had not established the risk of a threat to the public interest in the field of international relations concerning the undisclosed parts of the document relating to the legal basis. On appeal, the CJEU[64] confirmed this interpretation. The information on the choice of the legal basis provided in the Council document was unlikely to undermine the negotiating position of the EU and, more broadly, EU international relations.

The European Parliament does not have the power to initiate the suspension or termination of an international agreement under Article 218 TFEU.

from the Commission to the Council to authorise the opening of negotiations between the European Union and Australia, Canada and the US. Para 9 states that 'bilateral memorandums of understanding between Member States and the USA, alongside negotiations between the EU and the USA, are contrary to the principle of loyal cooperation between the EU institutions; urges the Council to provide further information and legal clarity on the situation regarding the legal base and competence of bilateral memorandums of understanding between Member States and the USA concerning information exchanges related to PNR data', OJ 2012, C 74/E/8.

61 This agreement was made necessary by the fact that in 2010 the provider of financial data to US authorities implemented a new messaging architecture, consisting of two processing zones – one zone in the US and the other in the European Union. Previously, this company had stored all relevant financial messages on two identical servers, located in Europe and the US. In order to ensure the continuity of the TFTP, the US had to conclude an international agreement with the European Union. COM(2013) 843 final, p. 2.

62 See infra.

63 T-529/09 *In'tVeld v Council*, ECLI:EU: T:2012:215. The GC only partially annulled the Council's decision refusing access to information.

64 C-350/12 P *Council v In't Veld*, ECLI:EU:C:2014:2039.

In October 2013, the Parliament exerted pressure on the Commission to suspend the TFTP as a result of the disclosure of the US mass surveillance programmes in June 2013.[65] Yet, since the Commission was convinced by the US that there was not a breach of the agreement, the request to suspend was rejected and the Parliament did not have any legal means by which to oppose the assessment of the Commission.

After the rejection of the TFTP in 2009, the Parliament has kept a watchful eye on the negotiation process of agreements designed to prevent terrorism and other forms of crime. This has meant that the Commission and the Council have had to compromise with the Parliament on the content of several bilateral agreements. Such a power cannot be directly inferred from the right to be immediately informed in all the stages leading to the conclusion of an international agreement, provided for by Article 218(10) TFEU.[66]

As hinted at above, the conclusion of PNR agreements is exemplary of the Parliament's major role in shaping EU relations with third countries. The cooperation with the US has played a crucial role in influencing the EU strategies to counter terrorism. Before the Lisbon Treaty, the EU had been quite uncritical in adopting the US techniques incorporated in the legislation adopted between 2001 and 2002, as a reaction to 9/11. In May 2010, the Parliament postponed its vote on the request for consent on the existing PNR agreements with the US and Australia. It demanded that the existing PNR agreements with Canada, Australia and US be renegotiated (5 May 2010).

The approval of the PNR agreements was fraught with difficulties because of the Parliament's concerns over European citizens' insufficient guarantees of data protection. Among all agreements with the transatlantic partners and Australia, that with the US met the strongest opposition by the Parliament. Special points of concern were the excessively long data retention periods, the use of the most privacy-intrusive transmission methods of travellers data to non-EU-recipients,[67] the possibility of data mining

65 Parliament resolution of 23 October 2013 on the suspension of the TFTP agreement as a result of US National Security Agency surveillance (P7_TA(2013)0449).

66 H. Hijmans and A. Scirocco, 'Shortcomings in EU Data Protection in the Third and Second Pillars: Can the Lisbon Treaty Be Expected to Help?' (2009) 46 *Common Market Law Review* 1522.

67 Internet-based communication of data can be made through different methods. The 'push system' is the method that encroaches less on the right to data protection and is the one favoured by the EU institutions when agreements providing exchange of information between EU flight companies and the competent border authorities of third countries are concerned. Under this system, the communication of information is initiated by the publisher or central server (data controller) and therefore it can be seen as deliberate transfer of data. In the pull system, the transmission of the information is initiated by the recipient (the third country interested in the receiving the data). European Data Protection Supervisor, 'The Transfer of Personal Data to Third Countries and International Organizations by the EU', 14 July 2014, p. 7, https://secure.edps.europa.eu/EDPSWEB/webdav/site/mySite/shared/Documents/Supervision/Papers/14-07-14_transfer_third_countries_EN.pdf (accessed 2 May 2015).

and flaws in the redress provisions with respect to European citizens.[68] As a result, the negotiation of the text of the agreement was prolonged in order to assuage Parliament's concerns. In 2010, as a result of this institution's pressure, the Commission for the first time laid down a set of general criteria that would form the basis of future negotiations on PNR agreements with third countries.[69]

Shortly after the Parliament decision to postpone the vote on the PNR agreement, the Commission recommended to the Council to authorise the opening of negotiations for an 'umbrella agreement' between the EU and the USA on protection of personal data when transferred and processed for the purpose of preventing, investigating, detecting or prosecuting criminal offences, including terrorism, in the framework of police cooperation and judicial cooperation in criminal matters.[70] It is clear that the Parliament's work was central to this decision. This institution asked the Commission not to initiate any new sectoral agreements or arrangements for the transfers of personal data for law enforcement purposes with the US as long as this framework agreement has not entered into force.[71]

The Parliament finally approved the PNR with the US and, although a few Member States were not thoroughly convinced of the terms of the agreements, the latter finally entered into force in 2012.

Although in no case has the Parliament prevented the conclusion of an international agreement with the US and other transatlantic partners, this institution has influenced the content of the agreements and has used all instruments at its disposal when the final texts did not satisfy legal safeguards on data protection.[72] In November 2014, the Parliament has also sought an advisory opinion from the CJEU on the EU-PNR agreement with Canada.[73] The critical opinion of the European Data Protection supervisor on the

68 European Parliament resolution of 12 July 2007 on the PNR agreement with the United States of America, P6_TA(2007)0347.

69 COM(2010) 492 Communication from the Commission on the global approach to transfers of Passenger Name Record (PNR) data to third countries, 22 September 2010, p. 3.

70 The European Council had invited the Commission to propose a recommendation for the negotiation of a data protection and, where necessary, data-sharing agreement for law enforcement purposes with the US in the Stockholm programme 'An Open and Secure Europe Serving and Protecting Citizens', 2010, point 2.5.

71 European Parliament resolution of 12 March 2014 on the US NSA surveillance programme, surveillance bodies in various Member States and their impact on EU citizens' fundamental rights and on transatlantic cooperation in Justice and Home Affairs (2013/2188(INI)), para 58.

72 By contrast the negotiation of the agreement with Australia was smooth on account of the good level of cooperation between the Parliament, Commission and Council. See Eckes, supra note 59, pp. 14–15 for more details on the Australian agreement.

73 The Parliament argues that there is legal uncertainty as to whether the draft agreement is compatible with the provisions of the Treaties (Article 16) and the Charter of Fundamental Rights of the European Union (Articles 7, 8 and 52(1)) as regards the right of individuals to protection of personal data. In addition, it questions the choice of legal basis, i.e., Articles 82(1)(d) and 87(2)(a) TFEU rather than the provision on data protection. See the European Parliament resolution of 25 November 2014 on seeking an opinion from the Court of Justice on the compatibility with the Treaties of the Agreement between Canada and the European Union on the transfer and processing of PNR data.

necessity and proportionality of the PNR schemes[74] as well as the CJEU's annulment of the data retention Directive[75] were undoubte\2dly influencing factors here.

An important source that broadens the information available to the Parliament to influence the negotiation of international agreements (outside the CFSP) is the inter-institutional agreement between the Parliament and the Council concerning the forwarding to and handling by the European Parliament of classified information held by the Council on matters other than in the area of the Common Foreign and Security Policy.[76] As a result of this, the Parliament will be able to get access to classified documents. However, this agreement has an important limitation: the documents classified by third parties cannot be disclosed.[77]

A further technique used by the Parliament to steer the negotiation of important data protection agreements is to threaten not to consent to international agreement under negotiation in domains outside the AFSJ. For example, after the revelations on mass surveillance programmes, the Parliament threatened not to give its consent to the EU–US Transatlantic Trade and Investment Partnership so long as the blanket mass surveillance activities and the interception of communications in EU institutions and diplomatic representations were not completely abandoned and an adequate solution was found for the data privacy rights of EU citizens, including administrative and judicial redress.[78]

Next, the Parliament has been able to halt the adoption of internal legislation that replicated the security strategy of third countries actively cooperating with the EU in counterterrorism, such as the US. This is the case of the so-called EU Passenger Name Record (PNR) system for the surveillance of air travel. There is a strong support at intergovernmental level for an EU system for collecting and processing PNR data by the EU Member States. This instrument is seen by the counterterrorism coordinator as a valuable tool against the threat posed by terrorists travelling from and into the EU and within the EU.[79]

74 The European Data Protection Supervisor (EDSP) has always been critical of the PNR agreements with third countries. The EDPS has not seen convincing elements showing the necessity and proportionality of the massive and routine processing of data of non-suspicious passengers for law enforcement purposes. See Executive Summary of the Opinion of the European Data Protection Supervisor on the proposals for Council decisions on the conclusion and the signature of the agreement between Canada and the European Union on the transfer and processing of passenger name record data, para 3 (OJ 2014, C 24/51).

75 Joined Cases *Digital Rights Ireland Ltd* (C-293/12) *v Minister for Communications, Marine and Natural Resources and Others and Kärntner Landesregierung* (C-594/12) and *Others*, ECLI:EU:C:2014:238.

76 OJ 2014, C 95/1.

77 D. Curtin, 'Official Secrets and the Negotiation of International Agreements: Is the EU Executive Unbound?' (2013) 50 *Common Market Law Review* 453.

78 European Parliament resolution of 12 March 2014 on the US NSA surveillance programme, cit, para 74.

79 Annual report on the implementation of the EU Counter-Terrorism Strategy, 2012, doc. no. 16471/1, 23 February 2012, p. 28.

In June 2014, revelations on the number of EU nationals, defined as 'foreign fighters', who leave the EU to fight in Syria or Iraq has caused the European Council to consider the adoption of an EU-PNR scheme as an important instrument to dissuade, detect and disrupt suspicious travel of these persons. As a result, it called the Council and the European Parliament to finalise work on the EU Passenger Name Record proposal before the end of 2014.[80] The idea of creating an in-house PNR scheme had been in discussion for quite some time. An attempt to set up an EU-PNR scheme has been made by the Commission upon request of the European Council since 2007.[81] This proposal became a proposal for a Directive after Lisbon.[82] However, its approval was halted by a negative vote of the LIBE Committee of the Parliament that questioned the necessity and proportionality of this new instrument in April 2013.[83] It is not sure, however, that the Parliament will be able to resist internal intergovernmental pressure[84] as well as the UNSC requests made to UN members with Resolution 2178 of September 2014 and finally the emotional shock of the Paris terrorist attacks of 2015. The concerned resolution calls upon the latter:

> to require airlines to provide advance passenger information to the appropriate national authorities in order to detect the departure from, entry into, or transit through their territory of individuals previously identified as falling within the scope of the resolution (para 9). States should furthermore prevent the movement and travel of terrorists through effective

80 'The European Council Guidelines may well constitute therefore a strategic attempt to re-inject "intergovernmentalism" or to bring back the old EU Third Pillar working habits of the JHA Council to the entire new institutional fabric of the EU AFSJ.' S. Carrera and E. Guild, 'The European Council's Guidelines for the Area of Freedom, Security and Justice 2020: Subverting the "Lisbonisation" of Justice and Home Affairs?' (2014) 13/14 *CEPS Essays* 6.

81 Discussions on the introduction of an 'EU PNR scheme' started after the European Council of 25–26 March 2004 invited the Commission to bring forward a proposal on an EU common approach on the use of PNR data for law enforcement purposes. See Proposal for a Council framework Decision on the use of Passenger Name Record (PNR) for law enforcement purposes, COM(2007) 654, of 6 November 2007.

82 In January 2010, the Council asked the Commission to present a proposal for an EU PNR. The European Commission put forward a new proposal for a Directive on EU-PNR on 2 February 2011.

83 www.statewatch.org/news/2014/nov/ep-eu-pnr-prel.pdf (accessed 30 May 2016).

84 The conclusions of the European Council of 30 August 2014 state: 'The European Council strongly believes that determined action is required to stem the flow of foreign fighters. It calls for the accelerated implementation of the package of EU measures in support of Member States efforts, as agreed by the Council since June 2013, in particular to prevent radicalisation and extremism, share information more effectively – including with relevant third countries, dissuade, detect and disrupt suspicious travel and investigate and prosecute foreign fighters. In this context, the European Council calls on the Council and the European Parliament to finalise work on the EU Passenger Name Record proposal before the end of the year.'

border control and close monitoring of the issuance of identity papers and travel documents (para 2).

A new wave of counterterrorism measures including an EU-PNR are likely to be adopted in the coming months.

A further interesting development of the Parliament's institutional practice concerns its decision to take a stand in situations in which the border between EU and national security is blurred. When the *Guardian* and the *Washington Post* revealed the existence of Prism in June 2013,[85] the Parliament instructed the Committee on Civil Liberties, Justice and Home Affairs to conduct an in-depth inquiry on the mass surveillance programme and its impact on human rights of EU citizens. The position was taken that the notion of 'internal security' should be interpreted in a restrictive manner and therefore issues related to mass surveillance programmes are not the sole competence of Member States.[86] Whereas at intergovernmental level there were no strong reactions to the 2013 revelations, the Parliament was very critical of Member States. It called all EU Member States and 'in particular, the United Kingdom, France, Germany, Sweden, the Netherlands and Poland to ensure that their current or future legislative frameworks and oversight mechanisms governing the activities of intelligence agencies are in line with the standards of the European Convention on Human Rights and European Union data protection legislation'.[87]

Finally, the Parliament has harshly criticised counterterrorism practices that strictly pertain to national security. A good example is illustrated by the abduction, detention without trial, secret prisons and torture of suspected terrorists that occurred on the EU territories of some Member States. A number of individual rights are breached by these illegal practices that concern national security. Despite Article 4(2) TEU, the Parliament has been quite vocal in criticising them and criticising the Council's silence on Member States' involvement in the CIA programme.[88] It has demanded full investigations into the alleged degree of involvement of Member States[89] with the US authorities, notably the CIA. The position of the Parliament is that these practices amount to serious breaches of the principles and values on which

85 This is the National Security Agency's programme enabling the mass surveillance of individuals through the direct access to the central servers of internet companies.

86 European Parliament resolution of 12 March 2014 cit. para 16.

87 Ibid., para 22 (see also paras 25, 26 and 29).

88 See the European Parliament Resolution of 11 September 2012 on alleged transportation and illegal detention of prisoners in European countries by the CIA: follow-up of the European Parliament TDIP Committee report (2012/2033(INI)), P7_TA(2012)0309.

89 Finland, Denmark, Portugal, Italy, the United Kingdom, Germany, Spain, Ireland, Greece, Cyprus, Romania, Poland and Lithuania, collaborated with the US. See Resolution of 11 September 2012, supra note 88, para 17.

the European Union is based and that the issuing of a recommendation pursuant to Article 7 TEU is not out of the question.

4 The evolution of data protection in the context of EU–US cooperation

Information exchange between law enforcement authorities is one of the tools used by the EU to counter terrorism, including in relations with third countries. As the LIBE Committee emphasises: 'In general, the EU system on transfers of personal data to third countries is based on the principle of the continuity of protection, so as to avoid that the protection granted in the EU is lost, eroded or denied just because the data are transferred to a third country.'[90]

As shown in the previous section, the Parliament consented to a new PNR agreement with the US after a long negotiating process. Does the new agreement ensure a higher level of data protection and enhanced due process rights for passengers coming from the EU?

The new EU–US agreement is considered an improvement on its predecessors from a rule of law perspective. Indeed, the main provisions and safeguards are set out largely in the text of the EU–US agreement itself and not in a non-legally binding act.[91] In addition, the retention period of data in an active database is shortened; the 'push' instead of the 'pull' method[92] (as envisaged by the agreement of 2004) will be used by carriers to transfer PNR data to the US Department of Home Security. A number of deficiencies remain. For example, the purpose limitation principle is stricter than in the 2007 text. It is thus possible to use 'PNR for the purposes of preventing, detecting, investigating, and prosecuting not only terrorist offences and related crimes', but also 'other crimes that are punishable by a sentence of imprisonment of three years or more and that are transnational in nature'. In previous versions of the agreements, the 'other crimes' had to be serious[93] and there was no reference to the number of years of imprisonment. The use of sensitive data (information revealing racial or ethnic origin, political opinions, religious or philosophical beliefs, trade union membership, or data concerning the health or sex life of the individual) is not prohibited as such but is possible in exceptional cases and the US also maintains discretion as to whether a transfer of PNR to competent government authorities of third countries may take place or not. Let us come to judicial redress for the use of PNR data, one of the most contentious issues for the Parliament. It is possible for any individual, including EU citizens, whose personal data and

90 LIBE Committee, Electronic Mass Surveillance of EU Citizens, 2014, p. 83.

91 V. Mitsilegas, *The Criminalisation of Migration in Europe: Challenges for Human Rights, and the Rule of Law* (Springer, 2015), p. 26.

92 See supra note 67.

93 Note the contrast with the EU–Australia agreement requiring the crime to be serious.

personal information has been processed and used in a manner inconsistent with the Agreement to seek effective administrative and *judicial* redress (emphasis added). The problem is that it is US law that defines the conditions of the exercise of these rights.

Moving on to consider the EU–US TFTP, does the agreement encompass safeguards for individuals in line with European standards? The answer of the Commission is positive: the first joint review and the second joint review of the implementation of the EU–US TFTP Agreement by the Commission have verified that the comprehensive safeguards included in the Agreement, in particular those related to personal data protection, function properly. 'The practical and to date more experienced application of the EU–US TFTP Agreement has showed that the original concerns at the time of initial analysis of an EU system have been addressed by the effective set of safeguards embedded in the Agreement.'[94]

It should be recalled that the weak standards in terms of data protection were at the basis of the Parliament's substantive refusal to approve the conclusion of the agreement. However, this institution did not question the need to cooperate with the US and to use TFTP. So much so that the agreement was renegotiated and approved by the Parliament in July 2010. The text of the agreement was not much different from the one rejected in 2009. The Parliament's position was criticised for this.[95] In order to avoid a second TFTP incident, the communication channels between the Parliament and the Commission in the negotiation of international agreements were kept open in the area of counterterrorism. It is true that the data protection standards for European citizens were improved after the agreement was renegotiated. For example, the administrative and legal redress for EU citizens in the US is possible; an independent observer appointed by the European Commission is based in Washington, DC, to oversee, along with SWIFT personnel, the extraction of SWIFT data.[96] However, eventually the Parliament was convinced of the need to consent to the agreement by economic factors rather than from its strengthened data protection standards.[97]

Let us now turn to the 'umbrella agreement' whose negotiation was concluded in September 2015. The Commission proposed the signature of this agreement to the Council in April 2016.[98] The negotiated Treaty was

94 Commission staff working document, SWD(2013)488 final, of 27 November 2013, p. 12.

95 A. Ripoll Servent and A. Mackenzie, 'The European Parliament as a "Norm Taker"? EU–US Relations after the SWIFT Agreement', (2012) 17 *European Foreign Affairs Review* 72.

96 Commission staff working document, SWD(2013)488 final, of 27 November 2013, p. 12.

97 An element that convinced the Parliament to vote in favour is that the failure of an agreement would have harmed European air carriers. M. Quesada Gàmez and E. Mincheva, 'No Data Without Protection? Rethinking Transatlantic Information Exchange for Law Enforcement Purposes', in P.J. Cardwell, *EU External Relations Law and Policy in the Post-Lisbon Era* (Springer, 2012), p. 299.

98 See proposal for a Council decision on the signing, on behalf of the European Union, of an agreement between the United States of America and the European Union on the

supposed to restore the trust between EU Member States and the United States after the 2013 revelations of mass surveillance programmes of EU citizens by the US and some Member States. The agreement was conceived by the EU as a tool to strengthen the rights of EU citizens. The Parliament had asked that the Treaty under negotiation provided effective and enforceable administrative and judicial remedies for all EU citizens in the US without any discrimination.[99] Indeed, the right to judicial review was not guaranteed by the US Privacy Act of 1974 (limiting such a right to US citizens and legal permanent residents) to EU citizens. However, the way the two Parties saw the agreement clashed.[100]

Does the proposed agreement actually reinforce the level of data protection standards for EU data subjects in the information flows between the EU and the US? The Judicial Redress Act was signed by Obama in February 2016 so as to provide some forms of judicial redress for EU citizens. Probably, had it not been for the revelations of 2013, the Commission would not have managed to convince the US negotiator to commit to change its legislation. As a result of the new US legislation, the legal safeguards that EU citizens enjoy when their personal data are in the hands of the US authorities are improved. Under the text of the new agreement, the right to administrative[101] and judicial[102] redress is strengthened for EU citizens. In this respect, the agreement satisfies one of the most important of Parliament's requests submitted during the negotiation of the agreement and achieves one of the objectives of President Junker's political guidelines. However, it should be noted that the US revised legislation does not guarantee absolute equality between US and EU citizens. For example, the latter do not have a right to sue for damages caused by wrongful government determinations and it is subject to the extensive caveats that exist for law enforcement agencies.[103]

protection of personal information relating to the prevention, investigation, detection, and prosecution of criminal offences, COM(2016) 238, final, 29 April 2016.

99 See European Parliament resolution of 12 March 2014, supra note 86, para 57.

100 There was a clash of views on the objectives of the agreement between the EU and the US side. It seems that the latter saw it as a way to set in stone that the EU largely accepted US data privacy standards as adequate and thus made the negotiation of future data-sharing agreements easier in the law enforcement arena. By contrast, the EU side considered the agreement as an opportunity to gain for EU citizens the right of judicial redress in the US. K. Archick, 'US–EU Cooperation Against Terrorism' (2013) *CRS Reports for Congress*.

101 Under Article 18 of the agreement, EU citizens are entitled to seek administrative review when the competent authority refuses to correct inaccurate information or the information is improperly processed.

102 Under Article 19 of the agreement, 'any citizen of a Party is entitled to seek judicial review with regard to: a) denial by a competent authority of access to records containing his or her personal information; b) denial by a competent authority of amendment of records containing his or her personal information; and c) unlawful disclosure of such information that has been wilfully or intentionally made, which shall include the possibility of compensatory damage'.

103 F. Bignami, *The US Legal System on Data Protection in the Field of Law Enforcement: Safeguards, Rights and Remedies for EU Citizens* (Study for the LIBE Committee, 2015), p. 33.

A further development occurred in February 2016 when the Parliament's Legal Service issued an opinion at the request of the LIBE Committee,[104] raising a number of concerns as to the compatibility of the proposed agreement with EU law. One of them concerned the lack of judicial redress in the new US legislation for persons coming within the scope of EU law.[105] The position of the Court in the *Schrems* case,[106] delivered in October 2015, shortly after the 'umbrella agreement' was unveiled, seems to be in the background of the Parliament's Legal Service opinion. In this case, the Court declared the so-called 'adequacy decision'[107] invalid and forced the Commission to adopt a new one. In this ruling, the Court states that 'legislation not providing for any possibility for an individual to pursue legal remedies in order to have access to personal data relating to him, or to obtain the rectification or erasure of such a data, does not respect the essence of the fundamental right to effective judicial protection'.[108]

Finally, it is worth highlighting that the Parliament's Legal Service considers the 'umbrella agreement' as 'an alternative form of adequacy decision', which will have primacy over the EU secondary legislation. In the light of the points briefly mentioned here, it is not definite that the Parliament will eventually approve the text of this agreement.

5 UN–EU cooperation on counterterrorism: constitutional challenges and the role of the CJEU

Under Article 21(1) TEU, the EU is bound to 'promote multilateral solutions to common problems, in particular in the framework of the United Nations'.[109] The threat posed to international security by entities and individuals financing terrorism is one such problem. The UNSC resolutions adopted in the aftermath of the 2001 terrorist attacks in the US are another external source of EU counterterrorism measures. The UN 'has exercised a high degree of influence over the EU as far as the financing of terrorism is

104 This letter, dated 14 January 2016, was leaked by Statewatch. See http://statewatch.org/news/2016/feb/ep-legal-opinion-umbrella.pdf (accessed 20 May 2016).

105 Under Article 19 of the Treaty, judicial redress against certain decisions of the competent authority is reserved to EU citizens. The same possibility is not offered to persons not having EU citizenship who come within the scope of EU law. This is in conflict with Article 16 TFEU and Article 8 of the Charter of Fundamental Rights. Indeed, under the mentioned sources of EU law, the right to protection of personal data is available to 'everyone', including people residing in the EU, without possessing the nationality of one of the Member States (and hence EU citizenship). Other concerns raised by the text of the agreement are here omitted.

106 C-362/14, *Schrems v Data Protection Commissioner*, ECLI:EU:C:2015:650.

107 This is Commission decision no. 2000/520/EC of 26 July 2000 pursuant to Directive 95/46 on the adequacy of the protection provided by the safe harbour privacy principles.

108 Para 95.

109 Article 21(1) TEU.

concerned'.[110] The EU has implemented the UNSC Resolution 1267(1999) as subsequently modified, which enables a Committee of the Security Council to freeze the funds and other financial resources of Osama bin Laden, the Taliban and individuals and entities associated with the Al-Qaeda network.[111] The EU joined multilateral efforts to prevent the financing of international terrorism, a phenomenon that threatens international peace and security,[112] and adopted freezing orders against the persons or associations included on the Al-Qaeda sanction list.[113] These means were recognised by the GC as the most effective to achieve the goal of curbing financial support to terrorism.[114] The most recent organisation added to the list of terrorists associated with Al-Qaeda is Boko Haram and another splinter group.[115]

In addition, the EU has created its own fund-freezing regime in order to give effect to UNSC Resolution 1373 (2001) setting out a parallel regime of sanctions to combat terrorism by all means, in particular the financing thereof.[116] Under this system, the EU has been able to freeze the funds of persons, groups or entities financing terrorism, other than persons affiliated with the Al-Qaeda network.[117]

Although the EU is bound to strengthen international security, in accordance with the purposes and principles of the United Nations Charter,[118] the Court of Justice has questioned the way these principles were interpreted by the 1267 Committee of the Security Council, without explicitly acknowledging it.[119] In a few cases, EU measures implementing UNSC resolution belonging to both categories of sanction regimes[120] were successfully challenged

110 S. Léonard and C. Kaunert, 'Combating the Financing of Terrorism Together? The Influence of the United Nations on the European Union's Financial Sanctions Regime', in O. Costa and K.E. Jorgensen, *The Influence of International Institutions on the European Union: A Framework for Analysis* (Palgrave Macmillan, 2012), p. 133.
111 As of 2011, the 1267 Committee administers the sanction regime against Al-Qaeda and associated individuals and entities; Resolution 1988 (2011) sets up a separate committee to oversee sanctions against the Taliban and any individual, group, undertaking and entity designated as or associated with the Taliban.
112 Cases C-402/05 P and C-415/05 P, supra note 2, para 363, and Cases C-539/10 P and C-550/10 P *Al-Aqsa v Council*, ECLI:EU:C:2012:711, para 130.
113 Council Common Position 2002/402/CFSP of 27 May 2002.
114 Cases C-539/10 P and C-550/10 P *Al-Aqsa v Council*, ECLI:EU:C:2012:711, para 125.
115 See http://europeansanctions.com/category/Nigeria (accessed 30 May 2015).
116 The basic rules were defined in the Common Position 2001/931/CFSP of 27 December 2001, OJ 2001, L 344/93 and by Regulation 2580/2001, OJ 2001, L 344/70.
117 European Commission, Restrictive Measures in Force (Article 215 TFEU) 5 December 2014, http://eeas.europa.eu/cfsp/sanctions/docs/measures_en.pdf.
118 Article 21(2)(c) TEU.
119 It should be noted that the Court denies that its case law contrasts with the practice of the 1267 Committee. See Judgment of 18 July 2013 in joined Cases C-584/10 P, C-593/10 P and C-595/10 P, *Commission et al v Yassin Abdullah Kadi* (hereafter '*Kadi II*'), ECLI:EU:C:2013:518, para 299.
120 For a list of relevant cases see C. Eckes, 'The Legal Framework of the European Union's Counter-Terrorist Policies: Full of Good Intentions?', in C. Eckes and T. Konstadinides

before the Court.[121] It may be acknowledged that the Court of Justice has never put the Member States and the EU in a state of non-compliance with international law.[122] However, the fact remains that the implementation of the UNSC resolutions in the EU is subject to limits that the Court has devised, as a result of the *Kadi* line of cases. So, while it is certain that the EU observes international law, it is less certain that the EU, through its Court, 'strictly' observes it, as is required by Article 3(5) TEU.

It should be noted that after the Lisbon Treaty, all Union acts, including those related to CFSP, must respect human rights within the limits defined at EU level. The duty to respect fundamental rights is imposed, in accordance with Article 51(1) of the Charter of Fundamental Rights of the European Union, on all the institutions and bodies of the Union, even in the context of Article 215 TFEU, which provides judicial safeguards.

As a result, the strengthening of the CFSP dimension of counterterrorism has not *per se* implied that the EU was unconstrained by the Charter. Indeed, Article 275 TFEU makes it clear that the Court has jurisdiction to exercise judicial control over restrictive measures adopted in the context of CFSP and to guarantee that fundamental rights are respected in relation to these measures.[123]

Given the impact that restrictive measures have on the rights of the designated persons and of their family members, a small number of these measures were impugned by the listed persons before the Court. In a number of judgments starting from the *Kadi* ruling of 2008 (*Kadi I*),[124] the CJEU has made clear that the concerned EU Regulations[125] are not immune from judicial review and must comply with fundamental human rights. The judiciary was asked to strike a balance between the requirements of the fight against international terrorism, on the one hand, and due process rights (the right of defence and the right to an effective judicial protection) as well as substantive rights (the right to the protection of property). In the cases in which the

(eds.), *Crime within the Area of Freedom, Security and Justice: A European Public Order*, (Cambridge University Press, 2011), pp. 138–140.

121 The most recent example is the annulment of the listing of Hamas. The Court considered that the Council decision to list was not based on an assessment of the decision of a national authority but on information derived from the press and the internet. Judgment of 17 December 2014, T-400/10 *Hamas v European Commission*, ECLI:EU:T:2014:1095, para 131.

122 This is emphasised by J. Larik, 'EU Counter-Terrorism and the "Strict Observance of International Law": Sewing the Seamless Coat of Compliance', in M. Avbely, F. Fontanelli, G. Martinico (eds.), *Kadi on Trial* (Routledge, 2014), p. 39.

123 Hillion, supra note 13, p. 92.

124 Cases C-402/05 P and C-415/05 P, supra note 2.

125 Regulation (EC) 1190/2008 of 28 November 2008 amending for the 101st time Council Regulation (EC) 881/2002 imposing certain specific restrictive measures directed against certain persons and entities associated with Osama bin Laden, the Al-Qaeda network and the Taliban, OJ 2008, L 322/25.

challenged measure implemented a UNSC resolution targeting the Al-Qaeda network, the EU acts were found to breach the right to effective judicial protection, the right to defence and the right to property, which are enshrined in the EU Charter. On these grounds, the Court annulled the challenged Regulation.[126]

In the cases in which the annulment actions were related to the EU-listing system, the Court considered that the Council decision to freeze funds (or to maintain a name on the list of persons whose assets were to be frozen) did not comply with the duty to state reasons and was not sufficiently detailed.[127]

The reactions to *Kadi I* were sharply divided. On the one hand, the Court was praised for considering these rights as supreme EU values, trumping any other obligations stemming from the EU Treaty. As Hendry put it: 'The Court of Justice of the European Union's (CJEU) decision in *Kadi* can be taken to represent its overt declaration to be a human rights actor in its own right.'[128] Thus, the ruling of 2008 and its progeny may be seen as paradigmatic of the autonomy of the EU legal order from the UN system. The Court is seeking to establish itself as the final arbiter and guarantor of the rights of individuals within the Union when the latter counters the threat of terrorism in cooperation with the UN. However, a number of observers have also criticised the stance taken by the Court. Indeed, it undermines the uniform application of the UNSC resolutions and eventually such an approach weakens the authority of this body in countering terrorism.[129]

Although Mr Kadi was relisted, the strong stand by the CJEU, as well as repeated calls by EU Member States and NGOs to adopt due process standards as well as a criminal justice approach, have influenced the UNSC's position.[130] For instance, the legal standards of the listing procedure of the 1267 Committee were improved and the office of Ombudsperson was established. Between July 2010 and April 2015, the Ombudsperson examined 57 cases and most of them led to delisting decisions.[131]

126 Persons who were in the same factual and legal situation of Mr Kadi successfully challenged Regulation 881/2002. See T-318/01 *Othman v Council*, ECLI:EU:T:2009:187, Joined Cases C-399/06 P and C-403/06 P *Hassan and Ayadi v Council and Commission*, ECLI:EU:C:2009:748; T-135/06 to T-138/06 l *Faqit and others v Council*, ECLI:EU:T:2010:412.

127 For example, see Case T-228/02 *Organisation des Modjahedines du Peuple d'Iran v Council*, ECLI:EU:T:2008:7 'the OMPI judgment' and Case T-327/03 *Stichting Al-Aqsa v Council*, ECLI:EU:T:2007:211.

128 J. Hendry, 'Kadi in sight of autopoiesis', in Avbely et al., supra note 122, p. 64.

129 See for critical comments on *Kadi I*, S. Poli and M. Tzanou, 'The Kadi Rulings: A Survey of the Literature' (2009) 28 *Yearbook of European Law* 533. See also G. de Búrca, 'The European Court of Justice and the International Legal Order after *Kadi*' (2009) 51 *Harvard International Law Journal* 1; K.S. Ziegler, 'Strengthening the Rule of Law, but Fragmenting International Law: The Kadi Decision of the ECJ from the Perspective of Human Rights' (2009) 9 *Human Rights Law Review* 288.

130 J. Wouters and S. Duquet, 'The United Nations, the European Union and Multilateral Action against Terrorism', in Govaere and Poli, supra note 13, p. 390.

131 See www.un.org/en/sc/ombudsperson/status.shtml (accessed 30 May 2016).

After *Kadi I*, the Court has continued to broadly interpret the procedural rights of the individuals listed by EU measures. In *Abdulrahim*,[132] the Court annulled the GC's ruling and stated that a Libyan national who challenged his listing as a terrorist, and subsequently had been delisted, maintained an interest in bringing proceedings under Article 263 TFEU. Indeed, the recognition of the illegality of the contested act cannot, as such, compensate for material harm or for interference with his private life; yet, it is nevertheless capable of rehabilitating him or constituting a form of reparation for the non-material harm that he has suffered by reason of that illegality. The Court sided with the individual unlawfully designated and underlined the opprobrium and suspicion that accompany the public designation of persons as being associated with a terrorist organisation.

The substantive rights of family members of a person designated as a terrorist were defended in *The Queen (on the application of M. and Others)*.[133] Here, the Court narrowly defined the scope of the freezing orders. The principle of legal certainty prevents that the payment of social security or social assistance benefits (such as income support, disability living allowance, child benefit, housing benefit and council tax benefit) to a spouse of a suspected terrorist can be included in the freezing orders. Indeed, this kind of economic resource, which is available to third parties, even if closely connected to the suspected terrorist, cannot be used to finance terrorist activities.

After the ruling of 2008, Mr Kadi was re-inserted in the list of terrorists. Indeed, the Commission had complied with the Court's ruling by disclosing to the person concerned a summary of the reasons underlying his inclusion on the list of suspected terrorists at UN level. Yet, the evidence and the information at the basis of the statement of reasons were not revealed on grounds of confidentiality. This led to a new application for annulment. This time the GC upheld the action[134] but the Council, the Commission and the UK introduced an appeal.

Eventually, in October 2012, the 1267 Sanctions Committee decided to delist Mr Kadi after considering his delisting request and the report produced by the Ombudsperson. This development concluded his sanction saga after 12 years of legal battles. Yet, this did not deprive of interest the pending appeal before the Court. Indeed, Mr Kadi was only one of the persons whose funds were frozen.

On 18 July 2013, the Court rejected the appeal against the General Court ruling. The Court confirms the principle of full judicial review on the legality of the decision to include (or confirm the inclusion) of the name of a person on the list of terrorists. On the merit, the judicature holds that Mr Kadi did

132 C-239/12 P *Abdulbasit Abdulrahim v Council of the European Union*, ECLI:EU:C:2014:238.

133 In case C-340/08, *The Queen (on the application of M. and Others) v Her Majesty's Treasury*, ECLI:EU:C:2010:232.

134 The General Court had annulled Commission Regulation (EC) No 1190/2008 of 28 November 2008 imposing certain specific restrictive measures directed against certain persons and entities associated with Osama bin Laden, the Al-Qaeda network and the Taliban

not have access to the information and evidence relied on against him and at the basis of the listing decision. Respect for the rights of the defence and the right to effective judicial protection requires that the competent Union authority discloses to the individual concerned that evidence. The statement of reasons sent by the 1267 Committee did not contain enough information. The obligation to state reasons laid down in Article 296 TFEU entails that the individual, specific and concrete reasons why the competent authorities consider that the individual concerned must be subject to restrictive measures should be disclosed to him. It is up to the EU institutions to impartially examine whether the reasons for listing are well founded. The Court lays down a sort of code of procedural conduct that the EU institutions must respect in managing the system of restrictive measures. This code dictates the rules that EU institutions should observe both before the listed person challenges the listing decision and after judicial action is introduced against that act. The assumption of the Court is that the EU institutions enjoy a certain degree of autonomy in managing the system of restrictive measures. Yet, this is not the case.

The Court emphasises that an in-depth analysis on the evidence is made necessary by the lack of procedural safeguards that continues to taint the UN sanction system generally and stresses that the unsatisfactory way in which that system works is also recognised by the ECHR. As Fontanelli put it: 'All issues [in *Kadi II*] arise from the gulf between the duties of the EU and the UN bodies' lack of duties.'[135] The conclusion of the Court is that none of the allegations presented against the appellant was such as to justify the adoption, at European Union level, of restrictive measures against him.[136]

The autonomy of the EU legal order is the principle underpinning this judgment, although that word was not even mentioned in the ruling.[137] It is contended that the position of the Court gives substance to the right of effective judicial protection of the listed person; this is all the more necessary in a situation in which, despite improvements in the listing procedure, the 1267 Committee does not respect this right. Yet, the position that the Court sets for itself as supreme guarantor of human rights in the financing of terrorism is temporary. In particular, when the listing procedure will work in such a way as to give the listed persons the possibility to defend themselves before the European Union competent authority, the Court will no longer have reasons to annul the listing decisions. Waiting for this to happen, the EU institutions are required to closely assess the

insofar as that measure concerns Mr Kadi. See T-85/09 *Yassin Abdullah Kadi v Commission*, ECLI:EU:T:2010:418

135 F. Fontanelli, 'Kadieu: Connecting the Dots: From Resolution 1267 to Judgment C-584/10 P: The Coming of Age of Judicial Review', in Avbely et al., supra note 122, p. 12.

136 Para 163.

137 G. Martinico, 'The Autonomy of EU Law: a Joint Celebration of Kadi II and Van Gend en Loos', in Avbely et al., supra note 122, p. 164.

evidence before them.[138] When in doubt, the decision to list should not be made. Ultimately, the Court scrutinises whether the evidence is sufficiently detailed. The fact that the information and evidence justifying the listing is confidential is not held to be in itself sufficient to screen the measure, implementing the UN freezing decision, from judicial appraisal.

To sum up, in *Kadi II*, the Court forges a sort of 'EU's temporary autonomy' from the UN in protecting due process human rights. The Court is willing to subject to judicial scrutiny the restrictive measures, implementing UNSC decisions, only as long as the UN system does not assure human standards equivalent to that available at EU level.[139] This approach does not show a willingness to isolate the EU from the UN; rather, the solution of a temporary disconnection is opted for as the 'necessary evil', waiting for the UN to play its part in affording greater safeguards to individuals.

6 Conclusions

In this chapter, a number of institutional and substantive changes were highlighted with respect to the external dimension of counterterrorism. First of all, the Parliament has substantially increased its influence on the content of EU agreements designed to counter terrorism and other forms of crime with respect to the pre-Lisbon era. As a result, the democratic accountability of the Commission and the Council in the exercise of their external powers in the AFSJ is greater than it was at the time the external dimension of the AFSJ was coined in the Hague Programme (2004). In addition, the Parliament has contributed to make security-oriented agreements with the US more respectful of human rights by defending the right to data protection. The 'umbrella agreement' with the US improves data protection standards for EU citizens, although it does not grant to them the same rights of judicial redress of US citizens. Certainly, human right concerns are not the top priority of the Commission and the Council in the negotiation and conclusion of international agreements with powerful powers, such as the US. However, the data protection concerns rank higher in the agenda of the EU executives than in the past, when the EU lacked data protection standards in the framework of the third pillar. Perhaps one limit of the Parliament's advocacy for human rights is that it concerns EU citizens' rights rather than those of third-country nationals.

What contribution has the Court of Justice made to the external dimension of the AFSJ? On the one hand, the judiciary has contributed to a decrease in the democratic accountability of the EU institutions when they enact freezing orders against natural or legal persons suspected of financing terrorism.

138 *Kadi II*, supra note 119, para 137.

139 On the equivalent protection in the Kadi line of cases, see M. Marchegiani, 'Il Principio di Protezione Equivalente nel Caso Kadi', (2014) *Diritto dell'Unione Europea* 169.

This has happened as a result of its judgment in case C-130/10, locating the bulk of these measures in the CFSP context rather than in that of the AFSJ. At the same time, the judiciary has seized the new opportunities offered by the Lisbon Treaty to appraise whether the EU institutions respect the rule of law in the context of the EU counterterrorism policy. The Court of Justice has made the adoption of the restrictive measures subject to its full judicial review. In addition, it has reinforced the due process rights of listed persons, since they are not adequately protected at UN level. The CJEU has promoted a right-oriented approach to restrictive measures, *de facto* challenging the strict observance of international law principles deriving from the UN Charter. An important limit of the case law on restrictive measures with a counterterrorism purpose is that 'it remains impossible to accurately assess the level of protection of human rights that the CJEU are likely to offer once that the problems with due process are remedied'.[140] Moreover, the Court's contribution to upholding the rule of law in the UN-driven counterterrorism action is limited to a few cases and is not sufficient to improve the deficiencies in terms of human rights protection of the UN sanction machinery.

It is now appropriate to answer the question asked in the introduction. Is the EU credible when it states that the 'War on Terror' cannot justify human rights violations if one looks at the external dimension of the AFSJ? Although the EU's engagement in respecting human rights in its counterterrorism action is not as solid as it is rhetorically stated,[141] classifying the EU's attempts to give substance to this proclamation as 'empty words'[142] does not do justice to the efforts and activity of both the European Parliament and the Court of Justice.

140 C.C. Murphy, *EU Counterterrorism Law: Pre-emption and the Rule of Law* (Hart Publishing, 2012), p. 135.

141 'Respect for fundamental rights and the rule of law is at the heart of the EU's approach to counter terrorism [...]; the Commission is dedicated to ensure that all tools that are deployed in the fight against terrorism fully respects fundamental rights.' See COM(2010) 386 of 20 July 2010, point 2.5.1.

142 Amnesty International, *The EU and Human Rights* (2009), p. 4.

16 Is there a transatlantic security strategy?

Area of Freedom, Security and Justice law and its global dimension

*Maria Fletcher and Ester Herlin-Karnell**

1 Introduction

The European Union is currently facing a number of challenges ranging from the financial crisis, to the refugee crisis, which escalated in 2015, to the increased terror threat in Europe. Each of these challenges includes prominent security elements and, given these globalised times, they also each relate to the *external* dimension of the EU as an Area of Freedom, Security and Justice (AFSJ). Tackling these challenges involves continued interaction with the United States of America (US), often with the latter setting the agenda. The transatlantic dimension of the AFSJ cuts across several dimensions of the EU legal landscape such as aspects of Common Foreign and Security Policy law[1] and financial markets regulation and is increasingly important for the external understanding of EU law. While much has been written on the EU–US relationship,[2] considerably less has been written on the transatlantic dimension of AFSJ law, which is instructive because of what it tells us about the constitutional structure of the AFSJ project; that is, its internal and external character, and how the external landscape shapes the internal agenda.[3] The AFSJ as a legal landscape is characterised by the 'hybridity' of legal sources

* Both authors wish to express their gratitude to Claudio Matera for his helpful feedback and insights, which have improved this chapter. Any errors remain the responsibility of the authors.

1 See Chapter 15 by Poli in this volume.

2 For example, F. Bignami, European versus American liberty: a comparative privacy analysis of antiterrorism data mining (2007) *Boston College Law Review* 609; D. Cole and F. Frabbini, Bridging the transatlantic divide? The United States, the European Union, and the protection of privacy across borders (2016) *ICON* 220; D. Curtin and E. Fahey, *A Transatlantic Community of Law: Legal Perspectives on the Relationship between the EU and US Legal Orders* (Cambridge University Press, 2014); D. Jancic, The role of the European Parliament and the US Congress in shaping transatlantic relations: TTIP, NSA surveillance, and CIA renditions (2016) *Journal of Common Market Studies* 1; E. Kica and R.A. Wessel, Transnational arrangements in the governance of emerging technologies, in E. Stokes, D. Bowman and A. Rip (eds.), *Embedding and Governing New Technologies: A Regulatory, Ethical & Societal Perspective* (Pan Stanford Publishing, 2016); C. Gómez-Jara Díez, *Federal European Criminal Law* (Intersentia, 2015).

3 See Chapter 15 by Poli in this volume.

on the one hand (national norms, EU norms and global norms), and by high politics in terms of Member States' objections to the enterprise of EU integration in such sensitive policy domains on the other hand. The external aspect is helpful for viewing the development and formation of the AFSJ more specifically. The events of 9/11 and the increased global terror threat have had a double effect on the EU's crime and security agenda. On the one hand they have largely shaped and facilitated the adoption of key EU criminal measures such as the European Arrest Warrant (EAW). On the other hand, they have also demonstrated how closely connected the internal/external EU governance structure is in this area, as the threat of terrorism transgresses the territorial borders of the EU.

This chapter will examine the AFSJ through the lens of a particularly prominent and influential external relationship; that of the EU and the US. It will reveal the prominent yet complex security identity and rationale of the EU and how that shapes the internal face of the AFSJ and also makes it receptive to external, often US, but increasingly global, dialogues and regulatory frameworks. Within this security context and at both the internal and external levels, the influence of a market rationale is apparent, if contested. More recently, the transatlantic partnership is navigating the stormy waters of rights protection in an era of massive cyber data flows and often controversial surveillance techniques. Albeit fragile, the emerging picture here is one of the EU as the (rare) dominant partner, and the EU within the transatlantic context, at the forefront of potentially developing genuinely global standards and regulatory blueprints.

The chapter is structured as follows. It begins by investigating the prominent and driving rationales of the AFSJ and the transatlantic aspects thereof. In particular it will demonstrate how the internal AFSJ dimension of the EU and indeed the transatlantic relationship is deeply connected to both a *security* rationale (Section 2) and a *market* rationale (Section 3). Specific elements of EU–US cooperation with regard to the fight against terrorism will be referenced by way of illustration; namely terrorist financing and money-laundering.[4] These are particularly interesting examples of where the US has largely led and shaped the global agenda and where the EU can be said to have largely absorbed those US norms and to some extent also cross-loaded between the regimes.[5] The next part of the chapter will focus upon the regulation of cyberspace and in particular the challenges posed by data surveillance regimes and data protection in the EU–US context (Section 4). In the light of recent CJEU cases of *Digital*

4 Note that this chapter does not address the transatlantic dimension of asylum and migration.

5 See, for example, L. Quaglia, *The EU and Global Securities Markets Regulation* (Oxford University Press, 2014).

Rights[6] and the *Schrems*,[7] we consider whether the EU might itself become the norm-setter and global standard-bearer on data protection and privacy matters, including in the crime/law enforcement and hence AFSJ context. Finally, the chapter concludes by discussing key challenges arising from this important yet complex and evolving relationship for the future (Section 5).

2 The EU's security identity and the transatlantic context

As part of its mission of establishing an AFSJ – and if reading Article 67 TFEU literally – the EU is committed to ensuring a high level of security. Certainly, the AFSJ has emerged as a largely security-driven agenda, often influenced by the causes and politics on the other side of the Atlantic.[8] Indeed, following the terrorist attacks of 11 September 2001, transatlantic counterterrorism efforts have been buoyed up by a greater flow of personal and financial data across the Atlantic and by unparalleled intelligence sharing.[9] As Sara Poli explains in her chapter, the EU's presence on the security stage has for a long time been turbulent,[10] not only because of the thin legal basis that has often been employed as legislative justification for EU action, but also and particularly because of the apparent one-sided focus on preventative measures to increase the internal security of the EU.[11] A prime example of EU security regulation has been in the fight against money-laundering and the financing of terrorism, as well as the more general fight against organised crime.[12] But there are many other examples, too. The recent directive on the freezing and confiscation of criminal assets is just one of the latest endeavours in the EU's internal security strategy.[13] The European Cybercrime Centre,[14] established

6 Case C-293/12, *Digital Rights Ireland and Seitlinger and Others*, Judgment of the Court (Grand Chamber) of 8 April 2014, nyr.
7 Case C-362/14, *Maximillian Schrems v Data Protection Commissioner*, Judgment of the Court (Grand Chamber) of 6 October 2015, nyr.
8 See, for example, the debate on the EU-PNR directive. On the use of Passenger Name Record data for the prevention, detection, investigation and prosecution of terrorist offences and serious crime, COM(2011) 32 final.
9 Jancic, supra note 2.
10 See Chapter 15 by Poli in this volume.
11 See, for example, M. Den Boer, *Preventive Empires: Security Dynamics At Multiple Levels of Governance* (Amsterdam Law Forum, 2011), p. 102.
12 See, for example, M. Bergstrom, Money laundering, in V. Mitsilegas, M. Bergstrom and T. Konstadinides (eds.), *Handbook on EU Criminal Law* (Edward Elgar, 2016), chapter 16.
13 Directive 2014/42/EU of the European Parliament and of the Council of 3 April 2014 on the freezing and confiscation of instrumentalities and proceeds of crime in the European Union.
14 Communication from the Commission to the Council and the EP – Tackling Crime in our Digital Age: Establishing a European Cybercrime Centre, COM(2012) 140 final. See also the informative website at Europol, www.europol.europa.eu/ec3 (accessed 30 May 2016).

by Europol with the mandate to 'strengthen the law enforcement response to cybercrime in the EU and to help protect European citizens, businesses and governments' is another. This Centre and indeed all of these examples demonstrate, the 'powerfulness' of the security concept in terms of legal reasoning and action in this internal context.

What then are the consequences of the security dogma in contemporary AFSJ law? For many years now there has been an almost exclusive concentration on prevention and that is not unique to the EU, as the global War on Terror has demonstrated security's very wide-ranging and dangerously broad potential for justifying action. A crucial issue is that although society has to be kept secure, the security agenda can easily and always be manipulated to fit 'what is needed in a democratic society'.[15] Moreover, Helena Carrapiço and Benjamin Farrand[16] elsewhere in this volume, illustrate that a key challenge in the EU regulation of cybercrime is how to achieve a balance between security requirements and business efficiency imperatives, an issue the Commission acknowledges in its 2013 Cyber Security Strategy, where it is stated that private actors still lack effective incentives to provide reliable data on the existence or impact of security threats and to embrace a risk-management culture or to invest in security solutions to keep the internet 'safe'. The involvement of private actors in the EU security landscape raises the further question of the accountability of the current regime and the level of human rights protection as the EU progresses into the global digital sphere.[17]

In descriptive terms, the legal set up of the AFSJ is rather straightforward albeit tilted towards a security-dominated agenda. The provision of Article 67 TFEU makes it clear that the Union shall constitute an AFSJ with respect for fundamental rights and the different legal systems and traditions of the Member States. Moreover, it reads that the Union shall ensure absence of internal border controls as well as a high level of security.[18] In addition, Article 67 TFEU stipulates that the EU shall frame an external border control that is fair towards third-country nationals and based on solidarity between Member States. Article 71 TFEU requires a standing committee to be set up within the Council in order to improve and strengthen operational cooperation on internal security within the Union. Although focused on practical implementation of strategy rather than being involved in the legislative procedure, the Standing Committee on Internal Security (COSI), established

15 See, for example, C. Murphy, *EU Counter Terrorism* (Hart Publishing, 2012), p. 231.

16 Chapter 18.

17 On AFSJ agencies see, for example, M. Busuioc, D. Curtin and M. Groenleer, Agency growth between autonomy and accountability: the European Police Office as a 'living institution' (2011) 18(6) *Journal of European Public Policy* 848.

18 Article 67 TEFU also reads that the EU shall take measures to prevent and combat crime, racism and xenophobia, and through measures for coordination and cooperation between police and judicial authorities and other competent authorities, as well as through the mutual recognition of judgments in criminal matters and, if necessary, through the approximation of criminal laws.

shortly after the Treaty of Lisbon, lends weight to the prominence of the 'internal security' objective in the AFSJ by virtue of it being an additional, formal institutional layer.

Despite being located in the TFEU, there are external elements to most AFSJ policies such as the operation of the EU asylum and migration system as well as the fight against terrorism and organised crime. In addition, the Lisbon Treaty strengthens the EU's preventive focus in the AFSJ in that Article 84 TFEU states that the European Parliament and the Council may establish measures to promote and support the action of Member States in the field of crime prevention, excluding any harmonisation of the laws and regulations of Member States. It is difficult, however, to assess the importance of this statement, since Article 83 TFEU provides a rather sweeping competence for the EU in criminal matters. Not only for crimes such as money-laundering, organised crime and drug trafficking, but also for any other crime policy area that is relevant for the effective implementation of existing Union policies. Surely this includes a preventive aspect.

The security concept is by itself a vague concept. Again as Poli explains in her chapter in this volume, in the EU context, security has traditionally been regarded as an external relations issue in the Common Foreign and Security Policy (CFSP) or the Common Security and Defence Policy (CSDP), or as an internal market issue by means of derogation from EU law (public policy, public security and so on).[19] This implies a European internal security space interacting with the external space. Indeed, it has been said that the notion of security knows no borders,[20] and this seems particularly true in the EU context, where there is no clear division between internal and external security. For example, national security remains the competence of the Member States (Articles 4(2) TEU and 72 TFEU). Hence, the question to be asked is whether such a clear distinction can be made between internal and external security, given that there is clearly an external dimension to the AFSJ and vice versa. This issue is important, of course, as it has implications for the Court's jurisdiction, which is largely excluded from the TEU.

While the EU's interest in transatlantic cooperation may at present seem predominantly focused on the contested Transatlantic Trade and Investment Partnership (TTIP),[21] the trade and investment agreement that is currently being negotiated between the US and the EU, cooperation with the US is ongoing in connection with its anti-terrorist strategies, and this continues to be an important trendsetter for AFSJ law as we shall see in Section 3 below. Indeed, it was this transatlantic context that triggered the externalisation of the AFSJ.[22]

19 See, for example, Article 45(3) and (4) TFEU.

20 *The EU Internal Security Strategy*, 17th Report of Session 2010–2012, House of Lords European Union Committee, HL Paper 149.

21 http://ec.europa.eu/trade/policy/in-focus/ttip (accessed 26 May 2016).

22 There are currently seven EU–US agreements covering justice and home affairs issues that fall under the AFSJ umbrella: Europol (exchange of data); extradition; mutual assistance;

Given this, one might expect to see more developed EU thinking on where transatlantic AFSJ relations fit into the AFSJ landscape. However, this is not apparent from the AFSJ programmes, and is perhaps not really feasible given the scattered AFSJ landscape characterised by hybridity and continually shaped in response to external events and emerging global norms. Although it is commonly emphasised today that the AFSJ needs to be balanced, how this is to be done in concrete terms is still largely unresolved. In the transatlantic context, the security concept, particularly in the context of the fight against terrorism is largely tied to the market rationale. This in turn raises familiar yet unresolved questions about the appropriate level of human rights protection in AFSJ law as well as the dividing line/relationship between the AFSJ and the internal market. Here we see in broad terms how the transatlantic security relationship exposes conceptual and legal gaps and challenges in the EU's AFSJ. The next section will look at the market rationale in more detail and consider why it matters for the transatlantic dimension.

3 The market rationale as underpinning the transatlantic and global security strategy

Central to the EU–US security dialogue is the fight against terrorism and terror financing in the concrete market context. For example, the US has advocated a rigorous stance towards money-laundering, which predates those of the EU and has influenced the international structure as well as the EU agenda.[23] In the US, the fight against organised crime was the starting point for a much broader criminal law project; the US anti-money-laundering policy is inherently linked with its continuing fight against the sale and distribution of illegal narcotics in the 1970s and 1980s.[24] This seems a similar picture to that of the EU genesis of criminal law; after all, much of EU criminal law came about through the need to tackle the threat of organised crime. In addition, the EU has been largely influenced by the international responses to serious crime and the recommendations issued by the Financial Action Task Force (FATF).[25] As pointed out by Lucia Quaglia, the combination of strong US regulatory capacity and weak EU regulatory capacity prior to the 2000s, meant that in that period, the EU passively incorporated part of its securities market legislation from the US.[26] After the strengthening of EU and US regulatory capacity following the financial crisis, these jurisdictions

PNR (Passenger Name Record); SWIFT (all financial transactions, commercial and personal); Container Security Initiative (CSI); Eurojust.

23 N. Ryder, *Money Laundering: An Endless Cycle* (Routledge, 2015), chapter 3.

24 Ibid.

25 See, for example, http://ec.europa.eu/dgs/home-affairs/what-we-do/policies/organized-crime-and-human-trafficking/index_en.htm (accessed 26 May 2016).

26 L. Quaglia, *The EU and Global Securities Markets Regulation* (Oxford University Press, 2014), chapter 4.

are in the process of actively and passively cross-loading parts of their new regulatory templates.[27]

The EU generally follows the FATF lead and has done so since 2001. Accordingly, when the FATF updated its recommendations in February 2012, one year later the EU announced its proposal for a new Directive. The Fourth Money Laundering Directive was adopted in May 2015 and offers a good example of the incorporation of external norms to the EU framework.[28]

As Nicholas Ryder points out, independently of the FATF guidelines the US is at the forefront of the global fight against money-laundering but this is not surprising given the amount of laundered money that is transferred through its banking system.[29] In particular, the terrorist attacks of 9/11 resulted in a reinterpretation of money-laundering by the international community and nation-states. Moreover, according to Ryder the issue of reverse money-laundering (clean money used for dirty purposes) was viewed by George Bush as a bigger threat to the US than money-laundering, thus illustrating the threat posed by money-laundering to a country's national security. This resulted in the introduction of the US Patriot Act (2001) and a wide range of new measures to tackle the threat posed by reverse money-laundering. In addition to the international legislative measures introduced by the UN and EU, we have also seen an increase in the use of international best practices and industry guidelines. Specifically, a number of international private-sector bodies have recommended the implementation of 'best practices' to combat money-laundering.[30] This seems to indicate that the international playing field with regard to the fight against financial crime and terror financing is largely shaped by the US as the trendsetter for the EU to follow.[31]

The US could therefore be seen as a key actor in the anti-money-laundering and anti-terror movement, and has arguably largely shaped the EU's responses in this area.[32] In addition, the US's response to the financial crisis by going after white-collar criminals may have influenced the EU's approach to the need to fight market abuse effectively.[33]

27 Ibid.

28 Directive of the European Parliament and of the Council on the Prevention of the Use of the Financial System for the Purpose of Money Laundering and Terrorist Financing, Directive (EU) 2015/849.

29 Ryder, supra note 23, chapter 3.

30 This includes, for example, the Basel Committee on Banking Supervision, the Wolfsberg Group, the Offshore Group of Banking Supervisors, the Financial Stability Forum of Offshore Financial Centres, the International Organization of Securities Commissions and the Egmont Group of Financial Intelligence Units. See Ryder, supra note 23, chapter 2.

31 Ibid.

32 L. Quaglia, *The EU and Global Securities Markets Regulation* (Oxford University Press, 2014); Ryder, supra note 23.

33 E. Herlin-Karnell, White-collar crime and European financial crises: getting tough on EU market abuse (2012) 37 *European Law Review* 487.

The EU's strategy to fight irregularities in the market should be seen in the light of the history of the debate on the market abuse regime and the question as to why the suppression of financial crimes is relevant in EU law.[34] The underlying theme of the EU's involvement in the fight against financial crime is to boost investor confidence and thereby contribute to the establishment of the internal market. Certainly, financial crimes together with organised crime have since the early days of the EU constituted the main criminal law threat to the establishment of the internal market and have, until 9/11 when the fight against terrorism became a higher priority, formed the core of the EU's approach to criminal law.[35] Added to this, there was, of course, no explicit supranational legislative competence for the EU in criminal law matters prior to the Lisbon Treaty.[36]

The claim of the EU legislator has been that the rulebook needs changing so as to increase investor confidence in the market and this market is related to the AFSJ domain and security regulation. For example, in the Commission's Communication on 'Driving European Recovery',[37] the Commission referred to the High Level Group, which stressed the importance of confidence, which was taken for granted in well-functioning financial systems but had been lost in the present crisis.[38] The idea is that if people do not feel secure and trust the EU, they will not use the EU market. Therefore, the reorganisation of this system focused on the importance of the enhancement of market integrity and investor protection where the reformation of the sanctions system was seen as a crucial part of this strategy.[39] Through the Lamfalussy Process and the legislative activity that followed at the EU level, several scholars have studied the process of European financial integration in terms of regulatory convergence that has taken place since 2000.[40] Yet how this scholarship is being translated to the AFSJ framework involving criminal law regulation is a difficult question.

Moreover, one of the most prominent bilateral EU–US agreements in the security domain is the Terrorist Finance Tracking Programme (EU–US

34 On financial crimes in global context, see N. Ryder, *The Financial Crisis and White Collar Crime* (Edward Elgar, 2014).

35 See, for example, the opening chapter in S. Peers, *EU Justice and Home Affairs* (Oxford University Press, 2011).

36 See, for example, ibid.; V. Mitsilegas, *EU Criminal Law* (Hart Publishing, 2009); M. Fletcher, R. Lööf and B. Gilmore, *EU Criminal Law* (Edward Elgar, 2008); S. Mettinen, *EU Criminal Law* (Routledge, 2013); E. Herlin-Karnell, *The Constitutional Dimension of EU Criminal Law* (Hart Publishing, 2012); A. Klip, *EU Criminal Law* (Beck, 2015).

37 COM/2009/0114 final.

38 The High Level Group of Financial Supervision in the EU, http://ec.europa.eu/internal_market/finances/docs/de_larosiere_report_en.pdf (accessed 26 May 2016).

39 Directive on criminal sanctions for insider dealing and market manipulation, COM(2011) 654 final, adopted 4 February 2014.

40 E. Grossman and P. Leblond, European integration: finally the great leap forward (2011) 49 *Journal of Common Market Studies* 413.

TFTP) Agreements,[41] which arose to address legal concerns arising out of revelations that the USA CIA was running a secret programme whereby it obtained financial messaging data in order to track terrorist financing.[42] The EU–US TFTP specifically concerns EU–US cooperation and the collection of data in the fight against terrorism and its financing. However, much like the EU–US Passenger Name Record Agreement,[43] pursuant to which the EU acquiesces to US law requiring airlines flying into the USA to send to US authorities a wide range of personal data on all passengers travelling (so-called 'PNR' data), these agreements have generated much criticism on account of privacy concerns and their limitations on legal redress, in particular, their uneven application of US law to EU citizens, who cannot fully realise their rights to redress and review.[44] Despite this, given the proven effectiveness of the US TFTP – in generating significant intelligence that has been beneficial for both the US and EU States in the fight against terrorism since its creation shortly after the terrorist attacks of 11 September 2001[45] – a similar internal EU system, to be known as EU Terrorist Finance Tracking System (EU TFTS) has been formally considered. However, after assessment, the Commission reported in 2013 that, at that stage, the case to present a proposal for an EU TFTS was not clearly demonstrated.[46] A different story is recorded for the internalisation of the US PNR transfer model in EU law; the EU PNR initiative, presumed dead due to wide-ranging human rights concerns, was resurrected following the *Charlie Hebdo* events in January 2015 and a directive agreed shortly after the Paris and Brussels terror attacks in late 2015.[47] Its compatibility with (at least) human rights law remains to

41 Agreement between the European Union and the United States of America on the processing and transfer of financial messaging data from the European Union to the United States for the purposes of the Terrorist Finance Tracking Program, 27 July 2010, OJ L 195/5 and Council Decision of 28 June 2010 on the signing on behalf of the Union of the agreement between the European Union and the United States of America on the processing and transfer of financial messaging data from the European Union to the United States for the purposes of the Terrorist Finance Tracking Program (TFTP) 2010/411/EU 2010 OJ L195/1.

42 Bank data is sifted by US in secret block to terror, *The New York Times* (23 June 2006).

43 See latest in force; Agreement between the United States of America and the European Union on the use and transfer of passenger name records to the United States Department of Homeland Security, OJ L215/5, 11 August 2012. The EU, since originally adopting the US agreement has also concluded PNR agreements with Canada and Australia.

44 E. Fahey, Transatlantic cooperation in criminal law, in Mitsilegas et al., supra note 12, p. 535. Also note that at the time of writing, the EU PNR Directive has been agreed by the Council and the European Parliament and is awaiting publication in the Official Journal. Finalised text of Directive in Council Doc. 2011/0023 (COD) LEX 1670, 27 April 2016.

45 See Joint review report of TFTP Provided Data pursuant to the EU–US TFTP Agreement by Commission and US Treasury Department SEC (2011) 438 final, 30 March 2011.

46 COM(2011) 429 final, Brussels, 13 July 2011, COM(2013) 842 final, Brussels, 27 November 2013.

47 N. Vavoula, *Back from the Dead and Standing on Travellers' Doorstep: The Case of the EU PNR Directive*, Open Democracy, 9 February 2016. At the time of writing, the EU PNR Directive has been agreed by the Council and the European Parliament and is awaiting

be tested, since it essentially introduces a system of generalised surveillance (over EU citizens and third-country nationals alike) that may fall foul of the standards of data protection and privacy defended by the CJEU and discussed below. Privacy rights in the context of data sharing and surveillance emerge as a battleground in both EU–US and internal EU contexts. Regulation of information society is a challenge of our time.

4 Regulating cyberspace: surveillance and data protection

The EU is no newcomer to regulation of the internet; it has regulated internet-related questions such as tracking 'cookies' since 2002 through the Directive on Privacy and Electronic Communications, which establishes that the user must consent to the use of cookies.[48] The EU also regulates spam and it is done through the consumer law framework, E-commerce Directive, again indicating the multi-legal dimension and strong market focus to this area.[49] The E-commerce Directive was amended in 2009, following the adoption of the Lisbon Treaty, to include criminal law sanctions.[50] But criminal law measures are only obligatory where conduct in the sending of spam falls within the ambit of Council Framework Decision on attacks against information systems[51] or the Council of Europe Convention of Cybercrime.[52] Considerably more robust is the regulation of cybercrime *stricto sensu*. For example, the 2013 Directive on attacks on information systems is the most important EU measure to date. It essentially reproduces the offences set out in the 2005 Framework Decision it replaced (illegal access to information systems, illegal system interference and illegal data interference), adds additional offences (such as illegal interception) and includes a broader range of penalties (i.e., imprisonment). The Directive brings the EU legislative response closer to the Cybercrime Convention, which sets out to harmonise national laws on

publication in the Official Journal. Finalised text of Directive in Council Doc. 2011/0023 (COD) LEX 1670, 27 April 2016.

48 Directive 2002/58/EC, OJ L201/37.

49 E-commerce Directive 2002/58/EC OJ L201/37 and see S. Summers, C. Schwarzenegger and F Young, *The Emergence of EU Criminal Law, Cyber Crime and the Regulation of the Information Society* (Hart Publishing, 2014), p. 215.

50 Directive 2009/136/EC of the European Parliament and of the Council of 25 November 2009 amending Directive 2002/22/EC on universal service and users' rights relating to electronic communications networks and services, Directive 2002/58/EC concerning the processing of personal data and the protection of privacy in the electronic communications sector and Regulation (EC) No 2006/2004 on cooperation between national authorities responsible for the enforcement of consumer protection laws.

51 2005/222/JHA, now replaced by Directive 2013/40/EU.

52 2001 Convention on Cybercrime, which entered into force in June 2004, CETS No. 185. The Convention is the first international treaty on crimes committed via the internet and other computer network. Its main objective, set out in the preamble, is to pursue a common criminal policy aimed at the protection of society against cybercrime, especially by adopting appropriate legislation and fostering international cooperation.

the criminalisation of cybercrime, but – according to some scholars – only marginally so.[53] Perhaps the problem for the EU is that although Article 83 TFEU provides for a more self-standing competence – to harmonise national criminal law in 'computer crime' – the regulation of cybersecurity is primarily done though the consumer law *acquis* and the establishment of the internal market. There is, in short, no real political justification at present at EU level for the regulation of cybercriminal law outside the market domain, mainly because of the lack of a common consensus in the Member States of the content of the regulation.[54]

It will be recalled that the internet is not only the largest repository of information, but also the largest marketplace today.[55] Naturally this means that it is also one of the most vulnerable crime scenes and one where the EU is increasingly active on the legislative front. EU–US cooperation on cyber security dates back to the 2010 EU–US summit, with the creation of a Working Group on Cyber Security and Cybercrime. The Working Group established a basis for transatlantic cyber engagements and, in addition, an increasing number of international cyber debates have raised the need for ever-closer consultations on major policy positions between strategic partners.

On the question of data sharing and its regulation, the common view is that positions of the EU and the US differ considerably; broadly, the EU upholds privacy while the US focuses on security. It has recently been suggested that the differences between the EU and US are often overstated.[56] The point made is that the EU system is not perfect, and that the NSA surveillance scandal and Snowdon revelations in recent years have at least prompted the US to review its system. Certainly, reports concerning the extent of the large-scale intelligence collection programmes in the US raised serious fundamental rights concerns at the EU and Member State level and have led to a period of intensified EU–US cooperation on the regulation of data transfers – in both the commercial and criminal law enforcement domains. This is significant, especially in an era when the EU is itself undergoing a comprehensive reform of data protection rules in the EU and when there is increasing recognition that the globalised nature of data flows calls for a strengthening of individual's data-protection rights internationally. The potential for the EU to play a leadership role in shaping the transatlantic arrangements and thus to emerge as a global standard-bearer on data protection is clear. Certainly, the Commission has not shied away from assuming such a role, and, as will become clear, the EU boasts a robust legal framework around data protection and privacy rights. Moreover, principles of data protection have been

53 www.europarl.europa.eu/meetdocs/2014_2019/documents/libe/dv/7_conv_budapest_/7_conv_budapest_en.pdf (accessed 30 May 2016). See also Summers et al., supra note 50.

54 Ibid.

55 Summers et al., supra note 49.

56 Cole and Frabbini, supra note 2.

developed and reinforced by the EU judiciary in a number of surveillance cases in recent times.

It is well-known that in times of crisis we are often asked to trade liberty and privacy for security.[57] The importance of a secure society is undeniable but the problem in the EU has always been how to balance this desire with the other Treaty-based promises of freedom and justice. One could then imagine that this particular balance is of greater significance at the EU level than the national level and asks some difficult governance questions. Therefore the pertinent task for the EU in navigating these contested and competing issues is how to uphold legal safeguards and the rule of law as the backbone for action at the *supra*-national level, including with relations with third countries.

Indeed, already in 2007, Bignami argued:

> With respect to personal data processing by government actors, the US legal framework is far less demanding than the European one. As for the private sector, an all-encompassing category for 'all types of personal data' does not exist in the United States. Rather, uses of specific types of personal data are regulated, including health information, video store records, financial information, and so on. By contrast, in European law, all personal data processing is treated as potentially problematic, even when undertaken by private actors.[58]

The most important change resulting from the Lisbon Treaty in this regard is, of course, the inclusion of Article 16 TFEU. That provision not only contains an individual right for the data subject to the protection of his or her personal data, but it also obliges the European Parliament and Council to provide for data protection in all areas of European Union law. Article 16 TFEU mirrors Article 8 of the Charter of Fundamental Rights, which also proclaims the right to data protection. In addition, Declaration 21 attached to the Lisbon Treaty states that specific rules on the protection of personal data and the free movement of such data in the fields of judicial cooperation in criminal matters and police cooperation based on Article 16 TFEU may prove necessary because of the specific nature of these fields.

This constitutional protection of personal data by the EU represents the most prominent and important divergence in approach compared to the US.[59] While data protection and privacy are fundamental rights in the EU

57 A. Moore, Privacy, security and government surveillance, WikiLeaks and the new accountability (2011) *Public Affairs Quarterly* 141.

58 F Bignami, European versus American liberty: a comparative privacy analysis of antiterrorism data mining (2007) *Boston College Law Review* 609.

59 F. Boehm, *A Comparison between US and EU Data Protection Legislation for Law Enforcement Purposes: A Study for the European Parliament LIBE Committee (2015)*, available at www.europarl.europa.eu/RegData/etudes/STUD/2015/536459/IPOL_STU(2015)536459_EN.pdf.

and are also applicable in the law enforcement context, there is no equivalent protection in the US.[60] Commenting on the US surveillance regime, Alec Walen explains that:

> today the US National Security Agency has nearly unlimited authority to spy upon citizens of foreign countries while they are outside the United States and that such targeting of non-U.S. citizens, without any hint of individualized suspicion either of criminal wrongdoing or of being a threat to national security, would be constitutionally prohibited under the Fourth Amendment.[61]

However, as Walen points out, the dominant view in the American legal community is that there is nothing constitutionally wrong, or even suspect, about such targeting of non-resident aliens. For example, in *United States v Verdugo-Urquidez*, US authorities were able to carry out searches in Mexico allegedly in breach of the Fourth Amendment, which was – according to the US Supreme Court majority – not applicable as the searches were carried out outside the territory of the EU.[62]

Given these broad divergences, even while there might be common ground to seek to agree binding frameworks for the exchange of commercial information[63] and law enforcement information[64] while ensuring that the protection of data protection and privacy are guaranteed, the extent to which and methods by which individual rights should feature and be secured within joint initiatives has been and continues to be contentious. Enter the Court of Justice of the EU.

A recent important decision where the principle of proportionality was applied to strike down a key piece of EU law on pre-emptive surveillance – the Data Retention Directive[65] – is the *Digital Rights*[66] case. This Directive

60 Ibid.

61 A. Walen, Fourth Amendment rights for nonresident aliens (2015) 16(5) *German Law Journal* 1131.

62 *United States v Verdugo-Urguidez*, 494.US.259 (1990), discussed in Cole and Frabbini, supra note 2.

63 Even prior to *Schrems*, in response to the 2013 US surveillance revelations, the Commission published a Communication about making the Safe Harbour safer; Communication on the Functioning of the Safe Harbour from the perspective of EU Citizens and Companies Established in the EU, COM(2013) 847 final, 27 November 2013.

64 An EU US High Level Contact Group, established in November 2006, to consider exchange of law enforcement data and privacy and personal data protection reported in 2009 that a binding international agreement was the best option. HLCG Report, Brussels, 23 November 2009, 15851/09, JAI 822 DATAPROTECT 74 USA 102.

65 Directive 2006/24/EC of the European Parliament and of the Council of 15 March 2006 on the retention of data generated or processed in connection with the provision of publicly available electronic communications services or of public communications networks and amending Directive 2002/58/EC, Data Retention Directive (annulled).

66 *Digital Rights Ireland and Others* C-293/12 and C-594/12.

had previously been challenged by Ireland on the grounds that it had been adopted pursuant to the internal market legal basis, Article 114 TFEU (ex 95 EC). Ireland argued that this legal basis was not appropriate since the sole objective of the Directive, or at least its principal objective, concerned the investigation, detection and prosecution of crime. The Court firmly rejected the challenge by asserting its view the that 'centre of gravity' of the measure indeed related to the functioning of the internal market and the removal of obstacles to trade.[67] The Court did not test the measure against subsidiarity or proportionality, as Ireland had not invoked these principles. Yet in its recent judgment concerning the same Directive and the challenge raised by NGO *Digital Rights*,[68] the Court adopted a different stand and annulled the Directive on the grounds of breach of proportionality. It held that the Directive had a too sweeping generality that was not nuanced enough and therefore breached the basic right of data protection as set out in Article 8 of the Charter. The Directive authorised the gathering of data and far-reaching surveillance mechanisms in order to ensure the effective fight against crime. Not even Article 52 of the Charter, which grants exceptions to the Charter rights on the grounds of proportionality, could justify the measure without any limitation or differentiation or exception being made in the light of the objective of fighting against serious crime.[69]

This significant judicial intervention and the fundamental rights benchmark that it set prompted a political response, both to urgently review current and draft EU legislation on data protection and to intensify transatlantic dialogue around US law on pre-emptive surveillance.[70] It will be recalled that the EU–US transatlantic partnership was already on rocky ground following the 2013 revelations by Edward Snowden of the existence and scale of the US intelligence mass surveillance programme, Prism. This had prompted the EU Commission to urgently set out an action plan to 'restore trust in data transfers', which called for the adoption of the proposed EU data protection reform package, making the Safe Harbour safer (see below) and the strengthening of data protection safeguards for law enforcement cooperation by concluding negotiations on the so-called 'Umbrella Agreement'.[71] While negotiations on each of these three actions might have intensified following the *Digital Rights* ruling, it was not until after another significant intervention by the CJEU in October 2015, that concrete conclusions are recorded.

67 Case C301/06 [2009] ECR I593.

68 Case C-293/12 and C-594/12, *Digital Rights,* judgment of 8 April 2014, nyr.

69 Ibid.

70 See V. Mitsilegas, The value of privacy in an era of security: embedding constitutional limits on preemptive surveillance (2014) 8(1) *International Political Sociology* 104; V. Mitsilegas, The transformation of privacy in an era of pre-emptive surveillance (2015) 20 *Tilburg Law Review* 35–57.

71 Commission Communication on Rebuilding Trust in EU–US Data Flows, COM(2013)846 final, 27 November 2013.

Not unlike its approach in the *Kadi* case,[72] where the Court of Justice set to safeguard values when interacting with the international stage, the Grand Chamber of the CJEU in *Schrems*,[73] ruled in essence that US law allows US intelligence services to access the personal data of EU citizens without sufficient privacy safeguards as a matter of EU law. Mr Schrems, an Austrian national residing in Austria, had complained to the national Data Protection Commissioner asking the latter to prohibit Facebook Ireland Ltd from transferring his personal data to the USA for storage on servers, because US law and practice did not ensure adequate protection of personal data against the surveillance activities of public authorities. The EU law in question was the so-called Commission 'Adequacy Decision' 2000/520, adopted pursuant to Article 25 of the Data Protection Directive 95/46. Under Directive 95/46 the transfer of personal data outside the European Economic Area to a third country is only permissible where the third country in fact ensures an 'adequate level of protection'. The Commission may find that a third country meets this standard by reason of its domestic law or international commitments and taking account of all the circumstances surrounding the data transfer. The Adequacy Decision of 2000 indeed confirmed that the US Department of Commerce's US–EU Safe Harbour Framework provided the requisite standard of protection in EU law. Pursuant to this framework, organisations that voluntarily *self-certify* to the US Department of Commerce that they comply with their 'safe harbour privacy principles' were *presumed* to meet an adequate level of protection.

Therefore, it is perhaps remarkable that the CJEU, some 16 years on, declared the Adequacy Decision invalid. It did so, 'without there being any need to examine the content of the safe harbour principles'[74] on the basis that the Commission had not stated in the Adequacy Decision that the United States in fact 'ensured' an adequate level of protection by reason of its domestic law or its international commitments.[75] Indeed the Court noted that the Decision lays down that, inter alia, 'national security' has primacy over the safe harbour principles and therefore enables interference with an individuals' fundamental rights on that basis. Two features of US law were highlighted as particularly problematic in relation to fundamental rights from the point of view of EU law. First, the 'generalised' nature of access to data or 'bulk'

72 Court of First Instance (CFI), Case T-315/01, *Yassin Abdullah Kadi v Council of the European Union and Commission of the European Communities* [2005] ECR II-3649; European Court of Justice (ECJ), Case C-402/05 P, *Yassin Abdullah Kadi v Council of the European Union and Commission of the European Communities* [2008] ECR I-5351; General Court, Case T-85/09, *Yassin Abdullah Kadi v European Commission*, judgment of 30 September 2010, *Kadi II*, Joined Cases C-584/10 P, C-593/10 P and C-595/10 P, judgment of 18 July 2013, nyr.

73 C-362/14 *Schrems v Data Protection Commissioner*, Judgment of Court (Grand Chamber) 6 October 2015, nyr.

74 *Schrems*, para 98.

75 Ibid., para 97.

surveillance permitted to public authorities by US law[76] and, second, the absence of legal remedies available to individuals to *have access to their personal data, or to obtain the rectification or erasure of such data.*[77]

The *Schrems* case in fact proved timely and important in the context of the calls to reform US privacy law (Privacy Act 1974), which limited rights of redress against the federal government for unauthorised disclosure of personal information to US citizens and legal residents. The establishment of adequate redress rights, in particular judicial redress, for European data subjects under US privacy was firmly established as a condition for making progress on data transfer agreements. In 2014, EU Commission President Juncker made clear in his Political Guidelines: 'The United States must [...] guarantee that all EU citizens have the right to enforce data protection rights in US courts, whether or not they reside on US soil. Removing such discrimination will be essential for restoring trust in transatlantic relations.'[78] The judgment in *Schrems* was important in this ongoing reform agenda because it essentially underscored the need for such reform and provided further guidance on the conditions that the reforms should fulfil. It clearly also intensified the spotlight on all parties to make progress on reaching agreements; indeed, just months later, on 24 February 2016, President Obama signed into law the Judicial Redress Act of 2015 (HR 1428). This Act is essentially intended to ensure that EU citizens – not only American citizens[79] – have the right to enforce data protection rights in the US courts. More specifically, it would do this by permitting citizens of 'certified states' to bring civil actions against US federal agencies and obtain civil remedies 'in the same manner and to the same extent and subject to the same limitations, including exemptions and exceptions', as US citizens, for certain violations of the Privacy Act of 1974 (5 USC §552a).[80] In other words it allows EU citizens – as citizens of 'certified states' – to sue the United States for unlawful disclosure of personal information – under the terms of the Privacy Act – obtained in connection with international law enforcement efforts.

Although described as an 'historic achievement' by EU Commissioner for Justice Věra Jourová,[81] and as unblocking the path towards the EU–US data transfer agreements in the commercial (replacement of the Safe Harbour clause known as the 'Privacy Shield') and law enforcement ('Umbrella Agreement') spheres, commentators have been quick to point out its

76 Ibid., para 94.

77 Ibid., para 95.

78 Published 15 July 2014, https://ec.europa.eu/priorities/sites/beta-political/files/juncker-political-guidelines_en.pdf (accessed 26 May 2016).

79 http://useu.usmission.gov/re-022416.html (accessed 30 May 2016).

80 Section 2(c) Judicial Redress Act of 2015. The Privacy Act of 1974 is the primary US statute imposing privacy obligations on the federal government.

81 http://europa.eu/rapid/press-release_STATEMENT-16-401_en.htm (accessed 30 May 2016).

shortcomings.[82] In particular, it actually preserves fewer, and not equivalent, rights to EU citizens than US nationals[83] and, crucially, the Privacy Act permits agencies to exempt a system of records from the access and redress provisions on grounds of national security. Since the NSA have already taken advantage of this exemption, the Privacy Act provides no meaningful redress to targets of NSA surveillance.[84]

Despite this critique, just days after the entry into force of the Judicial Redress Act, and alongside its Communication on restoring trust,[85] the Commission made publicly available the texts that will put in place the Privacy Shield[86] and published the text of the negotiated (but by then not yet signed) EU–US Umbrella Agreement. It furthermore announced that the reform of EU data protection rules had been finalised – namely, the General Data Protection Regulation[87] and the Data Protection Directive for the police and criminal justice sector[88] – thereby emphasising the importance of the adoption of this internal package to the external trust-building exercise.

At the time of writing, neither the Privacy Shield – a package running to 132 pages and comprising a revised 'adequacy decision', Privacy Principles and official representations and commitments from various US governmental agencies – nor the Umbrella Agreement is formally in force, although the Umbrella Agreement was signed by the EU and US on 2 June 2016.[89] Both agreements, in their draft form, have come under scrutiny and found

82 See, for instance, https://iapp.org/news/a/the-judicial-redress-act-a-path-to-nowhere; https://papersplease.org/wp/2016/02/25/why-the-judicial-redress-act-is-worthless; www.lawfareblog.com/redress-nsa-surveillance-devil-details (accessed 30 May 2016).

83 See Chapter 15 by Poli in this volume.

84 5 USC § 552a(k). 32 CFR § 322.7(a).

85 Transatlantic Data Flows: Restoring Trust through Strong Safeguards, COM(2016) 117 final, Brussels, 29 February 2016.

86 Press release of 29 February 2016, http://europa.eu/rapid/press-release_IP-16-433_en.htm (accessed 30 May 2016). The Privacy Shield documents include a draft revised 'adequacy decision' and the Privacy Shield Principles companies have to abide by, as well as written commitments by the US government (to be published in the US Federal Register) on the enforcement of the arrangement, including assurance on the safeguards and limitations concerning access to data by public authorities.

87 Regulation (EU) 2016/679 of the European Parliament and of the Council of 27 April 2016 on the protection of natural persons with regard to the processing of personal data and on the free movement of such data, and repealing Directive 95/46/EC (General Data Protection Regulation) COM(2016) 117 final, Transatlantic Data Flows: Restoring Trust through Strong Safeguards.

88 Directive (EU) 2016/680 of the European Parliament and of the Council of 27 April 2016 on the protection of natural persons with regard to the processing of personal data by competent authorities for the purposes of the prevention, investigation, detection or prosecution of criminal offences or the execution of criminal penalties, and on the free movement of such data, and repealing Council Framework Decision 2008/977/JHA.

89 Agreement between the United States of America and the European Union, on the protection of personal information relating to the prevention, investigation, detection, and prosecution of criminal offenses, Brussels 28 May 2016, doc. 8557/16.

to be wanting on various grounds. On the EU–US Privacy Shield, many argue that even with more robust oversight, review and enforcement, individual redress avenues for EU data subjects – a suspension clause and assurances on the safeguards and limitations concerning access to data by public authorities for law enforcement purposes – the proposed adequacy decision will suffer the same fate, if challenged before the CJEU, as the Safe Harbour scheme it has been designed to replace.[90] Key concerns relate to the nature and scope of US government access to European citizens' data, and the effectiveness of the four individual redress mechanisms laid out in the Privacy Shield package – particularly the independence of the proposed new Privacy Shield Ombudsperson in the US State Department.[91] It will be recalled that these issues were precisely the concerns that led to the invalidity finding by the CJEU in *Schrems*. The EU–US Umbrella Agreement has also been criticised on data protection and fundamental rights grounds[92] and the European Data Protection Supervisor, while welcoming the intention behind the agreement, called for three essential improvements to it, to avoid any breach of the EU Charter of Fundamental Rights, in particular of Articles 7, 8 and 47; first, clarification that all the safeguards apply to all individuals, not only EU nationals; second, ensuring judicial redress provisions are effective within the meaning of the Charter; and third, clarification that transfers of sensitive data in bulk are not authorised.[93] None of these suggested improvements made it into the Umbrella Agreement signed by the parties on 2 June and therefore the likelihood of judicial challenge on these bases is high.

The Umbrella Agreement does not itself provide a legal basis for transfer of personal data to the US. Rather, by establishing a framework of data protection principles and safeguards when data is transferred for criminal law enforcement purposes between the US and EU or between the US and EU Member States, it supplements data protection safeguards in existing and

90 See, for instance, https://iapp.org/news/a/privacy-shields-validity-debated-in-european-parliament (accessed 30 May 2016); M. Tzanou, The Commission's draft EU–US Privacy Shield adequacy decision: a shield for transatlantic privacy or nothing new under the sun, 12 April 2016, EU Law Analysis Blog, http://eulawanalysis.blogspot.co.uk (accessed 30 May 2016). Also note that the European Data Protection Authorities (the so called 'Article 29 Working Party') has expressed concerns that the Privacy Shield does not fully comply with four essential guarantees that should be respected whenever personal data are transferred between EU and third countries and intra-EU. See Statement of the Article 29 Working Party on the Consequences of the *Schrems* judgment, 3 February 2016, http://ec.europa.eu/justice/data-protection/article-29/press-material/press-release/art29_press_material/2016/20160203_statement_consequences_schrems_judgement_en.pdf (accessed 30 May 2016).

91 A concern raised inter alia by the European Ombudsman, www.ombudsman.europa.eu/en/resources/otherdocument.faces/en/64157/html.bookmark (accessed 30 May 2016).

92 See the Note by the Fundamental Rights European Experts Group (FREE), www.statewatch.org/news/2015/oct/eu-usa-umbrella-freegroup-Korff-complete-text.pdf (accessed 30 May 2016).

93 EDPS Opinion 1/2016 of 12 February 2016, https://secure.edps.europa.eu.

future data transfer agreements or national provisions authorising such transfers. In other words, it provides a safety net of protections and safeguards that will complement (in the sense of 'enhancing') *existing* agreements – both bilateral agreements between EU Member States and the US and EU–US agreements such as PNR, TFTP and Europol – on the basis of which personal data is sent to the US for law enforcement purposes. The scope[94] is formulated on a 'data transfer basis', that is to say, 'it covers, in principle, all data transfers for criminal law enforcement purposes between the EU and US, regardless of the nationality or place of residence of the data subject concerned'.[95] It will not cover transfers of personal data (or other forms of cooperation) between the US and the Member State's authorities responsible for safeguarding national security.[96] Suffice to say here that grey areas in the scope of the Umbrella Agreement make the need to analyse the interaction between this instrument, the Privacy Shield and the recently adopted EU data protection legislation all the more important.

Standing back from all of these recent developments, there can be no doubting that security and market-enhancing imperatives have been central to progress. For instance, political authorities on both sides of the Atlantic have been explicit that the uncertainty created by the invalidation of Safe Harbour, and the need to rely on and establish alternative legal solutions (e.g., model contracts and standard contractual clauses) stymies transatlantic commerce and the global digital economy. There is a strong market dimension to these matters and with it the risk that a consequentialist approach to efficiency output might prevail over the intrinsic value of data protection as such.

It therefore seems likely that the question of data protection and privacy rights in the context of the EU and indeed EU–US cooperation will remain contested for some time to come. The trust-building exercise underway must be welcomed but taken seriously, nurtured and sustained by parties on both sides of the Atlantic and even then, there is a long road ahead for the EU–US on this issue – the stakes are surely high, and the involvement of the EU judiciary almost inevitable.

Many questions remain unresolved for the EU of course; including the 'meta'-query of the extent to which market-enhancing objectives should inform law and policy in (at least) the AFSJ sphere and more specific regulatory questions such as whether the EU should regulate separately on

94 Article 3, Umbrella Agreement.

95 See Explanatory Memoranda of the Proposal for a Council Decision on the protection of personal information relating to the prevention, investigation, detection, and prosecution of criminal offenses, Brussels, 29 April 2016, COM(2016) 238 final. Note that, although this statement suggests that the personal scope therefore includes all data subjects, not only EU citizens, provisions in the agreement relating to non-discrimination (Article 4) and judicial redress (Article 19) refer to 'nationals' and 'citizens' of a Party respectively.

96 Article 3, Umbrella Agreement.

surveillance and prevention for the purposes of criminal investigations and police activities, recalling that the Court in *Schrems* has set a convincing standard in relation to a non-criminal law context. And shouldn't the rules and the proportionality tests differ context to context? Surveillance in investigations versus indiscriminate mass surveillance. This last distinction does not yet seem to be tackled by the EU as policymaker.

5 Challenges for the future – what direction for AFSJ law? Final remarks on the transatlantic tide

Given the position of the US and the EU as the most dynamic and important actors in counterterrorism, the potential for this relationship to generate priorities, frameworks and norms, for good or for ill, that might be mirrored in other parts of the world and indeed globally, is clear. We have seen that, in most instances, the relationship might be described as unequal, resulting in one-way traffic for processes of norm assimilation and policy transfer. Acquiescence with US demands has, in several key instances, led to a voluntary imitation and borrowing of policies at the EU level.[97]

Recently, the Commission has explicitly asserted the EU's normative potential on the global scene by saying that the recently agreed package of data protection measures at EU and EU–US level 'will enable the EU to step up its efforts to promote and develop international privacy and personal data protection standards'.[98] Therefore, contrary to the securitisation of the AFSJ, which was largely driven by the US norms being absorbed into EU law, the EU (judiciary) appears as a norm-maker with regard to data protection standards and the right to privacy. This appears similar to the *ETS* case on emission trading in the environmental policy field. In the *ETS* case, the Court of Justice set out to make a powerful statement on the importance of environmental protection, even when such concerns extend beyond the borders of Europe and confirmed a norm exportation approach rather than a norm importation.[99]

The EU's internal governance structure – with different institutions representing differing interests – does lend itself to internal wrangling and division. It will be interesting to see if and how the EU judiciary shapes the EU and EU–US landscape in the coming months and years on the question of

97 J. Argomaniz, When the EU is the 'norm-taker': the Passenger Name Records Agreement and the EU's internalisation of US border security norms (2009) 31(1) *Journal of European Integration* 119, at 132.

98 Transatlantic Data Flows: Restoring Trust through Strong Safeguards, COM(2016) 117 final, Brussels, 29 February 2016 at 3.

99 Case C-366/10 *Air Transport Association of America v Secretary of State for Energy and Climate Change* [2011] I-1133.

individual rights in the context of data transfers and if its rulings might penetrate more deeply – downwards and upwards to national and international fora.

From a political perspective, by speaking with 'one voice', the EU surely enhances its credibility and capacity as a unitary actor to engage and negotiate as a more equal partner in the transatlantic dialogue. Although this is challenging given the EU institutional dynamics at play, it is perhaps almost utopian if one considers the extent of variable geometry mechanisms enshrined in the EU's constitutional settlement in the AFSJ field. And yet it is notable that considerable legal coherence has been maintained by the EU in its legal cooperation with the US in the AFSJ sphere. Indeed, far from flexing their opt-out muscles, recent practice indicates that the UK and Ireland are firmly committed to the EU project of intensifying international cooperation with the US in matters dealing with criminal justice and policing measures.[100] A similar picture is evident in the financial crimes area and financial crimes where the UK, despite its many 'objections' to the EU closer cooperation project, has been one of the main proponents for the adoption of new EU measures in the fight against white-collar crime.

Common regulatory responses concerning cyberspace are more difficult to achieve. That said, legal responses to the challenges of pre-emptive surveillance have largely focused on data protection, and Mitsilegas highlights the wider potential offered by the 'right to privacy' as a legal principle.[101] This might sound an oxymoron in the era of Facebook and social media. Yet (at least on the EU level), such a right might be capable of more effectively addressing the reconfiguration of the relationship between the individual and the state caused by pre-emptive surveillance and shaping efforts towards achieving a global privacy framework that are developing apace.[102] Its value has certainly been highlighted more recently by judiciaries on the European stage (as we saw above) and the national stage, making courts – as opposed to legislators – the key institutional actors in reconfiguring the security–privacy constitutional struggle. As also noted above, crucial in the EU context has become the principle of proportionality and how it balances the constitutional concerns of the EU in upholding the rule of law and a high level of human rights protection. And, moreover, the

100 The UK and Ireland have also chosen to opt in to EU measures that apparently mirror EU–US arrangements (e.g., PNR). See further, J.S. Vara and E. Fahey, Transatlantic relations and the operation of AFSJ flexibility, in S. Blockmans (ed.), *Differentiated Integration in the EU: From the Inside Looking Out* (Centre for European Policy Studies, 2014).

101 Mitsilegas, The value of privacy, supra note 70; Mitsilegas, The transformation of privacy, supra note 70.

102 See, for instance, www.opendemocracy.net/digitaliberties/valsamis-mitsilegas/developing-global-privacy-regime-in-age-of-mass-surveillance-four-key-principles (accessed 26 May 2016). The Global Privacy Summit 2016 hosted by the International Association of Privacy Professional (IAPP) attracted thousands of delegates and significant press coverage.

question as to when these rights can be set aside to fight crime and terrorism effectively.[103]

Recent transatlantic developments in the context of data protection and privacy are important and welcome. The EU might be credited with confirming that privacy has not been and should not be sacrificed on the altar of the digital/information age and that it remains an important fetter on the activities of both private parties and States in all contexts, including in the pursuit of security. However, early indications suggest that the Privacy Shield and Umbrella Agreement do not go far enough in protecting rights and this perhaps ultimately reveals the failure on the part of the EU to affirm once and for all the relationship between the internal market and the AFSJ. Also, one wonders how influential the EU can be when so much of EU integration seems uncertain, and in the face of a growing propensity for governments in the EU (let alone the US) to legislate on a national level in favour of mass surveillance and police surveillance practices.[104] As for the future, it might be that more legislative approximation at the EU level is the most effective way to achieve appropriate safeguards in the regulation of surveillance. More certain is that judiciaries at all levels in Europe will shape the landscape in the coming years. With US presidential elections and the possible exit of the UK from the EU on the horizon,[105] transatlantic trade and security relations face uncertain times, underscoring once again the external challenges that (can and do) impact upon AFSJ law.

In conclusion there is no 'transatlantic security strategy' as such and certainly not one that can be labelled 'AFSJ'. Indeed, transatlantic relations on global security-related phenomenon apparently exacerbate the EU's security identity crisis, reveal unsolved tensions about the relationship between the internal market and AFSJ, and question the internal legal integrity and capacity of the EU to respond to transversal phenomena, such as the regulation of cyberspace. But the EU–US relationship remains an influential and at times 'laboratory-like environment' in the context of new and emerging global cooperatives and regulatory frameworks. Transatlantic cooperation in this sense does have an important and unique dynamic and is as rich and varied as it is challenging.

103 On the *Digital Rights* case and proportionality in AFSJ constitutional context, see E. Herlin-Karnell, *Justice and Justification in Europe's 'Area of Freedom, Security and Justice'*, WZB Centre for Global Constitutionalism, discussion paper (2015), SP SP IV 2015–805, www.econstor.eu/bitstream/10419/121485/1/838036619.pdf (accessed 30 May 2016). There is no specific discussion of 'proportionality' in *Schrems*, but the Court does reference the *Digital Rights* case, thereby creating a strong presumption that similar reasoning applies. The Court in *Schrems* referred to the US 'generalised' mass surveillance practices and the absence of legal remedies for EU citizens as compromising/not respecting the 'essence of' Article 7 and 47 of the EU Charter.

104 The UK Investigatory Powers Bill will force the storage of internet browsing records for 12 months and authorise the bulk collection of personal data. Two hundred senior lawyers signed an open letter to the *Guardian* on 14 March 2016 criticising the Bill for constituting mass surveillance and compromising the right to privacy, www.theguardian.com/world/2016/mar/14/investigatory-powers-bill-not-fit-for-purpose-say-200-senior-lawyers.

105 President Barack Obama has made public his concerns that UK's exit from the EU would be harmful for the USA.

Part VI

Legal challenges of network governance within the Area of Freedom, Security and Justice

17 Understanding JHA agencies in context

Where does Eurojust lie in the constitutional architecture of the Area of Freedom, Security and Justice?

*Irene Wieczorek**

1 Introduction

At least nine agencies can be counted operating as justice and home affairs (JHA) agencies.[1] Among these, the ones that are more involved in the criminal justice dimension are Europol, the European Police College (CEPOL), the Judicial Cooperation Unit of the EU (Eurojust) and the proposed European Public Prosecutor's Office (EPPO). This contribution aims to place and discuss the criminal justice agencies in the broad context of the constitutional architecture of the Area of Freedom, Security and Justice (AFSJ). For reasons of space, it focuses only on the *judicial* cooperation side, as opposed to *police* cooperation, thus it discusses Eurojust, and it incorporates some reflections on the possible establishment of the EPPO. The chapter considers two fundamental constitutional debates normally associated with the developments of the AFSJ: the tension between intergovernmental cooperation (sovereign states deciding to cooperate transnationally, yet on the basis of national law) and supranational integration (entrusting supranational bodies with the task of addressing transnational phenomena, operating according to supranational EU law);[2] and the tension between repression of crime and protection of fundamental rights.[3] This chapter will

* The author is a PhD student at the Vrije Universiteit Brussels and at the Université Libre de Bruxelles. She would like to thank Angelo Marletta for his precious cooperation in the drafting of this chapter. She was also an intern at the legal service of Eurojust, and at the Italian Desk from October 2011 to March 2012. She would like to thank Laura Surano and Filippo Spiezia for their guidance during her internship.

1 The JHA agencies are CEPOL, EASO, EIGE, EMCDDA, eu-LISA, Eurojust, Europol, FRA and Frontex. The term 'JHA agencies' is referred to in the institutions' official publications, as well as in EU official documents. See, by way of example, Council doc. 5968/13.

2 This tension relates to the problem of where power is allocated as between the centre and the periphery, which is arguably endemic to any multilevel polity. P. Craig, 'Subsidiarity: a political and legal analysis' (2012) 50(S1) *JCMS* 73.

3 On the balance between repression of crime and protection of fundamental rights within the Area of Freedom, Security and Justice, see A.H. Gibbs, 'Reasoned "balance" in Europe's Area of Freedom, Security and Justice' (2011) 17(1) *European Law Journal* 121.

look at Eurojust through these constitutional axes and it will identify where it is placed in each of them. It discusses intergovernmental and supranational elements within Eurojust's composition, accountability and functioning; followed by an analysis of the fundamental rights protection as envisaged by Eurojust's legal framework. Finally, the chapter broadens the scope of the discussion by jointly considering Eurojust and the related establishment of an EPPO, while keeping the focus on the two constitutional axes mentioned above.

Eurojust's legal framework has evolved over time. The legal framework for Eurojust is contained in the Eurojust Decision adopted in 2002,[4] and subsequently amended in 2003[5] and 2009.[6] The Treaty of Lisbon envisages, at Article 85 TFEU, the possibility to significantly amend the legal framework for Eurojust, and the Commission proposed in 2013 a regulation that would substitute the current decision.[7] This chapter refers to the current legal framework, while mentioning, where relevant, the innovations proposed by the draft regulation.

2 Eurojust and the tension between intergovernmental cooperation and supranational integration

Eurojust is the judicial cooperation unit of the EU. Its mission is that of facilitating judicial cooperation between national authorities when dealing with cross-border crimes, and seeking judicial assistance from one other. It provides efficient channels of communication between national magistrates, and a pool of expertise on judicial cooperation and cross-border crimes. The discussion on the establishment of Eurojust started in 1999 with Tampere,[8] and a few years later the 9/11 attacks then worked as catalysts for establishing the work of this judicial cooperation unit. The Decision formally creating Eurojust,[9] was then approved in the context of fight against cross-border crime and in particular the fight against terrorism. The following paragraphs examine the interactions and tensions between intergovernmental and supranational features of Eurojust, first with reference to its composition and structure (Section 2.1); then within its accountability system (Section 2.2); and finally within the actual competences of Eurojust (Section 2.3).

4 Decision 2002/187/JHA.
5 Decision 2003/659/JHA.
6 Decision 2009/426/JHA. Hereinafter, I will refer to the article of the 2002 decision as consolidated in 2009 (consolidated text). The consolidated text of the decision can be found at www.eurojust.europa.eu/doclibrary/Eurojust-framework/ejdecision/Consolidated%20version%20of%20the%20Eurojust%20Council%20Decision/Eurojust-Council-Decision-2009Consolidated-EN.pdf.
7 COM(2013) 535 final.
8 Tampere, Council Conclusions of 15 and 16 October 1999, pt. 46.
9 Supra note 6.

2.1 *The intergovernmental and supranational dimension of Eurojust's composition and governance structure*

As established by the relevant Council Decision, Eurojust is an agency with legal personality, composed of 28 national members, one from each of the EU's 28 Member States.[10] The National Members form the College of Eurojust, which is responsible for the operation and organisation of Eurojust. Eurojust may fulfil its tasks as a College or through one or more National Members. National Members are judges, prosecutors or police officers who are seconded from their respective national legal systems on a temporary basis.[11] This structure necessarily reflects an intergovernmental approach. Nonetheless, National Members and the College are also supported by an important Administration, including, for instance, the legal service, the case analysis unit, the college secretariat and headed by the Administrative Director.[12] Contrary to the College, the administration of Eurojust is composed of EU staff, subject to EU staff regulations.[13] This adds a supranational element to the composition of Eurojust. One could speculate as to whether different educational and professional backgrounds might have an impact on the mindset of the persons working within Eurojust, and on how they perceive the function and the potential of Eurojust.[14] National magistrates are more likely to have a national educational background, and might have previously worked in domestic contexts. This might give them a more intergovernmental mentality, envisaging Eurojust as merely a facilitator of transnational investigations carried out by sovereign national authorities.[15] Conversely, EU staff may more likely have a background in EU studies, and have previously worked in other EU institutions, such as the Commission services, or the Parliament administration. Members of the EU staff might thus be more likely to develop a more supranational vision of Eurojust, envisaging a future development for the agency as a supranational investigative body. Whether different mindsets within Eurojust might have an impact on the actual functioning of the agency obviously depends on the allocation of tasks among National Members, the College and the Administration.

10 The consolidated version of Council Decision 2002/187/JHA.

11 Article 33(1).

12 Article 2(8).

13 Article 30.

14 Sociological studies exist on the fact that Eurojust was conceived mainly as a facilitator between national authorities, rather than an actual supranational investigative and prosecutorial body, due to the pragmatic mindset, and culture of compromise, which was widespread among policymakers in the JHA area at the time. A Megie, 'The origins of EU authority in criminal matters: a sociology of legal experts in EU policy-making' (2014) 21(2) *Journal of European Public Policy* 241.

15 There are, however, important exceptions. Michele Coninsx, national member for Belgium, and current president of Eurojust, has long been an advocate of a stronger Eurojust with more autonomous powers. See for instance, M. Coninsx, 'Editorial' (2013) 14 *ERA-Forum* 174.

Admittedly, the Administration is conceived as subordinate to the College of National Members, it is entrusted with purely administrative and managing aspects, and it is, in principle, not directly involved in the operational work of Eurojust,[16] thus in principle it has little impact on the actual functioning of the agency. However, one should note that the Administration has been progressively more involved in the actual casework.[17] For instance, the Case Management System was introduced,[18] with the task of analysing information, identifying links between cases, and searching for trends. This might allow for identifying links between various cases and suggest embryonic transnational integrated enforcement strategies.[19] Furthermore, frequent contacts, which can take place within a permanent agency, such as Eurojust, and good interpersonal relations between various professionals working in Eurojust, who allegedly share a different understanding of the potential of the agency, can also lead to exchange of ideas, and possibly to the development of a common, potentially more supranational, vision of it.[20] Finally, persons working within Eurojust, including members of the Administration are free to – and in fact do – express their vision of Eurojust on a personal basis; for instance, through academic publications.[21] This could have an impact on future policy-shaping.[22]

16 Articles 29(4) and 30(3). One should note that the College also holds some managerial tasks in addition to its operational ones (Articles 10 and 29(5)).

17 M. Busuioc and M. Groenleer, *Beyond Design – The Evolution of Europol and Eurojust*, Amsterdam Law School Legal Studies Research Paper, No. 2011-09, p. 12, http://acelg.uva.nl/publications/working-papers/overview.html.

18 Article 15, Council Decision 2009/426/JHA. The case management unit is entrusted with the task of providing quality strategic reporting, for example the Eurojust Annual Report, the EU Serious and Organised Crime Threat Assessment (SOCTA) and the EU Terrorism Situation & Trend Report (TE-SAT), as well as enhancing the judicial dimension of the EU policy cycle, and producing reports on priority crime areas. See www.eurojust.europa.eu/about/structure/administration/Pages/case-analysis.aspx.

19 Eurojust is not *per se* in charge of devising EU integrated enforcement strategies on how to fight cross-border crimes, since the EU does not have operational competence to define how investigations should be carried out in specific cases, how much resource to allocate, what investigative measures to envisage and so forth. Nonetheless, in the context of the Eurojust meetings among national authorities, these might informally agree on common enforcement strategies.

20 The idea that interpersonal contact can shape mindsets was already recalled with respect of creating mutual trust by fostering interpersonal contacts between National Members of Eurojust. J. Vlastnik, 'Eurojust: a cornerstone of the Federal Criminal Justice System in the EU?', in F. Geyer and E. Guild, *Security versus Justice? Police and Judicial Cooperation in the European Union* (Ashgate, 2008).

21 See, for instance, the call of Catherine Deboyser, current head of Eurojust's legal service, for stronger binding powers for Eurojust in the context of resolution of conflicts of jurisdiction: C. Deboyser, *Eurojust Role in Matters of Choice of Forum*, in M. Luchtman (ed.), *Choice of Forum in Cooperation Against Financial Crime* (Elevent International Publishing, 2013).

22 In a different context, Cornelis De Jong, member of the LIBE Committee at the Parliament, has acknowledged that policymakers are strongly influenced by academic research. C. De

2.2 *The intergovernmental and supranational dimension of Eurojust's political and financial accountability system*

The accountability system of Eurojust also demonstrates intergovernmental and supranational features. Eurojust is, primarily, politically accountable to the Council, to which it must submit its annual report, including detailed information on the implementation of the budget.[23] Moreover, the president of Eurojust appears before the Council to present the annual report and to answer questions,[24] and the Council in turn responds by presenting its conclusions. Eurojust will then have to explain in the following annual report how it implemented the Council's conclusions.[25] This tight relationship with the Council necessarily enhances the influence that an intergovernmental body can have on the Eurojust priorities and agenda. Nevertheless, one should note that the Eurojust annual report is currently also forwarded to the European Parliament (EP), which is directly elected by EU citizens, and is as such a more supranational institution. The EP nonetheless does not enjoy the same right 'to react'.[26] Yet, if the proposed regulation[27] on Eurojust is approved as it stands, the EP will also be entitled to present observations and conclusions, and it may request the president of the College to appear before it to answer questions.[28] Additionally, the EP would be entitled to receive the results of studies and strategic projects elaborated or commissioned by Eurojust, working arrangements concluded with third parties and the annual report of the European Data Protection Supervisor.[29] Notably, the annual report would also have to be forwarded to the Commission and the Court of Auditors, which are both EU institutions with a strong supranational character and, in the case of the Commission, a pro-integration inclination.[30]

In relation to financial accountability, the role of the EP and the Commission, and thus the supranational element, is even more accentuated. Eurojust was the first third-pillar agency to be financed from the (then) Community budget.[31] This means that the EP must receive and approve the budget proposal.[32] Eurojust is then subject to a complex internal and external

Jong, 'The European Parliament Resolution of 22 May 2012 on a EU approach to criminal law', in A. Weyembergh and F. Galli (eds.), *Approximation of Substantive Criminal Law in the EU: The Way Forward* (Editions de l'Universite de Bruxelles, 2013).

23 Article 32(1).

24 Ibid.

25 See 2014 Eurojust annual report, p. 69. The report is available at www.eurojust.europa.eu/doclibrary/corporate/eurojust%20Annual%20Reports/Annual%20Report%202014/Annual-Report-2014-EN.pdf.

26 Article 32(2).

27 Supra note 7.

28 Article 55(2) of the proposed regulation.

29 Article 55(3) of the proposed regulation.

30 Article 14 of the proposed regulation. Remarkably it should also be sent to National Parliaments, Article 55(4) of the proposed regulation.

31 Article 35(2).

32 Article 314 TFEU.

audit system involving both the Commission and the Court of Auditors, to which Eurojust becomes accountable.[33]

2.3 *The intergovernmental versus supranational dimension of Eurojust's powers*

Here we move from what Eurojust *is* to what it *does*. The powers of Eurojust can be roughly divided in to four categories: the initiative function; the guidance function; the monitoring function; and the external relations function.[34] The initiative function concerns the powers of Eurojust to interfere with national investigations and to potentially trigger prosecution at a national level. Given their importance, especially with respect to the supranational versus intergovernmental dichotomy, Section 2.3.1 is entirely devoted to these. The guidance function of Eurojust concerns its competence to enact non-binding opinions on how to solve conflicts of jurisdiction; the monitoring function of Eurojust concerns its privileged position to monitor the effective implementation of judicial cooperation instruments; and the Eurojust external relations function concerns the capacity of Eurojust to conclude agreements with third countries. These three additional powers form the focus of Section 2.3.2.

2.3.1 *Eurojust powers of initiative*

2.3.1.1 EUROJUST POWERS VIS-À-VIS NATIONAL AUTHORITIES

Eurojust is intended to stimulate, improve and support judicial cooperation between Member States.[35] Articles 6 and 7 of the Eurojust Decision list a number of measures Eurojust can suggest for national authorities to undertake, which range from undertaking an investigation or prosecution of specific acts, to coordinating investigations.[36] Eurojust's requests are, however, non-binding,[37] even though Member States must state the reason for their non-compliance.[38] The degree of compliance with these requests is quite, albeit not entirely, satisfactory.[39]

As far as the powers of each national member, their definition is left to national legislation.[40] Nonetheless, the Eurojust Decision requires that

33 Article 37.

34 Monar describes them as such. J. Monar, 'Eurojust's present and future role at the frontline of European Union criminal justice cooperation' (2013) 14 *ERA-Forum* 187.

35 Article 3.

36 Article 6(1)(a) and Article 7(1)(a). Notably this list includes both arguably initiative powers, even if non-binding, and guidance powers.

37 Article 8.

38 Ibid.

39 Council of the European Union: Eurojust Strategic Seminar: New Perspectives in Judicial Cooperation, document 14428/11 of 21 September 2011.

40 Article 9a(2).

a minimum set of powers is granted to national members, which include some autonomous powers. Among these are a number of powers to facilitate or directly intervene in national investigations. These latter are classified as 'ordinary powers', 'powers exercised in agreement with a competent national authority' and 'urgent powers'. The first set of powers, ordinary powers, includes those to transmit and support the circulation of information between national authorities, and to request supplementary information from national authorities.[41] The second set of powers, powers exercised in agreement with national authorities, include the power to perform, upon request of national authorities, tasks that the latter are normally entrusted with, such as issuing judicial cooperation requests or decisions, or the power to order investigative measures.[42] Finally, national members must, on an urgent basis, have the power to authorise and coordinate controlled deliveries or execute a judicial cooperation request, without the authorisation of a competent authority, if it is impossible to identify and contact the national authority in time.[43] This last power represents the first embryonic autonomous power of Eurojust as an EU operational body, and not just as a facilitator of national authorities' cooperation. Nonetheless, given the sensitivity of this innovation, the Decision admits derogations from this rule if it would be contrary to 'constitutional rules' or to the 'fundamental aspects of the criminal justice system'.[44]

Briefly, beside the limited exception in urgent cases, Eurojust's current initiative powers do not extend as much as to be autonomous supranational investigative powers. The final decision on whether to undertake investigative measures remains with national authorities.

2.3.1.2 ARTICLE 85 TFEU AND THE 2013 COMMISSION PROPOSALS

Interestingly, the Lisbon Treaty opened the door for further enhancing Eurojust National Members' autonomous powers. Article 85(1) TFEU defines Eurojust's mission, and then it lists the powers that *may* be granted to it via the new regulation. These include the power to initiate criminal investigations, or propose the initiation of prosecution conducted by competent national authorities, especially concerning offences against the financial interests of the EU; the power to coordinate the investigations and prosecutions Eurojust has the power to initiate; the strengthening of judicial cooperation in criminal matters in close cooperation with the European Judicial Network, and that this strengthening may also include resolution of conflict of jurisdiction.

In short, the Lisbon Treaty allows for a qualitative leap for Eurojust, which could develop from a service provider agency, a *facilitator* of nationally based

41 Article 9b.
42 Article 9c.
43 Article 9d.
44 Article 9g.

investigations, to be an actual *coordinator* of transnational investigations, and even an EU agency with actual operational decision-making power to initiate investigations *proprio motu*.[45]

Nevertheless, in the proposed regulation, the Commission made the choice not to implement the part of Article 85 TFEU concerning Eurojust's autonomous binding investigative powers.[46] If the regulation on Eurojust is adopted as such, the main novelties regarding the powers of the National Members will only concern the possibility to issue and execute judicial cooperation requests autonomously and not, as currently, only with the authorisation of national authorities.[47] Moreover, National Members will also have the power to order investigative measures autonomously, but only in urgent cases. Finally, and not uncontroversially, the proposed regulation abolishes the so-called 'national safeguard clause' (Article 9(e)). In short, while the powers of National Members would undoubtedly be enhanced, the Commission did not opt for the qualitative leap in terms of attributing to Eurojust fully autonomous and thus supranational investigative powers. This cautious approach of the Commission as to Eurojust's supranational powers needs to be read in conjunction with the choice of the Commission to separately table the very ambitious EPPO proposal, which is considered later in the chapter.[48]

2.3.2 Guidance, monitoring and external relations powers of Eurojust

In addition to its initiative power, Eurojust holds some complementary guidance, monitoring and external relations powers. Interestingly, these functions are envisaged both within the Eurojust Decision and in some mutual recognition instruments, insisting, in particular, on the guidance function of Eurojust.[49] The College exercises its guidance role through coordination meetings, where Eurojust National Members and relevant judicial authorities are invited. In this framework, Eurojust has the power to enact non-binding opinions to solve possible conflicts of jurisdiction,[50]

45 A. Weyembergh, 'Coordination and initiation of investigations and prosecutions through Eurojust' (2013) 14 *ERA-Forum* 179.

46 K. Ligeti and A. Weyembergh, 'The European Public Prosecutor's Office: certain constitutional issues', in L.H. Erkelens, A.W.H. Meij and M. Pawlik (eds.), *The European Public Prosecutor's Office: An Extended Arm or a Two-Headed Dragon?* (Asser Press/Springer, 2013), p. 60.

47 Article 8(1) of the proposed regulation.

48 The choice seems to have been to negotiate one controversial proposal at the time. Section 4 of this chapter will elaborate further on this.

49 The Directive on the European Investigation Order generally recalls the function of Eurojust as a useful platform to transfer investigation orders (preamble recital 13 of Directive 2014/41/EU). The European Arrest Warrant especially points out the guidance role that Eurojust can play when two arrest warrants have been issued for the same person (Article 16(1) Framework Decision 2002/584/JHA).

50 Article 7(2).

or to address difficulties executing judicial cooperation requests.[51] Far from being a mere setting to solve disagreement, in practice the College uses these meetings also to steer the national colleagues involved towards more effective cooperation strategies. Monar argues that in light of these powers, and in light of the practice, which sees more and more Member States seeking and following Eurojust's guidance, the agency has gone far beyond the mere task of *assisting* national authorities, towards a more *steering* function of national investigations.[52] This arguably starts shifting the focus from a pure service-provider role for Eurojust to assist intergovernmental cooperation, to a more active European role pushing for, if not integrated then at least coordinated EU-wide investigations and prosecutions.

As far as the monitoring function goes, Eurojust is placed in a privileged position to assess the degree of implementation of judicial cooperation instruments. For instance, Eurojust must be informed of the setting up of Joint Investigation Teams (JITs),[53] and of any delay in the execution of European Arrest Warrant (for which Member States have to give reason).[54] In this sense, it can exercise a soft policing function, which is of a supranational nature, going beyond its mere role as a facilitator. Moreover, it can and has provided strategic analysis on the functioning of the European Arrest Warrant in the field of combatting trafficking in human beings, and with respect to JITs.[55] In both areas, it has also provided some specific recommendations.[56] This policy-shaping function is similarly of a supranational nature.

Finally, concerning the external relations function, Eurojust is authorised to conclude agreements with third countries and international organisations concerning exchange of information (including personal data) and the secondment of liaison officers or liaison magistrates to Eurojust. Moreover, Eurojust can also post liaison magistrates to third countries. It was observed that this international reach of Eurojust, and the fact that it is seen more and more as the point of reference for European judicial cooperation in Europe by third states and third parties, enhances its supranational role. Monar argues that this has:

51 Article 7(3).

52 Monar, supra note 34, p. 192.

53 Article 13(5).

54 Article 17(7).

55 See Monar, supra note 34, pp. 193, 195. On the information-gathering and policy-shaping role of Eurojust, see J. Parkin, *EU Home Affairs Agencies and the Construction of EU Internal Security*, CEPS Paper No. 53/December 2012.

56 For example, in November 2012 Eurojust adopted a strategic Report on 'Eurojust's action against trafficking in human beings' including a number of recomendations. These were duly taken into account by the Council and resulted in changes being made to the Council's 'operational action plan' against trafficking in human beings. See Council of the European Union, Follow-up to Strategic report on 'Eurojust's action against trafficking in human beings', doc. 6053/13.

> given Eurojust an international role and stature which goes … beyond a merely supporting function of cooperation between the member states, that … in this respect Eurojust can be regarded as a borderline case between a European Union criminal justice area based on cooperation and one approaching integration.[57]

To conclude on Eurojust's powers, the answer to the question whether Eurojust can currently *act* supranationally must be overall negative. Within the current legal framework, it does not enjoy autonomous investigative powers; however, some marginal supranational elements can be identified in the complementary, guidance, monitoring and external relation functions. Having scrutinised Eurojust's position along the axis 'intergovernmental cooperation versus supranational integration', the next section turns to the other tension that interests the AFSJ, namely 'repression versus protection'.

3 Eurojust and the tension between crime repression and fundamental rights protection

Eurojust is conceived as a *judicial cooperation* unit aimed at assisting Member States in the fight against cross-border crime. As a consequence, by definition it enhances the EU tools to *repress* crime.[58] Nonetheless, it is interesting to enquire as to what legal protection exists specifically for those fundamental rights, which might be potentially affected by Eurojust's decisions. Considered first is the right to data protection (Section 3.1), and then the right to judicial review of Eurojust's decisions (Section 3.2).

3.1 Eurojust data protection regime

The Lisbon Treaty recognised for the first time at Article 16 TFEU the right to data protection as an independent right that needs to be respected in all EU law fields. The Article leaves it to secondary law to detail the specific rules that would govern the protection of individuals with regard to the processing of personal data, but it clearly imposes that compliance with these norms should be effectively monitored by independent authorities. The Eurojust legal framework envisages some detailed data protection rules for the data they gather from national authorities.[59] A Data Protection Officer is included among Eurojust's administrative staff, and is under the direct authority of

57 Monar, supra note 34, p. 195.

58 Some authors even suggested that a Eurodefensor should be created as a mirror organisation to Eurojust composed by defence lawyers, but this proposal had no follow-up. B. Schünemann (ed.), *A Programme for European Criminal Justice Ein Gersamtkonzept für die Europäische Strafrechtspflege* (Carl Heymanns Verlag, 2006).

59 For the legal regime concerning data regarding Eurojust staff, see specifically the 'Rules of Procedure on the processing and protection of personal data at Eurojust' approved by the College of Eurojust, 2005/C 68/01.

the College.[60] Its competence is that of monitoring the respect of the data protection rules and it may refer data protection queries to the College or even to an independent external supervisory body known as the Joint Supervisory Body (JSB). This latter body is entrusted with the task of taking final and binding decisions on controversial cases of data processing by Eurojust. The JSB is composed of judges appointed by each Member State who are not members of Eurojust, and it has only three permanent members.[61]

Other norms on data protection are included in the agreements between Eurojust and other agencies or third parties. For instance, Europol and Eurojust signed an agreement on exchange of information, which entered into force in 2010.[62] The agreement refers to each agency's data protection regime, and it requires that the information should be used only for the aim it was transmitted for (principle of purpose).[63] Finally, Eurojust has also concluded agreements for exchange of information with third countries, such as, among others, the US or the Principality of Liechtenstein.[64] Most of these agreements include a basic standard clause that reads 'the parties recognize that the handling and processing of personal data they acquire from each other is of critical importance to preserving confidence in the implementation of this agreement'.[65] Remarkably, there is no body entrusted with monitoring the compliance with these rules. It is only specified that oversight of the implementation of the agreement is the competence of the administrative and judicial authorities of each party.[66] Since data protection regimes do vary, that means so too does the degree of rights protection.

Lastly, personal data exchanges may take place in the framework of JITs set up by Eurojust with third states. In these two last contexts, the legal framework for data protection remains more or less uncharted.[67]

60 Article 17.

61 Article 23.

62 www.eurojust.europa.eu/doclibrary/Eurojust-framework/agreements/Agreement%20between%20Eurojust%20and%20Europol%20%282010%29/Eurojust-Europol-2010-01-01-EN.pdf.

63 Article 13, paras 1 and 2 of the agreement.

64 Agreement with the US, www.eurojust.europa.eu/doclibrary/Eurojust-framework/agreements/Agreement%20Eurojust-USA%20%282006%29/Eurojust-USA-2006-11-06-EN.pdf; agreement with the Principality of Liechtenstein, www.eurojust.europa.eu/doclibrary/Eurojust-framework/agreements/Agreement%20on%20Cooperation%20between%20Eurojust%20and%20the%20Principality%20of%20Liechtenstein%20%282013%29/Eurojust-Liechtenstein_2013-06-07_EN.pdf.

65 See Articles 9–17 of the US agreement, and Articles 12–17 of the agreement with Liechtenstein.

66 See Article 19 of the Eurojust–US agreement.

67 P. de Hert and V. Papakonstantinou, *The Data Protection Regime Applying to the Inter-Agency Cooperation and Future Architecture of the EU Criminal Justice and Law Enforcement Area*, Study for the LIBE Committee, p. 25. The Study is available at www.europarl.europa.eu/RegData/etudes/STUD/2014/510001/IPOL_STU%282014%29510001_EN.pdf.

The current Eurojust data protection regime, albeit articulated, has not been judged up to the standards set by the Lisbon Treaty. De Hert and Papakonstantinou especially observe that the JSB does not meet the independence and effectiveness standard a supervisory authority should have according to Article 16 TFEU, given the fact that its permanent staff is limited, only three members sit permanently in the body, and all its members are nonetheless appointed by Member States.[68] What would be required is a fully equipped independent supervisory authority.[69] In addition to that, one should note that the JSB decisions are binding, and there is arguably no possibility of judicial redress against them (on this, see the next paragraph).[70] Finally, the same authors also observe that given the fragmentation of the legal framework and the lack of a common supervisory body 'there is effectively no way of knowing what happens to personal data once they exit the EU boundaries'.[71]

The Commission's proposal on Eurojust entrusts the European Data Protection Supervisor (EDPS) with the task of monitoring and supervising Eurojust's processing of personal data,[72] and it eliminates the JSB. The EDPS is an independent permanent and fully equipped EU body, established back in 2001 with the general task of addressing personal data processing executed by Community institutions.[73] Due to its structure, the EDPS would meet the effectiveness and independence standards envisaged by the Treaty of Lisbon.[74] The Commission also details the rules on data exchange between Eurojust and other EU agencies, offices and third states and the monitoring of the respect thereof. What still would need to be defined, however, is the relationship between the legal regime set by the Eurojust regulation, and the other instruments currently negotiated within the data protection package.[75]

3.2 *Judicial review of Eurojust decisions*

A second fundamental rights issue connected to the functioning of Eurojust is that of judicial review of Eurojust's decision potentially affecting the position of individuals.[76] A first example is that of national members deciding

68 Ibid., p. 32.
69 Ibid.
70 Article 23(8) of the 2002 Eurojust Decision as amended by 2009/426/JHA.
71 De Hert and Papakonstantinou, supra note 67, p. 25. See further Chapter 15 by Poli in this volume.
72 Supra note 7, see Articles 28(2), 28(4), 29(2), 31(2), 32(4), 32(7) as far as the monitoring function, and Article 36 on the possibility to lodge a complaint before the EDPS for failure to comply with the relevant requirements on data processing.
73 Regulation (EC) No 45/2001.
74 De Hert and Papakonstantinou, supra note 67, p. 25.
75 Ibid.
76 The Court of Justice has stated that the right to access a Court to have judicial review of decisions affecting individual legal positions is directly connected to the right to a fair trial, which is established in Article 6 of the European Convention on Human Rights and

in urgent cases, or with the authorisation of national authorities, to execute in relation to their Member State a request for, or a decision on, judicial cooperation. These decisions might imply carrying out invasive investigative activity, such as searches, in execution of a European Investigative Order. Also capable of affecting the position of individuals are the decisions taken by the College in the framework of its managerial function; that is, administrating the functioning of the Agency, concerning, for instance, tendering, or recruitment matters.

In both cases, the judicial review of Eurojust's decision can take place under the proceedings of annulment before the Court of Justice. Indeed, the Treaty of Lisbon has amended Article 263 TFEU entitling the Court to review also 'the legality of acts of bodies, offices or agencies of the Union intended to produce legal effects vis-à-vis third parties'. Before the Treaty entered into force, EU primary law did not explicitly recognise the possibility to review agencies' decisions, while some case law acknowledged this possibility for certain first-pillar agencies.[77] A case was brought on this point specifically concerning a managerial decision of Eurojust's board, *Eurojust v Spain*.[78] Here, the Court managed to avoid the abstract legal question of the reviewability of third-pillar agencies' acts, and it reasoned that the applicant had sufficient means of redress under the Eurojust staff regulations.[79] The controversy has nonetheless been fixed now with the Lisbon Treaty.

Some interesting observations can be made on the specific case in which National Members take decisions liable to affect the position of individuals, while acting with the authorisation of national authorities. In this case, the question is whether the legal effects of the investigative measure carried out by the National Member in observance of a judicial cooperation request must be attributed to the authorisation of the national authority, or to the act of the individual national member. If one considers the decision as an act of the national members, it has to be clarified if it is an act of national judiciary or of Eurojust. This is relevant to assess whether national or European judiciary should be entrusted to review them. Admittedly, Article 9c of the 2009 Eurojust Decision states that national members act in their capacity as members of competent national authorities, which points in the direction of considering them national decisions. Yet, in the proposed 2013 regulation, this specification interestingly disappears.[80] Vervaele and Luchtman observe that one could make the argument that in this case, the decisions

Fundamental Freedoms, and Article 47 of the EU Charter of Fundamental Rights. See in particular Case C-222/84, *Johnston*, 1986 ECR 01651; Case C-222/86, *Heylens*, 1987 ECR 04097; Case C-97/91, *Borelli v Commission*, 1992 ECR 06313.

77 See for instance T–411/06, *Solgema*.

78 C-160/03, *Eurojust v Spain*.

79 Case C-160/03, p. 42.

80 Supra note 7, Article 8.

are directly attributable to Eurojust, and should thus be reviewed by the Court.[81]

Finally, it is remarkable that no judicial redress is offered against the decision of the JSB on the matter of data protection. As mentioned above, the JSB provides final and binding decisions on disputes on how Eurojust treats personal data.[82] These are thus likely to have an impact on the legal position of individuals, and especially on whether their right to data protection has been respected. Nevertheless, given that the JSB does not enjoy legal personality, it is unclear whether its decision could be challenged before the Court of Justice through an annulment procedure.[83] If the new reform for Eurojust enters into force as it is drafted at present, the mission of data protection will be given to the EDPS, whose decisions are undoubtedly reviewable before the Court of Justice.[84]

4 The broader subject of EU enforcement of criminal law

This section broadens the perspective and puts Eurojust in relation with the proposal for the European Public Prosecutor's Office. In particular, it focuses on the role these two agencies might have in the enforcement of EU criminal law.[85]

4.1 The alternative between a more powerful Eurojust and a European Public Prosecutor's Office

Right after Article 85 TFEU on Eurojust, Article 86 TFEU grants the EU the competence to establish a European Public Prosecutor's Office (EPPO).[86] This would be a body directly entrusted with autonomous investigative and prosecutorial powers.[87] Article 86 TFEU imposes a unanimity requirement

81 J. Vervaele and M. Luchtman, 'European agencies for criminal justice and shared enforcement (Eurojust and the European Public Prosecutor's Office)' (2014) 10(5) *Utrecht Law Review* 138.

82 Article 23(8).

83 Article 263 TFEU states that the Court should have the competence to review acts of the Institutions and of Offices and Bodies of the European Union. In its case law, the Court has denied its competence to review the decision of a body that did not enjoy legal personality, nor had any managing functions independent from EU Institutions. (Case T–395/11, paras 68–71). From this it could be inferred *a contrario* that legal personality and independence were the two requirements for bodies and offices to qualify for Article 263 TFEU proceedings. The JSB is in the odd position of having to exercise an independent supervisory function from within Eurojust, while not enjoying any legal personality.

84 Article 32(3) of Regulation 45/2001.

85 On the place of agencies within the AFSJ, and especially on their power to impose sanctions, see E. Herlin-Karnell, *Is Administrative Law Still Relevant? How the Battle of Sanctions has Shaped EU Criminal Law*, Jean Monnet Working Paper 25/14, http://jeanmonnetprogram.org/wp-content/uploads/2015/04/JMWP-25-Karnell.pdf.

86 For a full analysis of the EPPO proposals to date, see Chapter 7 by Conway in this volume.

87 Article 86(2) TFEU.

for the establishment of an EPPO; however, if this cannot be reached, it envisages the possibility to adopt the regulation by a special fast-track enhanced cooperation procedure.[88] Notably, Article 86 TFEU is framed as granting the *option* for the EU to act. It states that the Council *may* establish an EPPO, but it is not bound to do so. In 2013, next to the proposal on Eurojust mentioned above,[89] the Commission also tabled a proposal on the EPPO.[90]

Reading the two proposals jointly, some scholars have argued that the choice of the Commission not to implement the part of Article 85 TFEU where autonomous investigative and prosecutorial powers are given to Eurojust was a strategic one, namely that of investing more negotiation efforts in having the EPPO established, rather than enhancing Eurojust's powers.[91] The Commission had the possibility to empower Eurojust so that autonomous *investigative* powers would exist for *all* the crimes for which Eurojust is competent. This would have meant a limited advancement in terms of EU powers (only autonomous investigative powers), but for a great number of crimes, given that the material scope of action of Eurojust is quite large.[92] Moreover, there would have been more chances to have a uniform legislation across Europe, given that Article 85 TFEU does not envisage unanimity requirements, nor the fast-track enhanced cooperation option for approving the Eurojust regulation, as does Article 86 TFEU for the EPPO. Nonetheless, the Commission decided to drop this option, and to pursue the objective of further EU powers, namely granting the EPPO both *investigative* and *prosecutorial* powers, which are stronger powers than Eurojust holds at present or could have under Lisbon, but allegedly in a more reduced number of areas. The EPPO competence is indeed limited to the crimes against the financial interests of the EU and the ancillary offences to these,[93] even if admittedly, Article 86 TFEU envisages the possibility to expand this competence to serious and cross border crimes via Council unanimous decision. If the proposal on the EPPO[94] is approved as it stands, this would mean more EU powers, but for a fewer number of crimes. Moreover, it would also mean, at least for the time being, stronger EU powers but vis-à-vis fewer than 28 Member States, as there is good reason to believe that the EPPO will be first be approved by enhanced cooperation.[95]

88 Article 86(1) TFEU.
89 Supra note 7.
90 COM(2013)534 final.
91 Ligeti and Weyembergh, supra note 46, p. 60.
92 The material scope of Eurojust is defined at Article 4, with reference to Europol's scope. It includes a significant number of serious crimes, which include all those mentioned at Article 83 TFEU.
93 See Article 86 TFEU.
94 Supra note 87.
95 The EPPO proposal received strong opposition from certain national parliaments, some of which declared themselves against the establishment of an EPPO *per se*. On this, see

Reading the Eurojust and the EPPO proposal jointly, it is interesting to reflect on the Commission's agenda for integration in the area of enforcement of criminal law, and the fundamental rights' implications of the Commission's approach.

4.2 The Commission's strategic push for integration choice and its implications for fundamental rights

The Commission has apparently chosen to suggest the establishment of the EPPO while limiting substantively these new EU powers. Despite these limits, these are important and quite revolutionary changes that would, to an unprecedented extent, breach the veil of sovereignty in the field of criminal justice adjudication in the EU. And there are reasons to believe that the establishment of the more limited EPPO is just the starting point of a bigger integration project, which will develop by a spillover effect. As currently proposed, in terms of material scope of action, the EPPO is conceived as a body for the fight against crimes affecting the financial interests of the EU. However, in light of the complex nature of criminal networks, and the often interconnected character of crimes, it seems plausible that the clause allowing the EPPO to investigate and prosecute ancillary crimes will be heavily relied upon, expanding the actual scope of the EPPO to cases of organised crime, inherently linked to fraud or money-laundering.[96] Moreover, given the growing cross-border character of criminality, it is also plausible that in the future the EPPO will have to seek cooperation from States that are not party to it, in a similar manner to what happens now with Eurojust and the contact points in third countries. This might eventually push for the further extension of the EPPO functioning to the whole of the EU, on the blueprint of what happened with Schengen. This might also count as a spillover effect. Briefly, the establishment of the EPPO might imply more than it seems at present. As a consequence, the choice of the Commission not to implement the wider possibilities offered for the supranationalisation of Eurojust's powers and to focus on the EPPO might indeed be a strategic one, aiming at achieving further integration as a result of a spillover effect.

If one adheres to the hypothesis of the EPPO as a vanguard for further integration, one can obviously question the opportunity of pushing for more integration by effect of a practical spillover.[97] While all Member States might

I. Wieczorek, 'The EPPO draft regulation passes the first subsidiarity test: an analysis and interpretation of the Commission's hasty approach to national parliaments' subsidiarity arguments' (2015) *German Law Journal*.

96 The Meijers Committee has expressed its perplexity in connection to the ancillary jurisdiction of the EPPO. See the note of 25 September 2013, available at: www.commissie-meijers.nl/sites/all/files/cm1315_note_meijers_committee_on_eppo.pdf.

97 It has been observed that integration within the AFSJ is often justified on the basis of a spillover argument. More particularly, that the AFSJ was justified functionally, as a way

agree on a general objective to jointly fight cross-border crime and crimes affecting the financial interests of the EU, not all might consider this objective so important as to establish a European supranational enforcement body. Yet, if the EPPO is approved, despite its apparent limited geographical and material scope, Member States that were contrary to its adoption might be forced to cooperate for practical reasons, and more crimes would need to be included due to the nature of current complex cross-border criminality. One might then wonder if it would not have been more advisable, and more 'honest' from a policy perspective, to first openly discuss how to gradually push operational integration further in all the areas where the EU has legislative competence, and to evaluate if the full exploitation of Eurojust's potential would not have been enough.

In any case, given the Commission's resolution to go down the road of stronger vertical integration for – at least for the time being – a limited number of crimes and of Member States, one should also note that more invasive powers come with higher fundamental rights responsibility. While to address the topic extensively would be beyond the scope of this chapter, it suffices to mention as a final remark, that the debate concerning judicial review of Eurojust's decision is only enhanced in the framework of the EPPO.[98]

5 Conclusion

This chapter has contextualised the EU's judicial cooperation agencies within the constitutional architecture of the Area of Freedom, Security and Justice. It chose as relevant constitutional themes for the AFSJ – through which to read the legal framework and the functioning of these agencies – the tension between intergovernmentalism and supranationalism; and the tension between crime repression and the respect of fundamental rights.

A first superficial conclusion would be that Eurojust is an agency whose functioning and philosophy is mainly inspired by intergovernmentalism and that contributes to the enhancement of the repressive side of the AFSJ. Yet, what this chapter has hopefully provided is a more sophisticated reading of the matter, illustrating how elements of supranationalism exist within the structure and the functioning of Eurojust. Moreover, it has discussed the legal framework for the protection of fundamental rights directly affected by Eurojust's decisions, as in the case of the right to data protection, and of judicial review. It has highlighted how the Lisbon Treaty has sensitively improved the protection of judicial review, and how the framework for data protection still presents some weaknesses, which are nonetheless addressed by the proposed regulation on Eurojust. If one then reads Eurojust jointly

to overcome the shortcomings of the free market, rather than as a goal in itself as such. M. Fletcher, R. Lööf and B. Gilmore, *EU Criminal Law and Justice* (Edward Elgar, 2009), p. 26.

98 On this extensively see Vervaele and Luchtman, supra note 81, pp. 140ff.

with the EPPO proposal, one can appreciate how the Commission is pushing in the direction of deeper integration. The necessary caveat is that deeper integration requires a fuller reflection on EU fundamental rights protection. Obviously, how the relationship between Eurojust and the EPPO will unfold, and how this will impact on the allocation of powers between Member States and the EU within the AFSJ and the protection of fundamental rights is still to be seen, given that the negotiations are still ongoing. Interestingly enough, and to conclude, the new strategic guidelines for the AFSJ[99] provide some insightful element at least on Eurojust. The role of the agency is mentioned as that of a *coordinator*, and not only as a *facilitator*, very much in line with the approach in the 2013 proposed regulation, implementing the novelties of Article 85 TFEU.[100] Moreover, the potential of Eurojust as a pool of expertise that could be useful to foster mutual trust is also mentioned.[101] This arguably points in the direction of an agency with a proper supranational role, fully integrated in the general project of building an Area of Freedom, Security and Justice, rather than a simple platform easing contacts between judicial authorities coming from different Member States.

99 Conclusions of the European Council of 26 and 27 June 2014, EUCO 79/14. For a comment on these see E. Herlin-Karnell, 'All roads lead to Rome: the new AFSJ package and the trajectory to Europe 2020' (2014) *EUCrim*.

100 Part 10 of the Conclusions.

101 Part 11 of the Conclusions.

18 The European Union's fight against cybercrime

Policy, legal and practical challenges

Helena Carrapiço and Benjamin Farrand

1 Introduction

When science-fiction writer William Gibson first dreamt about what cyberspace could look like,[1] he was far from imagining that his concept would become one of the most essential dimensions of our societies. Within 30 years, cyberspace evolved from a graphic representation of all computerised data in a sci-fi novel to being 'the dominant platform for life in the 21st century'.[2] From laptops to smartphones and common house appliances, the range of devices connecting individuals and enabling data transfer has not only grown exponentially, but it has also become considerably diverse. According to Europol, there were 8.7 billion devices connected to the internet in 2012, a figure that had grown to 10 billion in 2014, and is projected to increase to 50 billion by 2020.[3] The Internet of Things[4] alone is expected to connect 26 billion devices by 2020, according to the Digital Single Market Strategy.[5] The coming into being of cyberspace and its widespread adoption have been openly welcomed and cheered, given its perceived contribution to

1 W. Gibson, *Neuromancer* (Harper Voyager, 1982).

2 Hammersley, as cited in P.W. Singer and A. Friedman, *Cybersecurity and Cyberwar: What Everyone Needs To Know* (Oxford University Press, 2014), p. 15.

3 Europol, 'EC3 First Annual Report' (2014); Europol, 'iOCTA: The Internet Organised Crime Threat Assessment' (2014).

4 The Internet of Things is 'where physical objects are seamlessly integrated into the information network, and where the physical objects can become active participants in business processes [... and] might also serve as backbone for ubiquitous computing, enabling smart environments to recognize and identify objects, and retrieve information from the Internet to facilitate their adaptive functionality'. In other words, the Internet of Things is the capacity of physical appliances (such as an oven or a car) to transmit data within a given network. The risks associated with it were recently visible in a *Wired* experiment where a Jeep Cherokee was remotely hacked, leading to the recall of 1.4 million cars in the US according to A. Greenberg, 'Hackers Remotely Kill a Jeep on the Highway – With Me in It', *Wired* (21 July 2015), www.wired.com/2015/07/hackers-remotely-kill-jeep-highway (accessed 31 May 2016); BBC Technology News, 'Fiat Chrysler Recalls 1.4 Million Cars after Jeep Hack' (24 July 2015), www.bbc.co.uk/news/technology-33650491 (accessed 31 May 2016).

5 European Commission, 'Commission Staff Working Document: A Digital Single Market Strategy, for Europe–Analysis and Evidence' SWD(2015) 100 65.

economic and social development.[6] In order to promote such technological advancements and the respective positive outcomes, the EU started by approaching cyberspace as an area where competition and access to the free market should be ensured[7]. Soon, however, the EU realised that this area also had the potential for grave societal harm.[8] Given the world's degree of digital interdependence regarding communication, commercial transactions and critical infrastructures, policymakers and citizens, in general, have come to perceive cyberspace as in need of protection from possible abuse from criminals, terrorist groups and rogue states. Namely, at the European Union level, this cyber security awareness has resulted in a push towards further understanding the risks involved in cyberspace, as well as developing policy and legislative measures aimed at improving its resilience. Together with cyber defence and network and information infrastructure protection, cybercrime has been very much at the forefront of the European Union's cyber security policy and legislative interest. These three areas have come to form the pillars of the European Union's Cyber Security Strategy, which was issued in 2013.[9] However, unlike cyber defence, the prioritisation of the fight against cybercrime has been based on a large number of well-documented incidents and on a perception of large-scale vulnerability of both companies and individuals:

> The threat is very much a real one. The number of cyber attacks in the world is on the rise and the cost of cybercrime is skyrocketing. [...] This is a shared agenda between the EU institutions, Member States and the industry. Without all of us taking responsibility we will pay a very high price.[10]

Nevertheless, there are significant difficulties for the EU in establishing a coordinated and precise response to the challenges presented by cybercrime and cyber-attacks. This poses considerable problems for the realisation of the EU as an Area of Freedom, Security and Justice (AFSJ). Under Article 67 Treaty on the Functioning of the European Union (TFEU), the AFSJ is to be facilitated through actions of cooperation and coordination, up to and including, under Article 67(3), the approximation of criminal laws. However, a lack of conceptual clarity, legal uncertainty and reliance on network governance

6 Ibid.

7 S. Summers et al., *The Emergence of EU Criminal Law: Cyber Crime and the Regulation of the Information Society* (Hart Publishing, 2014).

8 See generally I. Hosein and J. Eriksson, 'International Policy Dynamics and the Regulation of Dataflows', in J. Eriksson and G. Giacomello (eds.), *International Relations and Security in the Digital Age* (Routledge, 2010).

9 European Commission and High Representative of the European Union for Foreign Affairs and Security Policy (HREU), 'Cybersecurity Strategy of the European Union: An Open, Safe and Secure Cyberspace', JOIN(2013) 1, 7 February 2013.

10 Cecilia Malmström, 'It's Time to Take Cyber Criminals Offline' (2011) SPEECH/11/260.

with reluctant private stakeholder involvement (with subsequent implications for cooperation and coordination) serves to create a significant gap between the expectations, competences and outcomes of the EU in this field of endeavour. This in turn leads to the question of whether the AFSJ truly exists when considering the issue of cybercrime. The present chapter begins by exploring the policy and legal architecture of the European Union's discursive construction of cybercrime, by emphasising the link between its threat perception and its proposed policies. However, as this chapter will go on to demonstrate, the ambiguity of the term 'cybercrime' in policy has led to a level of legal uncertainty, both when considering contestation over the reach of cybercrime as a broad field (including computer-facilitated crimes), as well as inconsistent national implementation of legislation pertaining to cybercrime narrowly defined (as attacks upon information systems). A clear gap between policy expectations and legal competences is, however, rendered visible and identified, in which the practical implications of these policy and legal uncertainties upon the implementation of the EU's cybercrime strategy will be explored. In particular, based on information asymmetries and a limited capacity to act, the EU has relied upon the establishment of coordinating agencies and private-sector engagement in order to ensure that cybercrime is effectively countered through information provision and ensuring the resilience of information systems to attack. Such a strategy, however, is hindered by uncertainties and ambiguities regarding the competing aims of specialisation and a holistic approach to cyber security, while subject to significantly constrained budgets, and a certain reluctance of stakeholders involved in this form of networked governance to share information.

2 The EU's fight against cybercrime: idealised outcomes, uncertain definitions?

For the European Union, cybercrime has been identified as one of the most challenging threats it is currently faced with; as stated by the then-Commissioner for Home Affairs in 2012: 'Cybercrime is an attack on basic societal values and citizens' security.'[11] According to the 2013 EU Cybersecurity Strategy, the considerable societal and economic development provided by digital technologies is currently at risk as a result of State-sponsored, terrorist and criminal attacks.[12] The Cybersecurity Strategy was written based on an understanding that 'information and communications technology has become the backbone of our economic growth and is a critical resource which all economic sectors rely on'.[13] Cybercrime, according to this strategy, constitutes a significant threat, not only to the

11 Cecilia Malmström, 'Public–Private Cooperation in the Fight against Cybercrime' (2012) SPEECH/12/409.

12 European Commission and HREU, supra note 9, p. 3.

13 Ibid., p. 2.

continued development of these technologies and their perceived capacity to substantially contribute to economic growth in the EU, but also to consumer confidence in using currently existing e-commerce platforms. Cybercrime itself, however, is not presented as a new phenomenon, although its rapidly expanding capacity for disruption is regarded as having achieved previously unthinkable levels due to the widespread adoption of digital communications technologies: cybercriminals are now able to 'conduct crime against large numbers of victims across different countries simultaneously with minimum effort and risk'.[14] Attracted by the EU's wealthy, but also internet-dependent economy,[15] cybercrime is now understood as having the capability to endanger not only the financial sector, but also the lives of ordinary citizens and society as a whole. According to the iOCTA, Europol's report on internet-enabled crimes, the trends in this area suggest that the problem has escalated beyond 'mere' economic damage, given the diversification in the scope and nature of the attacks and their victims.[16] Given its unique nature, cyberspace has led to the development of a distinct ecosystem, the rules of which differ substantially from those in the physical world. Criminals are not only capable of conducting transnational attacks from a distance and in a simultaneous fashion, but they are also aided by the difficulty in attribution of such attacks. As a result, what used to be a small-scale criminal community has become a large industry, driven by a services-based criminal business model, worth between $300 billion and $1 trillion, with an alleged 1 million new victims emerging every day.[17] On the basis of this understanding, it comes as little surprise that the EU and its Member States have put such emphasis on prioritising the fight against cybercrime: 'The EU must speed up the fight against cybercrime. [...] If we are to put an end to [...] the golden age of cybercrime and take the cyber criminals offline, we need more action from Member States as well as from the industry.'[18]

Cybercrime has, albeit indirectly, been a concern for the EU since the early 1990s.[19] Although the first development in the area of computer crime in Europe was the 1976 Council of Europe Conference on Criminological aspects of Economic Crime, with the proposal of creating different categories

14 Europol, 'iOCTA', supra note 3, p. 3.

15 In 2013, 75 per cent of the EU's population had regular access to the Internet, compared to 39 per cent in the rest of the world. This figure increases to 90 per cent of the population when referring to Nordic countries – Europol, 'iOCTA', supra note 3, p. 17.

16 Europol, 'iOCTA', supra note 3, p. 11.

17 See McAfee, 'The Economic Impact of Cybercrime and Cyber Espionage' (Center for Strategic and International Studies, 2013); Symantec, 'Norton Report 2013' (2013), http://go.symantec.com/norton-report-2013 (accessed 31 May 2016).

18 Malmström, supra note 10, p. 2; see also D. Avramopoulos, 'Commissioner Avramopoulos Presents European Agenda on Security at European Parliament' (2015) SPEECH/15/4885.

19 See M.G. Porcedda, 'Translantic Approaches to Cybersecurity and Cybercrime', in P. Pawlak (ed.), *The EU–US Security and Justice Agenda in Action* (Chaillot Papers, 2011).

of computer crime, serious attention would only start to be devoted to this area with attempts to complete the single market.[20] The rationale behind such a move was that if Member States adopted diverging regulatory approaches to the digital world, criminals might take advantage of legal loopholes, such as the differences in legal definitions and sentences. Largely basing itself on the work developed by the Council of Europe and the OECD, the European Community started to highlight the need to address computer security in order to remove obstacles to the pursuit of an e-common market, in its 1993 *White Paper on Growth, Competitiveness and Employment*.[21] Until the end of the 1990s, such efforts were mainly focused on self-regulation, focusing in particular on the protection of intellectual property and personal data. According to the 1993 White Paper, information and communication technologies were seen as essential to the continued development of economies and the completion of the single market.[22] Similarly, the Bangemann report also referred to the importance of safeguarding information technologies, as a competitive force with the potential to create numerous jobs.[23]

The EU's interest in cybercrime thus started off as an economic concern, related to the advancement of the single market through ensuring consumer protection, and subsequently trust, in electronic commerce. The transition from an economic rationale to a security one only occurred towards the end of the 1990s, when the Commission requested a comprehensive study on computer crime.[24] According to the latter, Europe was becoming increasingly vulnerable to attacks aimed at its information infrastructures. Such a scenario was made worse by the differences between national laws in terms of protection against breaches of privacy, hacking and illegal content. Fearful of the emergence of computer crime havens, with the potential to disrupt the development of the single market, the European Commission proposed that future action be based on international cooperation.[25] The European Council was particularly receptive to the Commission's report, having included, for the first time, in its conclusions the need to deal with high-tech crime.[26] As a follow-up, the Council proposed *eEurope 2002*, an action

20 See S. Schjolberg, 'The History of Global Harmonization on Cybercrime Legislation: The Road to Geneva', *Cyber Crime Law* (2008), www.cybercrimelaw.net/documents/cybercrime_history.pdf (accessed 31 May 2016).

21 Porcedda, supra note 19.

22 European Commission, 'Growth, Competitiveness, Employment: The Challenges and Ways Forward into the 21st Century' White Paper COM(93) 700.

23 European Commission and Bangemann Group, 'Europe and the Global Information Society: Recommendations of the High-Level Group on the Information Society to the Corfu European Council' (1994) S.2/94.

24 U. Sieber, *Legal Aspects of Computer-Related Crime in the Information Society* (University of Würzburg, 1998).

25 S.M. Kierkegaard, 'EU Tackles Cyber Crime', in L.J. Janczewski and A.M. Colarik (eds.), *Cyber Warfare and Cyber Terrorism* (IGI Global, 2007).

26 European Council Presidency, 'Conclusions, Tampere European Council 15 and 16 October 1999'.

plan focused on creating the most dynamic knowledge-based economy in the world, using a more secure internet as its basis.[27] In line with the action plan, the Commission produced another report on improving the security of information infrastructures and combating computer-related crime.[28] The latter suggested developing a coordinated approach to these issues, including the setting of minimum standards, the harmonisation of national definitions, the approximation of legislation and the development of joint instruments.[29] In 2001, European States proposed to adopt a common approach to tackle cybercrime with the signing of the Council of Europe's *Convention on Cybercrime*, which remains, to this date, the most important piece of international law signed and ratified by European States in this area. Although created within the context of the Council of Europe, the European Union urged Member States to ratify and implement the Treaty. The first legally binding EU instrument in this area was only adopted in 2005, under the format of the Council Framework Decision on *Attacks against Information Systems*. This timely hiatus reveals that, although considered, cyber security was not, until 2005, part of the EU's security priorities. As an example of that, the 2003 European Security Strategy was strangely silent on the topic.

From the mid-2000s to 2014, the EU has significantly changed its stance on cybercrime, not only by treating it as a relevant political issue, but also by creating numerous institutions and policies to help tackle cyber insecurities. Although, the major breakthrough came with the approval of the EU Cyber Security Strategy in March 2013, other measures had been put in place before that, particularly regarding critical information infrastructure protection (CIIP) and police cooperation. The creation of the European Network and Information Security Agency (ENISA) in 2004 is probably the most illustrative measure taken in this area, as it is aimed at improving the level of Network and Information Security (NIS) and at contributing to the development of an NIS culture within the Union. As explained by ENISA's executive director, Udo Helmbrecht, the agency understands its role as a 'pace-setter' for information security in the EU, by promoting awareness regarding how cyber-attacks (of state or criminal origin) can affect critical information infrastructures (CIIs). As such, it serves as a hub for the exchange of information and best practices between the key stakeholders in this area: Member States, EU institutions and the private sector. As for cybercrime, the creation of the European Cybercrime Centre (EC3) within Europol in 2012 was a major step towards the consolidation of an EU approach to cybercrime. Operational since January 2014, EC3 is responsible for coordinating the EU's response to cybercrime, to serve as the European cybercrime information focal point, to

27 Council of the European Union, 'eEurope 2002: An Information Society for All' (2000).

28 European Commission, 'Creating a Safer Information Society by Improving the Security of Information Infrastructures and Combating Computer-Related Crime' COM(2000) 890.

29 F. Mendez, 'The European Union and Cybercrime: Insights from Comparative Federalism' (2005) 12 *Journal of European Public Policy* 509.

act as an experts' forum, to provide support to individual Member States in their cybercrime investigations, and to become the collective voice of cybercrime investigators across law enforcement.[30] Despite working in previously distinct areas, ENISA and EC3 are part of a growing trend to understand different dimensions of cybersecurity as being interconnected.

In order to better understand the legal and political challenges of regulating cybercrime in the EU, it is important to consider the definition of the term as used by the EU. In general, the prefix 'cyber' alludes to a set of activities related to the use of computers and electronic networks.[31] More specifically, cybercrime usually refers to a large set of different criminal activities where computers and information systems constitute either the primary tool of the attack or their main target. The first EU document to include a deeper reflection on the concept of cybercrime, and subsequently develop its definition further, was the 2007 Communication 'Towards a General Policy on the Fight against Cyber Crime',[32] which noted the multiplication of similar terms to designate computer-related crimes and argued in favour of a single definition: 'cybercrime is understood as criminal acts committed using electronic communications networks and information systems or against networks and systems.'[33] According to this same document, such a definition covers three types of criminal activities: traditional forms of crime committed through electronic means, the publication of illegal content, and crimes against electronic networks. This definition is in line with the ones discussed in the academic literature,[34] which essentially distinguishes between two forms of cybercrime: those referring to the facilitation of traditional illegal activities through digital means (such as the exchange of child abuse images, or identity theft), and those that are aimed at information networks (namely, the usage of botnets[35] for spam or for distributed denial of service attacks[36]).[37]

30 European Commission, 'Tackling Crime in Our Digital Age: Establishing a European Cybercrime Centre' COM(2012) 140.

31 S. Fafinski, W. Dutton and H. Margetts, *Mapping and Measuring Cybercrime* (Oxford Internet Institute, 2010) Forum Discussion Paper 18, p. 8.

32 European Commission, 'Towards a General Policy on the Fight against Cyber Crime' COM(2007) 267.

33 Ibid., p. 2, see also European Commission and HREU, supra note 9.

34 See, for example, D.S. Wall, *Cybercrime: The Transformation of Crime in the Information Age* (Polity Press, 2007); N. Barrett, *Traces Of Guilt* (Corgi, 2009); R.G. Smith, P. Grabosky and G. Urbas, *Cyber Criminals on Trial* (Cambridge University Press, 2011).

35 Botnets are a collection of internet-connected computers that have been taken over (often without the knowledge of their users) to perform malicious activities such as spread spam or viruses.

36 A distributed denial of service attack consists in the attempt to render a given online server inaccessible to regular users by bombarding it with access requests. The server usually overloads and shuts down.

37 S.W. Brenner, 'Cybercrime: Rethinking Crime Control Strategies', in Y. Jewkes (ed.), *Crime Online* (2nd edn, Routledge, 2011).

However, the academic literature also emphasises that the concept of cybercrime remains elusive and essentially contested.[38] Indeed, 'cybercrime' as a term appears to be used interchangeably with concepts such as 'computer crime' (as used by the EU in Article 83 TFEU, as will be discussed in the next section), 'high-tech crime' and 'information-age crime'.[39] Clough describes it as a 'generic term used to describe the role of technology in the commission of crimes'.[40] This conceptual diversity creates a certain ambiguity that is deleterious to a unified AFSJ policy being developed and followed by the EU and its composite Member States: 'there are no universally accepted definitions of computer crime [and] high technology crime. Each of these terms have different meanings to criminal justice professionals around the world.'[41] The position has not noticeably improved with the publication of the EU's Cybersecurity Strategy.[42] On the topic of cybercrime, the Strategy states that 'cybercriminals are using ever more sophisticated methods for intruding into computer systems, stealing critical data or holding companies to ransom',[43] indicating that the EU considers cybercrime in a narrow context – however, in a footnote on the same page, the Strategy states that cybercrime 'commonly refers to a broad range of different criminal activities where computers and information systems are involved either as a primary tool or as a primary target',[44] including both attacks on information systems *and* facilitation of offences such as identity theft and content-related offences such as distribution of child abuse materials. As we shall demonstrate in the next section, the broad 'umbrella' concept of cybercrime in the EU's policy space has led to uncertainty issues in the legal implementation of these policies.

3 The EU's legal actions concerning cybercrime: idealised laws amid uncertain competences?

As has been stated in the above section, the EU's policies in this field have been developed in the direction of ensuring a coordinated, informed and uniform approach to cybercrime. However, as this section of the chapter will demonstrate, these goals are faced with a significant hurdle in light of legal uncertainties regarding the limits of the competence of the EU in this field, as well as with regard to the interpretation of existing laws. A considerable amount has been written on the general competences of the EU in the field of

38 Wall, supra note 34.

39 Brenner, supra note 37, p. 13.

40 J. Clough, 'The Council of Europe Convention on Cybercrime: Defining "Crime" in a Digital World' (2012) 23 *Criminal Law Forum* 363, at p. 371.

41 M. Goodman, 'International Dimensions of Cybercrime', in S. Ghosh and E. Turrini (eds.), *Cybercrimes: A Multidisciplinary Analysis* (Springer, 2011), p. 320.

42 European Commission and HREU, supra note 9.

43 Ibid., p. 3.

44 Ibid.

criminal law prior to the entry into force of the Lisbon Treaty, which for the purposes of brevity will not be reproduced in full here.[45] Subsequent to the entry into force of the Lisbon Treaty, the EU now has an explicit competence for legislating in the field of 'computer crime', giving the EU 'fresh opportunities to develop EU criminal law legislation'.[46] The Commission considers that offences regarded as 'Euro-crimes', designated as such due to their perceived serious and cross-border nature, are best handled at the EU level, rather than through national responses.[47] Indeed, under Article 83(1) of the TFEU, the Parliament and Council may, under the ordinary legislative procedure, 'establish minimum rules concerning the definition of criminal offences and sanctions in the areas of particularly serious crime with a cross-border dimension resulting from the nature or impact of such offences or from a special need to combat them on a common basis'. One of these areas of competence, listed in Article 83(1), is that of 'computer crimes'. The term 'computer crimes', however, is not defined, raising questions regarding the extent of the competences of the EU in this field.

Prior to the Treaty of Lisbon, 'computer crime' was not specifically mentioned as being within the law-making competence of the EU, with Article 31(e) TEU (Nice Consolidated Version) referring only to the approximation of rules concerning the constituent elements of criminal acts and to penalties in the fields of organised crime, terrorism and illicit drug trafficking. However, the Tampere Council Conclusions published in October 1999 made it clear that the European Council considered that 'common definitions, incrimination and sanctions' should be pursued in fields such as 'high tech crime'.[48] This view was reiterated by the Commission in a Communication in 2001, in which it was stated that in light of the developments brought by the 'information society' and the increased prevalence of internet usage for communication and commerce, these 'infrastructures have become a critical part of our economies [... resulting in] the need for [...] a comprehensive policy initiative [...] improving the security of information

45 See in particular, however, V. Mitsilegas, *EU Criminal Law* (Hart Publishing, 2009). See also A. Klip, *European Criminal Law: An Integrative Approach* (Intersentia, 2009); F. Calderoni, *Organized Crime Legislation in the European Union: Harmonization and Approximation of Criminal Law, National Legislations and the EU Framework Decision on the Fight Against Organized Crime* (Springer, 2010); H. Xanthaki, 'Eurojust: Fulfilled or Empty Promises in EU Criminal Law' (2006) 8 *European Journal of Law Reform* 175; E. Herlin-Karnell, 'Recent Developments in the Area of European Criminal Law' (2007) 14 *Maastricht Journal of European and Comparative Law* 15; Summers et al., supra note 7.

46 European Commission, 'Towards an EU Criminal Policy: Ensuring the Effective Implementation of EU Policies through Criminal Law' COM(2011) 573, p. 3.

47 Ibid., p. 5; see also C. Harding and J.B. Banach-Gutierrez, 'The Emergent EU Criminal Policy: Identifying the Species' (2012) 37(6) *European Law Review* 758, at pp. 763–764; A. Hinarejos, 'Integration in Criminal Matters and the Role of the Court of Justice' (2011) 36 *European Law Review* 420, at p. 423.

48 European Council, supra note 37, para 48.

infrastructures and combating cybercrime'.[49] The Communication, however, and somewhat unhelpfully, states that computer-related crime, the term then used, 'is addressed in the broadest sense, as any crime that in some way or other involves the use of information technology'.[50] Similarly, the Convention on Cybercrime,[51] which the Commission noted was being finalised as the Communication was published[52] and which Fahey comments has acted as a significant external norm influencing the EU approach to cyber security,[53] is also somewhat imprecise. According to the accompanying Explanatory Report, the internet was perceived as facilitating cross-border trade, communication and further technological development, but also as contributing towards 'the emergence of new types of crime as well as the commission of traditional crimes by means of new technologies'.[54] Furthermore, the potential for serious, transnational criminal activity to be facilitated by the internet, regardless of national borders or legal systems, led to the Council of Europe conclusion that a unified international response was required.[55]

The Convention, however, does not explicitly define 'cybercrime', instead providing for a broad and disparate set of offences linked only by the fact that a computer may either be used or targeted by an alleged offender – categorised as 'offences against the confidentiality, integrity and availability of computer data and systems',[56] 'computer-related offences',[57] 'content-related offences'[58] and 'offences related to infringements of copyright and related rights'.[59] A significant legal challenge for the combatting of cybercrime within the EU's AFSJ is that 'cybercrime' is an ill-defined and overly broad concept as used in the Convention,[60] which has the result of creating an atmosphere of legal uncertainty. With regard to the infamous 'vehicles in the park' example given by Hart,[61] vagueness of categorisation and ambiguity can lead to significant issues with the identification and implementation of legal standards. As Beck argues, ambiguity 'arises when the boundaries of meaning are indistinct and it cannot be said with certainty if the application of a word is correct or not'.[62] The fact that the terms 'cybercrime',

49 European Commission, supra note 9, p. 2.
50 Ibid., p. 12.
51 Council of Europe, 'Convention on Cybercrime, CETS No.185, Budapest 23 November 2001'.
52 European Commission, supra note 9, p. 15.
53 E. Fahey, 'The EU's Cybercrime and Cyber-Security Rulemaking: Mapping the Internal and External Dimensions of EU Security' (2014) 5 *European Journal of Risk Regulation* 46, at p. 48.
54 Convention on Cybercrime, Explanatory Report, para 5.
55 Ibid., paras 5–6.
56 Convention on Cybercrime, Articles 2–6.
57 Ibid., Articles 7–8.
58 Ibid., Article 9.
59 Ibid., Article 10.
60 Fahey, supra note 53, pp. 47–48.
61 H.L.A. Hart, *The Concept of Law* (3rd edn, Oxford University Press, 2012).
62 G. Beck, *The Legal Reasoning of the Court of Justice of the EU* (Hart Publishing, 2013), p. 56.

'computer crime' and 'high-tech crime' are all apparently interchangeable, as well as the ambiguity about whether in the context of the Lisbon Treaty the use of computer crime refers specifically to a narrow definition of offences against computer systems, or to a broader set of 'computer-related offences' as with the Convention on Cybercrime, poses a significant challenge to the development of a coherent cybercrime law-making strategy on the part of the Commission.[63] Furthermore, overly broad and ambiguous definitions within the context of criminal law generally raise concerns regarding the legitimacy of criminal law responses, as well as both the likelihood of effective prosecutions and fair trials.[64]

The position has not noticeably improved with the publication of the EU's Cybersecurity Strategy,[65] with a lack of confidence being expressed regarding the development of a concise legal definition. Commenting on the Strategy, the European Data Protection Supervisor remarked that the definition provided is still 'quite vague and broad [...,] there is not yet a single legal framework providing for a comprehensive definition of the offences that are being referred to by the term "cybercrime" '.[66] The areas of 'cybercrime' regulation as broadly defined are disparate, with different underlying logics and levels of acceptability; while the distribution of child-abuse materials is almost universally accepted as a serious crime necessitating a law enforcement response, the issue of copyright infringement online (another form of content-related offence) is far more contested.[67] A Framework Decision on combating child exploitation and abuse content[68] was uncontroversial regarding the need to protect children from sexual exploitation, and to create a unified response to

63 On this point, see also I. Walden, 'Harmonising Computer Crime Laws in Europe' (2004) 12 *European Journal of Crime, Criminal Law and Criminal Justice* 321.

64 For example, see the concerns regarding the Counter-Terrorism Act 2008 in the UK, and the possibility of imprisonment based upon broad definitions of 'terrorist financing', which are based upon the decision of the Treasury in E. Herlin-Karnell, *The Constitutional Dimension of European Criminal Law* (Bloomsbury Publishing, 2012); see also A. Weyembergh, 'Approximation of Criminal Laws: The Constitutional Treaty and the Hague Programme' (2005) 42 *Common Market Law Review* 1567.

65 European Commission and HREU, supra note 9.

66 European Data Protection Supervisor, 'Opinion on the Joint Communication Cybersecurity Strategy of the European Union and on the Commission Proposal for a Directive Concerning Measures to Ensure a High Common Level of Network and Information Security Across the Union', Brussels, 14 June 2013, pp. 7–8.

67 See, for example, B. Farrand, *Networks of Power in Digital Copyright Law and Policy: Political Salience, Expertise and the Legislative Process* (Routledge, 2014); C. Geiger, 'The Rise of Criminal Enforcement of Intellectual Property Rights ... and Its Failure in the Context of Copyright Infringements on the Internet', in S. Frankel and D.J. Gervais (eds.), *The Evolution and Equilibrium of Copyright in the Digital Age* (Cambridge University Press, 2014); B. Farrand and H. Carrapiço, 'Copyright Law as a Matter of (Inter)National Security? The Attempt to Securitise Commercial Infringement and Its Spillover onto Individual Liability' (2012) 57 *Crime, Law and Social Change* 373.

68 Framework Decision 2004/68/JHA, 'On Combating the Sexual Exploitation of Children and Child Pornography'.

the existence of child abuse material on the internet.[69] A 2011 Directive has replaced this Framework Decision[70] after a relatively speedy legislative process in which objections raised were limited solely to matters of technical substance rather than the intent and reasoning of the legislation.[71] With regard to the criminalisation of copyright infringement online, however, there has been substantial disagreement as to whether the conduct should be considered as criminal, particularly when the act of infringement is conducted by an individual end-user. The Information Society Directive[72] is the EU's central legislative act in the field of copyright law, containing the key provisions on the exploitation, protection and infringement of copyright. The infringement of copyright has traditionally been conceived as an issue of civil wrong, with the result that the main remedy for infringement has taken the form of an award of civil damages rather than criminal sanction.[73] However, in 2005, the Commission published a strongly worded Communication proposing criminal sanctions for commercial-scale copyright infringement, arguing that 'the increasing use of the Internet enables pirated products to be distributed instantly around the globe [... and that] this phenomenon appears to be increasingly linked to organised crime',[74] ostensibly placing the issue of copyright infringement both within the EU's competences for criminal law as well as the domain of 'cybercrime' broadly defined. Nevertheless, despite attempts to introduce a Directive imposing criminal sanctions for intellectual property rights infringement in 2005, Member States such as the UK and the Netherlands stated strong reservations to the Directive as proposed, and the European Parliament considered the proposal too broad, vague and unconcerned with protections for end-users.[75] The proposal was ultimately

69 European Commission, 'Combating Trafficking in Human Beings and Combating the Sexual Exploitation of Children and Child Pornography' COM(2000) 854 final/2 3.

70 Directive 2011/92/EU, 'Of the European Parliament and of the Council of 13 December 2011 on Combating the Sexual Abuse and Sexual Exploitation of Children and Child Pornography, and Replacing Council Framework Decision 2004/68/JHA' (2011).

71 See, for example, European Data Protection Supervisor, 'Opinion on the Proposal for a Directive of the European Parliament and of the Council on Combating the Sexual Abuse, Sexual Exploitation of Children and Child Pornography, Repealing Framework Decision 2004/68/JHA' (2010) Brussels, para 16; J. Monar, 'Justice and Home Affairs' (2012) 50 *Journal of Common Market Studies* 116.

72 Directive 2001/29/EC, 'Of the European Parliament and of the Council of 22 May 2001 on the Harmonisation of Certain Aspects of Copyright and Related Rights in the Information Society' (2001).

73 C. Geiger, 'Introduction', *Criminal Enforcement of Intellectual Property: A Handbook of Contemporary Research* (Edward Elgar, 2012), p. 1; D. Kioupis, 'Criminal Liability on the Internet', in I.A. Stamatoudi (ed.), *Copyright Enforcement and the Internet* (Kluwer Law International, 2010).

74 European Commission, 'Proposal for a European Parliament and Council Directive on Criminal Measures Aimed at Ensuring the Enforcement of Intellectual Property Rights' COM(2005) 276 2.

75 Geiger, supra note 67, p. 120.

withdrawn in 2010, for reasons including concern over the legality of its introduction and the lack of competence for criminal law harmonisation under the auspices of former Article 95 EC (now Article 114 TFEU) in the (EC) Community Pillar.[76] The Anti-Counterfeiting Trade Agreement, an international agreement concerning the protection of intellectual property rights was also rejected by the European Parliament in light of large-scale protests throughout the EU concerning the internet-based enforcement of copyright through actions such as web-blocking, and concerns over the criminalisation of individuals for downloading infringing content,[77] indicating that the inclusion of copyright infringement online within a general understanding of cybercrime is highly contentious.

Even focusing upon cybercrime narrowly defined as offences against computer systems, there are significant challenges to the development of a unified legal position, which the EU is now seeking to rectify. One such example can be found in legislation concerning attacks on information systems. In 2005, the EU implemented a Framework Decision on attacks against information systems.[78] The purpose of this Framework Decision, according to recital 1, was to 'improve cooperation between judicial and other competent authorities, including the police and other specialised law enforcement services', in order to combat attacks on information systems, ranging from illegal access[79] to illegal system[80] and data interference.[81] In its review of the implementation of the Framework Decision, however, the Commission noted it had been implemented in many different ways in the Member States, with the result that comparisons between the legal concepts and expressions used in each was difficult.[82] On this basis, a uniform approach to cybercrime (narrowly defined) was not achieved. According to the European Parliament, substantial differences between EU Member States on the interpretation of obligations under the Directive, along with general uncertainty regarding the definition of cybercrime, are impacting upon *legal* certainty and the protection of individuals.[83] Returning to the Commission review, Member States such as Austria and Finland were identified as having not fully complied with aspects of the Framework Decision regarding illegal access,[84] and concern was expressed that

76 Farrand, supra note 67, p. 47.

77 See generally B. Farrand, 'Lobbying and Lawmaking in the European Union: The Development of Copyright Law and the Rejection of the Anti-Counterfeiting Trade Agreement' (2015) 35 *Oxford Journal of Legal Studies* 487.

78 Framework Decision 2005/222/JHA, 'On Attacks against Information Systems'.

79 Ibid., Article 2.

80 Ibid., Article 3.

81 Ibid., Article 4.

82 European Commission, 'Report Based on Article 12 of the Framework Decision of 24 February 2005 on Attacks against Information Systems' COM(2008) 448, p. 3.

83 European Parliament, 'Fighting Cybercrime and Protecting Privacy in the Cloud' (Directorate General for Internal Policies) PE 462.509 (2012) 11.

84 European Commission, 'Report Based on Article 12 of the Framework Decision of 24 February 2005 on Attacks against Information Systems', supra note 82, pp. 4–5, 7.

seven Member States had failed to communicate *any* implementation measures.[85] Finally, the Commission commented that new technological developments, including the use of botnets to attack information systems, had not been considered at the time that the Framework Decision was drafted, with a need to combat these types of attack as well as mandate tougher minimum criminal penalties given the increased prevalence of such attacks.[86] In 2010, the Commission published a Proposal for a Directive on attacks against information systems,[87] in which the above-mentioned concerns were reiterated,[88] as well as the fact that the reporting of attacks was often 'inadequate, partly because some crimes go unnoticed, and partly because the victims (economic operators and companies) do not report crimes for fear of getting a negative reputation and of their future business prospects being affected by the public exposure of their vulnerabilities'.[89] According to Norton, only 21 per cent of cybercrime victims report the crime to the police.[90] For this reason, the updating of the Framework Decision was justified, both in terms of necessity and legal basis, identified as Article 83(1) TFEU.[91] The Framework Decision was repealed and replaced by the Directive on attacks against information systems in 2013,[92] which added additional offences of illegal data interception[93] and 'production, sale, procurement for use, import, distribution or otherwise making available' of tools used to facilitate attacks on information systems.[94] Also of note is that whereas Article 6 of the Framework Decision required Member States to instate maximum penalties of at least one to three years imprisonment, the Directive in Article 9 requires maximum penalties of at least two years, increasing to five years in cases where the attack is committed within the framework of a criminal organisation, causes serious damage or is targeted at a critical infrastructure information system.

While this Directive appears to be a good step towards a more uniform and coordinated approach to cybercrime, there are some concerns with the Directive. In particular, illegal access under Article 3 of the Directive will now be considered as an offence 'where committed by infringing a security measure', a requirement not stated in Article 3 of the Framework Decision.

85 Ibid., p. 10.
86 Ibid., p. 10.
87 European Commission, 'Proposal for a Directive on Attacks against Information Systems and Repealing Council Framework Decision 2005/222/JHA' COM(2010) 517.
88 Ibid., pp. 2–3.
89 Ibid., p. 3.
90 Symantec, 'Norton Report 2012' (2012), http://now-static.norton.com/now/en/pu/images/Promotions/2012/cybercrimeReport/2012_Norton_Cybercrime_Report_Master_FINAL_050912.pdf (accessed 6 October 2015).
91 Ibid., p. 8.
92 Directive 2013/40/EU, 'On Attacks against Information Systems and Replacing Council Framework Decision 2005/222/JHA' (2013).
93 Ibid., Article 6.
94 Ibid., Article 7.

This additional requirement is problematic, as neither the Proposal nor the finalised Directive define 'security measure', leaving open the possibility of substantial differences between the Member States on how this is to be interpreted and implemented in national law.[95] The second problem is that even should the Directive have the effect of approximating national laws, it does little to resolve the other problem identified in the Directive proposal, namely inadequate reporting of attacks on information systems. This duty to inform of possible attacks on information systems is included in the 'Telecoms Package',[96] which mandates under Article 13a(3) that Member States should ensure that 'undertakings providing public communications networks or publicly available electronic communications services notify the competent national regulatory authority of a breach of security or loss of integrity that has had a significant impact on the operation of networks or services'. Again, however, a difficulty in establishing a common EU framework for combatting cybercrime is the potential for legislation to be rendered outdated by technological developments; the Telecoms Package, while applying to internet service providers, does not appear to apply to online service providers such as Google, or social media platforms such as Facebook or Twitter. The Commission has stated it would pursue a renewed and reinforced policy for the protection on information systems, and would 'foster multi-stakeholder dialogue and self-regulation of European and global service providers (e.g. social networking platforms, mobile communications providers)'.[97] On this basis, the Commission proposed a Directive on Network Information Security (NIS),[98] under which Article 14 would require the disclosure of information regarding a security incident, defined as 'any circumstance or event having an actual adverse effect on security' under Article 3(4). As recital 30 indicates, 'criminal activities are in many cases underlying an incident', linking the issue of information system protection to the cybercrime agenda specifically. This Directive, which was approved in August 2016, contributes toward improving the legal requirements pertaining to the disclosure of security incidents that have been identified as a weakness of the EU's cybercrime agenda. Furthermore, as will be discussed in the next section, overly broad definitions of cybercrime, as well as the division of

95 On this point, see also P.M.F. Freitas and N. Gonçalves, 'Illegal Access to Information Systems and the Directive 2013/40/EU' (2015) 29 *International Review of Law, Computers & Technology* 50, at pp. 59–60.

96 Directive 2009/140/EC, 'Amending Directives 2002/21/EC on a Common Regulatory Framework for Electronic Communications Networks and Services, 2002/19/EC on Access To, and Interconnection of, Electronic Communications Networks and Associated Facilities, and 2002/20/EC on the Authorisation of Electronic Communications Networks and Services' (2009).

97 European Commission, 'A Digital Agenda for Europe' COM(2010) 245 final/2, pp. 17–18.

98 European Commission, 'Proposal for a Directive of the European Parliament and of the Council Concerning Measures to Ensure a High Common Level of Network and Information Security across the Union' COM(2013) 48 final.

the cybercrime dimension from the NIS protection dimension, have practical implications for the implementation of these laws and policies.

4 Expectations unrealised: how conceptual uncertainty impacts nodes in networked cybercrime governance

As has been discussed in the previous two sections, there is considerable uncertainty not only regarding the definition of cybercrime, but also the extent of the legal competences that the EU possesses in regulating cybercrime. In particular, the coexistence of an umbrella approach at the policy level aimed at increasing cyber resilience, and of a 'division of labour' approach at the legal and institutional level, has led to further problems with the implementation of the EU's policy goals in this area. This creates incoherence in the EU's cybercrime agenda, resulting not so much in an expectations–outcomes gap, but rather in an extended expectations–competences–outcome gap. This section will discuss how this gap has impacted on two dominating forms of governance present within the cybercrime field: the agencification and the privatisation of cybercrime governance.

Where the first form is concerned, the EU has promoted the use of agencies as a form of governance since the 1990s. EU agencies were created to provide a higher degree of professionalism, neutrality and credibility to the process of policymaking.[99] Although this model initially emerged within the single market, it quickly expanded to other policy areas, namely the AFSJ.[100] Despite justice and home affairs agencies having originally been created to support the work of Member States and to promote cooperation among national authorities,[101] their role seems to be evolving in the direction of further centralisation and regulation.[102] As a result, we have been witnessing a greater willingness of EU agencies to become involved both in the development and in the implementation of justice and home affairs policies. The field of cybercrime is no exception to this trend. As mentioned

99 G. Majone, 'The Credibility Crisis of Community Regulation' (2000) 38 *JCMS: Journal of Common Market Studies* 273; G. Majone, 'The New European Agencies: Regulation by Information' (1997) 4 *Journal of European Public Policy* 262; R. Dehousse, 'Regulation by Networks in the European Community: The Role of European Agencies' (1997) 4 *Journal of European Public Policy* 246.

100 H. Carrapiço and F. Trauner, 'Europol and Its Influence on EU Policy-Making on Organized Crime: Analyzing Governance Dynamics and Opportunities' (2013) 14 *Perspectives on European Politics and Society* 357; M. Busuioc, D. Curtin and M. Groenleer, 'Agency Growth between Autonomy and Accountability: The European Police Office as a "Living Institution"' (2011) 18 *Journal of European Public Policy* 848; H. Ekelund, 'The Agencification of Europe: Explaining the Establishment of European Community Agencies' (PhD Thesis, University of Nottingham 2010).

101 J. Monar, 'The Dynamics of Justice and Home Affairs: Laboratories, Driving Factors and Costs' (2001) 39 *JCMS: Journal of Common Market Studies* 747.

102 Carrapiço and Trauner, supra note 100.

in the second section of this chapter, the EU developed a network of specialised agencies to deal with specific aspects of cybercrime. Departing from the perceived need to protect information networks, the EU proposed the creation of ENISA in 2004 in view of promoting resilience mechanisms. A second body, EC3, which is part of Europol, would quickly join ENISA in 2013 as part of the cybersecurity institutional architecture focusing on police cooperation to fight different forms of cybercrime. Both agencies are considered as essential actors within this architecture: as an example, in 2014, the then-vice-president of the European Commission responsible for the Digital Agenda said that 'faced with so much uncertainty and worry, we need a tough leader, able to give intellectual command, and authoritative advice. ENISA is well placed to do that.'[103] Regarding the EC3, the Commissioner for Home Affairs mentioned, also in 2014, that 'during the short period in which the Centre has been active, it has already gained a well-deserved reputation in the EU and beyond the Union's borders [...] We have to make sure that the EC3 can continue to be at the forefront of the fight against cybercrime in the EU.'[104]

Furthermore, these agencies are also considered as essential actors because they are understood as the most efficient way to govern this field.[105] As underlined by the General Affairs' Council of June 2013, ENISA and EC3 are central to the operational level of the EU's fight against cybercrime.[106] Despite the EU's growing reliance on agencies dealing with cybercrime, it is possible to identify a number of problems with this form of governance, contributing to their difficulty in reaching the EU's policy goals. In particular, these problems are related to a contradictory model of agencification as a form of governance, and lack of appropriate resources. Where the first problem is concerned, and as mentioned in the second and third sections of this chapter, the agencies have been tasked with supporting Member States' actions and cooperation in this field, on the basis of specific mandates and division of labour. At the same time as the EU is promoting this technical and specialised model of governance, it is also endorsing the idea that the fight against cybercrime can only be truly effective if we acknowledge the idea that all areas of cybersecurity are interconnected. The EU's Cybersecurity Strategy is a particularly good illustration of this approach, as it equates efficiency with policy and institutional coherence. Proposed by the Commissioner for Home

103 N. Kroes, 'Facing the Future: Making Our Online Economy Trustworthy, Reliable and Resilient' (2014).

104 C. Malmström, 'An Intense First Year for the European Cybercrime Centre' (2014).

105 Council of the European Union, 'Council Conclusions Concerning an Action Plan to Implement the Concerted Strategy to Combat Cybercrime' (2010) 3010th General Affairs Council Meeting.

106 European Commission and High Representative of the European Union for Foreign Affairs and Security Policy, 'Cybersecurity Strategy of the European Union: An Open, Safe and Secure Cyberspace' JOIN(2013) 1 18.

Affairs, the Commissioner for Digital Agenda and the High Representative for Foreign Affairs and Security Policy, the 2013 Strategy considers that we need to go beyond the existing fragmented approach to cybersecurity, represented in part by the three disparate actors involved in proposing the new approach. The different national and European actors present in this field are thus encouraged to think beyond their traditional remits and to expand their existing cooperation. As a result, ENISA and EC3 find themselves at the forefront of two potentially contradictory models of governance: a specialisation one and a holistic one. The coexistence of these two models has so far yielded mixed results with, for example, a formal agreement being signed between ENISA and EC3 in 2014, but cooperation having so far been limited to the organisation of information workshops.[107]

The realisation of EU cybercrime policies is also impacted by the availability of agency resources. On the one hand, the EU is very much aware of the cost that cybercrime is imposing on society. Industry evaluates the total yearly bill for cybercrime at $113 billion, with 1.5 million victims per day.[108] On this basis, the EU wishes to become an important cybersecurity actor characterised by a strong and efficient cybercrime policy. On the other hand, it has so far failed to translate this desire into a serious investment in resources, namely for agencies such as ENISA and EC3. In 2015, ENISA had an annual budget of €10.1 million, out of which €5 million was used to cover the salaries of its limited staff of 60 people.[109] As a result of this very limited investment, the director of operations declared in 2015 that ENISA's 'coverage of technological change is minimal. I have one, perhaps two people who are experts in clouds. I have one person in industrial control systems. That's quite a weak basis for the future.'[110] EC3 is in a similar situation with a €7 million budget, corresponding to a very small part of Europol's budget of €94 million.[111] In fact, the creation of EC3 within Europol in 2013 was quite challenging from a budgetary perspective, given that the agency was not attributed any additional funding and had to divert the necessary amounts and staff members from other units to run EC3.[112] EC3's first Annual Report actually questions 'whether – in terms of staffing – EC3 will be able to cope with the steep increase of its workload'.[113]

107 Interview conducted by Carrapiço with an EC3 official in November 2013 at the Hague.
108 Symantec, supra note 17, p. 1 (estimate based on 24 countries).
109 ENISA, 'Statement of Estimates 2014' (2014), www.enisa.europa.eu/about-enisa/accounting-finance/files/annual-budgets/enisa-2014-annual-budget (accessed 14 October 2015).
110 Purser, as quoted in C. Stupp, 'EU Cybersecurity Agency Lacks Funds for Research on Major Tech Issues', *EurActiv* (31 July 2015), www.euractiv.com/sections/infosociety/eu-cybersecurity-agency-lacks-funds-research-major-tech-issues-316729 (accessed 31 May 2016).
111 N. Rial, 'EU Cybercrime Centre Opens Its Doors', *New Europe* (9 January 2013), http://neurope.eu/article/eu-cybercrime-centre-opens-its-doors (accessed 31 May 2016).
112 Interview conducted by Carrapiço with EC Official in November 2013 at the Hague.
113 EC3, 'First Year Report' (2014), p. 15.

The Commission has tacitly admitted that a top-down 'command and control' governance approach is infeasible when trying to combat cybercrime, but nor is a 'pure' agencification model of governance deemed to be wholly effective. Instead, the EU relies, in the field of cybersecurity, on a networked mode of governance. Such an approach to the issue is not unusual in the EU, and has been a major pillar of EU governance since the Commission's 2001 White Paper.[114] This is largely based upon a perception that the involvement of stakeholders ensures greater input legitimacy of the EU as regulator, as well as facilitating greater deliberation, transparency in decision-making and accountability.[115] Furthermore, the development of public–private partnerships as a phenomenon has been based on an understanding among policymakers that private enterprises better understand their business than public regulators, with a significant information asymmetry meaning that private actors are better placed to regulate within specific spheres.[116] In an environment of political and legal uncertainty, the EU has sought to rely on the expertise provided by private stakeholders as a means of addressing the shortcomings of their approach and the limited capacities of EC3 and ENISA. The Commission has legislated for a network-governance structure incorporating private stakeholders as sources of expertise and information, with agencies such as EC3 and ENISA then acting as coordination and information-sharing bodies. As early as 2007, the Commission stated that in order to achieve the goal of improving the resilience of computer systems (including against cyber-attacks), 'close cooperation between enforcement authorities, network operators and ISPs at national level is also needed'.[117] While Member States are considered as retaining the ultimate responsibility for defining CII-related policies, 'their implementation depends on the involvement of the private sector, which owns or controls a large number of CIIs'.[118] So too, the Commission reasons, should the private sector take an active role in combatting cybercrime; only through building trust and confidence between the private sector and law enforcement will it be possible to 'to fight and better protect against cybercrime [... and] to arrive at a better measurement of the cybercrime landscape in real time as well as to strive

114 European Commission, 'European Governance: A White Paper' COM(2001) 428.

115 S. Borrás and K. Jacobsson, 'The Open Method of Co-Ordination and New Governance Patterns in the EU' (2004) 11 *Journal of European Public Policy* 185.

116 A. Ogus, 'Rethinking Self-Regulation' (1995) 15 *Oxford Journal of Legal Studies* 97, at pp. 97–98; see also D. Levi-Faur, 'The Regulatory State and Regulatory Capitalism: An Institutional Perspective', in D. Levi-Faur (ed.), *Handbook on the Politics of Regulation* (Edward Elgar, 2013); P.D. Culpepper, *Quiet Politics and Business Power: Corporate Control in Europe and Japan* (Cambridge University Press, 2011).

117 European Commission, 'Commission Staff Working Document Annex to the European Electronic Communications Regulation and Markets (12th Report)' SEC(2007) 403 71.

118 European Commission, 'Critical Information Infrastructure Protection: "Protecting Europe from Large Scale Cyber-Attacks and Disruptions: Enhancing Preparedness, Security and Resilience"' COM(2009) 149, p. 5.

for more effective dismantling of cybercrime networks'.[119] This understanding is reiterated in Directive 2013/40/EU on attacks against information systems, where at recital 23 it is stated that cooperation between the public and private sectors 'is of great importance in preventing and combating attacks against information systems'. However, the Commission goes one step further, insofar as the private sector is not only responsible for reporting of incidences, but also in the identification and diffusion of resilience standards. In the Communication of CIIP, the Commission expressed hope that a multi-stakeholder governance model, facilitated by ENISA, could 'foster the involvement of the private sector in the definition of strategic public policy objectives as well as operational priorities and measures'.[120] As a document published by ENISA in 2012 demonstrates, the standards applied to ensuring information security and integrity are based heavily upon a set of 20 industry standards in use in the EU telecommunications market.[121] Information-sharing of private-sector best practices is seen as the basis for ensuring resilience against cyber-attacks, with the proposed Directive on NIS recital 33 stating: 'Standardization of security requirements is a market-driven process. To ensure a convergent application of security standards, Member States should encourage compliance or conformity with specified standards to ensure a high level of security at Union level.' Nevertheless, such an approach is dependent upon the private sector (and, in particular, online service providers such as social media platforms and search engines) to be willing to share such information, both relating to best practices, and with regard to the disclosure of incidences of cyber-attacks. As stated in the preceding section, there has been reticence among affected undertakings to provide information to law enforcement bodies regarding attacks upon their systems, in part due to concerns regarding negative publicity. Indeed, Johnson states in regard to cyber-attacks that 'most commercial organisations will only provide anonymous summaries of minor adverse events to these agencies – in some cases; even this would be refused unless there are reciprocal benefits from the further exchange of security information by competitors'.[122] Ultimately, 'one of the future challenges in many countries will be to achieve a balance between security requirements and business efficiency imperatives',[123] an issue the

119 European Commission, 'Tackling Crime in Our Digital Age: Establishing a European Cybercrime Centre', supra note 30, p. 7.

120 European Commission, 'Critical Information Infrastructure Protection: "Protecting Europe from Large Scale Cyber-Attacks and Disruptions: Enhancing Preparedness, Security and Resilience"', supra note 118, p. 6.

121 ENISA, 'Shortlisting Network and Information Security Standards and Good Practices' (2012), p. 4.

122 C.W. Johnson, 'Architectures for Cyber-Security Incident Reporting in Safety-Critical Systems', in A. Masys (ed.), *Disaster Management: Enabling Resilience* (Springer International Publishing, 2015), p. 134.

123 CEPS Task Force, 'Protecting Critical Infrastructure in the EU' (2010) Centre for European Policy Studies, p. 32.

Commission acknowledges in its 2013 Cyber Security Strategy, where it is stated that 'private actors still lack effective incentives to provide reliable data on the existence or impact of NIS incidents, to embrace a risk-management culture or to invest in security solutions'.[124] This ultimately creates something of a paradox in the EU's cybercrime policies – in order to ensure effective protection from cyber-attacks, the EU relies upon private-sector cooperation in information collection as a means of addressing an expertise asymmetry existing in the field; information, unfortunately, that the private sector has little commercial interest in providing.

5 Concluding remarks

The objective of this chapter was to provide a comprehensive overview of the challenges that the EU faces in combatting cybercrime, not only from a legal perspective, but also in terms of the policy choices made, and the practical implications of the governance model based in part on agencies and in part on public–private stakeholder cooperation. As this chapter has demonstrated, the issue of cybercrime is a difficult one to both conceptualise, and to separate from the associated dimension of cybersecurity and in particular policies concerning cyber-resilience. The use of cybercrime as an umbrella concept, including both a broad dimension of crimes facilitated *through* computer systems, as well as a narrow dimension of attacks *upon* computer systems, leads to a conceptual ambiguity that has translated into an uncertain EU legal framework. This has resulted both in contestation regarding the limits of cybercrime as a legal phenomenon and whether it should apply to issues such as copyright infringement, and in uneven implementation due to the open and uncertain definitions in legislation, leading to varied implementations of Framework Decisions and Directives on attacks on information systems at the national level. Finally, by having a legal distinction between cybercrime and cyber-resilience reflected in the Directive on attacks against information systems on the one hand, and a proposed Directive on NIS on the other, the EU has created a division between two arguably indivisible dimensions of cybersecurity. As a result, while each issue is handled by a separate and distinct agency, the EU has sought to encourage coordination and information-sharing between these agencies, as well as between private sector actors. However, limited cooperation between EC3 and ENISA, coupled with a reluctance on the part of private actors to divulge information that could be commercially sensitive or detrimental to business practices, means that the levels of cooperation thus far are limited. This has been further compounded by the limited resources of the cybersecurity agencies, leading to a situation in which the EU has weakened capacities as

124 European Commission and High Representative of the European Union for Foreign Affairs and Security Policy, supra note 106, p. 6.

a cybersecurity actor. In order to further explore these challenges, it will be interesting to analyse whether the implementation of the EU's strategies may lead in the future to an increased coherence of both policies and institutional competences in the field of cybersecurity, as well as a better defined and more legally certain concept of 'cybercrime'. A separate line of research could explore the competing modes of governance, one based in agencification and the other in networked public–private partnership, in order to assess how the influence of the different actors over policy and best practice standards in the field of cybercrime may evolve.

Bibliography

Avramopoulos, D., 'Commissioner Avramopoulos Presents European Agenda on Security at European Parliament' (2015) SPEECH/15/4885

Barrett, N., *Traces Of Guilt* (Corgi, 2009)

BBC Technology News, 'Fiat Chrysler Recalls 1.4 Million Cars after Jeep Hack' (24 July 2015), www.bbc.co.uk/news/technology-33650491 (accessed 6 October 2015)

Beck, G., *The Legal Reasoning of the Court of Justice of the EU* (Hart Publishing, 2013)

Borrás, S. and Jacobsson, K., 'The Open Method of Co-Ordination and New Governance Patterns in the EU' (2004) 11 *Journal of European Public Policy* 185

Brenner, S.W., 'Cybercrime: Rethinking Crime Control Strategies', in Y. Jewkes (ed), *Crime Online* (2nd edn, Routledge, 2011)

Busuioc, M., Curtin, D. and Groenleer, M., 'Agency Growth between Autonomy and Accountability: The European Police Office as a "Living Institution"' (2011) 18 *Journal of European Public Policy* 848

Calderoni, F., *Organized Crime Legislation in the European Union: Harmonization and Approximation of Criminal Law, National Legislations and the EU Framework Decision on the Fight Against Organized Crime* (Springer, 2010)

Carrapiço, H. and Trauner, F., 'Europol and Its Influence on EU Policy-Making on Organized Crime: Analyzing Governance Dynamics and Opportunities' (2013) 14 *Perspectives on European Politics and Society* 357

CEPS Task Force, 'Protecting Critical Infrastructure in the EU' (2010) Centre for European Policy Studies

Clough, J., 'The Council of Europe Convention on Cybercrime: Defining "Crime" in a Digital World' (2012) 23 *Criminal Law Forum* 363

Council of Europe, 'Convention on Cybercrime, CETS No.185, Budapest 23 November 2001'

Council of the European Union, 'eEurope 2002: An Information Society for All' (2000)

Council of the European Union, 'Council Conclusions Concerning an Action Plan to Implement the Concerted Strategy to Combat Cybercrime' (2010) 3010th General Affairs Council Meeting

Culpepper, P.D., *Quiet Politics and Business Power: Corporate Control in Europe and Japan* (Cambridge University Press, 2011)

Dehousse, R., 'Regulation by Networks in the European Community: The Role of European Agencies' (1997) 4 *Journal of European Public Policy* 246

Directive 2001/29/EC, 'Of the European Parliament and of the Council of 22 May 2001 on the Harmonisation of Certain Aspects of Copyright and Related Rights in the Information Society' (2001)

Directive 2009/140/EC, 'Amending Directives 2002/21/EC on a Common Regulatory Framework for Electronic Communications Networks and Services, 2002/19/EC on Access To, and Interconnection Of, Electronic Communications Networks and Associated Facilities, and 2002/20/EC on the Authorisation of Electronic Communications Networks and Services' (2009)

Directive 2011/92/EU, 'Of the European Parliament and of the Council of 13 December 2011 on Combating the Sexual Abuse and Sexual Exploitation of Children and Child Pornography, and Replacing Council Framework Decision 2004/68/JHA' (2011)

Directive 2013/40/EU, 'On Attacks against Information Systems and Replacing Council Framework Decision 2005/222/JHA' (2013)

EC3, 'First Year Report' (2014)

Ekelund, H., 'The Agencification of Europe: Explaining the Establishment of European Community Agencies' (PhD Thesis, University of Nottingham 2010)

ENISA, 'Shortlisting Network and Information Security Standards and Good Practices' (2012)

ENISA, 'Statement of Estimates 2014' (2014) www.enisa.europa.eu/about-enisa/accounting-finance/files/annual-budgets/enisa-2014-annual-budget (accessed 14 October 2015)

European Commission, 'A Digital Agenda for Europe' COM(2010) 245 final/2

European Commission, 'Combating Trafficking in Human Beings and Combating the Sexual Exploitation of Children and Child Pornography' COM(2000) 854 final/2

European Commission, 'Commission Staff Working Document: A Digital Single Market Strategy, for Europe–Analysis and Evidence' SWD(2015) 100

European Commission, 'Commission Staff Working Document Annex to the European Electronic Communications Regulation and Markets (12th Report)' SEC(2007) 403

European Commission, 'Creating a Safer Information Society by Improving the Security of Information Infrastructures and Combating Computer-Related Crime' COM(2000) 890

European Commission, 'Critical Information Infrastructure Protection: "Protecting Europe from Large Scale Cyber-Attacks and Disruptions: Enhancing Preparedness, Security and Resilience"' COM(2009) 149

European Commission, 'European Governance: A White Paper' COM(2001) 428

European Commission, 'Growth, Competitiveness, Employment: The Challenges and Ways Forward into the 21st Century' White Paper COM(93) 700

European Commission, 'Proposal for a Directive of the European Parliament and of the Council Concerning Measures to Ensure a High Common Level of Network and Information Security across the Union' COM(2013) 48 final

European Commission, 'Proposal for a Directive on Attacks against Information Systems and Repealing Council Framework Decision 2005/222/JHA' COM(2010) 517

European Commission, 'Proposal for a European Parliament and Council Directive on Criminal Measures Aimed at Ensuring the Enforcement of Intellectual Property Rights' COM(2005) 276

European Commission, 'Report Based on Article 12 of the Framework Decision of 24 February 2005 on Attacks against Information Systems' COM(2008) 448

European Commission, 'Tackling Crime in Our Digital Age: Establishing a European Cybercrime Centre' COM(2012) 140

European Commission, 'Towards a General Policy on the Fight against Cyber Crime' COM(2007) 267

European Commission, 'Towards an EU Criminal Policy: Ensuring the Effective Implementation of EU Policies through Criminal Law' COM(2011) 573

European Commission and Bangemann Group, 'Europe and the Global Information Society: Recommendations of the High-Level Group on the Information Society to the Corfu European Council' (1994) S.2/94

European Commission and High Representative of the European Union for Foreign Affairs and Security Policy, 'Cybersecurity Strategy of the European Union: An Open, Safe and Secure Cyberspace' JOIN(2013) 1

European Council Presidency, 'Conclusions, Tampere European Council 15 and 16 October 1999'

European Data Protection Supervisor, 'Opinion on the Proposal for a Directive of the European Parliament and of the Council on Combating the Sexual Abuse, Sexual Exploitation of Children and Child Pornography, Repealing Framework Decision 2004/68/JHA' (2010) Brussels

European Parliament, 'Fighting Cybercrime and Protecting Privacy in the Cloud' (Directorate General for Internal Policies) PE 462.509 (2012)

Europol, 'EC3 First Annual Report' (2014)

Europol, 'iOCTA: The Internet Organised Crime Threat Assessment' (2014)

Fafinski, S., Dutton, W. and Margetts, H., *Mapping and Measuring Cybercrime* (Oxford Internet Institute, 2010) Forum Discussion Paper 18

Fahey, E., 'The EU's Cybercrime and Cyber-Security Rulemaking: Mapping the Internal and External Dimensions of EU Security' (2014) 5 *European Journal of Risk Regulation* 46

Farrand, B., *Networks of Power in Digital Copyright Law and Policy: Political Salience, Expertise and the Legislative Process* (Routledge, 2014)

Farrand, B., 'Lobbying and Lawmaking in the European Union: The Development of Copyright Law and the Rejection of the Anti-Counterfeiting Trade Agreement' (2015) 35 *Oxford Journal of Legal Studies* 487

Farrand, B. and Carrapiço, H., 'Copyright Law as a Matter of (Inter)National Security? The Attempt to Securitise Commercial Infringement and Its Spillover onto Individual Liability' (2012) 57 *Crime, Law and Social Change* 373

Framework Decision 2004/68/JHA, 'On Combating the Sexual Exploitation of Children and Child Pornography'

Framework Decision 2005/222/JHA, 'On Attacks against Information Systems'

Freitas, P.M.F. and Gonçalves, N., 'Illegal Access to Information Systems and the Directive 2013/40/EU' (2015) 29 *International Review of Law, Computers & Technology* 50

Geiger, C., 'Introduction', in *Criminal Enforcement of Intellectual Property: A Handbook of Contemporary Research* (Edward Elgar, 2012)

Geiger, C., 'The Rise of Criminal Enforcement of Intellectual Property Rights … and Its Failure in the Context of Copyright Infringements on the Internet', in S. Frankel and D.J. Gervais (eds.), *The Evolution and Equilibrium of Copyright in the Digital Age* (Cambridge University Press, 2014)

Gibson, W., *Neuromancer* (Harper Voyager, 1982)
Goodman, M., 'International Dimensions of Cybercrime' in S. Ghosh and E. Turrini (eds.), *Cybercrimes: A Multidisciplinary Analysis* (Springer, 2011)
Greenberg A, 'Hackers Remotely Kill a Jeep on the Highway – With Me in It', *Wired* (21 July 2015), www.wired.com/2015/07/hackers-remotely-kill-jeep-highway (accessed 6 October 2015)
Harding, C. and Banach-Gutierrez, J.B., 'The Emergent EU Criminal Policy: Identifying the Species' (2012) 37(6) *European Law Review* 758
Hart, H.L.A., *The Concept of Law* (3rd edn, Oxford University Press, 2012)
Herlin-Karnell, E., 'Recent Developments in the Area of European Criminal Law' (2007) 14 *Maastricht Journal of European and Comparative Law* 15
Herlin-Karnell, E., *The Constitutional Dimension of European Criminal Law* (Bloomsbury Publishing, 2012)
Hinarejos, A., 'Integration in Criminal Matters and the Role of the Court of Justice' (2011) 36 *European Law Review* 420
Hosein, I. and Eriksson, J., 'International Policy Dynamics and the Regulation of Dataflows', in J. Eriksson and G. Giacomello (eds.), *International Relations and Security in the Digital Age* (Routledge, 2010)
Johnson, C.W., 'Architectures for Cyber-Security Incident Reporting in Safety-Critical Systems', in A. Masys (ed.), *Disaster Management: Enabling Resilience* (Springer International Publishing, 2015)
Kierkegaard, S.M., 'EU Tackles Cyber Crime', in L.J. Janczewski and A.M. Colarik (eds.), *Cyber Warfare and Cyber Terrorism* (IGI Global, 2007)
Kioupis, D., 'Criminal Liability on the Internet', in I.A. Stamatoudi (ed.), *Copyright Enforcement and the Internet* (Kluwer Law International, 2010)
Klip, A., *European Criminal Law: An Integrative Approach* (Intersentia, 2009)
Kroes, N., 'Facing the Future: Making Our Online Economy Trustworthy, Reliable and Resilient' (2014)
Levi-Faur, D., 'The Regulatory State and Regulatory Capitalism: An Institutional Perspective', in D. Levi-Faur (ed.), *Handbook on the Politics of Regulation* (Edward Elgar, 2013)
Majone, G., 'The New European Agencies: Regulation by Information' (1997) 4 *Journal of European Public Policy* 262
Majone, G., 'The Credibility Crisis of Community Regulation' (2000) 38 *Journal of Common Market Studies* 273
Malmström, C., 'It's Time to Take Cyber Criminals Offline' (2011) SPEECH/11/260
Malmström, C., 'Public–Private Cooperation in the Fight against Cybercrime' (2012) SPEECH/12/409
Malmström, C., 'An Intense First Year for the European Cybercrime Centre' (2014)
McAfee, *The Economic Impact of Cybercrime and Cyber Espionage* (Center for Strategic and International Studies, 2013)
Mendez, F., 'The European Union and Cybercrime: Insights from Comparative Federalism' (2005) 12 *Journal of European Public Policy* 509
Mitsilegas, V., *EU Criminal Law* (Hart Publishing, 2009)
Monar, J., 'The Dynamics of Justice and Home Affairs: Laboratories, Driving Factors and Costs' (2001) 39 *Journal of Common Market Studies* 747
Monar, J., 'Justice and Home Affairs' (2012) 50 *Journal of Common Market Studies* 116

Ogus, A., 'Rethinking Self-Regulation' (1995) 15 *Oxford Journal of Legal Studies* 97

Porcedda, M.G., 'Transatlantic Approaches to Cybersecurity and Cybercrime', in P. Pawlak (ed.), *The EU–US Security and Justice Agenda in Action* (Chaillot Papers, 2011)

Rial, N., 'EU Cybercrime Centre Opens Its Doors', *New Europe* (9 January 2013), http://neurope.eu/article/eu-cybercrime-centre-opens-its-doors (accessed 14 October 2015)

Schjolberg, S., 'The History of Global Harmonization on Cybercrime Legislation: The Road to Geneva', *Cyber Crime Law* (2008), www.cybercrimelaw.net/documents/cybercrime_history.pdf (accessed 6 October 2015)

Sieber, U., *Legal Aspects of Computer-Related Crime in the Information Society* (University of Würzburg, 1998)

Singer, P.W. and Friedman, A., *Cybersecurity and Cyberwar: What Everyone Needs To Know* (Oxford University Press, 2014)

Smith, R.G., Grabosky, P. and Urbas, G., *Cyber Criminals on Trial* (Cambridge University Press, 2011)

Stupp, C., 'EU Cybersecurity Agency Lacks Funds for Research on Major Tech Issues', *EurActiv* (31 July 2015), www.euractiv.com/sections/infosociety/eu-cybersecurity-agency-lacks-funds-research-major-tech-issues-316729 (accessed 14 October 2015)

Summers, S. et al., *The Emergence of EU Criminal Law: Cyber Crime and the Regulation of the Information Society* (Hart Publishing, 2014)

Symantec, 'Norton Report 2012' (2012), http://now-static.norton.com/now/en/pu/images/Promotions/2012/cybercrimeReport/2012_Norton_Cybercrime_Report_Master_FINAL_050912.pdf (accessed 6 October 2015)

Symantec, 'Norton Report 2013' (2013), http://go.symantec.com/norton-report-2013 (accessed 6 October 2015)

Walden, I., 'Harmonising Computer Crime Laws in Europe' (2004) 12 *European Journal of Crime, Criminal Law and Criminal Justice* 321

Wall, D.S., *Cybercrime: The Transformation of Crime in the Information Age* (Polity Press, 2007)

Weyembergh, A., 'Approximation of Criminal Laws: The Constitutional Treaty and the Hague Programme' (2005) 42 *Common Market Law Review* 1567

Xanthaki, H., 'Eurojust: Fulfilled or Empty Promises in EU Criminal Law' (2006) 8 *European Journal of Law Reform* 175

19 Entrenching the Area of Freedom, Security and Justice

Questions of institutional governance and judicial control

Henri de Waele

1 Introduction: the 'fragility of goodness' in the AFSJ

As the preceding chapters have already explicitly or implicitly confirmed, the present and future challenges for establishing an enduring Area of Freedom, Security and Justice (AFSJ) are manifold. In itself, the AFSJ venture transformed remarkably quickly from a proud ambition at the entry into force of the Treaty of Amsterdam, to a virtual reality at the entry into force of the Treaty of Lisbon.[1] For sure, in comparison, the obstacles for attaining the desired objectives seemed much greater in the previous settings that stretched from 1993 to 2009, let alone in the even humbler arrangements that were constructed in the more distant past. With the benefit of hindsight then, it is little cause for surprise that the principled intergovernmental approach, characterised, inter alia, by executive dominance, a feeble set of policy instruments and courts largely devoid of jurisdiction, failed to deliver. With the 'Lisbonised' setup, however – or so it is trumpeted – the era of trials and tribulations has finally been brought to a close.[2]

Has it indeed? Arguably, while the means and methods may have advanced tremendously in the past five years, the number of issues to be tackled has not diminished; and in quality terms, these issues have not become intrinsically easier to address. Moreover, earlier fracture lines have engrained themselves, if not expanded, due to the introduction of an unprecedented potential for differentiation between the Member States; and the tensions between the main supranational actors have, alas, not automatically evaporated either.[3] Therefore, while it may well be claimed that all EU policies in the field are 'normal' now,[4] this does not alter the fact that a particular spirit continues to

1 See respectively Article 61 TEC and Article 67 TFEU.

2 S Peers, 'Mission Accomplished? EU Justice and Home Affairs Law after the Treaty of Lisbon' (2011) 48 *Common Market Law Review* 661.

3 Similarly M. Fletcher, 'EU Criminal Justice: Beyond Lisbon', in C. Eckes and T. Konstadinides (eds.), *Crime within the Area of Freedom, Security and Justice* (Cambridge University Press, 2011) 10.

4 'A New Chapter for Cross-border Criminal Justice', Speech by First Vice-President Frans Timmermans, 13 November 2014, http://europa.eu/rapid/press-release_SPEECH-14-1701_en.htm.

permeate the domain. On the one hand, this can be explained *ratione materiae*, as the AFSJ pertains to the specific (and specifically sensitive) subject-matter of criminal justice and police cooperation. On the other hand, the institutional methods locked-in here are predicated on the combination of minimum standards and mutual recognition, rather than on harmonisation as the default option.

On both counts, the growing differences between the Member States, pursuant to the increasing size and heterogeneity of the EU, could be considered problematic.[5] At the same time, the idea in this domain is precisely to leave sufficient room for those differences, instead of resorting to the most convenient practice of 'legislating them away'. Indeed, while mutual recognition and approximation of national law do complement one another, provisions such as Article 67 and Article 82 TFEU demonstrate that on key matters in the AFSJ, the latter is contingent on the former.[6] In other words, although the domain has now truly opened itself up to European integration, proper heed must be taken of its idiosyncrasies, in order to attain the scheduled objectives. An impervious copy-pasting of the tried-and-tested *communautaire* methods even threatens to prove counterproductive, sparking *dis*integration of the field. This illustrates the 'fragility of goodness' in the AFSJ: for when the Area's special flavour is insufficiently appreciated, its overarching interests are easily put in jeopardy, and the ways for serving these likely to remain suboptimal.[7]

Conversely, however, in matters of compliance, obviously no more quarter is to be given here than elsewhere. Take, for instance, the Framework Decisions on the mutual recognition of judicial decisions on custodial sentences or measures involving deprivation of liberty, on probation decisions and alternative sanctions, and on supervision measures as an alternative to provisional detention.[8] Together, they seek to establish a coherent body of legislation facilitating the transfer of prisoners and detainees across the EU. In pre-alert communications identifying more than a dozen countries that have failed to adopt the necessary transposition measures, the Commission has pointed out that these 'laggards' also cause a terrible nuisance for other

5 C. Eckes and T. Konstadinides, 'Introduction', in C. Eckes and T. Konstadinides (eds.), *Crime within the Area of Freedom, Security and Justice* (Cambridge University Press, 2011) 2.

6 Fletcher, supra note 3, p. 33.

7 Naturally, long before the official establishment of the 'third pillar', there have been Community measures that straddled the border between the internal market and flanking policies on the policing, enforcement or criminalisation of the relevant rules. Even when recast and adopted under the new Title V TFEU, these occasionally continue to exhibit their old EC colours. See, for example, E. Herlin-Karnell, 'European Criminal Law as an Exercise in EU "Experimental" Constitutional Law' (2013) 20 *Maastricht Journal of European and Comparative Law* 442, at p. 460.

8 Respectively Framework Decision 2008/909/JHA, OJ [2008] L327/27; Framework Decision 2008/947/JHA, OJ [2008] L337/102, and Framework Decision 2009/829/JHA, OJ [2009] L294/20.

Member States, since those who have duly implemented cannot benefit from the envisaged assistance and collaboration modalities in their relations with the latter.[9] They might need to resort to the cumbersome, outmoded international legal assistance instruments instead, significantly increasing the risk of double jeopardy.[10] As emphasised by the current Commissioner for (inter alia) the rule of law, the AFSJ's mutual recognition instruments are cooperation instruments, which means they cannot work properly if they are not implemented by every country concerned.[11] Once again however, the contents of such instruments (including the way they are construed by the judiciary) must then duly reflect the (potentially divergent) domestic needs and preferences. Whenever it does come to harmonisation of national criminal laws, the underlying policy must be genuinely well-considered, and the coherence of the national systems maintained to the furthest possible degree. Compliance, after all, only follows on from legitimacy (in the sense of the perceived 'right to rule').[12] Here then, any desire to secure such legitimacy militates especially in favour of principles such as subsidiarity and *ultima ratio*, which form part of the Union's normative core.[13] Consequently, in this respect as well, when one resolves to successfully manage and develop the AFSJ, the 'good' in good governance requires adhering to a rather more elaborate set of benchmarks.

For the Court of Justice, even years after entry into force of the Lisbon Treaty, the assumption that a 'business-as-usual' attitude suffices in the handling of police and justice topics must still be quite tempting. Undoubtedly, the expiry of the transitional regime on 1 December 2014 has added fuel to that fire. In the post-Amsterdam era, judgments such as *Gözötük*, *Pupino* and *Segi* already showcased how the ECJ was reluctant to switch tracks, transposing familiar concepts and arguments without visible qualms.[14] Nevertheless, the judiciary cannot afford to don blinkers today any more than the political institutions can, if only due to the exigencies of individual human rights protection. Yet, the existence of sophisticated albeit unseasoned instruments

9 Report from the Commission to the European Parliament and the Council on the implementation by the Member States of the Framework Decisions 2008/909/JHA, 2008/947/JHA and 2009/829/JHA on the mutual recognition of judicial decisions on custodial sentences or measures involving deprivation of liberty, on probation decisions and alternative sanctions and on supervision measures as an alternative to provisional detention, COM(2014) 57 final.

10 E. de Capitani, 'Metamorphosis of the Third Pillar: The End of the Transition Period for EU Criminal and Policing Law', http://eulawanalysis.blogspot.co.uk/2014/07/metamorphosis-of-third-pillar-end-of.html.

11 Timmermans, supra note 4.

12 R. Flathman, 'Legitimacy', in R.E. Goodin, P. Petitt and T. Pogge (eds.), *A Companion to Political Philosophy*, Vol. II (Wiley-Blackwell, 2007) 678.

13 P. Asp, 'European Criminal Law: Challenges for the Future', in M. Bergström and A.J. Cornell (eds.), *European Police and Criminal Law Co-operation* (Hart Publishing, 2014) 61–62.

14 Joined Cases C-187/01 and C-385/01 *Criminal proceedings against Hüseyin Gözütok and Klaus Brügge*; Case C-355/04 P, *Segi v Council*; Case 105/03 *Criminal proceedings against Maria Pupino*.

like the European Arrest Warrant (EAW), or the intricate balancing exercises called for by the binding Charter of Fundamental Rights (CFR), entail that the probability of stepping on the toes of the other actors involved (not least the Member States) is greater than ever. That accession to the ECHR has been put on ice for a while longer could at first glance seem to offer relief.[15] Nonetheless, since no amount of self-proclaimed autonomy guarantees that the ECJ will hold exclusive jurisdiction in a hermetically isolated sphere, the conundrum with both the national and the Strasbourg courts is bound to intensify rather than abate. Conversely, in the present constellation, it may be argued that the task to entrench the AFSJ lies primarily with the judges at the Kirchberg, for they are to ensure as never before that the freedom, security and justice instruments composed by the Union's political institutions comply with the main tenets of the rule of law. Of course, this also renders desirable a maximum of legal accountability of the Union's bodies, offices and agencies in this realm – i.e., concomitant, unfettered judicial control over their actions. Simultaneously, however, it has rarely been harder for the Court to preserve or indeed pursue the common 'good', to do the 'right' thing: criticisms of its role and output are mounting, zeroing in hard and fast from multiple corners at once.[16] Previously, there appeared to be a greater 'failure tolerance' with regard to its market integration jurisprudence, considering the benevolent views in *la doctrine*, and the relatively marginal resistance of national courts. Now that the angle has shifted to a non-economic domain, the room for a similar dogged posture is palpably on the wane. Finally, throw into the mix the logistical and organisational challenges posed by the Court's convoluted Chamber system, raising the spectre of inconsistency, together with the (much more frequently invoked) preliminary reference procedure.[17] This wretched combination of a fragmented decision-making, rising workload, and greater urgency is likely to affect the quality of the Court's case law at a time it can least afford it. In sum, while the Union's judiciary is expected to uphold at final instance the refined contextual standards for good governance in the AFSJ, its own position has incrementally become more fragile too: how it performs the task as 'watchdog of correctness' in this continuum

15 Opinion 2/13, *Draft-Agreement on Accession of the European Union to the European Convention on Human Rights.*

16 For example, G. Conway, *The Limits of Legal Reasoning and the European Court of Justice* (Cambridge University Press, 2012); G. Beck, *The Reasoning of the Court of Justice of the EU* (Hart Publishing, 2012); M. Adams, H. de Waele, J. Meeusen and G. Straetmans (eds.), *Judging Europe's Judges* (Hart Publishing, 2013); compare also the exceedingly hostile stances of the Czech *Ústavní soud* and German *Bundesverfassungsgericht* in view of perceived '*ultra vires*' judgments.

17 N. Nic Shuibne, 'A Court Within a Court: Is it Time to Rebuild the European Court of Justice?' (2009) 34 *European Law Review* 173; M. Bobek, 'Talking Now? Preliminary Rulings in and from the New Member States' (2014) 15 *Maastricht Journal of European and Comparative Law* 781.

is subjected to unrelenting scrutiny, and open to wide contestation, despite Article 19 TEU's lofty prose.[18]

The current chapter purports to explore some salient governance challenges arising in the contemporary AFSJ, without any pretension of exhaustiveness. Linking in with the preceding observations, it first engages with the political-institutional dimension (Section 2), focusing in consecutive order on issues of decision-making (Section 2.1), accountability and regulatory quality (Section 2.2), and monitoring and enforcement (Section 2.3). We subsequently turn to the judicial dimension (Section 3), commencing with a generic reflection on the role of the CJEU in this area (Section 3.1), followed by some reflections on the type of horizontal and vertical power struggles faced by the Court (Section 3.2), spilling over into an assessment of its task and demeanour in the safeguarding of fundamental rights (Section 3.3). Finally, we conclude with an appraisal of the main choices that have been made in shaping the AFSJ so far, flagging several decision points that are yet to be confronted (Section 4).[19]

2 Institutional governance of the AFSJ: looking back and thinking forward

2.1 Decision-making and support-garnering – balancing the 'ins' and 'outs'

As remarked above, the institutional governance approach in the AFSJ is predicated on fostering mutual recognition and setting minimum standards, rather than the customary (*communautaire*) preference for harmonisation. In this respect, the political agenda of the Tampere European Council (1999) has left a more substantial and contentious legacy than many initially assumed. That cautious approach emanated from a broader underlying, still ongoing resistance of the Member States to shift powers from the national to the European level; so long as the number of commonly agreed EU standards supplanting domestic ones is kept to a minimum, their sovereignty is less impinged.[20] The Stockholm Programme (2009) suggested a closer alignment of the domestic systems nevertheless, inter alia, when it comes

18 'The Court of Justice of the European Union shall ensure that in the interpretation and application of the Treaties the law is observed.'

19 This contribution does not engage with aspects of external relations law; magisterial discussions are available in the form of, inter alia, R.A. Wessel, L. Marin and C. Matera, 'The External Dimension of the EU's Area of Freedom, Security and Justice', in C. Eckes and T. Konstadinides (eds.), *Crime within the Area of Freedom, Security and Justice* (Cambridge University Press, 2011) 272; C. Eckes, 'External Relations Law: How the Outside Shapes the Inside', in D. Acosta Arcarazo and C.C. Murphy (eds.), *EU Security and Justice Law* (Hart Publishing, 2014) 186; see also M. Cremona, J. Monar and S. Poli (eds.), *The External Dimension of the European Union's Area of Freedom, Security and Justice* (Peter Lang, 2011).

20 V. Mitsilegas, *EU Criminal Law* (Hart Publishing, 2008) 321.

to the definition of criminal offences and sanctions. In the wake of the *Environmental crimes* and *Ship-source pollution* rulings, which proffered a tentative opening, the entry into force of the Lisbon Treaty solidified the needed competencies.[21] Even now, however, the approximation of national law is regarded as anything but the default option; and perhaps the support for this is more on the wane now than ever before.[22] Simultaneously, in the post-Lisbon era, decision-making in the Council is to proceed on the basis of qualified-majority voting (QMV), which has raised the potential for minority dissenters to be overruled and made to swallow proposed uniform regulatory frameworks. Indeed, since 2009 the bulk of AFSJ measures have been adopted through the ordinary legislative procedure. Interestingly, however, up until now, this has not led to many heated showdowns or disgruntled remonstrations in the Council; in most cases, the Member States managed to reach consensus, with no contestant so far announcing or attempting to pull the 'emergency brake'. Moreover, on average it has proven possible to reach agreement within the Council within a commendable 6–12 months after the launching of the proposal.[23] Cooperation with the European Parliament does not appear to run any less smoothly, with agreements on draft AFSJ measures being reached with rising frequency at first reading. This has not prevented a handful of protracted clashes, inter alia, on the Schengen Borders Package, where a compromise was found only after the dispute had been brought before the ECJ.[24] All the same, the Parliament's elevation to co-legislator in the domain did not turn it into the over-assertive, markedly less cooperative partner that was expected by some.[25] Naturally, these are but early days – and the general tranquillity might easily be ascribed to the fact that none of the recently adopted measures envisaged to substantively overhaul the national criminal, police or immigration law regimes (nor, for that matter, the civil or family law regimes).

We notice a different, but equally endemic tension along the vertical axis, looking through the lens of subsidiarity. Since the AFSJ constitutes an area of shared competence, the latter principle may exert its full force.[26] Already before Stockholm, Council Conclusions emphasised the need to give it

21 Case C-176/03 *Commission v Council* (Environmental crimes); Case C-440/05 *Commission v Council* (Ship-source pollution).

22 Commission Communication, 'The EU Justice Agenda for 2020: Strengthening Trust, Mobility and Growth within the Union', COM(2014) 144 final; European Council Conclusions, Brussels, 26/27 June 2014, EUCO 79/14.

23 S. Peers, 'Justice and Home Affairs Law since the Treaty of Lisbon: A Fairy-Tale Ending?', in D. Acosta Arcarazo and C.C. Murphy (eds.), *EU Security and Justice Law* (Hart Publishing, 2014) 33.

24 Case C-55/10, *Parliament v Council and Commission* (Schengen Borders Code).

25 J.J. Rijpma, 'Institutions and Agencies: Government and Governance after Lisbon', in D. Acosta Arcarazo and C.C. Murphy (eds.), *EU Security and Justice Law* (Hart Publishing, 2014) 59.

26 Article 4(2)(j) TFEU and Article 5(3) TEU.

adequate attention when contemplating the introduction of common EU standards.[27] This message was subsequently picked up by the Commission and the Parliament.[28] In the present constellation, in line with the revised Protocol, and as underscored by Article 69 TFEU, the parliaments of the Member States have emerged as highly vocal protagonists. In addition, especially for the AFSJ, the threshold for objecting to a draft legislative act is lowered from one-third to one-quarter of the votes allotted to them.[29] At the end of 2013, this facilitated the second successful challenge on record, targeting the proposed establishment of the European Public Prosecutor's Office (EPPO). In accordance with the precepts of the Protocol, the 'yellow card' issued by 14 chambers of national parliaments prompted a review from the side of the Commission, despite the fact that the voiced concerns had actually little to do with subsidiarity *sensu stricto*. While the Commission ultimately decided against abandoning the proposal altogether, this episode risks setting a spiky precedent for the future – urging the Union legislator to suspend, rethink or even withdraw measures (however well-considered), in face of poorly substantiated complaints.[30] It may also unhelpfully open up the floor for playing out the 'national identity' card in situations where the quality, necessity and (greater) comparative efficiency of the relevant legislation stand wholly beyond doubt.[31]

The realisation of an EU-wide Area of Freedom, Security and Justice is considerably hampered by the presence of opt-outs. In many eyes, the United Kingdom's arrangement has to be qualified as the most disconcerting, enabling it to 'take a mallet to a still-drying frieze'.[32] At the individual level, the repercussions can be harrowing. Take the case of the European Arrest Warrant, where countries such as Germany, Spain or Italy are bound to surrender a person to the UK under an EAW, whereas EU law does not require the UK to offer him any legal assistance or aid whatsoever.[33] Even

27 Council Conclusions on guidelines for future criminal law in EU legislation, Brussels, 30 November 2009.

28 Commission Communication, 'Towards an EU criminal policy' COM(2011) 573 final; European Parliament resolution of 22 May 2012 on an EU approach to criminal law (2010/2310/INI).

29 Protocol (no. 2) on the application of the principles of subsidiarity and proportionality [2010] OJ C83/206, Article 7(2).

30 Commission Communication, 'On the review of the proposal for a Council Regulation on the establishment of the European Public Prosecutor's Office with regard to the principle of subsidiarity, in accordance with Protocol No 2', COM(2013) 851 final.

31 E. Herlin-Karnell, 'Constitutional Principles in the Area of Freedom, Security and Justice', in D. Acosta Arcarazo and C.C. Murphy (eds.), *EU Security and Justice Law* (Hart Publishing, 2014), pp. 50–51.

32 C.C. Murphy and D. Acosta Arcarazo, 'Rethinking Europe's Freedom, Security and Justice', in D. Acosta Arcarazo and C.C. Murphy (eds), *EU Security and Justice Law* (Hart Publishing, 2014) 7.

33 The UK having opted out of Directive 2013/48/EU on the right of access to a lawyer in criminal proceedings and in European Arrest Warrant proceedings, and on the right to have a third party informed upon deprivation of liberty and to communicate with third persons

when the further extension of such 'variable geometry' was the price to pay for abolishing the old third pillar,[34] the upshot is a Dalíesque picture that bewilders insiders and outsiders in equal measure. Perhaps the selective partaking of Ireland and Denmark causes fewer headaches, but there remains a definite randomness to their pre-emptive lack of support for some AFSJ initiatives, regardless of the latter's rationale or effects. Thankfully, such sentiments could be gaining traction, with consecutive Danish governments contemplating to relinquish the prerogatives in the near future.[35] On the other hand, for the sake of completeness, we should also point to an undeniably positive side of opt-outs that has manifested itself quite vigorously in recent years: namely, how decision-making at the Union level has become somewhat *less* complicated by virtue of the fact that the countries concerned do not bother to erect blockades against measures they are detached from *ab initio*.

2.2 *Enhancing accountability and regulatory quality*

As known, the AFSJ suffered from an accountability deficit right from its inception. Possibly the most galling expression of this was the absence of democratic scrutiny over the adoption of legislative instruments. The elevated position of the Parliament, noted above, largely remedied this flaw. In the Maastricht era, it was 'consulted and immediately forgotten'.[36] The contrast with the present could hardly be greater. At the same time, whereas the ordinary legislative procedure is now of general application here, the significant number of occasions where a special procedure must be resorted to should not be overlooked; and in many of these, the scrutiny powers of MEPs is unfortunately more limited.[37] Equally, the revamped Treaty setup conjures up a distorted picture in that it fails to convey the phenomenal, incommensurable importance of the European Council. Thus, in practice, the much-lamented executive dominance from days of old has far from dissipated.[38] Since the entry into force of the Lisbon Treaty, crucial political choices appear to have been transferred to the European Council, side-lining all other institutions; for example, with regard to the Internal Security Strategy

and with consular authorities while deprived of liberty, OJ [2013] L294/1, Directive 2010/64/EU of the European Parliament and of the Council of 20 October 2010 on the right to interpretation and translation in criminal proceedings, OJ [2010] L280/1, as well as the prospective Directive on provisional legal aid for suspects or accused persons deprived of liberty and legal aid in European arrest warrant proceedings, COM(2013) 824 final.

34 Timmermans, supra note 4.

35 Although the December 2015 referendum defied many predictions by not producing a favourable majority, requiring yet another tailor-made alternative to ensure Denmark's continued involvement in Europol.

36 H.G. Nilsson, 'Foreword', in M. Bergström and A.J. Cornell (eds.), *European Police and Criminal Law Co-operation* (Hart Publishing, 2014) vi.

37 See, for example, Article 75 TFEU, Article 83(1) TFEU, Article 87(3) TFEU.

38 Fletcher, supra note 3, p. 19.

and the Anti-Drugs Strategy (documents displaying a passion for dubiously generic approaches).[39] The Council, in turn, has increasingly delegated a fair share of priority-setting to the Standing Committee on Internal Security (COSI), to the exclusion of the Commission as well as the Parliament.[40] Article 71 TFEU exacerbates the lack of oversight, by merely obliging COSI to share and forward information on its proceedings.[41]

Arguably, it was precisely the lack of democratic input in the old-style AFSJ that produced instruments with avoidable flaws. Good intentions notwithstanding, the vaunted 'War on Terror' incited the EU executive to forge ahead with extra haste in the mid-2000s, presenting us with such contentious measures as the EAW and the Prüm package. Nowadays, rulings such as *Digital Rights Ireland* have reinforced the idea that the *acquis* built up under the third pillar does not entirely pass muster, pitted against modern fundamental rights and rule of law standards.[42] According to a House of Lords report, in order to reach unanimity, much of that *acquis* was agreed at the lowest common denominator, often resulting in a frightfully poor quality of drafting.[43] On the other hand, we must note that in the past five years, a number of measures have been revised and ameliorated, among which are the rules on market abuse, the confiscation of criminal assets and counterfeiting of the euro.[44] More are guaranteed to be spruced up soon under the 'Smart Regulation/REFIT' agenda that has of late received a firm impetus, with the Commission's first vice-president being entrusted with that dedicated portfolio.[45] As regards imminent new rules – for instance, on the rights of underage suspects, privacy and data protection, or the countering of cybercrime – it is imperative that concerns of the public-at-large, channelled *in*

39 E. De Capitani, 'The New Guidelines for the Area of Freedom, Security and Justice: Some Critical Comments', http://eulawanalysis.blogspot.nl/2014/06/the-new-guidelines-for-area-of-freedom.html. On this tendency see also more generally H. de Waele, 'Strained Actorness: The "New" European Council in Theory and Practice', in E. Fahey (ed.), *The Actors of Post-National Rule-Making* (Routledge, 2015) 91.

40 Rijpma, supra note 25, p. 75.

41 The same lack of democratic input holds for the provision on the evaluation of AFSJ policies *sensu lato*, Article 70 TFEU.

42 Joined Cases C-293/12 & C-594/12, *Digital Rights Ireland Ltd v Minister for Communications, Marine and Natural Resources and Others and Kärntner Landesregierung and Others.*

43 House of Lords, European Union Committee, 13th Report of Session 2012–13, 'EU Police and Criminal Justice Measures: The UK's 2014 Opt-out Decision', HL Paper 159, at p. 37.

44 Regulation 596/2014 on market abuse, OJ [2014] L173/1; Directive 2014/42/EU on the freezing and confiscation of instrumentalities and proceeds of crime in the European Union, OJ [2014] L127/39; Regulation 1210/2010 concerning authentication of euro coins and handling of euro coins unfit for circulation, OJ [2010] L339/1.

45 See Commission Communication 'Smart Regulation in the European Union', COM(2010) 543 final; Commission Communication 'EU Regulatory Fitness', COM(2012) 746 final; Commission Communication 'Regulatory Fitness and Performance Programme (REFIT): State of Play and Outlook', COM(2014) 368 final.

partim through the Parliament, are taken very seriously indeed. This precept retains every topicality, as those concerns might still be all too easily overlooked, particularly (but not exclusively) in the course of the special legislative procedure.[46] This aspect ought to have been addressed in the strategic agenda for the next five years that was laid down by the European Council in 2014, but was not.[47] The chance to stymie the aforementioned concerns – for example, by explicitly spelling out the need for a strengthened *ex ante* and *ex post* evaluation of these rules – was sorely missed. Hence, the executive appears to have left ample room for novel confrontations with the judiciary – confrontations that could just as easily be avoided.

A joint statement and common approach promulgated by the Parliament, Commission and Council in July 2012 addressed the specific need to enhance the accountability of the Union's agencies.[48] In this respect, however, it was the 'Lisbonisation' of the AFSJ that delivered supremely welcome improvements, by binding them to the EU Fundamental Rights Charter and rendering their decisions susceptible for actions for annulment at the Court of Justice.[49] In the day-to-day management and support of police and justice cooperation, Europol and Eurojust play a prominent part. In the monitoring and evaluation of their activities, Articles 85 and 88 TFEU have granted national parliaments a role alongside MEPs, thus ostensibly handing wide scrutiny powers to directly elected representatives. Yet again, it is pivotal that these are exercised rigorously throughout, in order to transcend the vapid paper promises. An excellent opportunity has arisen in the context of the projected reform of Europol. The Parliament is advocating here, inter alia, that it be given the right to interrogate the agency's executive director, and second an observer to its Management Board. If these demands were to be met, they should inspire it to turn up the heat on other bodies and offices as well – also vis-à-vis an overbearing political institution such as the European Council.[50] For that same reason, whereas the launching of a European Public Prosecutor's Office is commendable, at least, for its expected contribution to

46 For example Art 75 TFEU on the implementation of the administrative counterterrorism framework, designed as a *pas-de-deux* between the Commission and the Council. By way of compensation, national parliaments in multiple Member States were previously granted a scrutiny reserve on the approval of JHA instruments in the Council; in the Netherlands, however, this democratic safeguard was abolished at the ratification of the Lisbon Treaty.

47 European Council Conclusions, Brussels, 26/27 June 2014, EUCO 79/14; on this see also, for example, S. Carrera and E. Guild, 'The European Council's Guidelines for the Area of Freedom, Security and Justice 2020: Subverting the 'Lisbonisation' of Justice and Home Affairs?', CEPS Essay No 13/14, July 2014.

48 Joint Statement and Common Approach of the European Parliament, the Council of the EU and the European Commission on decentralised agencies, Brussels, 18 June 2012.

49 Art 263(1) TFEU: 'The Court of Justice of the European Union [...] shall also review the legality of acts of bodies, offices or agencies of the Union intended to produce legal effects vis-à-vis third parties.'

50 See European Parliament, Committee on Civil Liberties, Justice and Home Affairs, Report on the proposal for a regulation of the European Parliament and of the Council on the European Union Agency for Law Enforcement Cooperation and Training (Europol) and

transparency and accountability at both the European and the national levels, its creation cannot be considered a success if a maximum of democratic checks and balances were not to be installed on its practical operation.

2.3 *Optimising monitoring and enforcement*

In order for the mutual recognition paradigm to succeed, as a matter of logic, the standards upheld by the Member States cannot be too dissimilar. In relation to the rule of law and the protection of fundamental rights, it is nowadays sadly open to question whether all EU countries toe the same line.[51] This affects the very constitutional fabric of the AFSJ, besides striking at the heart of the 'ever-closer union' ideology. At the same time, the powers of the institutions to pinpoint and counter systemic threats to the EU's values fall woefully short. Already the Barroso Commission identified the need to bridge the gap between the available political persuasion and targeted infringement procedures on the one hand, and the 'nuclear option' of Article 7 TEU on the other. In 2014, it unveiled a new initiative that basically boils down to an early-warning mechanism; it introduces a structured dialogue between 'Brussels' and the Member State concerned, seeking to prevent the escalation of systemic threats to the rule of law, prior to a possible request to suspend the culprit's voting rights in the Council.[52] The proposal has been slammed by academics as too feeble to have any meaningful impact, and by the Council for breaching the principle of conferred powers.[53] The latter devised an alternative 'rule of law dialogue', predicated 'on the principles of objectivity, non-discrimination and equal treatment of all Member States', and to be 'conducted on a non partisan and evidence-based approach'.[54] Despite the rhetoric, this proposal does not put in place an effective monitoring and enforcement architecture that mediates between the ordinary infringement procedure and the 'nuclear option'. Consequently, in Europe we continue to lack a supranational *locus* where the quality of the national freedom, security and justice regimes is assessed critically, and (if need be) denounced.[55]

repealing Decisions 2009/371/JHA and 2005/681/JHA (Rapporteur: Agustín Díaz de Mera García Consuegra), Brussels, 7 February 2014, PE 513.116v02-00.

51 See, for example, Editorial Comments, 'Hungary's New Constitutional Order and "European Unity"' (2012) 49 *Common Market Law Review* 871.

52 Commission Communication, 'A New EU Framework to Strengthen the Rule of Law', Brussels, 19 March 2014, COM(2014) 158 final/2.

53 See, for example, A. von Bogdandy and M. Ioannidis, 'Systemic Deficiency in the Rule of Law: What It Is, What Has Been Done, What Can Be Done' (2014) 51 *Common Market Law Review* 59; D. Kochenov and L. Pech, 'Upholding the Rule of Law in the EU: On the Commission's "Pre-Article 7 Procedure" as a Timid Step in the Right Direction', EUI Working Paper RSCAS 2015/24.

54 Conclusions of the Council and the Member States meeting within the Council on ensuring respect for the rule of law, Brussels, 16 December 2014, doc. no. 16936/14.

55 Not even the Council of Europe's Venice Commission, which mainly operates as a consultative organ, qualifies as such.

Conversely, neither the Strasbourg nor the Luxembourg Court have shied away from exposing and condemning poignant deficiencies in the domestic treatment of migrants and asylum-seekers.[56] These judgments have severely dented the principle of mutual trust, sapping the foundations on which (inter alia) the European Arrest Warrant and the reciprocal recognition of judicial decisions have been based.[57] The Commission and the Council are therefore well advised to move beyond the symbolic, and urgently deploy all necessary means to reverse the internal decay and prevent further erosion – lest the AFSJ follow a similar crisis trajectory as the Eurozone. For the Commission, this inevitably necessitates a prudent utilisation of its discretionary competences under Articles 258–260 TFEU, and a concomitantly careful allocation of its scarce resources.[58] Paradoxically, the extension of its monitoring and enforcement powers in the AFSJ per 1 December 2014 has imposed greater constraints on the Commission's limited budget and manpower, making the desired energetic vigilance comparatively harder to attain – let alone its ability to undertake supplementary tasks.

3 Judicial control in the AFSJ: between the devil and the deep blue sea

3.1 The role of the judiciary – of measure and nuance

What is the role and what are the boundaries for the Court of Justice in this peculiar continuum? It has been argued that, compared to its past performance, an atypical demeanour is warranted, since integration in the criminal law sphere is a very different process from market integration. In particular, the peculiar function and ambit of individual rights suggest that the ECJ is to behave as a restraining force, instead of attempting to push things ahead.[59] From an institutional choice perspective, the legislature would thus appear to be the more appropriate driver.[60] Indeed, whereas it has been argued in close conjunction that 'integration through law' in the EU has, to

56 ECtHR, *Hirsi Jamaa and Others v Italy*, App. No. 27765/09; ECtHR, *MSS v Belgium and Greece*, App. No. 30696/09; ECJ, Joined Cases C-411/10 and C-493/11, *NS v Secretary of State for the Home Department* and *ME and Others v Refugee Applications Commissioner and Minister for Justice, Equality and Law Reform*.

57 I. Canor, 'My Brother's Keeper? Horizontal *Solange*: "An Ever Closer Distrust Among the Peoples of Europe" (2013) 50 *Common Market Law Review* 388; A Kornezow, 'The Area of Freedom, Security and Justice in the Light of EU Accession to the ECHR: Is the Break-up Inevitable?' (2012–2013) 12 *Cambridge Yearbook of European Legal Studies* 227.

58 For ideas on how to improve on the status quo in holistic fashion, see H. de Waele, 'Advancing the Supranational Compliance Debate: New Directions in the Enforcement of EU Law' (2014) 4 *The Lawyer Quarterly* 1.

59 A Hinarejos, 'Integration in Criminal Matters and the Role of the Court of Justice' (2011) 36 *European Law Review* 420.

60 Ibid, p. 427.

date, mostly been rights-focused, that paradigm has been put on its head in the realm of criminal law – since the emphasis lies there on facilitating the exercise of state power, rather than the bestowing of rights onto individuals.[61] Although one may subscribe to that point of view to a considerable degree, the supply of AFSJ legislation has been burgeoning impressively, and by now a vast number of instruments seems to provide the Court at least some leeway to buttress individual rights in the same way as in its classic market integration jurisprudence. Besides, not just the quantity of such measures has been on the rise, but the total collection of rights conferred onto individuals has therewith grown massively too.[62] In result, the cases in which a stronger or wider interpretation of those instruments is both possible and apposite are quickly becoming far less exceptional than scholars initially assumed.[63]

Even before the 'Lisbonisation' of the field, there was every indication that the Court regarded criminal law as yet another tool that could be mobilised to attain Community objectives.[64] The introduction into the old third pillar of doctrines from the first (indirect effect, among others) pointed quite obviously in the direction of conceptual harmonisation.[65] All the same, the ECJ, unlike in the 1950s, is not faced with a blank canvas here; for while an internal market was then a *terra incognita*, Member States already long ago drew up their own visions of how freedom, security and justice are to be constituted. Unhelpfully, the waters between them remain very deep, owing for instance to the Manichean dichotomies of common law versus civil law, and of investigatory versus accusatorial systems – let alone their diverse takes on crime and punishment as societal phenomena.[66] In itself, this offers an additional reason to argue that the *communautaire* ideology does not adequately map onto the AFSJ we know today – if ever it did.

Nevertheless, the exercise of judicial *control* has grown to be a matter of vital concern, meaning that in the Court's activities, the scrutiny of acts for whether they duly respect individual rights ought to take pride of place. A traditional role of the judiciary is after all to counterbalance the (in modern

61 T. Tridimas, 'Foreword', in V. Mitsilegas, *EU Criminal Law* (Hart Publishing, 2008) v.

62 For example, Directive 2012/13/EU on the right to information in criminal proceedings, OJ [2012] L142/1; Directive 2012/29/EU establishing minimum standards on the rights, support and protection of victims of crime, OJ [2012] L315/57; Directive 2013/48/EU of 22 October 2013 on the right of access to a lawyer in criminal proceedings and in European Arrest Warrant proceedings, and on the right to have a third party informed upon deprivation of liberty and to communicate with third persons and with consular authorities while deprived of liberty, OJ [2013] L294/1.

63 Hinarejos, supra note 59, p. 427.

64 Mitsilegas, supra note 20, p. 323.

65 M. Fletcher, R. Lööf and B. Gilmore, *EU Criminal Law and Justice* (Edward Elgar, 2008) 18.

66 Murphy and Acosta Arcarazo, supra note 32, p. 12; J.R. Spencer, 'EU Criminal Law', in C. Barnard and S. Peers (eds.), *European Union Law* (Oxford University Press 2014), pp. 753–755.

times increasingly dominant) executive.[67] True, post-Lisbon, the democratic pedigree of AFSJ acts has much improved in general; but as flagged above, the Parliamentary struggle goes on to come up against an overbearing European Council. Hence, it is to be applauded that the Court has been putting itself to task with visible ambition. In so doing, it, inter alia, harangued the deficiencies of the Dublin Regulation, lambasted pernicious trends in the criminalising of irregular migrants and beefed up the scope of protection of the Qualification Directive.[68] In this regard then, the ECJ has hitherto found good form in navigating these uncharted waters, placing warning beacons and throwing out lifelines where necessary.

In one respect, the demands placed on the Court in the AFSJ are certainly *not* different than usual: its output should be of the highest quality, which in turn presupposes, above all, a maximum of consistency. To that end, it needs to flesh out and unflinchingly maintain an acceptable set of principles guiding its interpretation, and back up its decisions with an impeccably persuasive reasoning. Whenever the Court formulates tenets of 'higher law', the outcomes in particular cases should conform faithfully to those principles.[69] So far, unsurprisingly, effectiveness has played a starring role. That principle was, for example, neatly connected to the operation of the European Arrest Warrant in the *Lopes da Silva Jorge* case, and in an amplified form in *Melloni* and *Jeremy F.*[70] In *Lopes da Silva Jorge*, the Court ruled that Member States may not automatically exclude non-nationals from the possibility to refuse to surrender a person against who an EAW is issued, but need to take into account the degree of integration of an EU citizen from another country residing on its territory. In *Melloni*, as well as *Jeremy F.*, the ECJ rejected the reading of Article 53 CFR as a blank opt-out, restricting the possibility for national authorities to apply domestic standards of protection. Similarly, the Court ruled in *El Dridi* that Member State authorities are to take proper heed of the objectives of the Returns Directive in their removal and repatriation policies.[71] Thereby, it narrowly circumscribed their discretion and powers with regard to the measures of coercion that may be imposed against illegally residing third-country nationals. Going back further, we saw the

67 L.F.M. Besselink, 'The Parameters of Constitutional Conflict after Melloni' (2014) 39 *European Law Review* 542.

68 See Joined Cases C-411/10 and C-493/11, *NS v Secretary of State for the Home Department* and *ME and Others v Refugee Applications Commissioner and Minister for Justice, Equality and Law Reform*; Case C-465/07, *Meki Elgafaji and Noor Elgafaji v Staatssecretaris van Justitie*; Case C-329/11, *Alexandre Achughbabian v Préfet du Val-de-Marne*; Case C-357/09 PPU, *Said Shamilovich Kadzoev (Huchbarov)*; Joined Cases C-199/12, C-201/12 & C-200/12, *Minister voor Immigratie en Asiel v X and Y*, and *Z v Minister voor Immigratie en Asiel*.

69 Fletcher et al., supra note 65, p. 13.

70 Case C-42/11, *João Pedro Lopes da Silva Jorge*; Case C-399/11, *Stefano Melloni v Ministerio Fiscal*; Case C-168/13, *Jeremy F. v Premier Ministre*.

71 Case C-61/11 PPU, *Hassen El Dridi, alias Soufi Karim*.

principle of effectiveness in vivid action in the *Environmental crimes* case law, which enlarged the erstwhile Community's competence to engage in the criminalisation of certain types of behaviour.[72] Considering the breadth and ambiguity of the principle, we know from EC history that its deployment can have unexpected ramifications, radically transforming the nature of the obligations that relevant actors believed they had undertaken.[73] Although the principles of legality and conferral of powers are two other mainstays of European constitutional law, in practice, these have hardly managed to constrain the ECJ's creative jurisprudence. Yet, in the AFSJ, legality and conferral of powers ought to rank among the *nec plus ultra*; this is especially so in the criminal law department, which traditionally purports to counter the dangers of 'Orwellian overstretch'.[74] This reinforces the need to rein in the effectiveness principle wherever it threatens to favour the goals of the EU measures to the detriment of individual rights. Fortunately, the Court has shown itself far from impervious to these demands, making it clear that it is ill-disposed to interpreting the EU's powers in criminal law any broader than those in other fields.[75] Simultaneously, perhaps it then also ought to proceed less squeamishly when it has the chance to augment the effectiveness of a measure so as to ameliorate the position of those persons that the rules at stake actually aim to benefit.[76]

In the future, the striking of the right balance between individual rights on the one hand and effectiveness on the other might well prove to be a structural difficulty for the Court, hampering its ability to adopt the most 'correct' posture. In the internal market realm, as mentioned earlier, the two interests often went hand-in-hand. Conversely, in the AFSJ, the desire to increase the 'bite' of the Union (inter alia, to prevent impunity) stands at odds with the desire of (potential) suspects to be spared from overly zealous prosecutions. Cases such as *Jeremy F.* and *Spasic* provide illustrations of this conundrum: in the former, the ECJ was willing to ride roughshod over the claimant's procedural rights where this served the effectiveness of the EAW, while in the latter, an invocation of the CFR could not avert a stretched interpretation of the Convention implementing the Schengen Agreement that led to a curtailing of the protection of the *ne bis in idem* principle.[77] In fact, the Schengen system as such leaves little room for a sustained approach based on 'unity' or 'effectiveness', built as it is on the conflicting rationales of free movement and

72 Case C-176/03 *Commission v Council* (Environmental crimes).

73 See, for example, Joined Cases C-6 & C-9/90, *Andrea Francovich and Danila Bonifaci and Others v Italy*.

74 E. Herlin-Karnell, 'Effectiveness and Constitutional Limits in European Criminal Law' (2014) 5 *New Journal of European Criminal Law* 267, at p. 272.

75 See most notably Case C-43/12, *Commission v Parliament and Council* (Traffic offences information Directive).

76 Case C-122/13, *Paola C. v Presidenza del Consiglio dei Ministri*.

77 Case C-168/13, *Jeremy F. v Premier Ministre;* Case C-129/14 PPU, *Criminal proceedings against Zoran Spasic*.

security.[78] Here then, tilting to the one side seems to be no more preferable than keeling over to the other.

Primarily therefore, the role of the Court in the AFSJ is to exercise judicial control over the Union institutions and national public authorities, an activity that naturally comprises both the interpretation and the review of acts adopted.[79] Thereby, it may endeavour to guarantee the effectiveness of the latter, so long as the rights of individuals are not affected to a degree that cannot be justified, in light of overriding principles that particularly hold sway in the field of criminal justice.[80] In order to deliver quality, it needs to adjudicate with a maximum of consistency. Paradoxically, however, consistency is best served by a measure of flexibility, instead of a persistent privileging of effectiveness over individual rights, or vice versa. The ECJ's output over the past five years indicates that here and there, adjustments to its practice are still warranted. While functioning as a check on the political institutions, the Court would do well to avoid an excessive arrogation of power, unless it does not mind catching extra flak; for that reason, it pays to keep a close watch on the views of the legislature and the executive, and absorb these in its own vision. Legally, it enjoys the last word in matters of interpretation indeed; but that does not mean that it possesses exclusive expertise across the board.[81] The record of Member States' compliance with AFSJ law, which has been nebulous in the old third pillar, stands to gain from such a measured and nuanced strategy as well.

3.2 *Preserving the horizontal and vertical* **séparation des pouvoirs**

A specific challenge for the Court resides in issues of demarcation along the horizontal and vertical axes, where, equally, adjudication has to take shape with good measure and nuance. Fortunately, with the final collapse of the Maastricht temple, the Court has been released from carrying out the cumbersome 'border patrol' missions in the sphere of police and justice cooperation.[82] All the same, since 2009, it has already been repeatedly asked to decide turf-wars between the Parliament, Council and Commission in

78 G. Cornelisse, 'What's Wrong with Schengen? Border Disputes and the Nature of Integration in the Area without Internal Borders' (2014) 51 *Common Market Law Review* 770.

79 Save for the review of the validity or proportionality of operations carried out by the police or other law enforcement services of a Member State or the exercise of the responsibilities incumbent upon Member States with regard to the maintenance of law and order and the safeguarding of internal security (excluded by Article 276 TFEU).

80 Legality, conferred powers, and derived principles such as transparency, non-retroactivity and protection of legitimate expectations.

81 G. Davies, 'Legislative Control of the European Court of Justice' (2014) 51 *Common Market Law Review* 1608.

82 A. Hinarejos, *Judicial Control in the European Union* (Oxford University Press, 2009), pp. 113–114; A. Engel, 'Delimiting Competences in the EU: CFSP versus AFSJ Legal Bases' (2015) 21 *European Public Law* 47.

various constellations – nowadays framed as legal basis disputes that are to be resolved in purely *communautaire* fashion, in adherence to its trusted 'centre of gravity' methodology. In these horizontal tussles, few surprises have emerged so far, with the main players having largely shared the spoils. In the saga of the Schengen Borders Package, for example, the ECJ chose to run with the hare and hunt with the hounds, by annulling the offending decision yet not laying down a restrictive *Diktat* on what constitutes the 'essential elements of a legislative act'; a Solomonic verdict that went down well with the opposing sides.[83] For now, this leaves in abeyance more spectacular suits, in which the Parliament (for instance, in follow-up to the previous *PNR* litigation) could attempt to tie the hands of the executive further.[84]

Along the vertical axis, the Court looks set to be confronted with subsidiarity questions with increasing frequency. As noted above, in the AFSJ, the threshold for objecting against a draft legislative act is just one-quarter of the votes allotted to national parliaments.[85] Moreover, Article 8 of the Protocol invites Member States to turn to the Kirchberg directly whenever they believe a legislative act was adopted that breaches the subsidiarity principle. The EPPO dossier makes clear how intensely that principle has become fudged with that of proportionality.[86] In all likelihood, this rising confusion brings us closer to the moment when the Union's judiciary shall indeed be requested to untie the knot. Where the ECJ managed to dodge or trivialise the issue in the pre-Lisbon period, it will have to engage with it head-on shortly, delineating the efficient and the comparatively less efficient level(s).[87]

Straddling the horizontal and vertical dimension are the opt-outs secured by a small selection of countries – before Lisbon covering immigration, asylum and civil law, but since then also stretching out to police and criminal law cooperation. Hitherto, these have not presented themselves to the Court as notable spots of bother. The alleged British/Polish exemptions on the Fundamental Rights Charter were rendered meaningless in *NS*, neutering their status to mere clarifications of the existing provision on the Charter's

83 Case C-355/10, *Parliament v Council and Commission* (Schengen Borders Code); see on this M. den Heijer and E. Tauschinsky, 'Where Human Rights Meet Administrative Law: Essential Elements and Limits to Delegation' (2013) 9 *European Constitutional Law Review* 514.

84 Joined Cases C-317/04 and C-318/04, *Parliament v Council and Commission* (Passenger name records).

85 Protocol (No. 2) on the application of the principles of subsidiarity and proportionality [2010] OJ C83/206, Article 7(2).

86 For an empirically founded critique, see E. Mastenbroek et al., *Engaging with Europe: Evaluating National Parliamentary Control of EU Decision-Making*, a study commissioned by the Dutch House of Representatives, www.houseofrepresentatives.nl/sites/www.houseofrepresentatives.nl/files/news_items/engaging_with_europe_report_of_findings_2nd_edition.pdf.

87 Case C-58/08, *The Queen, on the application of Vodafone Ltd and Others v Secretary of State for Business, Enterprise and Regulatory Reform.*

scope of application (Article 51).[88] Whereas the general non-participation in Schengen of Ireland and the United Kingdom is here to stay, these countries have not managed to entirely remove themselves from the ECJ's interpretation of the relevant rules and decisions on (urgent) preliminary references – if only because they continue to take part in the Schengen Convention on police and judicial cooperation in criminal matters and the Schengen Information System (SIS II).[89] Pending their full entry, Cyprus, Romania, Bulgaria and Croatia find themselves in a comparable halfway house – being bound to decisions, and confronted with their repercussions, on a subject-matter they do not yet fully take part in. Conversely, the UK did succeed in ring-fencing a sizeable chunk of the AFSJ by its decision to opt out of 130 'ex-third pillar' measures, and opt back into 35 of these.[90] Thereby, however, it has plainly accepted the Court's jurisdiction in key areas that include suspects' rights, cross-border criminal investigations, and the fight against human trafficking. In contrast, Denmark retains its wholesale opt-out with regard to the AFSJ, with the exception of those measures building upon the Schengen *acquis*. Nevertheless, neither the UK nor Denmark will be able to immunise themselves from the side-effects obliquely penetrating their legal orders, by virtue of the rights and obligations the Union judiciary may derive from the (integrally binding) EU Fundamental Rights Charter.[91] Although the Court is thus legally entitled to exercise jurisdiction in a number of cases that politicians believe to lie outside its grasp, many non-lawyers are prone to overlook these finer points. For the Union's judiciary, it will consequently be hard to dispel the impression that it is overstepping the boundaries here.

3.3 Taking fundamental rights seriously

Let us lastly zoom in further on the question of the power divide between the Union and the Member States from a fundamental rights perspective. Brighter sides, darker sides and several shades of grey are discernible here. Undeniably positive for natural persons is that the EU's newly binding Charter offers greater protection vis-à-vis the European Convention of Human Rights, by virtue of the fact that the former applies without reservation in migration and tax cases, whereas the latter does not. On top of this, the CFR contains a

88 Joined Cases C-411/10 and C-493/11, *NS v Secretary of State for the Home Department* and *ME and Others v Refugee Applications Commissioner and Minister for Justice, Equality and Law Reform*, para 120.

89 Which, as the Court has made clear longer ago, does not mean that they can contest the adoption of decisions with regard to those parts of the Schengen *acquis* they have contracted out of: see Case C-482/08, *United Kingdom v Council*.

90 See 'UK notification according to Article 10(4) of Protocol No 36 to TEU and TFEU', Brussels, 26 July 2013, Council doc. no. 12750/13. Despite a chaotic session in the House of Commons in November 2013, where a legally binding vote was only taken on 11 of these measures, the decision gained full effect on 1 December 2014.

91 In the same sense, Herlin-Karnell, supra note 7, p. 455.

whole gamut of provisions that are not to be found elsewhere, safeguarding, inter alia, the position of children, the elderly and the disabled.[92] This opulence considerably relieves the predicament of the European Court of Justice, for it allows for an assertively autonomous interpretation, even when (in accordance with Article 52(3) CFR) it is to take its cue from the precedents set by the European Court of Human Rights (ECtHR).[93] In the short to medium term, the ECJ also happily escapes from the vicissitudes of the co-respondent mechanism, having stalled (if not sunk) the intended full-blown integration into Strasbourg's jurisdiction.[94]

For the Member States and their citizens, the Court's *Melloni* ruling has sparked off a concurrently pernicious development. According to this judgment, Article 53 CFR bars national authorities and courts from applying domestic standards of protection when this undermines those included in the Charter, and/or when the primacy, unity and effectiveness of EU law are in danger of being compromised. Here, it was especially the *effet utile* of the EAW that had to prevail, standing in the way of a generous reading of the suspect's basic rights. In extrapolation of *Melloni*, domestic fundamental rights that seek to limit a person's criminal liability appear to stand just as little chance, pitted against the exigencies of effective enforcement and Union loyalty. The upshot is a compulsory levelling down of national constitutional guarantees, opening up the floor for novel conflicts with the Member States' constitutional courts.

We noted above how the Court's judgment in *NS* enjoined Member States to decrease the level of mutual trust in asylum cases. In the process, it signalled an erosion of the principle of mutual recognition in police and judicial criminal matters.[95] The Court was given the chance to initiate a reverse in *Radu*, with AG Sharpston launching a persuasive argument that mutual recognition is best constricted by the benchmarks enshrined in the CFR. The ECJ, however, declined to transpose its *NS* reasoning to the EAW, notwithstanding the manifestly defective conditions in which victims were to be surrendered from the one country to the other.[96] So, mutual recognition gets to stand in opposition to, and conveys the impression of trumping a due respect for fundamental rights – evincing a creed of 'effectiveness *über alles*'.[97] Lest it

92 Side-stepping for the moment the elusive distinction between 'rights' and 'principles' that is insufficiently demystified by Article 52(5) CFR, or the Explanations relating to the Charter of Fundamental Rights, OJ [2007] C303/17.

93 See, for example, Case C-279/09, *DEB Deutsche Energiehandels- und Beratungsgesellschaft mbH v Bundesrepublik Deutschland*, paras 35–52; Case C-398/12, *Criminal proceedings against M.*, paras 37–41; but see also Kornezow, supra note 57, p. 227.

94 Opinion 2/13, *Draft Agreement on Accession of the European Union to the European Convention for the Protection of Human Rights and Fundamental Freedoms.*

95 Murphy and Acosta Arcarazo, supra note 32, pp. 11–12.

96 Case C-396/11, *Proceedings relating to the execution of European Arrest Warrants issued agains Ciprian Vasile Radu; see also Case C-60/12, Proceedings concerning the enforcement of a financial penalty issued against Marián Baláž.*

97 See Besselink, supra note 67, p. 541.

adjust its course in forthcoming judgments, there are no prizes for guessing the likely impact on the Member States' compliance rate.

Albeit then that the Union's judiciary refuses to chain itself to external supervision, the Court has to take its own 'Bill of Rights' structurally seriously sooner rather than later, if it wants to preserve the coherence of the AFSJ.[98] This impels it to occasionally derogate from EU secondary law, even when this undercuts its primacy, unity and effectiveness. After all, if the *effet utile* were to blindly triumph over all other concerns here, that would flatly contradict the *Kadi* message of an autonomous legal order that is in a league of its own, precisely for attaching primordial value to the protection of fundamental rights.[99]

4 Conclusion: faithful choices, fateful decisions

Quo vadis, Area of Freedom, Security and Justice? In conclusion, a first thing that deserves to be underscored is how massively the position of the Parliament, Court and Commission has of late evolved – an evolution that has already left an invariably positive imprint on the formation of the relevant secondary rules. Many of the extant (substantially doubtful) measures that were adopted under the old JHA/PJCC pillars have meanwhile been substituted, are undergoing, or are scheduled to undergo revision. Overall, it is easy to perceive an unstoppable trend towards stronger institutional governance, judicial control, jointly resulting in an expansion of individual rights. This vindicates the faithful choices made by the *pères-fondateurs* of the Lisbon Treaty – culminating in the present, broadly agreeable equilibrium.

The preceding paragraphs have highlighted a selection of salient questions that the Union's political institutions and judiciary are poised to resolve, or are currently still grappling with: judicious decision-making and support garnering, enhancing accountability and regulatory quality, optimising monitoring and enforcement of the *acquis*, exercising judicial control with good measure and nuance, preserving the horizontal and vertical *séparation des pouvoirs*, while taking fundamental rights seriously. The overarching, issue that the political institutions as well as the Court have to sort out pertains to the long-term direction of the AFSJ: for do they aim to steer and shape the Area's development, or merely oversee the initiatives and support the needs of the Member States?[100] The legislation enacted up until now displays a preference for horizontal over vertical solutions: most of it does not mean to introduce a harmonised set of rules or subject domestic authorities to new central bodies, but to assist them in addressing the pertinent

98 For a recent show of confidence, see, however, Case C-562/13, *Centre public d'action sociale d'Ottignies-Louvain-La-Neuve v Moussa Abdida.*

99 Joined Cases C-402/05 P and C-415/05 P, *Kadi and Al Barakaat International Foundation v Council and Commission.*

100 Rijpma, supra note 25, p. 76.

subjects.[101] Dilemmas abound nevertheless, for instance with regard to the imposition of criminal penalties: in some instances the EU places its faith in the Member States to determine the right level, in others it sees an overriding need for approximation.[102] By the same token, for the longest time, Member States themselves were thought capable of ensuring effective, proportionate and dissuasive sanctions to safeguard inter alia the Union's financial interests – whereas now, relentless energy is invested in the creation of a European Public Prosecutor's Office. If the political institutions find it difficult to adhere to a coherent macro-strategy here, that evidently leaves space for the ECJ to step in; yet its decisions are equally likely to fall short, and readily attract criticism – not least from national (constitutional) courts.[103] This scenario is particularly problematic in the AFSJ, a continuum comprising substantive and procedural norms that *ratione materiae* ought to possess a minimum of ambiguity.

With the expiry of Lisbon's institutional transitional arrangements on 1 December 2014, rendering all national courts competent to submit preliminary references, and enabling the Commission to pursue infringement cases across the board, the ECJ has its work cut out for it anyway. True, the avalanche predicted earlier has not materialised[104] and any imminent explosion of its docket could be considered improbable; on the one hand, because two-thirds of the Member States had decided to opt-in on its jurisdiction pre-Lisbon, and on the other, because the pack of measures established post-Lisbon was not subjected to limitations from its inception. Still, the Court could easily find itself inundated by waves of Commission infringement proceedings; or a flood of references relating to Framework Decisions (in particular the European Arrest Warrant) that hitherto proved inadmissible. Moreover, since virtually all EAW cases involve persons in custody, these will need to be fast-tracked through the *procédure préjudicielle d'urgence* – casting doubts on the special PPU Chamber's ability to cope. Keeping in mind the imperative need to maintain decisional coherence, alongside the cardinal dictum that justice delayed is justice denied, pleas for a comprehensive redesigning of the Union's judicial architecture no longer seem as far-fetched as they once did.[105] This challenge, alongside a cornucopia of others, demonstrates that while the Area of Freedom, Security and Justice has supposedly already been constituted by the present Treaties, with regard to its actual realisation, embedding and entrenchment, we have, in fact, only just begun.

101 Spencer, supra note 66, p. 754.
102 V. Mitsilegas, 'EU Criminal Law Competence after Lisbon: From Securitised to Functional Criminalisation', in D. Acosta Arcarazo and C.C. Murphy (eds.), *EU Security and Justice Law* (Hart Publishing, 2014) 125.
103 Righteous warning shots were fired from academia in the 2011 'Manifesto on European Criminal Policy', discussed in Asp, supra note 13, pp. 60–62.
104 Peers, supra note 23, p. 34.
105 Nic Shuibne, supra note 17, p. 173.

Bibliography

Adams, M., de Waele, H., Meeusen, J. and Straetmans, G. (eds.), *Judging Europe's Judges* (Hart Publishing, 2013)

Asp, P., 'European Criminal Law: Challenges for the Future', in M. Bergström and A.J. Cornell (eds.), *European Police and Criminal Law Co-operation* (Hart Publishing, 2014) 53

Beck, G., *The Reasoning of the Court of Justice of the EU* (Hart Publishing, 2012)

Besselink, L.F.M., 'The Parameters of Constitutional Conflict after Melloni' (2014) 39 *European Law Review* 531

Von Bogdandy, A. and Ioannidis, M., 'Systemic Deficiency in the Rule of Law: What It Is, What Has Been Done, What Can Be Done' (2014) 51 *Common Market Law Review* 59

Canor, I., 'My Brother's Keeper? Horizontal *Solange*: "An Ever Closer Distrust Among the Peoples of Europe"' (2013) 50 *Common Market Law Review* 383

De Capitani, E., 'The New Guidelines for the Area of Freedom, Security and Justice: Some Critical Comments', http://eulawanalysis.blogspot.nl/2014/06/the-new-guidelines-for-area-of-freedom.html

De Capitani, E., 'Metamorphosis of the Third Pillar: The End of the Transition Period for EU Criminal and Policing Law', http://eulawanalysis.blogspot.co.uk/2014/07/metamorphosis-of-third-pillar-end-of.html

Carrera, S. and Guild, E., 'The European Council's Guidelines for the Area of Freedom, Security and Justice 2020: Subverting the "Lisbonisation" of Justice and Home Affairs?', CEPS Essay No 13/14, July 2014

Conway, G., *The Limits of Legal Reasoning and the European Court of Justice* (Cambridge University Press, 2012)

Cornelisse, G., 'What's Wrong with Schengen? Border Disputes and the Nature of Integration in the Area without Internal Borders' (2014) 51 *Common Market Law Review* 741

Cremona, M., Monar, J. and Poli, S. (eds.), *The External Dimension of the European Union's Area of Freedom, Security and Justice* (Peter Lang, 2011)

Davies, G., 'Legislative Control of the European Court of Justice' (2014) 51 *Common Market Law Review* 1579

Eckes, C., 'External Relations Law: How the Outside Shapes the Inside', in D. Acosta Arcarazo and C.C. Murphy (eds.), *EU Security and Justice Law* (Hart Publishing, 2014) 186–206

Eckes, C. and Konstadinides, T., 'Introduction', in C. Eckes and T. Konstadinides (eds.), *Crime within the Area of Freedom, Security and Justice* (Cambridge University Press, 2011) 1

Editorial Comments, 'Hungary's New Constitutional Order and "European Unity"' (2012) 49 *Common Market Law Review* 871

Flathman, R., 'Legitimacy', in R.E. Goodin, P. Petitt and T. Pogge (eds.), *A Companion to Political Philosophy*, Vol. II (Wiley-Blackwell, 2007) 678

Fletcher, M., 'EU Criminal Justice: Beyond Lisbon', in C. Eckes and T. Konstadinides (eds.), *Crime within the Area of Freedom, Security and Justice* (Cambridge University Press, 2011) 10

Fletcher, M., Lööf, M. and Gilmore, B., *EU Criminal Law and Justice* (Edward Elgar, 2008)

Herlin-Karnell, E., 'Integration in Criminal Matters and the Role of the Court of Justice' (2011) 36 *European Law Review* 420

Herlin-Karnell, E., 'European Criminal Law as an Exercise in EU "Experimental" Constitutional Law' (2013) 20 *Maastricht Journal of European and Comparative Law* 442

Herlin-Karnell, E., 'Constitutional Principles in the Area of Freedom, Security and Justice', in D. Acosta Arcarazo and C.C. Murphy (eds.), *EU Security and Justice Law* (Hart Publishing, 2014) 38

Herlin-Karnell, E., 'Effectiveness and Constitutional Limits in European Criminal Law' (2014) 5 *New Journal of European Criminal Law* 267

Hinarejos, A., *Judicial Control in the European Union* (Oxford University Press, 2009)

Hinarejos, A., 'Integration in Criminal Matters and the Role of the Court of Justice' (2011) 36 *European Law Review* 420

Kochenov, D. and Pech, L., 'Upholding the Rule of Law in the EU: On the Commission's "Pre-Article 7 Procedure" as a Timid Step in the Right Direction', EUI Working Paper RSCAS 2015/24

Kornezov, A., 'The Area of Freedom, Security and Justice in the Light of EU Accession to the ECHR: Is the Break-up Inevitable?' (2012–2013) 12 *Cambridge Yearbook of European Legal Studies* 227

Mastenbroek, E. et al., *Engaging with Europe: Evaluating National Parliamentary Control of EU Decision-making*, a study commissioned by the Dutch House of Representatives, www.houseofrepresentatives.nl/sites/www.houseofrepresentatives.nl/files/news_items/engaging_with_europe_report_of_findings_2nd_edition.pdf.

Mitsilegas, V., *EU Criminal Law* (Hart Publishing, 2008)

Mitsilegas, V., 'EU Criminal Law Competence after Lisbon: From Securitised to Functional Criminalisation', in D. Acosta Arcarazo and C.C. Murphy (eds.), *EU Security and Justice Law* (Hart Publishing, 2014) 110

Murphy, C.C. and Acosta Arcarazo, D., 'Rethinking Europe's Freedom, Security and Justice', in D. Acosta Arcarazo and C.C. Murphy (eds.), *EU Security and Justice Law* (Hart Publishing, 2014) 1

Nic Shuibne, N., 'A Court Within a Court: Is It Time to Rebuild the European Court of Justice?' (2009) 34 *European Law Review* 173

Nilsson, H.G., 'Foreword', in M. Bergström and A.J. Cornell (eds.), *European Police and Criminal Law Co-operation* (Hart Publishing, 2014) v

Peers, S., 'Mission Accomplished? EU Justice and Home Affairs Law after the Treaty of Lisbon' (2011) 48(3) *Common Market Law Review* 661

Peers, S., 'Justice and Home Affairs Law since the Treaty of Lisbon: A Fairy-Tale Ending?', in D. Acosta Arcarazo and C.C. Murphy (eds.), *EU Security and Justice Law* (Hart Publishing, 2014) 17

Rijpma, J.J., 'Institutions and Agencies: Government and Governance after Lisbon', in D. Acosta Arcarazo and C.C. Murphy (eds.), *EU Security and Justice Law* (Hart Publishing, 2014) 54

Spencer, J.R., 'EU Criminal Law', in C. Barnard and S. Peers (eds.), *European Union Law* (Oxford University Press, 2014) 751

Tridimas, T., 'Foreword', in V. Mitsilegas, *EU Criminal Law* (Hart Publishing, 2008) v

Wessel, R.A., Marin, L. and Matera, C., 'The External Dimension of the EU's Area of Freedom, Security and Justice', in C. Eckes and T. Konstadinides (eds.), *Crime within the Area of Freedom, Security and Justice* (Cambridge University Press, 2011) 272

de Waele, H., 'Advancing the Supranational Compliance Debate: New Directions in the Enforcement of EU Law' (2014) 4 *The Lawyer Quarterly* 1

de Waele, H., 'Strained Actorness: The "New" European Council in Theory and Practice', in E. Fahey (ed.), *The Actors of Post-National Rule-Making* (Routledge, 2015) 91

Index

For Product Safety Concerns and Information please contact our EU
representative GPSR@taylorandfrancis.com
Taylor & Francis Verlag GmbH, Kaufingerstraße 24, 80331 München, Germany

www.ingramcontent.com/pod-product-compliance
Ingram Content Group UK Ltd.
Pitfield, Milton Keynes, MK11 3LW, UK
UKHW020025200926
475702UK00014B/2057

* 9 7 8 0 3 6 7 1 9 3 4 5 4 *